Training and Development in Public and Private Policy

The International Library of Management
Series Editor: Keith Bradley

Titles in the Series:

Training and Development in Public and Private Policy

Edited by

Peter Cappelli

Professor of Management
The Wharton School of the University of Pennsylvania

Dartmouth
Aldershot · Brookfield USA · Hong Kong · Singapore · Sydney

Published by
Dartmouth Publishing Company Limited
Gower House
Croft Road
Aldershot
Hants GU11 3HR
England

Dartmouth Publishing Company
Old Post Road
Brookfield
Vermont 05036
USA

British Library Cataloguing in Publication Data
Training and Development in Public and Private Policy.
(International Library of Management)
 I. Cappelli, Peter II. Series
 658.3

Library of Congress Cataloging-in-Publication Data
Training and development in public and private policy. / edited by Peter Cappelli.
       p. cm. — (The International library of management)
     Includes bibliographical references and index.
     ISBN 1-85521-353-2
       1.Occupational training. 2. Employees—Training of. 3. Manpower
planning. 4. Adult education. I. Cappelli, Peter. II. Series.
HD5715.T7 1994
658.3'125—dc20   93-37289
                                                                                                              CIP

ISBN 1 85521 353 2

Printed in Great Britain by Galliard (Printers) Ltd, Great Yarmouth

Contents

PART VII DEVELOPMENT

Acknowledgements

The editor and publishers wish to thank the following for permission to use copyright material.

Academic Press Inc. for two figures from 'On Data-Limited and Resource-Limited Processes' by D.A. Norman and D.B. Bobrow in *Cognitive Psychology*, **7**, (1975).

Academy of Management for the essay: John F. Mathieu and Russell L. Leonard Jr. (1987), 'Applying Utility Concepts to a Training Program in Supervisory Skills: A Time-Based Approach', *Academy of Management Journal*, **30**, pp. 316–35.

Administrative Science Quarterly for the essay: James N. Baron, Alison Davis-Blake and William T. Bielby (1986), 'The Structure of Opportunity: How Promotion Ladders Vary Within and Among Organizations', *Administrative Science Quarterly*, **31**, pp. 248–73.

Alfred A. Knopf Inc. for the specified figure from *The Seasons of A Man's Life* by Daniel J. Levinson et al. Copyright © 1978 by Daniel J. Levinson. Reprinted by permission of Alfred A. Knopf Inc.

American Management Association for the essay: Edgar H. Schein (1975), 'How 'Career Anchors' Hold Executives to Their Career Paths', *Personnel*, **52**, p. 11–24. Copyright © 1975 American Management Association, New York. All rights reserved.

American Psychological Association for the essays: Elaine S. Elliott and Carol S. Dweck (1988), 'Goals: An Approach to Motivation and Achievement', *Journal of Personality and Social Psychology*, **54**, pp. 5–12; Ruth Kanfer and Phillip L. Ackerman (1989), 'Motivation and Cognitive Abilities: An Integrative/Aptitude-Treatment Interaction Approach to Skill Acquisition', *Journal of Applied Psychology*, **74**, pp. 657–90; Gary P. Latham and Colette A. Frayne (1989), 'Self-Management Training for Increasing Job Attendance: A Follow-up and a Replication', *Journal of Applied Psychology*, **74**, pp. 411–16; Michael J. Burke and Russell R. Day (1986), 'A Cumulative Study of the Effectiveness of Managerial Training', *Journal of Applied Psychology*, **71**, pp. 232–45; Daniel J. Levinson (1986), 'A Conception of Adult Development', *American Psychologist*, **41**, p. 3–13; Robert A. Cooke and Denise M. Rousseau (1984), 'Stress and Strain From Family Roles and Work-Role Expectations', *Journal of Applied Psychology*, **69**, pp. 252–60. Copyright © by the American Psychological Association. Reprinted by permission.

BSA Publications Limited for the essay: Wolfgang Streeck (1989), 'Skills and the Limits of Neo-Liberalism: The Enterprise of the Future as a Place of Learning', *Work, Employment & Society*, **3**, pp. 89–104.

Elsevier Science Publishers B.V. for the essay: Ann P. Bartel and Frank R. Lichtenberg (1987), 'The Comparative Advantage of Educated Workers in Implementing New Technology', *The Review of Economics and Statistics*, **69**, pp. 1–11.

JAI Press Inc. for the essay: Donald O. Parsons (1990), 'The Firm's Decision to Train', *Research in Labor Economics*, **11**, pp. 53–75.

National Institute of Economic and Social Research for the essay: Hilary Steedman, Geoff Mason and Karin Wagner (1991), 'Intermediate Skills in the Workplace: Deployment, Standards and Supply in Britain, France and Germany', *National Institute Economic Review*, **136**, pp. 60–76.

Oxford University Press for the essay: David Finegold and David Soskice (1988), 'The Failure of Training in Britain: Analysis and Prescription', *Oxford Review of Economic Policy*, **4**, pp. 21–53. By permission of Oxford University Press.

Personnel Psychology Inc for the essays: Marilyn E. Gist (1989), 'The Influence of Training Method on Self-Efficacy and Idea Generation Among Managers', *Personnel Psychology*, **42**, pp. 787–805; Timothy T. Baldwin and J. Kevin Ford (1988), 'Transfer of Training: A Review and Directions for Future Research', *Personnel Psychology*, **41**, pp. 63–105; Timothy T. Baldwin, Richard J. Magjuka and Brian T. Loher (1991), 'The Perils of Participation: Effects of Choice of Training on Trainee Motivation and Learning', *Personnel Psychology*, **44**, pp. 51–65.

Series Preface

The International Library of Management brings together in one series the most significant and influential articles from across the whole range of management studies. In compiling the series, the editors have followed a selection policy that is both international and interdisciplinary. The articles that are included are not only of seminal importance today, but are expected to remain of key relevance and influence as management deals with the issues of the next millennium.

The Library was specifically designed to meet a great and growing need in the field of management studies. Few areas have grown as rapidly in recent years, in size, complexity, and importance. There has been an enormous increase in the number of important academic journals publishing in the field, in the amount published, in the diversity and complexity of theory and in the extent of cross-pollination from other disciplines. At the same time, managers themselves must deal with increasingly complex issues in a world growing ever more competitive and interdependent. These remarkable developments have presented all those working in the field, whether they be theorists or practitioners, with a serious challenge. In the absence of a core series bringing together this wide array of new knowledge and thought, it is becoming increasingly difficult to keep abreast of all new important developments and discoveries, while it is becoming ever-more vital to do so.

The International Library of Management aims to meet that need, by bringing the most important articles in management theory and practice together in one core, definitive series. The Library provides management researchers, professors, students, and managers themselves, with an extensive range of key articles which, together, provide a comprehensive basis for understanding the nature and importance of the major theoretical and substantive developments in management science. The Library is the definitive series in management studies.

In making their choice, the editors have drawn especially from the Anglo-American tradition, and have tended to exclude articles which have been widely reprinted and are generally available. Selection is particularly focused on issues most likely to be important to management thought and practice as we move into the next millennium. Editors have also prefaced each volume with a thought-provoking introduction, which provides a stimulating setting for the chosen articles.

The International Library of Management is an essential resource for all those engaged in management development in the future.

KEITH BRADLEY
Series Editor
The International Library of Management

Introduction

The longstanding division between the study of training and development decisions made by firms and the study of government training and development programmes is eroding as we better understand the relationship between employer decisions and public policy concerns such as skill levels and economic competitiveness. The essays in this volume were chosen from personnel psychology, labour economics and sociology in an attempt to span that division by addressing general issues that face all training and development decisions. These issues include the factors that govern skill requirements and subsequent training needs, the characteristics that determine how training programmes can be financed, the effectiveness of different training methods, and the overall results of training and development programmes.

Training and Development in Public and Private Policy

Scholars from a wide variety of fields have been interested in issues associated with work-related skills. But, in general, their interests have never merged: personnel psychologists assessed skills and designed training systems; labour economists studied the returns from training and the incentives for acquiring it, while sociologists considered access to skills and the jobs they supported. In addition to these disciplinary divides, there has been perhaps an even greater separation between the study of these issues within individual firms and the policy analysis of the government's role in developing skills.

The rising importance of skill questions both to firms and to nations is breaking down these divisions by asking questions that cut across them.

For employers, the importance of skill and the arrangements for acquiring it are being driven by the development of 'resource-based' models that explain the competitiveness of individual firms on the basis of competencies or resources that competitors cannot easily imitate. The breakdown of market barriers and the ease with which technology transfers across competitors increasingly suggest that the most important competencies for firms are those that reside in their employees and management systems. The skills of employees, including management skills, appear central to firm competencies and, in turn, to firm competitiveness.[1]

More important, nations are discovering that their economic competitiveness – or lack thereof – may be linked to the capabilities of workforces and systems for providing skills. Especially in manufacturing, Japanese firms that use high-performance work systems of the kind pioneered by Toyota have become models for competitors elsewhere, and those high-performance work systems demand a workforce with higher skills. The system of on-the-job training and employee development within Japanese firms gets much of the credit for making those work systems possible. Similarly, the German apprenticeship system is cited as fundamental to that nation's high-skill, high-quality industrial production.[2]

Especially in the UK and the US, concern that workforce skill levels are below those of competitor nations is an important factor driving revisions of education and training systems.[3] These countries have developed a somewhat common set of responses that involve identifying necessary skills, establishing credentials to determine which workers have those skills, and helping support systems that produce them.

My interest in training and development stems from this public policy concern. It is impossible to develop public policy to improve skills in the economy as a whole unless it is grounded in an understanding of the training and development process that exists within individual employers. There seems to be an almost complete divorce between the policy discussion, which is centred in fields like labour economics, education and sociology, and the longstanding study of employer training and development practices centred in personnel psychology. (Indeed, the phrase 'Training and Development' is most typically used to define a subfield of personnel psychology.) Personnel psychologists have largely been left out of the policy debate, with the consequence that the discussion often seems completely ignorant of the findings in the 'Training and Development' (T&D) field.

Perhaps the main purpose of this volume, therefore, is to bring the policy and employer-based fields of training and development closer together. Policy-oriented scholars might find the readings about practices within firms an interesting introduction to decision making in the firm, and personnel experts similarly might be interested in the broader context and economic implications of training and development policies. The readings are designed for researchers and thoughtful practitioners who are interested in a conceptual overview of contemporary issues, and not in a practical or applied discussion of training and development. Anyone looking for a guide to the nuts and bolts of running a training and development programme should immediately drop this book and turn to the number of practitioner handbooks (e.g., Nadler and Nadler 1990) that examine those issues.

A Very Short Overview of Training and Development

Campbell, Dunnette, Lawler and Weick (1970) describe training and development as learning experiences that are planned by an organization for its members in order to help pursue the organization's goals. 'Training' usually refers to learning experiences needed for one's current job and 'development' to learning experiences needed to prepare one for some position in the future. Even with this tightly-drawn definition – and arguments abound as to whether it is tight enough – there are numerous complications concerning boundaries with other fields.

One of these boundary conflicts is with adult education. The topics of T&D often include basic academic skills taught in schools. What makes it training and development, as opposed to adult education, is presumably that it is organized by one's employer. But education, standard-setting, certification and continuing training can be provided by organizations other than the employer. Many highly specific vocational courses are offered by schools, unions and associations, and these courses may be required by employers. Occupations as diverse as aviation, accounting and nursing require job-related course work to maintain competencies that is offered by outside agencies. Even training that takes place within the organization can be provided by some other agency or group. Apprenticeship programmes, for example, are typically governed (at least in part) by unions or government agencies even when the training is delivered by the employer. Even a brief look across economic systems suggests that the same set of skills can be acquired from very different providers. In Germany and the Scandinavian countries, for example, metal-working skills might typically be acquired through apprenticeship programmes administered outside of individual firms; in Japan, that same set of skills is commonly learned within the firm; in the US, they might more typically be provided by proprietary and vocational schools.

The potential providers of skills can overlap and, in some cases, actually compete. It is an interesting question, explored below, as to how employers choose among competing providers of skill.[4] When employers control – and especially pay for – the learning experiences, a unique set of concerns is created, mainly associated with the context of training: how topics are chosen, how programmes are funded, and how they fit in with other organizational goals. These issues are explored in the papers contained in this volume.[5]

Historically, training and development programmes were limited by the fact that organizations themselves were primitive. Other than the church and the military, few organizations before the industrial revolution were substantial enough to provide systematic learning experiences. Often those that existed were simply 'learning by doing' and by observing. Apprenticeship programmes were the dominant arrangements for learning job-related skills, and these operated outside the context of individual employers. The earliest industrial operations often 'outsourced' the planning of any learning opportunities to supervisors who acted like contractors – hiring, firing and training their own work crews.

Unions were as likely to provide training and development opportunities as employers. In major industries like railroads, jobs and learning experiences were structured according to craft categories where unions often controlled the acquisition of skills. Indeed, it was easier for craft unions in particular to fund training because unions could recoup the costs through membership dues over a working lifetime, even if members changed employers (Cappelli 1989).

Even the rise of large-scale industrial operations did not by itself generate significant employer-provided T&D. What drove the modern concern for T&D were arguments suggesting how it might benefit the employer to provide learning experiences that could not be provided either by unions or by learning through observation. Perhaps the most important of these was offered by Frederick Taylor's theories. T&D was part of the general effort to identify and break down skills and then teach employees the narrow behaviours necessary to perform jobs in the manner dictated by scientific management's system of work design.

The planning demands of wartime economies and the military's development of personnel systems – primarily selection devices that were then matched with training – drove the next expansion of T&D. These practices began being transferred from military to civilian industries during World War I and accelerated during World War II. After those lessons had transferred, however, the new thrust in training and development was in the public policy arena. Attention in the US focused on providing basic skills for the unemployed as a means of getting them into the workforce. Policy interest in the UK also centred on job training schemes to address unemployment for school-leavers. In Scandinavia, especially in Sweden, policy involvement with training was much more extensive – an important component of the welfare state – but was still seen largely as a benefit provided by the government to help workers who were out of the labour force to get back in or to help them change careers.[6]

The development during the 1980s that refocused employers' attention on human resources practice in general, and training and development in particular, was the concern about lagging competitiveness, especially as compared to the high-performance work systems associated with Japanese manufacturing firms. In the US in particular, arguments about improving firm and national economic competitiveness focused on employer practices, especially new production strategies and systems for organizing work. Innovations such as Total Quality Management and Statistical Process Control, Employee Involvement/Empowerment, and customer-orientated management became the new routes to success. All made new demands on worker skills. Training and development that provided those skills therefore became a necessary condition for achieving competitiveness. And the status of T&D as a topic increased.

Themes

If the purpose of this volume is to integrate employer-based research and policy-oriented issues associated with training and development, then the main task is to set out a road map showing what the issues are and how they fit together. That requires establishing the context in which training and development decisions operate.

One way to begin a taxonomy is to think about what is left out of the highly-defined 'Training and Development' field within personnel psychology. Researchers in this area are unusually disposed to decry its research direction, especially the lack of theory.[7] More generally, the complaint applied to the broader discipline of personnel and industrial/organizational psychology is its inward focus and difficulty in relating to wider issues – theories, variables, topical problems – associated with other fields (see Zedeck and Cascio 1984).

It is no surprise that this field centres on those training and development issues that are of interest to psychologists, issues primarily associated with the effects of programmes on individual behaviour. This orientation provides only one cross-sectional slice (albeit a very important slice) through the issues associated with training and development. For example, although it is certainly acknowledged that training takes place in the context of organizations and that issues associated with organizations therefore affect training and development (see Hinrichs 1976), other fields have focused much more clearly on such issues. And factors beyond the organization – such as markets and government policy – are even less likely to be considered.

The glory of personnel psychology's research on training and development centres on application: how to design and evaluate training and development programmes. But other issues logically come first, six of which are identified and discussed below.

Choosing the Skills

What determines the knowledge, skills and abilities that workers need? Campbell (1988) notes that figuring out what should be learned is far more important – and difficult – than all the other issues associated with training. The 'Needs Assessment' literature in personnel psychology is very efficient in identifying what is required once particular jobs are designed.[8] The assumption in this literature is that the characteristics of the jobs are given, and that needs assessment is a technical exercise – often a complicated one – that identifies what should be learned by analysing the combination of individual attributes, job demands and projected changes in the organization and workforce.

It is very clear from other fields, however, that the design of jobs and the demands that they make on workers are themselves choice variables. Some of the variance in the design of jobs concerns choices of technology, where capital and technology can be used as a substitute for worker skills. But there is considerable variance in requirements even for jobs using the same technology. Machinists using numerically controlled machines, for example, in some cases do the programming of those machines themselves, but in other cases do not (see, e.g., Kelley 1990).

To further complicate the problem, it appears that the choices of work design are related to the skills available in the existing workforce and in the outside labour market; employers may decide to design work in ways that 'deskill' or reduce job requirements where the existing skill base is poor. One of the factors thought to justify the rise of Taylorism, for example, was the low level of skills of the newly-arrived immigrant workforce. An extensive literature in sociology and industrial relations describes how the power of work groups and unions shapes choices governing skill requirements (see, e.g., Hyman and Streeck 1989). There is also some evidence that labour market conditions may affect the skill requirements chosen by employers (Cappelli 1993). Conversely, there is a growing argument, noted below, that the choices of work design and skill levels may affect the competitiveness of individual firms and, ultimately, of nations.

The first three chapters in this volume examine the factors that determine the choice of skill levels. MacDuffie and Kochan begin by showing how work design issues associated with production strategies drive training and related human resource decisions in manufacturing. More important, they find no increase in terms of organizational performance associated with higher levels of training unless it is matched to production strategies that take advantage of it: the match between training and production and not training *per se* provides the increase in performance. Schuler and Jackson find that training and related human resource practices vary not only within organizations by occupation (organizational level), but also across organizations based on strategies associated with product life-cycles. Their arguments in Chapter 2 reinforce the general point that training and development decisions are ultimately driven by organization-level decisions.

Finally, Finegold and Soskice argue that there is something like an equilibrium in economies between production decisions and skill provision: a low level of skills in the economy helps push firms towards low-skill, low-quality production techniques which, in turn, reduce the incentives for the society to turn out workers with high skills. These choices, it is argued, have an important impact on the competitiveness of economies and on standards of living. The argument builds from Piore and Sable's (1984) assertion that high-wage industrial economies will need to seek out differentiated market niches based on quality to avoid the competition from low-wage economies in markets dominated by lower-skill assembly line production. It is an argument with substantial policy ramifications that has since spread to the US (see *America's Choice* 1990).

Choices for Getting Skills

Once the decisions about work design have been made, how should employers get the necessary knowledge, skills and abilities into the organization? One option is for an employer to train and develop them from within the firm, the option focused on in the personnel psychology literature. Another option is to hire workers who already have the requisite skills from outside or to subcontract the function to a supplier whose staff has those skills. This is the 'make or buy' choice. Still another option is for the training and development to be done outside the firm – the training and development organized as well as delivered outside – through apprenticeship systems, vocational courses, vendors, etc.

The answers to these questions, at least at present, turn largely on financial incentives for employers, characteristics of labour markets, and the availability of outside institutions that provide training. In his classic contribution (Chapter 4), Becker describes the relationship between training and the outside labour market and explains, for example, that employers are reluctant to fund training that creates general skills useful to other employers because it is difficult to recoup the costs: because these workers are now worth more elsewhere, the employer has to raise their wages, offsetting the productivity gains from training, or lose them to other employers. In Chapter 5, Parsons focuses on the different ways that employers can make training pay, especially on-the-job training, and reviews the empirical evidence pioneered by Mincer (1962) on how such training is provided. His arguments help lead us into the discussion below of the necessary conditions for providing training. He notes, for example, how turnover reduces the incentives for employers to invest in training and how the inability to enforce most employment contracts and the difficulty workers have in borrowing to finance their own training hamper the ability to finance training – an important public policy issue.

Streeck follows by waving a red flag right in the nose of the economics profession with the assertion that employers cannot by themselves provide the worker training that they will inevitably need, nor will they be able to purchase it in the market. He argues that governments will need to intervene and force firms to provide higher levels of training than appears to be in their immediate interest. The argument follows Becker's observations about the problems employers have in funding general training and adds two assertions: firms will need even higher levels of general skills in the future, and those skills can in practice be acquired only in work settings.

Much of this argument turns on empirical issues similar to those discussed by Finegold and Soskice: what higher levels of skills do new production systems need, how general are those skills, and how much of the economy is affected by them? The problem of providing more general skills training may require government intervention, with creating incentives for employers to provide it through programmes like apprenticeships being the most likely type of intervention. The kind of market-based analysis used by Becker and Parsons provides a first step to thinking about how those incentives could be created.

The reading from the Office of Technology Assessment's report on worker training (Chapter 7) provides a quick comparison of alternative systems associated with different national training models. The discussion focuses on Japan and Germany's very different systems, each of which is fundamental to their national economic success. Both create high levels of skill and smooth the transition between school and work. But Japan's system keeps skills and training focused within individual firms, while Germany's apprenticeship system, administered independently of individual firms, creates more general skills with credentials that can be traded in labour markets (the Streeck argument). Perhaps the most important lesson from this reading is the need to understand the complex financial, governmental and social conditions that make these systems possible, conditions that make it difficult to transplant similar arrangements to other countries. The Japanese system, for example, relies on complementary employment practices and a work culture that substantially reduces turnover; the German system benefits from a long tradition of employer participation in apprenticeships, as well as agreements not to hire away each other's apprentices.[9]

How Do People Learn?

Once an employer decides to provide training and has determined the content of the training programme, then the issue is how best to do it. The place to begin that discussion is with the question of how people learn, certainly one of the most important and interesting issues in training and development. It is an area where instructional psychology and personnel psychology greatly overlap and where the development of new cognitive models is making a powerful contribution.[10] Perhaps the central question in this area is, what determines the motivation to learn? Elliott and Dweck's essay (Chapter 8) shows how the characteristics of goals and the way that they are structured determine 'helpless' or 'mastery-oriented' responses to learning situations. Goals framed in terms of performance outcomes focus attention on one's ability; indications of poor performance create a sense of inadequacy that may cause one to withdraw effort. Goals framed in terms of how much one has learned, in contrast, do not focus attention on ability. Indications of poor performance or slow progress, therefore, are less likely to be interpreted as failures that require defensive responses such as giving up.

Kanfer and Ackerman (Chapter 9) examine the interaction between motivation and ability as it affects performance. They argue that different learning tasks make different demands on one's attention. Efforts to raise motivation through goal setting, for example, may actually have negative consequences for performance in situations that do not demand a great deal of attention because it interferes with task practice.[11] Their study provides a good example of rigorous evaluation design as well as illustrating how complicated the factors affecting motivation and performance can be.[12]

Policy discussions of training sometimes ignore altogether any inquiry into how people learn. Programmes that consider the motivation to learn at all invariably do so strictly in terms of financial incentives: paying trainees to participate, helping to ensure a financial payoff at the end (the expectancy model in psychology), etc. These chapters and the ones below help to suggest how much more complicated the issue of motivation is and may help to encourage the incorporation of cognitive issues into the design of training programmes.

What Training Methods Work Best?

As noted above, most of the public policy discussion of T&D implicitly assumes that people learn in order to receive rewards – behaviour modification. To counter that preoccupation, the readings in this section focus more on the developing cognitive models of training.[13] For example, behavioural modelling – observing the behaviours of a model who performs some activity – has been both a popular research topic and a powerful technique in the training and development area. There is some evidence, however, that it may be much less useful for conveying more complicated, cognitive behaviours, especially those that vary. It can also be an expensive technique that only works for behaviours that can be observed (see Robertson 1990 for a review). Cognitive modelling – reflecting on self-instructional statements that provide codes for appropriate behaviour – circumvents many of these problems, and Gist's study (Chapter 10) illustrates its usefulness in improving performance in the complex task of generating ideas.

In the next selection, Latham and Frayne indicate the power of another cognitive technique, goal setting, as a training device. They show how simple and inexpensive training in self-regulatory behaviour – setting goals, monitoring one's own progress – led to important improvements in work attendance that persisted over time. Techniques like these develop one's 'self-efficacy', the sense of being able to cope with problems effectively. The results of this study are particularly important, given that employers' main complaints about the quality of new workers concern behaviours such as attendance and not vocational skills (see Cappelli 1992a).

Burke and Day's paper (Chapter 12) summarizes the results of prior research on several popular training methods, along with differences in content, in the context of training managers. Their results suggest, for example, that the lecture/discussion format typically used in university education has about the lowest overall effectiveness. Their paper also illustrates the use of meta-analysis, a popular technique in personnel psychology for aggregating statistical results across studies (see Schmidt 1992 for a discussion).

Other interesting topics under the heading of training methods not covered in the readings in this volume include simulations and games, where the illusion of reality is strong enough to induce realistic responses and, in turn, to make the transfer of the training easier (see the discussion of training transfer below). Keys and Wolfe (1990) provide a thorough review of this area, including the results associated with specific games. Studies of new instructional technologies dominate the remaining topics in training methods (see Pursell and Russell 1991 for an overview).

What Conditions Support Training?

The papers above by Schuler and Jackson and Parsons began the discussion of the factors needed to make even an excellent programme of training succeed. One could even consider some of these factors (such as the need to retain trainees) as necessary conditions for effective programmes. Again, because the economics and policy-related research focuses so heavily on incentives to encourage education and training, it may be a useful balance to concentrate here on cognitive factors that help to support training.

The survey paper by Baldwin and Ford (Chapter 13) begins with the central propositions of training design that facilitate transfer. The notion of 'identical elements' – that transfer works best where the training and transfer settings are most similar – provides one explanation for the finding in labour economics that on-the-job training appears to be the most effective format in terms of wage gains (see Barron et al. 1989). The importance of teaching general principles, as opposed to specific skills, in facilitating transfer is directly relevant to debates about how curricula in schools should be reformulated to improve job performance (see the SCANS 1992 report). The paper goes on to examine supportive practices in the work environment that reinforce training transfer, such as the climate or culture of the organization and the behaviour of leaders. The interest in leadership behaviour may have been cooled somewhat by the lack of apparent relationships between support provided by supervisors and training effectiveness (see Russell et al. 1985).

The Effects of Training

Closely related to the issue of transfer of training are attempts to identify the overall effect of training. This topic represents perhaps the biggest divide between the policy and personnel psychology fields. As Latham (1988, p. 561) argues, 'Psychologists ... need to "stick to their knitting" and not be persuaded to regress to a search for reliable and valid outcome measures. ... Behavior, rather than an economic construct, is in most instances the dependent variable of interest in organizational psychology.' Most of the personnel psychology readings in this volume include assessments of training effects in terms of changes in the behaviour of trainees. The policy and business communities, in contrast, are desperate to know whether training can affect the performance of organizations. The evidence from personnel psychology about how training changes the behaviour of trainees (i.e., do they learn the tasks?) does not necessarily answer that question.[14]

The paper by Baldwin, Magjuka and Loher (Chapter 14) shows another cognitive factor that affects training success. The participation of trainees in choices concerning their training substantially improved their performance. More important, where their choices were thwarted, the performance was worse than if they were given no choices at all. (Universities whose students are often 'closed out' of elective courses should take note.) The attention given to 'empowerment' and to increasing worker participation in organizations makes these conclusions especially relevant.

The research on transfer of training – whether what is learned in training actually gets used on the job – focuses heavily on the conditions that support training. Whether training is transferred to the workplace is distinct from whether the training programme 'worked'; that is, whether trainees learned the desired skills or behaviours. When learning does not transfer to the job, it is both a financial burden for employers and a public policy concern. For example, the fact that grades in school are not good predictors of success on the job may in part reflect a problem of transfer between school learning and work behaviours (see Cappelli 1992b). The fact that the complaints about the performance of school leavers are loud even for highly-trained, practically-oriented students from business schools suggests that transfer, and not a lack of training *per se*, is the centre of the problem.

Research in labour economics typically measures training effectiveness by investigating whether wages have increased. This measure gets closer to the effects on organizations if one accepts the assumption that wages (in the absence of unions and related wage-setting institutions) reflect an employer's assessment of the importance and contribution of workers, and that training will not cause wages to go up unless it improves performance. Brown's study (Chapter 15) represents one of the best efforts at relating training and wages. It concludes that on-the-job training accounts for most of the wage growth for employees over their working life, even after controlling for tenure. This result is an important counter to previous findings – that wage growth was primarily due to seniority rules that rewarded tenure and not necessarily increasing productivity (Medoff and Abraham 1980).

Mathieu and Leonard (Chapter 16) present a study of the impact of training that uses 'utility concepts' accounting techniques for translating behaviours into money values. Their analysis shows impressive financial returns over time associated with a supervisory training programme. However, the main importance of their study here is to illustrate how to assess the effects of training on *employers* rather than on individuals. Lack of knowledge about how to make these calculations may explain why so few employers seem to have any idea of the benefits gained from their training programmes.

These two readings also help illustrate differences in the ways that psychologists and economists test hypotheses. Personnel psychologists, who typically collect their own data, are much more likely to rely on experimental designs to control for confounding factors; labour economists, who typically use existing data (generally national probability samples) cannot influence experimental designs and rely instead on statistical techniques to provide controls.

In Chapter 17, Bartel and Lichtenberg find evidence that more educated workers are better at implementing new technologies because they adapt and learn more quickly, characteristics that are especially important when new technologies are introduced. Their arguments apply to a range of learning activities – including various training arrangements – even though their data can only capture formal education. The attention given to the increasing pace of change in the world economy and, in turn, within organizations, makes this conclusion particularly relevant. Whether the higher capabilities of more educated workers are caused by additional education or whether such individuals seek out more education (the human capital vs screening debate in labour economics) cannot be answered by this data because it examines different cross-sections of workers over time. Either way, the results also suggest that firms, and perhaps nations as well, whose competitiveness turns on implementing new technologies have a special need to employ educated workers, reinforcing the point made by earlier papers concerning the relationship between training decisions and business strategies.

The comparative studies of skills, work organization and economic performance conducted by the National Institute of Economic and Social Research over the past decade have suggested that British firms have both lower performance and lower skills than their European competitors. These findings have played an exceptionally powerful role in shaping British policy discussions, especially as trade within the European Community has become more open. The essay by Steedman, Mason and Wagner (Chapter 18) continues the National Institute approach of case study comparisons, but focuses on 'intermediate skills' associated with technicians and supervisors rather than on the more typical craft skills. They find that British firms have adapted to the lower supply of intermediate skills available in Britain by producing the same products with fewer highly-skilled workers and supervisors than their European competitors. Instead, engineers and other employees with 'graduate skills' get drawn into shopfloor production decisions to solve problems that are addressed by skilled workers in other countries.

These arguments are especially important given evidence that technical or intermediate skills are becoming both more important to industrial economies and more scarce (Barley 1992). The recent 'downsizing' efforts in many companies, that focus on eliminating supervisors and other lower-level managers, may also contribute to intermediate skill shortages that will require different systems of work organization. The Steedman, Mason and Wagner study has become the focus of some controversy as it seems to imply that different mixes of skills can be used to achieve the same ends, thus contradicting the Finegold and Soskice argument made earlier. Shackleton (1992) uses this conclusion to argue that if employers can adapt successfully to a workforce with lower levels of skills, then there is little reason to invest in expanding those skills. The key issue, of course, is how successful the adaptations to lower skills really are. Steedman (1993) argues that the British systems are less effective, in particular because they use more expensive labour.

Development

One can think of development as taking the notion of training and making it dynamic; improving one's abilities and skills in order to take on new, more challenging tasks in the future. Development only makes sense, therefore, if there is reason to believe that more challenging tasks await one in the future. One of the reasons that development is typically associated with management jobs is because in the US and the UK, where this literature has developed, only employees in management jobs could expect to have careers, a sequence of jobs over a working lifetime that offered tasks that were different and typically of increasing challenge.

The first point to note, therefore, is that there is unlikely to be any development unless there is some career path. Many highly-skilled occupations, such as lawyers or accountants in professional firms, have little need for development because they do not have careers in the sense of changing tasks. They may need training to maintain skills, but have less need to develop significantly different skills.

Here the concept of an internal labour market (ILM) is essential. Without some arrangement like an ILM for moving employees across tasks and jobs, there is no need for development.[15] The study of mobility within organizations has become especially important in organizational sociology where the longstanding interest in social mobility has been turned inside the firm. The general topic of careers and development is one of the most multi-disciplinary fields in the employment area (see the papers in Arthur, Hall and Lawrence (1989) for examples).

Chapter 19 by Baron, Davis-Blake and Bielby investigates the characteristics of promotion opportunities within organizations and finds that a number of organizational characteristics essentially serve as conditions that support promotion ladders. Most important for this discussion, they also find evidence that development causes job ladders, that jobs seem to be organized into promotion hierarchies in order to support on-the-job training and the acquisition of firm-specific skills.[16]

Once the context for development is given, the psychologists again take the research lead with studies that focus on individual concerns. Much of this research has its roots in the field of adult development. Here the argument is that adults experience predictable changes as they age that create different needs. One goal of careers and development programmes in employment, therefore, is to match up with and meet the changing needs of employees as they age. Levinson's essay (Chapter 20) provides a good summary of what is known about adult development and makes an argument for some stability in careers, a contrast especially to the 'fast-track' career development programmes that emphasize rapid change.[17]

Schein adds a further wrinkle to the issue of career development in Chapter 21 with empirical results suggesting that differences across individuals in their values, needs and personalities cause them to gravitate towards certain jobs and stay there. These 'career anchors' may represent an important constraint on the ability of organizations to 'develop' employees.

An issue of increasing importance at the nexus between organizational demands and individual development is potential conflict between work and family. The paper by Cooke and Rousseau (Chapter 22) investigates two competing hypotheses: (1) that family roles provide a diversion and outlet for work-related stress and (2) that the addition of family roles that may compete with work roles helps create stress. They find that the demands of families generally increase stress, although they also find that, after controlling for the physical and emotional demands of family life, having a family is associated with better physical well-being. (See the papers in Zedeck (1992) for current issues associated with careers and family.)

As noted above, research on managers dominates the field of development. One of the more interesting development issues in this area is the debate about competencies, whether management students in particular should learn specific skills and competencies or general knowledge and administrative concepts associated with graduate school programmes (see Wexley and Baldwin 1986 for a review). This debate is very similar to the one in progress in general education. The SCANS (1992) recommendations in the US, for example, are closer to the skills or competency-based view than to a back-to-basics academic approach. Another interesting issue is the use of sophisticated assessment and feedback, provided through programmes such as assessment centres, as part of development exercises (see Keys and Wolfe 1988 for a review).

A final challenge to the field of development is the continuing pressure on organizations to 'downsize', especially to reduce the number of layers or levels of management. These changes clearly reduce both the need and the opportunity for development programmes. Even more important is the change in expectations, driven by employers, that career development is a responsibility of the employer at all. Reductions in promises of job security are frequently accompanied by rhetoric suggesting that employees should be responsible for their own career development. In some cases the argument is even made that a reasonable career progression will take them outside their current employer. If these changes are permanent, it will indeed be different to think of individuals and not firms as the purchasers of T&D programmes. One of the main beneficiaries of such a change would be schools of business, especially the degree and certification programmes that already market directly to individuals.

Conclusion

The topic of training and development is becoming more important to employers, unions and nations. But the questions now being asked are different than in the past. The topic is debated at higher levels and the questions reflect choices associated with the broader issue of skill: what level of skill should the organization choose; should that level be 'made' through training and development or bought from the outside; if decided upon, what arrangements can make it financially feasible. We then return to the more traditional questions about how best to design T&D programmes. Here, many of the lessons from cognitive-oriented research have yet to find their way into the mainstream practice of T&D.

In the public policy discussion of training, the demand is increasingly for programmes that will influence these private choices of employers because of the sense that some options are better for society and the economy than others. Understanding first what the 'better' choices are, and second what goes into making those choices, is central to any effort to influence them. Finally, for training programmes that are provided directly by the government, the design lessons from T&D research within organizations needs rather desperately to be applied. These issues cut across the subfields of research in the broad T&D area, and I believe that efforts to look across these subfields represents the first way forward.

Notes

1. Cappelli and Singh (1993) describe the implications of this resource view of firms for human resources.
2. A good description of high-performance work systems and of their dominance can be found in Office of Technology Assessment (1990), Chapter 7 in this volume.
3. See Office of Technology Assessment (1990) and Central Policy Review Staff (1980) for examples of these arguments at government level in the US and UK respectively.
4. There are other options as well, such as reducing the skills required to perform jobs. Cappelli and Pil (1993) identify empirically other options that employers in the US pursue, such as deskilling jobs.
5. Programmes designed to prepare people for jobs with different employers are excluded from consideration here. The most important of these programmes are those aimed at helping displaced workers get new jobs, on which there is a considerable body of research (see Leigh 1990 for a survey). The fact that the trainees in these programmes are not employees, and that the organizers are not employers, makes the experience so fundamentally different as to demand an entirely separate discussion. Examples of programmes at the interface between training as defined here and adult education would include work-based learning where the trainee is in a firm but is not an 'employee', as in German apprenticeships.
6. See Jacoby (1985) and Sheldrake and Vickerstaff (1987) for historical accounts of the rise of training within US and UK firms respectively. Lynch (1992) offers a contemporary review of training practices across countries.
7. See, for example, reviews by Campbell (1971), Goldstein (1980), Wexley (1984) and Campbell (1988).
8. For a good review of needs analysis procedures, see Goldstein (1991).
9. There are varieties of training arrangements within countries as well. Ferman et al. (1990) survey the especially broad range of training structures within the US.
10. See Pintrich et al. (1986) for an exhaustive review of instructional psychology research.
11. For a good summary of current research on motivation in general, see Kanfer (1991).
12. Readers interested in the general topic of how individuals respond to training could refer to Tannenbaum et al.'s (1991) findings that meeting trainees' expectations increased their commitment and motivation after training, even when controlling for attitudes towards training. Noe and Schmitt (1986) also conclude that trainees' sense of involvement with their job predicts learning and behaviour change. Noe (1986) reviews research on individual attributes and their relationship to training effectiveness, although many of the more interesting studies have been later. Tannenbaum and Yukl (1992) offer a summary of the more recent research.
13. For a review of training models, see Latham (1993).
14. There are, of course, strong alternative views in the field. See, e.g., Cascio (1991).
15. Surely this explains the lack of research interest in 'development' for employees in production jobs where the expectation is that they will be doing roughly the same job as long as they stay with the organization. Production jobs in countries like Japan, where internal promotion is important even at the production level, obviously provide an alternative model. Indeed, Japanese employers do offer something like development programmes for production workers.
16. Among the more interesting developments in this area are studies that examine how the demographic characteristics of organizations affect turnover and, in turn, career opportunities. See, for example, Wagner, Pfeffer and O'Reilly (1984).
17. Feldman (1988) provides a good description of the pros and cons of fast-track programmes.

References

America's Choice: High Skills or Low Wages? (1990), Rochester, NY: National Center on Education and the Economy.

Arthur, Michael B., Douglas T. Hall and Barbara S. Lawrence (eds) (1989), *Handbook of Career Theory*, Cambridge: Cambridge University Press.

Barley, Stephen R. (1992), 'The New Crafts: The Rise of the Technical Labor Force and its Implications for the Organization of Work', Philadelphia: National Center on the Educational Quality of the Workforce, University of Pennsylvania.

Barron, John M., Dan A. Black and Mark A. Loewenstein (1989), 'Job Matching and On-the-Job Training', *Journal of Labor Economics*, 7, pp. 1–19.

Campbell, J.P. (1971), 'Personnel Training and Development', *Annual Review of Psychology*, 22, pp. 565–602.

Campbell, J.P. (1988), 'Training Design for Performance Improvement' in J.P. Campbell and R.J. Campbell (eds), *Productivity in Organizations: Frontiers of Industrial and Organizational Psychology*, San Francisco: Jossey-Bass, pp. 177–216.

Campbell, J.P., M.D. Dunnette, E.E. Lawler and K.E. Weick (1970), 'Managerial Behavior, Performance, and Effectiveness', New York: McGraw Hill.

Cappelli, Peter (1989), 'The Role of Unions in Improving Workforce Quality, Labor Market Efficiency, and Effective Employee Management' in *Investing in People: A Strategy to Address America's Workforce Crisis*, Background Papers Vol. II, Washington, D.C.: US Department of Labor, Commission on Workforce Quality and Labor Market Efficiency.

Cappelli, Peter (1992a), 'How Should We Assess College Students? Lessons from Industry', *Change*, November.

Cappelli, Peter (1992b), 'Is the "Skills Gap" About Attitudes?', Philadelphia: National Center on the Educational Quality of the Workforce.

Cappelli, Peter (1993), 'Are Skill Requirements Rising? Evidence for Production and Clerical Jobs', *Industrial and Labor Relations Review*, 46, pp. 515–30.

Cappelli, Peter and Habir Singh, 'Integrating Strategic Management and Strategy in Human Resources' in David Lewin, Olivia Mitchell and Peter Sherer (eds) (1993), *New Frontiers in Human Resources*, Madison, WI: Industrial Relations Research Association.

Cappelli, Peter and Fritz Pil (1993), 'Strategies for Developing a Skilled Workforce: Explaining Employer Choices', Philadelphia: National Center on the Educational Quality of the Workforce.

Cascio, Wayne (1991), *Costing Human Resources: The Financial Impact of Behavior in Organizations*, Boston: Kent PWS.

Central Policy Review Staff (1980), 'Education, Training, and Industrial Performance', London: HMSO.

Feldman, Daniel C. (1988), *Managing Careers in Organizations*, Glenview, IL: Scott Foresman.

Ferman, Louis et al. (1990), *New Developments in Worker Training: A Legacy for the 1990's*, Madison, WI: Industrial Relations Research Association.

Ferman, Louis et al. (1991), *Joint Training Programs: A Union-Management Approach to Preparing Workers for the Future*, Ithaca, NY: ILR Press.

Goldstein, I.L. (1980), 'Training in Work Organizations', *Annual Review of Psychology*, 31, pp. 229–72.

Goldstein, I.L., E.P. Braverman and H.W. Goldstein, 'The Use of Needs Assessment in Training Systems Design' in K. Wexley (ed.) *ASPA/BNA Handbook of Human Resource Management: Developing Human Resources*, 5, Washington, D.C.: BNA Books, pp. 5–35.

Goldstein, I.L. (1990), 'Training System Issues in the Year 2000', *American Psychologist*, 45, pp. 134–43.

Hinrichs, J.R. (1976), 'Personnel Training' in M.D. Dunnette (ed.), *Handbook of Industrial and Organizational Psychology*, Chicago: Rand-MacNally, pp. 829–60.

Hyman, Richard and Wolfgang Streeck (1989), 'New Technology and Industrial Relations', Oxford: Basil Blackwell.

Jacoby, Sanford (1985), *Employing Bureaucracy*, New York: Columbia University Press.

Kanfer, R. (1991), 'Motivation Theory and Industrial and Organizational Psychology' in M.D. Dunnette and L.M. Hough (eds), *Handbook of Industrial and Organizational Psychology*, 1, Palo Alto, CA: Consulting Psychologists' Press, pp. 75–170.

Kelley, Maryellen (1990), 'New Process Technology, Job Design, and Work Organization', *American Sociological Review*, 55, pp. 191–208.

Keys, Bernard and Joseph Wolfe (1988), 'Management Education and Development: Current Issues and Emerging Trends', *Journal of Management*, **14**, pp. 205–29.

Keys, Bernard and Joseph Wolfe (1990), 'The Role of Management Games and Simulations in Education and Research', *Journal of Management*, **16**, pp. 307–36.

Kochan, Thomas A. and Peter Cappelli (1984), 'The Transformation of the Industrial Relations/Personnel Function' in Paul Osterman (ed.), *Internal Labor Markets*, Cambridge, MA: MIT Press, for a shorter account.

Latham, G. (1988), 'Human Resource Training and Development', *Annual Review of Psychology*, **39**, pp. 545–82.

Latham, G.P. (1993), 'Behavioral Approaches to the Training Process' in Irving L. Goldstein (ed.), *Training in Organizations*, Pacific Grove, CA: Brooks-Cole.

Leigh, Duane E. (1990), *Does Training Work for Displaced Workers? A Survey of Existing Evidence*, Kalamazoo, MI: W.E. Upjohn Institute for Employment Research.

Lynch, Lisa M. (1992), 'A National Training Agenda: Lessons from Abroad', Washington, D.C.: Economic Policy Institute.

Medoff, James E. and Katharine G. Abraham (1980), 'Experience, Performance, and Earnings', *Quarterly Journal of Economics*, **95**, pp. 703–36.

Mincer, Jacob (1962), 'On the Job Training: Costs, Returns, and Some Implications', *Journal of Political Economy*, **70**, Supplement, pp. 50–79.

Nadler, Leonard and Bruce Nadler (1990), *The Handbook of Human Resource Development*, New York: Wiley.

Noe, Raymond E. (1986), 'Trainees' Attributes and Attitudes: Neglected Influences on Training Effectiveness', *Academy of Management Review*, **11**, pp. 736–49.

Noe, Raymond E. and Neal Schmitt (1986), 'The Influence of Trainee Attitudes on Training Effectiveness: Test of a Model', *Personnel Psychology*, **39**, pp. 497–523.

Office of Technology Assessment (1990), *Worker Training*, Washington D.C.: US Congress.

Pintrich, Rual R., David R. Cross, Robert B. Kozma and Wilbert J. McKeachie (1986), 'Instructional Psychology', *Annual Review of Psychology*, **37**, pp. 611–51.

Piore, Michael J. and Charles F. Sabel (1984), *The Second Industrial Divide*, New York: Basic Books.

Pursell, E.D. and J.S. Russell (1991), 'Employee Development' in K. Wexley (ed.), *ASPA/BNA Handbook of Human Resource Management: Developing Human Resources*, **5**, Washington, D.C.: Bureau of National Affairs, pp. 5–76.

Robertson, I.T. (1990), 'Behavioral Modelling: Its Record and Potential in Training and Development', *British Journal of Management*, **1**, pp. 117–25.

Russell, J.S., J.R. Terborg and M.L. Powers (1985), 'Organizational Performance and Organizational Level Training and Support', *Personnel Psychology*, **38**, pp. 849–63.

Secretary's Commission on Achieving Necessary Skills (SCANS) (1992), *Learning a Living: A Blueprint for High Performance*, Washington, D.C.: GPO.

Schmidt, Frank L. (1992), 'What Do Data Really Mean? Research Findings, Meta-Analysis, and Cumulative Knowledge in Psychology', *American Psychologist*, **47**, pp. 1173–81.

Shackleton, J.R. (1992), *Training Too Much? A Skeptical Look at the Economics of Skills Provision in the U.K.*, London: Institute of Economic Affairs.

Sheldrake, J. and S. Vickerstaff (1987), *The History of Industrial Training in Britain*, Aldershot, Gower Publishing.

Steedman, Hillary (1993), 'Do Work-force Skills Matter?', *British Journal of Industrial Relations*, **31**, pp. 285–92.

Tannenbaum, S.I. and G. Yukl (1992), 'Training and Development in Work Organizations', *Annual Review of Psychology*, **43**, pp. 399–441.

Tannenbaum, S.I., J.E. Mathieu, E. Salas and J.A. Cannon-Bowers (1991), 'Meeting Trainees' Expectations: The Influence of Training Fulfillment on the Development of Commitment, Self-Efficacy, and Motivation', *Journal of Applied Psychology*, **76**, pp. 759–69.

Wagner, Gary W., Jeffrey Pfeffer and Charles A. O'Reilly, III (1984), 'Organizational Demography and Turnover in Top-Management Groups', *Administrative Science Quarterly*, **29**, pp. 74–92.

Wexley, K.N. (1984), 'Personnel Training', *Annual Review of Psychology*, **35**, pp. 519–51.

Wexley, K.N. and Timothy T. Baldwin (1986), 'Management Development', *Journal of Management*, **12**, pp. 277–94.

Zedeck, S. (ed.) (1992), *Work and Family Issues*, San Francisco: Jossey-Bass.

Zedeck, S. and Cascio, W.F. (1984), 'Psychological Issues in Personnel Decisions', *Annual Review of Psychology*, **35**, pp. 461–518.

Part I
Choosing the Skills

[1]

DO U.S. FIRMS UNDERINVEST IN HUMAN RESOURCES?

DETERMINANTS OF TRAINING IN THE WORLD AUTO INDUSTRY

JOHN PAUL MACDUFFIE
Wharton School, University of Pennsylvania

THOMAS A. KOCHAN
Massachusetts Institute of Technology

September 1993

It has now become commonplace to hear arguments that restoring the health of the U.S. economy and the competitiveness of American firms requires a major increase in investments in human resources (Cyert and Mowery, 1987; Marshall, 1987; Walton, 1987; Office of Technology Assessment, 1990) Indeed, it might be argued that issues of human resource strategy more than ever occupy a central and highly visible place in corporate strategy and in national policy debates.

Correspondingly, for some time academics have been urging human resource management researchers to move to a more strategic level of theory building and empirical research by investigating the determinants of human resource policies, their interrelationships with other aspects of organizational policy and practice, and their consequences for performance (Dyer, 1988; Fombrun, Tichy, and Devanna, 1984; Schuler, 1989; Kochan, Katz, and McKersie, 1986). Yet, to date, neither the increased visibility of human resources in national debates nor the calls for new approaches have produced a significant body of research that addresses the broad policy, theoretical, and empirical questions of interest.

This paper reports on one aspect of a research project that attempts to move in this direction. It investigates the often asserted but heretofore untested argument that U.S. firms underinvest in training and human resource development of workers relative to their key international competitors (Dertouzos, Solow, and Lester, 1989) and tests alternative explanations for the differences in cross-firm and cross-national training investments observed in the data.[1] We consider four hypotheses related to training differentials, two based on national-level characteristics and two that operate at the firm level; the firm-level hypotheses are valuable in explaining national variation to the extent that firm choices covary at the national level. Our data are drawn from an international sample of 70 automobile assembly plants collected as part of a long term international motor vehicle research project (Womack, Jones, and Roos, 1990).

In the following sections, we first set forth the four hypotheses, with particular emphasis on the hypothesis we favor -- that training investments are derived from the set of larger choices that firms make about their business/production strategy and overall human resource (HR) system. We develop the argument that in automotive assembly, training levels will be higher among firms choosing to adopt a "flexible production" strategy, which is more dependent on worker contributions to quality and continuous improvement than traditional mass production. We then elaborate on the "organizational logic" of flexible production and the role of training in such a production system. Next, we perform statistical analyses to see which of the four hypotheses best explains training differentials in the assembly plant sample. A final section then draws implications from our results for the broader human resource research and policy agenda.

POTENTIAL DETERMINANTS OF TRAINING

Why would we expect to see variations in the level of investment in training across firms and/or across national settings? We will consider four different explanations for this variation: 1) national-level comparative advantage with respect to human resources; 2) national-level cultural and/or institutional proclivities; 3) new or advanced technologies that require training for new skills; and 4) firm-level strategic choices about how to organize technical and human capabilities within an overall production system.

The macro-level competitiveness debates have done a rather good job in stating the basic comparative advantage proposition. Training is important to firms in the U.S. and other advanced economies because they cannot compete successfully with low wage countries on labor costs. Therefore, they must seek comparative advantage from product quality, flexibility, innovation, and product differentiation (Piore and Sabel, 1984), which in turn requires developing and utilizing a high quality labor force. The first hypothesis, therefore, is that firms in advanced industrial economies such as the U.S., Japan, and most of Western Europe would be expected to train

3

more than firms located in low wage newly-industrializing countries. Since the required skills are often highly firm-specific, this hypothesis would hold even if one assumes that a higher base of skills is provided by the educational system in these countries than in the low wage countries.[2]

But among advanced economies, why do we believe there is variation, and particularly variation that puts U.S. firms at a disadvantage? The second national-level hypothesis focuses on macro level differences in either "culture" or the broad features of the industrial relations system that emerge from a country's history and institutional context. Japan, for example, is argued to invest more because the decision by large Japanese firms to provide "lifetime employment" for its core employees makes labor a fixed rather than variable cost. This increases the benefit of human capital investments, particularly for firm-specific skills, and conversely, because seniority wages and internal promotion norms reduce the risk that training investments will be lost due to worker turnover. (Aoki, 1984; Koike, 1988; Shimada, 1983) Germany is said to invest more because of a national industrial and educational policy that provides apprenticeship training during the secondary school years to aid students with the school-to-work transition. (Casey, 1986; Streeck et al., 1987; Wever, Berg, and Kochan, 1992)

The third hypothesis operates at the industrial or firm level, and takes a "technological upgrading" view. The argument is that moving to high technology (either information technology in the office or robotics in the factory) will require more highly skilled "knowledge workers" who will in turn require high levels of training in order to capture the maximal benefits from the technology. (Adler, 1986) The opposite hypothesis -- that technological change leads to a net reduction in skills and hence a reduced need for training -- has also been advanced, as part of the "upskilling vs. downskilling" debate. (Attewell, 1987) Empirical evidence to date is generally inconclusive; automation results in some upskilling and some downskilling, across occupations and different industry contexts. (Cappelli, 1993; Attewell, 1992; Kelley, 1990) These findings have stimulated a variety of contingency versions of the hypothesis that technology is the driving force for training investments, giving a large role to the strategic choices made by the firm about how technology should be utilized and managed.[3]

The fourth hypothesis operates at the level of the firm and suggests that training investments are dependent on firm-level choices about business and production strategy rather than exogenous factors such as macro-economic context, national culture, or new technologies. This hypothesis draws upon what business strategy researchers call the "resource-based view of the firm" (Teece, Pisano, and Shuen, 1990), and provides a valuable way to conceptualize the strategic role of human resources. (Cappelli and Singh, 1993) From this perspective, business and production strategies emerge from (and henceforth influence the development of) a firm's "core capabilities" -- the knowledge of products and processes and relationships with suppliers and customers that convey sustainable competitive advantage. These capabilities are grounded in the firm-specific skills of employees, which provides an incentive for both on-the-job and off-the-job training.

It also draws on two other perspectives found in recent literature on the link between human resource practices and economic performance: 1) that "bundles" of interdependent HR practices, rather than individual practices, are the appropriate level of analysis for understanding the link to performance; (Arthur, 1992; Cutcher-Gershenfeld, 1991) and 2) that these HR "bundles" or systems must be integrated with the firm's business strategy to be effective. (Majchrzak, 1988; Kochan, Cutcher-Gershenfeld, and MacDuffie, 1991; Snell and Dean, 1992). Combining these viewpoints, the fourth hypothesis asserts that the level of training is derived from the requirements of the overall business/production strategy and the broad "bundle" or system of HR policies -- beyond training -- adopted by the firm.

In the context of the automotive industry, we argue that changes in manufacturing strategies from mass production to flexible production bring with them the need for much greater investments in human capabilities. Thus firms using flexible production systems tend to implement "bundles" of HR practices to generate the skill and motivation the production system needs. (MacDuffie, 1993) A high investment in training is likely to be part of the HR system that complements flexible production. From this perspective, as firms move towards flexible production, they will have a greater incentive to invest in training, irrespective of the national context or level of technology. We will develop this hypothesis below by describing the "organizational logic" of flexible production in the automotive industry -- the context for this study -- and the role of training under this production strategy.

THE "ORGANIZATIONAL LOGIC" OF FLEXIBLE PRODUCTION

Flexible production organizes both technical capabilities and human capabilities differently than mass production, with direct implications for training. The "organizational logic" of flexible production <u>reduces</u> the technical system's ability to function in the face of contingencies (problem conditions) through the minimization of buffers of all kinds -- thus reducing slack, increasing task interdependence, and raising the visibility of problems -- and <u>expands</u> human capabilities, so that people can deal effectively with these problem conditions and achieve improvements in the production system.

Under mass production, the realization of economies of scale is of paramount importance, so buffers (e.g. extra inventories or repair space) are added to the production system to protect against potential disruptions, such as sales fluctuations, supply interruptions, and equipment breakdowns. Such buffers are seen as costly under flexible production because they hide production problems. As long as inventory stocks are high, a defective part has no impact on production, because it can simply be scrapped and replaced with another part. But when inventories are very low, as with a Just-in-Time inventory system, a bad part can cause the production system to grind to a halt, creating a tremendous incentive to improve parts quality. The minimization of buffers serves a cybernetic or feedback function, providing valuable information about production problems for improvement activities. (Ono, 1988; Schonberger, 1982)

Under the philosophy of continuous improvement that characterizes flexible production, problems identified through the minimization of buffers are seen as opportunities for organizational learning[4] (Ono, 1988; Imai, 1986). Ongoing problem-solving processes on the shop floor, alternating between experimentation with procedural change and the careful standardization of each improved method, yield a steady stream of incremental improvements. (Tyre and Orlikowski, 1992) In a sense, the "buffering" capability to cope with change shifts from the technical system to the human system. (Adler, 1992; Cole, 1992; MacDuffie, 1991)

Implementing this continuous improvement philosophy requires a multiskilled and committed workforce. In order to identify and resolve quality problems as they appear, workers must have both a conceptual grasp of the production process and the analytical skills to identify the root cause of problems. To develop such skills and knowledge, flexible production utilizes a variety of multiskilling practices, including work teams, quality circles, job rotation within a few broad job classifications, and the decentralization of quality responsibilities from specialized inspectors to production workers. Furthermore, to insure that workers are motivated to contribute the attentiveness and analytical perspective necessary for effective problem-solving, flexible production is characterized by such "high commitment" human resource policies as employment security; compensation that is partially contingent on performance and a reduction of status barriers between managers and workers. (Shimada and MacDuffie, 1986)

TRAINING UNDER FLEXIBLE PRODUCTION

Unlike mass production, which is premised on the assumption that production work involves little skill and requires little training, flexible production sees production workers as skilled problem-solvers who must be adequately prepared for their task through effective training. One consequence is that flexible production requires a high level of competency in reading, math, reasoning, and communication skills. If the existence of these skills is not reliably guaranteed by the public educational system, flexible production plants are likely to screen carefully for these skills, or to provide remedial training. (Sako, 1992) Under mass production, these skills are rarely established as criteria for production jobs.

Under flexible production, the majority of training in technical skills is carried out by the firm, through a lengthy period of on-the-job training (OJT). (Koike, 1988) In contrast, mass production firms tend to provide off-the-job technical training in classroom settings, often provided by equipment vendors or corporate staff. These latter firms view the classroom approach as superior to OJT, which under mass production has traditionally had a connotation of brief, informal training, e.g. a new hire who is given a few hours of instruction from a co-worker and then "learns the ropes" through unstructured observation and imitation. By comparison, OJT in flexible production plants involves trainers who work intensively with new hires, at first demonstrating, then coaching, and who stay on the shop floor after initial training to show workers how to handle non-routine problem conditions. (Ford, 1986)

This approach to OJT is a very effective way to convey tacit knowledge about jobs, and leads to high retention of knowledge, both because of its experiential approach and because individuals acquire skills very close to the time when they will need to use them. OJT continues as employees move across jobs through job rotation or promotion. Only after an individual reaches a relatively high-level of skill does more advanced "off-the-job" classroom training take place. Advanced technical training is provided to all employees rather than some, and matched to the existing skill base of the individual -- a customized process that the firm is in a much better position to carry out than outside educational institutions because of its proximity to task requirements and employee needs, and its generally superior technical expertise. (Cole, 1992).

Finally, training in these flexible production plants aims to teach not only substantive knowledge but also processes of problem-solving and learning. (Imai, 1986; Lillrank and Kano, 1990) This is conveyed through the modeling behavior of employees who already thoroughly understand these processes and the broader production system. Furthermore, this training, together with policies of employment continuity, reinforce the message that the firm is willing to invest heavily in its employees. Thus the largely intra-firm approach to training bolsters the cultural norms of reciprocal obligation that help maintain employee commitment and motivation under flexible production. (Dore, 1992)

Thus, having a workforce that is multiskilled, adaptable to rapidly changing circumstances, and with broad conceptual knowledge about the production system is critical to the operation of a flexible production system. The learning process that generates these human capabilities is an integral part of how the production system functions, not a separate training activity. This implies that the demand for training is a function of the extent to which a flexible production system, which is heavily dependent on workforce skills, is deployed. It further implies that the alternate mass production logic may not be associated with high levels of training because it is designed to operate at a much lower threshold of workforce skill.

COMPETING HYPOTHESES

The four competing hypotheses on training we are testing can be summarized as follows:

H1. Investments in training result from national comparative advantage with respect to human resources. Specifically, firms in the advanced industrial economies (U.S., Japan, and most of Western Europe) that cannot compete on the basis of low labor costs will invest more in training than "low wage" newly-industralized countries.

H2. Investments in training result from the education/training institutional infrastructure that exists in different countries for cultural and/or historical reasons. Specifically, firms located in Japan and Germany (among other European countries) will invest more in training than firms located in the U.S. and newly-industrialized countries.

H3. Investments in training result from the extent to which the firm has implemented advanced automation. Specifically, firms with higher levels of robotics will invest more in training than firms with fewer or no robots.

H4. Investments in training are an interrelated part of the firm's choices about business/ production strategy and the overall human resource system. Specifically, firms that utilize a flexible production system will invest more in training than firms that utilize a mass production system.

As noted above, we favor the fourth hypothesis, but expect that there may be partial support for multiple hypotheses. Thus it is worth noting what kind of evidence would disconfirm each of these hypotheses. The sample consists entirely of auto assembly plants, which controls for industry and for the basic technology and complexity of the production task (compared with auto component plants or production tasks from other industries). To disconfirm the first hypothesis, assembly plants in newly-industrialized countries must train as much or more than assembly plants in the advanced industrialized countries. It would also weaken, but not disconfirm, the first hypothesis if substantial training differentials exist within the advanced industrialized countries. To disconfirm the second hypothesis, plants in the U.S. or in newly industrialized countries must train as much or more than plants in Japan or Germany (Europe). Disconfirming the third hypothesis would require that plants without robots train as much or more than plants with robots. It would weaken but not disconfirm this hypothesis if plants with equal amounts of robots trained different amounts. Finally, disconfirming the fourth hypothesis would require that traditional mass production plants train as much or more than flexible production plants.

Under certain conditions, these hypotheses overlap. If training varies for reasons that apply at the national level of analysis (H1 and H2) but the firm-level variables of automation and type of production organization (H3 and H4) also covary at a national level, it will be difficult to say which factor is responsible for the differences in training level. But to the degree that there is high variation in both dependent and independent variables within regions, distinguishing among these hypotheses will be much simpler.

EMPIRICAL EVIDENCE

Sample and Variables

Our data are from the International Assembly Plant Study, carried out through the International Motor Vehicle Program at M.I.T. This survey of 70 assembly plants from 24 companies in 17 countries worldwide sought to uncover the determinants of manufacturing performance, defined as labor productivity (hours per vehicle) and quality (defects per 100 vehicles). Details on this study, including the methodology for these outcome measures and the operationalization of control variables, can be found in Krafcik, 1988; Krafcik and MacDuffie, 1989; MacDuffie, 1991; and MacDuffie and Krafcik, 1992. Here only the main dependent and independent variables will be described in detail. Data analyses are carried out for the 57 plants in the sample for which we have complete data for these variables.

Training Effort. This dependent variable is based on the number of hours of off-the-job and on-the-job training received by new and experienced (over 1 year of employment) production workers. These are the employees most likely to receive different training treatment in the different situations captured by the four hypotheses -- particularly in auto assembly, where production work has traditionally been seen as unskilled (or marginally semi-skilled) work requiring little training. Since new hires typically receive much more training than experienced production workers receive annually, training hours for these two groups are standardized by conversion to z-scores before being added together to form the Training Effort measure. To aid interpretability, the summed z-scores are rescaled so that 0 represents the plant with the lowest training effort in the sample, and 100 the plant with the highest effort.

One caveat with an effort-based measure of training is that more training is not always better than less training. The Training Effort measure does not distinguish between different topics or different methods of training. As such, it measures only overall training effort and cannot address questions about what kinds of training in what areas are most effective.

Production Organization Measures. To operationalize the "organizational logic" of flexible and mass production systems, two measures related to a plant's production organization are developed: Use of Buffers and HR System. Each is an index made up of multiple variables, described below, that are standardized by conversion to z-scores before being additively combined. Each index is then transformed for easier interpretability, on a scale from 0 to 100 where 0 is the plant with the lowest score in the sample and 100 the plant with the highest score. Reliability tests for each index show a Cronbach's alpha score of .63 for Use of Buffers and .80 for HR System.

i) Use of Buffers: This index measures a set of production practices that are indicative of overall production philosophy with respect to buffers (e.g. incoming and work-in-process inventory), with a low score signifying a "buffered" system and a high score signifying a "lean" system. It consists of three items:

* the space (in square feet) dedicated to final assembly repair, as a percentage of total assembly area square footage

* the average number of vehicles held in the work-in-process buffer between the paint and assembly areas, as a percentage of one shift production

* the average level of inventory stocks, in days for a sample of eight key parts, weighted by the cost of each part.

ii) HR System: This index captures how work is organized, in terms of both formal work structures and the allocation of work responsibilities, the participation of employees in production-related problem-solving activity, and HR policies that affect the "psychological contract" between the employee and the organization, and hence employee motivation and commitment. A low score for this index indicates an HR system that is "low-skill" and "low-commitment" in orientation, while a high score indicates a "multiskilling", "high-commitment" orientation. It consists of seven different items:

* the percentage of the workforce involved in "on-line" work teams and "off-line" employee involvement groups.

* the number of production-related suggestions received per employee and the percentage implemented.

* the extent of job rotation within and across teams.

  (0 = no job rotation, 1 = infrequent rotation within teams, 2 = frequent rotation within teams, 3 = frequent rotation within teams and across teams of the same department, 4 = frequent rotation within teams, across teams and across departments.);

* the degree to which production workers carry out quality tasks.

  (0=functional specialists responsible for all quality responsibilities; 1, 2, 3, 4 = production workers responsible for 1,2 ,3 or 4 of the following tasks: inspection of incoming parts, work-in-process, finished products; gathering Statistical Process Control data).

* the hiring criteria used to select employees in three categories: production workers, first line supervisors, and engineers.

  (the sum of rankings of the importance of various hiring criteria for these three groups of employees, with low scores for criteria that emphasize the fit between an applicant's existing skills and job requirements ("previous experience in a similar job") and high scores for criteria that emphasize openness to learning and interpersonal skills ("a willingness to learn new skills" and "ability to work with others")

* the extent to which compensation system is contingent upon performance.

   (0 = no contingent compensation; 1 = compensation contingent on corporate performance; 2 = compensation contingent on plant performance, for managers only; 3 = compensation contingent on plant performance or skills acquired, production employees only; and 4 = compensation contingent on plant performance, all employees.)

* the extent to which status barriers between managers and workers are present.

   (0 = no implementation of policies that break down status barriers and 1,2,3,4 = implementation of 1,2,3, or 4 of these policies: common uniform, common cafeteria, common parking, no ties);

Robotic Index. This variable indicates the extent to which advanced technology is used in a plant. It measures the number of robots, defined as programmable equipment with at least three axes of movement, in the weld, paint, and assembly departments of an assembly plant, adjusted for plant scale. This is one of two alternate technology variables used in the larger study. The other, Total Automation, covers the entire automation stock of a plant, measuring the percentage of direct production steps in the welding, paint, and assembly areas that are automated. While Total Automation is more comprehensive, it does not distinguish the age or type (e.g. programmable vs. dedicated) of automation. Thus the Robotic Index is more appropriate for testing the technology hypothess, given that training needs are said to increase most when new, programmable technology is implemented. [5]

Control Variables. Four other measures of the plant's production system are used here as controls. **Plant Scale** is defined as the average number of vehicles built during a standard, non-overtime day, adjusted for capacity utilization. **Model Mix Complexity** measures the mix of different products and product variants produced in the plant. It includes the number of distinct

platforms, models. body styles, drive train configurations (front-wheel vs. rear-wheel drive), and

export variations (right-hand vs. left-hand steering). The **Parts Complexity** index includes three

measures of parts variation -- the number of engine/transmission combinations, wire harnesses,

and exterior paint colors -- that affect the sequencing of vehicles, the task variability facing

production workers, and material handling requirements; and three measures -- the number of

total parts to the assembly area, the percentage of common parts across models, and the number

of suppliers to the assembly area -- that affect the administrative/coordination requirements for

dealing with suppliers. **Product Design Age.** is the weighted average number of years since a

major model change introduction for each of the products currently being built at each plant, and

serves as a partial proxy for manufacturability in the assembly area, under the assumption that

products designed more recently are more likely to have been conceived with ease of assembly

in mind than older products.

Table 1 and Table 2 about here

Regional Differences in Training Effort

Table 1 shows regional means for actual training hours for newly-hired and experienced

production workers. and Table 2 shows regional means for the Training Effort index, together with

the results of t-tests for statistically signficant differences in scores for this dependent variable.[6]

These latter means provide the basis for evaluating the first two hypotheses concerning national-

level training differentials. Plants in the Newly-Industrialized Countries train more than U.S.-

owned plants in North America and than plants in Australia, suggesting that the hypothesis linking

higher levels of training to advanced industrialized economies is not supported. The very high differentials in training effort among the three most industrialized groups of plants (in the U.S., Europe, and Japan) calls both the first and second hypotheses into question.[7] This variation suggests that the determinants of training go well beyond wage rates, since wage differentials among the U.S., Japan, and Europe are much less than the training differentials.

Examination of Japanese-owned plants in North America and U.S.-owned plants in Europe also challenges the hypothesis that the national infrastructure for education and training determines training levels, since both sets of "transplants" offer different amounts of training than locally-owned plants; the J/NA plants train more than US/NA plants, and US/Eur plants train less than Eur/Eur plants. Another sign that training differentials reflect firm-level rather than national-level factors is the lack of significant difference in training effort between J/J and J/NA plants and between U.S./NA and U.S./Eur plants. These findings suggest that H1 and H2 are not supported, although a full test of national-level factors requires controls for other variables, as below.

Tables 3 and 4 about here

Regression Analyses

Table 3 contains descriptive statistics and Table 4 reports the results of regression analyses with the Training Effort index as the dependent variable. The first equation is the "base case" for testing firm-level hypotheses. It tests the third hypothesis directly, by including the Robotic Index and the four control variables. Equations 2-4 test the fourth hypothesis about flexible production systems, in three stages. Equations 2 and 3 test for the direct effects of the two production organization indices: first adding the Use of Buffers index and then adding the HR System index. Equation 4 tests the claim that these two aspects of the production system are integrated by adding a "Buffers by HR System" interaction term. Equation 5 then adds dummy variables for the regional groups identified in Tables 1 and 2, to see whether they have significant explanatory power when controlling for the other variables; the U.S.-owned plants in North America dummy variable is omitted to make it the comparison group.[8]

The first equation has an adjusted R^2 of .029 and is not statistically significant. Coefficients for the Robotic Index and the control variables are indistinguishable from zero. This disconfirms Hypothesis 3 about the relationship between advanced automation and training effort. Clearly, plants with similar levels of robotics have very different training policies. The second equation, including the Use of Buffers index, has an adjusted R^2 of .095 and is statistically significant; the index is significant at the 95% confidence level and has the expected sign, with more training associated with smaller buffers of inventory and repair space, consistent with the hypothesis about flexible production.

The third equation adding the other production organization index, HR System, has an adjusted R^2 of .199, a significant increase from Equation 2. With HR System and Use of Buffers both in the equation, only the former index is significant, at the 99% confidence level. This is not surprising, given the high correlation (r = .64) between the two indices. This finding is also consistent with evidence from other analyses (not presented here) that some plants begin the transition to flexible production by reducing buffers but do not make corresponding changes in their HR policies (at least initially.)

Equation 4 includes the interaction term, Buffers by HR System, to test whether the hypothesized integration of production policies and HR policies helps explain training levels better than the individual indices. The adjusted R^2 of this equation is .237, which represents a statistically significant increase over Equation 3. Here only the interaction term is statistically significant (at the 95% significance level) and the individual indices are not. This is strongly supportive of the integration and bundling arguments about flexible production, and provides the strongest evidence confirming Hypothesis 4.

Finally, Equation 5, which includes the regional dummy variables, has an adjusted R^2 of .38, which is a statistically significant increase over Equation 4. The Buffers by HR System interaction term retains the same significance level. Of the regional dummy variables, only those for European-owned plants in Europe and for Newly-Industrialized Countries are significant, with positive coefficients. In other words, both of these regional groups provide higher levels of training than their approach to the production system -- closer to mass production than flexible production -- would predict. But the regional dummies for Japanese-owned plants, both in Japan and in North America, U.S.-owned plants in Europe, and Australian plants are not significant once controls for the production system are included. The Japanese-owned plants appear to train a lot because they rely heavily on flexible production, while the U.S.-owned plants in Europe and the Australian plants appear to train very little because they follow traditional mass production practices and philosophies.

These results provide some limited support for the view that differences in national practices affect the level of training, even aside from differences in production systems. In Europe, in particular, many countries have strong public policy support for extensive training, with the German apprenticeship model as the most notable example. But European plants have not, for the most part, moved very far towards the implementation of flexible production principles. One explanation is that the volume producers in Europe (Volkswagen, Fiat, Renault) have used the past fifteen years to move closer to the high volume, standard product approach of mass production -- a goal that proved elusive in earlier years, when production volumes were low and craft methods more strongly entrenched. (Womack et al., 1990) So the education and training infrastructure in European countries may help produce an ample **supply** of skills in the workforce but the **demand** for the skills is limited due to following mass production principles. The one caveat to this interpretation, as noted above, is the low level of training by U.S.-owned plants in

Europe. Perhaps these plants are bound by corporate policies set in the U.S., and are exempted from (or resistant to) instititutional pressures in their host countries to boost training. This finding requires further investigation.

The case of the Newly-Industrialized Countries is equally intriguing. Plants in these low-wage countries, where absenteeism and turnover are typically high, are not expected to offer much training. However, this finding is consistent with observations that some auto assembly plants in these countries, particularly Mexico and Korea, have achieved quality (if not productivity) levels comparable to those in the advanced industrialized countries, and that they have been willing to make unusually high investments in training (if not wages) to be able to achieve these results. (Womack et al., 1990) It would be valuable to know more about the decisions to invest in training -- whether these firms believe that they will recoup some of the cost in lower turnover, greater attentiveness to quality, and a higher level of work effort, or whether they are given incentives to train by national governments as part of an economic development policy.

CONCLUSIONS AND IMPLICATIONS

These results support the popular hypothesis that U.S. firms do invest less in the development of human resources than their Japanese and European competitors. Moreover, this gap will not be automatically closed by greater investments in high technology. Training levels have virtually no relationship with the level of technology in these assembly plants, nor with a plant's scale, product mix, or parts complexity. Instead, these results suggest two factors that drive investments in training -- the production strategy employed by the organization and some characteristics of the national environment of the parent firm.

The significance of the production organization indices, both separately and in interaction, suggests that one way to encourage training in U.S. firms is to support the diffusion of flexible production models that demand greater training. This raises a variety of issues about supply vs. demand for skills and training. The case of Europe shows that the presence of relatively high levels of training is not automatically associated with the adoption of flexible production systems. So public policies that boost the supply of skills through mandated training, in the absence of action by firms to adopt new approaches to organizing work, may not improve the demand (and hence utilization) of skills. On the other hand, if firms move towards flexible production and are not able to find an adequate supply of workers with the necessary skills in reading, math, and analytical problem-solving, the implementation of new work structures may be slowed or firms may have to assume the cost of remedial training.

This analysis suggests that the provision of a high level of basic skills through the public education system (and the related institutions of adult education) should be the top priority of U.S. public policy in the training area. Beyond that, public policy should focus on encouraging the demand for skills. For example, any government incentives or subsidies for training could be made contingent on firms changing their approach to organizing work and their human resource policies. In addition, the federal government could promote workplace models that both develop human capabilities (through training and new work structures) and strive to retain skilled employees through appropriate incentive systems and employment continuity policies.

While public policy may be able to encourage the adoption of new ways of organizing work, this analysis implies that firm choices about business and/or production strategy will still be the primary determinant of training effort. The example of Japanese-owned plants in North America and U.S.-owned plants in Europe, both of which train at very different levels than other plants located in the same region, reveals how strong the influence of corporate-wide training policies is, compared with national-level institutional pressures.

Competing forces will determine whether corporate strategies towards training in the auto industry are likely to change in coming years. Since 1989, when these data were collected, a number of factors have caused U.S. auto firms to boost their training. The presence of joint training funds established through collective bargaining between each of the Big Three and the UAW has guaranteed a steady flow of funding for training production workers and skilled trades. (Ferman, Hoyman, Cutcher-Gershenfeld, and Savoie, 1990) The U.S. companies have also been influenced by the success of the Japanese transplants, whose use of flexible production and high training investment has been widely publicized. In addition, there is a widespread perception that the "high-tech" strategy used by General Motors in the mid-1980s failed to boost plant performance because few changes were made in production strategy and human resource policies to complement the technology investment.

However, there is reason to question whether recent rhetoric about increased training from the U.S. auto companies will result in sustained investments in training over time. Training effort in the U.S., even in companies that train heavily, is typically closely related to corporate profitability. This is due in part to accounting conventions that treat training as a variable cost rather than as an investment, so that cutbacks in training have an immediate positive impact on the bottom line. Current economic conditions in the industry favor training, with the Big Three enjoying a resurgence in sales and market share, due to the adoption of flexible production methods that have improved quality and efficiency, attractive new products, the dominance of high-demand market segments (e.g. minivans) and pricing restraint at a time when exchange rates are forcing Japanese competitors to raise prices. But training plans are still often scaled back in the face of production deadlines and financial pressures. While joint training funds with the union have institutionalized auto industry training to some degree, these funds came close to depletion during the 1991-92 industry turndown. The next period of financial difficulty will provide the best test of whether or not the U.S. auto companies are truly commited to adopting flexible production systems, with their high training requirements.

European and Japanese company policies towards training should also be instructive to observe in the coming years. Japanese companies are facing extreme difficulties, due to a slump in their domestic market, overinvestments in new plant capacity, difficulties in finding and retaining production workers, and widespread criticisms of the social costs of flexible production (e.g. traffic congestion from Just-in-Time inventory deliveries, long working hours and high levels of overtime due to "no buffer" staffing policies). These conditions and the accompanying financial losses (including the first assembly plant closing since WWII) are putting considerable pressure on the "lifetime employment" policy of the large auto companies, which supports high levels of training by insuring that training investments are not lost through employee turnover. It is not clear yet whether Japanese companies will reverse either their commitment to flexible production or their high levels of training in the face of these pressures. At least at their U.S. facilities, companies such as Honda have reacted to slumping sales by resisting layoffs and **boosting** worker training.

European companies are also confronted with slack market demand, but otherwise face very different conditions than U.S. and Japanese companies. The success of Japanese plants, first in the U.S. and more recently in the U.K., and of Japanese entries into the luxury market have convinced many European companies (and unions) that they are seriously uncompetitive in manufacturing performance and must make the transition to flexible production as soon as possible. Here the high level of training in European companies is regarded as an important asset that might speed the transition process, particularly compared to U.S. companies that train much less. If this proves to be true, it will no doubt influence the training debate within the U.S. Thus the actions of Japanese and European firms, as well as U.S. firms, will reveal much about the future determinants of training effort in this competitive and turbulent international industry.

NOTES

1. We will use the term "cross-national" in this paper to include both comparisons across individual countries (e.g. U.S. vs. Japan) and across regional groupings of countries (e.g. Europe vs. Newly Industrialized Countries).

2. From this perspective, one should expect the educational system of the advanced industrialized countries to produce graduates with a high level of basic skills that can then be further developed through firm training. Given the current furor about the problems of the U.S. educational system, it is clear that this hypothesis does not always hold. Nevertheless, with respect to training, this hypothesis would anticipate an even higher level of training in order to compensate for any deficits in the educational system. This leaves unresolved the claim by some U.S. companies that the poor educational system prevents them from finding the skilled employees necessary for the high value-added strategy.

3. Two variants of this contingency view are important here, but they are difficult to untangle empirically. The first variant hypothesizes that technology does have some determinant effect on skill requirements and training, i.e. all firms that increase automation levels also increase training, even though at any given level of technology, some firms may choose to train more than others. The second variant rejects the idea of any technological determinism and hypothesizes that managerial choice about organizational structure, work organization, and control systems alone will affect skill requirements and hence training, i.e. that firms increasing their automation level are as likely to decrease skill requirements (and training) as to increase them. The dilemma empirically is how to distinguish between situations where firms reduce training despite automation that does increase skill requirements from situations where more automation reduces both skill levels and training. The former situation could be attributed to managerial incompetence or ideology, and could be distinguished from the latter over time by mortality rates, on the presumption that such firms will be less competitive than firms that use the technology more wisely. Objective measures of skill as well as measures of training and performance would be needed to distinguish between these variants.

4. This philosophy has become institutionalized in a problem-solving procedure known as the "five whys", in which one identifies the "root cause" of a problem by asking repeatedly what lies behind its most immediately obvious manifestations. The false starts and dead ends that are part of the search for the "root cause" are seen as valuable in themselves, to develop broad knowledge about the overall production system. (Cole, 1992)

5. The two measures are very highly correlated ($r = .81$), since plants with above-average scores for Total Automation have generally directed most of their recent technology investment towards robotic technology. The results reported below, using the Robotic Index variable, are nearly identical when the Total Automation measure is used.

6. Examination of the distribution of the Training Effort variable shows that five plants are outliers above the sample mean -- two Japanese-owned plants in Japan; one European-owned plant in Europe; and two plants in Newly-Industrialized Countries. These outliers account for the high standard deviation for these three regional groupings, and undoubtedly affect the regional means as well. Since we have no reason to believe that the data from these plants are incorrect, we judged that it was better to include them when calculating the sample mean, rather than excluding

them. We do test to see whether the outliers affect the regression analyses, as reported below.

7. While there is variation with the group of plants in Europe, it appears to be based on the company rather than the country. This is particularly striking with respect to Germany, which is often described as having very high levels of training. The two German plants in the sample train less than some plants in France, Belgium, Sweden, and Italy. Indeed, the level of variation within many of the regional groupings is impressively high. The standard deviation for Japanese-owned plants in Japan is higher than that for European-owned plants in Europe, even though both groups have outlier plants, as indicated in note #6.

8. Due to the presence of outliers in the distribution of training effort, these analyses were repeated using log training effort as the dependent variable. The results were unchanged.

TABLE 1

Regional Means for Training Hours for Production Workers

	Jpn/Jpn	Jpn/NA	US/NA	US/Eur	Eur/Eur	NIC	Aust
Newly-Hired Production Workers (hours in first 6 months)	364	225	42	43	178	260	40
Experienced Production Workers (hours per year for those with over 1 year of experience)	76	52	31	34	52	46	15
n	8	4	14	4	10	11	6

Jpn/Jpn =   Japanese-owned plants in Japan

Jpn/NA =   Japanese-owned plants in North America

US/NA =   U.S.-owned plants in North America

US/Eur =   U.S.-owned plants in Europe

Eur/Eur =   European-owned plants in Europe

NIC =   Newly-Industrialized Countries (Korea, Mexico, Taiwan, Brazil)

Aust =   Australia

TABLE 2

Regional Means for Training Effort Index

(Sum of z-scores for training hours for new & experienced production workers,
rescaled from 0 to 100)

Region	Mean	S.D.	n
Japanese-owned plants in Japan (Jpn/Jpn)	$49.1^{3,4,7}$	28.6	8
Japanese-owned plants in N. Amer. (Jpn/NA)	$31.5^{3,4,7}$	8.2	4
U.S.-owned plants in N. America (US/NA)	$12.5^{1,2,5,6}$	8.0	14
U.S.-owned plants in Europe (US/Eur)	$13.6^{1,2}$	12.7	4
European-owned plants in Europe (Eur/Eur)	$28.5^{3,7}$	20.8	10
All Newly Industrialized Country plants (NIC)	$31.0^{3,7}$	31.8	11
All Australian plants (Aust)	$6.0^{1,2,5,6}$	3.9	6

1 = Mean significantly different from Japanese-owned plants in Japan

2 = Mean significantly different from Japanese-owned plants in N. America

3 = Mean significantly different from U.S.-owned plants in N. America

4 = Mean significantly different from U.S.-owned plants in Europe

5 = Mean significantly different from European-owned plants in Europe

6 = Mean significantly different from NIC plants

7 = Mean significantly different from Australian plants

Significance level for all t-tests is $p < .05$.

TABLE 3

Descriptive Statistics for Regression Analyses
(n=57)

Variable	Mean	S.D.
Training Effort	24.7	23.7
Scale	936	651
Model Mix Complexity	30.6	21.2
Parts Complexity	56.5	23.5
Product Design Age	4.7	3.3
Robotic Index	2.2	2.0
Use of Buffers	58.7	22.4
HR System	33.6	26.3
Buffers by HR System	371.3	626.4
Jpn/Jpn dummy	0.14	0.35
Jpn/NA dummy	0.07	0.26
US/Eur dummy	0.07	0.26
Eur/Eur dummy	0.17	0.38
NIC dummy	0.19	0.40
Australia dummy	0.10	0.31

TABLE 4

Regression Model for Training in the Automobile Industry
(standard error in parentheses)

Variable	1	2	3	4	5
Scale	.008 (.006)	.005 (.006)	.007 (.005)	.007 (.006)	.002 (.005)
ModelMix Complexity	.129 (.170)	.021 (.171)	.018 (.161)	.034 (.157)	.066 (.158)
Parts Complexity	-.124 (.176)	-.077 (.171)	-.151 (.163)	-.204 (.162)	-0.369** (.173)
AgeCar	-1.46 (1.13)	.004 (1.28)	-.318 (1.21)	-.545 (1.18)	-1.89 (1.21)
Robotic Index	.432 (2.01)	.536 (1.94)	-1.50 (1.97)	-1.58 (1.92)	-1.18 (2.08)
Use of Buffers	---	.384** (.176)	.076 (.199)	.112 (.196)	.231 (.202)
HR System	---	---	.422*** (.154)	.206 (.191)	.105 (.220)
Buffers by HRSys	---	---	---	.012** (.006)	.016** (.008)
Jpn/Jpn Dum	---	---	---	---	1.53 (22.9)
Jpn/NA Dum	---	---	---	---	-2.03 (14.8)
U.S./Eur Dum	---	---	---	---	11.6 (12.4)
Eur/Eur Dum	---	---	---	---	26.7*** (9.7)
NICDum	---	---	---	---	21.9*** (9.3)
AustDum	---	---	---	---	-11.9 (10.5)
Adj. R^2	.029	.095	.199	.237	.380
F for equation	1.3	2.0*	2.9***	3.2***	3.5***
F for change in R^2 from preceding equation	---	4.8**	7.5***	3.4*	2.9**

* = Statistically significant at .10 level; ** = statistically significant at .05 level; *** = statistically significant at .01 level

References

Adler, Paul S. 1986. "New Technologies, New Skills." California Management Review 29: 9-28.

Adler, Paul S. 1992. "The 'Learning Bureaucracy': New United Motor Manufacturing, Inc." In Research in Organizational Behavior, edited by Barry M. Staw and Larry L. Cummings. Greenwich, CT: JAI Press.

Aoki, Masahiko. 1984. "Aspects of the Japanese Firm." In The Economic Analysis of the Japanese Firm, edited by Mashiko Aoki, pp. 259-64. Amsterdam: North Holland.

Attewell, Paul. 1987. "The Deskilling Controversy." Work and Occupations 14 (3):323-46.

Attewell, Paul. 1992. "Skill and Occupational Changes in U.S. Manufacturing." In Technology and the Future of Work, edited by Paul S. Adler, pp. 46-88. New York: Oxford University Press.

Arthur, Jeffrey B. 1992. "The Link Between Business Strategy and Industrial Relations Systems in American Steel Minimills." Industrial and Labor Relations Review 45: 488-506.

Cappelli, Peter. 1993. "Are Skill Requirements Rising? Evidence from Production and Clerical Jobs." Industrial and Labor Relations Review 46: 515-530.

Cappelli, Peter and Harbir Singh. 1992. "Integrating Strategic Human Resources and Strategic Management." In Research Frontiers in Industrial Relations, edited by Peter Sherer, David Lewin, and Olivia Mitchell, pp. 165-192. Madison, WI: Industrial Relations Research Association series.

Casey, Bernard. 1986. "The Dual Apprenticeship System and the Recruitment and Retention of Young Persons in West Germany." British Journal of Industrial Relations (March).

Cole, Robert A.. 1992. "Issues in Skill Formation and Training in Japanese Manufacturing." In Technology and the future of work, edited by Paul S. Adler, pp. 187-209. New York: Oxford University Press.

Cutcher-Gershenfeld, Joel. 1991. "The Impact on Economic Performance of a Transformation in Workplace Relations." Industrial and Labor Relations Review 44: 241-260.

Cyert, Richard M. and David C. Mowery 1986. Technology and Employment. Washington, D.C.: National Academy Press.

Dertouzos, Michael, Robert Solow, and Richard Lester. 1989. Made in America. Cambridge: MIT Press.

Dore, Ronald P. 1992. "Japan's Version of Managerial Capitalism." In Transforming Organizations, edited by Thomas A. Kochan and Michael Useem, pp. 17-27. New York: Oxford University Press.

Dyer, Lee. 1988. "A Strategic Perspective on Human Resource Management." In Human Resource Management: Evolving Roles and Responsibilities, edited by Lee Dyer, pp 1-35. Washington, D.C.: BNA Books.

Ferman, Louis A., Michele Hoyman, Joel Cutcher-Gershenfeld, and Ernest J. Savoie, eds. 1990. New Developments in Worker Training: A Legacy for the 1990s. Madison, WI: IRRA.

Fombrun, Charles, Noel M. Tichy, and Mary Anne Devanna. 1984. Strategic Human Resource Management. New York: Wiley.

29

Ford, G. W. 1986. Learning from Japan: The Concept of Skill Formation. <u>Australian Bulletin of Labor</u> 12 (2):119-127.

Imai, Kenichi. 1986. <u>Kaizen</u>. New York: Free Press.

Kelley, Mary Ellen. 1990. "New Process Technology, Job Design, and Work Organization: A Contingency Model." <u>American Sociological Review</u> 55: 191-208.

Kochan, Thomas A., Harry C. Katz, and Robert McKersie. 1986. <u>The Transformation of American Industrial Relations</u>. New York: Basic Books.

Kochan, Thomas A., Joel Cutcher-Gershenfeld, and John Paul MacDuffie. 1991. "Employee Participation, Work Redesign, and New Technology: Implications for Manufacturing and Engineering Practice." In <u>Handbook of Industrial Engineering</u>, second edition, edited by Gavriel Salvendy, pp. 798-814. New York: John Wiley.

Koike, Kazuo 1988. <u>Understanding Industrial Relations in Modern Japan</u>. London: MacMillan Press.

Krafcik, John F. 1988. "Comparative Analysis of Performance Indicators at World Auto Assembly Plants." Unpublished masters' thesis, Sloan School of Management, M.I.T.

Krafcik, John F. and John Paul MacDuffie. 1989. "Explaining High Performance Manufacturing: The International Assembly Plant Study." Working Paper, International Motor Vehicle Program, M.I.T.

Lillrank, Paul and Kano, Noriaki. 1989. <u>Continuous Improvement: Quality Control Circles in Japanese Industry</u>. Ann Arbor, MI: Center for Japanese Studies, University of Michigan.

MacDuffie, John Paul. 1993. "Human Resource Bundles and Manufacturing Performance: Flexible Production Systems in the World Auto Industry." Unpublished paper, Wharton School, University of Pennsylvania.

MacDuffie, John Paul. 1991. "Beyond Mass Production: Flexible Production Systems and Manufacturing Performance in the World Auto Industry." Unpublished doctoral dissertation, Sloan School of Management, M.I.T.

MacDuffie, John Paul and Krafcik, John F. 1992. "Integrating Technology and Human Resources for High Performance Manufacturing." In <u>Transforming Organizations</u>, edited by Thomas A. Kochan and Michael Useem, pp. 209-225. New York: Oxford University Press.

Majchrzak, Ann. 1988. <u>The Human Side of Factory Automation</u>. San Francisco: Jossey-Bass.

Marshall, Ray. 1987. <u>Unheard voices</u>. New York: Basic Books.

Office of Technology Assessment. 1990. <u>Worker Training: Competing in the New International Economy</u>. Washington, D.C.: Government Printing Office.

Ono, Taiichi. 1988. <u>Workplace Management</u>. Cambridge, MA: Productivity Press.

Piore, Michael and Charles Sabel. 1984. <u>The Second Industrial Divide</u>. New York: Basic Books.

Sako, Mari. 1992. "Training, Productivity, and Quality Control in Japanese Multinational Companies: Preliminary Studies in Britain and Germany." Unpublished manuscript, London School of Economics.

Schonberger, Richard. 1982. <u>Japanese Manufacturing Techniques</u>. New York: Free Press.

Schuler, Randall S. 1989. "Strategic Human Resource Management and Industrial Relations." Human Relations 42, 157-84.

Shimada, Haruo. 1983. "Japanese Industrial Relations - A New General Model?" In Contemporary Industrial Relations in Japan, edited by T. Shirai, pp. 5-23. Madison, WI: University of Wisconsin Press.

Shimada, Haruo and MacDuffie, John Paul. 1986. "Industrial Relations and 'Humanware': Japanese Investments in Automobile Manufacturing in the United States." Working Paper, Sloan School of Management, M.I.T.

Snell, Scott A. and James W. Dean Jr. 1992. "Integrated Manufacturing and Human Resource Management: A Human Capital Perspective." Academy of Management Journal 35: 467-504.

Streeck, Wolfgang et al. 1987. "The Role of Social Partners in Vocational Training and Further Training in the Federal Republic of Germany." IIM/LMP Working Paper, Wissenschaftszentrum, Berlin.

Teece, David J., Gary Pisano, and Amy Shuen. 1990. "Firm Capabilities, Resources, and the Concept of Strategy: Four Paradigms of Strategic Management." Unpublished paper, University of California at Berkeley.

Tyre, Marcie and Wanda Orlikowski. 1992. "Windows of Opportunity: Temporal Patterns of Technological Adaptation in Organizations", forthcoming in Organization Science.

Walton, Richard E. 1987. Innovating to Compete. San Francisco: Jossey-Bass.

Wever, Kirsten, Peter Berg, and Thomas A. Kochan 1992. Labor, Business, Government, and Skills in the U.S. and Germany: The Role of Institutions. Unpublished paper.

Womack, James P., Daniel Jones, and Daniel Roos. 1990. The Machine That Changed the World. New York: Rawson-MacMillan.

ABSTRACT

Do U.S. Firms Underinvest in Human Resources?
Determinants of Training in the World Auto Industry

        This paper investigates the common assertion that U.S. firms underinvest in training relative to their key international competitors. We test four alternative explanations for differences in training effort found in the data, drawn from an international sample of 70 automobile assembly plants. We find the strongest support for the view that the level of training is derived from the requirements of the business/production strategy and the overall "bundle" of human resource policies -- beyond training -- adopted by the firm.

The authors gratefully acknowledge the financial support of the International Motor Vehicle Program and the Leaders for Manufacturing Program at M.I.T. We are also appreciative of helpful comments from Peter Cappelli and Paul Osterman.

[2]

Organizational Strategy and Organization Level as Determinants of Human Resource Management Practices

Randall S. Schuler and Susan E. Jackson, *New York University*

Executive Summary

In a previous article in Human Resource Planning, Schuler (1987) offered several propositions relating human resource management (HRM) practices to organizational strategy. This article reports the empirical results of a study designed to examine some of those propositions. Specifically, the relationships between HRM practices and three types of organizational strategy are reported, namely: growth, extract profit and turnaround.

To assess whether HRM practices vary systematically across organizations pursuing different business strategies, we studied 304 business units. Empirical examination of Schuler's (1987) propositions indicates that HRM practices are used differently by organizations that differ in their strategies. By and large, these differences are consistent with the propositions presented. In addition, further analysis revealed that greater differences in HRM practices are found within organizations than across organizations, regardless of strategy. That is, organizations are likely to use rather different HRM practices with employees at different levels.

Our results suggest that as organizations change strategies they are likely to change HRM practices. This raises significant questions for the HR planner, not the least of which are "Which practices will be needed for the next strategy?" "What is the next strategy?" and "How can the change in HRM practices be made with the least disruption and in the fastest time possible?" The fact that HRM practices often differ dramatically by level also raises several issues. Significant questions for the HR planner to address here include: "How can we manage the inequity that is likely to occur from treating employees differently across levels in the organization?" and "Are the differences in HRM practices really necessary or should we think of gradually eliminating some of the differences?"

In an earlier article Schuler (1987) offered several propositions relating HRM practices to organizational strategy. Due to the lack of empirical data, the propositions were offered to stimulate future research. The purpose of this article is to report results from a study designed to empirically test several of Schuler's propositions.

This research project was graciously funded by the Human Resource Planning Society. The results in no way reflect the opinions or positions of the HRPS.

HRM Practices

In relating HRM practices (planning, staffing, appraising, compensating, and training and development) to organizational strategy there is the presumption that HRM practices vary across organizations (Pfeffer and Cohen, 1984; Cohen and Pfeffer, 1986). For example, for some organizations to be effective it may be more useful to rely upon external sources to recruit top management while for others it may be more useful to rely upon internal sources (Business Week, 1986 pp. 94-95). However, it is also likely that some practices are invariant across organizations. For example, regardless of whether organizations recruit internally or externally they may all find it is most useful to select individuals using valid (as opposed to invalid) selection tests.

When we began this study, we knew of no scales or questionnaires that systematically measured variations in HRM practices. Consequently, we developed items based on Schuler's (1987) literature review. Exhibit 1 summarizes Schuler's discussion. A perusal of Exhibit 1 suggests a great many HRM practices proposed to vary across organizations with different strategies. Examples of how some of these HRM practices were measured are provided in the section below on Methodology.

Schuler's propositions relating HRM practices to organizational strategy presume that the successful implementation of different strategies requires different roles to be played by the employees and requires them to exhibit different characteristics. For example, organizations pursuing a growth strategy may need employees who are willing to take risks and who are comfortable with modest levels of change and uncertainty. However, organizations pursuing an extract profit strategy may need employees who are more predictable in their behaviors, less innovative and more willing to live with rules, procedures and structure.

Cost and market considerations provide further rationale for proposing a link between strategy and HRM practices (Kochan and Chalykoff, 1987). Accordingly, it is useful to review here the cost and market considerations for each organizational strategy. Note that the literature from which the following review is drawn assumes that organizational strategy covaries with product life cycles.

In the growth product life cycle stage a relatively tight labor market exists and labor costs tend to be given a low priority (Piore and Sabel, 1984; Galbraith, 1985; Kochan and Barrocci, 1985; Kochan, McKersie and Cappelli, 1984; Milkovich, Dyer and Mahoney, 1983). This is because firms in the early states of growth need technical talent to transform into marketable products the ideas of the founder or the basic technological breakthrough that gave rise to the new business (Kochan and Chalykoff, 1987). Given that technical skills are so critical and in such short supply, and that internal sources of supply are almost nonexistent, the attraction and retention of talented individuals becomes essential. Because wage rates in this scenario are likely to be high already (and often tied to the firms' profitability and employees' skills), firms are more likely to attract essential talent by differentiating themselves from the competition rather than by paying higher rates. Presumably, such differentiation can be attained by using innovative, nontraditional HRM practices including employment security, high levels of employee participation in decisions and close involvement in HRM (Kochan and Chalykoff, 1987). The management of conflict and provisions for due process are handled through employer-provided grievance procedures, including meetings with managers and ombudsman services (Balfour, 1984). Part-time workers and subcontractors may be used to provide job security for workers in case of economic downturns. Employee participation in decision making is encouraged through quality circles, employee involvement groups and participation teams (Kochan and Chalykoff, 1987).

As firms move into the maturity stage, attracting highly skilled individuals is no longer as high a priority. Firms in the mature stage have an extensive internal labor market and extensive training and development programs. Thus, firms in this stage should develop pay systems designed to retain rather than to attract talent. Wages here are likely to be less dependent on the firm's profitability and employee skills, and more dependent on job classifications and the cost of living. Jobs tend to be narrowly defined

EXHIBIT 1
Human Resource Management Practice Menus

Planning Choices

Informal	. . . .	Formal
Loose	. . . .	Tight
Short Term	. . . .	Long Term
Explicit Analysis	. . . .	Implicit Analysis
Narrow Jobs	. . . .	Broad Jobs
Segmental Design	. . . .	Integrative Design
Low Employee Involvement	. . . .	High Employee Involvement

Staffing Choices

Internal Sources	. . . .	External Sources
Narrow Paths	. . . .	Broad Paths
Single Ladder	. . . .	Multiple Ladders
Explicit Criteria	. . . .	Implicit Criteria
Limited Socialization	. . . .	Extensive Socialization
Closed Procedures	. . . .	Open Procedures

Appraising Choices

Loose, Incomplete Integration	. . . .	Tight, Complete Integration
Behavioral Criteria		Results Criteria
Purposes: Development, Remedial, Maintenance		
Low Employee Participation		High Employee Participation
Short-Term Criteria	. . . .	Long-Term Criteria
Individual Criteria	. . . .	Group Criteria

Compensating Choices

Low Base Salaries	. . . .	High Base Salaries
Internal Equity	. . . .	External Equity
Few Perks	. . . .	Many Perks
Standard, Fixed Package	. . . .	Flexible Package
Low Participation	. . . .	High Participation
No Incentives		Many Incentives
Short-Term Incentive	. . . .	Long-Term Incentive
No Employment Security		High Employment Security
Hierarchical	. . . .	Egalitarian

Training and Development

Short Term		Long Term
Narrow Application		Broad Application
Spontaneous, Unplanned	. . . .	Planned, Systematic
Individual Orientation	. . . .	Group Orientation
Low Participation	. . . .	High Participation
Extensive Organizational Structure	. . . .	Minimal Organization Structure

Adapted from R.S. Schuler, "Human Resource Management Choices and Organizational Strategy," In R.S. Schuler, S.A. Youngblood, and V. Huber (eds.), *Readings in Personnel and Human Resource Management*, 3e. (St. Paul: West Publishing, 1987).

ORGANIZATIONAL STRATEGY AND ORGANIZATION LEVEL AS
DETERMINANTS OF HUMAN RESOURCE MANAGEMENT PRACTICES **127**

and employee participation may be limited. Economic downturns are handled by employee layoffs. Conflict resolutions and due process under collective bargaining is the grievance procedure with third party arbitration (Kochan and Chalykoff, 1987).

The growth and the mature product life cycle stages parallel the growth and the extract profit strategies rather well, but there is less of a parallel between the decline stage and the turnaround strategy. It has been suggested, however, that entry into the decline stage is a precipitating event for a turnaround strategy. On this basis, characteristics of the decline stage are relevant in making predictions about the relationships between human resource practices and organizational strategy (Ferris, Schellenberg and Zammuto, 1984).

Firms in the decline stage have to deal with the existence of an excess number of employees. Although many of these employees may be qualified to perform well, some have to be separated. Thus, sound performance appraisal data can be critical at this stage, for a crucial issue to be resolved is how to select out those individuals least likely to help the organization survive. Cost constraints in this stage are severe and there is likely to be extreme pressure on wages and salaries. Because an attempt at a turnaround in this stage is apt to be regarded as a crisis, the direction the leadership will take is uncertain. Top management may decide either to centralize the decision making or to decentralize the decision making (Milburn, Schuler and Watman, 1983a;b)—either is equally likely.

Organizational Strategies

There are numerous conceptualizations of organizational strategy (Hofer and Davoust, 1977; Wissema, Van Der Pol and Messer, 1980; Tichy, Fombrun and Devanna, 1982; Wright, 1974; and Hax, 1985). Critical to the conceptualization used here and shown in Exhibit 2 are descriptions of the business characteristics associated with each strategy. These are critical because they suggest which employee characteristics are necessary to meet the strategic demands and because they are consistent with the descriptions made of analogous product life cycle stages. It is on the basis of these business and employee characteristics that HRM practices are presumed to vary with strategy.

EXHIBIT 2
Corporate Strategy and Business Concerns

Dynamic Growth Strategy: Here risk taking on projects is modest. There is a constant dilemma between doing current work and building support for the future. Policies and procedures are starting to be written as there is a need for more control and structure for an ever expanding operation.

Extract Profit Strategy: The focus here is on maintaining existing profit levels. Modest cost cutting efforts and employee terminations may be occurring. Control systems and structure are well developed along with an extensive set of policies and procedures.

Turnaround Strategy: The focus of this strategy is to save the operation. Although cost cutting efforts and employee reductions are made, they are short term programs for long run survival. Worker morale may be somewhat depressed.

The strategy conceptualization used here is based upon the work of Gerstein and Reisman (1983). Gerstein and Reisman identified the managerial characteristics a selection system should consider, but they did not systematically identify all the HRM practices for each strategy type, nor did they include a discussion of nonmanagerial employees. Using Gerstein and Reisman's organizational strategies, Schuler (1987) framed several propositions for HRM practices for all managerial and nonmanagerial employees. The propositions examined here include those related to dynamic growth, extract profit and turnaround strategies as defined in Exhibit 2. Consequently there are three sets of propositions related to organizational strategy:

Proposition 1. For the *dynamic growth strategy*, necessary employee characteristics include the need for flexibility and adaptability, a high task orientation, a longer term outlook and some degree of creativity. Accordingly, the proposition is that:

(a) The HRM practices will permit employees to participate in decisions impacting their job and job conditions. There will be some difficulty in specifying career paths and jobs because operations are relatively new and just taking shape.

(b) Performance appraisal will be used more for developmental than evaluative purposes, and group as well as individual criteria will be used.

(c) Some degree of job and employment security will also be provided (Cummings, 1984; Carroll and Schneier, 1982; Miller, 1984; Lawler, 1984; McGill, 1984; Milkovich, et al., 1983; Fombrun, et al., 1984).

(d) Because there is much to do in the short term, training is apt to be less, and what training *is* given will not emphasize future needs.

Proposition 2. The *extract profit strategy* is facilitated by employees focusing on generating high quantities of output, having short term orientations and being comfortable with highly repetitive and low-risk behaviors. Specifically, the proposition is that:

(a) HRM practices will focus on narrowing employee discretion and participation in job decisions, and will reflect a short term perspective.

(b) Employees will have a greater awareness of what to do and there will be greater emphasis on individual rather than group criteria for performance appraisal.

(c) Promotion paths and career paths will be rather extensive, and internal equity and cost of living increases are likely to be provided so as to reduce turnover and retain key people. In addition, pay levels may be higher to help in the efforts to retain employees (Pfeffer and Cohen, 1984).

(d) Training will be more future oriented given the time to do it and the margins to fund it (Kochan and Chalykoff, 1987; Burgelman, 1983; Benston and Schuster, 1983; London and Stumpf, 1982; Stumpf and Hanrahan, 1984; and Carroll and Schneier, 1983).

Proposition 3. For the *turnaround strategy*, organizations need employees who have high organizational identification, will engage in rapidly paced, short-term activities for the benefit of the longer-term possibilities, and are willing to be adaptable and work in close cooperation with others. Specifically, the proposition is that:

(a) The HRM practices will emphasize formality and modest employee

involvement. Job descriptions will be clearly written to ensure
employees are doing exactly what is needed.

(b) In turn, performance appraisals will be formalized because the results
may be needed to implement staff reductions fairly and legally.

(c) Pay levels are likely to be low but stock is likely to be offered in
order to retain employees and motivate them.

(d) Training will focus on short term needs to the extent it is done at all
(Ferris, et al., 1984; Milburn, et al., 1983).

Note that although employee characteristics and business characteristics are used
to explain the relationship between HRM practices and organizational strategy, they
are not examined directly in this study. Organizational level *is* examined in this study,
however. Organizational level is used for the last proposition.

Organizational Level

Organizational level is included in the study because of Thompson's (1967) work
on organizational design and theory. According to Thompson, organizations seek to
buffer their "cores" from the uncertainties of the external environment as much as
possible. In most organizations, the core is the production center - the place where
products are produced or services actually rendered. Although there may be a few
management people in the core, typically most core employees are nonmanagement.
When organizations attempt to buffer their cores they are minimizing the impact of the
environment on nonmanagerial employees; they are also buffering nonmanagerial
employees from the impact of the organizations' efforts (strategies) to deal with the
environment. As employees (managerial or nonmanagerial) become more removed
from the core they become more susceptible to the environment and so they are more
significantly affected by the organization's strategy. Consequently, in looking at the
relationships between HRM practices and organization strategy, it is useful to account
for organizational level, i.e., where the employees are in the organization. Accordingly,
the last proposition to be examined here is:

Proposition 4: The relationships between organizational strategy and HRM practices
described in Propositions 1-3 will be stronger for top management employees and will
diminish through the lower management levels. That is, the effects of strategy will be
stronger for HRM practices related to higher level employees, and will be weaker for
nonmanagerial employees, especially those working in the core of the organization.

Methodology

Study Participants

Data to test Propositions 1 through 4 were gathered by means of two survey
questionnaires. The two sets of respondents were the HR managers and the line
managers. In this research project 304 HR managers completed the questionnaire. Upon
return of the questionnaire the HR managers were contacted and asked to provide
the names and addresses of the head line manager in their business unit. Approximately
two-thirds did this. The line managers so named were sent the second and shorter
questionnaire. Approximately 75% (150) of the line managers returned a completed
questionnaire. In cases where an organization had several relatively independent
divisions (50%), the survey questions were answered for only one of the divisions.
Thus the data gathered described single business units.

Represented in our sample are many types of business units, including
manufacturers of consumer products (21%), manufacturers of industrial/commercial
products (34%), service providers (32%), and retail and wholesale distributors (13%).

The primary markets served by these business units ranged in scope from regional (31%), to national (49%) and international (20%). The founding dates ranged from 1776 to 1985 (median = 1950; S.D. = 13.5 yr.). The number of full time employees in the business units studied ranged from 5 to 40,000 (median = 415; S.D. = 4429.6). Finally, 60% of the business units had no union representation. Among the 40% with some union presence, there was great variation in both number of unions represented (1 to 56) and number of employees who were union members (2 to 20,000). The fact that our study includes a very heterogeneous mix of business units means that any pattern of results we report can be assumed to be broadly generalizable across many types of businesses.

Measures

Respondents completed extensive questionnaires that included questions about the basic characteristics of the business units and items designed to assess (a) organizational strategy; (b) human resource management practices; (c) organizational level; and (d) product life cycle stage.

Organizational strategy was measured by asking the line manager or the HR manager to indicate which strategy best describes what the unit is doing. Three choices were presented:

- Dynamic Growth Strategy
- Extract Profit Strategy
- Turnaround Strategy

These are defined in Exhibit 2.

HRM practices were measured with numerous items, some of which are shown in Exhibits 3 through 5. Items were developed under the presumption that different practices are going to be used in different companies, and that different practices are more effective than others depending upon the strategy and the competitive methods being used. Not all HRM practices are expected to vary or be more effective in different types of companies, so some HRM practices were not measured. For example, for effective employee selection all companies are likely to use validated selection tests. Whether or not companies use validated selected tests was, therefore, not expected to depend upon the business characteristics being measured in this project and so was not assessed.

Organizational level was operationalized here to consist of four major levels of employees. These four major levels are shown in Exhibits 3 through 5 and consist of (a) the top three levels of management, (b) other management, (c) nonexempt salaried employees, and (d) hourly employees. Although large organizations may be expected to have more than four distinct levels of employees in the organization, the use of these four categories of employees was thought likely to cover the business units in our sample. This is also consistent with other treatments of organizational issues (Benston and Schuster, 1983).

Product life cycle stage was determined by asking respondents to indicate the percentage of sales that come from products in each of the following stages of the product life cycle:

Introduction: Primary demand for product just starting to grow; product still unfamiliar to many potential users.

Growth: Demand growing at 10% or more annually in real terms; technology and competitive structure still changing.

Maturity: Product familiar to vast majority of prospective users; technology and competitive structure reasonably stable. Real growth ranges 0% to 10%.

Decline: Product viewed as a commodity; weaker competitors beginning to exit. Real growth is negative.

Only the final three stages were used in this study and only to confirm the existence of the assumed relationship between product life cycle stage and organizational strategy.

Data Analysis

Although there were two sets of respondents (HR managers and line managers) in the study, not all respondents answered the same questions. In fact, the line manager questionnaire was considerably shorter than that of the HR manager. A significant difference between the two was that only the HR manager responded to the human resource practices measures. Responses from HR managers were used in conjunction with line manager responses to questions about organizational strategy and product life cycle stage. Thus the analysis here uses data from two different sets of respondents. This reduces the likelihood of response bias and also results in rather conservative estimations of the relationships between the organizational strategy and human resource management practices.

Using the two sets of respondents, the data were analyzed for the first three propositions by calculating the percent of employees for whom the various HRM practices were provided. These percentages were calculated only for those HRM practices relevant to the propositions.

Results

The results of the four propositions are presented here. Before discussing the four propositions it is important to note that there was a high relationship between organizational strategy and product life cycle stage, supporting an important assumption underlying all the propositions. Thus, firms pursuing a growth strategy had 30% sales coming from products in the growth stage, compared to 15% for other firms. Firms pursuing an extract profit strategy had 70% of sales coming from mature products, compared to 50% for other firms. And, firms pursuing a turnaround strategy had 18% of sales from products in the decline stage, compared to 10% for other firms.

Proposition 1: The Dynamic Growth Strategy

Nature of the Jobs. Proposition 1 proposed that HRM practices for the dynamic growth strategy would reflect some difficulty in specifying job characteristics because the business unit is just beginning to organize and structure itself. This condition makes it difficult to write clear job descriptions and for all employees to know exactly what to do. The results shown in Exhibit 3 suggest that this is the case for our sample.

Item 7 in the "Nature of the Jobs" section indicates that only about 70 percent of hourly, non-exempt salaried, and most management employees know exactly how to perform their jobs effectively. This is in contrast to 84 percent of those employees in the extract profit strategy. Due to the rapid pace of change likely to be occurring in the growth strategy, the career aspirations of employees are not widely known by others in the organization (items 8 and 9). As Exhibits 4 and 5 show, knowledge of career aspirations is higher in firms pursuing other types of strategies.

Performance Appraisal. Proposition 1 also predicted that performance appraisal would be used more for developmental purposes than for evaluation purposes. A comparison of items 4 and 5 in the "Performance Appraisal" section supports this prediction. Also supported is the prediction that the criteria used would be more short-term oriented than longer-term oriented (item 11).

Compensation. The results in items 4 and 5 under "Compensation" support the proposition that some degree of employment and/or job security would be provided. Note that while security is greater here than in firms pursuing a turnaround strategy, there is little difference between these firms and those pursuing an extract profit strategy.

Training and Development. Another prediction was that training and development would tend to focus more on the short-term needs than on the longer-term needs given that the organization is just getting going and still does not have the luxury to peer too far down the road. Item 1f in the "Training and Development" section appears to support this prediction. In the same section items 2 and 3 appear to suggest that even in the short term, little training is provided, especially in comparison with the same items in Exhibit 5 for the turnaround strategy.

EXHIBIT 3
HRM Practices in Firms Pursuing a Growth Strategy

	% Employees this is true for			
Nature of the Jobs	Top Mgt	Other Mgt	Non-exempt Salaried	Hourly
7. Employees know exactly what it takes to do the job effectively.	76%	71%	68%	70%
8. Employees career aspirations within the company are known by their immediate supervisors.	73%	68%	55%	40%
9. Employees who desire promotion have more than one potential position they could be promoted into.	37%	45%	53%	53%
Performance Appraisal				
3. Employees have a significant say about the criteria on which they are appraised.	63%	57%	33%	20%
4. The primary objective of appraisals is to improve performance.	72%	74%	74%	64%
7. Performance appraisals are very informal. There is little written documentation.	20%	10%	8%	21%
5. The primary objective of appraisals is documenting performance deficiencies in order to justify reprisals (e.g., transfers, layoffs).	10%	11%	13%	14%
10. The employee's performance appraisal results reflect the performance of many people other than the appraisee.	49%	48%	17%	19%
11. Appraisals focus primarily on projects or assignments that take...				
...less than 6 months to do.	22%	38%	60%	71%
...6 to 12 months to do.	52%	51%	39%	26%
...12-24 months to do.	19%	11%	3%	3%
...2 years or more.	9%	3%	0%	0%
Total =	100%	100%	100%	100%

EXHIBIT 3
HRM Practices in Firms Pursuing a Growth Strategy (Continued)

	Top Mgt	Other Mgt	Non-exempt Salaried	Hourly
Compensation				
4. *Job* security is almost guaranteed.	36%	35%	35%	38%
5. *Employment* security is almost guaranteed.	31%	32%	29%	32%
9. Employees have a cafeteria-style fringe benefits package (indirect compensation).	33%	35%	22%	16%
15. Employees receive compensation that has been deferred for 2 or more years.	28%	13%	12%	6%
Training and Development				
1. During the past 12 months, how many employees in your firm/division attended training programs designed to:				
d. teach skills for other jobs within the firm in order to increase *lateral* mobility.	7%	14%	11%	14%
e. teach skills for other jobs within the firm in order to increase promotability.	9%	16%	13%	13%
f. teach skills for jobs that do not yet exist, in anticipation of future company needs.	5%	6%	3%	4%
2. The typical employee received how many hours of training during the past 12 months (exclude new hires)?	32 hours	34 hours	23 hours	10 hours
3. The typical new hire received how many hours of training during the past 12 months?	36 hours	66 hours	48 hours	46 hours

Proposition 2: The Extract Profit Strategy

Proposition 2 predicted that HRM practices would be designed to facilitate an extract profit strategy. The data for this proposition are shown in Exhibit 4. The data reveal support for many of the predictions.

Nature of the Jobs. It was found that more than 80% of the employees know exactly what to do on their jobs and that career paths and career concerns are rather extensive. This is in keeping with the notion that a well developed internal labor market facilitates an extract profit strategy (Osterman, 1984; Pfeffer and Cohen, 1984). The results, however, were not as strong as predicted, as revealed by the responses to items 7 through 9.

EXHIBIT 4
HRM Practices in Firms Pursuing An Extract Profit Strategy

	% Employees this is true for			
Nature of the Jobs	Top Mgt	Other Mgt	Non-exempt Salaried	Hourly
1. Employees actively participate in writing their job descriptions.	77%	72%	50%	26%
7. Employees know exactly what it takes to do the job effectively.	83%	81%	79%	84%
8. Employees' career aspirations within the company are known by their immediate supervisors.	76%	72%	59%	47%
9. Employees who desire promotion have more than one potential position they could be promoted into.	47%	54%	54%	61%
Performance Appraisal				
4. Employees have a significant say about the criteria on which they are appraised.	62%	55%	35%	21%
7. Performance appraisals are very informal. There is little written documentation.	23%	8%	14%	27%
10. The employee's performance appraisal results reflect the performance of many people other than the appraisee.	50%	44%	13%	4%
Compensation				
2. Employees' pay is determined primarily by market rates for similar jobs.	72%	80%	79%	71%
3. Employees' pay is determined primarily by comparison to comparable jobs within the firm/division.	23%	29%	34%	35%
11. Cost of living increases are routinely given.	10%	11%	15%	35%
12. The amount earned during each pay period is determined primarily by an incentive plan rather than by a guaranteed-income plan.	7%	6%	4%	11%

EXHIBIT 4
HRM Practices in Firms Pursuing An Extract Profit Strategy (Continued)

Training and Development	Top Mgt	Other Mgt	Non-exempt Salaried	Hourly
1. During the past 12 months, how many employees in your firm/division attended training programs designed to:				
c. teach skills that will be needed in their job in the near future.	25%	27%	22%	21%
d. teach skills for other jobs within the firm in order to increase *lateral* mobility.	12%	12%	12%	9%
e. teach skills for other jobs within the firm in order to increase promotability.	14%	19%d	13%	13%
2. The typical employee received how many hours of training during the past 12 months (exclude new hires)?	27 hours	34 hours	23 hours	24 hours
3. The typical new hire received how many hours of training during the past 12 months?	41 hours	81 hours	90 hours	65 hours

Performance Appraisal. It was also predicted that performance appraisal criteria would be more individual than group-oriented and item 10 in the "Performance Appraisal" section supports this. Similar results were found for the dynamic growth and turnaround strategies.

Compensation. Because of the high relationship between the extract profit strategy and the mature product life cycle stage, it is not surprising that the pay practices reflected compensation rates tied to the market and increases derived mostly from guaranteed sources (items 2 and 11 in the "Compensation" section). Again, however, similar results were found in the other two strategies.

Training and Development. Consistent with the high relationship between extract profit and the mature stage is the fact that there are many hours of training for current and future needs. Organizations in the extract profit stage have more time and money to carry off extensive training programs. The results of items 2 and 3 in the "Training and Development" section appear to support this. These results indicate a substantially higher amount of training than in the other two strategies.

Proposition 3: The Turnaround Strategy

Nature of the Jobs. Proposition 3 applies to the organizations with a turnaround strategy. To facilitate this strategy it was predicted that job requirements would be well known. The results in item 7 under the "Nature of the Jobs" section suggests this was not the case. In fact, in comparison with the other two strategies, the employees in the turnaround strategy were least aware of what it takes to do their jobs effectively.

Performance Appraisal. It was also predicted that performance appraisals would be highly formalized. The results of items 6 and 7 support this prediction. In addition, these results show that performance appraisal formality is highest in the turnaround strategy compared with the other two strategies.

EXHIBIT 5
HRM Practices in Firms Pursuing a Turnaround Strategy

Nature of the Jobs	% Employees this is true for			
	Top Mgt	Other Mgt	Non-exempt Salaried	Hourly
1. Employees actively participate in writing their job descriptions.	67%	56%	31%	13%
7. Employees know exactly what it takes to do the job effectively.	65%	60%	67%	61%
8. Employees' career aspirations within the company are known by their immediate supervisors.	79%	71%	60%	45%

Performance Appraisal				
3. Employees have a significant say about the criteria on which they are appraised.	68%	56%	28%	16%
6. Performance appraisals are very formalized. Forms are filled out and processed at regular intervals.	84%	90%	94%	73%
7. Performance appraisals are very informal. There is little written documentation.	16%	10%	2%	8%

Compensation				
4. Job security is almost guaranteed.	29%	18%	23%	37%
5. Employment security is almost guaranteed.	38%	27%	26%	29%
6. Employees are stockholders.	47%	41%	31%	33%
9. Employees have a flexible fringe benefits package (indirect compensation).	12%	7%	6%	0%
14. Pay rates currently are 15% or more below the rates of our major competitors.	14%	15%	18%	20%

EXHIBIT 5
HRM Practices in Firms Pursuing a Turnaround Strategy (Continued)

Training and Development	Top Mgt	Other Mgt	Non-exempt Salaried	Hourly
1. During the past 12 months, how many employees in your firm/division attended training programs designed to:				
c. teach skills that will be needed in their job in the near future.	8%	23%	14%	12%
d. teach skills for other jobs within the firm in order to increase *lateral* mobility.	6%	9%	10%	8%
e. teach skills for other jobs within the firm in order to increase promotability.	6%	14%	14%	8%
f. teach skills for jobs that do not yet exist, in anticipation of future company needs.	4%	4%	2%	2%
2. The typical employee received how many hours of training during the past 12 months (exclude new hires)?	25 hours	28 hours	12 hours	12 hours
3. The typical new hire received how many hours of training during the past 12 months?	18 hours	51 hours	32 hours	26 hours

Compensation. Because the use of this strategy may turn on an organizational crisis, and thus be attended by cash flow problems, it was predicted that pay rates would be relatively low and that stock would be provided employees as a means of motivating and retaining them. In the "Compensation" section, items 6, 11 and 14 support these predictions. In contrast with the dynamic growth and extract profit strategies, in the turnaround strategy more employees were stockholders, more employees were being paid 15 percent or more below the major competitors and fewer employees were receiving cost of living increases.

Training and Development. To facilitate a turnaround strategy it was predicted that there would be limited training and most of it would be for current job needs. Little training would be provided to enhance the internal mobility of employees. The corroborating evidence for this is in the "Training and Development" section, items 1c-1f. Items 2 and 3 in the Training section indicate that there is relatively little training and development. In comparison to the other two strategies, training and development is lowest in the turnaround strategy.

Proposition 4: Differences Across Employees at Different Levels
The results relevant to Proposition 4, concerning the relationship between organizational level and HRM practices, are shown in Exhibits 3-5. Within each of these exhibits, the relevant data are the columns that reflect the organizational level of the employees, from the top three levels of management to hourly employees. For example, in Exhibit 5, item 1 under "Nature of the Jobs" shows that employee participation in

writing job descriptions increases dramatically in going from the bottom to the top level. In Exhibit 3, item 10 under "Performance Appraisal" shows that the group has an influence on performance, and the amount of group influence increases to the top three levels of management. The same trend is descriptive for item 3 under "Performance Appraisal," i.e., with increased level there is more employee input in the performance appraisal criteria. Also as predicted, the developmental purpose of appraisal increases from the bottom to the top management levels. Not consistent with the predictions are the numbers for item 7 under "Nature of the Jobs." The results show that the degree to which employees know how to do the job remains constant regardless of organizational level. The degree of consistency in support for Proposition 4 remains the same for the three strategies (Exhibits 3-5).

Discussion And Implications

The results here suggest there are predictable relationships between organizational strategy and human resource management practices. Unfortunately these results do not prove that organizations systematically selected particular practices to match their strategy. The past few years have witnessed a rapid proliferation of alternative human resource management practices (Kochan and Cappelli. 1983; Beer and Spector, 1984). This has resulted in part from attempts by firms to try anything to make their employees more productive and from the recognition that different practices are needed in different types of businesses (Dyer. 1984; Miles and Snow. 1984a). As stated by Reginald H. Jones, former chairman and CEO of General Electric company:

When we classified . . . (our) . . . businesses, and when we realized that they were going to have quite different missions, we also realized we had to have quite different people running them (Fombrun. 1982, p. 46).

Consequently, some firms have started to select not only people but entire sets of HRM practices on the basis of what they need from employees (Miles and Snow. 1984b) particularly as they are related to various organizational strategies (Kochan and Chalykoff. 1987). In so doing they are significantly altering the conditions of employment. And firms are finding it more imperative to change strategies more rapidly than before, although not always in smooth and systematic ways (Miller and Friesen, 1980; DiMaggio and Powell, 1983). Whether or not these changes will result in more effective organizations remains to be determined. Although it was implied in this study and those of others (e.g., Miles and Snow, 1984b) that a fit between HRM practices and organizational strategy is likely to be more effective than a lack of fit, this remains to be empirically examined. Work by Schuster (1984) however, indicates that some compensation policies in high technology firms are associated with greater effectiveness than other compensation policies. Similar results were reported by Kerr (1982; 1985). Schuster's work also highlights the importance of other factors in the effectiveness of firms besides HRM practices. Strong leadership and culture of performance are just two of many additional factors (Lawler, 1984). This should be kept in mind by human resource managers in the process of promoting a change in HRM practices. Also to be kept in mind is the potentially large impact of any change in HRM practices on the employees.

As firms begin to think in terms of matching HRM practices to their strategy, employees will face ever-changing employment relationships. A significant implication that follows is that employees of a single firm will be exposed to different sets of HRM practices during the course of employment. Consequently, workers will be asked to exhibit different characteristics and will be exposed to several different conditions of employment thus altering conditions of employment and conditions of the internal labor market (Osterman. 1984: Doeringer and Piore, 1971). Unclear at this time are answers to questions such as: How feasible or desirable is it for workers to continually change? What can firms do to aid the adjustment to change? What should firms do if workers fail to change? Will the need to change HRM practices be uniform across all levels of the firm? What will be the reaction of workers, unions and government?

While it is difficult to predict the exact answers to these questions, it is unlikely that firms will be able to proactively and singly change HRM practices unless they have significant power (Cooke, 1985). The very act of changing HRM practices may not only require a significant degree of power but also cause a further shift of power (Cooke, 1985). Given a relative balance of power, cooperation among the interested parties, such as between the United Auto Workers and the Saturn Division of General Motors, may be more typical. Government intervention is also a possibility if firms elect to move operations when employees resist changes in HRM practices. State laws already exist in Wisconsin, Maine and Massachusetts constraining certain forms of plant/office closings. Consequently, the attempts by firms to change their HRM practices are likely to occur in a rather dynamic context (Osterman, 1984).

Another human resource implication of changing HRM practices is that firms with more than one business are likely to have more than one set of HRM practices. Thus, a single firm with several businesses may have different conditions of employment to the extent that it has businesses (divisions or plants) operating with different life cycle stages and pursuing different organizational strategies. Here enter the challenges of treating employees equitably across divisions regarding issues such as career development, equal opportunity and compensation. Similar challenges present themselves when just looking within a division across organizational levels. As reported under Proposition 4, there are substantial differences in HRM practices across levels. Inconclusive at this time is whether or not smaller differences across levels are associated with greater effectiveness. While high technology firms arìd Japanese firms report fewer hierarchical differences, it is difficult to tell if this is a major reason for their effectiveness. The trend in restructuring and downsizing in U.S. corporations, however, appears to be diminishing hierarchical differences and improving performance.

In summary, this article highlights a great many challenges and opportunities facing the human resource planner specifically and the human resource manager more generally. There are challenges to be met and opportunities to be seized. Systematically linking and proactively managing human resource practices with the needs and concerns of the business in one way to do both.

References

Balfour, A. "Five types of Non-union Grievance Systems." *Personnel, 61*, March-April 1984, pp. 67-76.

Beer, M. and Spector, B. "Transformations in Human Resource Management." Unpublished paper, Harvard University Graduate School of Business Administration, 1984.

Bentson, M. A. and Schuster, J. R. "Executive Compensation and Employee Benefits." In S. J. Carroll and R. S. Schuler (eds.), *Human Resources Management in the 1980s* (Washington, D.C.: The Bureau of National Affairs 1983).

Burgelman, R. "Corporate Entrepreneurship and Strategic Management: Insights from a Process Study." *Management Science*, December 1983, pp. 1349-1364.

Carroll, S. J., Jr. and Schneier, C. E. *Performance Appraisal and Review Systems.* (Glenview, IL: Scott, Foresman and Company 1982).

Cohen, Y. and Pfeffer, J. "Organizational Hiring Standards." *Administrative Science Quarterly*, 1986, *31*, pp. 1-24.

Cooke, W. N. "Toward a General Theory of Industrial Relations." In D. B. Lipsky and J. M. Douglas (eds.), *Advances in Industrial and Labor Relations.* (Greenwich, CT: JAI Press 1985).

Cummings, L. L. "Compensation, Culture, and Motivation: A Systems Perspective." *Organizational Dynamics*, Winter 1984, pp. 33-43.

DiMaggio, P. J. and Powell, W. W. "The Iron Cage Revisited: Institutional Isomorphism and Collective Rationality in Organizational Fields." *American Sociological Review*, 1983, *48*, pp. 147-160.

Doeringer, P. B. and Piore, M. J. *Internal Labor Markets and Manpower Analysis,* (Lexington, MA: D. C. Heath, 1971).

Ferris, G. R., Schellenberg D. A. and Zammuto, R. F. "Human Resource Management Strategies In Declining Industries." *Human Resource Management*, 1984, *23*, 381-394.

Fombrun, C "An Interview with Reginald Jones." *Organizational Dynamics*, Winter 1982, pp. 42-49.

Gerstein, M. and Reisman, H. "Strategic Selection: Matching Executives to Business Conditions." *Sloan Management Review*, Winter, 1983, pp. 33-49.

Hax, A. C. "A Methodology for the Development of a Human Resource Strategy." MIT working paper #1638-85, March, 1985.

Hofer, C. W. and Davoust, M. J. *Successful Strategic Management*. (Chicago, IL: A. T. Kearney, 1977).

Kerr, J. L. "Assigning Managers on the Basis of the Life Cycle." *Journal of Business Strategy*, 1982, pp. 58-65.

Kerr, J. L. "Diversification Strategies and Managerial Rewards: An Empirical Study." *Academy of Management Journal*, *28*, 1985, pp. 155-179.

Kochan, T. A. and Chalykoff, J. "Human Resource Management and Business Life Cycles: Some Preliminary Propositions." In A. Kleingartner and C. Anderson (eds.), *Human Resources and High Technology Firms*. (Lexington: Heath. 1987).

Kochan, T. A. and Barocci, T. A. *Human Resource Management and Industrial Relations*. (Boston: Little Brown & Company, 1985).

Kochan, T. A., McKersie, R. B. and Capelli, P. "Strategic Choice and Industrial Relations Theory." *Industrial Relations*, Winter 1984. pp. 16-39.

Lawler III, E. E. "The Strategic Design of Reward Systems." In R. S. Schuler and S. A. Youngblood (eds.), *Readings in Personnel and Human Resource Management*, 2nd edition. (St. Paul: West Publishing, 1984)

London, M. and Stumpf, S. A. *Managing Careers*. (Reading, Mass.: Addison-Wesley Publishing Company, 1982).

McGill, A. R. "Practical Considerations: A Case Study of General Motors." In C. Fombrun, N. M. Tichy, and M. A. Devanna (eds.) *Strategic Human Resource Management*. (New York: John Wiley & Sons, Inc., 1984).

Milburn, T. A., Schuler, R. S. and Watman, K. "Organizational Crisis Part I: Definition and Conceptualization." *Human Relations*, *36*, 1983a, 1141-1160.

Milburn, T. A., Schuler, R. S. and Watman. K. "Organizational Crisis Part II: Strategies and Responses." *Human Relations*, *36*, 1983b, 1161-1180.

Miles, R. E. and Snow, C. C. "Designing Strategic Human Resources Systems." *Organizational Dynamics*, 1984a, pp. 36-52.

Miles, R. E. and Snow, C. C. "Fit, Failure and The Hall of Fame." *California Management Review*, *26*, 1984b, pp. 10-28.

Milkovich, G., Dyer, L. and Mahoney, T. "The State of Practice and Research in Human Resource Planning." In S. Carroll and R. S. Schuler (eds.), *Human Resource Management in the 1980s*. (Washington, D. C.: Bureau of National Affairs, 1983).

Miller, A. and Camp, B. "Exploring Determinants of Success in Corporate Ventures." *Journal of Business Venturing*, 1984, 1, pp. 87-105.

Mills, D. Q. *The New Competitors*, (New York: The Free Press, 1985).

Osterman, P. (Ed.) *Internal Labor Markets*. (Cambridge, MA: London, 1984).

Piore, M. J. and Sabel, C. F. *The Second Industrial Divide*. (New York: Basic Books, 1984).

Peters, T. J. "Strategy Follows Structure: Developing Distinctive Skills." *California Management Review*, 1984, Spring, pp. 111-125.

Pfeffer, J. and Cohen, Y. "Determinants of Internal Labor Markets in Organizations." *Administrative Science Quarterly*, 1984, *29*, pp. 550-572.

Schuler, R. S. "Personnel and Human Resource Management Choices and Organizational Strategy." *Human Resource Planning*, 1987. *10*, pp. 1-17.

Stumpf, S. A. and Hanrahan, N. M. "Designing Organizational Career Management Practices to Fit Strategic Management Objectives." In R. S. Schuler and S. A. Youngblood (eds.), *Readings in Personnel and Human Resource Management*, 2nd edition. (St. Paul: West Publishing, 1984).

Schuster, J. *Management Compensation in High Technology Companies*. (Cambridge: Lexington Books, 1984).

Thompson, J. D. *Organizations in Action*. (New York: McGraw-Hill, 1967).

Tichy, N. M., Fombrun, C. J. and Devanna. M. A. "Strategic Human Resource Management." *Sloan Management Review*, 1982. *23*, pp. 47-61.

Wissema. J. G., Van Der Pol, H. W. and Messer, H. M. "Strategic Management Archetypes." *Strategic Management Journal*, 1980. *1*, pp. 37-47.

Wright. R. V. L. *A System for Managing Diversity*. (Cambridge, MA: Arthur D. Little, 1974).

[3]

OXFORD REVIEW OF ECONOMIC POLICY, VOL. 4, NO. 3

THE FAILURE OF TRAINING IN BRITAIN: ANALYSIS AND PRESCRIPTION

DAVID FINEGOLD
Pembroke College, Oxford

DAVID SOSKICE[1]
University College, Oxford

I. INTRODUCTION

In the last decade, education and training (ET) reform has become a major issue in many of the world's industrial powers. One theme which runs throughout these reform initiatives is the need to adapt ET systems to the changing economic environment. These changes include: the increasing integration of world markets, the shift in mass manufacturing towards newly developed nations and the rapid development of new technologies, most notably information technologies. Education and training are seen to play a crucial role in restoring or maintaining international competitiveness, both on the macro-level by easing the transition of the work force into new industries, and at the micro-level, where firms producing high quality, specialized goods and services require a well-qualified workforce capable of rapid adjustment in the work process and continual product innovation (see Fonda and Hayes in this issue).

This paper will highlight the need for policy-makers and academics to take account of the two-way nature of the relationship between ET and the economy. We will argue that Britain's failure to educate and train its workforce to the same levels as its international competitors has been both a product and a cause of the

[1] The authors would like to thank Kay Andrews, Geoffrey Garrett, Ken Mayhew, Derek Morris, John Muellbauer and Len Schoppa for helpful comments; and to acknowledge intellectual indebtedness to Chris Hayes and Prof. S. Prais. Research on comparative aspects of training was financed in part by a grant to D. Soskice from the ESRC Corporatist and Accountability Research Programme.

0266-903X/88$3.00 © 1988 OXFORD UNIVERSITY PRESS AND THE OXFORD REVIEW OF ECONOMIC POLICY LIMITED 21

OXFORD REVIEW OF ECONOMIC POLICY, VOL. 4, NO. 3

nation's poor relative economic performance: a product, because the ET system evolved to meet the needs of the world's first industrialized economy, whose large, mass-production manufacturing sector required only a small number of skilled workers and university graduates; and a cause, because the absence of a well educated and trained workforce has made it difficult for industry to respond to new economic conditions.

The best way to visualize this argument is to see Britain as trapped in a low-skills equilibrium, in which the majority of enterprises staffed by poorly trained managers and workers produce low-quality goods and services.[2] The term 'equilibrium' is used to connote a self-reinforcing network of societal and state institutions which interact to stifle the demand for improvements in skill levels. This set of political-economic institutions will be shown to include: the organization of industry, firms and the work process, the industrial relations system, financial markets, the state and political structure, as well as the operation of the ET system. A change in any one of these factors without corresponding shifts in the other institutional variables may result in only small long-term shifts in the equilibrium position. For example, a company which decides to recruit better-educated workers and then invest more funds in training them will not realize the full potential of that investment if it does not make parallel changes in style and quality of management, work design, promotion structures and the way it implements new technologies.[3] The same logic applies on a national scale to a state which invests in improving its ET system, while ignoring the surrounding industrial structure.

The argument is organized as follows: section two uses international statistical comparisons to show that Britain's ET system turns out less-qualified individuals than its major competitors and that this relative ET failure has contributed to Britain's poor economic record. Section three explores the historical reasons for Britain's ET problem and analyses the institutional constraints which have prevented the state from reforming ET. Section four argues that the economic crisis of the 1970s and early-1980s and the centralization of ET power undertaken by the Thatcher Administration have increased the possibility of restructuring ET, but that the Conservative Government's ET reforms, both the major changes already implemented and the Bill which has just passed through Parliament, will not significantly improve Britain's relative ET and economic performance. The fifth section proposes an alternative set of ET and related policies which could help Britain to break out of the low-skill equilibrium.

II. INTERNATIONAL COMPARISONS

i) Britain's Failure to Train

Comparative education and training statistics are even less reliable than cross-national studies in economics; there are few generally agreed statistical categories, wide variations in the quality of ET provision and qualifications and a notable lack of data on training within companies. Despite these caveats, there is a consensus in the growing body of comparative ET research that Britain provides significantly poorer ET for its workforce than its major international competitors. Our focus will be on differences in ET provision for the majority of the population, concentrating in particular on the normal ET routes for skilled and semi-skilled workers. This need not be technical courses, but may - as in Japan or the US - constitute a long course of general education followed by company-based training.

---

[2] 'Equilibrium' is not meant to imply that all British firms produce low-quality products or services, or that all individuals are poorly educated and trained. A number of companies (often foreign-owned MNCs) have succeeded in recruiting the educational élite and offering good training programmes.

[3] An excellent discussion of the differences in each of these dimensions between British and German companies is contained in Lane (1988).

D. Finegold and D. Soskice

The baseline comparison for ET effectiveness begins with how students in different countries perform during compulsory schooling. Prais and Wagner (1983) compared mathematics test results of West German and English secondary schools and found that the level of attainment of the lower half of German pupils was higher than the average level of attainment in England, while Lynn (1988, p. 6) reviewed thirteen- year-olds' scores on international mathematics achievement tests from the early 1980s and found that 'approximately 79 per cent of Japanese children obtained a higher score than the average English child'. The results are equally disturbing in the sciences, where English fourteen year-olds scored lower than their peers in all seventeen countries in a recent study (Postlethwaite, 1988).

This education shortfall is compounded by the fact that England is the only one of the world's major industrial nations in which a majority of students leave full-time education or training at the age of sixteen. The contrast is particularly striking with the US, Canada, Sweden and Japan, where more than 85 per cent of sixteen year-olds remain are in full-time education. In Germany, Austria and Switzerland, similar proportions are either in full-time education or in highly structured three or four-year apprenticeships. Britain has done little to improve its relative postion. It was, for example, the only member of the OECD to experience a decline in the participation rate of the sixteen-nineteen age group in the latter half of the 1970s. (OECD, 1985, p. 17) Although staying-on rates have improved in the 1980s - due to falling rolls and falling job prospects - Britain's relative position in the OECD rankings has not.

The combination of poor performance during the compulsory schooling years and a high percentage of students leaving school at sixteen has meant that the average English worker enters employment with a relatively low level of qualifications.

Workers' lack of initial qualifications is not compensated for by increased employer-based training; on the contrary, British firms offer a lower quality and quantity of training than their counterparts on the Continent. A joint MSC/NEDO study (1984, p. 90) found that employers in Germany were spending approximately three times more on training than their British rivals, while Steedman's analysis (1986) of comparable construction firms in France and Britain revealed that French workers' training was more extensive and less firm-specific. Overall, British firms have been estimated to be devoting 0.15 per cent of turnover to training compared with 1-2 per cent in Japan, France and West Germany (Anderson, 1987, p. 69). And, as we will show in Section four, neither individuals nor the Government have compensated for employers lack of investment in adult training.

ii) Why Train? The link between ET and Economic Performance

Britain's relative failure to educate and train its workforce has contributed to its poor economic growth record in the postwar period. While it is difficult to demonstrate this relationship empirically, given the numerous other factors which effect labour productivity, no one is likely to dispute the claim that ET provision can improve economic performance in extreme cases, i.e. a certified engineer will be more productive working with a complex piece of industrial machinery than an unskilled employee. Our concern, however, is whether marginal differences in the quality and quantity of ET are related to performance. We will divide the evidence on this relationship in two parts: first, that the short-term expansion of British industry has been hindered by the failure of the ET system to produce sufficient quantities of skilled labour; and second, that the ability of the British economy and individual firms to adapt to the longer-term shifts in international competition has been impeded by the dearth of qualified manpower.

A survey of the literature reveals that skill shortages in key sectors such as engineering and information technology have been a recurring problem for UK industry, even during times of high unemployment. The Donovan Commission (1968, p. 92) maintained that 'lack of skilled labour has constantly applied a brake to our economic expansion since the war', a decade later, a NEDO study (1978, p. 2) found that 68 per cent

OXFORD REVIEW OF ECONOMIC POLICY, VOL. 4, NO. 3

of mechanical engineering companies reported that output was restricted by an absence of qualified workers. The problem remains acute, as the MSC's first *Skills Monitoring Report* (May, 1986, p. 1) stated: 'Shortages of professional engineers have continued to grow and there are indications that such shortages will remain for some time, particulary of engineers with electronics and other IT skills.'

The shortages are not confined to manufacturing. Public sector professions, i.e. teaching, nursing and social work, which rely heavily on recruiting from the limited group of young people with at least five O-levels, are facing a skilled (wo)manpower crisis as the number of school-leavers declines by 25 per cent between 1985 and 1995. In the case of maths and science teachers, the shortages tend to be self-perpetuating, as the absence of qualified specialists makes it harder to attract the next generation of students into these fields (Gow, 1988, p. 4; Keep, 1987, p. 12).

The main argument of this paper, however, is that the evidence of skill shortages both understates and oversimplifies the consequences Britain's ET failure has on its economic performance. Skill shortages reflect the unsatisfied demand for trained individuals within the limits of existing industrial organization, but they say nothing about the negative effect poor ET may have on how efficiently enterprises organize work or their ability to restructure. Indeed, there is a growing recognition among industry leaders and the major accounting firms that their traditional method of calculating firms' costs, particularly labour costs, fails to quantify the less tangible benefits of training, such as better product quality and increased customer satisfaction (*Business Week*, 1988, p. 49).

There are, however, a number of recent studies which show the strong positive correlation between industry productivity and skill levels. Daly (1984, pp. 41-2) compared several US and UK manufacturing industries and found that a shift of 1 per cent of the labour force from the unskilled to the skilled category raised productivity by about 2 per cent, concluding that British firms suffered because 'they lacked a large intermediate group with either educational or vocational qualifications'. The specific ways in which training can harm firm performance were spelled out in a comparison of West German and British manufacturing plants (Worswick, 1985, p. 91): 'Because of their relative deficiency in shop-floor skills, equivalent British plants had to carry more overhead labour in the form of quality controllers, production planners . . . the comparative shortage of maintenance skills in British plants might be associated with longer equipment downtime and hence lower capital productivity.'

Likewise, employee productivity levels in the French construction industry were found to be one-third higher than in Britain and the main explanation was the greater breadth and quality of French training provision (Steedman, 1986).

While these studies have all centred on relatively comparable companies producing similar goods and services, a high level of ET is also a crucial element in enabling firms to reorganize the work process in pursuit of new product markets, what Reich has called 'flexible-system' production strategies (Reich, 1983, pp. 135-6). 'Flexible-system' companies are geared to respond rapidly to change, with non-hierarchical management structures, few job demarcations and an emphasis on teamwork and maintaining product quality. They can be located in new industries, i.e. biotechnology, fibre optics, or market niches within old industries, such as speciality steels and custom machine tools.

A number of recent studies have highlighted the role of training in 'flexible-system' production: in Japanese firms, Shirai (1983, p. 46) found that employees in 'small, relatively independent work groups . . . grasped the total production process, thus making them more adaptable when jobs have to be redesigned'. Streeck (1985) took the analysis one step further in his study of the European car industry, arguing that the high-quality training programmes of German automakers have acted as a driving force behind product innovation, as firms have developed more sophisticated models to better utilize the talents of their employees. Even in relatively low-tech industries, such as kitchen manufacturing, German

D. Finegold and D. Soskice

companies are, according to Steedman and Wagner (1987), able to offer their customers more customized, better-quality units than their British competitors because of the greater flexibility of their production process--a flexibility that is contingent on workers with a broad skill base.

III. WHY HAS BRITAIN FAILED TO TRAIN?

Economists normal diagnosis of the undersupply of training is that it is a public good or free ride problem: firms do not invest in sufficient training because it is cheaper for them to hire already skilled workers than to train their own and risk them being poached by other companies. While the public good explanation may account for the general tendency to underinvest in training, it does not explain the significant variations between countries' levels of training nor does it address the key public policy question: Given the market's inability to provide enough skilled workers, why hasn't the British Government take corrective action? To answer this question we will look first at why political parties were long reluctant to intervene in the ET field, and then, at the two major obstacles which policy-makers faced when they did push for ET change: a state apparatus ill-equipped for centrally-led reform and a complex web of institutional constraints which kept Britain in a low-skills equilibrium.

i) Political Parties

Through most of the postwar period, the use of ET to improve economic performance failed to emerge on the political agenda, as a consensus formed among the two major parties on the merits of gradually expanding educational provision and leaving training to industry. Underlying this consensus was an economy producing full employment and sustained growth, which covered any deficiencies in the ET system. The broad consensus, however, masked significant differences in the reasons for the parties' positions: For Labour, vocational and technical education were seen as incompatible with the drive for comprehensive schooling, while the Party's heavy dependence on trade unions for financial and electoral support prevented any attempts to infringe on union's control over training within industry (Hall, 1986, p. 85). In the case of the Conservatives, preserving the grammar school track was the main educational priority, while intervening in the training sphere would have violated their belief in the free market (Wiener, 1981, p. 110). An exception to the principle of non-intervention came during the war, when the Coalition Government responded to the manpower crisis by erecting makeshift centres that trained more than 500,000 people. When the war ended, however, these training centres were dismantled.

ii) The State Structure

One of the main factors which hindered politicians from taking a more active ET role was the weakness of the central bureaucracy in both the education and training fields. On the training side, it was not until the creation of the Manpower Services Commission (MSC) in 1973 (discussed in section four) that the state developed the capacity for implementing an active labour market policy. The staff of the primary economic policy-making body, the Treasury , 'had virtually no familiarity with, or direct concern for, the progress of British industry' (Hall, 1986, p. 62) and none of the other departments (Environment, Trade and Industry, Employment or Education and Science) assumed clear responsibility for overseeing training. There was, for example, a dearth of accurate labour market statistics, which made projections of future skill requirements a virtual impossibility (Reid, 1980, p. 30). Even if the state had come up with the bureaucratic capability to develop a coherent training policy, it lacked the capacity to implement it. Wilensky and Turner (1987, pp. 62-3) compared the state structure and corporatist bargaining arrangements of eight major industrialized nations and ranked the UK last in its ability to execute manpower policy.

OXFORD REVIEW OF ECONOMIC POLICY, VOL. 4, NO. 3

While responsiblity over education policy in the central state was more clearly defined, resting with the Department of Education and Science (DES), the historical decentralization of power within the educational world made it impossible for the DES to exercise effective control (Howell, 1980; OECD, 1975). Those groups responsible for delivering education, local authorities (Jennings, 1974) and teachers (Dale, 1983), were able to block reforms they opposed, such as vocationalism. The lack of central control was particularly apparent in the further education sector, an area accorded low priority by the DES until the 1970s (Salter and Tapper, 1981).

The main obstacle to ET reform, however, was not the weakness of the central state, which could be remedied given the right external circumstances and sufficient political will, but the interlocking network of societal institutions which will be explored in the following sections, beginning with the structure, or lack of it, for technical and vocational education and entry-level training.

iii) The ET System

Technical and work-related subjects have long suffered from a second-class status in relation to academic courses in the British education system (Wiener, 1981). The Norwood Report of 1943 recommended a tripartite system of secondary education, with technical schools to channel the second-quarter of the ability range into skilled jobs; but while the grammar schools and secondary moderns flourished, the technical track never accommodated more than 4 per cent of the student population. In the mid-1960s two programmes, the Schools Council's 'Project Technology' and the Association for Science Education's 'Applied Science and the Schools', attempted to build an 'alternative road' of engineering and practical courses to rival pure sciences in the secondary curriculum (McCulloch et al. 1985, pp. 139-55). These pilot experiments were short-lived due to: 1) conflicts between and within the relevant interest groups, 2) minimal co-ordination of the initiatives and 3) the absence of clearly defined objectives and strategies for implementing them (ibid., pp. 209-12).

The efforts to boost technical education were marginal to the main educational tranformations of the postwar period: the gradual shift from division at eleven-plus to comprehensives and the raising of the school-leaving age to fifteen, and eventually sixteen in 1972. The education establishment, however, was slow to come up with a relevant curriculum for the more than 85 per cent of each age cohort who were now staying longer in school, but could not qualify for a place in higher education. Success for the new comprehensives continued to be defined by students' performance in academic examinations (O- and A-levels), which were designed for only the top 20 per cent of the ability range (Fenwick, 1976) and allowed many students to drop subjects, such as mathematics and science, at the age of fourteen. The academic/ university bias of the secondary system was reinforced by the powerful influence of the public schools, which while catering for less than 6 per cent of students produced 73 per cent of the directors of industrial corporations (Giddens, 1979), as well as a majority of Oxbridge graduates, MPs and top education officials; thus, a large percentage of those charged with formulating ET policy, both for government and firms, had no personal experience of state education, much less technical or vocational courses.

The responsibility for vocational education and training (VET) fell by default to the further education (FE) sector. The 1944 Education Act attempted to provide a statutory basis for this provision, declaring that county colleges should be set up in each LEA to offer compulsory day-release schemes for fifteen-eighteen year-olds in employment. The money was never provided to build these colleges, however, with the result that 'a jungle' of different FE institutions, courses and qualifications developed (Locke and Bloomfield, 1982). There were three main paths through this 'jungle': the academic sixth form, the technical courses certified by independent bodies, such as City & Guilds, BTEC or the RSA, and 'the new sixth form' or 'young stayers on', who remain in full-time education without committing to an A-level or specific training course (MacFarlane Report, 1980). A host of factors curtailed the numbers pursuing the intermediate route: the relatively few careers requiring these qualifications, the lack of maintenance support for FE

D. Finegold and D. Soskice

students and the high status of the academic sixth, which was reinforced by the almost total exclusion of technical students from higher education.

The majority of individuals left education for jobs which offered no formal training. Those who did receive training were almost exclusively in apprenticeships. The shortcomings of many of these old-style training programmes, which trained 240,000 school-leavers in 1964, were well known: age and gender barriers to entry, qualifications based on time-served (up to seven years) rather than a national standard of proficiency and no guarantee of off-the-job training (Page, 1967). The equation of apprenticeships with training also had the effect of stifling training for positions below skilled level and for older employees whose skills had become redundant or needed updating.

In the early 1960s the combination of declining industrial competitiveness, a dramatic expansion in the number of school-leavers and growing evidence of skill shortages and 'poaching' prompted the Government to attempt to reform apprenticeships and other forms of training (Perry, 1976). The route the state chose was one of corporatist compromise and minimal intervention, erecting a network of training boards (ITBs) in the major industries staffed by union, employer and government representatives (Industrial Training Act, 1964). The ITBs' main means of overcoming the free-rider problem was the levy/grant system, which placed a training tax on all the companies within an industry and then distributed the funds to those firms that were training to an acceptable standard, defined by each board (Page, 1970).

The boards created a fairer apportionment of training costs and raised awareness of skill shortages, but they failed to raise substantially the overall training level because they did not challenge the short-term perspective of most companies. The state contributed no new funds to training and each board assessed only its industry's training needs, taking as given the existing firm organization, industrial relations system and management practices and thus perpetuating the low-skill equilibrium. Despite the Engineering ITB's pioneering work in developing new, more flexible training courses, craft apprenticeships remained the main supply of skilled labour until Mrs Thatcher came to power in 1979.

iv) Industrial/Firm Structure

Industry Type. One of the main reasons that British industry has failed to update its training programmes is the concentration of the country's firms in those product markets which have the lowest skill requirements, goods manufactured with continuous, rather than batch or unit production processes (Reich, 1983). An analysis of international trade in the 1970s by NEDO found that the UK performed better than average in 'standardized, price-sensitive products' and below average in 'the skill and innovation-intensive products' (Greenhalgh, 1988, p. 15). New and Myers' 1986 study of two hundred and forty large export-oriented plants confirmed that only a minority of these firms had experimented with the most advanced technologies and that management's future plans were focused on traditional, mass-production market segments.

Training has also been adversely effected by the long-term shift in British employment from manufacturing to low-skill, low-quality services. Manufacturing now accounts for less than one-third of British employment and its share of the labour market has been declining. The largest growth in employment is in the part-time service sector where jobs typically require and offer little or no training. The concentration of British service providers on the low-skill end of the labour market was highlighted in a recent study of the tourist industry (Gapper, 1988).

While the type of goods or services which a company produces sets limits on the skills required, it does not determine the necessary level of training. Recent international comparisons of firms in similar product markets (i.e. Maurice et al., 1986; Streeck, 1985) have revealed significant variations in training provision depending on how a company is organized and the way in which this organizational structure shapes the

OXFORD REVIEW OF ECONOMIC POLICY, VOL. 4, NO. 3

implementation of new technologies. In the retail trade, for instance, 75 per cent of German employees have at least an apprenticeship qualification compared with just two percent in the UK. The brief sections which follow will outline how, in the British case, the many, integrally-related components of firms' organizational structures and practices have combined to discourage training.

Recruitment. British firms have traditionally provided two routes of entry for young workers: the majority are hired at the end of compulsory schooling, either to begin an apprenticeship or to start a semi- or unskilled job, while a select few are recruited from higher education (HE) for management posts (Crowther Report, 1959). (Nursing is one of the rare careers which has sought students leaving further education (FE) at the age of 18.) As a result, there is little incentive for those unlikely to gain admittance to HE to stay on in school or FE. Indeed, Raffe (1984, Ch. 9) found that Scottish males who opted for post-compulsory education actually had a harder time finding work than their peers who left school at sixteen. Vocational education is perceived as a low status route because it provides little opportunity for career advancement and because managers, who themselves typically enter employment without practical experience or technical training, focus on academic examinations as the best means of assessing the potential of trainees.

Job design and scope. After joining a company, employees' training will depend upon the array of tasks they are asked to perform. Tipton's study (1985, p. 33) of the British labour market found that 'the bulk of existing jobs are of a routine, undemanding variety' requiring little or no training. The failure to broaden individuals' jobs and skill base, i.e. through job rotation and work teams, has historically been linked to craft unions' insistence on rigid demarcations between jobs, but there is some evidence that these restrictive practices have diminished in the last decade. The decline in union resistance, however, has been counterbalanced by two negative trends for training: subcontracting out skilled maintenance work (Brady, 1984) and using new technologies to deskill work (Streeck, 1985). The latter practice is particularly well documented in the automobile industry, where British firms, unlike their Swedish, Japanese and German rivals, have structured new automated factories to minimize the skill content of production jobs, instead of utilizing the new technology to increase flexibility and expand job definitions (Scarbrough, 1986). Tipton concludes (p. 27): 'the key to improving the quality of training is the design of work and a much needed spur to the movement for the redesign of work . . . may lie in training policies and practice'.

Authority Structure. In the previous section we used job design to refer to the range of tasks within one level of a firm's job hierarchy (horizontal scope); how that hierarchy is structured - number of levels, location of decision-making power, forms of control - will also effect training provision (vertical scope). *A Challenge to Complacency* (Coopers and Lybrand, 1985, pp. 4-5) discovered that in a majority of the firms surveyed, line managers, rather than top executives, are generally responsible for training decisions, thereby hindering long-term manpower planning. British firms also lack structures, like German work councils, which enable employees to exercise control over their own training.

Career/Wage Structure. A company's reward system, how wages and promotion are determined, shapes employees' incentives to pursue training. While education levels are crucial in deciding where an employee enters a firm's job structure, these incentives are low after workers have taken a job because pay and career advancement are determined by seniority not skill levels (George and Shorey, 1985). This disincentive is particularly strong for the growing number of workers trapped in the periphery sector of the labour market (Mayhew, 1986), which features part-time or temporary work, low wages and little or no chance for promotion.

Management. Linking all of the preceding elements of firm organization is the role of management in determining training levels. The poor preparation of British managers, resulting from a dearth of technical HE or management schools and a focus on accounting rather than production, is often cited as a reason for the lack of priority attached to training in Britain (i.e. Davies and Caves, 1987). A recent survey of over 2,500 British firms found that less than half made any provision at all for management training

D. Finegold and D. Soskice

(Anderson, 1987, p. 68). In those firms which do train, managers tend to treat training as an operating expense to be pared during economic downturns and fail to incorporate manpower planning into the firm's overall competitive strategy. For managers interested in career advancement, the training department is generally seen as a low-status option (Coopers and Lybrand, 1985, pp. 4-5). And for poorly qualified line managers, training may be perceived as a threat to their authority rather than a means of improving productivity. It is important, however, to distinguish between bad managers, and able ones who are forced into decisions by the institutional structure in which they are operating. We will explore two of the major forces impacting on their decisions, industrial relations and financial markets, in the following sections.

v) Financial Markets

The short-term perspective of most British managers is reinforced by the pressure to maximize immediate profits and shareholder value. The historical separation of financial and industrial capital (Hall, 1986, p. 59) has made it harder for British firms to invest in training, with its deferred benefits, than their West German or Japanese competitors, particularly since the City has neglected training in its analysis of companies' performance (Coopers and Lybrand, 1985). Without access to large industry-oriented investment banks, British firms have been forced to finance more investment from retained profits than companies in the other G5 nations (Mayer, 1987).

vi) Industrial Relations

Just as the operation of financial markets has discouraged training efforts, so too the structure, traditions, and common practices of British industrial relations have undermined attempts to improve the skills of the work force. The problem must be analysed at two levels: a) the inability of the central union and employer organisations to combine with government to form a co-ordinated national training policy; and b) the historical neglect of training in the collective bargaining process.

Employer Organizations. The strength of the CBI derives from its virtual monopoly status - its members employ a majority of Britain's workers and there is no competing national federation. But while this membership base has given the CBI a role in national training policy formulation, the CBI lacks the sanctions necessary to ensure that employers implement the agreements which it negotiates with the Government. The power lies not in the central federation, nor in industry-wide employers' associations, but in individual firms. The CBI's views on training reflect its lack of control, as Keep (1986, p. 8), a former member of the CBI's Education, Training and Technology Directorate, observes: 'The CBI's stance on training policy . . . was strongly anti-interventionist and centred on a voluntary, market-based approach. Legislation to compel changes in training policy . . . was perceived as constituting an intolerable financial burden on industry.'

This free-market approach, combined with the absence of strong local employer groups, like the West German Chambers of Commerce, has left British industry without an effective mechanism for overcoming the 'poaching' problem. Among the worst offenders are the small and medium-sized firms, poorly represented in the CBI, which lack the resources to provide broad-based training.

Trade Unions. There are four key, closely connected variables which determine the effectiveness of a central union federation in the training field (Woodall, 1985, p. 26). They are: degree of centralisation, financial membership and organisation resources, degree of youth organisation and structure and practice of collective bargaining. Woodall compared the TUC with European central union federations and found it weak along all of these axes. Like the CBI, it could exert a limited influence on government policy, but it lacked the means to enforce centrally negotiated initiatives on its members.

The TUC has had to deal with 'the most complex trade union structure in the world', (Clegg, 1972, p. 57)

OXFORD REVIEW OF ECONOMIC POLICY, VOL. 4, NO. 3

while having little control over its affiliated unions. And whereas the German central union federation, the DGB, claims 12 per cent of its member unions' total receipts, the TUC has received less than 2 per cent and devotes only a small fraction of these resources to training. This inattention to education and training is reflected in unions lack of involvement in the transition from school to work. Britain's major youth organisations, the National Union of Students and Youthaid, grew outside the formal union structure and have often criticized the labour movement for failing to address the needs of the nation's school-leavers, particularly the unemployed. The unco-ordinated nature of British collective bargaining, with agreements varying from coverage of whole industries to small portions of a particular factory, and the lack of central input in the negotiations further hinder TUC efforts to improve training provision. The combination of these factors prompted Taylor (1980, p. 91) to observe that 'by the standards of other Western industrialised nations, Britain provides the worst education services of any trade union movement.'

Although we have broken down this analysis into separate sections for conceptual clarity, it is essential to view each element as part of a historically evolved institutional structure which has limited British ET. In the next part we will examine how the economic crisis of the 1970s destabilized this structure, creating the opportunity for the Thatcher Government's ET reforms.

IV. MRS THATCHER'S EDUCATION AND TRAINING POLICIES

During the 1970s a confluence of events brought an end to the reluctance of central government to take the lead in ET policy-making. The prolonged recession which followed the 1973 oil shock forced the Labour Government to cut public expenditure, necessitating a re-examination of educational priorities. This reassessment came at a time when the education system was drawing mounting criticism in the popular press and the far Right's 'Black Papers' for allegedly falling standards and unchecked teacher progressivism (CCCS, 1981). The response of the then Prime Minister, Callaghan, was to launch the 'Great Debate' on education in a now famous speech at Ruskin College, Oxford in October 1976, where he called on the ET sector to make a greater contribution towards the nation's economic performance (*TES* 22/10/76, p. 72).

The increase in bipartisan political support for vocational and technical education was matched by a strengthening of the central state's capacity to formulate ET policy. The Manpower Services Commission (MSC), a tripartite quango funded by the Department of Employment, was established in 1973 to provide the strong central organization needed to co-ordinate training across industrial sectors which was missing from the industrial training board structure. In practice, however, the ITBs were left to themselves, while the MSC concentrated on the immediate problem of growing youth unemployment. The Commission supervised the first substantial injection of government funds into training, beginning with TOPS (Training Opportunities Scheme) and later through YOP (Youth Opportunities Programme). The rapid increase in government spending, the MSC budget rose from £125 million in 1974-5 to £641 million in 1978-9, did little to improve skills, however, since the funds were concentrated on temporary employment, work experience and short-course training measures and the demands for quick action precluded any long-term manpower planning.

Spurred on by its new rival, the MSC, the DES set up the Further Education Unit (FEU) in 1978, which produced a steady stream of reports that helped shift educational opinion in favour of the 'new vocationalism', (i.e. *A Basis for Choice*, 1979). The Department teamed up with the MSC for the first time in 1976 to launch the Unified Vocational Preparation (UVP) scheme for school-leavers entering jobs which previously offered no training. Although this initiative never advanced beyond the early pilot phase, it set a precedent for subsequent reform efforts.

D. Finegold and D. Soskice

The state structure was in place for the new Thatcher Government to transform the ET system. The first half of this section will outline three distinct phases in the Conservatives' ET reform efforts (see Table

Table 1: Mrs Thatcher's Education and Training Policies

Phase/Date	Characteristics	Programmes		
		Education	Youth Training	Adult Training
I. Preparation 1979-81	Market orientation Weaken resistance Lack overall strategy	Budget cuts	Apprenticeship collapse	Dismantle ITBs
II. NTI 1982-86	Focus on 14-18s Concern with youth unemployment Enterprise economy Increase central control	TVEI Pilot-National Programme in 4 yrs	YTS/ITeCs NCVQ YOP;1 yr YTS; 2 yr YTS YTS apprentice route	TOPS/JTS/CP TOPS-new JTS Focus on adult unemployment
III. Expansion 1987-	Education-new priorities Adults - first attempt at coherence.	GERBIL/CTCs TVEI extension or extinction?	Weaken MSC Compulsory YTS NCVQ finish in 1991.	Weaken MSC Training for employment 600,000 places; no new money.

1), examining how the Government has avoided many of the pitfalls which plagued past efforts at change, while the latter portion will argue that these reforms, while leading to significant shifts in control over ET, will not raise Britain's relative ET performance.

i) Phase 1: Preparation

It is only in retrospect, that the first few years of the Thatcher Administration can be seen as an effective continuation of the movement towards greater centralization of ET power. At the time, Government economic policy was dominated by the belief that controlling the money supply and public expenditure were the keys to reducing inflation and restoring competitiveness. Education and training accounted for approximately 15 per cent of the budget and thus needed to be cut if spending was to be curtailed. The cuts included: across the board reductions in education funding, a drop in state subsidies for apprenticeships and the abolition of seventeen of the twenty-four training boards (one new one was created), despite the opposition of the MSC. The financial rationale for the cuts was underpinned by the then strongly held view of the Government that training decisions were better left to market forces.

The net effect of these cuts, coming at the start of a severe recession in which industry was already cutting back on training, was the collapse of the apprenticeship system. The number of engineering craft and technician trainees, for example, declined from 21,000 to 12,000 between 1979 and 1981, while construction apprentice recruitment fell by 53 per cent during the same period (from EITB and CITB in TUC Annual Report, 1981, pp. 434-5). The destruction of old-style apprenticeships, combined with the Government's attacks on trade unions' restrictive practices through industrial relations legislation, meant that when the state eventually chose to reform initial training within companies, there was only minimal resistance from organized labour and employers.

OXFORD REVIEW OF ECONOMIC POLICY, VOL. 4, NO. 3

ii) Phase II: 'The New Training Initiative'

By 1981 the deepening recession and the dramatic rise in youth unemployment which it caused compelled the Government to reassess its non-interventionist training stance. While the Conservative's neo-liberal economic philosophy offered no immediate cure for mass unemployment, it was politically essential to make some effort to combat a problem which the polls consistently showed to be the voters' primary concern (Moon and Richardson, 1985, p. 61). This electoral need was highlighted in a Downing Street Policy Unit paper from early 1981:

> 'We all know that there is no prospect of getting unemployment down to acceptable levels within the next few years.(Consequently) we must show that we have some political imagination, that we are willing to salvage something - albeit second-best - from the sheer waste involved.' (Riddell, 1985, p. 50.)

What this 'political imagination' produced was the New Training Initiative (NTI) (1981), whose centerpiece, the Youth Training Scheme (YTS), was the first permanent national training programme for Britain's school-leavers. YTS replaced YOP, which had begun as a temporary scheme in 1978 to offer a year's work experience and training to the young unemployed. In just four years, however, YOP had swelled to more than 550,000 places, and as the numbers grew so did the criticism of the programme for its falling job-placement rates and poor quality training. YTS attempted to improve YOP's image by upgrading the training content, 'guaranteeing' a year's placement with at least thirteen weeks off-the-job training to every minimum age school-leaver and most unemployed seventeen year-olds and more than doubling the programme's annual budget, from £400 to £1,000 million.

Despite these improvements, the scheme got off to a difficult start, with a national surplus of close to 100,000 places, as school-leavers proved reluctant to enter the new programme. In response, the MSC implemented a constant stream of YTS reforms: the scheme was lengthened from one to two years, with off-the-job training extended to twenty weeks, all sixteen and seventeen year-olds, not just the unemployed, were made eligible, some form of qualification was to be made available to each trainee, and monitoring and evaluation were increased by requiring all training providors to attain Approved Training Organisation (ATO) status. While the majority of YTS places continue to offer trainees a broad sampling of basic skills ('foundation training') and socialization into a work environment, some industries, such as construction, engineering and hairdressing, have used the scheme to finance the first two years of modernized apprenticeships.

The other major ET reform originating in this period was the Technical and Vocational Education Initiative (TVEI), launched by the Prime Minister in November 1982. TVEI marked the Thatcher Administration's first attempt to increase the industrial relevance of what is taught in secondary schools, through the development of new forms of teacher training, curriculum organisation and assessment for the fourteen-eighteen age group. Under the direction of MSC Chairman David (now Lord) Young, the Initiative grew extremely rapidly, from fourteen local authority pilot projects in 1983 to the start of a nationwide, £1 billion extension just four years later. Lord Young conceived TVEI as a means of fostering Britain's 'enterprise economy', by motivating the vast majority of students who were not progressing to higher education: 'The curriculum in English schools is too academic and leads towards the universities. What I am trying to show is that there is another line of development that is equally respectable and desirable which leads to vocational qualifications . . . ' (*Education*, 19 Nov. 1982, p. 386).

This line of development was extended into the FE sector in 1985 with the introduction of the Certificate of Pre-Vocational Education (CPVE), a one-year programme of broad, work-related subjects for students who wished to stay on in full-time education, but were not prepared for A-levels or a specific career path.

D. Finegold and D. Soskice

In 1985 the Government set up a working group to review Britain's increasingly diverse array of vocational qualifications. The De Ville Committee's Report (1986) led to the establishment of the National Council for Vocational Qualifications (NCVQ) which has the task of rationalizing all of the country's training qualifications into five levels, ranging from YTS to engineering professionals, with clear paths of progression between stages and national standards of proficiency. The Council, which is scheduled to complete its review in 1991, will be defining broad guidelines for training qualifications into which the courses of the independent certification bodies (i.e. RSA, BTEC, City and Guilds) can be slotted.

Taken together these initiatives represent a dramatic reversal in the Government's approach to ET. The scope and pace of reform was made possible by the centralization of power in the hands of the MSC, an institution which has proved adept at securing the co-operation required to implement these controversial changes. In the case of YTS, the MSC has thus far retained trade union support, despite protests from over one-third of the TUC's membership that the schemes lead to job substitution and poor-quality training (*TUC Annual Reports*, 1983-86), because the TUC leadership has refused to give up one of its last remaining channels for input into national policy-making.

The MSC has also become a major power in the educational world because it offered the Conservatives a means of bypassing the cumbersome DES bureaucracy (Dale, 1985, p. 50). The Commission was able to convince teachers and local authorities, who had in the past resisted central government's efforts to reform the curriculum, to go along with TVEI through the enticement of generous funding during a period of fiscal austerity and the use of techniques normally associated with the private sector, such as competitive bidding and contractual relationships (Harland, 1987). Its influence over education increased still further in 1985, when it was given control over 25 per cent of non-advanced further education (NAFE) funding, previously controlled by the LEAs. This change has, in effect, meant that the MSC has the power to review all NAFE provision.

iii) Phase III: Expanding the Focus

The constantly changing nature of ET policy under Mrs Thatcher makes it hazardous to predict future developments, but early indications are that education and training reform will continue to accelerate in her third term. The combination of a successful economy (low inflation, high growth and falling unemployment) and a solid electoral majority has enabled the Conservatives to turn their focus toward fundamental social reform. As a result, the narrow concentration of ET policy on the fourteen-eighteen age group appears to be broadening to include both general education (The Great Education Reform Bill (GERBIL), 1987) and adult training (Training for Employment, 1988).

The 1987 Conservative Election Manifesto signalled the emergence of education reform as a major political issue. While GERBIL is primarily an attempt to raise standards by increasing competition and the accountability of the educational establishment, a number of its provisions will impact on the vocational education and training (VET) area: the National Curriculum, which will ensure that all students take mathematics and science until they reach sixteen; City Technical Colleges, which may signal the beginning of an alternative secondary school track, funded directly by the DES with substantial contributions from industry; the removal of the larger Colleges of Further Education (CFEs) and Polytechnics from LEA control, freeing them to compete for students and strengthening their ties with employers; and increased industry representation on the new governing body for universities, the UFC (University Funding Council).

At the same time, the Government has begun restructuring adult training provision. Over the previous eight years, the MSC concentrated on reducing youth unemployment, while financing a succession of short-duration training and work experience programmes for the long-term unemployed: TOPS (Training Opportunities Scheme - short courses normally based in CFEs), JTS, and new-JTS (Job Training

OXFORD REVIEW OF ECONOMIC POLICY, VOL. 4, NO. 3

Scheme - work placement with minimal off-the-job training for eighteen-to-twenty-fours), and the CP (Community Programme - state-funded public work projects). In February 1988 the Government's White Paper, *Training for Employment*, introduced a plan to combine all of these adult initatives into a new £1.5 billion programme that will provide 600,000 training places, with initial preference given to the eighteen-to-twenty-four age group. To attract the long-run unemployed into the scheme the Government is using both carrot and stick: a training allowance at least £10 above the benefit level, along with increases in claimant advisors and fraud investigators to ensure that all those receiving benefit are actively pursuing work.

The new scheme will be administered by the Training Commission, the heir to the MSC. The Employment Secretary surprised both critics and supporters when he announced that the Government's most effective quango would come to an end in 1988. The new Training Commission lacks the MSC's employment functions, which have been transfered to the DoE, and its governing board structure has been altered to give industry representatives, some now appointed directly rather than by the CBI, effective control. The changes seem to indicate that the Thatcher Government no longer feels the need to consult trade unions and wants to play down the role of the CBI in order to push forward its training reforms.

The Government has also started to devote a limited amount of resources to broadening access to ET for those already in employment. The DES is expanding its PICKUP (Professional, Industrial and Commercial Updating) Programme, which is now spending £12.5 million a year to help colleges, polytechnics and universities tailor their courses more closely to employers' needs. And in 1987, the MSC provided start-up money for the Open College, which along with Open Tech uses open-learning techniques to offer individuals and employers the chance to acquire new skills or update old ones.

iv) **Problems with Mrs Thatcher's ET Policies**

While Mrs. Thatcher has brought about more radical and rapid changes in the ET system than any British leader in the postwar period, there are a number reasons to doubt whether her reforms will succeed in closing the skills gap which has grown between Britain and its major competitors. Rather than detail the shortcomings of specific programmes, we will focus on two major flaws in this Government's ET policy: the lack of coherence and weakness in the many initiatives designed to change the transition from school to FE or employment (reforms for the fourteen-eighteen age group) and the absence of an adult training strategy and sufficient funding to facilitate industrial restructuring.

The Transition from School to Work. Oxford's local education authority has coined a new term, 'GONOT'. GONOT is the name of a committee set up to coordinate GCSE, OES, NLI, OCEA and TVEI,[4] just some of the reforms introduced by the Government since 1981 for the fourteen-eighteen age group. The need to create abbreviations for abbreviations is symptomatic of the strains which the Conservatives' scatter-shot approach to ET policy has placed on those charged with implementing the reforms. The case of TVEI provides a clear illustration of the difficulties created by this incoherence.

When TVEI was first announced one of its primary objectives was to improve staying-on rates. This goal has since been de-emphasized, however, because TVEI's sixteen-eighteen phase comes into direct conflict with YTS. Students have a dual incentive to opt for the narrower training option: first, because YTS offers an allowance, while TVEI does not, and second, because access to skilled jobs is increasingly

----

[4.] These initials stand for: General Certificate of Secondary Education (GCSE), Oxford Examination Syndicate (OES), the New Learning Initiative (NLI) -- part of the Low-Attaining Pupils Programme (LAP), Oxford Certificate of Educational Achievement (OCEA) -- part of the Record of Achievement Initiative and, of course, TVEI.

D. Finegold and D. Soskice

limited to YTS apprenticeships. The failure of the MSC to co-ordinate these programmes is evident at all organizational levels, from the national, where the headquarters are based in different cities, to the local, where the co-ordinators of the two initiatives rarely, if ever, come into contact.

The success of individual TVEI pilot schemes is also threatened by recent national developments. Local TVEI consortia, for example, have built closer ties between schools and the FE sector to rationalize provision at sixteen-plus, a crucial need during a period of falling student numbers. But these consortia are in jeopardy due to GERBIL's proposals for opting out, open enrollment and the removal of the larger Colleges of Further Education (CFEs) from LEA control, which would foster competition rather than co-operation among institutions. Likewise, TVEI's efforts to bridge traditional subject boundaries and the divide between academic and vocational subjects are in danger of being undermined by the proposed national curriculum with its individual subject testing and the failure to include academic examinations (GCSE and A-level) in the National Review of Vocational Qualifications (DeVille Report, 1986, p. 4).

These contradictions stem from divisions within the Conservative Party itself. Dale (1983) identifies five separate factions, industrial trainers, populists, privatizers, old-style Tories and moral educationalists, all exercising an influence on Thatcher's ET policies. Do the Conservatives, for instance, want to spread technical and vocational subjects across the comprehensive curriculum (the TVEI strategy) or ressurrect the old tripartite system's technical school track (the City Technical College route)? Another conflict has emerged in the examination sphere, where modular forms of assessment pioneered under TVEI and GCSE, which are already improving student motivation and practical skills (HMI, 1988), have been stifled by Conservative traditionalists, such as the Minister of State at the DES Angela Rumbold, insisting on preserving the narrow, exclusively academic focus of A-levels and university admissions (Gow, 1988, p. 1). The splits within the Party were highlighted in a leaked letter from the Prime Minister's secretary to Kenneth Baker's secretary, indicating Mrs Thatcher's reservations concerning the forms of assessment proposed by the Black Committee to accompany the National Curriculum (Travis, 1988, p. 1).

Emerging from this unco-ordinated series of reforms appears to be a three-tiered, post-compulsory ET system (Ranson, 1985, p. 63) which will not significantly raise the qualifications of those entering the work force: At the top, higher education will continue to be confined to an academic élite, as the White Paper 'Higher Education - Meeting the Challenge' (1987) projects no additional funds for HE in the next decade, despite growing evidence of graduate shortages; the middle rung of technical and vocational courses in full-time FE seems equally unlikely to expand, given that the Government refuses to consider educational maintenance allowances (EMAs) and that the extension funding for TVEI appears inadequate to sustain its early successes (Dale, 1986); the basic training route, then, will remain YTS, a low-cost option which has not succeeded in solving the skills problem (Deakin and Pratten, 1987; Jones, this issue). As of May 1987, more than half of all YTS providers had failed to meet the quality standards laid down by the MSC (Leadbeater, 1987). And though the quality of training may since have improved, organizations are finding it increasingly difficult to attract school-leavers on to the scheme, as falling rolls lead to increased competition among employers for sixteen year-olds to fill low-skill jobs (Jackson, 1988).

Restructuring/Adult Training. As we have shown (section 2.2), the capacity for continuously updating the skills of the work force is a key factor in the process of industrial restructuring, either at firm or national level. But in the rush to develop new ET initiatives for the fourteen-eighteen sector, the Conservatives have neglected the largest potential pool of trainees: adults in employment. The Government has not secured sufficient extra resources from any of the three basic sources of funding for post-compulsory ET, the state, individuals or companies, to finance a major improvement in British ET performance.

The largest increase in expenditure has come in the state sector, but it is crucial to examine where the money was spent. Although the MSC's budget tripled (to £2.3 billion) during the Conservatives' first two terms, only just over 10 percent of these funds were spent on adult training, the vast majority on the

OXFORD REVIEW OF ECONOMIC POLICY, VOL. 4, NO. 3

long-term unemployed. Those courses, like TOPS, which did offer high-quality training geared to the local labour market, have been phased out in favour of the much-criticized JTS and new-JTS, which offer less costly, lower-skill training (Payne, 1988). This emphasis on quantity over quality was continued in the new 'Training for Employment' package, which proposes to expand the number of training places still further without allocating any new resources. Mrs Thatcher's efforts to improve training within companies have been largely confined to a public relations exercise designed to increase 'national awareness' of training needs (*Training for Jobs*, 1984). Former MSC Chairman Bryan Nicholson made the Government's position clear: 'The state is responsible for education until an individual reaches sixteen. From sixteen to eighteen, education and training are the joint responsibility of industry and government. But from eighteen on, training should be up to the individual and his employer.' (Press Conference at People and Technology Conference, London, November, 1986.)

The Conservatives, however, have had little success in convincing the private sector to assume its share of responsibility for training. While the MSC has been gradually placing a greater portion of YTS funding on employers, the bulk of the cost is still met by the state. In fact, an NAHE study (1987) revealed that private training organizations were making a profit off the MSC's training grants. The Government may be regretting its decision to do away with the one legislative means of increasing employers' funding for training, as this remark made last year by Nicholson indicates: 'Those industries who have made little effort to keep the grand promises they made when the majority of ITBS were abolished should not be allowed to shirk forever.' (Clement, 1986, p. 3)

Mrs Thatcher has made somewhat more progress in her attempts to shift the ET burden on to individuals, who can fund their own ET either through direct payments (course fees, living expenses) or by accepting a lower wage in exchange for training. The state has compelled more school-leavers to pay for training by removing sixteen and seventeen year-olds from eligibility for benefits and then setting the trainee allowance at a level well below the old apprenticeship wage. It has also forced individuals staying on in full-time education to make a greater financial contribution to their own maintenance costs through the reduction of student grants, a policy which seems certain to accelerate with the introduction of student loans.

These measures, however, are not matched by policies to encourage adults to invest their time and money towards intermediate or higher-level qualifications. This failure can be traced to three sources: lack of opportunity, capital and motivation. The state's assumption of the full costs of higher education (HE), among the most expensive per pupil in the world, has resulted in a strictly limited supply of places. Those individuals who wish to finance courses below HE level suffer both from limited access to capital and a tax system which, unlike most European countries, offers employees no deductions for training costs (DES, 1988). But the main reason for workers' reluctance to invest in their own training is that the Government has done nothing to alter the basic operation of British firms which, as we saw in section three, are not structured to reward improvements in skill levels.

This underinvestment in ET raises the question: If it is true that training is critical to economic restructuring and that Mrs Thatcher has failed to improve Britain's poor ET record, why has the UK grown faster than all the major industrial nations, except Japan, over the last eight years? Part of the answer lies in the Conservatives' success in creating more efficient low-cost production and services economy. A series of supply-side measures, weakening Wage Councils and employment security legislation, subsidizing the creation of low-wage jobs (the Young Workers Scheme) and attacking trade unions, have improved labour mobility and company profitability. Training programmes, like YTS, have played a pivotal role in this process, providing employers with a cheap means of screening large numbers of low-skilled, but well-socialized young workers (Chapman and Tooze, 1986). The liberalization of financial markets, with the resultant pressure on firms to maximize short-term profits, and the explosion of accountancy-based management consultancy (*Business Week*, June 1988) have further reinforced industry's cost-cutting approach. The irony is that while Britain is striving to compete more effectively with low-cost producers

D. Finegold and D. Soskice

such as South Korea and Singapore, these nations are investing heavily in general education and training to enable their industries to move into flexible, high technology production.

V. POLICIES FOR THE FUTURE.

This section suggests in broad terms what policies could remedy the insufficiencies of our system of education and training. It covers both those in the sixteen to twenty age group and the (far larger) adult labour force. We take the quantitative goal to be the broad level which the Japanese, German and Swedes have achieved, namely where about 90 per cent of young people are in full-time highly-structured education and training until nineteen or twenty. And, less precisely, that major improvements take place in the training of those already in the workforce, both by the employer and externally. Training of managers, in particular of supervisers, is treated in relation to these goals.

What type of education and training? There is broad agreement about the need to raise ET standards and levels, but less about its content. This reflects the failure of the (opposed) ET methodologies of the post-war decades: manpower planning, on the one hand, and human capital theory, on the other. Manpower planning has proved too inflexible in a world in which long-run predictions about occupational needs can seldom be made. And the rate of return calculations underlying human capital approaches to optimal training provision have foundered on the difference between social and market valuations. While both approaches have a role to play when used sensibly, few practitioners would see either as sufficient to determine the content of ET.

Reform of education and training is seen in this section as part of the process of 'managing change'. This context argues for three general criteria as determining the content of education and training.

First, the uncertainty of occupational needs in the future requires *adaptability*. Many people in the labour force will have to make significant career changes in their working lives, which will require retraining. There is some agreement that successful retraining depends on a high level of general education and also on previous vocational training. Moreover, as much training for new occupations covers skills already acquired in previous ET (e.g. computing skills), a modular approach to training is efficient.

Second, ET needs to equip workers with the skills required for *innovation in products and processes* and the *production of high quality goods and services*. One implication is that participation in higher education will have to steadily increase. And there is a more radical implication, as Hayes and others have stressed: effective innovation and quality production requires participation: that means that workers and managers should acquire not just technical competence, but also the social and managerial skills involved in working together. We may need increasingly to blur the distinction between management ET and worker ET. The implications are various: a high level of general education, sufficiently broad that young people are both technically competent and educated in the humanities and arts; strong emphasis on projects, working together and interdisciplinary work; vocational education and training which provides management skills as well as technical understanding. More generally, ET should be designed to reduce class barriers (not only as a good in itself, but also) because of the requirements of innovation and high-quality production.

Third, ET must be *recognisable* and *useful*, so that employers want to employ the graduates of the ET system and young people and adults want to undertake ET. There is a potential tension here with the previous paragraph. For the abilities stressed there are at present only demanded by a minority of companies. Vocational education is thus a compromise between the characteristics needed in the longer term and the skills and knowledge which companies can see as immediately useful to them. A second

OXFORD REVIEW OF ECONOMIC POLICY, VOL. 4, NO. 3

implication of the need for recognition and usefulness is that there be a widely agreed and understood system of certification, based on acceptable assessment.

Much policy discussion, sensibly, concerns potential improvements within the broad context of the existing framework of ET provision within the UK. As a result less thought has been given to the wider transformations which we believe the management of change and the move to a high skills equilibrium imply. The discussion of this section thus takes a longer-term perspective.

There are five interdependent parts to these recommendations for reform: reforming ET provision for the sixteen to twenty age group; training by companies; individual access to training; the external infrastructure of ET; and the macro-economic implications of a major ET expansion.

i) The Education and Training of Sixteen to Twenty Year-Olds

The focus of this section is on how incentives, attitudes, institutions and options can be changed so that young people will choose to remain in full-time education and training until the age of nineteen or twenty, rather than entering the labour market or YTS at age sixteen.

For two reasons the next decade offers a window for reform which was not previously open. First, the demographic decline in the sixteen-plus age cohort will mean a drop of nearly a third over the next ten years in the numbers of young people aged between sixteen and nineteen. It will therefore be an ideal period for bringing our system into line with that of other advanced countries. For the resource cost, although considerable, of a substantial increase in the ET participation ratio of sixteen to nineteen year-olds will be significantly less than in the past decade.

The second reason was spelt out in section four. The institutional constraints against change are in two ways significantly weaker now than a decade or two decades ago. Unions at national level, far from seeking to frustrate change, would support it in this area; they would see it as a means of regaining membership, rather than a threat to the bargaining position of existing skilled workers. The education system (teachers, LEAs, educationalists, teachers unions) no longer sees itself as having the right to determine education policy alone; central government has far stronger control over it than in the past, and this will increase over the next decade as opting out develops; the larger CFEs will no longer be run by LEAs; teachers unions are moving away from the belief that they can successfully oppose government to the view that they need to cultivate wider alliances, including industry; and educationalists today are far more aware of the role which schools can play in helping children to get employment. In addition political parties are no longer constrained as they were (say) two decades ago in formulating policy in these areas.

What basic requirements are implied for a sixteen to twenty ET system by the discussion in the introduction above? Five should be stressed:

— Good general education, covering both technical subjects and the humanities.

— This should be designed to encourage interaction (project etc.) and reduce social class differences.

— Rising percentage over time going into HE, and ease of switching between more vocational and more academic routes.

— Structured vocational training for those not going on to HE, with acquisition of broad skills, including communications and decision-making competences.

— Modularisation and certification.

D. Finegold and D. Soskice

Despite the 'window of opportunity'" how feasible is the sort of major change envisaged? Aside from the question of financing, formidable problems will need to be resolved:

(a) Young people have the option at sixteen to remain in full-time education. About 65 per cent choose not to. Raising the legal minimum school leaving age to eighteen is politically not a possibility, and in any case it is desirable that young people should choose to stay on. How are incentives to be structured and attitudes changed to raise the staying-on rate to above 80 per cent?

(b) Relatively few businesses are currently capable of providing high-quality training. And, while employer organisations are becoming more committed to involvement in ET, effective action on their part will require a co-ordinating capacity which is beyond their present power or resources.

(c) In comparison to other countries with well-developed vocational training systems the UK lacks an effective administrative structure and a major research and development capacity.

Of these constraints the first must be overcome. It will be argued in this section that the involvement of employers and their organisations and a proper state infrastructure will be needed to achieve both this and the ET desiderata set out above. To see why this is the case, we look first at why sixteen year-olds choose to leave education and training, and with this in mind, examine the experience of sixteen-twenty ET in other countries.

Why do such a large proportion of young people choose to join the labour market or YTS at sixteen? There are two main reasons. The first is financial. On YTS or social security young people get a small income. If they remain in full-time education they receive nothing (their parents receiving child benefit). There are therefore strong inducements to leave full-time education at sixteen. The demographic shrinking of the sixteen-plus age group (while it will make reform easier) will, in the absence of reform, strengthen the incentive to leave; this is because employers are accustomed to recruiting from this age group, directly or nowadays through YTS, since it provides relatively cheap and pliable labour, so that relative earnings at sixteen-plus may be expected to rise.

In the second place, staying on in full-time ET has not been seen as a bridge to stable employment. The best route to employment for most sixteen year-olds today is via YTS, which is used by many employers as a screening device for the choice of permanent employees. YTS trainees who show themselves to be co-operative have a high probability of securing permanent employment; and that probability will rise as the demographic decline in the sixteen-plus age cohort sets in.

Foreign experience can give an idea of different possible systems of sixteen-twenty ET, as well as alerting to some of the problems.

— One country often cited as an exemplar is the US. About 75 per cent of the relevant age group graduates from high school by age eighteen after a broadly based course, more academically geared for those going on to HE, more vocational for those going directly into the labour market. Over 40 per cent go on to two year junior colleges or university, producing a remarkably educated population. But there are problems with the education and training of those who do not go on to HE. In many areas, lack of co-ordinated employer involvement has meant there is no clear bridge between education and employment. The 'Boston compact', under which a group of companies guaranteed training and employment against for good high school performance, acknowledged this need. And lack of involvement by companies in sixteen to twenty ET has limited firms' provision of training for manual workers and low-level white collar workers.

— France has a more highly structured system of initial vocational training. Less able children can go to vocational schools from fourteen to eighteen, and end with craft-level qualifications. More emphasis in the future is being placed on the various higher-level vocational *baccalaureat* courses, from

OXFORD REVIEW OF ECONOMIC POLICY, VOL. 4, NO. 3

sixteen to nineteen, which turns out technician engineers with managerial skills. Compared with the UK, both routes are impressive, especially the second. But, as in the US, there is limited employer involvement. One consequence is staying-on rates at sixteen-plus well below the Northern European and Japanese, and a higher rate of youth unemployment. A second is limited training for manual workers in companies.

— In the Germanic (Germany, Austria, Switzerland) system, those going on to higher education spend two years from sixteen to eighteen in a high school before taking the *abitur*. Those working for vocational qualifications become apprenticed at sixteen for three or four years and follow a highly structured, carefully monitored system of on-the-job and off-the-job training and education, with external exams on both practical and theoretical subjects.

— In the Scandanavian (Norway, Sweden) system, young people remain in the same college between sixteen and eighteen, specialising in vocational or academic areas; vocational education is then completed in vocational centres post-eighteen.

— Denmark has been actively experimenting with post-sixteen ET in the last two decades. The Danes have been moving towards a system in which all young people remain within the same educational institution between sixteen and eighteen, more or less a tertiary college. If they choose the vocational route, they move into a two year apprenticeship at eighteen, for which much work will have already been covered in the college.

Both the Germanic and Scandinavian systems succeed in attaining very high participation rates for thw sixteen-eighteen age groups, and in delivering high-quality vocational training as well as good general education. There are, however, arguments against both Germanic and Scandinavian systems as the optimal model for the UK, despite the fact that both systems are greatly superior to our own. The main argument against applying the Scandinavian system to the British context is that Britain lacks the infrastructure to make it work: the close involvement of employer organisations with the public system of vocational education. Moreover, there is powerful union and state pressure on companies to maintain training standards.

The Germanic system also has disadvantages, in part because it would be based too strongly on employers if transplanted to the UK. There are four reasons why we should be wary of advocating a German-type division at sixteen between academic education and an employer-based three or four-year apprenticeship:

— The greater the employer involvement (unless restrained by powerful employer organisations and unions as in Germany), the more the apprenticeship will reflect the short term needs of the employer. This is illustrated by the otherwise excellent EITB engineering apprenticeship scheme in the UK: broken into modules, employers select those modules most relevant to their own needs, rather than to the longer-term needs of the trainee.

— Few UK employers are in a position to run quality three or four year apprenticeships; but these would be needed across the board in public and private sectors, and in industry and services.

— If young people were to move into employer-based apprenticeships at sixteen, it would *de facto* close them off from higher education.

— Equally, by dividing the population at sixteen, the opportunity to reduce class distinctions would not be taken.

How, then, should sixteen-twenty ET evolve in the future? We believe a system very roughly along Danish lines is the most feasible model to aim for, given the current UK position.

D. Finegold and D. Soskice

(1) *A common educational institution from sixteen to eighteen.* Apart from the Germanic countries, the US and Scandanavia, as well as Japan (more or less), have a common institution from sixteen to eighteen. France and Denmark have both been moving towards it as a matter of conscious choice. It is an obvious vehicle for encouraging a rising percentage of young people to go on to higher education at eighteen. Equally it has a necessary part to play in reducing class differences.

(2) *Accelerated apprenticeships post-eighteen: the bridge to employment.* The Germanic and Scandinavian systems, and Japan and South Korea, provide at least four years of ET post-sixteen. This could be done in the UK by short, highly structured apprenticeships, which would at the same time build clear bridges to employment. If further training was carried out mainly in vocational schools post-eighteen, this bridging perception would be less clear; of course, vocational schools would be important post-eighteen, since UK companies would require considerable help if they were to provide high-quality training. The next section 5.2 discusses how companies could develop high-quality training capacities: it is evident that if they can the benefits would go beyond sixteen-twenty ET; the need for companies in both public and private sectors to develop effective training capacities is central to the management of change.

(3) *Linking post-eighteen apprenticeships with pre-eighteenET.* In order for two-year apprenticeships to be of high quality, considerable preparatory work towards them will need to have been completed pre-eighteen. It is also important to make clear to students the link between what is expected from them in the sixteen-eighteen period and their subsequent training opportunities. Preparatory work covers both general and vocational education. The role of a good general education, covering technical subjects and the humanities, has already been stressed, as has the parallel need for vocational education to include the acquisition of broad skills including communications and decision-making competences, with emphasis on developing individual initiative and team-work through projects. Vocational education will also be focused in part on the chosen apprenticeship area. Thus, for those who choose it at sixteen, there will be a 'vocational' route, with specific and general requirements for particular apprenticeship areas.

(4) *Modules and certification.* Vocational qualifications would be awarded and HE entrance requirements satisfied by successfully completed modules. In the case of HE the modules would all be taken in the common institution; it would be natural to think of AS levels as module-based (the original intention), and that the major part of the most common route to satisfying HE entrance requirements would consist in completing the modules needed to gain so many AS levels. To gain a vocational qualification, and to fulfil the condition for entry to an apprenticeship, a substantial proportion of the necessary modules could and should be completed pre-eighteen. A modular system in a single institution provides considerable flexibility. Most students would choose early on a vocational or an HE route; but if some proportion of AS modules were allowed for vocational qualification purposes and some proportion of vocational modules for entry into HE, those students who wished to do so could keep their options open for longer. Modules could also be used to broaden HE entry requirements, and to increase the general education component in vocational qualification. There might in addition be a case for a college graduation diploma, as in many countries, based on successful completion of modules.

(5) *Employer co-ordination and involvement.* A high degree of employer co-ordination and involvement will be needed to make this system work. That is the positive lesson of Northern Europe. Local co-ordination is necessary to link 'training' employers with educational institutions and with students. At a regional and national level, employer involvement is needed to help develop curricula, monitoring of 'trainers', assessment procedures, and so on. This will require more powerful employer organisations, nationally, sectorally and locally than the UK has now. How this might be achieved is further discussed below.

(6) *Role of unions.* Many 'training' employers, especially in the public sector, are unionised, so that union co-operation will be needed. Union involvement in curriculum development and the like will also be

OXFORD REVIEW OF ECONOMIC POLICY, VOL. 4, NO. 3

important in balancing the power of employer organisations. This again is a lesson from the experience of Sweden and Germany.

(7) *Local and national government.* Government has played a key role in providing a coherent framework for the sixteen-twenty ET system at local, regional and national level in each of the countries discussed, with the exception of the US. The UK lacks institutional coherence in this area, and has only a limited research and policy-making capacity.

(8) *Education maintenance allowance and financial incentives.* A central purpose of the reform strategy suggested above has been to construct a clear bridge from education to employment so that young people stay within a well-structured ET system from the age of sixteen to nineteen or twenty. This is in line with the instrumental view of education taken by most young people who leave at sixteen (Brown, 1987). But to be successful in raising the sixteen-plus participation rate, it is also necessary to ensure that leaving at sixteen is less attractive than staying on. This will require, first, an educational maintenance allowance for those who stay on, at least equal to state payments for those who leave. More fundamentally, it raises the question of reducing employer incentives to hire sixteen year olds, and convincing them to stop seeing the sixteen-plus age group as its main recruiting ground for unskilled and semi-skilled labour (Ashton & Maguire, 1988). This is discussed in the next section.

ii) Developing the Training Capacity of Employers

International comparisons suggest that UK employers devote a smaller share of value added to training expenditures than any other major advanced country. For radical reform to be successful, the attitude of employers will have to change, as has been seen in the discussion in the last section of post-sixteen ET and restructuring: specifically, the development by employers of a training capacity is necessary for a system of accelerated apprenticeships. In addition to sixteen-twenty ET, a training capacity is needed for restructuring within organisations for training and retraining existing employees.

In looking at restructuring, it is useful to distinguish between retraining by the existing employer, which will be referred to as internal retraining, and retraining elsewhere, primarily in state/union/employer-organisation or private vocational training centres. This will be referred to as external retraining and will be discussed below. Roughly the internal/external retraining distinction corresponds to that between internal (e.g. changing product composition within a company) and external (e.g. closures/running down an industry) restructuring.

With internal restructuring companies meet declining demand by product innovation. In countries where product innovation strategies are emphasised they are associated with reliable sources of long-term finance, and long-term relations with suppliers which the company does not wish to disrupt. More important, they are associated with internal training capacities in companies, a retrainable workforce with on-the-job flexibility and a high perceived cost to making workers redundant (Streeck et al., 1985; Sorge and Streeck, 1988; Hotz-Hart, 1988). The high perceived cost may arise from legal requirements, as in Germany, or collective bargaining power, as in Sweden, or from a basic communitarian view of the enterprise, as in Japan (Dore, 1987). Cost reduction strategies under these circumstances will tend to focus on reducing capital or material or financing costs, rather than labour saving changes. Again, retraining capacities are critical.

In the UK much more use has been made of external restructuring. This reflects the lack of the characteristics described in the last paragraph as associated with internal restructuring in countries such as Germany, Japan and Sweden. Instead the UK is characterised by:

D. Finegold and D. Soskice

(i) The organisation of production around relatively standardised goods and services, with low skill requirements and cost-cutting rather than technically competent management; aggravated by:

— the public goods problem; and

— the pressure of financial institutions and, in the public sector, cash limits against long-term investment activity.

(ii) The lack of pressure from employees to maintain training; and the ease with which companies can make workers redundant without being required to consider product innovation and retraining as alternative ways of maintaining employment.

(iii) The lack of an effective infrastructure. Few sectors of the economy have well developed training structures, with worked out systems of certification, training schools, and information and counselling for companies. Employers organisations are weak, and unions are seldom equipped to provide good training services to their members.

The difficulties involved in increasing company expenditure on training and ensuring it is of the right quality are thus substantial. In a longish-term perspective two general points may be made:

— The increase in the educational level of young people entering the labour force and a different attitude to adult education and training will make it easier for companies to move to a higher skills equilibrium.

— Policies to change company behaviour on training should be one part of a co-ordinated strategy to help companies focus on marketing, product innovation, new technology, high-quality production, and provision of long-term finance. Education and training policies should be closely linked to industrial and regional policies; but to trace out these links would be beyond the scope of this paper. Four main policy directions are set out here: how they might be financed, where not implicit, is discussed below.

(1) *Financial incentives.* There is little question that companies in both public and private sectors need financial incentives (positive or negative) if they are significantly to increase their training activities. This is because, for the foreseeable future, there will be a divergence between private and public returns because of the public good problem and the low-skills equilibrium. (The general strategy advocated in this paper is designed to reduce the divergence over time, but specific incentives will be necessary until then.)

The form of the incentives is critical. A minimum legal requirement is unlikely to be productive, at least by itself. It might take one of two forms: a requirement to spend a certain minimum percentage of value added or payroll on training; and/or a requirement to carry out certain types of training, e.g. to take so many apprentices, with a significant enough penalty to gain compliance. One problem with both approaches is that some companies may be better placed to carry out effective training than others. In addition, the minimum percentage approach (by itself) says nothing about who gets trained: in France this approach led to senior managers being sent to expensive hotels in the French Pacific to learn English. And the 'minimum number of apprentices' approach poses formidable quality problems.

A sensible approach, at least to start with, is to give financial incentives to companies (private and public) who are prepared to train and undergo the monitoring and other conditions necessary to ensure both quality and coverage (i.e. that training covers apprenticeships and semi-skilled workers as well as managers, etc.). The further conditions are discussed in the next paragraph. These incentives would not need to be uniform across industries, regions or types of training.

OXFORD REVIEW OF ECONOMIC POLICY, VOL. 4, NO. 3

(2) *Meisters and certification.* How are we to ensure that companies train to the right quality and over the desired coverage? In Japan, Germany and similar countries, the role of the supervisor in both industry and services is different to the UK superviser, (see e.g. Prais and Wagner, 1988). In those countries supervisors (in German *'meister'*) are technically skilled as well as playing a management role; moreover they have major responsibility for training. In the German system, they have themselves to pass a rigorous training after having gained a technician or craft-level qualification. The above suggests ideas along the following lines:

(a) A distinction should be drawn between certified skills and non-certified skills. This would be similar to the distinction between marketable and firm-specific skills. In practical terms it would reflect those that the NCVQ included as certifiable.

(b) Companies wishing to participate in the training of employees for certified skills would be required to employ certified 'training supervisers', i.e. similar to German *meisters.*

(c) The Government could then negotiate with employer organisations tariffs for different certified skills, and use this as one means of influencing the size and distribution of training. Those companies would then get automatic payments for certified training, subject to periodic inspections and subject to satisfactory results of trainees in external assessment.

In summary, financial incentives should be used, not just to produce a desired amount of training, but also to ensure that companies acquire a training capacity and supervisory staff with a professional commitment to training.

(3) *Changing the age structure of hiring.* Specific disincentives will be needed to dissuade businesses from hiring sixteen-eighteen year olds over the next decade.

(4) *Employee representation.* Again, as in Northern Europe, it is sensible to give employees a role in decision-making on training within companies. They have an interest in the acquisition of certified skills. For this role to be effective, decisions on training would need to be codetermined between management and employees. In addition, continental experience suggests that employee representatives need union expertise if they are to challenge low-spending management with any chance of success.

In particular, it is important to enable employees to challenge management decisions on redundancies. In the German model, management is required to reach an agreement with the works council on how redundancies are to be dealt with. The cost to management of not reaching an agreement means that managers emphasise innovation and retraining in their long-term planning.

(5) *External infrastructure.* Both (2) and (3) impose strong demands on an external infrastructure. Companies will in practice rely heavily on the advice of employer organisations, whom they can trust at least to give advice in the interest of the sector they represent, if not in the interest of the individual company. Employees need the advice of unions if they are to challenge company decisions on training and redundancies. Public or tripartite bodies will be required to provide R & D on training technology and labour market developments (e.g. skill shortages); to run a system of certification; and to provide training where it is needed to complement company training. How this can be done is discussed in 5.4.

iii) A Culture of Lifetime Education and Training.

There is an apparent lack of interest by adults in the UK in continuing education and training. In countries with good training systems, a strong belief by individuals in the benefits of ET reinforces the system: parents can see the value of education and training for their children; employees put pressure on laggardly employers to provide training; the public good problem which companies face is reduced by individuals

D. Finegold and D. Soskice

paying for the acquisition of marketable skills. Yet in the UK little adult training takes place which is not paid for by the employer; this is in particular the case for unskilled and semi-skilled employees and for the unemployed. Why is human capital theory wrong in asserting that individuals will be prepared to pay for the acquisition of marketable skills? Why especially is this the case when vacancies for skilled jobs coexist with high unemployment and insecure semi-skilled employment?

In the first place, individuals seldom have access to financial resources sufficient to finance any extended period of vocational training:

(a) Borrowing. Financial institutions are reticent about lending without security for training, except for a few cases where returns from the training are high. This is not particular to UK financial institutions. Banks in most countries will not lend for ET purposes to individuals, unless the loans are guaranteed or subsidised or unless the bank has close connections and knowledge of a community. This likely reflects both moral hazard and adverse selection problems.

(b) There is limited access to state subsidy for most adult vocational training, particularly for maintenance, but also for tuition. Individual expenditure on training is in general not tax deductible. The unemployed likewise have limited access to funds: their retraining possibilities seldom relate to those areas in which there are vacancies.

(c) Major reductions in income are seldom feasible for those who are employed; *a fortiori* for those who are unemployed.

Secondly, the individual return from much vocational training is not high. There are several reasons for this:

(a) The low-skills equilibrium organisation of work means that the marginal productivity of skills for individual workers is below what it would be in an economy where a large enough proportion of the workforce was skilled to permit a high-skills pattern of work organisation.

(b) For a large proportion of the workforce (manual and low-level white-collar) there reflects the organisation of work discussed. Second, differentials for skilled workers were heavily compressed in the 1970s, and though they have widened since, they are still not high in comparison to high-skill countries. (Prais and Wagner, 1988.)

(c) A large proportion of the workforce does not have the basic education required to proceed to craft-level vocational training; so a major prior investment is necessary.

(d) The existing system of certification is unhelpful, as the NCVQ has emphasised. Aside from being confusing, it fails to give employers real guarantees in many areas as to the competences of the certified employee, because of the lack of proper assessment procedures. In addition, and more important, portability is limited. In the modern economy skills obsolesce. The acquisition of new skills should not involve returning to square one, as it frequently does today.

(e) Finally, for those who are currently employed, and wish independently to take leave to pursue education or training, there is seldom a guarantee that they will be able to keep their job.

This means that major self-financed training or retraining is not seen as a realistic possibility, if it is considered at all, by most unskilled or semi-skilled workers or those who are unemployed. Moreover, with the exceptions of a few unions who provide good counselling services, little advice is available.

(1) *A comprehensive external training system.* Those who seek, or might be persuaded to seek, external training fall into two categories with some overlapping: people with clear goals and courses in mind, adequate previous education and training, but held back by unavailability of finance or employment insecurity; and the unskilled, semi-skilled and unemployed with little belief in the possibility of effective retraining. For both groups adequate financing is necessary. There is a strong case for formalising a system

OXFORD REVIEW OF ECONOMIC POLICY, VOL. 4, NO. 3

of education credits for adults. These credits would be intended for training not covered by companies. The general question of financing is considered below, but it should be noted here that if individuals had their own 'training accounts', into which education credits were put, these credits could be added to by saving, perhaps topped-up by public funding. For most people in the second group, additional financing will be necessary, since it will not be reasonable to expect them to save enough. It is of great importance that those threatened by redundancy or made redundant are given sufficient resources for long periods of ET. Along Swedish lines, a reasonable income might be conditioned on in effect a contract to train for a given range of skills in which there are vacancies or in which employment is likely.

For this group, much more is required than financing. Also needed are counselling, an information system covering vacancies and future areas of demand, structured basic education if necessary, training and retraining facilities (though they might be in the private sector and hired by the state), and a support system to facilitate mobility if needed. How an external retraining system might be set up is discussed in the next section.

(2) *Returns to skills.* This is an important problem to which there are few easy solutions. We argued above for policies to encourage the development of a supervisory grade with technical qualifications: if successful, that would help the concept of a career ladder based on skills. It is harder for the government to intervene in the process of wage determination, and widen skill differentials even if there is case for doing so. In our view, the more sensible approach is to give incentives to employers to increase training, on the one hand, and to develop an external training policy to help redundant and potentially redundant workers, who have less need of incentives to acquire skills, on the other.

iv) Institutional Infrastructure

Radical reform of ET requires a more effective institutional infrastructure than presently exists. Our view is that radical reform is not a simple political option, but one requiring major institutional changes which will be difficult to bring about in the UK, at least if reform is to realise its full potential. This returns the argument to those economic historians that our basic economic problems lie in our institutions.

It was argued in section four that the old constraining infrastructure has broken down; and that the Government has substituted increased centralised control via the MSC (as was) and the DES, combined with the use of contracts with training agencies. The centralisation of policy-making has not been accompanied by a significant expansion of the very limited research and information-gathering capacities of the MSC and the DES. A parallel can be drawn between this system and large conglomerates controlled by a small financially-oriented headquarters. The new system will become more pronounced as: (a) local education authorities have a diminished role in post-sixteen ET, with the removal of polytechnics and the larger CFEs from their control, with the decline in importance of TVEI, and with the possible opting out of secondary schools; (b) the wide variety of course-development, assessment and accreditation bodies are encouraged to behave more competitively; and (c) the NCVQ becomes more a body carrying out government instructions, especially in relation to certification of YTS trainees, than a forum in which different points of view, of the business community, of unions and of educationalists and trainers can be expressed.

The new system is hardly adequate for dealing with YTS and ATS; it has major drawbacks if it is to carry through radical reform. We will argue that a different system needs to be developed in which employers organisations, unions, educationalists and the regions should all ideally play a more important part; and in which the role of government should be more concerned with the provision of information, research and development, and coordination, than with unilateral policy-making.

D. Finegold and D. Soskice

(1) *The need for better information, R & D, and co-ordination.* The reforms discussed in the preceding sub-sections involve major course developments: for sixteen-eighteen year olds; for accelerated apprenticeships; for those at work; for *meisters*; for those undertaking external retraining; together with development of assessment procedures, certification and accreditation of examining bodies. It will be necessary to co-ordinate academic examining boards with vocational training institutions such as BTEC; and to co-ordinate the activities of the vocational institutions themselves. Also, it is important to allow experimentation and thus course development by individual teachers or trainers, and a mechanism is needed to permit the diffusion of best-practice innovations. All this demands a much greater role of government in the R & D and co-ordination process. This might perhaps be on the lines of regional labour market and regional education boards in Sweden.

For two broad reasons, a more effective ET system also requires involvement by the social partners (employers' organisations and unions) as well as educational institutions and the Government. The first is to ensure that policy-making is conducted in a balanced way, (2) below. The second is to bring about the participation of companies (3), and employees (4).

(2) *Multilateral participation in ET governance.* Running a complex ET system is a principal-agent problem. However clear the ideas of the Government (the principal) and however effective its own research and development activities, the co-operation of teachers and trainers as agents is essential to efficient course development, assessment, etc. But educators will have their own interests. (Japan is a case in point, where educationalists dominate the development of sixteen-eighteen education, business has no influence, and where rote learning still plays a major role.) A tempting solution is for governments to use expert civil servants as additional agents; of course it is important that government experts should be involved, but there is a danger: if detailed polcy-making is left to government experts and educationalists, the former may assimilate over time the goals of the latter, particularly if governments change.

A more effective solution is to balance the interests of educators against the interests of employers and those of employees. Hence the case for involving their representatives as additional agents, to bring about more balanced objectives. If this is to be successful, both employers' organisations and unions need expertise; here again Northern European experience, where the social partners have their own research institutions, in some cases financed by the state, is suggestive. Moreover, as employers' organisations and unions acquire expertise, so a common culture of understanding and agreement on a range of training issues gets built up by professionals on all sides. Thus the agents, with their different interests but shared culture, become players in a co-operative game over time in which compromise and flexibility are available to meet changing conditions. (For a broader use of this type of approach, see the insightful Lange, 1987.)

A similar case can be made for involving representatives of regions in addition to central government. For individual regions will have their own economic goals, and more political stability than central government. Again, effective involvement requires expertise. This reinforces the argument for regional labour market and regional education boards.

(3) *Employers' organisations and the participation of companies.* Most companies see no gain in participating in training in marketable skills and associated activities to a socially optimal degree. This is both because of the standard prisoner's dilemma problem and the low skills equilibrium. As a partial solution to both problems we suggested the use of financial incentives to encourage the building up of a training capacity within companies. Important though that is by itself, its effectiveness can be greatly enhanced through employers' organisations. First, getting companies to train in the right way is difficult for government, because of an assymetry of information: the company knows much more about how good its training is than the Government. Companies are often loathe to be monitored by, or give detailed information to, government, because they distrust the use to which the information will be put. Employers'

OXFORD REVIEW OF ECONOMIC POLICY, VOL. 4, NO. 3

organisations are in a better position to engage the co-operation of companies, because they are seen to be on the side of companies as a whole. Secondly, powerful employers' organisations, as in Germany, can sanction free-riders more cheaply than the Government. This is the case where employers' organisations distribute a range of valued services to companies, not necessarily just in the training area; and have a degree of discretion over their distribution. One of these services may be training advice; others might be in, say, export marketing. This gives the organisation potential sanctions, which might enable it, for instance, to organise local co-ordination of companies with respect to the bridge between education and employment; or to prod companies into increasing training activities.

(4) *Employees and unions.* Unions have several important roles to play in an effective ET system, as mentioned above. Here we want to stress the role of unions in promoting employee involvement in training decision-making. Such involvement is a critical component of high-skill economies. If it is to be effective, employees must be properly backed up by union advice and expertise.

Much of the argument of this sub-section is influenced by the study of why the Scandinavian and Germanic ET systems have been successful. There is an important research agenda here for the UK. We do not want to suggest the type of powerful employers organisations or union confederations in those countries, or regional government as in Germany is transplantable, it is not. But there is a strong case for giving muscle to employers' organisations and unions, and to regions and perhaps metropolitan areas, in the training field. Unions are moving in the UK (some much faster than others) to consider training as a core area of their interests. Business organisations are moving less fast, but in the right direction. Radical reform of ET will need a push by government. One possibility, for a radical reforming government, is to give the social partners the resources to develop major expertise in training. A second is to consider whether chambers of commerce can play a more significant role at local level, so as to enable them to develop local employer networks. Third, to consider the possibilities of regional labour market and regional education boards as quadripartite institutions, with educationalists and regional representatives as well as the social partners.

5. Macroeconomic and Financing Implications

The preceding four sub-sections have looked at the micro aspects of policies needed for transforming the post-sixteen education and training system. They have suggested how to change incentives facing individuals and organisations; how co-ordinating and providing institutions could be built up; and how training policies should be seen as part of a broader micro-economic strategy directed at changing ways in which companies operate. If successful these changes carry great benefits in terms of macro-economic performance. But to be successful they require a major injection of resources.

In a steady-state, the benefits can be assumed to outweigh the resource cost. But in the process of the transforming the system, resource costs would be likely to precede the benefits of additional resources. There is not the space in this article to discuss in detail the financing of this gap. But we want to make some brief points to indicate why we believe that increased expenditures in this area can be more easily managed than in many others.

The increased resources devoted to ET can be met in one or more of three ways:

— an increase in GDP;

— a reduction in other expenditures;

— an increase in imports.

There are two reasons why some part of the resource cost can be met by reduction in other expenditures. First, specific forms of taxation or quasi-taxation can be exploited with minimal economic damage.

D. Finegold and D. Soskice

— A training levy on companies who do not undertake certified training. It will be difficult for these companies to pass on the levy in the form of higher prices if some competitors are undertaking certified training and hence not paying the levy. And since most of the non-training companies are likely to be in the sheltered sector of the economy, any reduction in their activity levels as a result of the levy will have the beneficial effect of transferring business to training competitors.

— Individual training accounts. If individuals choose to contribute to an individual training account, it will come from a voluntary reduction in consumers expenditure.

Second, other government expenditures will be reduced:

— Reduction in government expenditures on YTS and other MSC related activities which would be phased out as a new system of sixteen-twenty ET developed.

— Reduction in government expenditures on education and training post sixteen as a result of demographic decline.

Thus some part of the necessary resources can be met from reduced expenditure elsewhere but without relying on an increase in general taxation. The damage caused by the latter is not only political, but also, via its inflationary potential, economic. But there are limits beyond which it may be unwise or impossible to push these reductions.

This means that the resources to finance a training programme will have to come in part from increased GDP and increased imports. The point to be made here is that the standard problems associated with an expansionary policy can be more easily handled within the context of a training programme than in other cases.

The first problem is that of inflation caused by the increased bargaining power of employees as employment rises. Appropriate increases in the skilled workforce can reduce inflationary pressures in two ways. Directly, it reduces skilled labour bottlenecks and the power of 'insiders' relative to outsiders. Indirectly, it facilitates wage restraint especially if unions are involved in the training institutions.

The second problem is financing the external deficit and the public sector deficit, at least without a fall in the exchange rate or a rise in the interest rate. Avoiding these consequences requires: that inflation does not increase; and that the increase in the PSBR and the external deficit are seen as eventually self-correcting. The last paragraph was concerned with inflation. A training programme can, more easily than most programmes involving increased government expenditure, be credibly seen as self-correcting in its effect on the PSBR and the external deficit.

VI. CONCLUDING REMARKS

The UK has long suffered from a low-skills equilibrium in which the ET system has delivered badly educated and minimally trained sixteen year-old school-leavers to an economy which has been geared to operate - albeit today more efficiently - with a relatively unskilled labour force. Some companies have broken out of this equilibrium with the aid of strategic managers, to see training and innovation as core activities. Most have not.

Despite the much-vaunted reforms of the ET system of the last few years, major improvements are unlikely to be brought about:

— The majority of children will still leave school at sixteen, and will gain a low-level training in YTS; referring to the certification of YTS by the NCVQ, Jarvis and Prais argued that it would lead to 'a

OXFORD REVIEW OF ECONOMIC POLICY, VOL. 4, NO. 3

certificated semi-literate under-class - a section of the workforce inhibited in job-flexibility, and inhibited in the possibility of progression'. *(Financial Times* , 1/7/88, quoting Jarvis and Prais, 1988.)

— There are no substantive policies to remedy the vacuum in training in most companies.

— There are no measures to undertake the depth education and training frequently needed in a rapidly restructuring world economy to enable those made redundant acquire relevant skills.

We have argued the case in section 5 for: full-time education to eighteen, with 'accelerated' apprentice-ships thereafter, for those not going on to higher education; building up training capacities within companies; and an external retraining system to deal with restructuring between companies and industries.

Instead of summarising these proposals, we want to underline certain points which have not always been adequately brought out in discussions of reform:

— It is important to think in terms of the incentives which face individuals, rather than make the mistake of some educators of just talking about institutions or educational innovations. But equally the economist's mistake, of treating of incentives as only financial, must be avoided. We lay stress on the idea of enabling individuals to see career progressions: thus importance is attached to the bridge from education to employment for sixteen to twenty year-olds.

— Companies should be seen not as profit-maximising black boxes, but as coalitions of interests, particularly among managers. We argue that, rather than incentives being used to increase the amount of training as such, they can more effectively be used if they increase a company's training capacity, by giving companies an incentive to train or hire meisters, or training supervisors. This produces a stake in training as a company activity.

— Along similar lines, employees should be given a role in training decision-making within the company. Here, there are lessons to be learned from industrial democracy procedures in Germany and Sweden. This reinforces the idea of groups within the company with a stake in training.

— More generally, the problem of moving companies from a low-skill to a high-skill equilibrium involves much more than training and education. It requires changes in management style, R & D, financing, marketing, etc. so training policy should be seen as part of a wider industrial strategy.

— Countries with successful ET systems devote substantial resources to research on education and training and labour market developments. In the UK today policy-making has become highly centralised but based on limited information and research.

— Successful countries also place great reliance on employers' organisations and unions. In the UK their role in the governance of training has been progressively reduced. If radical reform is to be successful, it will be important to build up the expertise and involvement of the social partners.

To conclude, the UK is becoming isolated among advanced industrialised countries. They have either attained or are targeting a far higher level of generalised education and training than is being considered here. This should be worrying enough in itself. What makes it more so, is the progress made by other countries with substantially lower labour costs: South Korea has currently 85 per cent in full-time education to the age of seventeen or eighteen, and over 30 per cent in higher education. *(Financial Times* ,30/6/88.)

REFERENCES

Anderson, A. (1987), 'Adult Training: Private Industry and the Nicholson Letter', in Education & Training UK 1987, Harrison, A. and Gretton, J.(eds.), *Policy Journals*, pp. 67-73.
Brady, T. (1984), *New Technology and Skills in British Industry*, Science Policy Research Unit.
Business Week (1988), 'How the New Math of Productivity Adds Up', pp. 49-55, June 6.

D. Finegold and D. Soskice

Callaghan, J. (1976), Ruskin College Speech, *Times Educational Supplement*, 22 October, p. 72.

Centre for Contemporary Cultural Studies (1981), *Unpopular Education*, London, Hutchinson.

Chapman, P. and Tooze, M. (1987), *The Youth Training Scheme in the UK*, Aldershot, Avebury.

Clegg, H. (1972), *The System of Industrial Relations in Great Britain*, Oxford, Basil Blackwell.

Clement, B. (1986), 'Industry Threatened over Training Lapses', *Independent*, p. 3, 29 November.

Coopers and Lybrand Associates (1985), *A Challenge to Complacency: Changing Attitudes to Training*, MSC/NEDO, Moorfoot, Sheffield.

Crowther Commission (1959), *15 to 18*, Report to the DES, HMSO.

Dale, R. (1983), 'The Politics of Education in England 1970-1983: State, Capital and Civil Society', Open University, unpublished.

— (1983), Thatcherism and Education, In Ahier, J. and Flude, M. (eds.), *Comtemporary Education Policy*, London, Croom Helm.

— (1985), The Background and Inception of TVEI, in Dale (ed.), *Education, Training and Employment*, Milton Keynes, Open University.

— (forthcoming), TVEI: From National Guidelines to Local Practice.

Daly, A. (1984), 'Education, Training and Productivity in the U.S. and Great Britain', NIESR no. 63, London.

Deakin, B. M. and Pratten, C. F. (1987), Economic Effects of YTS, *Department of Employment Gazette*, 95, 491-7.

Department of Education and Science (1987), Education Reform Bill, 20 November.

— (1988), *Tax Concessions for Training*, HMSO, May.

Department of Employment (1988), *Training for Employment*, HMSO no. 316, February.

Department of Education and Department of Education and Science, *Training for Jobs*, HMSO, Jan.

De Ville, H. G. et al. (1986), *Review of Vocational Qualifications in England and Wales*, Report to MSC and DES, April.

Donovan, Lord (1968), *Royal Commission on Trade Unions and Employers' Associations 1965-1968* Report, HMSO, London.

Dore, R. (1987), *Taking Japan Seriously*, Athlone Press, London.

Fenwick, I. G. K. (1976), *The Comprehensive School 1944-1970*, London, Methuen.

Gapper, J. (1987), '£500,000 scheme to boost training in tourist sector', *Financial Times*, 17 March.

George, K. D. and Shorey, J. (1985), 'Manual Workers, Good Jobs and Structured Internal Labour Markets', *British Journal of Industrial Relations*, 23:3, pp. 425-47, November.

Giddens, A. (1979), 'An Anatomy of the British Ruling Class', *New Society*, 4 October, pp. 8-10.

Gow, D. (1988), 'Fury at A-Level Rejection', *Guardian*, p. 1, 8 June.

Gow, D. (1988), 'Teaching Shortage Catastrophe Feared', *Guardian*, p. 4, 16 June.

— and Travis, A. (1988), 'Leak Exposes Thatcher Rift with Baker', *Guardian*, p. 1, 10 March.

Greenhalgh, C. (1988), *Employment and Structural Change: Trends and Policy Options*, mimeo, Oxford.

Hall, P. (1986), *Governing the Economy*, Oxford, Polity Press.

Harland, J. (1987), 'The TVEI Experience', in Gleeson, D. (ed.)*TVEI and Secondary Education*, Milton Keynes, Open University.

Hotz-Hart, B.. (1988), 'Comparative Research and New Technology: Modernisation in Three Industrial Relations Systems', in Hyman, R. and Streeck, W. (eds.) *New Technology and Industrial Relations*.

Howell, D.A. (1980), 'The Department of Education and Science: its critics and defenders', *Educational Administration*, 9, pp. 108-33.

Hyman, R. and Streeck, W. (eds.) (1988), *New Technology and Industrial Relations*, Oxford, Blackwells.

Independent (1986), 'Managers "a Decade Out of Date"', 11 December.

Jackson, M. (1988), 'More leavers shun youth training scheme', *Times Educational Supplement*, 19 February, p. 13.

OXFORD REVIEW OF ECONOMIC POLICY, VOL. 4, NO. 3

Jennings, R. E. (1977), *Education and Politics: Policy-Making in Local Education Authorities*, London, Batsford.

Keep, E. (1986), *Designing the Stable Door: A Study of how the Youth Training Scheme was Planned*, Warwick Papers in Industrial Relations No. 8, May.

— (1987), *Britain's Attempts to Create a National Vocational Educational and Training System: A Review of Progress*, Warwick Papers in Industrial Relations no.16, Coventry.

Lane, C. (1988), 'Industrial Change in Europe: the Pursuit of Flexible Specialisation', in *Work, Employment and Society*, forthcoming.

Lange, P. (1987). *The Institutionalisation of Concertation. International Political Economy*, WP no. 26, Duke University.

Leadbeater, C. (1987), 'MSC criticises standard of youth training', *Financial Times*, 13 May, p. 1.

Lynn, R. (1988), *Educational Achievement in Japan*, Basingstoke, MacMillan.

MSC (1981), *A New Training Initiative, a Consultative Document*, HMSO, May.

— (1986) *Skills Monitoring Report*, MSC Evaluation and Research Unit, Sheffield.

Maurice, M., Sellier, F. and Silvestre, J. J. (1986), *The Social Foundations of Industrial Power: A Comparison of France and West Germany*, Cambridge, MIT Press.

Mayer, C. (1987), 'The Assessment: Financial Systems and Corporate Investment', *Oxford Review of Economic Policy*, Winter.

Mayhew, K. (1986), 'Reforming the Labour Market', *Oxford Review of Economic Policy*, Summer.

McArthur, A. and McGregor, A. (1986), 'Training and Economic Development: National versus Local Perspectives', *Political Quarterly*, 57, 3, July-September, pp. 246-55.

McCulloch, G. et al. (1985), *Technological Revolution? The Politics of School Science and Technology in England and Wales since 1945*, London, Falmer.

Macfarlane, N. (1980), Education for 16-19 Year Olds, report to the DES and Local Authority Associations, HMSO, December.

Moon, J. and Richardson, J. (1985), *Unemployment in the UK*, Aldershot, Gower.

Morton, K. (1980), *The Education Services of the TGWU*, Oxford University, Ruskin College Project Report.

National Economic Development Council (1984), *Competence and Competition: Training in the Federal Republic of Germany, the United States and Japan*, London, NEDO/MSC.

— (1978), *Engineering Craftsmen: Shortages and Related Problems*, London, NEDO.

New, C. and Myers, A. (1986), *Managing Manufacturing Operations in the UK, 1975-85*. Institute of Manpower Studies.

Nicholson, B. (1986), Press Conference at People and Technology Conference. London, November.

OECD (1975), *Educational Development Strategy in England and Wales*, Paris.

— (1985), *Education and Training After Basic Schooling*, Paris.

Page, G. (1967), *The Industrial Training Act and After*, London, Andre Deutsch.

Perry, P. J. C. (1976), *The Evolution of British Manpower Policy*, London, BACIE.

Postlethwaite, N. (1988), 'English Last in Science', *Guardian*, 1 March.

Prais, S. J. and Wagner, K. (1983), Schooling Standards in Britain and Germany, London, NIESR Discussion Paper no. 60.

Raffe, D. (1984), *Fourteen to Eighteen*, Aberdeen University Press.

Rajan, A. and Pearson, R. (eds.) (1986), *UK Occupational and Employment Trends*, IMS, London, Butterworths.

Ranson, S (1985), 'Contradictions in the Government of Educational Change', *Political Studies*, 33, 1, pp. 56-72.

Reich, R (1983), *The Next American Frontier*, Middlesex, Penguin.

Reid, G. L. (1980), 'The Research Needs of British Policy-Makers', in McIntosh, A. *Employment Policy in the UK and the US*, London, John Martin.

Riddell, P. (1983), *The Thatcher Government*, Oxford, Martin Robertson.

Salter, B. and Tapper, T. (1981), *Education, Politics and the State*, London, Grant McIntyre.

Scarbrough, H. (1986). 'The Politics of Technological Change at BL.', in Jacobi, O. et al. (eds.)
    Technological Change, Rationalisation and Industrial Relations.
Sorge, A. and Streeck, W. (1988). 'Industrial Relations and Technological Change', in Hyman and
    Streeck (1988).
Steedman, H. (1986), 'Vocational Training in France and Britain: the Construction Industry', *NI
    Economic Review*, May.
Steedman, H. and Wagner, K. (1987), 'A Second Look at Productivity, Machinery and Skills in
    Britain and Germany', *NI Economic Review*, November.
Streeck, W. (1985), 'Industrial Change and Industrial Relations in the Motor Industry: An
    International Overview', Lecture at University of Warwick, 23/10/85.
Streeck et al. (1985). 'Industrial Relations and Technical Change in the British, Italian and German
    Automobile Industry'. IIM discussion paper 85-5, Berlin.
Taylor, R. (1980), *The Fifth Estate*, London, Pan.
Tipton, B. (1982), 'The Quality of Training and the Design of Work', *Industrial Relations Journal*,
    pp. 27-42, Spring.
TUC Annual Reports, 1980-1986.
Wiener, M. (1981), *English Culture and the Decline of the Industrial Spirit*, Cambridge, Cambridge
    University Press.
Wilensky, H. and Turner, L. (1987), *Democratic Corporatism and Policy Linkages*, Berkeley,
    Instititute of International Studies.
Woodall, J. (1985), 'European Trade Unions and Youth Unemployment', unpublished Kingston
    Polytechnic Mimeograph, London.
Worswick, G. D. (1985), *Education and Economic Performance*, Gower, Aldershot.

Part II
Choices for Getting Skills

[4]

INVESTMENT IN HUMAN CAPITAL: A THEORETICAL ANALYSIS[1]

GARY S. BECKER

Columbia University and National Bureau of Economic Research

I. INTRODUCTION

SOME activities primarily affect future well-being, while others have their main impact in the present. Dining is an example of the latter, while purchase of a car exemplifies the former. Both earnings and consumption can be affected: on-the-job training primarily affects earnings, a new sail boat primarily affects consumption, and a college education is said to affect both. The effects may operate either through physical resources, such as a sail boat, or through human resources, such as a college education. This paper is concerned with activities that influence future real income through the imbedding of resources in people. This is called investing in human capital.

The many ways to invest include schooling, on-the-job training, medical care, vitamin consumption, and acquiring information about the economic system. They differ in the relative effects on earnings and consumption, in the amount of resources typically invested, in the size of returns, and in the extent to which the connection between investment and return is perceived. But all improve the physical and mental abilities of people and thereby raise real income prospects.

People differ substantially in their economic well-being, both among countries and among families within a given country. For a while economists were relating these differences primarily to differences in the amount of physical capital since richer people had more physical capital than others. It has become increasingly evident, however, from studies of income growth[2] that factors other than physical resources play a larger role than formerly believed, thus focusing attention on less tangible resources, like the knowledge possessed. A concern with investment in human capital, therefore, ties in closely with the new emphasis on intangible resources and may be useful in attempts to understand the inequality in income among people.

The original aim of my study was to estimate the money rate of return to college and high-school education in the United States. In order to set these estimates in proper context I undertook a brief formulation of the theory of investment in human capital. It soon became clear to me, however, that more than a restatement was called for: while important and pioneering work had been done on the economic return to various

[1] I am greatly indebted to the Carnegie Corporation of New York for the support given to the National Bureau of Economic Research to study investment in education and other kinds of human capital. I benefited greatly from many discussions with my colleague Jacob Mincer, and also with other participants in the Labor Workshop of Columbia University. Although many persons offered valuable comments on the draft prepared for the conference, I am especially indebted to the detailed comments of Theodore Schultz, George Stigler, and Shirley Johnson.

[2] The evidence for the United States appears to show that the growth in capital per capita explains only a small part of the growth in per capita income and that the growth in "technology" explains most of it: On this see S. Fabricant, *Economic Progress and Economic Change: 34th Annual Report of the National Bureau of Economic Research* (New York: National Bureau of Economic Research, 1954).

occupations and education classes,[3] there have been few, if any, attempts to treat the process of investing in people from a general viewpoint or to work out a broad set of empirical implications. I began then to prepare a general analysis of investment in human capital.

As the work progressed, it became clearer and clearer that much more than a gap in formal economic analysis would be filled, for the analysis of human investment offered a unified explanation of a wide range of empirical phenomena which had either been given *ad hoc* interpretations or had baffled investigators. Among these are the following: (1) Earnings typically increase with age at a decreasing rate. Both the rate of increase and the rate of retardation tend to be positively related to the level of skill. (2) Unemployment rates tend to be negatively related to the level of skill. (3) Firms in underdeveloped countries appear to be more "paternalistic" toward employees than those in developed countries. (4) Younger persons change jobs more frequently and receive more schooling and on-the-job training than older persons do. (5) The distribution of earnings is positively skewed. especially among professional and other skilled workers. (6) Abler persons receive more education and other kinds of training than others. (7) The division of labor is limited by the extent of the market. (8)

The typical investor in human capital is more impetuous and thus more likely to err than is the typical investor in tangible capital. What a diverse and possibly even confusing array! Yet all these as well as many other important empirical implications can be derived from very simple theoretical arguments. The purpose of this paper is to set out these arguments in some generality, with the emphasis placed on empirical implications, although little empirical material is presented. My own empirical work will appear in a later study.

First, a lengthy discussion of on-the-job training is presented and then, much more briefly, discussions of investment in schooling, information, and health. On-the-job training is dealt with so elaborately not because it is more important than other kinds of investment in human capital—although its importance is often underrated—but because it clearly illustrates the effect of human capital on earnings, employment, and other economic variables. For example, the close connection between foregone and direct costs or the effect of human capital on earnings at different ages is vividly brought out. The extended discussion of on-the-job training paves the way for much briefer discussions of other kinds of investment in human beings.

II. DIFFERENT KINDS OF INVESTMENT

A. ON THE JOB

Theories of firm behavior, no matter how they differ in other respects, almost invariably ignore the effect of the productive process itself on worker productivity. This is not to say that no one recognizes that productivity is affected by the job itself; but the recognition has not been formalized, incorporated into economic analysis, and its implications worked out. We now intend to do just

[3] In addition to the earlier works of Smith, Mill, and Marshall, see H. Clark, *Life Earnings in Selected Occupations in the U.S.* (New York: Harper & Bros., 1937); J. R. Walsh, "Capital Concept Applied to Man," *Quarterly Journal of Economics*, February, 1935; M. Friedman and S. Kuznets, *Income from Independent Professional Practice* (New York: National Bureau of Economic Research, 1945); G. Stigler and D. Blank, *The Demand and Supply of Scientific Personnel* (New York: National Bureau of Economic Research, 1957); and T. W. Schultz, "Investment in Man: An Economist's View," *Social Service Review*, June, 1959.

INVESTMENT IN HUMAN CAPITAL: A THEORETICAL ANALYSIS   11

that, placing special emphasis on the broader economic implications.

Many workers increase their productivity by learning new skills and perfecting old ones while on the job. For example, the apprentice usually learns a completely new skill while the intern develops skills acquired in medical school, and both are more productive afterward. On-the-job training, therefore, is a process that raises future productivity and differs from school training in that an investment is made on the job rather than in an institution that specializes in teaching. Presumably, future productivity can be improved only at a cost, for otherwise there would be an unlimited demand for training. Included in cost are a value placed on the time and effort of trainees, the "teaching" provided by others, and the equipment and materials used. These are costs in the sense that they could have been used in producing current output if they were not used in raising future output. The amount spent and the duration of the training period depend partly on the type of training—more is spent for a longer time on an intern than on an operative—partly on production possibilities, and partly on the demand for different skills.

Each employee is assumed to be hired for a specified time period (in the limiting case this period approaches zero), and for the moment both labor and product markets are assumed to be perfectly competitive. If there were no on-the-job training, wage rates would be given to the firm and would be independent of its actions. A profit-maximizing firm would be in equilibrium when marginal products equaled wages, that is, when marginal receipts equaled marginal expenditures. In symbols

$$MP = W, \qquad (1)$$

where W equals wages or expenditures and MP equals the marginal product or receipts. Firms would not worry too much about the relation between labor conditions in the present and future partly because workers were only hired for one period, and partly because wages and marginal products in future periods would be independent of a firm's current behavior. It can therefore legitimately be assumed that workers have unique marginal products (for given amounts of other inputs) and wages in each period, which are, respectively, the maximum productivity in all possible uses and the market wage rate. A more complete set of equilibrium conditions would be the set

$$MP_t = W_t, \qquad (2)$$

where t refers to the tth period. The equilibrium position for each period would depend only on the flows during that period.

These conditions are altered when account is taken of on-the-job training and the connection thereby created between present and future receipts and expenditures. Training might lower current receipts and raise current expenditures, yet firms could profitably provide this training if future receipts were sufficiently raised or future expenditures sufficiently lowered. Expenditures during each period need not equal wages, receipts need not equal the maximum possible productivity, and expenditures and receipts during all periods would be interrelated. The set of equilibrium conditions summarized in equation (2) would be replaced by an equality between the *present values* of receipts and expenditures. If E_t and R_t represent expenditures and receipts during period t, and i the market discount rate, then the equilibrium condition can be written as

$$\sum_{t=0}^{n-1} \frac{R_t}{(1+i)^{t+1}} = \sum_{t=0}^{n-1} \frac{E_t}{(1+i)^{t+1}}. \quad (3)$$

where n represents the number of periods, and R_t and E_t depend on all other receipts and expenditures. The equilibrium condition of equation (2) has been generalized, for if marginal product equals wages in each period, the present value of the marginal product stream would have to equal the present value of the wage stream. Obviously, however, the converse need not hold.

If training were given only during the initial period, expenditures during the initial period would equal wages plus the outlay on training, expenditures during other periods would equal wages alone, and receipts during all periods would equal marginal products. Equation (3) becomes

$$MP_0 + \sum_{t=1}^{n-1} \frac{MP_t}{(1+i)^t}$$
$$(4)$$
$$= W_0 + k + \sum_{t=1}^{n-1} \frac{W_t}{(1+i)^t},$$

where k measures the outlay on training. If a new term is defined,

$$G = \sum_{t=1}^{n-1} \frac{MP_t - W_t}{(1+i)^t}, \quad (5)$$

equation (4) can be written as

$$MP_0 + G = W_0 + k. \quad (6)$$

Since the term k only measures the actual outlay on training it does not entirely measure training costs, for excluded is the time that a person spends on this training, time that could have been used to produce current output. The difference between what could have been produced, call this MP_0' and what is produced, MP_0, is the opportunity cost of the time spent in training. If C is defined

as the sum of opportunity costs and outlays on training, (6) becomes

$$MP_0' + G = W_0 + C. \quad (7)$$

The term G, the excess of future receipts over future outlays, is a measure of the return to the firm from providing training; and, therefore, the difference between G and C measures the difference between the return from, and the cost of, training. Equation (7) shows that marginal product would equal wages in the initial period only when the return equals costs, or $G = C$; it would be greater or less than wages as the return was smaller or greater than costs. Those familiar with capital theory might argue that this generalization of the simple equality between marginal product and wages is spurious because a full equilibrium would require equality between the return from an investment—in this case, made on the job—and costs. If this implied that $G = C$, marginal product would equal wages in the initial period. There is much to be said for the relevance of a condition equating the return from an investment with costs, but such a condition does not imply that $G = C$ or that marginal product equals wages. The following discussion demonstrates that great care is required in the application of this condition to on-the-job investment.

1. *General.*— Our treatment of on-the-job training produced some general results—summarized in equations (3) and (7)—of wide applicability, but more concrete results require more specific assumptions. In this and the following section two types of on-the-job training are discussed in turn: general and specific. General training is useful in many firms in addition to the firm providing it, as a machinist trained in the army finds his skills of value in steel and aircraft firms,

INVESTMENT IN HUMAN CAPITAL: A THEORETICAL ANALYSIS 13

or a doctor trained (interned) at one hospital finds his skills useful at other hospitals. Most on-the-job training presumably increases the future marginal product of workers in the firm providing it, but general training would also increase their marginal product in many other firms as well. Since in a competitive labor market the wage rates paid by any firm are determined by marginal productivities in other firms, future wage rates as well as marginal products would increase to firms providing general training. These firms could capture some of the return from training only if their marginal product rose by more than their wages. "Perfectly general" training would be equally useful in many firms and marginal products would rise by the same extent in all of them. Consequently, wage rates would rise by exactly the same amount as the marginal product and the firms providing such training could not capture any of the return.

Why, then, do rational firms in competitive labor markets provide general training, for why provide training that brings no return? The answer is that firms would provide general training only if they did not have to pay any of the costs. Persons receiving general training would be willing to pay these costs since training raises their future wages. Hence the cost as well as the return from general training would be borne by trainees, not by firms.

These and other implications of general training can be more formally demonstrated with equation (7). Since wages and marginal products are raised by the same amount, MP_t must equal W_t for all $t = 1, \ldots n - 1$, and therefore

$$G = \sum_{t=1}^{n-1} \frac{MP_t - W_t}{(1+i)^t} = 0. \qquad (8)$$

Equation (7) is reduced to

$$MP_0' = W_0 + C, \qquad (9)$$

or

$$W_0 = MP_0' - C. \qquad (10)$$

In terms of actual marginal product

$$MP_0 = W_0 + k, \qquad (9')$$

or

$$W_0 = MP_0 - k. \qquad (10')$$

The wage of trainees would not equal their opportunity marginal product but would be less by the total cost of training. In other words, employees would pay for general training by receiving wages below their current (opportunity) productivity. Equation (10) has many other implications, and the rest of this section is devoted to developing the more important ones.

Some might argue that a really "net" definition of marginal product obtained by subtracting training costs from "gross" marginal product must equal wages even for trainees. Such an interpretation of net productivity could formally save the equality between marginal product and wages here, but later I show (pp. 18–25) that it cannot always be saved. Moreover, regardless of which interpretation is used, training costs would have to be included in any study of the relation between wages and productivity.

Employees pay for general on-the-job training by receiving wages below what could be received elsewhere. "Earnings" during the training period would be the difference between an income or flow term, potential marginal product, and a capital or stock term, training costs, so that the capital and income accounts would be closely intermixed, with changes in either affecting wages. In other words, earnings of persons receiving on-the-job training would be net of

14   GARY S. BECKER

investment costs and would correspond to the definition of *net* earnings used throughout this paper, which subtracts all investment costs from "gross" earnings. Therefore, our departure with this definition of earnings from the accounting conventions used for transactions in material goods—which separate income from capital accounts to prevent a transaction in capital from *ipso facto*[4] affecting the income side—is not capricious but is grounded in a fundamental difference between the way investment in material and human capital are "written off." The underlying cause of this difference undoubtedly is the widespread reluctance to treat people as capital and the accompanying tendency to treat all wage receipts as earnings.

Intermixing the capital and income accounts could make the reported "incomes" of trainees unusually low and perhaps negative, even though their long-run or lifetime incomes were well above average. Since a considerable fraction of young persons receive some training, and since trainees would tend to have lower current and higher subsequent earnings than other youth, the correlation between current consumption and current earnings of young people[5] would not only be much weaker than the correlation with long-run earnings, but the

signs of these correlations might even differ.[6]

Doubt has been cast on the frequent assertion that no allowance is made in the income accounts for depreciation on human capital.[7] A depreciation-type item is deducted, at least from the earnings due to on-the-job training, for the cost would be deducted during the training period. Depreciation on tangible capital does not bulk so large in any one period because it is usually "written off" or depreciated during a period of time designed to approximate its economic life. Hence human and tangible capital appear to differ more in the time pattern of depreciation than in its existence,[8] and the effect on wage income of a rapid "write-off" of human capital is what should often be emphasized and studied.

Our point can be put differently and more rigorously. The ideal depreciation on a capital asset during any period would equal its change in value during the period. In particular, if value rose, a negative depreciation term would have

---

[4] Of course, a shift between assets having different productivities would affect the income account on material goods even with current accounting practices.

[5] I say "young people" rather than "young families" because as J. Mincer has shown (in a paper to be published in a National Bureau of Economic Research conference volume on labor economics), the labor-force participation of wives is positively correlated with the difference between husbands' long-run and current income. Participation of wives, therefore, makes the correlation between a family's current and a husband's long-run income greater than that between a husband's current and long-run income.

[6] A difference in signs is impossible in Friedman's analysis of consumer behavior because he assumes that transitory and long-run (that is, permanent) incomes are uncorrelated (see his *A Theory of the Consumption Function* [Princeton, N.J.: Princeton University Press, 1959]); we are suggesting that they may be *negatively* correlated for young persons.

[7] See, for example, A. Marshall, *Principles of Economics* (8th ed.; New York: Macmillan Co., 1949); C. Christ, "Patinkin on Money, Interest, and Prices," *Journal of Political Economy*, August, 1957, p. 352; and W. Hamburger, "The Relation of Consumption to Wealth and the Wage Rate," *Econometrica*, January, 1955.

[8] In a recent paper, R. Goode has argued (see "Educational Expenditures and the Income Tax," in Selma J. Mushkin [ed.], *Economics of Higher Education* [Washington: United States Department of Health, Education, and Welfare (forthcoming)]) that educated persons should be permitted to subtract from income a depreciation allowance on tuition payments. Such an allowance is apparently not required for on-the-job training costs; indeed, one might argue, on the contrary, that too much or too rapid depreciation is permitted on such investment.

INVESTMENT IN HUMAN CAPITAL: A THEORETICAL ANALYSIS 15

to be subtracted or a positive appreciation term added to the income from the asset. Since training costs would be deducted from earnings during the training period, the economic "value" of a trainee would at first increase rather than decrease with age, and only later would it begin to decrease.[9]

Training has an important effect on the relation between earnings and age. Suppose that untrained persons received the same earnings regardless of age, as shown by the horizontal line UU in Figure 1. Trained persons would receive lower earnings during the training period because training is paid for then, and higher earnings at later ages because the return is collected then. The combined effect of paying for and collecting the return from training in this way would be to make the age earnings curve of trained persons, shown by TT in Figure 1, steeper than that of untrained persons, the difference being greater the greater the cost of, and return from, the investment.

Not only does training make the curve steeper but, as indicated by Figure 1, also more concave; that is, the rate of increase in earnings is affected more at younger than at older ages. Suppose, to take an extreme case, that training raised the level of marginal productivity but had no effect on the slope, so that the marginal productivity of trained persons was also independent of age. If earnings equaled marginal product, TT would merely be parallel to and higher than UU, showing neither slope nor concavity. Since, however, earnings of trained persons would be below marginal productivity during the training

period and equal afterwards, they would rise sharply at the end of the training period and then level off (as shown by the dashed line $T'T'$ in Fig. 1), imparting a concave appearance to the curve as a whole. In this extreme case an extreme concavity appears; in less extreme cases the principle would be the same and the concavity more continuous.

Foregone earnings are an important, although neglected, cost of much human capital and should be treated on the same footing as direct outlays. Indeed, *all* costs appear as foregone earnings to workers

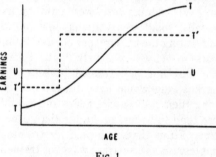

Fig. 1

receiving on-the-job training; that is, all costs appear as lower earnings than could be received elsewhere, although direct outlays, C, may really be an important part of costs. The arbitrariness of the division between foregone and direct costs and the resulting advantage of treating total costs as a whole[10] can be

[10] The equivalence between foregone and direct costs applies to consumption as well as to investment decisions. A household can be assumed to maximize a utility function

$$U(X_1, X_2, \ldots X_r),$$

$X_1, \ldots X_r$ being consumption goods, subject to the constraint

$$\sum_{i=1}^{r} p_i X_i = W \left(h - \sum_{j=1}^{r} h_j X_j \right) + y,$$

where p_i is the market price of the ith good, W the average wage rate, y non-wage income, h the total

16   GARY S. BECKER

further demonstrated by contrasting school and on-the-job training. Usually only the direct cost of school training is emphasized, even though the foregone cost is sometimes (as with college education) an important part of the total. A shift of training from schools to on the job would, however, reverse the emphasis and make all costs appear as foregone earnings, even when direct outlays were important.

Income maximizing firms in competitive labor markets would not pay the cost of general training and would pay trained persons the market wage. If, however, training costs were paid, many persons would seek training, few would quit during the training period, and labor costs would be relatively high. Firms that did not pay trained persons the market wage would have difficulty satisfying their skill requirements and would also tend to be less profitable than other firms. Firms that both paid for training and less than the market wage for trained persons would have the worst of both worlds, for they would attract too many trainees and too few trained persons.

These principles have been clearly demonstrated during the last few years in discussions of problems in recruiting military personnel. The military offers

---

number of hours available for either consumption or work, and h_j the number of hours required to consume a unit of the jth good. By transposing terms the constraint can be written as

$$\Sigma (p_i + W h_i) X_i = W h + y .$$

The total cost or price of consuming a unit of the ith good is the sum of two components: the market price or direct outlay per unit, p_i, and the foregone earnings per unit, $W h_i$. I expect to show in another paper that this formulation of household decisions gives extremely useful insights into a number of important economic problems, such as the choice between labor and "leisure," the effect of price control on prices, the role of queues, and the cause of differences among income classes in price elasticities of demand.

training in a wide variety of skills and many—such as piloting and machine repair—are very useful in the civilian sector. Training is provided during part or all of the first enlistment period and used during the remainder of the first period and hopefully during subsequent periods. This hope, however, is thwarted by the fact that re-enlistment rates tend to be inversely related to the amount of civilian-type skills provided by the military.[11] Persons with these skills leave the military more readily because they can receive much higher wages in the civilian sector. Net military wages for those receiving training are higher relative to civilian wages during the first than during subsequent enlistment periods because training costs are largely paid by the military. Not surprisingly, therefore, first-term enlistments for skilled jobs are obtained much more easily than are re-enlistments.

The military is a conspicuous example of an organization that both pays at least part of training costs and does not pay market wages to skilled personnel. It has had, in consequence, relatively easy access to "students" and heavy losses of "graduates." Indeed, its graduates make up the predominate part of the supply in several civilian occupations. For example, well over 90 per cent of United States commercial airline pilots received much of their training in the armed forces. The military, of course, is not a commercial organization judged by profits and losses and has had no difficulty surviving and even thriving.

What about the old argument that

[11] See *Manpower Management and Compensation* (Washington: Government Printing Office, 1957), Vol. I, Chart 3, and the accompanying discussion. The military not only wants to eliminate the inverse relation but apparently would like to create a strong positive relation because they have such a large investment in heavily trained personnel (see *ibid.*).

INVESTMENT IN HUMAN CAPITAL: A THEORETICAL ANALYSIS   17

firms in competitive labor markets have no incentive to provide on-the-job training because trained workers would be bid away by other firms? Firms that train workers are supposed to impart external economies to other firms because the latter can use these workers free of any training charge. An analogy with research and development is often drawn since a firm developing a process that cannot be patented or kept secret would impart external economies to competitors.[12] This argument and analogy would apply if firms were to pay training costs, for they would suffer a "capital loss" whenever trained workers were bid away by other firms. Firms can, however, shift training costs to trainees and have an incentive to do so when faced with competition for their services.

The difference between investment in training and in research and development can be put very simply. Without patents or secrecy, firms in competitive industries cannot establish property rights in innovations, and these innovations become fair game for all comers. Patent systems try to establish these rights so that incentives can be provided to invest in research. Property rights in skills, on the other hand, are automatically vested, for a skill cannot be used without permission of the person possessing it. This property right in skills is the source of the incentive to invest in training and explains why an analogy with unowned innovations is misleading.

2. *Specific.*—Completely general training increases the marginal productivity of trainees by exactly the same amount in firms providing the training as in other firms. Clearly some kinds of training increase productivity by a different amount in firms providing the training than in other firms. Training that increases productivity more in firms providing it will be called specific training. Completely specific training can be defined as training that has no effect on the productivity of trainees that would be useful in in other firms. Much on-the-job training is neither completely specific not completely general but increases productivity more in firms providing it and falls within the definition of specific training. The rest increases productivity by at least as much in other firms and falls within a definition of general training. The previous section discussed general training and this one will cover specific training. A few illustrations of the scope of specific training are presented before a formal analysis is developed.

The military offers some forms of training that are extremely useful in the civilian sector, as already noted. Training is also offered that is only of minor use to civilians: astronauts, fighter pilots, and missile men all illustrate this to a greater or lesser extent. Such training falls within the scope of specific training because productivity is raised in the military but not (much) elsewhere.

Resources are usually spent by firms in familiarizing new employees with their organization,[13] and the knowledge so acquired is a form of specific training because productivity is raised more in the firms acquiring the knowledge than in other firms. Other kinds of hiring costs, such as employment agency fees, the expenses incurred by new employees in finding jobs (what Stigler calls in his paper in this Supplement the "costs of

---

[12] These arguments can be found in Marshall, *op. cit.*, pp. 565–66, although he compares training to land-tenure systems.

[13] To judge by a sample of firms recently analyzed, formal orientation courses are quite common, at least in large firms (see H. F. Clark and H. S. Sloan, *Classrooms in the Factories* [New York: New York University Press, 1955], chap. iv).

search"), or the time employed in interviewing, testing, checking references, and in bookkeeping do not so obviously raise the knowledge of new employees, but they too are a form of specific investment in human capital, although not training. They are an investment because outlays over a short period create distributed effects on productivity; they are specific because productivity is raised primarily in the firms making the outlays; they are in human capital because they lose their value whenever employees leave. In the rest of this section I usually refer only to on-the-job specific training even though the analysis applies to all on-the-job specific investment.

Even after hiring costs are incurred, firms usually know only a limited amount about the ability and potential of new employees. They try to increase their knowledge in various ways—testing, rotation among departments, trial and error, etc.—for greater knowledge permits a more efficient utilization of manpower. Expenditures on acquiring knowledge of employee talents would be a specific investment if the knowledge could be kept from other firms, for then productivity would be raised more in the firms making the expenditures than elsewhere.

The effect of investment in employees on their productivity elsewhere depends on market conditions as well as on the nature of the investment. Very strong monopsonists might be completely insulated from competition by other firms, and practically all investments in their labor force would be specific. On the other hand, firms in extremely competitive labor markets would face a constant threat of raiding and would have fewer specific investments available.

These examples convey some of the surprisingly large variety of situations that come under the rubric of specific investment. This set is now treated abstractly in order that a general formal analysis can be developed. Empirical situations are brought in again after several major implications of the formal analysis have been developed.

If all training were completely specific, the wage that an employee could get elsewhere would be independent of the amount of training he had received. One might plausibly argue, then, that the wage paid by firms would also be independent of training. If so, firms would have to pay training costs, for no rational employee would pay for training that did not benefit him. Firms would collect the return from such training in the form of larger profits resulting from higher productivity, and training would be provided whenever the return—discounted at an appropriate rate—was at least as large as the cost. Long-run competitive equilibrium requires that the present value of the return exactly equals costs.

These propositions can be stated more formally with the equations developed earlier. According to equations (5) and (7) the equilibrium of a firm providing training in competitive markets can be written as

$$MP'_0 + G\left[\sum_{t=1}^{n-1} \frac{MP_t - W_t}{(1+i)^t}\right] \qquad (11)$$
$$= W_0 + C,$$

where C is the cost of training given only in the initial period, MP'_0 is the opportunity marginal product of trainees, W_0 is the wage paid to trainees, and W_t and MP_t are the wage and marginal product in period t. If the analysis of completely specific training given in the preceding paragraph was correct, W would always equal the wage that could be received elsewhere, $MP_t - W_t$ would be the full return in t from training given in 0, and G would be the present value of these returns. Since MP_0' measures the marginal product elsewhere and W_0 would measure the wage elsewhere of trainees, $MP_0' = W_0$. As a consequence $G = C$, or, in full equilibrium, the return from training equals costs.

Before claiming that the usual equality between marginal product and wages holds when completely specific training is considered, the reader should bear in mind two points. The first is that the equality between wages and marginal product in the initial period involves opportunity, not actual marginal product. Wages would be greater than actual marginal product if some productivity was foregone as part of the training program. The second is that, even if wages equaled marginal product initially, they would be less in the future because the differences between future marginal products and wages constitute the return to training and are collected by the firm.

All of this follows from the assumption that firms pay all costs and collect all returns. But could not one equally well argue that workers pay all specific training costs by receiving appropriately lower wages initially and collect all returns by receiving wages equal to marginal product later? In terms of equation (11), W_t would equal MP_t, G would equal zero, and $W_0 = MP_0' - C$, just as with general training. Is it more plausible that firms rather than workers pay for and collect and return from training?

An answer can be found by reasoning along the following lines. If a firm had paid for the specific training of a worker who quit to take another job, its capital expenditure would be partly wasted, for no further return could be collected. Likewise, a worker fired after he had

paid for specific training would be unable to collect any further return and would also suffer a capital loss. The willingness of workers or firms to pay for specific training should, therefore, closely depend on the likelihood of labor turnover.

To bring in turnover at this point may seem like a *deus ex machina* since it is almost always ignored in traditional theory. In the usual analysis of competitive firms, wages equal marginal product, and since wages and marginal product are assumed to be the same in many firms, no one suffers from turnover. It would not matter whether a firm's labor force always contained the same persons or a rapidly changing group. Any person leaving one firm could do equally well in other firms, and his employer could replace him without any change in profits. In other words, turnover is ignored in traditional theory because it plays no important role within the framework of the theory.

Turnover becomes important when costs are imposed on workers or firms, which are precisely the effects of specific training. Suppose a firm paid all the specific training costs of a worker who quit after completing it. According to our earlier analysis he would have been receiving the market wage and a new employee could be hired at the same wage. If the new employee were not given training, his marginal product would be less than that of the one who quit since presumably training raised the latter's productivity. Training could raise the new employee's productivity but would require additional expenditures by the firm. In other words, a firm is hurt by the departure of a trained employee because an equally profitable new employee could not be obtained In the same way an employee who pays for specific training would suffer a loss from being laid off because he could not find an equally good job elsewhere. To bring turnover into the analysis of specific training is not, therefore, a *deus ex machina* but is made necessary by the important link between them.

Firms paying for specific training might take account of turnover merely by obtaining a sufficiently large return from those remaining to counterbalance the loss from those leaving. (The return on "successes"—those remaining—would, of course, overestimate the average return on all training expenditures.) Firms could do even better, however, by recognizing that the likelihood of a quit is not fixed but depends on wages. Instead of merely recouping on successes what is lost on failures, they might reduce the likelihood of failure itself by offering higher wages after training than could be received elsewhere. In effect, they would offer employees some of the return from training. Matters would be improved in some respects but worsened in others, for the higher wage would make the supply of trainees greater than the demand, and rationing would be required. The final step would be to shift some training costs as well as returns to employees, thereby bringing supply more in line with demand. When the final step is completed firms no longer pay all training costs nor do they collect all the return but they share both with employees.[14] The shares of each depend on the relation between quit rates and wages, layoff rates and profits, and on other factors not discussed here, such as the cost of funds, attitudes toward risk, and desires for liquidity.[15]

If training were not completely specific, productivity would increase in other firms as well, and the wage that could be received elsewhere would also in-crease. Such training can be looked upon as the sum of two components, one completely general, the other completely specific, with the former being relatively larger the greater the effect on wages in other firms relative to the firms providing the training. Since firms do not pay any of completely general costs and only part of completely specific costs, the fraction of costs paid by firms would be negatively related to the importance of the general component, or positively related to the specificity of the training.

Our conclusions can be stated formally in terms of the equations developed earlier. If G is the present value of the return from training collected by firms, the fundamental equation is

$$MP' + G = W + C. \qquad (12)$$

If G' measures the return collected by employees, the total return, G'', would be the sum of G and G'. In full equilibrium the total return would equal total costs, or $G'' = C$. Let a represent the fraction of the total return collected by firms. Since $G = aG''$ and $G'' = C$, equation (12) can be written as

[14] Marshall was clearly aware of specific talents and their effect on wages and productivity: "Thus the head clerk in a business has an acquaintance with men and things, the use of which he could in some cases sell at a high price to rival firms. But in other cases it is of a kind to be of no value save to the business in which he already is; and *then his departure would perhaps injure it by several times the value of his salary*, while probably he could not get half that *salary elsewhere*" (*op. cit.*, p. 626). (My italics.) However, he overstressed the element of indeterminacy in these wages ("their earnings are determined . . . by a bargain between them and their employers, the terms of which are theoretically arbitrary" [*ibid.*, fn.]) because he ignored the effect of wages on turnover.

[15] The rate used to discount costs and returns is the sum of a (positive) rate measuring the cost of funds, a (positive or negative) risk premium, and a liquidity premium that is presumably positive since capital invested in specific training is very illiquid (see the discussion in Sec. IV, C).

INVESTMENT IN HUMAN CAPITAL: A THEORETICAL ANALYSIS   21

$$MP' + aC = W + C, \qquad (13)$$

or

$$W = MP' - (1 - a)C.^{16} \qquad (14)$$

Employees pay the same fraction of costs, $1 - a$, as they collect in returns, which generalizes the results obtained earlier. For if training were completely general, $a = o$, and equation (14) reduces to equation (10); if firms collected all the return from training, $a = 1$, and (14) reduces to $MP_0' = W_0$; if $0 < a < 1$, none of the earlier equations are satisfactory.

A few major implications of this analysis of specific training are now developed.

Rational firms pay generally trained employees the same wage and specifically trained employees a higher wage than they could get elsewhere. A reader might easily believe the contrary, namely, that general training would command a higher wage relative to alternatives than specific training does, since, after all, competition for persons with the latter is apt to be weaker than for those with the former. This view, however, overlooks the fact that general training raises the wages that could be received elsewhere while (completely) specific training does not, so a comparison with alternative wages gives a misleading impression of the *absolute* effect on wages of different types of training. Moreover, firms are not too concerned about the turnover of employees with general training and have no incentive to offer them a premium above wages elsewhere because the cost

of such training is borne entirely by employees. Firms are concerned about the turnover of employees with specific training, and a premium is offered to reduce their turnover because firms pay part of their training costs.

The part of specific training paid by employees has effects similar to those discussed earlier for general training: it is also paid by a reduction in wages during the training period, tends to make age-earnings profiles steeper and more concave, etc. The part paid by firms has none of these implications, since current or future wages would not be affected.

Specific, unlike general, training would produce certain "external" effects, for quits would prevent firms from capturing the full return on costs paid by them, and layoffs would do the same to employees. Note, however, that these are external *diseconomies* imposed on the employees or employers of firms providing the training, not external economies accruing to other firms.

Employees with specific training have less incentive to quit, and firms have less incentive to fire them, than employees with no or general training, which implies that quit and layoff rates would be inversely related to the amount of specific training. Turnover would be least for employees with extremely specific training and most for those receiving such general training that productivity was raised less in firms providing the training than elsewhere. These propositions are as applicable to the large amount of irregular quits and layoffs that continually occur as to the more regular cyclical and secular movements in turnover; in this section, however, only the more regular movements are discussed.

Consider a firm that experiences an unexpected decline in demand for its

---

16 If G'' did not equal C, these equations would be slightly more complicated. Suppose, for example, $G'' = G + G' = C + n$, $n \geq 0$, so that the present value of the total return would be greater than total costs. Then $G = aG'' = aC + an$, and

$$MP' + aC + an = W + C,$$

or

$$W = MP' - [(1 - a)C - an].$$

output, the rest of the economy being unaffected. The marginal product of employees without specific training—such as untrained or generally trained employees—presumably initially equaled wages, and their employment would be reduced to prevent their marginal productivity from falling below wages. The marginal product of specifically trained employees initially would have been greater than wages. A decline in demand would reduce these marginal products too, but as long as they were reduced by less than the initial difference with wages, firms have no incentive to lay off such employees. For sunk costs are sunk, and there is no incentive to lay off employees whose marginal product is greater than wages, no matter how unwise it was, in retrospect, to invest in their training. Thus workers with specific training seem less likely to be laid off as a consequence of a decline in demand than are untrained or even generally trained workers.[17]

If the decline in demand were sufficiently great so that even the marginal product of specifically trained workers was pushed below wages, would the firm just proceed to lay them off until the marginal product was brought into equality with wages? To show the danger here, assume that all the cost and return from specific training was paid and collected by the firm. Any worker laid off would try to find a new job, since nothing would bind him to the old one.[18] The firm might be hurt if a new job was found, for the firm's investment in his

training might be lost forever. If specifically trained workers were not laid off, the firm would lose now because marginal product would be less than wages but would gain in the future if the decline in demand proved temporary. There is an incentive, therefore, not to lay off workers with specific training when their marginal product is only temporarily below wages, and the larger a firm's investment the greater the incentive not to lay off such workers.

A worker collecting some of the return from specific training would have less incentive to find a new job when temporarily laid off than others would: he does not want to lose his investment. His behavior while laid off in turn affects his chances of being laid off, for if it were known that he would not readily take another job, the firm could lay him off without much fear of losing its investment.

The conclusion here can be briefly summarized. When one firm alone experiences an unexpected decline in demand, relatively few workers with specific training would be laid off, if only because their marginal product were initially greater than their wage. If the decline were permanent, all workers would be laid off when their marginal product became less than their wage and all those laid off would have to find jobs elsewhere. If the decline were temporary, specifically trained workers might not be laid off even though their marginal product were less than their wage because the firm would suffer if they took other jobs. The likelihood of their taking other jobs would be inversely related, and therefore the likelihood of their being laid off would be positively related, to the extent of their own investment in training.

The analysis can easily be extended to

---

[17] A very similar argument is developed by Walter Oi in "Labor as a Quasi-fixed Factor of Production" (unpublished Ph.D. dissertation, University of Chicago).

[18] Actually one need only assume that the quit rate of laid-off workers tends to be significantly greater than that of employed workers, if only because the cost of searching for another job is less for laid-off workers.

cover general declines in demand; suppose, for example, a general cyclical decline occurred. Let me assume that wages are sticky and remain at the initial level. If the decline in business activity were not sufficient to reduce the marginal product below the wage, workers with specific training would not be laid off even though others would be, just as before. If the decline reduced marginal product below wages, only one modification in the previous analysis is required. A firm would have a greater incentive to lay off specifically trained workers than when it alone experiences a decline because laid-off workers would be less likely to find other jobs when unemployment was widespread. In other respects the implications of a general decline with wage rigidity are the same as those of a decline in one firm alone.

The discussion has concentrated on layoff rates, but the same kind of reasoning shows that a rise in wages elsewhere would cause fewer quits among specifically trained workers than among others. For specifically trained workers initially receive higher wages than are available elsewhere and the wage rise elsewhere would have to be greater than the initial difference before they would consider quitting. Thus both the quit and layoff rate of specifically trained workers would be relatively low and fluctuate relatively less during business cycles. These are important implications than can be tested with the data available.

Although quits and layoffs are influenced by considerations other than investment costs, some of these, such as the presence of pension plans, are more strongly related to investments than may appear at first blush. A pension plan with incomplete vesting privileges[19] penalizes employees quitting before retirement and thus provides an incentive

—often an extremely powerful one—not to quit. At the same time pension plans "insure" firms against quits for they are given a lump sum —the non-vested portion of payments—whenever a worker quits. Insurance is needed for specifically trained employees because their turnover would impose capital losses on firms. Firms can discourage such quits by sharing training costs and the return with employees, but they have less need to discourage them and would be more willing to pay for training costs if insurance was provided. The effects on the incentive to invest in one's employees may have been a major stimulus to the development of pension plans.[20]

An effective long-term contract would insure firms against quits, just as pensions do, and also insure employees against layoffs. Firms would be more willing to pay for all kinds of training—assuming future wages were set at an appropriate level—since a contract, in effect, converts all training into completely specific training. A casual reading of history suggests that long-term contracts have, indeed, primarily been a means of inducing firms to undertake large investments in employees. These contracts are seldom used today in the United States.[21] and while they have declined in importance over time, they were probably always the exception here largely because courts have considered them a form of involuntary servitude.

[19] According to the National Bureau of Economic Research study of pensions, most plans still have incomplete vesting (see D. Holland's report in *A Respect for Facts: National Bureau of Economic Research Annual Report* [New York: National Bureau of Economic Research, 1960], pp. 44-46).

[20] In recent years pensions have also been an important tax-saving device, which certainly has been a crucial factor in their mushrooming growth.

[21] The military and entertainment industry are the major exceptions.

Moreover, any enforcible contract could at best specify the hours required on a job, not the quality of performance. Since performance can vary widely, unhappy workers could usually "sabotage" operations to induce employers to release them from contracts.

Some training may be useful neither in most nor only in a single firm but in a set of firms defined by product, type of work, or geographical location. For example, carpentry training would raise productivity primarily in the construction industry, and French legal training would be ineffective in the United States, with its different language and legal institutions. Such training would tend to be paid by trainees, since a single firm could not readily collect the return,[22] and in this respect would be the same as general training. In one respect, however, it is similar to specific training. Workers with training "specific" to an industry, occupation, or country are less likely to leave that industry, occupation, or country (via migration) than other workers, so their industrial, occupational, or country "turnover" would be less than average. The same result is obtained for specific training, except that a firm rather than an industry, occupation, or country is used as the unit of observation in measuring turnover. An analysis of specific training, therefore, is helpful also in understanding the effects of certain types of "general" training.

Although a discrepancy between marginal product and wages is frequently taken as evidence of imperfections in the competitive system, it would occur even in a perfectly competitive environment where there is investment in specific training. The investment approach provides a very different interpretation of some common phenomena, as can be seen from the following examples.

A positive difference between marginal product and wages is usually said to be evidence of monopsony power, and just as the ratio of product price to marginal cost has been suggested as a measure of monopoly power, so has the ratio of marginal product to wages been suggested as a measure of monopsony power. But specific training would also make this ratio greater than one. Does the difference between the marginal product and the earnings of major-league baseball players, for example, measure monopsony power or the return on a team's investment? Since teams do spend a great deal on developing players, some and perhaps most of the difference must be considered a return on investment even were there no uncertainty about the abilities of different players.[23]

Earnings might differ greatly among firms, industries, and countries and yet there may be relatively little worker mobility. The usual explanation would be that workers were either irrational or faced with formidable obstacles in moving. However, if specific[24] training were important, differences in earnings would be a misleading estimate of what "migrants" could receive, and it might be perfectly rational not to move. For example, although French lawyers earn less than American lawyers, the average French lawyer could not earn the average American legal income simply by migrat-

---

[22] Sometimes firms co-operate in paying training costs, especially when training apprentices (see *A Look at Industrial Training in Mercer County, N.J.* [Washington Bureau of Apprenticeship and Training, 1959], p. 3).

[23] S. Rottenberg ("The Baseball Players' Labor Market," *Journal of Political Economy*, June, 1956, p. 254) argues that the strong restrictions on entry of teams into the major leagues is prima facie evidence that monopsony power is important, but the entry or threat of new *leagues*, such as have occurred in professional basketball and football, is a real possibility.

[24] Specific, that is, to the firms, industries, or countries in question.

INVESTMENT IN HUMAN CAPITAL: A THEORETICAL ANALYSIS   25

ing to the United States, for he would have to invest in learning English and American law and procedures.[25]

In extreme types of monopsony, exemplified by an isolated company town, job alternatives for both trained and untrained workers are nil, and all training, no matter what the nature, would be specific to the firm. Monopsony combined with control of a product or an occupation (due, say, to anti-pirating agreements) converts training specific to that product or occupation into firm-specific training. These kinds of monopsony increase the importance of specific training and thus the incentive to invest in employees.[26] The effect on training of less extreme monopsony positions is more difficult to assess. Consider the monopsonist who pays his workers the best wage available elsewhere. I see no reason why training should have a systematically different effect on the foregone earnings of his employees than of those in competitive firms and, therefore, no reason why specific training should be more (or less) important to him. But monopsony power as a whole, including the more extreme manifestations, would appear to increase the importance of specific training and the incentive for firms to invest in human capital.

B. SCHOOLING

A school can be defined as an institution specializing in the production of training, as distinct from a firm that offers training in conjunction with the production of goods. Some schools, like those for barbers, specialize in one skill, while others, like universities, offer a large and diverse set. Schools and firms are often substitute sources of particular skills. The shift that has occurred over time in both law and engineering is a measure of this substitution. In acquiring legal skills the shift has been from apprenticeships in law firms to law schools, and in engineering skills from on-the-job experience to engineering schools.[27]

Some types of knowledge can be mastered better if simultaneously related to a practical problem; others require prolonged specialization. That is, there are complementarities between learning and work and between learning and time. Most training in the construction industry is apparently still best given on the job, while the training of physicists requires a long period of specialized effort. The development of certain skills requires both specialization and experience and can be had partly from firms and partly from schools. Physicians receive apprenticeship training as interns and residents after several years of concentrated instruction in medical schools. Or to take an example closer to home, a research economist not only spends many years in school but also a rather extensive apprenticeship in mastering the "art" of empirical and theoretical research. The complementarity with firms and schools depends in part on the amount of formalized knowledge available: price theory can be formally presented in a course, while a formal statement of the principles

[25] Of course, persons who have not yet invested in themselves would have an incentive to migrate, and this partly explains why young persons migrate more than older ones. For a further explanation see my discussion on p. 38; also see the paper in this Supplement by L. Sjaastad.

[26] A relatively large difference between marginal product and wages in monopsonies might measure, therefore, the combined effect of economic power and a relatively large investment in employees.

[27] State occupational licensing requirements often permit on-the-job training to be substituted for school training (see S. Rottenberg, "The Economics of Occupational Licensing" [paper given at the National Bureau of Economic Research Conference on Labor Economics, April, 1960]).

used in gathering and handling empirical materials is lacking.

Training in a new industrial skill is usually first given on the job, since firms tend to be the first to be aware of its value, but as demand develops, some of the training shifts to schools. For example, engineering skills were initially acquired on the job, and over time engineering schools have been developed.

A student does not work for pay while in school but may do so "after" or "before" school, or during "vacations." His earnings are usually less than if he were not in school since he cannot work as much or as regularly. The difference between what could have been and is earned is an important and indirect cost of schooling. Tuition, fees, books and supplies, unusual transportation and lodging expenses are other, more direct, costs. *Net* earnings can be defined as the difference between actual earnings and direct school costs. In symbols,

$$W = MP - k, \qquad (15)$$

where MP is actual marginal product (assumed equal to earnings) and k is direct costs. If MP_0 is the marginal product that could have been received, equation (15) can be written as

$$W = MP_0 - (MP_0 - MP + k)$$
$$= MP_0 - C, \qquad (16)$$

where C is the sum of direct and foregone costs and where net earnings are the difference between potential earnings and total costs. These relations should be familiar since they are the same as those derived for general on-the-job training, which suggests that a sharp distinction between schools and firms is not always necessary: for some purposes schools can be treated as a special kind of firm and students as a special kind of trainee. Per-

haps this is most apparent when a student works in an enterprise controlled by his school, which frequently occurs at many colleges.

Our definition of student net earnings may seem strange since tuition and other direct costs are not usually subtracted from "gross" earnings. Note, however, that indirect school costs are implicitly subtracted, for otherwise earnings would have to be defined as the sum of observed and foregoine earnings, and foregone earnings are a major cost of high school, college, and adult schooling. Moreover, earnings of on-the-job trainees would be net of *all* their costs, including direct "tuition" costs. Consistent accounting, which is particularly important when comparing earnings of persons trained in school and on the job, would require that earnings of students be defined in the same way.[28]

Regardless of whether all costs or merely indirect costs are subtracted from potential earnings, schooling would have the same kind of implications as general on-the-job training. Thus schooling would steepen the age-earnings profile, mix together the income and capital accounts, introduce a negative relative between the permanent and current earnings of young persons, and allow for depreciation on human capital. This supports our earlier assertion that an analysis of on-the-job training leads to general results that apply to other kinds of investment in human capital as well.

C. OTHER KNOWLEDGE

On-the-job and school training are not the only activities that raise real income primarily by increasing the knowledge at a person's command. Information

---

[28] Students often have negative net earnings and in this respect differ from most on-the-job trainees, although at one time many apprentices also had negative earnings.

INVESTMENT IN HUMAN CAPITAL: A THEORETICAL ANALYSIS   27

about the prices charged by different sellers would enable a person to buy from the cheapest, thereby raising his command over resources, or information about the wages offered by different firms would enable him to work for the firm paying the highest (see Stigler's paper in this Supplement, pp. 94–105). In both examples information about the economic system, of consumption and production possibilities, is increased as distinct from knowledge of a particular skill. Information about the political or social system—the effect of different parties or social arrangements—could also significantly raise real incomes.[29]

Let us consider in more detail investment in information about employment opportunities. A better job might be found by spending money on employment agencies and situation-wanted ads, using one's time to examine want ads, talking to friends and visiting firms, or in Stigler's language by "search." When the new job requires geographical movement, additional time and resources would be spent in moving.[30] These expenditures constitute an investment in information about job opportunities that would yield a return in the form of higher earnings than would otherwise have been received. If workers paid costs and collected the return, an investment in search would have the same implications about age-earnings profiles, depreciation, and the like as general on-the-job training and schooling, although it must be noted

that the direct costs of search, like the direct costs of schooling, are usually added to consumption rather than deducted from earnings. If firms paid costs and collected the return, search would have the same implications as on-the-job specific training.

Whether workers or firms pay for search depends on the effect of a job change on alternatives: the larger the number of alternatives made available by a change, the larger, not the smaller, the fraction of costs that have to be paid by workers. Consider a few examples. Immigrants to the United States usually found many firms that could use their talents, and these firms should have been reluctant to pay the large cost of transporting workers to the United States. In fact, immigrants almost always had to pay their own way. Even the system of contract labor, which we have seen is a means of protecting firms against turnover, was singularly unsuccessful in the United States and has been infrequently used.[31] Firms that are relatively insulated from competition in the labor market have an incentive to pay the costs of workers coming from elsewhere since they have little to worry about in the way of competing neighboring firms. In addition, firms would be willing partly to pay for search within a geographical area because some costs—such as an employment agency's fee—would be specific to the firm doing the hiring since they must be repeated at each job change.

D. PRODUCTIVE WAGE INCREASES

One way to invest in human capital is to improve emotional and physical health. In Western countries today earn-

---

[29] The role of political knowledge is systematically discussed in A. Downs, *An Economic Theory of Democracy* (New York: Harper & Bros., 1957), and more briefly in my "Competition and Democracy," *Journal of Law and Economics*, Vol. I (Fall, 1958).

[30] Studies of large geographical moves—those requiring both a change in employment and consumption—have tended to emphasize the job change more than the consumption change. Presumably money wages are considered to be more dispersed geographically than prices.

[31] For a careful discussion of the contract-labor system see C. Erickson, *American Industry and the European Immigrant, 1860–1885* (Cambridge, Mass.: Harvard University Press, 1957).

28　　　　　　　　　　GARY S. BECKER

ings are much more closely geared to knowledge than to strength, but in an earlier day, and elsewhere still, strength had a significant influence on earnings. Moreover, emotional health increasingly is considered an important determinant of earnings in all parts of the world. Health, like knowledge, can be improved in many ways. A decline in the death rate at working ages may improve earning prospects by extending the period during which earnings are received; a better diet adds strength and stamina, and thus earning capacity; or an improvement in working conditions—higher wages, coffee breaks, and so on—might affect morale and productivity.

Firms can invest in the health of employees through medical examinations, luncheons, or steering them away from activities with high accident and death rates. An investment in health that increased productivity to the same extent in many firms would be a general investment and would have the same effect as general training, while an investment in health that increased productivity more in the firms making them would be a specific investment and would have the same effect as specific training. Of course, most investments in health in the United States are made outside firms, in households, hospitals, and medical offices. A full analysis of the effect on earnings of such "outside" investment in health is beyond the scope of this paper, but I would like to discuss a relation between on-the-job and "outside" human investments that has received much attention in recent years.

When on-the-job investments are paid by reducing earnings during the investment period, less is available for investments outside the job in health, better diet, schooling, and other factors. If these "outside" investments were more pro-

ductive, some on-the-job investments would not be undertaken even though they were very productive by "absolute" standards.

Before I proceed further, one point needs to be made. The amount invested outside the job would be related to current earnings only if the capital market was very imperfect, for otherwise any amount of "outside" investment could be financed with borrowed funds. The analysis assumes, therefore, that the capital market is extremely imperfect, earnings and other income being a major source of funds.[32]

A firm would be willing to pay for investment in human capital made by employees outside the firm if it could benefit from the resulting increase in productivity. The only way to pay, however, would be to offer higher wages during the investment period than would have been offered since direct loans to employees are prohibited by assumption. When a firm gives a productive wage increase—that is, an increase that raises productivity—"outside" investments are, as it were, converted into on-the-job investments. Indeed, such a conversion is a natural way to circumvent imperfections in the capital market and the resultant dependence of the amount invested in human capital on the level of wages.

The discussion can be stated more formally. Let W represent wages in the absence of any investment, and let a productive wage increase costing an amount C be the only on-the-job investment. Total costs to the firm would be $\pi = W + C$, and since the investment cost is received by employees as higher wages, π would also measure total wages. The cost of on-the-job training is not

---

[32] Imperfections in the capital market with respect to investment in human capital are discussed in Sec. IV, *D*.

INVESTMENT IN HUMAN CAPITAL: A THEORETICAL ANALYSIS 29

received as higher wages, so this formally distinguishes a productive wage increase from other on-the-job investments. The term MP can represent the marginal product of employees when wages equal W, and G the gain to firms from the investment in higher wages. In full equilibrium.

$$MP + G = W + C = \pi. \quad (17)$$

Investment would not occur if the firm's gain was nil $(G = o)$, for then total wages (π) would equal the marginal product (MP) when there is no investment.

We have shown that firms would benefit more from on-the-job investment the more specific the productivity effect, the greater their monopsony power, and the longer the labor contract; conversely, the benefit would be less the more general the productivity effect, the less their monopsony power, and the shorter the labor contract. For example, a wage increase spent on a better diet with an immediate impact on productivity might well be granted,[33] but not one spent on general education with a very delayed impact.[24]

The effect of a wage increase on productivity depends on the way it is spent, which in turn depends on tastes, knowledge, and opportunities. Firms might exert an influence on spending by exhorting employees to consume good food, housing, and medical care, or even by requiring purchases of specified items in company stores. Indeed, the company

store or truck system in nineteenth-century Great Britain has been interpreted as partly designed to prevent an excessive consumption of liquor and other debilitating commodities.[35] The prevalence of employer paternalism in underdeveloped countries has been frequently accepted as evidence of a difference in temperament between East and West. An alternative interpretation suggested by our study is that an increase in consumption has a greater effect on productivity in underdeveloped countries, and that a productivity advance raises profits more there either because firms have more monopsony power or because the advance is less delayed. In other words "paternalism" may simply be a way of investing in the health and welfare of employees in underdeveloped countries.

An investment in human capital would usually steepen age-earnings profiles, lowering reported earnings during the investment period and raising them later on. But an investment in an increase in earnings may have precisely the opposite effect, raising reported earnings more during the investment period than later and thus flattening age-earning

[34] Marshall discusses delays of a generation or more and notes that profit-maximizing firms in competitive industries have no incentive to grant such wage increases.

"Again, in paying his workpeople high wages and in caring for their happiness and culture, the liberal employer confers benefits which do not end with his own generation. For the children of his workpeople share in them, and grow up stronger in body and in character than otherwise they would have done. The price which he has paid for labour will have borne the expenses of production of an increased supply of high industrial facilities in the next generation; but these facilities will be the property of others, who will have the right to hire them out for the best price they will fetch: neither he nor even his heirs can reckon on reaping much material reward for this part of the good that he has done" (*op. cit.*, p. 566).

[35] See G. W. Hilton, "The British Truck System in the Nineteenth Century," *Journal of Political Economy*, LXV (April, 1957), 246–47.

[33] The more rapid the impact the more likely that it comes within the (formal or de facto) contract period. Leibenstein apparently initially assumed a rapid impact when discussing wage increases in underdeveloped countries (see his "The Theory of Underemployment in Backward Economies," *Journal of Political Economy*, Vol. LXV [April, 1957]). In a later comment he argued that the impact might be delayed ("Underemployment in Backward Economies: Some Additional Notes," *Journal of Political Economy*, Vol. LXVI [June, 1958]).

30   GARY S. BECKER

profiles. The cause of this difference is simply that reported earnings during the investment period tend to be net of the cost of general investments and gross of the cost of a productive earnings increase.[36]

The productivity of employees depends not only on their ability and the amount invested in them both on and off the job but also on their motivation, or the intensity of their work. Economists have long recognized that motivation in turn partly depends on earnings because of the effect of an increase in earnings on morale and aspirations. Equation (17), which was developed to show the effect of investments outside the firm financed by an increase in earnings, can also show the effect of an increase in the intensity of work "financed" by an increase in earnings. Thus W and MP would show initial earnings and productivity, C the increase in earnings, and G the gain to firms from the increase in productivity caused by the "morale" effect of the increase in earnings. The incentive to grant a morale-boosting increase in earnings, therefore, would depend on the same factors as does the incentive to grant an increase used for outside investments. Many recent discussions of wages in underdeveloped countries have stressed the latter,[37] while earlier discussions often stressed the former.[38]

[36] If E represents reported earnings during the investment period and MP the marginal product when there is no investment, $E = MP - C$ with a general investment, $E = MP$ with a specific investment paid by the firm, and $E = MP + C$ with a productive earnings increase.

[37] See the papers by Leibenstein, *op. cit.*, and H. Oshima, "Underdevelopment in Backward Economies: An Empirical Comment," *Journal of Political Economy*, Vol. LXVI (June, 1958).

[38] For example, Marshall stressed the effect of an increase in earnings on the character and habits of working people (*op. cit.*, pp. 529–32, 566–69).

III. RELATION BETWEEN EARNINGS,
COSTS, AND RATES OF RETURN

Thus far little attention has been paid to the factors determining the amount invested in human capital. The most important single determinant is the profitability or rate of return, but the effect on earnings of a change in the rate of return has been difficult to distinguish empirically from a change in the amount invested. For investment in human capital usually extends over a long and variable period, so the amount invested cannot be determined from a known "investment period." Moreover, the discussion of on-the-job training clearly indicated that the amount invested is often merged with gross earnings into a single net earnings concept (which is gross earnings minus the cost or plus the return on investment).

In the following, some rather general relations between earnings, investment costs, and rates of return are derived. They permit one to distinguish, among other things, a change in the return from a change in the amount invested. The discussion proceeds in stages from simple to complicated situations. First, investment is restricted to a single period and returns to all remaining periods; then investment is permitted to be distributed over a known group of periods called the investment period. Finally, we show how the rate of return, amount invested, and the investment period can all be derived from information on net earnings alone.

Let Y be an activity providing a person entering at a particular age, called age zero, with a real net earnings stream of Y_0 during the first period, Y_1 the next period, and so on until Y_n is provided during the last period. The general term "activity" rather than occupation or

INVESTMENT IN HUMAN CAPITAL: A THEORETICAL ANALYSIS 31

another more concrete term is used to indicate that any kind of investment in human capital is permitted, not just on-the-job training but also schooling, information, health, and morale. By "net" earnings I continue to mean that tuition costs during any period have been subtracted and returns added to "gross" earnings during the same period (see discussion in Sec. II). "Real" earnings are the sum of monetary earnings and the monetary equivalent of psychic earnings. Since many persons appear to believe that the term "investment in human capital" must be restricted to monetary costs and returns, let me emphasize that essentially all my analysis applies independently of the division of real earnings into monetary and psychic components. Thus the analysis applies to health, an activity with a large psychic component, as well as to on-the-job training, an activity with a large monetary component. When psychic components dominate, the language associated with consumer durable goods might be considered more appropriate than that associated with investment goods, but to simplify the presentation, I use investment language throughout.

The present value of the net earnings stream in Y would be

$$V(Y) = \sum_{j=0}^{n} \frac{Y_j}{(1+i)^{j+1}}, \quad ^{39} \quad (18)$$

where i is the market discount rate, assumed for simplicity to be the same in each period. If X were another activity

providing a net earning stream of X_0, $X_1, \ldots X_n$, with a present value of $V(X)$, the present value of the gain from choosing Y would be given by

$$d = V(Y) - V(X)$$
$$= \sum_{j=0}^{n} \frac{Y_j - X_j}{(1+i)^{j+1}}. \quad (19)$$

Equation (19) can be reformulated to bring out explicitly the relation between costs and returns. The cost of investing in human capital equals the net earnings foregone by choosing to invest rather than choosing an activity requiring no investment. If activity Y requires an investment only in the initial period and if X does not require any, the cost of choosing Y rather than X is simply the difference between their net earnings in the initial period, and the total return would be the present value of the differences between net earnings in later periods. If $C = X_0 - Y_0$, $k_j = Y_j - X_j$, $j = 1, \ldots n$, and if R measures the total return, the gain from Y could be written as

$$d = \sum_{j=1}^{n} \frac{k_j}{(1+i)^j} - C = R - C. \quad (20)$$

The relation between costs and returns can be derived in a different and, for our purposes, preferable way by defining the internal rate of return,[40] which is simply a rate of discount equating the present value of returns to the present value of costs. In other words, the internal rate, r, is defined implicitly by the equation

---

[39] Our discussion assumes discrete income flows and compounding, even though a mathematically more elegant formulation would have continuous variables, with sums replaced by integrals and discount rates by continuous compounding. The discrete approach is, however, easier to follow and yet yields the same kind of results as the continuous approach. Extensions to the continuous case are straightforward.

[40] A substantial literature has developed on the difference between the income gain and internal return approaches. See, for example, Friedrich and Vera Lutz, *The Theory of Investment of the Firm* (Princeton, N.J.: Princeton University Press, 1951), chap. ii, and the articles in *The Management of Corporate Capital*, ed. Ezra Solomon (Glencoe, Ill.: Free Press, 1959).

$$C = \sum_{1}^{n} \frac{k_j}{(1+r)^j}, \qquad (21)$$

which clearly implies

$$\sum_{j=0}^{n} \frac{Y_j}{(1+r)^{j+1}} - \sum_{0}^{n} \frac{X_j}{(1+r)^{j+1}} \qquad (22)$$

$$= d = 0,$$

since $C = X_0 - Y_0$ and $k_j = Y_j - X_j$. So the internal rate is also a rate of discount equating the present values of net earnings. These equations would be considerably simplified if the return were the same in each period, or $Y_j = X_j + k$, $j = 1, \ldots n$. Thus equation (21) would become

$$C = \frac{k}{r}[1 - (1+r)^{-n}], \qquad (23)$$

where $(1+r)^{-n}$ is a correction for the finiteness of life that tends toward zero as people live longer.

If investment is restricted to a single known period, cost and rate of return are easily determined from information on net earnings alone. Since, however, investment in human capital is distributed over many periods—formal schooling is usually more than ten years in the United States, and long periods of on-the-job training are also common—the analysis must be generalized to cover distributed investment. The definition of an internal rate in terms of the present value of net earnings in different activities obviously applies regardless of the amount and duration of investment, but the definition in terms of costs and returns is not generalized so readily. If investment were known to occur in Y during each of the first m periods, a simple and superficially appealing approach would be to define the investment cost in each of these periods as the difference between net earnings in X and Y, total investment costs as the present value of these differences, and the internal rate would

equate total costs and returns. In symbols,

$$C_j^1 = X_j - Y_j, \qquad j = 0, \ldots m - 1,$$

$$C^1 = \sum_{0}^{m-1} C_j^1(1+r)^{-j},$$

and

$$C^1 = \frac{k}{r}\left[\frac{1 - (1+r)^{m-1-n}}{(1+r)^{m-1}}\right]. \qquad (24)$$

If $m = 1$, this reduces to equation (23).

Two serious drawbacks mar this appealing straightforward approach. The estimate of total costs requires a priori knowledge and specification of the investment period. While the period covered by formal schooling is easily determined, the period covered by much on-the-job training and other investment is not, and a serious error might result from an incorrect specification: to take an extreme example, total costs would approach zero as the investment period is assumed to be longer and longer.[41]

A second difficulty is that the differences between net earnings in X and Y do not correctly measure the cost of investing in Y since they do not correctly measure earnings foregone. A person who invested in the initial period could receive more than X_1 in period 1 as long as the initial investment yielded a positive return.[42] The true cost of an invest-

[41] Since

$$C^1 = \sum_{0}^{m-1} (X_j - Y_j)(1+r)^{-j},$$

$$\lim_{m \to n} C^1 = \sum_{0}^{n-1} (X_j - Y_j)(1+r)^{-j} = 0.$$

by definition of the internal rate.

[42] If C_0 was the initial investment, r_0 its internal rate, and if the return were the same in all years, the amount

$$X_1^1 = X_1 + \frac{r_0 C_0}{1 - (1+r_0)^{-n}}$$

could be received in period 1.

ment in period 1 would be the total earnings foregone, or the difference between what could have been received and what is received. The difference between X_1 and Y_1 could greatly underestimate true costs; indeed, Y_1 might be greater than X_1 even though a large investment was made in period 1.[43] In general, therefore, the amount invested in any period would be determined not only from net earnings in the same period but also from net earnings in earlier periods.

If the cost of an investment is consistently defined as the earnings foregone, quite different estimates of total costs emerge. Although superficially a less natural and straightforward approach, the generalization from a single period to distributed investment is actually greatly simplified. So let C_j be the foregone earnings in the jth period, r_j the rate of return on C_j, and let the return per period on C_j be a constant k_j, with $k = \Sigma k_j$ being the total return on the whole investment. If the number of periods was indefinitely large, and if investment occurred only in the first m periods, the equation relating costs, returns, and internal rates has the strikingly simple form of[44]

$$C = \sum_{0}^{m-1} C_j = \frac{k}{\bar{r}}, \qquad (25)$$

where

$$\bar{r} = \sum_{0}^{m-1} w_j r_j, \qquad w_j = \frac{C_j}{C},$$

and

$$\sum_{0}^{m-1} w_j = 1. \qquad (26)$$

Total cost, defined simply as the sum of costs during each period, would equal the capitalized value of returns, the rate of capitalization being a weighted average of the rates of return on the individual investments. Any sequence of internal rates or investment costs is permitted, no matter what the pattern of rises and declines, nor what form the investments take, be they a college education, an apprenticeship, ballet lessons, or a medical examination. Different investment programs would have the same ultimate effect on earnings whenever the average rate of return and the sum of investment costs were the same.[45]

Equation (25) can be given an interesting interpretation if all rates of return were the same. The term $k/\bar{r}$ would then be the value at the beginning of the mth period of all succeeding net earning differentials between Y and X discounted

---

[43] Y_1 is greater than X_1 if

$$X_1 + \frac{r_0 C_0}{1 - (1 + r_0)^{-n}} - C_1 > X_1,$$

or if

$$\frac{r_0 C_0}{1 - (1 + r_0)^{-n}} > C_1,$$

where C_1 is the investment in period 1.

[44] A proof is straightforward. An investment in period j would yield a return of the amount $k_j = r_j C_j$ in each succeeding period if the number of periods was infinite and the return was the same in each. Since the total return is the sum of individual returns,

$$k = \sum_{0}^{m-1} k_j = \sum_{0}^{m-1} r_j C_j = C \sum_{0}^{m-1} \frac{r_j C_j}{C} = \bar{r} C.$$

I am indebted to Helen Raffel for important suggestions which led to this simple proof.

[45] Note that the rate of return equating the present values of net earnings in X and Y is not necessarily equal to $\bar{r}$, for it would weigh more heavily than $\bar{r}$ does the rates of return on earlier investments. For example, if rates were higher on investments in earlier than later periods, the over-all rate would be greater than $\bar{r}$, and vice versa if rates were higher in later periods. The difference between the over-all internal rate for X and Y and $\bar{r}$ would be small, however, as long as the investment period was not very long and the systematic difference between internal rates not very great.

34   GARY S. BECKER

at the internal rate, r.[46] Total costs would equal the value also at the beginning of the mth period—which is the end of the investment period—of the first m differentials between X and Y.[47] The value of the first m differentials between X and Y must equal the value of all succeeding differentials between Y and X, since r would be the rate of return equating the present values in X and Y.

The internal rate of return and the

amount invested in each of the first m periods could be estimated from the net earnings streams in X and Y alone if the rate of return was the same on all investments. For the internal rate r could be determined from the condition that the present value of net earnings must be the same in X and Y, and the amount invested in each period seriatim from the relations[48]

$$C_0 = X_0 - Y_0, \quad C_1 = X_1 - Y_1 + rC_0$$
$$C_j = X_j - Y_j + r\sum_{k=0}^{j-1} C_k, 0 \le j \le m-1. \quad (27)$$

So costs and the rate of return can be estimated from information on net earnings. This is fortunate since the return on human capital is never empirically separated from other earnings and the cost of such capital is only sometimes and incompletely separated.

The investment period of education can be measured by years of schooling, but the period of on-the-job training, the search for information, and other investments is not readily available. Happily, one need not know the investment period to estimate costs and returns, since all three can be simultaneously estimated from information on net earnings. If activity X were known to have no investment (a zero investment period) the amount invested in Y during any period would be defined by

---

[46] That is,

$$\sum_{j=m}^{\infty} (Y_j - X_j)(1+r)^{m-1-j}$$

$$= k\sum_{m}^{\infty} (1+r)^{m-1-j} = \frac{k}{r}.$$

[47] Since, by definition,

$$X_0 - Y_0 = C_0, \quad X_1 - Y_1 = C_1 - rC_0,$$

and more generally

$$X_j - Y_j = C_j - r\sum_{k=0}^{j-1} C_k, \quad 0 \le j < m,$$

then

$$\sum_{j=0}^{m-1} (X_j - Y_j)(1+r)^{m-1-j}$$

$$= \sum_{j=0}^{m-1} \left(C_j - r\sum_{0}^{j-1} C_k\right)(1+r)^{m-1-j}$$

$$= \sum_{0}^{m-1} C_j\{(1+r)^{m-1-j} - r[1$$

$$+ (1+r) + \ldots + (1+r)^{m-2-j}]\}.$$

$$= \sum_{0}^{m-1} C_j = C.$$

The analytical difference between the naïve definition of costs advanced earlier and one in terms of foregone earnings is that the former measures total costs by the value of earning differentials at the beginning of the investment period and the latter by the value at the end of the period. Therefore, $C^1 = C(1+r)^{1-m}$, which follows from eq. (24) when $n = \infty$.

[48] If the rate of return was not the same on all investments there would be $2m$ unknowns—$C_0, \ldots C_m - 1$, and $r_0, \ldots r_{m-1}$—and only $m+1$ equations—the m cost definitions and the equation

$$k = \sum_{0}^{m-1} r_i C_i.$$

An additional $m - 1$ relation would be required to determine the $2m$ unknowns. The condition $r_0 = r_1 = \ldots = r_{m-1}$ is one form these $m - 1$ relations can take.

$$C_j = X_j - Y_j + r \sum_0^{j-1} C_k, \quad \text{all } j, \quad (28)$$

and total costs by

$$C = \sum_0^\infty C_j. \qquad (29)$$

The internal rate could be determined in the usual way from the equality between present values in X and Y, costs in each period from equation (28) and total costs from equation (29).

The definition of costs presented here simply extends to all periods the definition advanced earlier for the investment period.[49] The rationale for the general

[49] Therefore, since the value of the first m earning differentials has been shown to equal

$$\sum_0^{m-1} C_j$$

at period m (see n. 47), total costs could be estimated from the value of all differentials at the end of the earning period. That is,

$$C = \sum_0^\infty C_j = \sum_0^\infty (X_j - Y_j) \infty^{-1-j}.$$

Thus the value of all differentials would equal zero at the beginning of the earning period—by definition of the internal rate—and C at the end. The apparent paradox results from the infinite horizon, as can be seen from the following equation relating the value of the first f differentials at the beginning of the gth period to costs:

$$V(f, g) = \sum_{j=0}^{f-1} (X_j - Y_j)(1 + r)^{g-1-j}$$

$$= \sum_{j=0}^{f-1} C_j (1 + r)^{g-f}.$$

When $f = \infty$ and $g = 0$, $V = 0$, but whenever $f = g$,

$$V = \sum_0^{f-1} C_j.$$

In particular, if $f = g = \infty$, $V = C$.

definition is the same: investment occurs in Y whenever earnings there are below the sum of those in X and the income accruing on prior investments. If costs were found to be greater than zero before some period m and equal to zero thereafter, the first m periods would be the empirically derived investment period. But costs and returns can be estimated from equation (28) even when there is no simple investment period.

A common objection to an earlier draft of this paper is that the general and rather formal definition of costs advanced here is all right when applied to on-the-job training, schooling, and other recognized investments, but goes too far by also including as investment costs many effects that should be treated otherwise. For example, the protest runs, suppose that learning was essentially unavoidable in an activity Z, so that earnings "automatically" grows rapidly with experience. Since earnings in Z would tend to be lower than those in X at younger ages and higher later on, my approach would say that investment occurs in Z. Critics have argued that there really is no investment in Z since the rise in earnings results from *unavoidable* learning rather than from an attempt to improve skills, knowledge, or health. Although the argument is superficially plausible I am convinced it is as reasonable to say that investment in human capital occurs in Z as in activities requiring training or schooling. Indeed, an important virtue rather than defect in my concept of human capital is that learning—both on and off the job—is included along with training and schooling.

If Z were preferred to X the higher earnings at later ages presumably outweigh the earnings foregone initially. Similarly, a person entering an activity requiring much education is said to value the stream of future higher earnings more than the net earnings foregone initially. If the lower earnings due to education are called investment costs, the higher earnings investment returns, and if costs are related to returns by an internal rate of return, logical consistency and economic sense would require that similar concepts apply to learning. Thus the lower initial earnings of high-school graduates who enter occupations "with a future" have as much right to be considered investment, both from the social and private viewpoints, as do the lower net earnings of those enrolled in college. In general, since the private and social ranking of different economic activities depend only on their net earning streams, if one activity was said to require a given investment and to yield a given return, another activity with the same net earning stream must be said to require the same investment and yield the same return, no matter how they differ in other respects.

So much in defense of our approach. To estimate costs empirically still has required a priori knowledge that nothing is invested in activity X. Without such knowledge, only the *difference* between the amounts invested in any two activities with known net earning streams could be estimated from the definitions in equation (28). Were this done for all available streams the investment in any activity beyond that in the activity with the smallest investment could be determined.[50] The observed minimum investment would not be zero, however, if the rate of return on some initial investment was sufficiently high to attract everyone. A relevant question is, therefore: can the shape of the stream in an activity having zero investment be specified a priori so that the total investment in any activity can be determined?

The statement "nothing is invested in an activity" means only nothing would be invested after the age when information on earnings first became available; investment can have occurred before that age. If, for example, the data begin at age eighteen, some investment in schooling, health, or information surely must have occurred at younger ages. The earning stream of persons who do not invest after age eighteen would have to be considered, at least in part, as a return on the investment before eighteen. Indeed, in the developmental approach to child-rearing (discussed in Selma Mushkin's paper), most if not all of these earnings would be so considered.

The earning stream in an activity with no investment beyond the initial age (activity X) would be flat if the developmental approach was followed and earnings were said to result entirely from earlier investment.[51] The minimum investment could then be determined if an assumption was made about its rate to return. My discussion of the shape of the earning stream in X is, however, highly conjectural,[52] and further investigation may well indicate that another approach is preferable.

Our assumption that lifetimes are infinite, although descriptively unrealistic, is often a very close approximation. For example, I have shown elsewhere that the average rate of return on college education in the United States could

---

[50] The technique is applied and further developed by Mincer in his paper in this Supplement.

[51] If C measured the cost of investment before the initial age and r its rate of return, $k = rC$ would measure the return per period. If earnings were attributed entirely to this investment, $X_i = k = rC$, where X_i represents earnings at the ith period past the initial age.

[52] But note that empirical evidence indicates that age-earning profiles in unskilled occupations are very flat.

only be slightly raised if people remained in the labor force indefinitely. A finite earning period has, however, a greater effect on the rate of return of investments occurring at later ages, say after age forty; indeed, it helps explain why schooling and other investments are primarily made at younger ages.

An analysis of finite earning streams can be approached in two ways. One simply applies the concepts developed for infinite streams and says there is disinvestment in human capital when net earnings are above the amount that could be maintained indefinitely. Investment at younger ages would give way to disinvestment at older ages until no human capital remained at death (or retirement). This approach has several important applications and is used in parts of my study. An alternative that is more useful for some purposes lets the earning period itself influence the definitions of accrued income and cost. The income resulting from an investment during period j would be defined as

$$k_j = \frac{r_j C_j}{1 - (1 + r_j)^{j-n}}, \quad (30)$$

where $n + 1$ is the earning period, and the amount invested during j would be defined by

$$C_j = X_j - Y_j$$

$$+ \sum_{k=0}^{k=j-1} \frac{r_k C_k}{1 - (1 + r_k)^{k-n}}. \quad (31)$$

IV. THE INCENTIVE TO INVEST

A. NUMBER OF PERIODS

The discussion summarized in equations (28) and (31) shows how total costs, rates of return, and the investment period can be estimated from information on net earnings alone, and thus how the effect on earnings of a change in the amount invested can be distinguished empirically from the effect of a change in rates of return. Our attention now turns to the factors influencing the amount invested in different activities and by different persons. Economists have long believed that the incentive to expand and improve physical resources depends on the rate of return expected. They have been very reluctant, however, to interpret improvements in the effectiveness and amount of human resources in the same way, namely, as systematic responses or "investments" resulting in good part from the returns expected. In this section I try to show that an investment approach to human resources is a powerful and simple tool capable of explaining a wide range of phenomena, including much that has either been ignored or given *ad hoc* interpretations.

An increase in the lifespan of an activity would, other things the same, increase the rate of return on the investment made in any period. The influence of lifespan on the rate of return and thus on the incentive to invest is important and takes many forms. A few of these forms will now be discussed.

The number of periods is obviously affected by mortality and morbidity rates, for the lower they are, the longer the expected lifespan, and the larger the fraction of a lifetime that can be spent at any activity. The major secular decline of these rates in the United States and elsewhere may have increased the rates of return on investment in human capital,[53] thereby encouraging such investment. This conclusion is independent

[53] I say *may* because rates of return are adversely affected by the increase in labor force that would result from a decline in death and sickness. If the adverse effect was sufficiently great, a decline in death and sickness would reduce rates of return on human capital. I am indebted to my wife for emphasizing this point.

38   GARY S. BECKER

of whether the secular improvement in health itself resulted from investment; if so, the secular increase in rates of return would be part of the return to investment in health.

A relatively large fraction of younger persons are in school, enter upon on-the-job training, change jobs and locations, and add to their knowledge of economic, political, and social opportunities. The entire explanation of these differences between young and old persons may not be that the young are more interested in learning, more able to absorb new ideas, less tied down by family responsibilities, more easily supported by parents, or more flexible about changing their routine and place of living. One need not rely only on life-cycle effects on capabilities, responsibilities, or attitudes as soon as one recognizes, as we have throughout, that schooling, training, mobility, and the like are ways to invest in human capital and that younger people have a greater incentive to invest because they can collect the return over more years.[54] Indeed, a greater incentive would be present even if age had no effect on capabilities, responsibilities, and attitudes.

Although the unification of these different kinds of behavior by the investment approach is important evidence in its favor, other evidence is needed. A powerful test can be developed along the following lines.[55] Suppose that investment in human capital raised earnings for p periods only, where p varied between o and n. The size of p would be affected by many factors, including the rate of obsolescence since the more rapidly an investment became obsolete the smaller p would be. The advantage in being young would be less the smaller p was, since the effect of age on the rate of return would be positively related to p. For example, if p equaled two years, the rate would be the same at all ages except the two nearest the "retirement" age. If the investment approach was correct, the difference between the amount invested at different ages would be positively correlated with p, which is not surprising since an expenditure with a small p would be less of an "investment" than one with a large p, and arguments based on an investment framework would be less applicable. None of the life-cycle arguments seem to imply any correlation with p, so this provides a powerful test of the importance of the investment approach.

The time spent in any one activity is determined not only by age, mortality, and morbidity but also by the amount of switching between activities. Women spend less time in the labor force than men and, therefore, have less incentive to invest in market skills; tourists spend little time in any one area and have less incentive than residents of the area to invest in knowledge of specific consumption opportunities;[56] temporary migrants to urban areas have less incentive to invest in urban skills than permanent residents; and, as a final example, draftees have less incentive than professional soldiers to invest in purely military skills.

Women, tourists, and the like have to

---

[54] Younger persons would also have a greater incentive to invest if the cost of any investment rose with age, say, because potential and thus foregone earnings rose with age.

[55] This test was suggested by George Stigler's discussion of the effect of different auto-correlation patterns on the incentive to invest in information (see "The Economics of Information," *Journal of Political Economy*, Vol. LXIX [June, 1961], and his paper in this Supplement).

[56] This example is from Stigler, "The Economics of Information," *op. cit.*

find investments that increase productivity in several activities. A woman wants her investment to be useful both as a housewife and as a participant in the labor force, or a frequent traveler wants to be knowledgeable in many environments. Such investments would be less readily available than more specialized ones—after all, an investment increasing productivity in two activities also increases it in either one alone, extreme complementarity aside, while the converse does not hold; specialists, therefore, have greater incentive to invest in themselves than others do.

Specialization in an activity would be discouraged if the market were very limited; thus the incentive to specialize and to invest in oneself would increase as the extent of the market increased. Workers would be more skilled the larger the market, not only because "practice makes perfect," so often stressed in discussions of the division of labor,[57] but also because a larger market would *induce* a greater investment in skills.[58] Put differently, the usual analysis of the division of labor stresses that efficiency, and thus wage rates, would be greater the larger the market, and ignores the potential earnings period in any activity, while ours stresses that this period, and thus the incentive to *become* more efficient, would be directly related to market size. Surprisingly little attention has been paid to the influence of market size on the incentive to invest in skills.

[57] See, for example, Marshall, *op. cit.*, Bk. IV, chap. ix.

[58] If "practice makes perfect" means that age-earnings profiles slope upward, then according to my approach it must be treated along with other kinds of learning as a way of investing in human capital. The distinction above between the effect of an increase in the market on practice and on the incentive to invest would simply be that the incentive to invest in human capital is increased even aside from the effect of practice on earnings.

B. WAGE DIFFERENTIALS AND SECULAR CHANGES

According to equation (30) the internal rate of return depends on the ratio of the return per unit time to investment costs. A change in the return and costs by the same percentage would not change the internal rate, while a greater percentage change in the return would change the internal rate in the same direction. The return is measured by the absolute income gain, or by the absolute income difference between persons differing only in the amount of their investment. Note that absolute, not relative, income differences determine the return and the internal rate.

Occupational and educational wage differentials are sometimes measured by relative, sometimes by absolute, wage differences,[59] although no one has adequately discussed their relative merits. Marginal productivity analysis relates the derived demand for any class of workers to the ratio of their wages to those of other inputs,[60] so wage ratios are more appropriate in understanding forces determining demand. They are not, however, the best measure of forces determining supply, for the return on investment in skills and other knowledge is determined by absolute wage differences.

[59] See A. M. Ross and W. Goldner, "Forces Affecting the Inter-industry Wage Structure," *Quarterly Journal of Economics*, Vol. LXIV (May, 1950); P. H. Bell, "Cyclical Variation and Trend in Occupational Wage Differentials in American Industry since 1914," *Review of Economics and Statistics*, Vol. XXIII (November, 1951); F. Meyers and R. L. Bowlby, "The Interindustry Wage Structure and Productivity," *Industrial and Labor Relations Review*, Vol. VII (October, 1953); Stigler and Blank, *op. cit.*, Table 11; P. Keat, "Long-Term Trends in Occupational Wage Differentials," *Journal of Political Economy*, Vol. LXVIII (December, 1960).

[60] Thus the elasticity of a substitution is usually defined as the percentage change in the ratio of quantities employed per 1 per cent change in the ratio of wages.

40 GARY S. BECKER

Therefore neither wage ratios nor wage differences are uniformly the best measure, ratios being more appropriate in demand studies and differences in supply studies.

The importance of distinguishing between wage ratios and differences, and the confusion resulting from the practice of using ratios to measure supply as well as demand forces, can be illustrated by considering the effects of technological progress. If progress were uniform in all industries and neutral with respect to all factors, and if there were constant costs, initially all wages would rise by the same proportion and the prices of all goods, including the output of industries supplying the investment in human capital,[61] would be unchanged. Since wage ratios would be unchanged, firms would have no incentive initially to alter their factor proportions. Wage differences, on the other hand, would rise at the same rate as wages, and since investment costs would be unchanged, there would be an incentive to invest more in human capital, and thus to increase the relative supply of skilled persons. The increased supply would in turn reduce the rate of increase of wage differences and produce an absolute narrowing of wage ratios.

In the United States during much of the last eighty years, a narrowing of wage ratios has gone hand in hand with an increasing relative supply of skill, an association that is usually said to result from the effect of an *autonomous* increase in the supply of skills—brought about by the spread of free education or the rise in incomes—on the return to skill, as measured by wage ratios. An alternative interpretation suggested by our analysis is that the spread of education and the increased investment in other kinds of human capital were in large part *induced* by technological progress (and perhaps other changes) through the effect on the rate of return, as measured by wage differences and costs. Clearly a secular decline in wage ratios is not inconsistent with a secular increase in real wage differences if average wages were rising, and, indeed, one important body of data on wages shows a decline in ratios and an even stronger rise in differences.[62]

The interpretation based on autonomous supply shifts has been favored partly because a decline in wage ratios has erroneously been taken as evidence of a decline in the return to skill. While a decision ultimately can be based only on a detailed re-examination of the evidence,[63] the induced approach can be made more plausible by considering trends in physical capital. Economists have been aware that the rate of return on capital could be rising or at least not falling while the ratio of the "rental" price of capital to wages was falling. Consequently, although the rental price

[61] Some persons have argued that only direct investment costs would be unchanged, indirect costs or foregone earnings rising along with wages. Neutral progress implies, however, the same increase in the productivity of a student's time as in his teacher's time or in the use of raw materials, so even foregone earnings would not change.

[62] Keat's data for 1906–53 in the United States show both an average annual decline of 0.8 per cent in the coefficient of variation of wages and an average annual rise of 1.2 per cent in the real standard deviation. The decline in the coefficient of variation was shown in his study (*op. cit*); I computed the change in the real standard deviation from data made available to me by Keat.

[63] For those believing that the evidence overwhelmingly indicates a secular decline in rates of return on human capital, I reproduce Adam Smith's statement on earnings in some professions. "The lottery of the law, therefore, is very far from being a perfectly fair lottery; and that, as well as many other liberal and honourable professions, is, in point of pecuniary gain, evidently under-recompensed" (*The Wealth of Nations* [New York: Modern Library, 1937], p. 106). Since economists tend to believe that law and most other liberal professions are now over-compensated relative to non-professional work "in point of pecuniary gain," the return to professional work could not have declined continuously if Smith's observations were accurate.

INVESTMENT IN HUMAN CAPITAL: A THEORETICAL ANALYSIS   41

of capital declined relative to wages over time, the large secular increase in the amount of physical capital per man-hour is not usually considered autonomous, but rather induced by technological and other developments that, at least temporarily, raised the return. A common explanation based on the effects of economic progress may, then, account for the increase in both human and physical capital.

C. RISK AND LIQUIDITY

An informed, rational person would invest only if the expected rate of return was greater than the sum of the interest rate on riskless assets and the liquidity and risk premiums associated with the investment. Not much need be said about the "pure" interest rate, but a few words are in order on risk and liquidity. Since human capital is a very illiquid asset—it cannot be sold and is rather poor collateral on loans—a positive liquidity premium, perhaps a sizable one, would be associated with such capital.

The actual return on human capital varies around the expected return because of uncertainty about several factors. There always has been considerable uncertainty about the length of life, one important determinant of the return. People are also uncertain about their ability, especially younger persons who do most of the investing. In addition, there is uncertainty about the return to a person of given age and ability because of numerous events that are not predictable. The long time required to collect the return on an investment in human capital reduces the knowledge available, for required is knowledge about the environment when the return is to be received, and the longer the average period between investment and return the less such knowledge is available.

Informed observation as well as cal-culations I have made suggest that there is much uncertainty about the return to human capital.[64] The response to uncertainty is determined by its amount and nature and by tastes or attitudes. Many have argued that attitudes of investors in human capital are very different from those of investors in physical capital because the former tend to be younger,[65] and young persons are supposed to be especially prone to overestimate their ability and chance of good fortune.[66] Were this view correct, a human investment which promised a large return to exceptionally able or lucky persons would be more attractive than a similar physical investment. However, a "life-cycle" explanation of attitudes toward risk may be no more valid or necessary than life-cycle explanations of why investors in human capital are relatively young (discussed on pp. 37–38). Indeed, an alternative explanation of reactions to large gains has already appeared.[67]

[64] For example, Marshall said: "Not much less than a generation elapses between the choice by parents of a skilled trade for one of their children, and his reaping the full results of their choice. And meanwhile the character of the trade may have been almost revolutionized by changes, on which some probably threw long shadows before them, but others were such as could not have been foreseen even by the shrewdest persons and those best acquainted with the circumstances of the trade" (*op. cit.*, p. 571), and "the circumstances by which the earnings are determined are less capable of being foreseen [than those for machinery]" (*ibid.*).

[65] Note that our argument on p. 38 implied that investors in human capital would be younger.

[66] Smith said: "The contempt of risk and the presumptuous hope of success, are in no period of life more active than at the age at which young people choose their professions" (*op. cit.*, p. 109). Marshall said that "young men of an adventurous disposition are more attracted by the prospects of a great success than they are deterred by the fear of failure" (*op. cit.*, p. 554).

[67] See M. Friedman and L. J. Savage, "The Utility Analysis of Choices Involving Risk," reprinted in *Readings in Price Theory*, ed. G. J. Stigler and K. Boulding (Chicago: Richard D. Irwin, Inc., 1952).

42   GARY S. BECKER

D. CAPITAL MARKETS AND KNOWLEDGE

If investment decisions respond only to earning prospects, adjusted for risk and liquidity, the adjusted marginal rate of return would be the same on all investments. The rate of return on education, training, migration, health, and other human capital is supposed to be higher than elsewhere, however, because of financing difficulties and inadequate knowledge of opportunities. These will now be discussed briefly.

Economists have long emphasized that it is difficult to borrow funds to invest in human capital because such capital cannot be offered as collateral and courts have frowned on contracts which even indirectly suggest involuntary servitude. This argument has been explicitly used to explain the "apparent" underinvestment in education and training and also, although somewhat less explicitly, underinvestment in health, migration, and other human capital. The importance attached to capital market difficulties can be determined not only from the discussions of investment but also from the discussions of consumption. Young persons would consume relatively little, productivity and wages might be related, and some other consumption patterns would follow only if it were difficult to capitalize future earning power. Indeed, unless capital limitations applied to consumption as well as investment, the latter could be indirectly financed with "consumption" loans.[68]

Some other implications of capital market difficulties can also be mentioned:

[68] A person with an income of X and investment costs of Y ($Y < X$) could either use X for consumption and receive an *investment loan* of Y, or use $X - Y$ for consumption, Y for investment, and receive a *consumption loan* of Y. He ends up with the same consumption and investment in both cases, the only difference being in the names attached to loans.

1. Since large expenditures would be more difficult to finance, investment in (say) a college education would be more affected than in (say) short-term migration.

2. Internal financing would be common, and consequently wealthier families would tend to invest more than poorer ones.

3. Since employees' specific skills are part of the intangible assets or good will of firms and can be offered as collateral along with tangible assets, capital would be more readily available for specific than for general investments.

4. Some persons have argued that opportunity costs (foregone earnings) are more readily financed than direct costs because they require only to do "without," while the latter require outlays. Although superficially plausible, this view can easily be shown to be wrong: opportunity and direct costs can be financed equally readily, given the state of the capital market. If total investment costs were $800, potential earnings $1,000, and if all costs were foregone earnings, investors would have $200 of earnings to spend; if all were direct costs, they would initially have $1,000 to spend, but just $200 would remain after paying "tuition," so their *net* position would be exactly the same as before. The example can be readily generalized and the obvious inference is that indirect and direct investment costs are equivalent in imperfect as well as perfect capital markets.

While it is undeniably difficult to use the capital market to finance investments in human capital, there is some reason to doubt whether otherwise equivalent investments in physical capital can be financed much more easily. Consider an eighteen-year-old who wants to invest a given amount in equipment for a firm he is starting rather than in a college education. What is his chance of borrowing the whole amount at a "moderate" interest rate? Very slight, I believe, since he would be untried and have a high debt equity ratio; moreover, the collateral provided by his equipment would probably be very imperfect. He, too, would either have to borrow at high interest rates or self-finance. Although the difficulties of financing investments in human capital have usually been related to special properties of human capital, in large measure they seem also to beset comparable investments in physical capital.

A recurring theme is that young persons are especially prone to be ignorant of their abilities and of the investment opportunities available. If so, investors in human capital, being younger, would be less aware of opportunities and thus more likely to err than investors in tangible capital. I suggested earlier (pp. 37–38) that investors in human capital are younger partly because of the cost in postponing their investment to older ages. The desire to acquire additional knowledge about the return and about alternatives provides an incentive to postpone any risky investment, but since an investment in human capital is more costly to postpone, it would be made earlier and presumably with less knowledge than comparable non-human investments. Therefore, investors in human capital may not have less knowledge *because* of their age; rather both might be a *joint* product of the incentive not to delay investing.[69]

[69] Marshall (*op. cit.*, pp. 571–73) appears to argue that it is also intrinsically more difficult to acquire knowledge about the return from an investment in human capital.

The eighteen-year-old in our example who could not finance a purchase of machinery might, without too much cost, postpone the investment for a number of years until his reputation and equity were sufficient to provide the "personal" collateral required to borrow funds. Financing may prove a more formidable obstacle to investors in human capital because they cannot postpone their investment so readily. Perhaps this accounts for the tendency of economists to stress capital market imperfections when discussing investments in human capital.

V. SOME EFFECTS OF HUMAN CAPITAL

A. EXAMPLES

Differences in earnings among persons, areas, or time periods are usually said to result from differences in physical capital, technological knowledge, ability, or institutions (such as unionization or socialized production). Our analysis indicates, however, that investment in human capital also has an important effect on observed earnings because earnings tend to be net of investment costs and gross of investment returns. Indeed, an appreciation of the direct and indirect importance of human capital appears to resolve many otherwise puzzling empirical findings about earnings. Consider the following examples:

1. Almost all studies show that age-earnings profiles tend to be steeper among more skilled and educated persons. I argued earlier (pp. 14–15) that on-the-job training would steepen age-earning profiles and the analysis of Section III generalizes the argument to all human capital. Since observed earnings are gross of returns and net of costs, investment in human capital at younger ages would reduce observed earnings then and raise them at older ages, thus steepening

44   GARY S. BECKER

the age-earnings profile.[70]

2. In recent years students of international trade theory have been somewhat shaken by findings that the United States, said to have relative scarcity of labor and abundance of capital, apparently exports relatively labor-intensive commodities and imports relatively capital-intensive commodities. For example, one study found that export industries pay higher wages than import competing ones.[71]

An interpretation consistent with the Ohlin-Heckscher emphasis on the relative abundance of different factors argues that the United States has an even more (relatively) abundant supply of human than of physical capital. An increase in human capital would, however, show up as an apparent increase in labor intensity since earnings are gross of the return on such capital. Thus export industries might pay higher wages than import competing ones primarily because they employ more skilled or healthier workers.[72]

3. Several recent studies have tried to estimate empirically the elasticity of substitution between capital and labor. Usually a ratio of the input of physical capital to the input of labor is regressed on the wage rate in different areas or time periods, the regression coefficient being an estimate of the elasticity of substitution.[73] Countries, states, or time periods that have relatively high wages and inputs of physical capital also tend to have much human capital. Just as a correlation between wages, physical capital and human capital seems to obscure the relationship between relative factor supplies and commodity prices, so it obscures the relationship between relative factor supplies and factor prices. For if wages were high primarily because of human capital, a regression of the relative amount of physical capital on wages could give a seriously biased picture of the effect of factor proportions on wages.[74]

---

[70] According to eq. (28) earnings at age j can be approximated by

$$Y_j = X_j + \sum_{k=0}^{k=j-1} r_k C_k - C_j,$$

where X_j are earnings at j of persons who have not invested in themselves, C_k is the investment at age k, and r_k is its rate of return. The rate of increase in earnings would be at least as steep in Y as in X at each age and not only from "younger" to "older" ages if and only if

$$\frac{\Delta Y_j}{\Delta j} \geq \frac{\Delta X_j}{\Delta j},$$

or

$$r_j C_j \geq \frac{\Delta C_j}{\Delta j}.$$

This condition is usually satisfied since $r_j C_j \geq 0$ and the amount invested tends to decline with age.

[71] See I. Kravis, "Wages and Foreign Trade," *Review of Economics and Statistics*, Vol. XXXIII (February, 1956).

[72] This kind of interpretation has been put forward by many writers; see, for example, the discussion in W. Leontief, "Factor Proportions and the Structure of American Trade: Further Theoretical and Empirical Analysis," *Review of Economics and Statistics*, Vol. XXXIII (November, 1956).

[73] Interstate estimates for several industries can be found in J. Minasian, "Elasticities of Substitution and Constant-Output Demand Curves for Labor," *Journal of Political Economy*, LXIX (June, 1961), 261–70; intercountry estimates in Kenneth Arrow, Hollis B. Chenery, Bagicha Minhas, and Robert M. Solow, "Capital-Labor Substitution and Economic Efficiency," *Review of Economics and Statistics* (August, 1961); unpublished papers by Philip Nelson and Robert Solow contain both interstate and time-series estimates.

[74] Minasian's argument (*op. cit.*, p. 264) that interstate variations in skill level necessarily bias his estimates toward unity is actually correct only if skill is a perfect substitute for "labor." (In correspondence Minasian states that he intended to make this condition explicit.) If, on the other hand, human and physical capital were perfect substitutes the estimates would always have a downward bias, regardless of the true substitution between labor and capital. Perhaps the most reasonable assumption would be that physical capital is more complementary with human capital than with labor; I have not, however, been able to determine the direction of bias in this case.

INVESTMENT IN HUMAN CAPITAL: A THEORETICAL ANALYSIS 45

4. A secular increase in average earnings has usually been said to result from increases in technological knowledge and physical capital per earner. The average earner, in effect, is supposed to benefit indirectly from activities by entrepreneurs, investors, and others. Another explanation put forward in recent years argues that earnings can rise because of direct investment in earners.[75] Instead of only benefiting from activities by others, the average earner is made a prime mover of development through the investment in himself.[76]

B. ABILITY AND THE DISTRIBUTION OF EARNINGS

An emphasis on human capital not only helps explain differences in earnings over time and among areas but also among persons or families within an area. This application will be discussed in greater detail than the others because a link is provided among earnings, ability, and the incentive to invest in human capital.

Economists have long been aware that conventional measures of ability—intelligence tests or aptitude scores, school grades, and personality tests—while undoubtedly relevant at times, do not reliably measure the talents required to succeed in the economic sphere. The latter requires a particular kind of personality, persistence, and intelligence. Accordingly, some writers have gone to the opposite extreme and argued that the only relevant way to measure economic talent is by results, or by earnings themselves.[77] Persons with higher earnings would simply have more ability than others, and a skewed distribution of earnings would imply a skewed distribution of abilities. This approach goes too far, however, in the opposite direction. The main reason for an interest in relating ability to earning is to distinguish its effects from differences in education, training, health, and other such factors, and a definition equating ability and earnings *ipso facto* precludes such a distinction. Nevertheless, results are very relevant and should not be ignored.

A compromise might be reached through defining ability by earnings only when several variables had been held constant. Since the public is very concerned about separating ability from education, on-the-job training, health, and other human capital, the amount invested in such capital would have to be held constant. Although a full analysis would also hold discrimination, nepotism, and several other factors constant, a reasonable first approximation would say that if two persons have the same investment in human capital, the one who earns more is demonstrating greater economic talent.

Since observed earnings are gross of the return on human capital they are affected by changes in the amount and rate of return. Indeed, after the investment period earnings (Y) can be simply approximated by

$$Y = X + rC, \qquad (32)$$

[75] The major figure here undoubtedly is T. W. Schultz. Of his many articles see esp. "Education and Economic Growth" in *Social Forces Influencing American Education* (Sixtieth Yearbook of the National Society for the Study of Education, Part II [Chicago: University of Chicago Press, 1961]).

[76] One caveat is called for, however. Since observed earnings are not only gross of the return from investments in human capital but also are net of some costs, an increased investment in human capital would both raise and reduce earnings. Although average earnings would tend to increase as long as the rate of return was positive, the increase is less than it would be if the cost of human capital, like that of physical capital, was not deducted from national income.

[77] Let me state again that whenever the word "earnings" appears I mean real earnings, or the sum of monetary earnings and the monetary equivalent of psychic earnings.

where C measures total investment costs, r the average rate of return, and X earnings when there is no investment in human capital. If the distribution of X is ignored for now, Y would depend only on r when C was held constant, so "ability" would be measured by the average rate of return on human capital.[78]

The amount invested is not the same for everyone, nor even in a very imperfect capital market rigidly fixed for any given person, but depends in part on the rate of return. Persons receiving a high marginal rate of return would have an incentive to invest more than others.[79] Since marginal and average rates are presumably positively correlated[80] and since ability is measured by the average rate, one can say that abler persons would invest more than others. The end result would be a positive correlation between ability and the investment in human capital,[81] a correlation with several important implications.

[78] Since r is a function of C, Y would indirectly as well as directly depend on C, and therefore the distribution of ability would depend on the amount of human capital. Some persons might rank high in earnings and thus high in ability if everyone were unskilled, and quite low if education and other training were widespread.

[79] In addition, they would find it easier to invest if the marginal return and the resources of parents and other relatives were positively correlated.

[80] According to a well-known formula

$$r_m = r_a \left(1 + \frac{1}{e_a} \right).$$

where r_m is the marginal rate of return, r_a the average rate, and e_a the elasticity of the average rate with respect to the amount invested. The rates r_m and r_a would be positively correlated unless r_a and $1/e_a$ were sufficiently negatively correlated.

[81] This kind of argument is not new; Marshall argued that business ability and the ownership of physical capital would be positively correlated: "[economic] forces . . . bring about the result that there is a far more close correspondence between the ability of business men and the size of the businesses which they own than at first sight would appear probable" (*op. cit.*, p. 312).

One is that the tendency for abler persons to migrate, continue their education,[82] and generally invest more in themselves can be explained without recourse to an assumption that non-economic forces or demand conditions favor them at higher investment levels. A second implication is that the separation of "nature from nurture" or ability from education and other environmental factors is apt to be difficult, for high earnings would tend to signify both more ability and a better environment. Thus the earnings differential between college and high-school graduates does not measure the effect of college alone since college graduates are abler and would earn more even without the additional education. Or reliable estimates of the income elasticity of demand for children have been difficult to obtain because higher income families also invest more in contraceptive knowledge.[83]

The main implication, however, is in the field of personal income distribution. At least ever since the time of Pigou economists have tried to reconcile the strong skewness in the distribution of earnings and other income with a presumed symmetrical distribution of abilities.[84] Pigou's own solution, that property income is not symmetrically distributed, does not directly help explain the skewness in earnings. Subsequent attempts have largely concentrated on developing *ad hoc* random and other probabilistic mechanisms that have little

[82] The first is frequently alleged (see, for example, Marshall, *op. cit.*, pp. 199, 684). Evidence on the second is discussed in my forthcoming study for the National Bureau of Economic Research.

[83] See my "An Economic Analysis of Fertility" in *Demographic and Economic Change in Developed Countries* (Princeton, N.J.: Princeton University Press, 1960).

[84] See A. C. Pigou, *The Economics of Welfare* (4th ed.; London: Macmillan & Co., 1950), Part IV, chap. ii.

INVESTMENT IN HUMAN CAPITAL: A THEORETICAL ANALYSIS 47

relation to the mainstream of economic thought.[85] The approach presented here, however, offers an explanation that is not only consistent with economic analysis but actually relies on one of its fundamental tenets; namely, that the amount invested is a function of the rate of return expected. In conjunction with the effect of human capital on earnings this tenet can explain several well-known properties of earnings distributions.

By definition, the distribution of earnings would be exactly the same as the distribution of ability if everyone invested the same amount in human capital; in particular, if ability were symmetrically distributed, earnings would also be. Equation (32) shows that the distribution of earnings would be exactly the same as the distribution of investment if all persons were equally able; again, if investment were symmetrically distributed, earnings would also be.[86] If ability and investment both varied, earnings would tend to be skewed even when ability and investment were not, but the skewness would be small as long as the amount invested was statistically independent of ability.[87]

Our analysis has shown, however, that abler persons would tend to invest more than others, so ability and investment would be positively correlated, perhaps quite strongly. Now the product of two symmetrical distributions is more positively skewed the higher the positive correlation between them, and might be quite skewed.[88] The economic incentive given abler persons to invest relatively large amounts in themselves does seem

capable, therefore, of reconciling a strong positive skewness in earnings with a presumed symmetrical distribution of abilities.

Variations in X help explain an important difference among skill categories in the degree of skewness. The smaller the fraction of total earnings resulting

[86] Jacob Mincer ("Investment in Human Capital and Personal Income Distribution," *Journal of Political Economy*, Vol. LXVI [August, 1958]) concluded that a symmetrical distribution of investment in education implies a skewed distribution of earnings because he defines educational investment by school years rather than costs. If we follow Mincer in assuming that everyone was equally able, that schooling was the only investment, and that the cost of the nth year of schooling equaled the earnings of persons with $n - 1$ years of schooling, then, say, a normal distribution of schooling can be shown to imply a log-normal distribution of school costs, and thus a log-normal distribution of earnings.

The difference between the earnings of persons with $n - 1$ and n years of schooling would be $k_n = Y_n - Y_{n-1} = r_n C_n$. Since r_n is assumed to equal r for all n, and $C_n = Y_{n-1}$, this equation becomes $Y_n = (1 + r)Y_{n-1}$, and therefore

$$C_1 = Y_0$$

$$C_2 = Y_1 = Y_0(1 + r)$$

$$C_3 = Y_2 = Y_1(1 + r) = Y_0(1 + r)^2$$

$$C_n = Y_{n-1} = \ldots = Y_0(1 + r)^{n-1},$$

or the cost of each additional year of schooling increases at a constant *rate*. Since total costs have the same distribution as $(1 + r)^n$, a symmetrical, say a normal, distribution of school years, n, implies a log-normal distribution of costs and hence by eq. (32) a log-normal distribution of earnings. I am indebted to Mincer for a helpful discussion of the comparison and especially for the stimulation provided by his pioneering work. Incidentally, his article and the dissertation on which it is based cover a much broader area than has been indicated here.

[87] For example, C. C. Craig has shown that the product of two independent normal distributions is only slightly skewed (see his "On the Frequency Function of XY," *Annals of Mathematical Statistics*, VII [March, 1936], 3).

[88] Craig (*op. cit.*, pp. 9–10) showed that the product of two normal distributions would be more positively skewed the higher the positive correlation between them, and that the skewness would be considerable with high correlations.

[85] A sophisticated example can be found in B. Mandelbrot, "The Pareto-Levy Law and the Distribution of Income," *International Economic Review*, Vol. I (May, 1960). In a recent paper, however, Mandelbrot has brought in maximizing behavior (see "Paretian Distributions and Income Maximization," *Quarterly Journal of Economics*, Vol. LXXVI [February, 1962]).

from investment in human capital—the smaller rC relative to X—the more would the distribution of earnings be dominated by the distribution of X. Higher skill categories have a greater average investment in human capital and thus presumably a large rC relative to X. The distribution of "unskilled ability," X, would, therefore, tend to dominate the distribution of earnings in relatively unskilled categories while the distribution of a product of ability and the amount invested, rC, would dominate in skilled categories. Hence if abilities were symmetrically distributed, earnings would tend to be more symmetrically distributed among the unskilled than among the skilled.[89]

Equation (32) holds only when investment costs are small, which tends to be true at later ages, say after age thirty-five. Net earnings ar earlier ages would be given by

$$Y_j = X_j + \sum_0^{j-1} r_i C_i + (-C_j),$$

where j refers to the current year and i to previous years, C_i measures the investment cost of age i, C_j current costs, and r_i the rate of return on C_i. The distribution of $-C_j$ would be an important determinant of the distribution of Y_j since investment is large at these ages. Hence our analysis would predict a smaller (positive) skewness at younger than at

older ages because the presumed negative correlation between $-C_j$ and $\sum_0^{j-1} r_i C_i$ would counteract the positive correlation between ability and investment.

A simple analysis of the incentive to invest in human capital seems capable of explaining, therefore, not only why the over-all distribution of earnings is more skewed than the distribution of abilities, but also why earnings are more skewed among older and skilled persons than among younger and less skilled ones. The renewed interest in investment in human capital may provide the means of bringing the theory of personal income distribution back into economics.

VI. SUMMARY AND CONCLUSIONS

Most investments in human capital both raise observed earnings at older ages, because returns are added to earnings then, and lower them at younger ages, because costs are deducted from earnings then. Since these common effects are produced by very different kinds of human capital, a basis is provided for a unified and powerful theory. The analysis proceeded from a discussion of specific kinds of human capital, with greatest attention paid to on-the-job training because it clearly illustrates and emphasizes the common effects, to a general theory applying to any kind.

The general theory has a wide variety of important implications, ranging from interpersonal and interarea differences in earnings, to the shape of age-earning profiles, to the effect of specialization on skill. For example, since earnings are gross of the return on human capital, some persons may earn more than others simply because they invest more in themselves. And since "abler" persons tend to invest more than others, the distribution

---

[89] As noted earlier, X does not really represent earnings when there is no investment in human capital, but only earnings when there is no investment after the initial age (be it fourteen, twenty-five, or six). Indeed, the developmental approach to child-rearing argues that earnings would be close to zero if there was no investment at all in human capital. The distribution of X, therefore, would be at least partly determined by the distribution of investment before the initial age, and if it and ability were positively correlated, X might be positively skewed, even though ability was not.

of earnings could be very unequal and even skewed, even though "ability" were symmetrically and not too unequally distributed. To take another example, learning, both on and off the job, and other activities appear to have exactly the same effects on observed earnings as do education, training, and other traditional investments in human capital. We argue that a relevant concept should cover all activities with identical effects and show that the total amount invested in a generalized concept of human capital and its rate of return can be estimated from information on earnings alone.

Some investments in human capital do not affect earnings because costs are paid and returns are collected by the firms, industries, or countries using the capital. These "specific" investments range from hiring costs to executive training and are more important than is commonly believed. To take a couple of examples, we showed that the well-known greater unemployment among unskilled than skilled workers may result from the latter having more specific capital, or incompletely vested pension plans may be a means of insuring firms against a loss on their specific investments.

This paper has concentrated on developing a theory of investment in human capital, with an emphasis on empirical implications rather than on formal generalization. Of course, empirical usefulness is the only justification for any theory, and although I did not try to bring in even the quite limited evidence on the role of human capital, the empirical work reported in this volume, my own work, and that of many others support the view that investment in human capital is a pervasive phenomenon and a valuable concept. The next few years should provide much stronger evidence on whether the recent emphasis placed on this concept is just another fad or a development of great and lasting importance.

[5]

THE FIRM'S DECISION TO TRAIN

Donald O. Parsons

I. INTRODUCTION

Job training is a fundamental part of the total educational system in any industrialized economy, and the efficient provision of such training an important element in any comprehensive industrial strategy. In his classic study of on-the-job training, Jacob Mincer concluded a careful assessment of the aggregate importance of on-the-job training with the remark, "It is probably correct to say that, in the male half of the world, on-the-job training—measured in dollar costs—is as important as formal schooling" (Mincer. 1962. p.63). This paper provides a critical review of economic models of the firm's decision to train workers: what training is undertaken, where it is undertaken, and who finances it. In the final section. I consider ways in which the government can encourage the more efficient provision of on-the-job training.

Many critical job skills. for example, reading and mathematical skills. are not typically learned on the job, but are developed in a formal schooling environment. Presumably these attributes are almost universally demanded, so that economies of scale argue for collective provision. Many of these skills also have returns beyond any direct labor market returns, for example, an informed electorate. and are collectively provided (subsidized) for that reason as well. The

Research in Labor Economics. Volume 11. pages 53–75.
Copyright © 1990 by JAI Press Inc.
All rights of reproduction in any form reserved.
ISBN: 1-555938-080-2

efficiency of the schooling system in providing these skills is often questioned, but only modest variations or reform have been proposed, suggesting that the basic structure (publicly financed, specialized training centers) is perceived as reasonable.

Skills more directly linked to the job are more eclectically supplied, reflecting perhaps the diversity of the skills required. Some job skills are learned in formal job-training programs, either on-site or in specialized centers not unlike public schools, while others are the informal outcome of work activity (learning by doing). Imposing some sort of logical structure on these disparate activities has been an important contribution of economic analysis.

In the final analysis, training is an investment decision. The training process absorbs the worker's time as well as the time of coworkers and supervisors, various materials, and the indirect costs of mistakes made by the inexperienced worker. If the training is to be economically rational, these costs must be offset by the highest future productivity of the trained worker. Because these returns (and costs) are distributed over time, the financial aspects of the transactions are important as well. The financing of intensive on-the-job training activities is a serious obstacle to the efficient provision of a highly trained work force.

The distinction between the *training activity* itself and the *financing* of the training activity is an important one. The form of the training activity is in the first instance technological. What is the nature of the on-the-job learning mechanism? In what environment is the learning of job skills most cheaply provided: in the firm or in some specialized training program, for example, schools? The financing issue is fundamentally one of access to capital and is intimately related to the structure of the property rights system. The financing decision depends in an important way on the legal environment in which firm and worker exchange goods and services as well as promises of future exchanges. As in many economic decisions, the action decision (training) and the financing decision (who pays for the training) are intimately related.

The focus of this review is on the provision of job training to workers with no unusual training problems. The provision of job-training programs to seriously disadvantaged individuals is itself a major policy issue, possibly justifying extensive direct government intervention, but the direct government supply of trained (disadvantaged) workers is not a significant portion of the total supply of job skills in the economy. Job training in the United States has been overwhelmingly private, forged in a variety of ways among workers, firms, and unions. It is this market that is examined below.

The review proceeds in the following way. I first consider the nature of on-the-job training more precisely, emphasizing the role of the firm in the supply of on-the-job training opportunities. Two alternative models of on-the-job training are considered and a few implications for the efficient supply of training services are derived. In Section III, I develop the basic investment model of on-the-job training, the analytical structure that will be used to frame the discussions to follow. The economic logic of this human-capital paradigm is discussed at length because of its central role in forming the economist's conception of this market. In Section IV, conditions under which the free market will generate the efficient amount of on-the-job training are outlined. The discussion then proceeds to the important issue of why this market may fail to yield efficient results, most prominently the financing problem. The relationship of human capital finance to the deeper issue of property rights structures is explored: the right of contract has been socially abridged for a variety of reasons, both by design (bankruptcy laws) and by the inadvertent decisions of judges and juries. Analyses of variations on this fundamental problem comprise much of the remainder of this review, including the policy discussion of the final section. The potential for an alternative supply mechanism—employer training cooperatives—is critically examined.

II. THE FIRM AS SUPPLIER OF TRAINING OPPORTUNITIES

The distinction between schooling and on-the-job training is not always a clear one. The issue is more than one of academic vs. vocational skills. Vocational skills that are obvious candidates for on-the-job training, for example, carpentry, are often taught in public schools or in specialized training centers. In that sense, on-the-job training must be considered as part of a broader educational structure, with the observed mix of formal schooling and on-the-job training an equilibrium outcome. Neither is the issue simply one of the geographic locus of training. During the English industrial revolution, firms often provided traditional schooling activities to young workers, much as Hollywood provides tutors to young actors today and for the same reason: the convenient integration of work schedules and legal requirements for schooling. This is not what is normally implied by on-the-job training, which includes the notion of a paid or "on-the-clock" activity. In this review, on-the-job training refers to any activity undertaken on the job (during work hours) that increases the worker's subsequent productivity.

Given the diffuse nature of this definition, the physical training activity is difficult to conceptualize neatly. The standard investment model of on-the-job training, discussed at greater length in the next section, is simply an extension of a schooling model into a period of incomplete specialization in education (Mincer, 1962, 1974; Ben-Porath, 1967; Heckman, 1976; Rosen, 1976; Haley, 1976). Individuals who wish to undertake a human-capital investment program that involves less than complete time specialization in schooling are presumed to choose on-the-job training. Why such activities should be undertaken during paid hours is not obvious.

The implications of this view for the optimal geographic locus of training activities are few: the part-time schooling could be carried on in schools or in the firm. The usual balance between economies of scale (in training) and commuting costs would presumably affect the outcome. For example, one could imagine that, if a large number of individuals in the same workplace wanted to undertake the same course of study at the same time, transportation economies would lead to the activity being undertaken at the workplace. If the labor market is competitive, one could also imagine that the training activity would be provided efficiently, with the individual's own time and assorted other inputs combined in a rational fashion. The incomplete specialization model is in many ways like the Hollywood tutoring model; the training may occur at the workplace, but does not capture much of the interaction of work activity and learning that is commonly associated with the notion of on-the-job training.

An intuitively plausible alternative model of the learning process is the learning-by-doing or learning-as-a-by-product model. Evidence from the National Longitudinal Survey of Youth reveals that on-the-job learning is intimately related to what the individual does on the job, that is, in his or her occupation (Parsons, 1985). Among male youth in 1982 who had jobs and were not enrolled in school, approximately two-thirds of all professionals, managers, and craftsmen reported that their jobs had high learning content. In contrast, only one-third of laborers and service workers and only one-fourth of farm laborers reported that their jobs had high learning content. This suggests that much on-the-job learning is the by-product of work activities and not simply incomplete specialization in schooling.

The learning-by-doing model emphasizes the importance of the underlying work activity and also the notion of learning rather than training. In this vein, Rosen (1972) has stressed the unique supply characteristics of training in the workplace. Specifically, Rosen proposes that individuals be viewed as choosing among jobs based on a compensation bundle that includes both current wages and on-the-job training, which itself is determined by the technological characteristics of the job and on the firm's efficiency at providing such training. The interaction of these individual and employer choices yields the equilibrium level of on-the-job learning in the economy as well as the rate of return to the activity.

In many circumstances the distinction between these two training activity models is not an important one. In other circumstances, however, the differences may be pronounced. A key difference in the models is the implied degree of flexibility in the provision of learning opportunities. If firms are simply schools within the plant, the opportunities for on-the-job training should respond flexibly to shifts in worker demand. Conversely if such learning is primarily a by-product of work activities, then the firm may have much less flexibility in varying learning activities.

For example, as a by-product of work activity, the aggregate supply of on-the-job learning opportunities will be positively linked to the business cycle through new hires, etc. On-the-job learning will increase or decrease more or less in proportion to the expansion and contraction of employment opportunities. Conversely, formal schooling tends to be mildly countercyclical; when current business conditions are difficult, individuals are more likely to remain in school. If on-the-job training is, in fact, well characterized by an incomplete-specialization-in-schooling model, then one might expect to see a similar expansion of the training component of work when product demand contracts; the learning content of jobs should increase.

The focus on the supply characteristics of the training activity raises other issues as well. Specialization in the training function may occur across firms and industrial sectors; on-the-job training need not be conducted in the firm at which the worker is trained (Cho, 1983). If the process involves explicit, controllable training programs, specialization will only occur if the training function is characterized by increasing returns. If on-the-job training is largely learning by doing, however, the learning accumulated by a firm's employees at one point in time may bear no systematic relationship to the amount demanded subsequently. Individuals may find that they cannot use their newly acquired skills profitably in the current firm. In this case, learning may induce mobility.

Evidence for such specialization is reported by several investigators. Schiller (1986), for example, provides evidence that learning among new entrants to the labor force occurs disproportionately in small firms. These firms, on net, lose experienced workers to larger firms. Weiss (1985) attempts to resolve theory and evidence that (1) union workers are better trained than nonunion workers, but that (2) union workers are less likely to receive training (Mincer, 1983), by arguing that experienced, nonunion workers disproportionately migrate to unionized firms. I argue below (although this is no more than a conjecture) that the training provided in small firms is disproportionately in rudimentary job skills, especially work discipline and cooperation, and that intensive on-the-job training is primarily carried on in large firms, principally because of the ease of internal financing.

On the production side, on-the-job training can be viewed as simply another product of the firm. To the extent the final product market activities are efficiently organized, one could assume that the time of worker, supervisor, and coworkers and the related direct costs devoted to the training will in general be in efficient proportions and combined rationally into a final trained product. One unique problem that arises in the provision of training is obtaining the cooperation of coworkers (Reagan, 1988). The heart of the cooperative problem is that workers are being asked to train their own potential replacements. This is not a serious problem if the market is large and the trainers are specialists, but may be serious in internal labor markets in which the trainers are coworkers. The problem is an ancient one. Noncompetitive provisions were an important part of early apprenticeship contracts; the apprentice's right to compete with the master was often limited. For example, he could not establish a shop within a fixed range of the master's own shop. If the employees doing the training are closely monitored, this type of malfeasance may be limited. If the training personnel have a great deal of discretion, however, as would be the case in less-formal training programs, the problem may be an important one.

Reagan (1988) has argued that seniority rules on layoffs and promotions are in part an institutional way of reducing this obvious conflict of interest. I assume below that these institutional rules are in fact sufficient to enable the firm to produce the training activity efficiently, *given* the amount of training that is to be undertaken. In the next several sections, I develop more carefully the issue of the efficient *amount* of on-the-job training. The training specialization issue is considered again in Section VII, when the implications for training of the recent restructuring of the industrial base in the United States are derived.

III. ON-THE-JOB TRAINING: AN INVESTMENT PERSPECTIVE

The on-the-job training decision is one of a broad class of human capital investment decisions (Jacob Mincer, 1962, 1974). The heart of the decision calculus is as simple as it is powerful. The training activity typically involves a period in which the worker is not as productive as he or she might otherwise be. The training activity may involve other costs as well, including the diversion of supervisor and coworker time and energies to the training process, purchased training materials, and unusually high scrappage rates (or lost business opportunities at the management trainee level) due to a high incidence of mistakes. Set against these costs is the increase in worker productivity after the training period.

It will be useful to formalize the investment decision. Denote the workers' productivity flow in the absence of training as v_t, which when discounted at the interest rate r, promises lifetime wealth (W) of

$$W \text{ (no training)} = \int_0^\infty v_t\, e^{-rt}\, dt. \tag{1}$$

If productivity is fixed forever at a level v, that is $v_t = v$ for all t, the wealth formula takes on the simple form

$$W \text{ (no training)} = v/r. \tag{2}$$

Productivity is likely to decline at some point and indeed fall to zero at death or retirement, but the constant-productivity assumption underlying Eq. (2) may still be a useful approximation, especially if retirement is many years in the future or if the interest rate is high.

The training alternative also involves a time flow of productivity, say v_t^* and may include some direct costs of training at each instant, say d_t. The lifetime wealth implied by the training alternative is

$$W \text{ (Training)} = = \int_0^\infty (v_t^* - d_t)\, e^{-rt}\, dt. \tag{3}$$

If, for example, the training period is of duration T, during which the worker's productivity is v_0^* and direct training costs are d, and after which the worker's productivity is v_1^*, the worker's lifetime wealth in the training regime is

$$W \text{ (training)} = (1/r)[(v_0^* - d)(1 - e^{-rT}) + v_1^* e^{-rT}]. \tag{4}$$

The *efficiency criterion* is a simple one: the training activity should be undertaken if and only if the worker's productive wealth in the training regime equals or exceeds his or her productive wealth if untrained, where all wealth computations are undertaken at the social discount rate, say ρ. Formally this means that training is economically efficient if and only if

$$W \text{ (training} \mid r = \rho) \geq W \text{ (no training} \mid r = \rho), \tag{5}$$

or in the special case represented by Eqs. (2) and (4):

$$(1/\rho)[(v_0^* - d - v)(1 - e^{-\rho T}) + (v_1^* - v)e^{-\rho T}] \geq 0. \tag{6}$$

In the typical case in which $v_0^* < v$, and $d > 0$, the posttraining productivity v_1^* must exceed the untrained productivity by an amount sufficient to cover the foregone earnings $(v - v_0^*)$ and the direct training costs incurred during the training period T:

$$v_1^* \geq v + (v - v_0^* + d)(e^{\rho T} - 1). \tag{7}$$

As with any investment that yields returns over an extended period, the present value of the investment (and its economic efficiency) is sensitive to the interest rate that must be paid to finance the investment. The set of efficient training opportunities is likely to be seriously reduced in the high-interest-rate regime.

IV. TRAINING EFFICIENCY AND THE FREE MARKET

The question naturally arises, What institutional structure, if any, will generate the efficient job-training outcome? A free labor market composed of wealth-maximizing individuals will be efficient if:

1. the worker has access to capital at the social discount rate;
2. a large number of firms demand the skills developed; and
3. job changing is costless.

In such a world, the worker would receive at each instant a wage equal to his or her net productivity; assuming that the firm provides all training materials, the competitive wage at each instant t should be

$$w_t = \begin{cases} v_t & \text{if no training,} \\ \\ v_t^* - d_t & \text{if training.} \end{cases} \tag{8}$$

This market outcome has strong efficiency implications. The wealth-maximizing worker facing this wage structure would train when training is efficient, and would not train when training is inefficient. If the direct training costs are paid directly by the worker, the wage in the training alternative would not include an implicit charge for this material; the conclusion that the individual would choose efficiently among the alternatives is unchanged.

A model of this sort has provided the basis for a highly successful model of life cycle wages in the postschooling period. The pioneering work in this area, especially that of Mincer (1962, 1974), is based on this theoretical linkage between training and wage growth in a competitive spot market for labor services: in such a market, on-the-job learning leaves predictable patterns in the wage/experience profiles of young workers. The optimal time path of life cycle learning and earnings was first formally derived within a simple structural environment by Ben-Porath, and was extended and empirically implemented by Haley (1976), Heckman (1976), Rosen (1976), and others [see Weiss (1986) for a review of this literature]. Empirical implementation of these models requires strong assumptions on a variety of environmental and technological conditions. As a consequence, the simple log earnings function approximation to this process remains a standard estimating tool. For an excellent critical review of the standard model, see Hanushek and Quigley (1985).

Becker (1975) used a simple investment model to assess the efficiency of the provision of a college education in the United States. In particular, he found that the after-tax rate of return on a college education was comparable to that on physical capital, a strong indication of efficiency in the college market. Unfortunately the same analysis cannot be used to assess the aggregate efficiency of the market for on-the-job training. To understand why, it is necessary to sketch out briefly the standard wage model. In the standard log wage function, t years following school departure, the log wage can be represented by the approximation (ignoring individual subscripts)

$$\text{Log}(w_t) = \text{Log}(w_0) + rH_t - \Delta H_t + \epsilon_t, \qquad (9)$$

where w is the observed wage rate, H the stock of accumulated on-the-job learning capital, ΔH the current-period addition to that stock (current learning activity), and ϵ a random element. The initial postschooling wage $\text{Log}(w_0)$ is assumed to be a linear function of a variety of attributes:

$$\text{Log}(w_0) = X\beta, \qquad (10)$$

where X is a vector of personal productivity attributes, such as schooling and intelligence. With all variables directly observable, the coefficients as well as their standard errors can be estimated efficiently using ordinary least-squares techniques under common assumptions on the error term ϵ (iid normal). The coefficient r on the stock of human capital variable H can be interpreted as a rate of return on on-the-job training.

Unfortunately, the stock of on-the-job training is not directly observable. Instead. the model is normally implemented by assuming a simple investment pattern. In particular, assume that

$$H_t \equiv \sum_{i=0}^{t-1} \Delta H_i = \sum_{i=0}^{t-1} \lambda_i k_i, \tag{11}$$

where λ_i represents the individual's work intensity in period i. and k_i is the share of total human capital in period i devoted to learning activities. The standard treatment for male earnings is to impose the assumption that $\lambda_i = 1$ for all i and that on-the-job investment shares decrease at a linear rate with job market experience:

$$k_i = \kappa_0 - \kappa_1 E_i, \qquad 0 < \kappa_0 < 1, \quad \kappa_1 \leq 0, \tag{12}$$

where $E_i = i$ in this model. This investment structure induces a log wage model with experience and experience-squared terms, at least over the range of value for which k_i is feasible (positive):

$$H_i = \kappa_0 E_i + (\kappa_1/2)(E_i)^2. \tag{13}$$

In almost all empirical applications of this model in which the sample age intervals are sufficiently broad to permit precise estimation, log wage is estimated to be a positive, concave function of experience. Unfortunately. the rate of return on on-the-job training is not identified in this structure; it can only be jointly estimated with the share of training time parameters κ_i, unless individuals differ in work intensity λ (Hanushek and Quigley, 1985).

Direct measures of on-the-job learning permit a more persuasive test of the on-the-job-training hypothesis, but also fail to identify the critical rate of return on training parameter. In Parsons (1989), for example, an on-the-job learning variable is constructed from a question designed to elicit the respondent's self-perception of learning activities. The instrument had four categories of response, indexed by L_j, $j = 1,2,3,4$. with 4 denoting the highest learning condition. This instrument provides an alternative, *direct* measure of human capital investment and stock under competitive assumptions:

$$\Delta H_i = \sum_{j=1}^{4} \alpha_j L_{ji}, \tag{14}$$

and

$$H_t = \sum_{i=0}^{t-1} \sum_{j=1}^{4} \alpha_j L_{ji}. \tag{15}$$

Presumably $0 < \alpha_1 < \alpha_2 < \alpha_3 < \alpha_4$ if the self-assessment measures are valid. Since the no-job status is the base category, the empirical equivalence of the learning content of no job and of a no-learning job can be tested as the hypothesis that $\alpha_1 = 0$. Estimates of such a model are consistent with the basic on-the-job hypothesis (Parsons, 1989), but the rate of return measure is again not identified, being jointly estimated with α_i. The fact that the on-the-job-training hypothesis is broadly consistent with the observed pattern of postschooling wages does *not* imply that this training is efficiently provided. but rather that the market for on-the-job training is not fundamentally perverse.

Institutional features of the U.S. labor market raise the possibility that the market mechanism set out in Eq. (8) may not be feasible. The competitive-labor-market model suggests that equalizing or compensating differentials should exist, so that individuals in high-learning jobs (with the prospect of higher future wages) will receive lower current wages, much as individuals in formal schooling must forego current income. A variety of plausible institutional forces, however, may support wage rates above competitive levels, most obviously a legal wage minimum. A number of studies report evidence that on-the-job training is restricted by effective minimum wages (Fleisher. 1981); Leighton and Mincer, 1981; Hashimoto, 1982). Social forces may also limit the ability of workers to pay for job training through wage deductions during the training period. Lazear (1979), for example, has recently argued that affirmative-action pressures have had perverse effects on the provision of on-the-job training activities to black youth. In particular, he argues that average current wages are the most visible indicator of discrimination, so that employers have an incentive to shift black workers systematically into low-learning/high-current-wage jobs (under the standard equalizing differential argument). The logic of the argument depends on the specific observability assumption—that affirmative-action enforcers observe wages and not learning activities. This empirical assumption is not plausible for formal training programs. It seems unlikely that an employer under affirmative-action pressures would restrict entry by blacks into training programs. The insight may be valid, however, for more informal learning-by-doing activities for which no statistics or measurements are available.

Works by Barron et al. (1989), based on employer reports of training activity, and by Parsons (1989), based on self-reporting of on-the-job learning activity by workers. suggest that compensating differentials are not significant. The Barron et al. data contained only modest individual quality controls. and they attribute the absence of an observed compensating differential to unmeasured quality characteristics of trainees. The phenomenon is also observed in the Parsons study, however, which includes much richer individual controls, including the extensive aptitude and achievement information in the Armed Services Vocational Aptitude Battery.

In any case it is *theoretically* possible for the firm to work around the minimum-wage constraint by having the worker enter explicitly into a financial transaction (an explicit loan) that breaks the link between current wages and current training. Full payment of wages and a corresponding bill for the training, appropriately financed. should provide an equivalent solution to the investment problem. In the next section we shall see why this is not done.

V. THE FINANCING PROBLEM

Prominent among the sufficient conditions for the free market in on-the-job training to be efficient is the requirement that workers have access to capital at the social rate of discount. One would suspect that this condition does not hold empirically, even approximately. Workers undertaking substantial job-training investments are often young, with only insignificant capital holdings. Even among older workers, a substantial fraction of those considering substantial human-capital investments are displaced workers, many of whom have similar financial difficulties. If the training investment is a significant one, the financing problem may substantially increase the costs of undertaking the activity.

The incentive for the employer to supply its workers with some form of funds for training is evident. In this section. I first explore the nature of the borrowing problem that limits the worker's access to funds in general and then explain why the firm has a unique role as provider of the resources required to finance the training.

A. The Worker's Ability to Borrow: The Property Rights Issue

Obviously, limitations on worker credit are a serious problem if the worker is expected to finance a major investment activity. The amount of training activity will be less than the efficient level and the more-limited supply of trained workers will translate into higher costs to the firm. To consider solutions to the problem. it is necessary to understand more completely the nature of the borrowing difficulty; a property rights perspective is useful.

Consider a world of certainty with completely enforceable contracts, so that an individual who commits to a specified payment scheme is not able to avoid these payments. The financing of the training program in this environment is unlikely to be a problem: the least-cost provider would supply the funds, whether that provider is the worker, the firm, or a financial intermediary. and. ceteris paribus, the training-would be supported at least cost.

Two important processes arise that make financial contracts of this type incompletely enforced: default and bankruptcy. Individuals who die with debts exceeding assets do. in a sense. take it with them: their creditors are out of luck. Less-drastic means of avoiding repayment also exist. If the debt is sufficiently small or the costs of collection sufficiently high. then the creditor may write off a specific debt. Bankruptcy introduces social values into the debt collection mechanism. If the individual's debts exceed his or her assets, he or she may from time to time declare bankruptcy, distribute the assets proportionately among the creditors, and return to a zero net asset position. A special problem with human-capital investments is that the resulting capital is not viewed as an asset in this computation; such investments do not create their own collateral, they are an invitation to bankruptcy.

To illustrate the importance of the financing aspect, consider an historical example that illustrates the basic principles of the problem in an extreme way, the practice of indentured servants. In the colonial period, land and natural resources were abundant in the United States, but labor shortages were severe. A basic problem was the high cost of transportation from areas of relative labor surplus, the Old World, to areas of labor shortage, the New. The cost of passage in the early seventeenth century was almost one-and-one-half times the annual income per person in a laboring family (Galenson, 1981, p.230). Equally important was the financing. The individuals most likely to find migration to the New World economically attractive were those in the most unfavorable economic conditions, a group unlikely to have significant capital holdings to finance the cost of passage.

An institutional response to this problem was the development of the practice of indenturing servants. Individuals could purchase passage to the colonies by promising to work for a master for a fixed period of time, typically for four years or more, depending on skill and other personal characteristics. Indentured servants were a major source of labor in the colonial period; Galenson (1981, pp. 3–4) cites two accounts that claim that one-half to three-quarters of the immigrants to the colonies in the seventeenth century were indentured servants. Over time, slave labor came to dominate this market, but for an extended period of time this alternative, the long-term commitment of labor services, was the dominant institution for handling the problem of financing migration.

More than a simple labor contract was involved: "indentured servitude . . . involve[d] a stricter obligation than most forms of labor contract because the system provided for the enforcement of the agreement by requirement of specific performance of the work described in the contract" (Galenson, 1981, p.3). Commercial law developed around indentured-servants' contracts; they could be, and were, freely bought and sold for the duration of their indenture periods. The control problem with indentured servants was a serious one. Such contracts could not permit bankruptcy; few of these individuals had significant physical assets upon arrival to set against their transportation debt. The problem was deeper; the new arrivals had to be secured to their place of employment and motivated to work for another without the usual free-market incentives. In this natural-resource–abundant society, runaways were a problem. To assist in the enforcement of this type of contract, colonists were required to carry internal passports.

A modern and somewhat less exotic example is the government's funding of training of military officers, most prominently in military academies. These institutions provide an expensive college education at no cost to those selected to participate. Indeed, the various armed services pay attendees a substantial wage during the training period. At the end of the training period, attendees are very much in debt to the government. Payment again is by specific performance: the individual is required to serve a minimum length of time with the "firm," in this case one of the military services. The individual can also be funded to attend professional school, with an additional number of years added to his or her service requirement. The commitment is not subject to personal bankruptcy.

Both examples, the historical and the modern, illustrate (1) the basic problem of financing an expensive training activity, (2) the institutional responses to the problem—contracts with specific performance requirements, and (3) the difficulties that the response themselves generate—any long-term contract involves some limitation on the individual's freedom. Private employers today do not have the specific-performance option. Nonetheless, they have a unique role in providing personal financing to workers with modest capital. The nature of the lending mechanism and its limitations are developed next.

B.   The Unique Role of the Firm

The problem of funding human-capital investments with third-party loans is a serious one. Of particular importance here, the employer has an alternative debt repayment mechanism, one that provides for repayment despite the bankruptcy constraint, namely, job mobility costs. If mobility costs are high, the employer can invest in the worker, knowing that the worker cannot strategically respond by leaving the firm. The bankruptcy problem is preempted: the individual cannot go to court and have the debt erased. Mobility costs are an essential element in a variety of long-term implicit contracts, for example, if the firm supplies productivity insurance, either across the business cycle or across the life cycle (Bailey, 1974; Gordon, 1974; Azariadis, 1975; Freeman, 1977; Harris and Holmstrom, 1982). The firm cannot pay above-average wages when conditions are adverse without paying below-average wages when times are good, an arrangement that is only possible if mobility costs are significant. The limitations on this mechanism are clear. No individual is completely immobile; if the firm becomes a sufficiently large (implicit) creditor to the worker, the worker has an incentive to leave the firm and seek work elsewhere.

One interesting model combines on-the-job investment and the mobility process within a life cycle framework (Jovanovic, 1979). Jovanovic argues that the time profile of on-the-job learning will interact with expected mobility in a systematic way in an optimal investment program. Given the high turnover rates among new hires, perhaps due to job shopping over nonpecuniary aspects of the job, employers may not offer valuable training opportunities to new entrants until they have shown that they are stable and unlikely to leave the firm for an alternative employer [see also Lester (1954), Bishop (1985), and Parsons (1989)]. As a consequence, the life cycle profile of job learning intensity may *increase* early in the individual's career, not decline as assumed in the standard on-the-job-training model, Eq. (12). The Jovanovic hypothesis assumes that on-the-job learning activities include important worker/firm match–specific elements; the returns to on-the-job learning are partly (or wholly) dependent on the worker having a continuing relationship with the firm in which the investment takes place. By definition, interfirm mobility will completely depreciate the specific human capital. Similar results hold for general capital with positive mobility costs.

VI.   WORKER IMMOBILITY AND THE EMPLOYER HOLDUP PROBLEM

The employer has mechanisms for providing the worker with a loan that is not vulnerable to bankruptcy or to default in the usual sense. To the extent the worker's job mobility is limited by effective long-term employment contracts or by high transaction costs, the firm can finance the worker's training costs by paying the worker more than his or her productivity during the training period and then recovering the expenditures by paying the worker less than his or her productivity in the posttraining period. Both explicit long-term contracts and intrinsically high worker mobility costs introduce their own difficulties, however. A few of these are considered here, as are the market forces that ameliorate their effects.

Long-Term Employment Contracts

If it were possible to bind the worker to the firm, it would not be difficult in a static world to design a long-term employment contract that permits the employer to absorb some or all the training costs, if that is efficient. If the labor market in which the basic employment contract is negotiated is competitive, posttraining wages will be set at a level that just compensates the firm for its training outlays. The least-cost provider of capital in this relationship will absorb the majority, perhaps all, of the training costs as efficiency dictates.

Unfortunately, the world is dynamic, not static; conditions are constantly changing and in unpredictable ways. Complete worker immobility is almost surely inefficient in such a dynamic environment; an unexpected increase in the worker's productivity outside the firm or a sudden decline in the worker's productivity inside the firm calls for the reallocation of the worker to a more-productive work setting. Explicit mobility bonding schemes can in principle handle this problem [Mortensen, 1978; Hashimoto, 1981; see also the review in Parsons (1986)]. The party that wants to break the contract can be required to pay a penalty to the other party for the breach; properly designed in an ideal environment, such a bonding mechanism can induce efficient behavior.

The use of explicit bonding schemes in this case is limited by information problems, most obviously the identification of the party that precipitated the job change. This critical information may not be observable to an outside (enforcement) party. The worker may voluntarily leave the firm (quit), but only under (unobservable) pressure from the firm; conversely, the firm could lay off or fire the worker, but only after the worker became slack or malfeasant on the job. Hashimoto and Yu (1980) consider more efficient contracts with imperfect observability. The mobility bond is indexed to observable proxies correlated with separation culpability; the efficiency of the bond then is a function of the quality of the proxies.

Casual empiricism suggests that such elaborate mobility-bonding schemes are not often observed in practice, and that the difficulties in implementing explicit long-term contracts are serious ones. Whether this is the result of intrinsic problems in the approach or to legal problems of enforcement of long-term employment contracts is unclear. The legal enforcement of long-term contracts is at best fitful (Green, 1989). Enforcement depends in the main on interpretations by the various state court systems, which vary in their commitment to contractual agreements of this sort over time and across states. In general, courts seem reluctant to restrict the worker's freedom to seek alternative jobs.

High Mobility Costs

High interfirm mobility costs provide an alternative to enforceable long-term contracts. If it is expensive for the worker to relocate, then the firm can hope to pay the worker a wage less than productivity in the posttraining period without losing him or her to another firm. A concern naturally arises, however: What keeps the firm from extracting more than its share of training costs? Once the worker is in place, the potential for exploitation of immobile workers would seem a real one. What keeps the employer from squeezing all quasi-rents out of the worker? Of course, there exists a symmetry here: If the firm invests in the worker, the worker may attempt to extract a disproportionate share of the returns by threatening to leave the firm; such a threat becomes less credible the higher mobility costs, but it is never totally absent.

If the labor market in which the original job commitment is made is a competitive one, the firm could not expect to extract more than its share of training costs out of the worker, at least if the worker correctly anticipates the firm's posttraining wage behavior. If the worker anticipates that the employer is going to act exploitively in the posttraining period, then the worker will require a higher current wage from the firm. In a sense, the unreliable firm will be forced to accept a larger share of the investment. Conversely, if the firm anticipates that the worker is going to capture a disproportionate share of the rents, it will insist that the worker bear a greater share of the investment costs.

The efficiency problem is that the investment cost–sharing decision may be made, not on the basis of differential access to capital, but on the basis of expectations of future quasi-rent sharing. This problem has been considered at length in the employment-contracting literature. Specifically, a literature has developed considering the most extreme possibility of an employer–employee lockin, "firm-specific human capital," in which a skill *only* has value in one firm, presumably the firm in which the training occurs (Becker, 1975; Oi, 1962). More widely valued human capital with positive mobility costs can be considered a generalization of the specific human-capital model (mobility costs induce economic specificity).

Two approaches to implicit contracting and specific human-capital investment sharing have been proposed, both of which stress the anticipation of subsequent quasi-rent sharing in the determination of investment cost shares. The early literature—Becker, Oi, and also Parsons (1972)—focused explicitly on the interplay between the specific human-capital financing decision and job mobility. The worker is never completely immobile. Individual heterogeneity ensures that worker mobility is only a probability statement; some workers will stay, others leave, with only the proportion of stayers and movers in the workplace changing as compensation changes.

This literature explores a weak form of employment contract: wages are fixed (with mobility processes in mind) and firms and workers respond through layoffs and quits, respectively. In these models, the worker quits whenever outside productivity exceeds the (fixed) wage, and the firm lays off the worker whenever the wage exceeds inside productivity. Job separation is not fully efficient under this simple contract if outside and inside productivity are subject to random shocks due to product market demand fluctuations or technological shifts (Hashimoto, 1981; Parsons, 1986). The incentives of the two parties do not adjust optimally in this stochastic environment. Becker (1975) first proposed that there may be some optimal investment sharing between firm and worker that will minimize this inefficient separation. The financing of and returns to the investment will be shared between firm and worker because some investment by each reduces the incentives for unilateral withdrawal from the relationship by the other; investment sharing is a form of mobility bond. The investment sharing is not fully optimal, depending as it does on the bonding device, namely, the shapes of the quit and layoff functions as well as on more fundamental factors.

A second approach to investment cost sharing also places much emphasis on the forces that determine posttraining rent sharing (Grout, 1984). As in the turnover model, Grout argues that the worker and firm are forward looking, that they can anticipate the outcome of subsequent bilateral bargaining, and that they accept financial shares based on this perspective. He employs a bargaining model rather than a relative turnover model as the structure that underlies rent sharing in the posttraining period. Specifically, he assumes that a Nash bargaining model can be used to formalize the "solution" of the bargaining process. Bargaining models of this sort *assume* that the bargaining outcome has features consistent with some set of stylized facts. The Nash model, for example, assumes that the bargaining outcome meets an intuitively plausible fairness criterion. The efficiency problem is the same as in the turnover model—the sharing is driven by a process other than access to capital.

Reputational Enforcement of Implicit Contracts

The market itself may generate (partial) solutions to the "holdup" problem, especially through reputational forces. Employers, especially large employers, may find it profitable to behave as if they are legally bound to a contract, even when they are not. In the current case, the firm may behave *as if* it has a commitment not to exploit the worker once the worker is locked in to the firm. Despite the potential importance of these reputational forces, empirical evidence on the situations in which they are operative remains limited. The evidence indicates that reputational enforcement of implicit employment contracts is a large-firm phenomenon (e.g., Clark et al., 1986; Parsons, 1988).

VII.   SECULAR TRENDS IN WORK PLACE STRUCTURE: CONSEQUENCES FOR THE SUPPLY OF TRAINING

Recent industrial trends have favored smaller, nonunion workplaces (Blau, 1987; Farber, 1987; Parsons, 1988). The decline in the large-firm sector is largely attributable to the well-noted (relative) decline in manufacturing employment and the growth of the service sector. The economies of scale that induced the rapid growth of large industrial enterprises in earlier periods are apparently more limited in the service economy that has blossomed in the last two decades. This industrial restructuring is a long-term one: between 1970 and 1986, employment in the manufacturing sector declined as a share of total employment from 26.4 to 19.1% (U.S. Bureau of the Census, 1987, p. 379). Over the same time interval, employment in the service sector expanded from 25.9 to 31.3%. Even within industrial sectors, trends appear unfavorable to the growth of large enterprises. Although consistent time series data on recent trends in firm size *within* industries is unavailable, casual evidence suggests that firm size has declined within sectors as well as in aggregate, for example, the rise of minimills in the steel industry.

Reflecting in part this structural shift, the unionized sector of the labor market has shrunk dramatically. The decline in union representation in the workforce has been precipitous, with union membership dropping from 25.6% of non-agricultural employment in 1973 to 14.1% in 1985 (Farber, 1987). This decline again is only partly explained by sectoral shifts (Farber, 1987).

Less clear are the implications of this industrial restructuring for the provision of on-the-job training. As noted in Section II, it has been argued that training is disproportionately carried on in the nonunionized, small-firm sector. Schiller

(1986) reports that learning among new entrants to the labor force occurs disproportionately in small firms. These firms, on net, lose experienced workers to
larger firms. Mincer (1983) finds that union workers are less likely to receive
training than are nonunion workers.

Does this mean that the aggregate supply of trained workers is improved by
these recent sectoral shifts? I think not. I suspect that the preponderance of
training activities in small, nonunionized firms is limited to the provision of
relatively rudimentary job skills. Employment in a fast-food outlet, a common
entry level job, no doubt teaches the young person a number of useful job skills,
including the value of punctuality and cooperation. What is more difficult to
undertake efficiently in the small-firm setting is the training of highly skilled
craftspeople and operatives. The individual worker's problem in financing a
training program is likely to increase with the size of the investment. A highly
skilled machinist, under current limitations on contracting, may have serious
difficulty financing his or her investment. At the same time, the low mobility
costs implied by a large number of similar firms make the investment an unattractive one for the small employer to finance; the likelihood that the employer
will be able to capture a significant share of the training returns is small. If true,
the training of highly skilled workers may become a matter of increasing concern
in coming years.

VIII. PUBLIC POLICY ISSUES: SUPPORT FOR PRIVATE JOB TRAINING

The policy issue is an important one: how best to foster the efficient provision of
job training. I have argued above that the main problem is one of financing. The
firm typically has access to credit at rates substantially below those available to
most trainees. The firm cannot simply lend the worker the resources, however,
because of the possibility of bankruptcy and default. If the worker is relatively
immobile (has high job-changing costs), it may be possible for the firm to lend
resources implicitly to the worker through its wage policy, in a sense absorbing
the investment costs (and returns) itself. This avenue of finance is partly dependent on high job mobility costs, however, and especially in this period of sectoral
shifts toward smaller firms (and perhaps lower intrinsic mobility costs), consideration of alternative financing mechanisms is important.

Direct provision of training programs by the government is not likely to be
productive (beyond the provision of basic skills to seriously disadvantaged individuals). The main argument against direct government involvement is informational; the market is a complex one, with thousands of firms demanding thousands of skills and, in turn, supplying a corresponding number of job-training
opportunities. Knowing which services to offer and which to eliminate is an
immense coordinating task. Clearly this is a market in which decentralized
decision making is essential.

The issue is how to encourage and support job training at arms length, that is, with limited direct governmental micromanagement. An obvious solution is the public provision of job training loans to workers, comparable to educational-loan programs. To state the solution is to state the problem; the government student loan program has faced the same sort of problems that have beset the private capital market. Particularly among the young, access to a large amount of capital is an invitation to default and bankruptcy. More importantly, it is an invitation to fraud, of which this group, especially the least educated, are themselves likely to be victims. To the extent that job training is less well defined than is formal schooling, the invitation to deception and fraud by suppliers of training is increased. Without a fundamental change in the rules of the game, the problem is likely to be severe.

One recent public policy initiative, the compromise legislation to increase the minimum wage, is likely to have reduced the efficient functioning of the private on-the-job-training market. The minimum-wage increase is likely to be most damaging to the least skilled, those whose training wage would drop them below minimum-wage levels. The policy is likely to have had little impact on highly skilled workers, such as machinists, whose training wages are likely to be well above the minimum wage (although this fact may be changing with increased competition in this sector). In that sense, eliminating the minimum wage is only a partial step toward a more complete solution of the training problem, although perhaps an important one, given the social interest in the well-being of the least skilled.

Tax policy is another potential mechanism for governmental encouragement of job training in the private sector (Smolensky and Quigley, this volume). Current tax laws permit (require) training costs to be "expensed" rather than amortized over the life of the investment as with physical capital investments. If (1) the tax structure is not progressive and (2) the interest rate is positive, this tax system favors human-capital investments, whether undertaken by the firm or by the worker. The rate-of-return measurement problem (discussed in Section IV) makes a quantitative assessment of the impact of the tax structure on training activity difficult. While the use of tax policy to foster governmental nonrevenue objectives indirectly is currently out of fashion, this condition may eventually change.

Given that the financing problem is, at its core, a property rights issue, reformation of the contract system would seem to offer an alternative approach. The issue is a delicate one, however, since the limitations on the ability to contract—(1) the right to declare bankruptcy when debts exceed assets, and (2) the right to (relatively) unrestricted job mobility—are based on important social values. It is possible, however, that modest adjustments could be made in each that would facilitate the supply of credit to trainees. It may be enough to strengthen the worker's right to contract with the firm over a specific employment period, or at least a period in which the individual could not work for a competitor.

thereby encouraging worker–firm training relationships that are now partly, and imperfectly, cemented by positive mobility costs. Elimination of bankruptcy possibilities for a certain class of loans is another alternative, although the potential for creditor abuse of financial structure is a real one. In a sense, what is required is a refashioning of apprenticeship contracts.

The encouragement of employer training collectives for the development of skills specific to an industry or type of technology may also be useful. If a highly specialized skill is demanded by a relatively small number of employers, a training cooperative may be designed so that the employers (with their access to capital at lower cost) may have an incentive to finance the investment activity themselves. As argued at length above, employers will agree to finance investments in worker skills only if they are able to capture the returns on the investment through subsequent wage payments that are less than the worker's productivity (by an amount sufficient to compensate them for the training costs they incur). An agreement to share the costs of training in proportion to the employer's share of new-trainee hires would achieve the desired object *if* combined with a "no-raiding" agreement on previously hired workers. In the absence of such an agreement a charging mechanism based on the new hires of trainees would break down, with rational employers bidding up the wages of experienced workers to the value of marginal product, thereby eliminating the necessary payback period. A no-raiding agreement is unattractive for a variety of reasons: workers may want to change jobs, not because of wages, but because of changes in geographic preferences or personality conflicts with supervisors and coworkers.

An alternative charging mechanism that would permit workers to change jobs freely and at the same time protect the employer's investment in the worker would be an agreement by the employer to share training costs according to the *total* number of cooperatively trained workers currently on the employer's payroll. If aggregate training levels are stable over time, this charging scheme is efficient; employers could hire trained workers from other firms, but they would be responsible for the workers' training costs as well as for the workers' current wages. The employer's wage offer would therefore reflect the value of the worker's product less the appropriately amortized charge for the costs of training incurred by the cooperative. The worker would not be able to "capture" the gains in his or her productivity that resulted from the employers' joint investment in the worker.

The collective provision of training reduces the free-rider problem that makes the employer financing of training unprofitable. The level of interfirm cooperation required in the training cooperative, however, raises serious antitrust concerns. It may be necessary to give an explicit antitrust exemption to the activity if it is to be attractive to employers, perhaps along the lines of existing legislation designed to foster joint research and development activities among firms, the National Cooperative Research Act of 1984. Such a relaxation would not be likely to increase significantly the probability of a successful product market cartel, which is the primary focus of the antitrust laws.

The problem of an efficient training mechanism is an important one, especially in this period of intense international competition. Japanese employers, a major focus of competitive concern, are felt to have significant advantages in the provision of training opportunities, because of cultural biases against job mobility and toward greater industrial harmony (Hashimoto, 1989; Mincer and Higuchi, 1988). Whether these cultural factors are a cause or a consequence of the rapid, sustained growth of the Japanese economy is not clear. Nonetheless the concern is a significant one, given the importance of job training. Deeper consideration of the property rights system that both supports and retards the training process is warranted.

ACKNOWLEDGMENTS

This paper was funded under Purchase Order No. 99-9-4757-75-009-04 from the U.S. Department of Labor, Commission on Workforce Quality and Labor Market Efficiency. Opinions stated in this document do not necessarily represent the official position or policy of the U.S. Department of Labor, Commission on Workforce Quality and Labor Market Efficiency.

REFERENCES

Azariadis, Costas (1975), "Implicit Unemployment and Underemployment Equilibrium." *Journal of Political Economy* 83:1183–1202.

Bailey, Martin M. (1974), "Wages and Employment under Uncertain Demand." *Review of Economic Studies* xx:37–50.

Barron, John M., Dan A. Black, and Mark A. Loewenstein (1989), "Job Matching and On-the-Job Training." *Journal of Labor Economics* 7 (January):1–19.

Becker, Gary S. (1975), *Human Capital*. New York: Columbia University Press.

Ben-Porath, Yoram (1967), "The Production of Human Capital and the Life Cycle of Earnings." *Journal of Political Economy* 75 (August):352–365.

Bishop, John (1985), "Preparing Youth for Employment." Mimeo, The National Center for Research in Vocational Education, The Ohio State University, Columbus.

Blau, David M. (1987), "A Time-Series Analysis of Self-Employment in the United States." *Journal of Political Economy* 95 (June):445–467.

Cho, Woo (1983), "Promotion Prospects, Job Search, and the Quit Behavior of Employed Youth." Mimeo, The Ohio State University, Columbus.

Clark, Robert L., Steven C. Allen, and Daniel Sumner (1986). "Inflation and Pension Benefits." In Richard A. Ippolito and Walter W. Kolodrubetz (eds.), *Handbook of Pension Statistics 1985*. Chicago: Commerce Clearing House, Inc., pp. 177–250.

Farber, Henry S. (1987), "The Decline of Unionization in the United States: What Can Be Learned from Recent Experience?" NBER Working Paper No. 2267, Washington, D.C.

Fleisher, Belton, M. (1981), *Minimum Wage Regulation in Retail Trade*. Washington, DC: American Enterprise Institute.

Freeman, Smith (1977), "Wage Trends as Performance Displays Productivity Potential: A Model and Application to Academic Early Retirement." *Bell Journal of Economics* 8:419–443.

Galenson, David W. (1981), *White Servitude in Colonial America*. Cambridge: Cambridge University Press.

Gordon, Donald F. (1974), "A Neo-Classical Theory of Keynesian Unemployment." *Economic Inquiry* 12:431–459.

Green, Wayne E. (1989), "Courts Skeptical of 'Non-Compete' Pacts." *Wall Street Journal*, Wednesday, January 11:B1.

Grout, P. (1984), "Investment and Wages in the Absence of Binding Contracts: A Nash Bargaining Approach." *Econometrica* 52:449–461.

Haley, William J. (1976), "Estimation of the Earnings Profile from Human Capital Accumulation." *Econometrica* 44:1223–1238.

Hanushek, Eric A. and John M. Quigley (1985), "Life-Cycle Earning Capacity and the OTJ Investment Model." *International Economic Review* 26(June):365–385.

Harris, Milton and Bengt Holmstrom (1982), "A Theory of Wage Dynamics." *Review of Economic Studies* 49:315–333.

Hashimoto, Masanori (1981), "Specific Human Capital as a Shared Investment." *American Economic Review* 71:475–482.

––––––– (1982), "Minimum Wage Effects on Training on the Job." *American Economic Review* 72 (December):1070–1087.

––––––– (1989), "Employment and Wage Systems in Japan and Their Implications on Productivity: A Transaction-Cost Perspective." Paper presented at Brookings Institution Conference on Alternative Compensation Schemes.

Hashimoto, Masanori and Benjamin T. Yu (1980), "Specific Human Capital, Employment Contracts and Wage Rigidity." *Bell Journal of Economics* 11:536–549.

Heckman, James (1976), "A Life Cycle Model Of Earnings, Learning, and Consumption." *Journal of Political Economy* 84 (August, Supplement):S11–S44.

Jovanovic, Boyan (1979), "Firm-Specific Capital and Turnover." *Journal of Political Economy* 87 (December):1246–1260.

Lazear, Edward (1979), "The Narrowing of the Black–White Wage Differential Is Illusory." *American Economic Review* 69 (September):553–563.

Leighton, Linda and Jacob Mincer (1981), "Effects of Minimum Wages on Human Capital Formation." In Simon Rottenberg (ed.), *The Economics of Legal Minimum Wages*. Washington, DC: American Enterprise Institute, pp. 155–173.

Lester, Richard A. (1954), "Hiring Practices and Labor Competition." Industrial Relations Section Report, Princeton University, Princeton, NJ.

Mincer, Jacob (1962), "On-the-Job Training: Costs, Returns and Some Implications." *Journal of Political Economy* Suppl. 70 (October): 50–79.

––––––– (1974), *Schooling, Experience, and Earnings*. New York: Columbia Univ. Press, for NBER.

––––––– (1983), "Union Effects: Wages, Turnover, and Job Training." *Research in Labor Economics* Suppl. 2:217–252.

Mincer, Jacob and Yoshio Higuchi (1988), "Wage Structure and Labor Turnover in the United States and Japan." *Journal of the Japanese and International Economies* 2:97–133.

Mortensen, Dale (1978), "Specific Human Capital and Turnover." *Bell Journal of Economics* 9:572–586.

Oi, Walter Y. (1962), "Labor as a Quasi-Fixed Factor." *Journal of Political Economy* 70:538–555.

Parsons, Donald O. (1972), "Specific Human Capitol: Layoffs and Quits." *Journal of Political Economy* 80:1120–1143.

––––––– (1985), "Wage Determination in the Post-Schooling Period: The Market for On-the-Job Training." In R. D'Amico et al. (eds.), *Pathways to the Future*. Volume VI. Columbus: Center for Human Resource Research, Ohio State University, Chapter 7.

––––––– (1986), "The Employment Relationship: Job Attachment, Work Effect, and the Nature of

Contracts." In Orley Ashenfelter and Richard Layard (eds.), *Handbook of Labor Economics*. Amsterdam: North-Holland. pp. 789–848.

———— (1988), "The Provision of Private Pensions: An Equilibrium Approach." Mimeo, Ohio State University, Columbus.

———— (1989), "On-the-Job Learning and Wage Growth." Mimeo, Ohio State University, Columbus.

Reagan, Patricia (1988), "On-the-Job Training, Layoff by Inverse Seniority, and the Incidence of Unemployment." Mimeo, Ohio State University, Columbus.

Rosen, Sherwin (1972), "Learning and Experience in the Labor Market." *Journal of Human Resources* 7 (Summer):326–342.

———— (1976), "A Theory of Life Earnings." *Journal of Political Economy* 84 (August, Suppl.):S45–S68.

Schiller, Bradley R. (1986), "Early Jobs and Training: The Role of Small Business." Final Report on Contract SBA-9281-AER, Capital Research, Inc., Washington, DC.

Weiss, Yoram (1985), "The Effect of Labor Unions on Investment in Training." *Journal of Political Economy* 93 (October):994–1007.

———— (1986), "The Determination of Life Cycle Earnings: A Survey." In Orley Ashenfelter and Richard Layard (eds.), *Handbook of Labor Economics*. Amsterdam: North-Holland, pp. 603–640.

U.S. Bureau of the Census (1987), *Statistical Abstract of the United States: 1988*. 108th edition. Washington, DC: U.S. Government Printing Office.

[6]

Work, Employment & Society, Vol. 3, No. 1, pp. 89–104   March 1989

NOTES AND ISSUES
Skills and the Limits of Neo-Liberalism: The Enterprise of the Future as a Place of Learning*

Wolfgang Streeck

Introduction: Capitalism and Collective Production Factors

Political cycles often appear as perpendicular movements of collective energy and attention between bipolar choices, such as demand- and supply-side economics, 'Keynesianism' and 'Schumpeterianism', state and market, or equity and efficiency. Today the 1970s, to which we are said to owe our present predicaments, are identified with a syndrome of politicized demand management, distributive conflict, redistributive justice (or rather, in the eyes of some, injustice), and extensive regulatory state intervention. The 1980s, by comparison, are believed to have rediscovered the supply side and the need to pay attention to production as well as distribution; to restore competitiveness and efficiency – if necessary, at the expense of equity; and to unleash the innovative capacities of the market and of 'creative destruction' through 'deregulation'. A pervasive *Zeitgeist*, extending from convinced 'neo-liberals' well into the old mixed economy camp, tells us that regulation stifles innovation, impedes 'flexibility' and depresses efficiency, and that it therefore should be avoided wherever possible. Supply-side economics rules the day, and it is regarded by both its proponents and its adversaries as identical with deregulation and free marketeerism. This position is what I will try to challenge.

My argument will call upon a fundamental but today often suppressed insight of social theory: *that successful self-interested, utilitarian behaviour in market environments requires the presence of collective resources, common values and shared expectations that rationally acting individuals cannot normally generate, protect or restore even if they fully recognize their vital importance.* This is because such resources are in significant respects 'collective goods' which cannot be privately appropriated and to whose generation rational capitalist actors have therefore no, or no sufficient, incentives to contribute. As a consequence, the unbridled pursuit of self-regarding interests results in suboptimal outcomes not just for

---

*This paper is an abridged version of a contribution to a conference on 'Mutamenti del lavoro e trasformazione sociale', panel on 'Il ruolo dell'impressa nella societa di domani', Istituto Universitario di Studi Europei di Torino, Turin, 27 and 28 November, 1987.

Wolfgang Streeck is Professor of Sociology at the University of Wisconsin-Madison, USA.

the community at large but also for economically rational individuals themselves.

The political implications of this principle, could it be shown to apply to the capitalist firm in particular and the 'supply side' of the economy in general, are formidable. Capitalism, the freedom to pursue and appropriate private material gain, would have to be treated as a socio-economic arrangement that depends on foundations – physical-environmental, social, moral or other – which, since they cannot be privately owned, a capitalist economy is in constant danger of eroding and consuming; it would appear as a configuration of productive forces beset by a self-destructive dynamic from which it needs to be protected by social-regulatory institutions. To be able to take full advantage of economic opportunities, capitalists would have to be placed under constraints that would *simultaneously force and enable* them to make more efficient use of both 'private' and 'public', individual and collective production factors. Deregulation would therefore in the long run be self-defeating. Left to themselves, capitalists would be incapable of managing their affairs. What I want to argue is that, in significant respects, this is indeed the case, and perhaps today more so than ever. This is the reason why I think that at least in the more economically successful societies, the enterprise of the future will be embedded in a system of institutionally enforced social obligations, and why I think that societies that pay too much heed to fashionable pressures for deregulation may end up with significant deficits in economic performance.

The Economic and Political Significance of Skills

Before explaining in what sense the generation of skills can be and has to be conceived as the production of a collective good, let me briefly describe what I see as the key role of skills in today's political economy. Under the conditions of the 1980s European industrial societies can remain high-wage economies only if they become and remain high-skill economies, and they can cease to be high-wage economies only at the price of fundamental social conflict with entirely uncertain outcomes. (The exception to the second, not the first of the two propositions may be Britain.) By high-wage economy I mean not just one with a high *average* standard of living, like the United States, but also one with a relatively *even distribution* of incomes and life-chances – which implies and requires, among other things, a functioning system of social welfare. A high-wage economy in this sense can be said to have become part of the cultural and political identity of most European countries. Given the irreversible increase in competition and world market integration in the past decade, the preservation of this pattern demands rapid economic restructuring towards a less price- and more quality-competitive product range, which alone can yield the high returns that sustain high wages. Producing such products requires a high input of skills. The same is true for product diversification

SKILLS AND THE LIMITS OF NEO-LIBERALISM   91

and customization which also help remove production from the pressures of price competition. Technical innovation as such does not protect high wages, given that new technology can be used not only for moving an economy towards what we have elsewhere called 'diversified quality production' (Sorge and Streeck 1988), but also for rationalization of traditional mass production with massive shedding of labour and deskilling.

There is no need here to speculate which of the two possible adjustment paths and production patterns firms and managers would 'in principle' prefer: a *rationalised*, high-technology version of (neo)Taylorist mass production or a *modernized* industrial economy of diversified quality production. In part, such choices are likely to be affected by past experiences, especially by the kind of markets and product ranges in which a firm or industry has traditionally operated. But what is more important is that even if production along the lines of the second pattern was known to be more profitable, and even though restructuring in this direction would clearly save societies the economic costs of political conflict and institutional discontinuities likely to be associated with 'rationalization', firms may, in the absence of an adequate skill supply, have to opt for the latter — although this may mean a longdrawn, downhill, losing battle against competition from countries which, for some time to come, will find it much easier to operate low wage or dual economies. However, moving product ranges 'upwards' towards more diversified demands and high quality markets requires not only capital investment in research and development for better and more diversified products, but also human resource investment in new and higher skills. The latter, I will demonstrate, firms acting 'rationally' in a liberal political economy are only in exceptional cases able to achieve on their own, and it appears that the skills needed for industrial modernization have so peculiar collective goods properties that they cannot even be generated by unilateral state provision in the same way as, say, a predictable legal order.

It is at this point that firms are today faced with a perhaps unprecedented degree of ambivalence. This is because the solution of the skilling problem, which is a precondition of upward industrial restructuring, may simultaneously offer capital's traditional adversaries, the trade unions and their political allies, a solution to *their* problem of defending the European high-wage economy, at the very moment that the high and rigid wages that capital has had to accept in the past have for the first time come under serious pressure. The same human resource investment, that is, on which firms depend for the probably more profitable solution of their adjustment problems, may again underwrite the high and relatively uniform price of labour that trade unions have in the past been able to extract from capital. To the extent that such investment is unlikely to come about without authoritative intervention, firms may furthermore become dependent for the success of their restructuring strategies upon regulatory agencies which may use the opportunity to pursue political-egalitarian objectives together with and merged into economic ones. In the process, trade unions and Social-Democratic parties may find for themselves a new, firm basis from which to (re-)capture political power. And even if the production of skills for industrial modernization was managed, as it well might be, by conservative political forces, the role and status of the enterprise in society will at the end come to look rather different from what it is envisaged to be in the deregulation scenario.

Skill Generation as Collective Goods Production

Why is it that skill generation poses a problem in a market economy? Almost all countries today face skill shortages which stand in the way of the vitally important fast and broad diffusion of new micro-electronic technologies. But liberal societies like the United States and Britain where the market has traditionally played a dominant role seem to suffer more than, for example, Japan and, to an extent, West Germany with their heritage of community bonds and corporatist regulation. Differences like these have often given rise to the suspicion that it may not be enough for the formation of work skills to rely on the self-interest of individuals investing time, effort and money in acquiring the marketable qualifications that optimally fit their innate abilities, and of firms adding to the already existing skills of their workers those additional, job-specific skills they need to compete successfully in their product markets. Of course, liberal economists have always tried to attribute skill deficits to distortions of the pay-off matrix for firms and individuals caused by more or less well-meaning political intervention, and they have devoted much effort and intelligence to the question of how to generate an equilibrium skill supply by allocating the costs of training between individuals, firms and society as a whole (as represented by the state) so as to correspond to what rational individuals under free market conditions would agree upon if they could act on their interests. Without going into technical details, I would like to suggest that *this* is clearly *not* the problem, and that quite to the contrary market failure in skill formation is endemic and inevitable, for many reasons of which the following two are perhaps the most fundamental:

1. *Individuals have to acquire their basic work skills at a young age when they are least likely to accept the long deferral of gratifications that is the essence of 'investing'.* Deferring gratifications presupposes a degree of certainty as to what one is likely to need and value in the future; such certainty comes as part of a social and personal identity which young people, by definition, have yet to form. At the same time, it is precisely for their lack of such identity that young people are better able to learn than adults; the reason why one cannot teach an old dog new tricks is not that the dog is old, but that he wants to remain the kind of dog he has grown to be. Since skill acquisition and identity formation are so inextricably linked, precisely the most important, 'formative' learning in a person's life cannot possibly be conceived or motivated in terms of rational investment in the longer-term pursuit of individual interests. The

SKILLS AND THE LIMITS OF NEO-LIBERALISM 93

decision what kind of work skills one wants to acquire in order later to sell them in the labour market is inseparable from the decision what kind of person one wants to be; this, however, does not follow a logic of supply and demand – and cannot because, at the very least, this logic is itself part of the curriculum. Young people, the most prolific learners, thus lack crucial properties and capacities which the rational decision-making model held in so high regard by economists and liberals, neo or not, takes for granted.

Training, this implies, *is likely to be more successful and to generate a larger supply of skills where it is conceived as education rather than voluntary-rational-utilitarian investment.* What we are really talking about when we are discussing work skills is the presence and viability in the institutional core of an industrial society of what has been called 'preceptoral relations' – which differ from market relations precisely in that they are not and cannot be entered into voluntarily. Liberal utilitarianism, by urging people to be rationally concerned about payoffs and returns on investment, undermines such relations and erodes structures of authority without which a society's potential for learning and teaching is seriously reduced. Here again, utilitarian rationality may be self-defeating: he, or she, who learns only what he thinks he can use, may find little opportunity later to use what he has learned. Societies that treat learning as investment or, for that matter, as an entitlement or a 'citizen's right' will end up with fewer skills than societies where learning is treated as an obligation. In essence and with some modifications, this applies not only to young but also to older people. Compared to the overwhelming importance of this cultural factor, the arguments of revisionist institutional economists against market-led training systems – which emphasize the uncertain returns on an individual's training investment and the need for reassurance through adequate institutional arrangements that investments will pay off at some later day – pale into insignificance.

2. *Most firms will most of the time have a tendency to invest less in training than they should in their own interest.* The reason for this is a condition which is universal and essentially unremovable in Western societies: the free labour contract. As long as workers have the right to move from one firm to another, and as along as they do not feel socially obliged to stay with their employer for all their working lives if he wants to keep them, firms will always have to be concerned that their investment in training may not pay for them since the worker may leave before he has repaid his debts. Unlike in Japanese firms, training investment in Western firms can never be safely internalized as the skills imparted on a worker cannot be appropriated by the employer: to the contrary, they become the property of the worker which he may take with him when he leaves. The 'Western' view of the dignity of workpeople, and also the power of workers *vis-à-vis* their employers, depends to an important extent on this possibility. Unless we are willing to accept vertical bondage in closed internal labour markets as the organizing principle for the exchange of labour services in our economies, we will have to assume that firms will always tend to be reluctant investors in the skills of their workforce.

In effect, the fundamental uncertainty for employers recovering their train-ing expenses in an open labour market — rudimentary and incomplete as the latter may be — turns skills, from the viewpoint of the individual employer, into a *collective good*. If an employer provides training, he is no more than adding to a common pool of skilled labour which is in principle accessible to all other employers in the industry or the locality, many of which are his competitors. While the individual employer may well recognize the impor-tance of skilled workers for his enterprise, he also knows that if he incurs the expenses for their training, his competitors can easily 'poach' his trained workers by offering them a higher wage, with their overall labour costs still remaining below his. Since the rewards of his investment can so easily be 'socialized' whereas the costs remain his own, an employer in a competitive labour market will therefore be tempted not to train, or to train as little as possible, and 'buy in' needed skills from his competition. As these are likely to perceive their pay-off matrix in much the same way as he, they will probably prefer not to train either. As a result, there will be a chronic undersupply of skilled labour. The important point is that to arrive at this prediction, one does not have to assume that employers fail to recognize the importance of skills, or that they are not acting rationally. The point, rather, is that economic objectives, rational as they may be, often cannot be achieved by rational means alone, and that actors that are too rational and interest-conscious may well thereby 'outsmart themselves'. In this sense, I regard skills as an example of what I described at the outset as collective, social production factors which capitalist firms, acting according to the rational-utilitarian model, cannot adequately generate or preserve.

Of course, this is an ideal-typical model, and I am well aware that there are all kinds of modifications, exceptions and qualifications that need to be taken into account. For example, a firm may have a monopoly in its local labour market so that it can in practice expect to keep its skilled workers for a suffi-ciently long time to recover the costs of training. Or high-skill firms, since they operate in more lucrative product markets, may be able to pay higher wages than their labour market competitors, and thereby bind their workers to their present place of employment. Internal labour markets may evolve, as they so forcefully do in many countries today, where a benevolent long-term manpower and human resource management converges with highly firm-specific, idiosyncratic skill demands to keep workers from moving across firm boundaries. All this is possible, and in fact it happens frequently. Nevertheless, I maintain that there is evidence to the effect that voluntary investment in training, as guided by the imperatives of market rationality, will produce high skills only in exceptional cases, and even in these the result will likely be suboptimal. If training is left to the market, there will not be no training, and there will also be high-quality training, but the latter will be limited to isolated 'islands of excellence', and differences between firms will be enormous. Many firms that might do better economically if they had access to a sufficient supply of skilled labour, will not realize their full potential because they happen to be unable to internalize and privatize their skilled human resources. Moreover, even inside the 'islands of excellence' skill production will more often than not remain behind what it could and sometimes should be in the interest of the enterprise itself. Three reasons for this are paramount:

(1) Precisely in order to facilitate internalization of their investment returns, firms are likely to emphasize workplace-specific over general skills. If what workers learn from their employer can be used only in their present place of work, 'poaching' becomes difficult, and the bargaining power of workers does not increase in proportion with their skills. *Nota bene*, however, that the distinction between job-specific and general skills sounds easier to make than it is in practice. An employer who is anxious not to give away too many transferable skills, will probably fail to create enough non-transferable skills. Moreover, sometimes it is precisely general skills that are needed, skills that can be applied to a wide variety of tasks that are as yet unknown – for example, when a new 'basic technology' like micro-electronic circuitry is introduced in a wide range of products and processes, and in particular if this technology is used to increase product variety and process flexibility, as is presently the case in many firms under pressure from growing world market competition. In such a situation, excessive concern over the appropriation of skills, as with other collective goods, is bound to result in shortage of supply.

(2) A firm providing training according to its rational interests and present commercial objectives will often be tempted to save on training costs even if this goes at the expense of its own longer-term future. 'Opportunism', in the institutional economics sense, may damage not just others but also oneself. Under pressure from competition, firms may find it expedient, if they can, to reduce training costs even if they may be well aware that this may impair their future competitiveness. Similarly, firms in a crisis that come under pressure from their core workforce to protect their jobs will tend to cut their training programs as a first step towards cutting labour costs – unless there are other, countervailing forces making them do for 'non-rational' reasons what they should in their own interest be doing for rational ones.

This point can be illustrated by an example (Streeck 1987). When the crisis of the Western automobile industry broke out in the 1970s, firms in all major Western producer countries except one reduced their apprenticeship programs, cutting down their number of apprentices faster than their overall workforces. This was at a time when it was already clear that the dominating problem of the ongoing restructuring process was the mastery of the new production technologies, and that firms which did well on this would in future enjoy a major competitive advantage. The one exception was West Germany where in the same period the number of apprentices in the automobile industry increased in both relative and absolute terms. This was because in this country, the decision of a firm as to how many apprentices it takes in is to a large extent dependent on forces other than its management, such as the government, 'public opinion', the chambers of commerce and industry, the trade union and the works council. As fears were mounting in the 1970s of high youth unemployment, successful moral, political and legal pressures were brought to bear on German employers to extend their training programs. That German auto manufacturers had to yield to such pressures goes a long way towards explaining the superior technical and economic performance of that industry in the restructuring period and thereafter. Where only the market rules, present profitability, when 'the chips are down', counts more than future prospects for profitability. But where present profitability counts too much, there may be no future prospects at all – which is another way of saying that too much rationality may be irrational, and that rational action in order not to be self-defeating in the long run must be embedded in and guided by non-rational, 'social' or 'cultural' motives.

(3) Finally, there is also in large organizations an interest on the part of their management not to share too much knowledge with the workforce, so as to protect its own position of power and control. Such 'political' motives can easily be exaggerated, as they are, I believe, in the Bravermanian 'labour process' theory. When managerial interests in domination clash with interests in profitability, it is not by any means clear that the former will prevail. Nevertheless, sharing knowledge with somebody who occupies an inferior position in a hierarchy is difficult, and at least in Western countries there is likely to be a tendency to come out, if in doubt and especially if the costs are uncertain and will show only in the future, on the restrictive side: to do less rather than more and to keep to oneself as much as possible of what the German sociologist, Karl Mannheim, has so aptly called '*Herrschaftswissen*'. Again, trying to appropriate as a private good what is more efficient if treated as a collective good is likely to be dysfunctional from the perspective of the enterprise, but here too, perverse incentives to cheat on one's own longer-term interests may be overwhelming. Where firms, and superiors inside firms, feel they can make do without sharing the knowledge vested into the firm as an important part of its capital, they will as a rule try; the widespread adherence to Taylorist principles of work organization even in situations where non-Taylorist organizational forms have long proven superior is a clear indication.

There is no need to contest that there are situations in which the limited capacity of competing firms to generate work skills is not of great significance. Where firms can rely mostly on unskilled labour, such as in the mining industry, or where skills can be made redundant by Taylorist forms of work organization, such as in the mass production of standardized goods, it is quite conceivable that the deficits of a free market training regime will never make themselves felt. *But this*, I submit, *is precisely not the situation that obtains in the present period of industrial restructuring.* Not only do the new competitive conditions in world markets place a premium on high skills, favouring firms that can build a skilled workforce over those that cannot. What is more, it seems that what firms need today is not just skills but broad and unspecific skills; not just 'functional' skills dedicated to a specific purpose, as they can be created by instant 'refresher courses' or the replacement of one subject in a curriculum by another, but skills as a *generalized, polyvalent resource* that can be put to many different and, most importantly, *as yet unknown* future uses. Practitioners everywhere agree that the crucial work qualification today is the capacity to acquire more and new work qualifications – something which German labour market analysts call *Schluesselqualifikationen* ('key qualifications'). And there is also growing recognition that the new, highly capital-intensive production processes have created an increasing need for even more unspecific, 'extra-functional' skills, that are essentially of an attitudinal and behavioural kind and which include individual characteristics like diligence, attention to detail, thoroughness, and a willingness to carry responsibility.

Firms, that is to say, which want to be successful in today's changed economy, need not just the skills they need, but above all skills they do not – yet – need; they not only need what is functional in their present environment but, in a period of change, also what may become functional in uncertain and contingent future environments. Put dialectically, what is merely functional may be liable to become dysfunctional, and that which under the new conditions satisfies functional needs may be precisely what is not functionally defined. A liberal-voluntaristic training regime which is already endemically weak in generating specific, 'dedicated' skills, is likely to fall far short if it is asked to produce work skills as cultural resources which, from the viewpoint of rationally calculating individuals or firms, are bound to appear as 'excess qualifications'.

The Limits of State Provision and the Indispensable Contribution of the Enterprise

Nevertheless, it could be argued that while the market may not be very good at generating other than narrow, job-specific skills, this does not in itself constitute a case for social or political regulation of the behaviour of firms. Liberal doctrine does not in principle deny that there may be limits to what markets can do; as long as the resulting imperfections can be repaired by direct state provision, its *Weltbild* is still in order. One possible solution to the skilling deficiencies of markets – one which would be essentially compatible with a deregulation view of the 'enterprise of the future' – would be to delegate the production of 'general' work skills to the state school system while leaving the generation of 'specific' work skills to free contracts between workers and employers. In line with the liberal view of the state, this would keep intervention in markets to a minimum, and above all such intervention would be strictly limited to 'making markets work'. But plausible as this solution may look – and different versions of it have been adopted in a large number of countries – skills are a peculiar thing, and it seems that *not only the market finds it difficult to provide adequately for their formation but also the state.* There are other collective goods as well where market failure is not compensated by state success but rather coincides with state failure, and it is precisely where and when such goods become important for a society that the fundamental shortcoming of neo-liberalism as a political doctrine becomes most apparent: its self-limitation to two mechanistically opposed sources of social order, state and society, and its conceptualization of the latter as a system of voluntary-contractual exchange relations.

That schools are not an ideal place to create work skills, even and especially if such skills are desired to be broad and polyvalent, is one of the central premises underlying the West German industrial training system. Schools, in particular vocational schools, do play a legitimate and indispensable part in that system; but apprentices attend these schools only one day a week, and in the remaining time they are trained at the workplace. Among the reasons why this is likely to be a superior way of producing work skills, and why state provision of industrial training is neither attuned to the dynamics of the training process nor conducive to the kind of skills that are needed for successful upward restructuring, are the following:

(1) Many young people, and even more older ones, are not enthuasiastic about going to a school. While they may be willing to learn, they are not willing to accept being excluded for this purpose from the 'real life' of the workplace. It is widely accepted among German practitioners in industrial training and further training that '*Verschulung*' — the delegation of training to specialized schools — is more often than not pedagogically counterproductive. An important reason why especially young people may feel little motivation in a school to work hard enough to build up adequate work skills is that the potential reward — a 'real' job — is much less visible and much further removed there than in a workplace setting.

(2) Industrial training is not just the acquisition of manual or mental skills but it is also, and increasingly needs to be, a process of socialization in work-related values, in a culture and community of work in which extra-functional skills like reliability, the ability to hold up under pressure, and solidarity with others working at the same tasks are highly regarded and rewarded. To internalize value orientations, at work and elsewhere, people need role models; teachers, however, can serve this function only to a very limited extent and only for very few, selected roles. Unless one aspires to be a teacher oneself, work-related skills and orientations are acquired not from professional teachers but from more experienced peers in a place of work where technical competence can be blended into, and transmitted together with, attitudinal discipline and diligence.

(3) Learning requires doing. Work skills can be ultimately acquired only at work. Being told in a school how concrete is mixed and poured on a construction site is something quite different from living through the drama and the crises of fifteen or twenty-four hours of continuous, minutely timed

SKILLS AND THE LIMITS OF NEO-LIBERALISM   99

and tightly coordinated hard physical work. This is not to advocate 'on-job-training' if this means that somebody is hired to do a job and is expected to pick up by doing it what skills he may need. Learning there has to be, especially if skills are to be broad and flexible, and this, as we have said, demands preceptoral and not just contractual relations. But these must be integrated in the workplace and the work process, and they have to prove and legitimate themselves under the pressures of economy and time in an environment that is real and not artificial. A crucial role in this respect is played in the German system by the *Ausbilder*: the man or woman in a firm who is in charge of the training of apprentices. *Ausbilder* need a training licence which they receive only if they are themselves highly skilled, and in addition they often have to attend special courses and pass examinations for their training function; but only in rare cases do they work as full-time trainers, and normally they take part as all other employees in the firm's everyday production work.

Work skills, then, for motivational, cultural and cognitive reasons, seem to be best produced where they are used: at the workplace. State provision in specialized public organizations is not likely to do the job, especially if the result has to meet high demands like those imposed on high-wage countries by present world-market conditions. It seems that here as in many other areas, we are today experiencing what one could call *the limits of functional differentiation*. For a long time, received opinion in the West was that places of work and places of learning should best be kept neatly apart, and that if this was done, both learning and work would be optimally served. Today more and more people have come to doubt this, and such doubts extend far beyond the industrial part of the educational system. It is no accident that the Japanese way of skilling and the German 'dual system', which a few years ago would have been regarded as remnants of a less 'modern' past, are attracting growing attention. Much to our surprise, 'premodern' institutions with their higher mutual interpenetration of functions and social arenas often seem to perform better in a period of change and uncertainty than 'modern', functionally differentiated institutions. As our needs for work skills have increased, the future of training and industry may demand a reintegration of learning and work.

If all this is true, then the conclusion is clear: if we are to generate the high and broad skills that we require to preserve our specifically European 'culture of work' in spite of present economic exigencies, a direct and substantial contribution of the enterprise to industrial training is indispensable. Enterprises, in the West just as in the East, have to become *places of learning in addition to being places of production* as no other institution can do what they can to produce the urgently needed collective good of a large supply of work skills. But if this is so, then the neo-liberal proponents of a de-regulated economy have a problem. If only the firm can do what has to be done, the fact that, as we have seen, it does not have the rational motivation to do it voluntarily is bound to upset the purity of supply-side *Ordnungspolitik*. Only firms will do, *but not de-regulated firms*. If society wants skills, enterprises have to be drafted and mandated by regulating agencies to produce them. To substitute for the moral obligations and the close communitarian bonds that seem to both force and enable firms in Japan to impart excess skills on their workforces, institutions are needed in Western societies that constrain the rational self-seeking behaviour of firms and make the enterprise do its duty as a cultural institution. Just as skill formation in individuals requires education, skill formation in firms requires regulation. Deregulation, if driven too far, breeds inefficiency.

The Need for Regulation and the Continuing Viability of Democratic Corporatism

Firms, we have said, need to be drafted by society to serve as places of training. Where an open external labour market is part of a country's social and political heritage, and where broad and general skills are needed in addition to and as a basis for workplace-specific skills, common training standards and curricula need to be imposed on firms providing training; adherence to them must be carefully monitored; and ways have to be found to prevent firms from exiting the training system in protest against too demanding requirements. Moreover, as economies develop dynamically, mechanisms have to be devised to adjust curricula to technical and organizational change. Not least, safeguards must be developed to protect apprentices from exploitation by firms that use the integration of training and work to take advantage of their apprentices' productive contribution without providing them in turn with transferable skills, and general rules and procedures must be established for decisions on training licences, experimental curricula, examinations, and sanctions against firms that do not properly discharge their obligations. All this certainly applies to Western countries where training arrangements must take into account the existence of an open labour market and where there is a need to design formal-institutional equivalents, or at least supports, for informal-moral mechanisms of social control and integration. The West German training system offers ample illustration of the enormous institutional complexity that seems to be needed to perform this function with a degree of relative success.

Not that moral factors were absent or not important in the West. As recent German experience has shown, public exhortation is well able to motivate small and large firms to increase their training efforts beyond immediate needs in an attempt to accommodate a demographic surplus of school leavers. And there is little doubt that in certain artisanal communities, where training and the rituals of examination and admission are the focus of communal life and collective identity, a sense of moral obligation still plays a major part in the operation of industrial training. But even in these cases, Chambers often with statutory membership exist that regulate and supervise, educate and admonish,

SKILLS AND THE LIMITS OF NEO-LIBERALISM 101

and sometimes sanction the firms whose training efforts they are charged with guiding. Such organizations usually operate under some kind of state licence and public mandate, and just as in other areas, it seems that collective, or 'corporatist', self-governance of enterprises can safely function only if it is backed by some form of state support and legal facilitation. States, in turn, act primarily under political pressure, and since capitalists usually find it difficult to lobby the government to be disciplined, even if this would be in their own interest, regulatory intervention in the behaviour of firms is greatly advanced if a strong trade union movement presses for it at the national level.

This is not to say that capitalist firms could not in principle attempt to govern themselves, with or without state involvement. In fact, when it comes to training they may have a particularly strong motive for this, which is to do with another emerging collective goods property of skills. A major aspect of knowledge-intensive diversified quality production seems to be its tendency to give rise to close inter-firm alliances between equally highly skilled production units. To the extent that diversified quality production presupposes the possibility of entering into a large number of cooperative relationships with other firms, enterprises seeking their economic future in a production pattern of this kind will find it hard to operate successfully as isolated 'islands of excellence'. If one firm's skills cannot be adequately utilized without other firms commanding the same kind of skills, then firms become strongly interested in the technical capabilities of other firms — even though these may be their competitors for most of the time. Once again, the problem is appropriability in the sense that firms require skills that they cannot own, and that they therefore have no rational incentive to generate. Where the lack of skills of others becomes a bottleneck to one's own growth, the uneven development endemic in market-led training systems becomes economically suboptimal even from the perspective of the individual firm. To the extent that diversified quality production remains unstable unless it is embedded in an, often regional, ecology of similar firms, individual enterprises may become self-interested in collective, equal development, and economic interests may arise in collective behavioural regulation that the market as such cannot provide.

It may well be that at the end of the day, capitalist firms may not be motivated enough by their enlightened self-interest to begin to govern themselves as a collectivity — although we do see in a number of countries today that competing firms are beginning to set up joint, cooperative training centres for their workforces. But firms may be even more willing to act, and on a broader scale, if pressed to do so by a government which, while not intervening directly, indicates that it may unless firms themselves 'get their act together'. Trade union pressure would greatly help in this. To be sure, labour movements have mostly emphasized the contribution of training to equality rather than efficiency, and they have in particular been concerned with its distributional aspects. In the era of prosperity in the 1960s and 1970s, this has expressed itself in an almost exclusive concern with equal access and entitlement to education, often as a kind of advanced consumption – a perspective borrowed from the liberal middle classes. This, however, may be about to change. In the economic conditions of today, the role of education in achieving equality seems to have become a much more serious one. As the European high-wage economy is coming under growing pressure from its Asian competition, training may be discovered as a means of raising work skills to a level where they justify the high and relatively uniform price of labour imposed on European economies by collective bargaining and the welfare state. Otherwise, a clearing of labour markets may eventually take place at conditions that will not only undo most of the achievements of labour movements but also, very likely, labour movements themselves. The defence of the high level of equality that is vested in the high-wage pattern of European economies; the restructuring and revitalization of industrial economies to increase their competitiveness; and the generalization of both diversified quality production and advanced work skills beyond isolated islands of excellence may thus already have become one and the same thing. Equality pursued by labour movements under these premises may not be incompatible with the interests of capitalist firms in a supportive 'ecology of skills', and there is no reason in principle to preclude the possibility of joint action in the pursuit of such interests.

It is true that to many, in particular on the left, skills often appear as a primarily conservative concern, the popular image being one of employers pressing for 'pay incentives' for skilled workers and trade unions opposing 'elitism' and 'discretionary rewards'. But in reality the matter is far more complex. Not only have trade unions and Social-Democratic parties in the past attached great significance to learning at a time when the bourgeoisie still believed that the 'masses' were essentially unable to be educated (*Wissen ist Macht*, Knowledge is Power, being the slogan of the widespread educational activities that were organized by the German labour movement at the end of the last century, and there are equivalents to this in almost all industrial countries). What is more important in our context is that for a long time in the post-war era, it was the employers who did all they could to eliminate skills from the shopfloor under a Taylorist work regime, and it was often the unions which, mostly in vain, resisted the 'degradation of labour' that went with capitalist rationalization. Doubtless during the 'long boom', many unions have made their peace with Taylorism, as it not only seemed to be producing ever growing wages for everybody but in addition, working against the elitist minority of traditional craft workers, could be pictured as promoting equality. But today the situation is different, not only because now employers are beginning to regret their former policy of deskilling, but also because a comprehensive rebuilding of the skill base of Western economies may now have become the most promising means of defending and extending whatever degree of equality unions may have been able to achieve in the past. Should it not be possible to rediscover and revitalize in this situation the traditional commitment of the left to *Wissen und Koennen*, to knowledge and skills –

now that the two may have become even less separable than in the past? And should it not be possible also on this basis to establish a new pattern of *conflictual cooperation*, a new *historical compromise* with employers under which these would be *simultaneously constrained and enabled* to generate the kind of skills they need to survive in the highly competitive and volatile markets of the future?

It is not by chance that the West German industrial training system on which I now draw for empirical reference is a picture-book case of a democratic corporatist arrangement: democratic since it is embedded in a parliamentary democracy and since it includes strong and independent trade unions on, in principle, a co-equal basis. While market motives and processes play a significant and recognized part in the system, they are controlled by, and embedded in, what are essentially collective agreements between monopolistic employers associations and trade unions exercising, under a state licence, delegated public responsibility which enables them to impose effectively binding obligations upon their memberships. But while this is undoubtedly corporatist, it seems to have little in common with the political-distributional bargaining that was associated with the concept in the 1970s. It may be true that neo-corporatism may result in short-sighted appeasement of powerful special interests at the expense of long-term fiscal stability, the non-organized, taxpayers, future generations or whoever, and in this respect it may have deserved some of its present bad reputation. But it is also true that the 'public use of private organized interests', the 'private interest government' mode of regulating socio-economic relationships, is not inherently limited to the management of demand and the regulation of distributional conflict: it can also be applied to the problem of 'effective supply' and the generation of collective production factors. Indeed, one could argue that where democratic corporatism has been doing more economic harm than good, this was where it was confined to matters of demand and distribution, with self-governing groups sharing no responsibility for the supply side and efficient production.

In short, it may be premature to discard democratic corporatism just because the leading concerns of economic and social policy have shifted towards the supply side. On the contrary, I have tried to show that the apparently growing needs of Western capitalism firms for collective, non-appropriable production factors, like a rich supply of high and broad functional and extrafunctional skills, opens up political arenas where corporative self-government of social groups may be a superior mode of regulation compared to both state intervention and the free market. Why else should there be such a widespread interest in almost all Western countries today not only in workplace-based industrial training but also and simultaneously in trade union involvement in the governance of training systems? Democratic corporatism may have a future after all, and in particular in an area like training where it seems that both trade unions and employers may, for partly different and partly identical reasons, be about to discover a joint interest in jointly preventing market as well as state failure.

If a widespread, equal distribution of skills is becoming a precondition for economic success even for firms that are capable of generating a sufficient supply of work skills for themselves, then egalitarian interests on the part of trade unions in a generalization of advanced upgraded production patterns, in preventing social dualism and in defending the egalitarian elements of the European high-wage economy, may not only be compatible with the interests of capital, but their forceful articulation may be a precondition of such interests being realized.

References

Sorge, A. and Streeck, W. (1988) 'Industrial Relations and Technical Change: the Case for an Extended Perspective' in R. Hyman and W. Streeck (eds.), *New Technology and Industrial Relations*, Oxford: Blackwell.

Streeck, W. (1987) 'Industrial Relations and Industrial Change in the Motor Industry: an International View', *Economic and Industrial Democracy*, 8, 437–62.

Streeck, W., Hilbert, J., van Kevelar, K.H., Maier, F. and Weber, H. (1987) *The Role of the Social Partners in Vocational Training and Further Training in the Federal Republic of Germany*, Berlin: European Centre for the Development of Vocational Training (CEDEFOP).

Department of Sociology
University of Wisconsin
1180 Observatory Drive
Madison, Wisconsin 53706
USA

[7]

FOREIGN TRAINING SYSTEMS: HOW DOES THE UNITED STATES COMPARE?

In many other nations, including the Federal Republic of Germany (FRG) and Japan, public and private training systems function more effectively than in the United States. There is no question that these two countries, and several others, train their workers to higher average standards. Table 3-4 (an expanded version of table 1-5 in ch. 1) briefly compares U.S. and foreign education and training systems. (Because of the lack of reliable figures for the United States, OTA has not attempted to estimate training expenditures in other countries.)

The Competition: Training Systems Abroad

Germany and Japan pursue markedly different approaches to training. The contrast between the United States and Germany is particularly striking. The FRG not only has the best apprenticeship system of any major economy, jointly financed by public and private sectors, but policies and traditions that give status and respect to blue- and grey-collar work. In Germany, the prestige associated with a college education works against broad vocational

Box 3-A—Training in the Textile Industry[1]

Since the mid-1970s, U.S. textile firms have sought to meet international competition through automation, work reorganization, and greater product variety. Two decades ago, mills were organized for long runs of a few standard products. The workforce was largely unskilled or semiskilled. Recent work reorganizations, along with computer-based automation, have placed greater demands on employee skills. Some jobs now require operators to read manuals and enter or record information on electronic control panels.[2] Machine repair has become much more demanding.

Textile firms have had limited success in recruiting better educated workers. Forced to improve the skills of current employees, they have begun to implement training programs in basic skills and in grey-collar technical work.

Forces for Change

Since the mid-1970s, three sudden shocks have hit the U.S. textile industry. First, styles began to change at an accelerating pace. Many American textile suppliers had specialized in a limited range of standardized goods. Now apparel manufacturers (and retailers and consumers) demand variety even in denim; cotton "white goods" come in hundreds of styles rather than dozens. Survival has meant adaptation. Second, import competition has grown steadily more intense, not only from low-wage Asian economies (China, Korea, Hong Kong), but from mills based in Europe and Japan that concentrate on high-quality, high-fashion fabrics. Third, after several decades of relatively stable production technology, a wave of innovation hit. Water-jet and air-jet looms operate many times faster than traditional shuttle looms. Microprocessor-based controls enhance consistency and quality. Inexpensive computer systems track product flow.

Automation and Organizational Change

In earlier years, U.S. textile firms had sought to keep their costs competitive by moving to the Southeast, where organized labor was weak and wage rates low. Investments in the new generation of automated equipment helped the industry increase its productivity by 5 percent annually between 1975 and 1987, a much higher rate than for U.S. manufacturing as a whole. But imports also grew, and employment fell.

Some American firms, unable to compete either with cheap fabrics coming in from Asia or with high-fashion textiles entering from other advanced economies, began to search out market segments where their capital-intensive, vertically integrated plants would create advantages. They found them particularly in fabrics for home furnishings and in industrial textiles—categories that, together, accounted for 52 percent of U.S. textile production in 1980, 60 percent in 1985, and 63 percent in 1988. Within their chosen niches, firms began offering greater variety. One spinning mill went from three active styles to 35 in 2 years; another now offers 300 furniture fabrics rather than 100. These strategies depend on fine-tuning the flow of production: computers have literally revolutionized production planning and control in the mills, where they are now used for tracking in-plant inventories as well as handling ordering and invoices. Some firms have also reorganized by replacing traditional functional departments, one for each step in the production process, with product-oriented departments that carry out a lengthy sequence of operations for a given product class.

Work and Skills

Textile jobs were much the same in 1975 as in 1955. The work was repetitive, and, despite high levels of mechanization, largely manual. With the technological flux of the 1980s, jobs for operators, for maintenance and repair workers ("fixers"), and for supervisors have all changed. For instance, threads break far less often in spinning and weaving, so that operators now spend less time tying them back together—a task requiring dexterity and experience. Operators spend much more of their time monitoring automated equipment. Errors in such tasks as recording information and entering new instructions can have serious consequences; to minimize machine stoppages, operators must understand something of the production process and their place in it. Some companies

---

[1]Based on "Training and Competitiveness in U.S. Manufacturing and Services: Training Needs and Practices of Lead Firms in Textiles, Banking, Retailing, and Business Services," report prepared for OTA under contract No. L3-3560 by Lauren Benton, Thomas Bailey, Thierry Noyelle, and Thomas M. Stanback, Jr., Columbia University, February 1990, pp. 60-89. The productivity levels and market share figures in this box come from unpublished data of the American Textile Manufacturers Institute.

[2]For a complementary discussion focusing on apparel, especially in Europe, see Jonàthan Zeitlin and Peter Totterdill, "Markets, Technology and Local Intervention: The Case of Clothing," *Reversing Industrial Decline? Industrial Structure and Policy in Britain and Her Competitors*, Paul Hirst and Jonathan Zeitlin, eds. (Oxford, UK: Berg, 1989), pp. 155-190. In some apparel plants, each worker now has a keypad at his or her workstation for recording production flow information. Among other things, these systems automatically calculate each workers' pay on a piecework basis. Clive Cookson, "A Good Fit on the Factory Floor," *Financial Times*, June 6, 1990, p. 13.

are training operators to diagnose machine problems (e.g., stoppages) and enter a corresponding code from a multipage manual. They must use good sense in deciding when to call in a supervisor or fixer. They must also have the basic skills needed for looking up the codes and punching them in; if the plant is to run smoothly, operators must not only be able to diagnose equipment problems, but read and write—skills rarely needed in the old days. In some cases, even loom cleaners, who are among the lowest paid of mill workers, must be able to follow written instructions and punch numbers into a key pad.

In maintenance and repair, the balance has tipped still farther from manual toward mental skills. At one time, tinkering outside the workplace coupled with informal on-the-job training could suffice to earn a promotion from operator to fixer; lack of basic skills was no bar. Fixers could see how older machines worked; today, with invisible electronic logic replacing electro-mechanical controls, they need conceptual understanding. Textile firms are seeking graduates of 2-year associate degree programs, and increasing the formal training they give their technicians. Promotions of operators to the next level without formal training, once common, have become rare.

Upward Mobility

In earlier years, unskilled workers could enter the mills in service jobs (cleaning) or as laborers (unloading bales) and move upward through progressively more demanding positions. People with aptitude and interest could look forward to becoming operators, then fixers, perhaps eventually a supervisor. Most training was informal. Companies saw no need for a high school diploma. On-the-job experience would serve, whatever a person's formal education, given the unchanging nature of the work. These traditional job ladders have broken down. Most textile firms still post openings internally, and try to recruit from within, but they have had trouble finding enough qualified people internally to fill the growing need for fixers and technicians who can cope with the latest equipment.

Education and Training

The industry has trouble finding skilled workers in part because it is concentrated in the smaller cities and towns of the Southeast. Wages have always been low, and textile firms buffeted by cheap imports argue that they have little scope for raising them. The industry also seems trapped by its past practices of hiring unskilled, poorly educated workers. It now needs better educated employees, but can offer neither the image nor the wages nor the opportunities that would attract them.

Vocational schools and community colleges have been little help, in part because textile firms rarely tried to work with them in the past. Few community colleges have kept abreast of the industry's technical needs; students attend these schools in part to escape the mills. Of 75,000 students in 1985-86 taking technical courses in North Carolina community colleges, 5,000 were studying for occupations in demand in the textile industry, while 35,000 were preparing for office jobs in service industries.

Unable to hire from existing labor pools, textile firms have responded in three ways: 1) by seeking to improve basic skills in local labor pools, through participation in literacy programs and strengthened relationships with secondary schools; 2) through technical training, both internally and in conjunction with community colleges; and 3) by contracting for training provided by equipment manufacturers. Companies with workplace literacy programs have aggressively pursued funds from Federal and State programs. In South Carolina, for instance, the Governor's Initiative for Workforce Excellence has established literacy programs at several textile firms, including Milliken. The literacy initiative is playing a key role at Milliken's Kingstree, SC plant, which has installed 400 new weaving machines and begun reducing the number of job classifications from 38 to four. Employees must know three of the four new jobs to be promoted; an off-hours basic skills program helps them prepare.[3]

While community colleges rarely took the initiative in developing technical courses suited to the needs of the industry, they have been more responsive to firms asking for specialized programs; these help the schools attract students and justify State funding. Companies have also sent employees to training programs, typically several weeks long, offered by equipment manufacturers. Some firms have then used these courses as models for in-house training on other types of machinery.

New skill requirements caught most U.S. textile firms off guard. As companies discovered they could not recruit the workers they needed, they began turning to training. If these efforts—which remain in early stages—do not succeed, American textile firms stand to lose still more ground to imports.

---

[3] "Basic Skills Education in Business and Industry: Factors for Success or Failure," report prepared for OTA under contract No. L3-1765 by Paul V. Delker, January 1990, p. 41. On Milliken's overall labor force strategy, which includes reorganization around work groups, reductions in supervisory ranks, and tighter links with fewer suppliers, see "Pushing To Improve Quality," *Research-Technology Management*, May-June 1990, pp. 19-22.

Table 3-4—Worker Training Compared

	United States	Germany	Japan	Korea	Canada
Primary and secondary schooling	Local control contributes to wide range in course offerings and quality	Excellent for those in academic high school; generally good for others	High quality; uniform curriculum; emphasis on rote learning	Strong core curriculum and basic skills emphasis evident in international test scores	Wide range in quality
School-to-work transition	Left mostly to chance; some employers have ties with local schools	Apprenticeship for most non-college-bound youth	Personal relationships between employers and local schools	Employers recruit from vocational and academic high schools	Left mostly to chance; apprenticeships available for some young people
Vocational education					
Extent	Available in most urban areas	Near-universal availability	Limited; mostly assumed by employers	Widely available	Available in most urban areas
Quality	Wide range: poor to excellent	Uniformly good	Fair to good	Vocational high schools uniformly good	Wide range: poor to excellent
Adult education					
Extent	Moderate; community colleges offer widespread opportunities	Limited but growing	Widespread; self-study common	Limited	Widespread
Relationship to work	Relatively common	Nearly universal	Common	Common	Common
Employer-provided training					
Extent	Emphasis on managers and technicians	Widespread at entry level (apprenticeship) and to qualify for promotion	Widespread at all levels	Limited; employers rely on public vocational institutes	Limited[a]
Quality	Sometimes excellent, but more often weak or unstructured; many firms do not train	Very good	Very good	Generally poor	Not evaluated
Public policies	Federal role limited; State aid to employers growing	Governs apprenticeship; supports further training	Subsidies encourage training by small firms	Directive--some employers resist government policies	Limited, but growing; aid to trade association and union training efforts

[a]One estimate is that Canadian firms spend less than half as much per employee on formal training as do U.S. firms —*Success in the Works* (Ottawa, Ontario: Employment and Immigration Canada, April, 1989), p. 2.

SOURCE: Office of Technology Assessment, 1990.

training, but not nearly so strongly as in the United States.

In Japan, rigorous academic preparation coupled with extensive company training yields a highly qualified workforce. Firms and individuals absorb most of the costs of training. Stable, long-term employment relations, particularly in large corporations, mean that Japanese companies can invest in their workers with little fear of losing them. For employees, training is more than a means for advancement: in Japan, a host of subtle and not-so-subtle pressures encourage continuous, life-long learning.

Japanese and German managers embrace broad, ongoing training as a way to enhance productivity, quality, and competitiveness. Although the two countries rely on very different training systems, the net effect is much the same. Most workers have broad skills: they can do more than one job, and participate effectively in the ongoing search for better production methods. Because many U.S. employers fear they might lose skilled workers to another employer, or have to pay higher wages, company training is spotty (see ch. 5). In smaller firms, many employees receive no formal instruction; larger firms slant their training towards supervisors and managers. U.S. apprenticeship programs have been in decline (ch. 8), while other forms of vocational education and training have not picked up the slack. Although Japan's vocational education system is weak, pervasive employer-provided training makes up for this.

Germany: Apprenticeship as a Foundation

The strength of the German training system lies in its integration of training with education, in contrast to Japan, where schools and employers function independently to create a high-quality labor force. The vast majority of the German work force boasts formal training; 60 percent have completed an apprenticeship.[23] Today, these long-established programs have been reinforced with incentives for post-apprenticeship training.

The FRG Government works with trade associations and unions to define uniform national curricula and examinations for apprentices in over 400 occupations. Most apprenticeships last three years, combining on-the-job training (for a small wage) with at least 1 day per week of classroom instruction. Certification requires passage of written tests and demonstration of practical skills. Trade associations have always played a central role: beginning as a compulsory system of artisan guilds in the Middle Ages, Germany's apprenticeship system evolved into one jointly regulated by employers and government, "with the changeable consent of the unions."[24]

All apprentices must attend *Länder*-supported vocational schools 1 day per week. The structure of the rest of the week depends on the firm. In large companies, apprentices spend much of their time in training centers, often licensed and partially funded by *Länder* governments; these supplement vocational school curricula.[25] Apprentices in smaller companies spend more time on the factory floor, often interspersed with periods of a few days to several weeks at area training centers supported roughly half and half by local chambers of commerce and the Federal Ministry of Education and Science.

Training beyond the apprenticeship has traditionally taken the form of night classes delivered by local trade associations; governmental bodies often pay the bills. Employees who pursue such opportunities, and pass the required tests, can win certification as a master craftworker. Among other things, this qualifies him or her for promotion to foreman. Workers normally attend these courses on their own time (in the United States, first-line supervisors often get their training on company time). In addition, many certified apprentices go back to school, graduating from vocational institutes or even

[23]*Berufsbildungsbericht 1988* (Bonn: Federal Ministry of Education and Science), p. 64.

[24]Arndt Sorge and Malcolm Warner, *Comparative Factory Organisation* (Brookfield, VT: Gower, 1986), p. 192.

Although apprenticeships have existed in Germany for hundreds of years, they were not formalized and regulated until 1969. Two forces lay behind legislation passed at that time: 1) shortages of apprentices (young people had turned away from vocational training); and 2) labor union concern that apprentices were being exploited (working for low wages while learning relatively little). The 1969 law led to nationwide standards for each apprenticeable occupation, specifying both the content of training, and testing following completion of the three-year program. The Federal Vocational Training Institute develops curricula in consulation with unions and trade associations.

[25]Anthony P. Carnevale and Janet W. Johnston, *Training America: Strategies for the Nation* (Alexandria, VA: American Society for Training and Development and National Center on Education and the Economy, 1989), p. 27.

Germany's *Länder* correspond to our States.

Box 3-B—*Impacts of the German Training System on Productivity and Competitiveness: Two Examples*

Comparisons With British Industry[1]

A series of studies carried out by British investigators offers perhaps the most careful and comprehensive examination of the effects of training and skills on the performance of manufacturing firms ever undertaken. These studies demonstrate in striking fashion the impacts of the German training system on costs, productivity levels, and quality. Intended to help diagnose the competitive problems of British industry, the comparisons covered a set of quite different sectors: metalworking (45 companies producing small parts such as screws, springs, and drill bits); fitted kitchen furnishings (23 companies making such products as counter tops and cabinets); and women's clothing (22 matched plants). The results demonstrate that German firms perform better than their British counterparts because of their better trained workers.

The average labor productivity in German metalworking firms was more than 60 percent greater than in the British sample. About half the shopfloor workers in the German metalworking companies had earned apprenticeship or similar qualifications, compared with one-quarter in Britain. German furniture-making firms were 50-60 percent more productive, and turned out higher quality goods. In every German furniture company sampled, 90 percent or more of the shopfloor workers had, as their minimum qualification, certification following 3 years of training; in none of the British firms did more than 10 percent of the employees have any formal qualification. Higher skill levels in the German apparel industry helped firms move into short runs of specialized, high-quality clothing for export, while British firms continued to mass produce lower priced, standard goods for the domestic market. In the apparel sample, 80 percent of German maintenance workers had completed an apprenticeship program, while not a single British worker had earned any form of certification. Machinery breakdowns were far less frequent in the German plants.

Plant visits and surveys revealed no possible source for the differences except training. The British firms, for example, typically had comparable manufacturing equipment—indeed, had sometimes made heavier capital investments. But British workers and supervisors were unable to use their equipment as effectively.

Training in a German Machine Tool Firm[2]

When faced with stronger Japanese competition in the late 1970s, Scharmann, a machine tool manufacturer located near Dusseldorf, made worker training a central element in reshaping its corporate strategy. The firm decided to specialize in automated equipment for producing relatively large parts, rather than the standard tools emphasized by Japanese competitors. Scharmann won a major order from Caterpillar's Belgian factory in 1980, helping the company move in this new direction.

Scharmann was able to build on its own earlier experience. Like many machine tool builders, the company designs and fabricates much of its own production equipment. During the 1970s, the company had automated internally while trying to save on payroll costs by hiring unskilled workers (including several who had completed apprenticeships in unrelated fields like baking). When this effort failed, Scharmann decided to strengthen its apprenticeship program.

In the new program, a 16-year-old apprentice could expect to spend a day-and-a-half each week in one of Scharmann's own classrooms, another day at a nearby vocational school studying the principles of machine tools, plus 2 days at work in the company training center. After completion of the program, Scharmann sends selected workers to a technical college for 2 years of further study in industrial electronics. The company's unskilled work force has dropped from about 230 to fewer than 40 (of 800 total). Scharmann has been able to draw on its employee's

[1]This section summarizes the following articles, each from the noted issue of *National Institute Economic Review*: A. Daly, D.M.W.N. Hitchens and K. Wagner, "Productivity, Machinery and Skills in a Sample of British and German Manufacturing Plants," February 1985, pp. 48-61; Hilary Steedman and Karin Wagner, "A Second Look at Productivity, Machinery and Skills in Britain and Germany," November 1987, pp. 84-95; Hilary Steedman and Karin Wagner, "Productivity, Machinery and Skills: Clothing Manufacture in Britain and Germany," May, 1989, pp. 41-57. Also see the broader comparisons between British and German education/training practices likewise appearing in *National Institute Economic Review*: S.J. Prais and Karin Wagner, "Some Practical Aspects of Human Capital Investment: Training Standards in Britain and Germany," August 1983. pp. 46-65; S.J. Prais and Karin Wagner, "Schooling Standards in England and Germany: Some Summary Comparisons Bearing on Economic Performance," May 1985, pp. 53-76; S.J. Prais, "Educating for Productivity: Comparisons of Japanese and English Schooling and Vocational Preparation," February 1987. pp. 40-56; and S.J. Prais and Karin Wagner, "Productivity and Management: The Training of Foremen in Britain and Germany," February 1988, pp. 34-47.

[2]Ira Magaziner and Mark Patinkin, *The Silent War* (New York: Random House, 1989), pp. 120-136.

new skills to make the steady, incremental improvements in work methods and production practices necessary to achieve its cost and quality targets.[3]

[3]Comparisons of British and German machine tool producers matched by size have shown that a broadly-skilled work force, capable of both programming and maintaining automated equipment, helps German firms compete more effectively. *Comparative Factory Organization,* op. cit., footnote 24, p. 164.

universities. Among those who completed apprenticeships during the 1960's, nearly 20 percent have now either been certified as master craftworkers (9 percent) or graduated from a vocational institute or university (10 percent).

As international competition and the need for top-quality products has grown, more West German employers are offering on-the-job training, as well as paying for outside courses that may not be tied directly to certification as a master craftworker. Government support for such training has grown. At the same time, more German workers are enrolling in classes on their own time, sometimes at their own expense, sometimes with government assistance. For example, between 1980 and 1985, 23 percent of employed adults took at least one job-related course (other than courses to become a master craftworker), an increase over the 1974-79 period, when 20 percent did so.

German employers view completion of an apprenticeship as evidence of motivation and willingness to learn. Nearly half (43 percent during the 1980s) of certified craftsworkers find themselves in occupations other than those for which they apprenticed, but they are nevertheless much less likely to experience unemployment than unskilled workers.[26] Although a substantial fraction of apprentices leave the firm in which they train, nearly 80 percent of all firms with at least 20 employees participate in apprenticeship programs.[27] Growing numbers of German workers have also been participating in less traditional forms of continuing education and training—e.g., short courses in data processing, or sales and management.

Box 3-B summarizes an extensive series of comparisons between training and measures of costs, productivity, and competitiveness in German and British industy, as well as outlining changes in employment and training practices in a medium-sized German machine tool firm. The German-British comparisons demonstrate in convincing detail the shopfloor benefits that German manufacturing firms get from better trained workers.

Japan: Training Integrated With Work[28]

Employer-provided training in Japan contrasts sharply with that in the United States: large Japanese firms, and many smaller ones as well, pursue training with unmatched zeal. Managers and supervisors deliver much of the training—an approach that has paid substantial dividends by integrating ongoing learning into corporate cultures.

Japanese firms provide extensive training for both new recruits and seasoned hands. After hiring in, blue-collar workers in larger firms typically begin with a week or so in an off-the-job motivational program. These programs are intended to impart not only the essentials of their employer's history, organizational structure, and product lines, but its culture and "philosophy"—based, in many cases, on the thoughts of the original founder. Employees then rotate through several jobs, a few days at a time, so they can develop a broad view of the company's business. During this period, they get systematic on-the-job instruction, commonly making use of training manuals prepared by supervisors or by a work group (e.g., as part of quality circle activities). After a few weeks, each recruit is assigned to a group, beginning with simpler tasks under the supervision of an experienced employee.

Production workers as well as managers are taught to embrace the concept of continuous improvement (*kaizen*) and hence continuous learning as a foundation for economic success. Quasi-public

[26]*Berufsbildungsbericht 1988,* op. cit., footnote 23, p. 65.

[27]*Zur Finanzierung der Berufsausbildung* (Bonn: Kuratorium der deutschen Wirtschaft fuer Berufsbildung, 1985), p. 4. This was the percentage in 1983.

[28]This section is based on "Employee Training in Japan," report prepared for OTA under contract No. L3-4335 by David Cairncross and Ronald Dore, March 1990.

industry bodies, such as the Japan Management Association and the Japanese Efficiency Association, have provided training to blue-collar workers since the 1950s; in recent years, they have offered courses for managers as well. With the recent rapid expansion of foreign direct investment by Japanese firms, many companies (40 percent according to one survey) now provide language training, not only to managers and sales staff, but to technicians and other skilled workers. Increasingly, such employees may not only be asked to respond to technical inquiries from overseas but be sent abroad temporarily (e.g., to aid in new plant startups, or train foreign workers).

The distinctive Japanese approach to training is relatively recent. Following a period of conflict after the Second World War, industry and labor reached an accommodation. The mostly male core employees of large firms, especially skilled workers and supervisors, won the benefits of "lifetime" employment (and systematic training) in return for an end to labor strife. Although lifetime employment is by no means universal for Japanese workers, the precedents and practices set by the largest firms strongly influence employment and training practices throughout the economy.

American experts helped establish the Japan Productivity Center and the Japan Industrial Training Association to meet growing training needs, especially in smaller firms. The initial focus on training supervisors as instructors helped shape the practice of integrated on-the-job training that has proven so successful. As with Japan's adoption of quality control practices pioneered in the United States, these postwar training efforts first borrowed U.S. practices, then refined and extended them.

Smaller Japanese firms sometimes benefit from assistance that large corporations provide to associations of first-tier suppliers.[29] For example, each of the three largest construction companies in Osaka has helped its leading subcontractors establish a local training center. Government grants also channel financing to these training centers. Finally, small firms in Japan often pool training resources through producers' cooperatives.

Training in Japan tends to be structured in terms of content, although delivered by managers and supervisors rather than specialists—both on the shopfloor and during the day or two per year that employees typically spend in a classroom setting. Their role as trainer helps managers stay in touch with the shopfloor and keep workers informed of company plans. It is no surprise that Japanese managers have more confidence in the usefulness of training than their U.S. counterparts. Moreover, the benefit/cost ratio is higher in Japan because so much training takes place on the job with little loss of working time. Employees quickly grasp the connections between new skills and their everyday work. And, as noted in chapter 1 (see box 1-B), many Japanese workers get more hours of training than their American counterparts. Not only is training in Japan more effective, there is more of it.

Vocational Credentials and Status

Other countries also work harder than the United States to maintain the quality of vocational education programs, seeking to keep them attuned to the needs of the labor market and to overcome widespread biases in favor of academic education. For example, Germany, South Korea, and to a lesser extent Japan, use skill certification as an incentive and symbol of achievement. The governments of Japan and Korea also support young people who participate in skills competitions (box 3-C).

Unrealistic attitudes and overemphasis on college help explain the disappointing record of high school vocational education programs in the United States (see ch. 8). Although post-secondary vocational education has a somewhat better track record, many graduates of such programs find their newly acquired skills ill-suited to the job market. Germany, in contrast, has been quite successful in creating and maintaining respect for blue- and grey-collar work: the concept of vocation is deeply ingrained, the link between formal qualifications and occupational status far stronger than in most countries. After 10 years of schooling, as required by law, about 90 percent of West Germans continue in some sort of formal education/training program—either an apprenticeship (three-quarters of the 90 percent who continue), an academic high school in preparation for university (20 percent), or a vocational high

---

[29]One-quarter of small- and medium-sized manufacturing firms responding to a 1984 survey reported that an affiliated parent firm had helped them with training. "New Technology Acquisition in Small Japanese Enterprises: Government Assistance and Private Initiative," report prepared for OTA under contract No. J3-4950 by D.H. Whittaker, May 1989, p. 23.

Box 3-C—*National and International Skills Competitions*

In 1950, Spain initiated the International Vocational Training Competition (called the International Youth Skill Olympics, or IYSO, in the United States). Entrants, who must be under age 23, compete biannually in areas ranging from welding to graphic design. In 1989, more than 400 people from 21 countries participated.

From 1975, when a U.S. team first entered, until 1983, the Americans finished last. Teams from South Korea, Japan, and Taiwan earned the highest scores, while European countries with apprenticeship systems also did well. By 1985, a U.S. team reached the middle rank.[1]

IYSO results mirror government policies for the support of vocational education and training. Japan, Korea, and Taiwan, among others, support national and international skills competitions to help encourage young people to enter skilled trades. In each of these countries, a government training agency sponsors the IYSO team; American entrants have been sponsored by the Vocational Industrial Clubs of America, a private nonprofit group. In other countries, government training agencies coach the contestants, sometimes provide living allowances, and may provide cash prizes to winners at local, national, and international levels. Korea, for example, uses money from a payroll levy both to support public vocational institutes (as discussed later in the chapter) and to provide substantial cash awards to winners of national and international skill Olympics.[2]

---

[1]The American team finished 11th among 18 competing nations in 1985, 13th out of 19 three years later, and 13th of 21 in 1989. "International Youth Skill Olympics Fact Sheet," Vocational Industrial Clubs of America, January 1990.

[2]Winners at the national level get about $9,200, and are automatically certified as "Class II" craftsmen. Those who win in the IYSO contest get a sum twice as large, plus exemption from military duty, special housing privileges, and scholarships. The Korean Government also gives winners seed money for starting their own businesses. Although these rewards may not have changed the views of Korean parents and students, who place high values on a college education, they have undoubtedly spurred on the teams that have won seven IYSO competitions. See "Training of Private Sector Employees in South Korea," report prepared for OTA under contract No. L3-4180 by Joe W. Lee and Youngho Lee, March 1990, p. 90. (Most of the information on Korea elsewhere in the chapter comes from this report.)

---

school (the remaining 5 percent). Skill certification helps encourage young people to prepare for occupations ranging from bartender to machinist to office assistant.

In Japan, many more young people—some 95 percent—go on to an academic high school than in Germany. Of the 90 percent that graduate, two-thirds attend an academic or vocational post-secondary institution; the others enter the labor market immediately. Vocational credentials get less emphasis than in Germany, although Japan's Ministry of Labor (MOL) established a national testing system in 1959, declaring its intent to "raise the social status of blue-collar workers by giving public recognition to the skill level which they have achieved."[30] The MOL administers examinations covering 130 occupational skills, with industry bearing most of the testing costs. In addition, the Ministry of International Trade and Industry oversees a special set of tests for skills needed in the electronics industry. Many firms have also created internal certification procedures as incentives for their employees. Japan's testing and certification standards tend to be much more specialized than those in Germany, and ongo-

ing informal evaluations by supervisors carry more weight within a company than formal qualifications.

Other Examples: South Korea and Sweden

Like a number of developing Asian nations, Korea has made education and training a central element in economic planning. Over the past 20 years, 3-year vocational high schools and 1-year training institutes, established under government auspices, have helped train some 2.4 million workers, half of Korea's current workforce (about 60 percent of whom are high school graduates).

Korean training practices draw on the German example. As in Germany, the Korean Government has sought to counter bias against occupational rather than academic skills through testing and certification programs, and by requiring government bodies at both local and national levels to preferentially hire workers with such credentials. Even more than in the FRG, training in Korea has been driven by government policies. Companies have often been reluctant partners, although it seems plain that the remarkable performance of the Korean economy—where labor productivity has grown at an average

---

[30]Cited in "Employee Training in Japan," op. cit., footnote 28, p. 28.

Photo credit: National Training Fund,
Sheet Metal and Air Conditioning Industry

Student practicing flame cutting.

rate of 10-12 percent annually and exports at 25-30 percent—owes much to education and training.

In Sweden, as in most countries with well-developed training systems, high-quality general education provides the foundation. Vocational preparation in Sweden bears the stamp of the country's strong trade unions, closely allied with the Social Democratic party. Swedish unions have traditionally opposed apprenticeships in private companies, fearing that employers will stress narrow job- and firm-specific skills. Instead, Sweden relies heavily on school-based vocational education through "integrated upper secondary schools" that provide both liberal arts and vocational courses. The government has recently added a third year to the vocational track, during which students spend at least half their time in on-the-job training.[31] About 55 percent of Swedish young people graduate from high school with a vocational specialty, after which they can

expect extensive on-the-job training and easy access to adult education.

Educational Preparation

It is no news that education in the United States compares poorly with a number of our economic rivals—a sad irony given the historic U.S. commitment to free and universal schooling. Although the schooling system helped support industrialization during an earlier era, the United States has fallen behind during the last several decades. The most dramatic evidence comes from international comparisons on standardized tests (table 3-5). Not only did American 13-year-olds rank near the bottom in the latest such comparison, but if Japanese and Taiwanese students had been included, U.S. performance would no doubt have looked even worse. Other tests have shown similar results, with widening gaps between the performance of U.S. and foreign students as grade levels increase.[32]

Today, the best American high schools continue to graduate students well-prepared for elite colleges and professional careers. Many others offer a decent education to students with the initiative to take advantage of it. But the quality of instruction varies greatly across the Nation, and American schools, generally speaking, do a poor job of serving average and below-average students. This hurts not only the people who find themselves entering adulthood lacking basic skills and the willingness to work and to learn but the competitive ability of U.S. industry. Japan offers a sharp contrast, with a tightly controlled nationwide curriculum completed by most young people. While the regimented Japanese educational system has its own dark side, the bottom half of Japan's labor force may be the best qualified in the world.

Compensating in part for weaknesses in primary and secondary schooling, and in employer-provided training, the United States can claim a well-developed system of adult education. Enrollments have grown from 8 percent of all adult Americans as

---

[31]The schools, not the companies, control the content of this on-the-job training. "Working Classes," *The Economist*, Nov. 12, 1988, p. 18.

[32]Students in other countries might get higher average scores in the higher grades if poorer students are selected out for early exits into the labor market. However, Americans test poorly even in the primary grades. For instance, gaps in performance between American, Japanese, and Taiwanese children in reading and mathematics have been found to grow between the first and fifth grades. Harold W. Stevenson et al., "Mathematics Achievement of Chinese, Japanese, and American Children," *Science*, Feb. 14, 1986, pp. 693-699. In mathematics and science tests conducted by the International Association for the Evaluation of Educational Achievement (IAEEA) between 1983 and 1986, the relative rank of U.S. students fell, from low at ages 10 and 14, to almost always the lowest at age 17. Kenneth Redd and Wayne Riddle, "Comparative Education: Statistics on Education in the United States and Selected Foreign Nations," Congressional Research Service, November 1988, pp. 54, 57, 59. In the IAEEA tests, Japanese students were at or near the top in both age groupings.

Table 3-5—Rank Ordering in Mathematics and Science Tests at Age 13[a]

Mathematics	Science
South Korea (568)	South Korea (550)
Spain (512)	United Kingdom (520)
United Kingdom (510)	Spain (504)
Ireland (504)	**United States (479)**
United States (474)	Ireland (469)

[a]By average score (in parentheses) on the International Assessment of Mathematics and Science, administered during 1988 by the Educational Testing Service to random samples of about 1,000 students in each country (from both public and private schools). In addition to the countries listed, the tests were given in four Canadian provinces; because no aggregate results for Canada are available, that country has been omitted from the table.

SOURCE: A.E. Lapointe, N.A. Mead, and G.W. Phillips, *A World of Differences: An International Assessment of Mathematics and Science* (Princeton, NJ: Educational Testing Service, 1989).

directly. In Germany, however, a partnership of employer associations, labor unions, and Federal, *Länder*, and local governments designs, delivers, and pays for apprenticeship, and increasingly, further training. Area training centers, funded equally by the Federal Government and local chambers of commerce, provide short courses for certified craftworkers as well as apprentices. They house training advisors who work directly with companies to design and deliver both apprenticeship and upgrade training programs. In addition, some firms and workers receive direct subsidies for training from a Federal payroll tax levy. The FRG also encourages firms to provide advanced programs through direct subsidies, technical assistance, and regulations.

long ago as 1957, to 14 percent in 1984.[33] Still, some nations show up better. Canada, for example, estimates that a quarter of employed people over age 17 participated in adult education during 1983 (the latest available year); nearly half of those surveyed were enrolled in job-related courses, with nearly half of those courses provided by employers.[34]

Germany has an extensive system of adult education, offering advanced technical courses at convenient times and often at no out-of-pocket cost to the worker. And given the near-reverential view so many Japanese have of education, it is no surprise to find widespread and effective adult education in that country. Many Japanese companies encourage or require employees to take courses in off hours, while the government pays firms that help their employees with the costs. Nihon Denso, like many other larger companies, also pays its employees a small stipend (about two-thirds of the minimum wage) for the time they spend on home study or in off-site classes. Correspondence schools cover subjects from steelmaking to bookkeeping. Given that self-study is widely valued throughout their society, many Japanese need little encouragement from employers.

In recent years, Japanese policies have shifted from their earlier focus on pre-employment training to emphasize upgrading the skills of employed workers. For example, many of the Skill Training Centers that once trained young people as craft workers now function as schools offering short courses for employees of nearby firms. Government bodies at both national and prefectural (local) levels channel payments to individuals, companies, and industry groups (such as the associations of first-tier suppliers mentioned earlier). To be eligible for MOL funds, companies must first submit an Enterprise Skill Development Plan. Smaller firms qualify for larger subsidies—e.g., half the cost of hiring teachers and purchasing in-house training materials, versus one-third for bigger companies. In total, Japan's prefectures spend about two-thirds as much on training as the MOL, supporting vocational colleges, skill development and training centers, and testing and certification programs.

Government Policies

Policy choices underlie many of the contrasts summarized in table 3-4 and discussed above. In the United States, the Federal Government rarely seeks to influence company training or to support training

Other governments have also looked to industry and trade associations for delivery of training, especially to smaller firms. Canada and Australia provide technical assistance for identifying training needs and designing training programs for groups set up jointly by unions and trade associations. Korea offers a package of incentives—including construction financing, low-cost land, subsidies for instructors' salaries, and free training equipment—to or-

[33]Susan T. Hill, *Trends in Adult Education 1969-1984* (Washington, DC: Department of Education, Center for Education Statistics, 1987), pp. 6-7. These are the most recent data available, gathered as part of the May 1984 Current Population Survey. The 1957 data is from Ivan Charner and Bryna Shore Fraser, "Access and Barriers to Adult Education and Training," report prepared for OTA under contract, 1986, p. 46.

[34]M.S. Devereaux, *One in Every Five: A Survey of Adult Education in Canada*, (Ottawa: Statistics Canada and the Department of the Secretary of State, 1984), table 7, p. 18. (Somewhat lower participation by men than women evidently accounts for the title of this publication.).

ganizations such as the Korea Machinery Industry Association.

Payroll-Based Levies

West Germany and a number of other countries tax payrolls to help pay for training. The FRG's 4-percent payroll tax—half charged to the company, half to the employee—goes to the Federal Employment Institute. Most of the Institute's budget provides income support for unemployed workers, but about 15 percent is spent on three types of training: 1) post-apprenticeship programs; 2) training in new technologies; and 3) retraining of unemployed workers. Most payments go to workers individually.

On launching its program of support for further training in 1969, the West German Government expected that most funds from the levy would be used to help firms retrain employed workers to use new technology and meet growing international competition. However, as long-term unemployment has grown and persisted, a growing fraction of the money has been targeted to displaced workers—during 1988 and 1989, over half (55 percent) of the participants were unemployed. Many of the employed participants are studying for certification as master craftworkers, while others are enrolled in on-the-job training. In addition to the payroll levy, the German Government supports the area training centers discussed above. Another source of government assistance is the *Länder*, which provide tuition aid to some workers for outside courses. Some *Länder* now require firms to give employees 1 or 2 weeks per year of paid ''training leave'' to attend outside seminars.

In France, Korea, and several other countries, payroll taxes are used to encourage company training: if a firm's training expenditures equal or exceed the levy, no payment is required. French companies employing 10 or more workers must devote 1.2 percent of their payroll costs to employee training.[35] (Another 0.5 percent is collected for apprenticeship training.) Firms can meet this ''obligation to spend''

by providing training themselves, by contracting with outside providers, or by joining in a multifirm training fund. Government has little control over what is taught or who is selected for training; some French companies take these programs much more seriously than others.

Korea requires all firms with over 300 employees to either spend a certain percentage of payroll (varying with industry sector and firm size) for training or pay a tax. Most of the tax money goes to support the extensive system of public vocational training institutes that provide a year of pre-employment training for young people. In part because of stringent requirements on the type and amount of training necessary to avoid the levy, and in part because it was originally quite low, most Korean companies simply paid the tax, whether or not they provided any training. In the 1980s, with Korea's first wave of industrialization completed and the economy beginning to shift from labor-intensive industries such as textiles towards those requiring higher skills, the government passed new legislation. Current law makes it easier for companies to satisfy the government's requirements, while raising the levy substantially. As a result, many more Korean firms, including smaller enterprises, have established in-house training programs complying with government standards. Funds raised through the levy help pay for cooperative training programs involving companies and the public training institutes. In these programs, entering 15-year-olds get 3 years of training and must then spend 4 years working for the participating firm—a ''dual system'' modeled on German apprenticeships.

Older Workers

Among the major industrial nations, only the United States and Japan have implemented employment and training policies specifically for older workers.[36] Evaluations of U.S. programs funded under the Older Americans Act and the Job Training Partnership Act indicate that they have been suc-

[35]Olivier Bertrand, ''Employment and Education Statistics in the Service Sector in France,'' report prepared for the Organisation for Economic Cooperation and Development, July 1988.

Companies can include the wages of those in training as part of the required expenditures, which were set at 1.1 percent of payrolls until 1987. Any company spending less than the current 1.2 percent requirement is supposed to pay the difference to the treasury, but most firms report spending more. Indeed, the government's figures show that payroll percentages devoted to training have increased steadily since the law was passed in 1971, and now exceed 2.5 percent of payrolls. (For 1987, 2.5 percent of French payrolls would be equivalent to about $4.3 billion.)

[36]Canada's government does fund a National Labor Market Innovations Program that supports pilot programs for training and employing older workers. Mary Trueman, ''Training of Older Workers in Canada,'' ILO discussion paper, International Labour Office, Geneva, May 1989.

cessful in placing older workers in jobs.[37] Nonetheless, most American firms have been reluctant to train older workers, nor do Federal programs encourage them to. The aging of the U.S. labor force will no doubt force both corporate officials and government policymakers to pay more attention to these issues over the next decade or two (see ch. 8).

In Japan, the government has urged firms to continue training their older employees, providing special subsidies for companies that train workers aged 45 and up.[38] These and other measures are intended to encourage large Japanese companies to offer training as part of life-long career development plans, rather than "farming out" middle-aged workers at lower pay to subsidiaries.

Lessons From Abroad

In Germany, widespread participation by companies, government bodies, and labor unions has kept the training system responsive to shifting demands for skills. Both business and labor have a stake in the system; both understand the need to adapt to ongoing changes in technology and international competition.

Japan's experience shows that comprehensive training need not carry a high price tag. If American firms embedded training in day-to-day operations like Japanese firms, using first-line supervisors as instructors, some would find they spent less on training than they do now (once they had trained their supervisors). But such an approach, by itself, would not be enough. As many Japanese firms have discovered, automation means that on-the-job training must be supplemented with classroom instruction to develop the broader and deeper skills needed by those who work with the new equipment. Despite such limitations, the Japanese approach suggests that many American firms could benefit from structured, on-the-job training as part of the daily routine for supervisors and shopfloor workers.

In addition, the payroll levies adopted by a number of countries show that such policies can spur increases in employer-provided training. But these levies also have limitations. Korean companies viewed the original requirements as onerous; few complied, preferring simply to pay the tax. In

France, on the other hand, government allows companies a great deal of latitude, with the result that some "training" consists of junkets for top management.

CONCLUDING REMARKS

High levels of mobility in the U.S. labor market, driven by both supply (people seeking new or better jobs) and demand (new companies, established enterprises seeking new workers), create continuing needs for training. At a minimum, newly hired employees need an introduction to the workplace—what the job requires, how the company views task assignments and responsibilities. Over and above these routine activities, new workplace technologies and new organizational practices entail training or retraining. Finally, American companies increasingly find they must provide some basic skills training, in addition to instruction in particular tasks. In their efforts to cut costs, improve quality, and enhance flexibility, companies are also relying on training to help motivate employees.

Most of the new jobs created in the U.S. economy over the next several decades will be in the services; relatively few service products trade internationally. Small firms will create more jobs than large firms; few small companies face direct international competition, regardless of whether their products are goods or services. Even so, the link between skills and competitiveness is a vital one. Each and every industry counts, regardless of whether firms in that industry are exposed to international competition. The need for training and retraining is pervasive; it is not just a matter of meeting the needs of growing sectors, growing occupations, or sectors beset by international competition.

Under intense pressure, often from imports, to improve quality while at the same time lowering costs, many American companies are reevaluating the ways in which work gets done, making sweeping changes in workplace organization. Together with shifts in consumer preferences and in markets for producer goods and services, the pressures have already led to substantial restructuring in U.S. industry. Like labor market churning, these changes

---

[37] Harold L. Sheppard and Sara E. Rix, "Training of Older Workers in the United States," ILO discussion paper No. 31, International Labour Office, Geneva, 1989.

[38] Masako M. Osako, *Training of Older Workers in Japan* (Geneva: International Labour Office, 1989).

—the subject of the next chapter—add to the demand for training.

Better training cannot but help in rebuilding U.S. competitiveness. Indeed, it is one of the essential steps. Training has proven central in aggressive corporate strategies stressing quality, flexibility, and customer service, as well as cost and price. Dispersed computing power for automating the back offices of banks places new demands on workers, just like computers for managing the flow of production in a textile mill. Management style is at least as important as worker training itself in responding to these demands: when a firm reorganizes production, it will probably need to retrain supervisors along with shopfloor workers. In larger U.S. corporations, particularly multinationals, high-level executives increasingly see continuous training as a necessary investment for competitive survival—on a par with investments in plant and equipment.

Even so, it remains true that German and Japanese firms are more likely to view training as an investment, U.S. firms to see it as a cost. And more than ever before, the international economy pits American workers against those in other countries. If the U.S. labor force fares poorly in this head-to-head competition, American living standards will suffer. Unemployment levels may rise, particularly among the disadvantaged. American companies can move operations abroad. Few American workers have such alternatives.

Part III
How Do People Learn?

[8]

Goals: An Approach to Motivation and Achievement

Elaine S. Elliott and Carol S. Dweck
Laboratory of Human Development
Harvard University

This study tested a framework in which goals are proposed to be central determinants of achievement patterns. Learning goals, in which individuals seek to increase their competence, were predicted to promote challenge-seeking and a mastery-oriented response to failure regardless of perceived ability. Performance goals, in which individuals seek to gain favorable judgments of their competence or avoid negative judgments, were predicted to produce challenge-avoidance and learned helplessness when perceived ability was low and to promote certain forms of risk-avoidance even when perceived ability was high. Manipulations of relative goal value (learning vs. performance) and perceived ability (high vs. low) resulted in the predicted differences on measures of task choice, performance during difficulty, and spontaneous verbalizations during difficulty. Particularly striking was the way in which the performance goal–low perceived ability condition produced the same pattern of strategy deterioration, failure attribution, and negative affect found in naturally occurring learned helplessness. Implications for theories of motivation and achievement are discussed.

Past research (Diener & Dweck, 1978, 1980) documented and described two strikingly different reactions to failure. Despite previous success on a task, children displaying the "helpless" response quickly began to attribute their failures to low ability, to display negative affect, and to show marked deterioration in performance. In contrast, those with the mastery-oriented response did not focus on failure attributions; instead, they exhibited solution-oriented self-instructions, as well as sustained or increased positive affect and sustained or improved performance.

Although the research has clearly demonstrated these different patterns, the question that remains unanswered is why two groups of children who are completely equal in ability would react to failure in such discrepant ways—that is, why do helpless children react as though they have received an indictment of their ability, but mastery-oriented children react as though they have been given useful feedback about learning and mastery. These findings suggested that helpless and mastery-oriented children are pursuing different goals in achievement situations, with helpless children seeking to document their ability (but failing to do so) and mastery-oriented children seeking to

increase their ability (and receiving information on how to do so).

The purpose of our study was to experimentally test the hypothesis that different goals set up the observed helpless and mastery-oriented patterns.

Specifically, we propose that there are two major goals that individuals pursue in achievement situations: (a) performance goals, in which individuals seek to maintain positive judgments of their ability and avoid negative judgments by seeking to prove, validate, or document their ability and not discredit it; and (b) learning goals, in which individuals seek to increase their ability or master new tasks (Nicholls & Dweck, 1979). It is hypothesized that performance goals, which focus individuals on the adequacy of their ability, will render them vulnerable to the helpless response in the face of failure, setting up low ability attributions, negative affect, and impaired performance. In contrast, it is hypothesized that learning goals, which focus individuals on increasing their ability over time, will promote the mastery-oriented response to obstacles: strategy formulation, positive affect, and sustained performance.

To elaborate, one may view each goal as generating its own set of concerns and as creating its own framework for processing incoming information. Individuals who pursue performance goals are concerned with the measurement of their ability and can be seen as posing the question, Is my ability adequate? Subsequent events, such as failure outcomes, may be seen as providing information that is relevant to this question, leading some individuals (particularly those who may already doubt their ability) to low ability attributions and their sequelae.

In contrast, individuals who pursue learning goals are concerned with developing their ability over time and can be seen as posing the question, How can I best acquire this skill or mas-

This research was conducted in partial fulfillment of the requirement for the doctoral degree at the University of Illinois by Elaine S. Elliott.

We wish to thank the people who have contributed in various ways to this study. In particular, we would like to acknowledge Susan Harner for serving as experimenter and Mary Bandura for her input on drafts of this article.

Correspondence concerning this article should be addressed to Elaine Elliott, OSM Associates, 27 Grove Hill Avenue, Newtonville, Massachusetts 02160.

Journal of Personality and Social Psychology, 1988, Vol. 54, No. 1, 5–12
Copyright 1988 by the American Psychological Association, Inc. 0022-3514/88/$00.75

6   ELAINE S. ELLIOTT AND CAROL S. DWECK

Table 1

Summary of Goals and Predicted Achievement Patterns

		Predicted achievement pattern	
Goal value	Confidence (perceived level of ability[a])	Task choice	Response to difficulty
Performance goal is highlighted	High	Sacrifice learning and choose moderate or moderately difficult task to display competence	Mastery-orientation of effective problem-solving
	Low	Sacrifice learning and choose moderately easy task to avoid display of incompetence	Learned-helpless response of deterioration in problem-solving and negative affect
Learning goal is highlighted	High or low	Choose learning at risk of displaying mistakes to increase competence	Mastery-orientation of effective problem-solving

[a] A distinction is made between perceived current ability (perceived level of current skill) and potential ability (perceived capacity to acquire new skills). Perceived current ability was manipulated to be high or low. Perceived potential ability was manipulated to be high and constant across all conditions.

ter this task? Subsequent events, such as failure outcomes, may then provide information that is relevant to this question, leading individuals to alter their strategies or escalate their efforts. Here, even individuals with poor opinions of their current ability should display the mastery-oriented pattern, because (a) they are not focused on judgments of their current ability, (b) errors are not as indicative of goal failure within a learning goal, and (c) low current ability in a valued area may make skill acquisition even more desirable.

The specific hypotheses of our study are depicted in Table 1. It is predicted that when goals (performance or learning) and perceptions of current ability level (low or high) are induced experimentally, the following patterns will result: (a) Performance goals and high perceived ability will allow a mastery-oriented response (but will lead subjects to sacrifice learning opportunities that involve the risk of errors), (b) performance goals and low perceived ability will create the helpless response, and (c) learning goals and either high or low perceived ability will result in the mastery-oriented response to failure.

How, more specifically, might the performance goal–low perceived ability condition act to create debilitation? What are the particular mechanisms through which impairment occurs? Although these factors are not tested separately here, we suggest that this condition can in itself generate many of the different cognitive and affective factors that have been found to be associated with performance disruption during difficulty: (a) low ability attributions that lead to a loss of belief in the utility of effort (e.g., Ames, 1984; Diener & Dweck, 1978; Dweck, 1975); (b) defensive withdrawal of effort, given that continued effort may further document low ability (e.g., Frankl & Snyder, 1978; Leggett, 1986; Nicholls, 1976, 1984); (c) worry about goal failure that can divert attention from the task (e.g., Spielberger, Morris, & Liebert, 1968; Wine, 1971, 1982); (d) negative affect, such as anxiety or shame, that can motivate escape attempts (e.g., Weiner, 1972, 1982); and (e) blockage of intrinsic rewards from task involvement, solution-oriented effort, or even progress, due to threatened negative judgment (Deci & Ryan, 1980; Lepper, 1980; Lepper & Greene, 1978). Thus, *goal* may be a con-

struct that organizes these previously distinct cognitive and affective factors and helps us to understand the conditions under which they arise.

The focus of individuals who pursue learning goals (whether they believe their ability to be high or low) is on improving ability over time, not on proving current ability. As noted, obstacles will not as readily be seen to imply goal failure and will, therefore, not require defensive maneuvers, not as readily generate anxiety, and not detract from the intrinsic rewards shown to derive from involvement and progress on a valued task.

Method

Overview

There were four experimental contrasts: feedback that the child's current skill level on the experimental task was either low or high was crossed with task instructions that highlighted the value of either a performance (look competent) or a learning (increase competence) goal.

Children's beliefs about their current level of skill on the experimental task were manipulated via feedback on a pattern recognition task. Half the children were told that this task revealed that they currently had high ability and half were told that they currently had low ability for the experimental task. All were told that they had the capacity to acquire new knowledge or skills from the task.

In the second part of the study, another experimenter, who was unaware of the child's ability feedback, gave instructions that highlighted (relatively) either a learning or a performance goal (i.e., high value for learning and moderate value for performance vs. high value for performance and moderate value for learning). Half the children were assigned to each of the goal value conditions.

There were three dependent variables: choice of tasks, performance during difficulty, and spontaneous verbalizations during difficulty. All children were given a choice of tasks, each embodying one goal: (a) one described as a learning task (i.e., continued risks of mistakes and confusion during the acquisition process, but the task would promote skill development); and (b) another described as a performance task (i.e., nothing new would be learned, but the task would allow one to display or avoid display of one's skills by choice of three difficulty levels). In fact, all were given the same discrimination task, which was designed to allow comparison of groups on effectiveness of problem-solving strategies and on spontaneous verbalizations (e.g., attributions, expression of positive or negative affect, etc.).

Predictions for each of the experimental groups are summarized in Table 1.

Participants

The participants were 101 fifth-grade children (57 girls and 44 boys) from semirural schools. Roughly equal numbers of subjects had been randomly assigned to conditions, but due to time limits imposed by the school's schedules, several sessions could not be completed, resulting in unequal cell sizes: 15 girls and 12 boys in the learning goal–low ability condition, 14 girls and 10 boys in the learning goal–high ability condition, 13 girls and 10 boys in the performance goal–low ability condition, and 15 girls and 12 boys in the performance goal–high ability condition.

An additional 9 girls and 8 boys and 15 girls and 14 boys participated in the first and second pilot study, respectively.

Tasks and Procedures

Tasks and procedures for manipulating ability perceptions. A pattern recognition task adapted from Glanzer, Huttenlocher, and Clark (1963) was used to manipulate perceptions of ability. Each stimulus consisted of some combination of five geometric forms drawn in yellow or blue on a card. The subject was shown a card for 2 s and was then asked to recognize the pattern from among three alternative cards. Each subject was administered 10 cards. This task was sufficiently complex so that subjects were unsure of the correctness of their responses. This allowed the tester to give predetermined feedback on performance.

The experimenter instructed the children that their performance would indicate how good they presentlv were at this type of work and explained the details of the task. To ensure that children who would be receiving high ability feedback did not attribute their performances to good luck, children were told that even the kinds of guesses they made would indicate how they would do on the later work. Children were randomly assigned to the low and high ability feedback conditions.

All children were told that they had the capacity to acquire knowledge from the tasks to be presented by the experimenter. This was done in order to ensure that all children had high confidence in their ability to learn. Hence, if children sacrificed learning, it would be known that sacrifice of learning did not come from low confidence in learning. It could also be shown that learned helplessness occurs with the presence of a performance goal despite high confidence in ability to learn. In other words, a strong case is made if the learning option has a high expectancy and moderately high value (i.e., if there is a good alternative and it is not taken and not kept in mind for mastery purposes).

Tasks and procedures for highlighting goal value. After the children were given the instructions described above, the first experimenter introduced the second experimenter to the children and left the room with her materials. The next experimenter was blind to the children's ability conditions. She presented all children with two boxes: one described as containing the learning task and the other described as containing the performance task with its three levels of difficulty: moderately easy, moderate, and moderately difficult. The identical discrimination task had been placed in both boxes.

The presentation of the boxes was counterbalanced. (Differences between goal value manipulations are described below.) All children were given the following description of the tasks in the two boxes.

> *Performance task.* In this box we have problems of different levels. Some are hard, some are easier. If you pick this box, although you won't learn new things, it will really show me what kids can do.

> *Learning task.* If you pick the task in this box, you'll probably learn a lot of new things. But you'll probably make a bunch of mistakes, get a little confused, maybe feel a little dumb at times—but eventually you'll learn some useful things.

Under conditions that highlighted the value of the performance goal, children were told that their performance was being filmed and would be normatively evaluated by experts. It was assumed that the filming instructions would make the value of displaying competence high and that the general description of the learning task would make the value of increasing competence moderate.

Under conditions that highlighted the value of the learning goal, no film was mentioned. In addition to the general description of the learning task, children were told that the learning task might be a big help in school, because it "sharpens the mind" and learning to do it well could help their studies. It was assumed that this added information about the learning task would make the value of increasing competence high and that the mere presence of the experimenter would make the value of displaying competence moderate.

As can be seen, we made both goals available in each condition rather than presenting one goal per condition. This was done to mimic real-world choices in which the two goals are valued and available, and in which individuals must sacrifice one goal as a result of high value on the other. That is, the learning goal leads individuals to risk performance failure and the performance goal makes individuals sacrifice learning opportunities.

Procedures for measuring dependent variables. There were three dependent variables: task choice, problem-solving effectiveness during the discrimination task, and spontaneous verbalizations during the discrimination task.

Children's task choice preferences were taken after the manipulation of the goal. To ensure that children felt no demand from the experimenter to choose a particular task, children were told that different children like to choose different tasks and that she was only interested in what tasks children choose.

After children indicated preferences, all worked on the same discrimination task, which was found in both the learning and the performance boxes. For those who chose the learning box, instructions for the discrimination task were given immediately. For those who chose the performance task, the three levels were reviewed and the children were asked to indicate their two preferences. All children who chose the performance task were then given the "moderate" task, which could be presented as consonant with their choice in that it was either one of their two choices or could be described as the average of their two choices. This allowed comparison of the experimental groups when subjects believed that they were performing a task that allowed inferences about ability.

The discrimination task, used to measure problem-solving effectiveness and spontaneous verbalizations, was adopted from Diener and Dweck (1978). Each child was presented with four training problems and three test problems. A problem consisted of a deck of cards with each card displaying two figures that varied on three dimensions: color (e.g., red or blue), form (e.g., square or triangle), and symbol in the center of the form (e.g., dot or star; see Figure 1). At the beginning of each new deck of cards the experimenter named each of the six stimulus values and told the child only one was correct for the entire deck. Children pointed to the left or right figure and the experimenter said "correct" if the figure contained the stimulus value that was chosen for the deck.

To monitor hypothesis testing on Training Problems 3 and 4 and all test problems, the children received feedback about the correctness of their responses on every fourth card (Levine, 1966). A hypothesis was defined as the consistent selection of a particular stimulus property, such as the color red, over four trials prior to feedback. The cards were varied in a systematic fashion so that the child's hypothesis about the correct solution could be inferred unambiguously from his or her pattern of choices of the left or right side. For example, a child who is testing the hypothesis, "triangle," would choose cards in the sequence of left, left, right, left, as can be seen in Figure 1.

On the fourth training problem, the children were asked to begin "thinking out loud" (see Diener & Dweck, 1978) when they worked on the problems. They were told that we were interested in what kinds of things children think about while they do tasks of this nature. To dispel inhibitions about making task irrelevant statements, it was stressed that children think about many different kinds of things.

Because one goal of the study was to examine the effects of failure feedback on problem-solving strategies during the testing, rather than to test children's hypothesis use per se, each child was given extensive training prior to the test problems. The experimenter repeated a training problem until the child reached a criterion of six successive correct responses. A hint was provided each time the training deck was repeated (e.g., "The correct answer is one of the two shapes, either the square or triangle").

On the three test problems, the child received feedback after every fourth response and was asked to verbalize his or her thoughts. Each of the three test decks was gone through only once. This allowed the children to search for the solution but ensured that, given their strategy level, they would not have tested all possible solutions. The feedback always consisted of "wrong," thus permitting the monitoring of strategy change following continued failure feedback.

Children were very carefully debriefed to make sure that all left feeling proud of their performance. The second experimenter told them that they certainly did very well on her tasks. She also said that sometimes children who do poorly on the first task really do show a lot of talent, that it does not always indicate how well children will do. She added that because they had done such good work, she had even put in some problems that were intended for older children.

Two pilot studies were run to ensure the effectiveness of the ability manipulation and goal value manipulation. The pilot questions and results are presented in Table 2.

Results

Pilot Studies

Pilot Studies 1 and 2 revealed that the ability and the goal value manipulations were effective (Table 2).

Choice of Tasks

The number of children in each of the four conditions who chose the learning and the performance box was analyzed by means of a chi-square test. As expected, no significant effect was found for ability feedback. The data were collapsed across ability and a chi-square test was performed on the number of children who chose either the learning or the performance box in performance and learning conditions. As predicted, children more often chose the learning box (82.4%) when the utility of the knowledge was high and the performance box (66%) when the importance of evaluation was high, $\chi^2(1, N = 101) = 22.35$, $p < .001$.

The number of children in the high and low ability feedback conditions who chose each of the three difficulty levels was analyzed. The results supported our predictions. About 33% of the children who were given low feedback chose the moderately easy level and none of the children chose the moderately hard level. On the other hand, only 9% of the children who were given high feedback chose the moderately easy level and 14% chose the moderately difficult level, $\chi^2(2, N = 42) = 5.91$, $p = .05$.

Performance Measures

Classification of strategies. To assess the effectiveness of each group's problem-solving efforts, their hypotheses were classified as useful strategies (dimension checking and hypothesis checking, in descending order of sophistication) or as ineffectual strategies (stimulus preference, position alternation, and position preference, also in descending order of sophistication). Useful strategies are sequences of hypotheses that, when followed perfectly, will lead to problem solution. Ineffectual strategies are sequences of hypotheses that can never lead to problem solution (see Diener & Dweck, 1978, for a fuller description of strategies).

Training measures: Performance prior to failure. To determine the comparability of groups prior to the test trials, several ease-of-training measures were analyzed: number of hints, number of ineffectual hypotheses, and number of times children used dimension checking versus hypothesis checking during training. These training trial measures were not significant except for a single effect on Trial 2 and on Trial 3, and all differences were eliminated by the training trial immediately preceding the failure test trials.

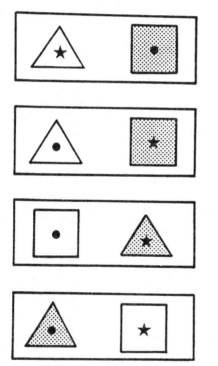

Figure 1. Example of four consecutive stimulus cards that allowed the tracking of a hypothesis over the no-feedback trials.

GOALS: AN APPROACH TO MOTIVATION AND ACHIEVEMENT   9

Table 2
Ability and Goal Value Manipulations

Pilot question	Manipulation	M	df	t
Right now, how good do you think you are on these tasks?	High present ability feedback	5.33	15	2.04**
	Low present ability feedback	4.37		
How good do you think you'll be at learning new things, developing new skills from these tasks?	High present ability feedback	5.00	15	.23
	Low present ability feedback	5.12		
How important is it to you that I (experimenter)/ experts think your work is good?	High evaluation	5.40	27	1.83**
	Moderate evaluation	4.54		
How important is it to you that you learn new things and develop new abilities from these tasks?	High skill utility instruction	6.23	27	1.54*
	Moderate skill utility instruction	5.40		

*$p < .10$. **$p < .05$.

An Ability × Goal interaction was found on Trial 2 for the number of hints, $F(1, 97) = 8.51$, $p < .005$, (mean number of hints was 0.1 for the performance goal–low perceived ability group, 0.7 for the performance goal–high perceived ability group, 0.5 for the learning goal–low perceived ability group, and 0.3 for the learning goal–high perceived group). A main effect on Trial 3 was also found for the stimulus preference hypothesis, with groups under the performance conditions ($M = .51$) using this ineffectual hypothesis more often than groups under the learning conditions ($M = .24$), $F(1, 94) = 4.08$, $p < .05$.

Strategy use on Trials 3 and 4 was also analyzed. A chi-square analysis was performed on the number of children in each condition using hypothesis checking versus dimension checking. No significant effects were found for Trials 3 or 4.

Test measures: Strategy change after failure. Analyses were performed to test for the predicted changes in strategy use from Test 1 to Test 3. To ensure that there were no baseline differences between groups on Test 1, a chi-square analysis was performed on the number of children in each condition using ineffectual hypotheses, hypothesis checking, or dimension checking. No significant differences were found between the low and high ability groups in the learning condition, $\chi^2(2, N = 51) = 1.72$, $p = .42$, nor in the performance condition, $\chi^2(2, N = 50) = 3.02$, $p = .22$.

Given no significant baseline differences in Test 1, children's strategies (ineffectual strategy use, hypothesis checking, or dimension checking) were classified as improving, remaining the same, or deteriorating on Test 1 versus Test 3 (Table 3).

As predicted, there were differences between low and high ability groups under performance but not under learning conditions, although this difference fell just short of significance. Under the performance condition, 43.5% of the low ability group deteriorated and only 8.7% improved from Test 1 to Test 3. In contrast, only 29.6% of the high ability children deteriorated, whereas 37.0% of them actually improved, $\chi^2(2, N = 50) = 5.47$, $p = .06$.

In addition to the chi-square, a McNemar test (Siegel, 1956) for the significance of change was used to test the significance of the observed changes for each of the four experimental groups. There were no significant changes from Test 1 to Test 3 for any group except the performance goal–low perceived ability group. These children showed a significant tendency to deteriorate in use of problem-solving strategies from Test 1 to Test 3, $\chi^2(1,$

$N = 23) = 4.08$, $p < .05$. These results replicated the Diener and Dweck (1978, 1980) findings for children with learned helplessness.

Verbalizations

Raters. Two independent raters, blind to the condition of each subject, categorized verbalizations according to the classification used by Diener and Dweck (1978). The mean interrater reliability for these categories was computed by using the conservative method of evaluating percentage agreements for each category separately. Only categories with mean interrater reliabilities greater than 80% were used in the study. These categories included statements of useful task strategy, statements of ineffectual task strategy, attributions, statements of negative affect, and solution-irrelevant statements. Only verbalizations on which there was agreement were used in the analyses.

Training. Verbalizations were recorded on the last training trial prior to failure trials. Analyses showed that as in the Diener and Dweck (1978) study, there were no verbalization differences among groups during training.

Testing. Contingency tables for verbalizations were analyzed with a chi-square or a Fisher's exact test. Several significant differences were found among the verbalizations of the different groups (Table 4). The attributional category includes statements that attribute performance on the task to lack or loss of

Table 3
Percentage of Low and High Ability Feedback Children in Each condition Whose Hypothesis-Testing Strategy Improved, Remained the Same, or Deteriorated Over the Three Failure Trials

Strategy status	Condition			
	Learning goal		Performance goal	
	Low	High	Low	High
Improved	22.2	20.8	8.7	37.0
No change	44.4	45.8	47.8	33.3
Deteriorated	33.3	33.3	43.5	29.6

Table 4
Percentage of Low and High Ability Children in Each
Condition Who Make Verbalizations
During the Failure Problems

	Condition			
	Learning goal		Performance goal	
Verbalizations	Low	High	Low	High
Statements of attribution	3.7	8.3	26.1	3.7
Statements of negative affect	3.7	0.0	30.4	3.7

ability, lack of effort, task difficulty, experimenter's unfairness, or lack of luck. An analysis of the number of children in each group who made attributional statements during the failure trials supported the original predictions. Under the learning condition there was no difference between low and high ability groups. Neither high nor low ability groups were likely to make attributions for failure. However, under the performance conditions there was a significant difference between low and high ability groups. Under the performance condition, children given low ability feedback more frequently made attributions for failure, whereas only 4% of the high ability feedback group made such an attribution (Fisher's exact test, $p = .03$).

Particularly noteworthy is that all of the children in the performance goal–low perceived ability group attributed failure to an uncontrollable cause. None attributed failure to lack of effort, a controllable and modifiable factor. Of the low ability group who made attributional statements, half attributed their failures to themselves. These statements reflected a perceived lack or loss of ability such as "I'm not very good at this" or "I'm confused." The remaining children in this group made statements that fit into various attributional categories including luck ("I accidentally picked the wrong one"), task difficulty ("This is hard and still getting harder"), and experimenter unfairness ("Seems like you're switching on me").

Analysis of verbalizations of negative affect also supported predictions. Under the learning condition, neither low nor high ability groups were likely to express negative affect during the failure trials. Under the performance condition, however, there was a significant difference between ability groups (Fisher's exact test, $p = .01$) as 30% of the low ability group expressed negative affect during the failure test trials. These included statements like "After this (problem), then I get to go?" "This is boring," "My stomach hurts," and "I'm going to hate this part" (stated prior to a "wrong" feedback). Only one child in the high ability group expressed negative affect during the failure test trials.

There were no differences among groups in the remaining verbalization categories: solution-irrelevant statements and statements of effective and ineffectual task strategy.

Similar to the learned helpless children in the Diener and Dweck (1978) study, verbalizations of the performance goal–low perceived ability group were characterized by attributions for their failure to uncontrollable factors and by statements of negative affect. In contrast, similar to the mastery-oriented chil-

dren of the Diener and Dweck study, verbalizations of the performance goal–high perceived ability condition and verbalizations of both high and low ability–learning goal conditions were marked by an absence of both attributions and negative affect during the failure trials.

Discussion

This study addressed the question of children's behavioral, cognitive, and affective patterns in achievement situations. When will children undertake challenging achievement tasks and exhibit the mastery-oriented response to difficulty? What underlies children's avoidance of challenging tasks and the more interfering, learned helpless response to failure? Why do these children allow little latitude for learning and focus prematurely on negative outcomes as a reflection of a personal deficit (i.e., low ability)?

The results of this study suggest that children's achievement goals are critical determinants of these patterns. When these achievement goals were fostered experimentally, the constellation of mastery-oriented and helpless achievement responses were created in their entirety. Specifically, when the value of the performance goal was highlighted and children believed they had low ability, they responded to feedback about mistakes in the characteristic learned helpless manner: making the attribution that mistakes reflected a lack of ability, responding to them with negative affect, and giving up attempts to find effective ways of overcoming those mistakes despite "ability to learn."

When the value of a performance goal was highlighted and children believed their current skills were high, they responded in a mastery-oriented manner in the face of obstacles. These children persisted in attempts to find solutions and did not make attributions for failure or express negative affect. Yet, like the performance-goal children who believed their current skills were low, performance-goal children with high perceived ability also passed up the opportunity to increase their skills on a task that entailed public mistakes.

In contrast to the condition in which the value of the performance goal was highlighted, when the learning goal value was salient, children's beliefs about their current skills were irrelevant in determining their achievement behavior. Regardless of whether they perceived their skills to be high or low, they sought to increase competence. That is, they opted for challenging tasks and did not forego opportunities to learn new skills, even with public errors. These children, regardless of their beliefs about their current skills, responded to failure in a mastery-oriented manner—their problem-solving strategies became more sophisticated.

Future studies are necessary to tease apart the aspects of the manipulations that affected the observed results. For example, our attempts to increase the salience of evaluation could have heightened concern about evaluation by adult experts or could have increased feelings of competition with peers. Regardless, we assume this would impact on the value of the performance goal. Dweck and Elliott (1983) considered other factors (e.g., intrinsic motivation and expectancies) that may influence goal values and confidence.

More generally, the results of our study suggest that learning and performance goals may be a very useful approach to understand achievement patterns (see also Dweck & Elliott, 1983; and Nicholls, 1984, for further discussion of this approach). Our research suggests that each of the achievement goals runs off a different "program" with different commands, decision rules, and inference rules, and hence, with different cognitive, affective, and behavioral consequences. Each goal, in a sense, creates and organizes its own world—each evoking different thoughts and emotions and calling forth different behaviors.

We believe this learning and performance goals framework has the potential to build and expand on past approaches to achievement behavior. Past studies may be classified into two categories: (a) approaches that focus on specific mediators of achievement, which include the attributional approach (Weiner, 1972, 1982; Weiner, Frieze, Kukla, Reed, Rest, & Rosenbaum, 1971), the evaluation anxiety approach (Mandler & Sarason, 1952; Sarason, Davidson, Lighthall, Waite, & Ruebush, 1960; Sarason & Mandler, 1952; Wine, 1971, 1982), and the social learning approach (Battle, 1965, 1966; V. C. Crandall, 1967, 1969; V. J. Crandall, 1963; V. J. Crandall, Katkovsky, & Preston, 1960); and (b) approaches that focus on general energizers of achievement behavior, which include the work within the need for achievement tradition (Atkinson, 1957, 1964; Atkinson & Feather, 1966; Heckhausen, 1967; McClelland, Atkinson, Clark, & Lowell, 1953).

Similar to researchers in the first category, we attempted to precisely delineate specific mediators and link these to specific achievement behaviors in testable ways. Our approach, however, puts specific motivational measures within a broader context of a more general theory of achievement goals and attempts to show how mediators such as attributions and anxiety follow from a focus on particular goals and how they represent part of a coherent pattern of mediators.

As to the second category of researchers who have attempted to measure the underlying motives by using global measures (such as the Thematic Apperception Test [Murray, 1938]) and then to use these to predict achievement behavior, we suggest these global motive measures may be viewed as the "grand sum" of the cognitive and affective measures that are found by researchers focusing on specific mediators. It may be that this property makes their approach useful for prediction (e.g., task choice) but less useful for understanding the specific motivational mediators and for precisely elucidating the pattern of individual and situational influences. Our approach, instead, suggests the ways in which goal orientation interacts with confidence to set in motion a sequence of specific processes that influence, in turn, task choice, performance, and persistence.

In conclusion, our experiment provides support for an approach to achievement behavior that emphasizes learning and performance achievement goals as the critical determinants of achievement patterns. It is suggested that this framework can provide a general, yet precise, context for systematically understanding the specific mediators of individual differences in and situational influences on motivational patterns. To the extent that performance and learning goals can be adopted with respect to any personal attribute and not just ability (to judge/validate the attribute vs. to develop the attribute), our framework may provide a useful tool for the general study of motivation.

References

Ames, C. (1984). Achievement attributions and self-instructions under competitive and individualistic goal structures. *Journal of Educational Psychology, 76*, 478–487.

Atkinson, J. W. (1957). Motivational determinants of risk-taking behavior. *Psychological Review, 64*, 359–372.

Atkinson, J. W. (1964). *An introduction to motivation.* Princeton, NJ: Van Nostrand.

Atkinson, J. W., & Feather, N. T. (Eds.). (1966). *A theory of achievement motivation.* New York: Wiley.

Battle, E. S. (1965). Motivational determinants of academic task persistence. *Journal of Personality and Social Psychology, 2*, 209–218.

Battle, E. S. (1966). Motivational determinants of academic competence. *Journal of Personality and Social Psychology, 4*, 634–642.

Crandall, V. C. (1967). Achievement behavior in the young child. In W. W. Hartup (Ed.), *The young child: Review of research* (pp. 165–185). Washington, DC: National Association for the Education of Young Children.

Crandall, V. C. (1969). Sex differences in expectancy of intellectual and academic reinforcement. In C. P. Smith (Ed.), *Achievement-related motives in children* (pp. 11–45). New York: Russell Sage Foundation.

Crandall, V. J. (1963). Achievement. In H. Stevenson (Ed.), *Child psychology: Sixty-second yearbook of the National Society for the Study of Education* (pp. 416–459). Chicago: University of Chicago Press.

Crandall, V. J., Katkovsky, W., & Preston, A. (1960). A conceptual formulation for some research on children's achievement development. *Child Development, 31*, 787–797.

Deci, E. L., & Ryan, R. M. (1980). The empirical exploration of intrinsic motivational processes. In L. Berkowitz (Ed.), *Advances in experimental social psychology* (Vol. 13, pp. 39–80). New York: Academic Press.

Diener, C. I., & Dweck, C. S. (1978). An analysis of learned helplessness: Continuous changes in performance, strategy, and achievement cognitions following failure. *Journal of Personality and Social Psychology, 36*, 451–462.

Diener, C. I., & Dweck, C. S. (1980). An analysis of learned helplessness: II. The processing of success. *Journal of Personality and Social Psychology, 39*, 940–952.

Dweck, C. S. (1975). The role of expectations and attributions in the alleviation of learned helplessness. *Journal of Personality and Social Psychology, 31*, 674–685.

Dweck, C. S., & Elliott, E. S. (1983). Achievement motivation. In E. M. Hetherington (Ed.), *Socialization, personality, and social development* (pp. 643–691). New York: Wiley.

Frankl, A., & Snyder, M. L. (1978). Poor performance following unsolvable problems: Learned helplessness or egotism? *Journal of Personality and Social Psychology, 36*, 1415–1423.

Glanzer, M., Huttenlocher, J., & Clark, W. H. (1963). Systematic operations involving concept problems. *Psychological Monographs, 77*, 1–14.

Heckhausen, H. (1967). *The anatomy of achievement motivation.* New York: Academic Press.

Leggett, E. (1986, April). *Individual differences in effort–ability inference rules: Implications for causal judgments.* Paper presented at the meeting of the Eastern Psychological Association, New York, NY.

Lepper, M. R. (1980). Intrinsic and extrinsic motivation in children: Detrimental effects of superfluous social controls. In W. A. Collins (Ed.), *Minnesota symposium on child psychology* (Vol. 14, pp. 155–214). Hillsdale, NJ: Erlbaum.

Lepper, M. R., & Greene, D. (Eds.) (1978). *The hidden costs of reward: New perspectives on the psychology of human motivation.* Hillsdale, NJ: Erlbaum.

Levine, M. (1966). Hypothesis behavior by humans during discrimination learning. *Journal of Experimental Psychology, 71*, 331–338.

Mandler, G., & Sarason, S. B. (1952). A study of anxiety and learning. *Journal of Abnormal and Social Psychology, 47,* 166–173.

McClelland, D. C., Atkinson, J. W., Clark, R. A., & Lowell, E. L. (1953). *The achievement motive.* New York: Appleton-Century-Crofts.

Murray, H. A. (1938). *Explorations in personality.* New York: Oxford University Press.

Nicholls, J. G. (1976). Effort is virtuous but it's better to have ability: Evaluative responses to perceptions of effort and ability. *Journal of Research in Personality, 10,* 306–315.

Nicholls, J. G. (1984). Achievement motivation: Conceptions of ability, subjective experience, task choice, and performance. *Psychological Review, 91,* 328–346.

Nicholls, J. G., & Dweck, C. S. (1979). *A definition of achievement motivation.* Unpublished manuscript. University of Illinois at Champaign-Urbana.

Sarason, S. B., Davidson, K., Lighthall, F., Waite, F., & Ruebush, B. (1960). *Anxiety in elementary school children.* New York: Wiley.

Sarason, S. B., & Mandler, G. (1952). Some correlates of test anxiety. *Journal of Abnormal and Social Psychology, 47,* 561–565.

Siegel, S. (1956). *Nonparametric statistics for the behavioral sciences.* New York: McGraw-Hill.

Spielberger, M., Morris, L., & Liebert, R. (1968). Cognitive and emotional components of test anxiety: Temporal factors. *Psychological Reports, 20,* 451–456.

Weiner, B. (1972). *Theories of motivation: From mechanism to cognition.* Chicago: Markham.

Weiner, B. (1982). An attribution theory of motivation and emotion. In H. Krohne & L. Laux (Eds.), *Achievement, stress, and anxiety* (pp. 223–245). Washington, DC: Hemisphere.

Weiner, B., Frieze, I. H., Kukla, A., Reed, L., Rest, S., & Rosenbaum, R. M. (1971). *Perceiving the causes of success and failure.* Morristown, NJ: General Learning Press.

Wine, J. D. (1971). Test anxiety and direction of attention. *Psychological Bulletin, 76,* 92–104.

Wine, J. D. (1982). Evaluation anxiety: A cognitive-attentional construct. In H. W. Krohne & L. Laux (Eds.), *Achievement, stress, and anxiety* (pp. 207–219). Washington, DC: Hemisphere.

Received June 18, 1985
Revision received February 26, 1987
Accepted April 16, 1987 ■

[9]

JOURNAL OF APPLIED PSYCHOLOGY MONOGRAPH

Motivation and Cognitive Abilities: An Integrative/Aptitude–Treatment Interaction Approach to Skill Acquisition

Ruth Kanfer and Phillip L. Ackerman
University of Minnesota

Two central constructs of applied psychology, motivation and cognitive ability, were integrated within an information-processing framework. This theoretical framework simultaneously considers individual differences in cognitive abilities, self-regulatory processes of motivation, and information-processing demands. Evidence for the framework is provided in the context of skill acquisition, in which information-processing and ability demands change as a function of practice, training paradigm, and timing of goal setting. Three field-based lab experiments were conducted with 1,010 U.S. Air Force trainees. In Experiment 1 the basic ability–performance parameters of the air traffic controller task and goal-setting effects early in practice were evaluated. In Experiment 2 goal setting later in practice was examined. In Experiment 3 the simultaneous effects of training content, goal setting, and ability–performance interactions were investigated. Results support the theoretical framework and have implications for notions of ability–motivation interactions and design of training and motivation programs.

Motivation and cognitive abilities represent two basic determinants of learning and work performance. Numerous studies have investigated the role of cognitive-intellectual abilities in predicting individual differences in job performance (for reviews, see Dunnette, 1976; Ghiselli, 1966; Hunter, 1986). Findings from this large amount of research show a substantial positive relationship between cognitive abilities and job performance (e.g., Hunter, 1986). From a different perspective, motivational theorists have focused on the effects of dispositions, environments, self-systems, and conative processing on task performance (e.g., Atkinson, 1957; Atkinson & Feather, 1966; Bandura, 1977; Kuhl, 1984, 1986; Locke, 1968; Weiner, 1986). Incentives, goal assignments, need achievement, expectancies, subjective valuation of outcomes, self-efficacy expecta-

tions, and a host of other noncognitive factors have been shown to influence goal choice, intended effort, task behavior, and work performance (for reviews, see Bandura, 1986; Campbell & Pritchard, 1976; Feather, 1982; Ilgen & Klein, 1988; R. Kanfer, in press; Lawler, 1973; Locke, Shaw, Saari, & Latham, 1981; Mitchell, 1974).

In addition to the independent effects of ability and motivation, several researchers have stressed the importance of *interactions* between ability and motivation determinants of performance (Gagné & Fleishman, 1959; Maier, 1955; Pinder, 1984; Vroom, 1964). The most common conceptualization of ability-motivation interactions in industrial and organizational psychology is that suggested by Vroom (1964), who indicated that when motivation is low, both low- and high-ability individuals demonstrate similar low levels of performance. However, when motivation is high, performance variability due to individual differences in ability will be more evident. As Vroom (1964) noted, this interaction has two implications for work settings. First, enhancing task motivation should exert a beneficial effect on performance among persons of both low and high ability. Second, when task motivation is high, the role of abilities in determining individual differences in performance should be more pronounced. That is, high-ability persons will show a proportionately greater performance improvement from an increase in motivation than will low-ability persons. Several studies (Fleishman, 1958; French, 1957; Wyatt, 1934, cited in Vroom, 1964) appear to demonstrate such interaction effects; other studies do not (e.g., Locke, 1965).

No unified approach currently exists for understanding the simultaneous effects of motivation and individual differences in abilities on task performance. Furthermore, Vroom's (1964) ability–motivation interaction hypothesis appears to address

Portions of this research were sponsored by the Air Force Office of Scientific Research and Project LAMP, under the auspices of the Air Force Human Resources Laboratory (Contract AFOSR-87-0234), with matching funds from the University of Minnesota Graduate School and College of Liberal Arts, to Ruth Kanfer and Phillip L. Ackerman. This research program is also supported in part by funds from the Office of Naval Research to Phillip L. Ackerman, Cognitive Science Contract N00014-86-K-0478.

We thank John P. Campbell, Frederick H. Kanfer, Richard E. Snow, and Antonette M. Zeiss for their helpful comments on earlier drafts of this article. We also wish to gratefully acknowledge Kim Pearson for his programming assistance, Debra S. Johnson for her assistance in task development and experiment pilot testing, the cooperation of the Learning Abilities Measurement Program in the collection of the data reported here, and especially the efforts of Dr. Valerie J. Shute.

Correspondence concerning this article should be addressed to Ruth Kanfer, Department of Psychology, University of Minnesota, Elliott Hall, 75 East River Road, Minneapolis, Minnesota 55455.

Journal of Applied Psychology, 1989, Vol. 74, No. 4, 657–690
Copyright 1989 by the American Psychological Association, Inc. 0021-9010/89/$00.75

performance variability due to abilities and motivation only after prerequisite skills have been learned. Little attention has been given to ability–motivation interactions during complex skill acquisition. The interactive effects of these constructs in complex skill acquisition may have implications for the development of training programs to maximize achievement among individuals of different aptitudes. In this article, we take advantage of recent advances in cognitive and information-processing psychology to provide a unified framework of cognitive ability and motivational determinants of complex skill acquisition. We report the results of three experiments that investigate hypotheses derived from this framework.

Previous Findings

Terborg (1977) reviewed 14 studies investigating ability–motivation interactions. He found a clear motivation–ability interaction effect in only 2 studies (Fleishman, 1958; French, 1957). Six studies provided mixed results (Galbraith & Cummings, 1967; Lawler, 1966; Lawler & Suttle, 1973; Locke, 1965; Porter & Lawler, 1968; Vroom, 1960) and 6 studies provided no evidence for ability–motivation interactions (Arvey, 1972; Dachler & Mobley, 1973; Gavin, 1970; Graen, 1967; Lawler & Porter, 1967; Mitchell & Nebeker, 1973).

Terborg noted several difficulties in drawing conclusions from the literature. He pointed out that the use of pre-experimental task performance as a measure of ability (e.g., Fleishman, 1958; Graen, 1967; Locke, 1965) runs the risk of potentially confounding ability with motivation. In addition, task effort was assessed indirectly in several studies that used estimates based on expectancy–value models of task effort (e.g., Arvey, 1972; Gavin, 1970; Mitchell & Nebeker, 1973). According to Terborg, the problem with such effort measures is that their adequacy depends on the validity of the expectancy–value theoretical model. Terborg noted increasing criticism of the assumptions underlying expectancy–value models of effort (e.g., Mitchell, 1982). Finally, a number of different motivational manipulations were used (e.g., n Ach in French, 1957; instructions in Fleishman, 1958). Although these manipulations appeared to affect intended effort, comparisons of performance effects are difficult given the hypothetically different effects the manipulations exert on motivational processes. Achievement motives, for example, influence effort as a joint function of perceived task difficulty and valence of task success. In contrast, explicit goal assignments may enhance effort by directing attention or altering the attractiveness of task success.

On the basis of his review, Terborg (1977) suggested that differences in task difficulty might further account for the mixed evidence obtained in previous studies. Terborg proposed that task difficulty would affect the demonstration of ability–motivation interactions by altering the relationships among the predictors and performance. In less difficult tasks, ability may represent a less potent predictor of performance than would motivation. In contrast, performance of more difficult task assignments may be substantially affected by the interactive effects of motivational processes and ability.

Terborg (1977) investigated the effects of task difficulty, effort, and ability in a simulated training program. Sixty subjects, responding to advertisements for temporary, part-time work, were hired to complete a series of programmed texts de-

signed to teach principles of electricity. To assess ability, Terborg used a composite index comprising five independent ability tests. Effort was operationalized as the percentage of time subjects spent working on the programmed text material. Time spent on text material was recorded on film. Task difficulty varied across two of the six programmed text segments.

Consistent with Terborg's hypotheses, ability and effort each exerted a significant independent effect on time to complete the materials and performance on a comprehensive examination. Comparison between performance levels for easy and difficult task segments provided mixed support for the moderating role of task difficulty in demonstration of ability–motivation interactions. A significant interaction between ability and motivation was found in the difficult task segment but not in the easier task segment. Terborg concluded that ability–motivation interaction effects on performance were likely to be most influential in tasks of moderate difficulty. He noted, however, that assessment of task difficulty was problematic and depended on the skills of the subject sample. Alternatively, we suggest that task difficulty be conceptualized in an information-processing framework. The material that was to be mastered in Terborg's study involved acquisition of complex skills over time. An information-processing framework enables investigation of ability–performance relations over the course of skill acquisition.

Toward a Unified Framework

As implied by Terborg (1977), a theoretical perspective for relating ability and motivation is necessary to explain and systematically investigate the nature and influence of ability–motivation interactions on performance. Previous empirical findings suggest that such a theory must address several issues. First, the theory must take into account critical characteristics of the task and indicate how these characteristics affect the potential contribution of abilities and motivation to task performance. Similarly, previous findings in the motivation literature often limit analysis to the effects of motivational factors on single trial performance rather than across a series of trials during which both motivation and abilities might exert dynamic effects on performance (e.g., persistence). Thus, less is known about the effects of motivational manipulations on skill acquisition, or learning. Although theories dealing with individual differences in abilities have long been concerned with the dynamic nature of ability–performance relations during learning, resolution of these issues has only recently appeared to be an attainable goal (e.g., see reviews by Ackerman, 1987; Cronbach & Snow, 1977; Fleishman, 1972; Gagné, 1989; Glaser, 1967; Snow, Kyllonen, & Marshalek, 1984). A unified theory of performance should thus take into consideration the effects of motivation and abilities during skill acquisition as well as in performance of well-learned tasks.

Second, an integrated approach must provide a common conceptual metric or some taxonomy for assessment of the relative contributions of ability and motivation determinants of performance (for taxonomic approaches, see Fleishman, 1975; Fleishman & Quaintance, 1984; Kyllonen & Shute, 1989; Melton, 1964). Such a metric may enable investigation of testable hypotheses about the interactive effects of the variables (above and beyond their independent effects). In addition, a common framework may ultimately provide practical recommendations about how much progress might be expected from motivational manipulations among lower ability persons during and after training.

Third, an integrated framework must include a full treatment of both abilities and motivation. Prior research has tended to focus on one or the other, depending on the investigator's primary concern. Treatment of both constructs is needed to ground the theory of performance in both domains and to ensure generalizability across contexts.

The problem of clarifying the interactive effects of abilities and motivation may be best viewed as a particular case of the broader challenge faced in attempting rapprochement of two historically disparate paradigms: experimental psychology (oriented toward identification of normative principles of behavior) and differential psychology (Cronbach, 1957, 1975; Snow, 1986, 1989). Recent theory and empirical research strongly suggest the potential advantages of such a framework (Snow, in press; e.g., see integrative approaches to personality and motivation by Humphreys & Revelle, 1984, or achievement motivation and information processing by Kuhl, 1986). Consistent with the path taken by these researchers, the theoretical foundation for our position lies in cognitive, information-processing models. In the following sections, we describe this foundation, map the effects of individual differences in abilities and motivational processes in a model-theoretic approach, and report three experiments designed to test several key hypotheses derived from the model.

Attention as a Core Construct

The construct of *cognitive resources* or *attentional resources* provides a theoretical linkage between ability and motivation and clarifies the influence of objective task characteristics on ability/motivation–performance relations. Theories of human information processing (e.g., Kahneman, 1973; Norman & Bobrow, 1975; Wickens, 1984) have defined attentional effort as cognitive resources of limited availability. A central concern for such theories is understanding the effects of various task characteristics on the relations between attentional effort and task performance.

The performance–resource function postulated by Norman and Bobrow (1975) provides a common metric for the effort–performance relation under a variety of information-processing task constraints, such as task difficulty. Norman and Bobrow proposed a performance–resource function based on the concepts of *resource limitations* and *data limitations*. Resource limitations refer to performance limits due to the amount of cognitive resources devoted to the task. Data limitations refer to the performance limits imposed by task characteristics. The performance–resource function depicts the relations between the amount of cognitive-attentional resources devoted to a task and the resulting level of performance on that task. The only explicit assumption about these functions is that they are monotonically increasing; that is, performance will not decrease when additional resources are devoted to the task. This assumption is consistent with research on the effects of environmental stressors—such as heat and noise—in which stressors are conceptualized as reducing the availability of attentional resources. Maximal attention devoted to a task, in this frame-

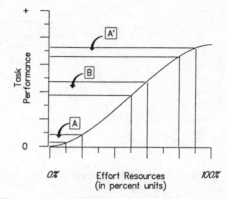

Figure 1. An example performance–resource function. The function is mostly resource-dependent, but is more so in segment B and less so in segments A and A'. (From "On Data-Limited and Resource-Limited Processes" by D. A. Norman and D. B. Bobrow, 1975, *Cognitive Psychology, 7,* p. 49. Copyright 1975 by Academic Press. Adapted by permission.)

work, is only possible during moderate levels of arousal (see, e.g., Hancock, 1986; Humphreys & Revelle, 1984).

In this perspective, a task is *resource-limited* when increases or decreases in the amount of attention devoted to the task result in measurable changes in objective task performance. Conversely, a task is said to be *data-limited* when changes in the amount of attention do not result in substantial changes in performance. Thus, information-processing demands associated with a task may be classified to indicate performance–resource functions that show tasks to be dependent on, or insensitive to, changes in attentional effort devoted to a task.

As shown in Figure 1, a task is *resource-dependent* whenever an increase (or decrease) in the amount of attention devoted to the task is accompanied by a change in level of performance. When performance is limited, not by allocation of attention, but by the nature of the task, the task is *resource-insensitive;* changes in attention result in minimal change to performance. In the hypothetical task depicted in Figure 1, there are two areas of relative resource insensitivity. At low levels of attention, there is essentially a threshold for any performance marginally above zero. At the upper range of attention, there is a situation of diminishing returns. At this point, increases from 90% to 100% attention result in small changes to performance. Note that the task is considered to be resource-dependent when the slope of this performance–resource function is steep.

Research in information-processing indicates that the performance–resource function is altered under several key situations (e.g., Norman & Bobrow, 1975; Wickens, 1984). For example, changes in task difficulty, by increasing the load on memory, are associated with making the performance–resource function increasingly resource-dependent. Conversely, when the task is simplified, the slope of the performance–resource function decreases (the task becomes resource-insensitive). Similarly, under conditions of skill acquisition, a task that is initially resource-dependent will ordinarily become progressively more

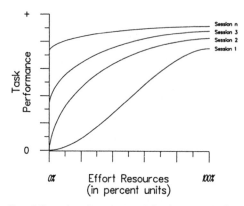

Figure 2. Changes in performance–resource functions as a result of sessions of practice. Although the performance–resource function is initially resource-dependent (Session 1), as the number of practice sessions increases, the task becomes more resource-insensitive (as the skill becomes proceduralized). (From "On Data-Limited and Resource-Limited Processes" by D. A. Norman and D. B. Bobrow, 1975, *Cognitive Psychology, 7*, p. 61. Copyright 1975 by Academic Press. Adapted by permission.)

resource-insensitive with task practice (Fisk & Schneider, 1983). As Figure 2 indicates, consistent task practice is associated with higher levels of performance and decreasing demands on attention (Norman & Bobrow, 1975).

Discrepancies obtained from previous findings on the effects of motivation on performance across a variety of tasks may in part result from differences in task performance–resource functions (R. Kanfer, 1986, 1987). If level of effort is conceptualized as the amount of attentional resources devoted to the task, increases in effort would be expected to yield increases in performance when tasks are characterized by steep slopes (resource-dependent tasks). When tasks are resource-insensitive, as might occur when the task is well-learned or extremely difficult, changes in attentional effort are predicted to yield only minor changes in task performance.

Skill Acquisition and Attention

The contribution of ability and motivation factors to task performance depends on the attentional demands imposed by the task. Learning theorists have historically described skill acquisition in terms of stage or phase designations delineating different aspects of the learning process (e.g., Bryan & Harter, 1899; Fitts & Posner, 1967; see Adams, 1987, for a review). Anderson (1982, 1983), for example, has used a "production system" perspective to suggest that skill acquisition can be segmented into the following three phases: declarative knowledge (Phase 1), followed by knowledge compilation (Phase 2), and, finally, procedural knowledge (Phase 3).[1]

Phase 1: Declarative Knowledge

Declarative knowledge is defined as "knowledge about facts and things" (Anderson, 1985, p. 199). The *declarative knowl-*

edge phase of skill acquisition appears to involve all of the requisite memory and reasoning processes that allow the performer to attain an understanding of the task requirements. The task content at this point often consists of the specification of task objectives (i.e., some end result of proficiency or task completion) and frequently includes instruction about the task, as would be exemplified by a lecture on a mechanical system or general principles for equipment operation. During this phase the performer may observe demonstrations of the task, may encode and store task rules, and may derive strategies for the task.

A critical feature of the declarative phase of skill acquisition is the substantial attentional resource demands imposed on the learner. At this level of skill acquisition, persons devote most, if not all, of their attention to understanding and performing the task. When confronted with additional information-processing requirements, as with the inclusion of a secondary task, persons are unable to adequately devote attention to the secondary task and to the learning of the criterion task simultaneously (e.g., see Nissen & Bullemer, 1987).

Performance in the declarative knowledge phase is slow and error prone. Once the person has come to an adequate cognitive representation of the task, he or she can proceed to the second stage, the knowledge compilation phase.

Phase 2: Knowledge Compilation

For tasks that allow for consistent information processing, performance speed and accuracy markedly improve over the course of practice (Fisk, Ackerman, & Schneider, 1987). During the *knowledge compilation* phase of skill acquisition, persons integrate the sequences of cognitive and motor processes required to perform the task. As various methods for simplifying or streamlining the task are tried and evaluated, performance generally becomes faster and more accurate than in the declarative knowledge phase. Anderson (1985) indicates that the process of knowledge compilation is analogically similar to the process of compiling interpretive computer source code (the actual program statements) to obtain object code (or machine-level code). As this compilation occurs for each task component, the declarative knowledge system, and thus the attentional apparatus, is relieved of the processes originally required to perform the task. As such, the attentional load on the learner is reduced as the task objectives and procedures are moved from short-term, or working memory, to long-term memory (Fisk & Schneider, 1983).

---

[1] In the domain of skill acquisition, it is useful to distinguish between two types of learning. One type (e.g., learning how to drive a car) we can refer to as a *terminal* or *closed-ended* skill. As one learns how to drive a car, the task starts out being quite difficult; one must keep in mind all of the components of the task (such as the speedometer, the rear view mirror, the turn signals, the fuel gauge, etc.). After sufficient practice, for instance, a few days, weeks, or months, these component skills become automatic. Once the skill is automatic, the majority of learning has taken place. These types of skills may be contrasted with *open-ended* skills. In open-ended skills (for example, in graduate education), lower order learning leads, of necessity, to the engagement of higher order learning. Skill learning, from the current perspective, refers to the individual component skills rather than to ultimate achievement on some higher order accomplishment.

When a competing task is added to the learning task during the knowledge compilation phase, performance on the learning task may not improve to the same degree as under single task conditions, but learning task performance appears to be less susceptible to interference from external attentional demands (Yeh & Schneider, 1985). Therefore, attentional resources may be diverted from the task, or used for processing other components of the entire skill, without the resulting substantial decrements associated with removal of attention when the learner is at the declarative knowledge phase of skill acquisition.

Phase 3: Procedural Knowledge

Procedural knowledge is defined as "knowledge about how to perform various cognitive activities" (Anderson, 1985, p. 199). This final phase of skill acquisition is reached when the individual has essentially automatized the skill and the task often can be efficiently performed with little attention. During Phase 3, the skill has been proceduralized such that once a stimulus is presented, the responses can often be prepared and executed without conscious mediation by the learner. After a substantial amount of consistent task practice, skilled performance becomes fast, accurate, and the task can often be performed with minimal impairment while attention is also being devoted to a secondary task (e.g., see Schneider & Fisk, 1982). Although improvements in performance during practice are still found at this final level of skill acquisition, practice functions at this stage are well described in terms of diminishing returns, in keeping with the Power Law of Practice (Newell & Rosenbloom, 1981).

Summary

From a performance–resource function perspective, information processing that requires the use of declarative knowledge implies a demand for attentional resources. During Phase 1 of skill acquisition, great demands are placed for cognitive-attentional effort. However, as a learner acquires skills (through knowledge compilation and proceduralization), the demands on the attentional system are markedly reduced, freeing resources for other activities. At asymptotic levels of skill acquisition (complete proceduralization), the task can be performed with few (if any) attentional resources. This level of skilled performance is characterized as *automatic*. Thus, when tasks of at least moderate difficulty demand the use of declarative knowledge, performance is essentially resource-dependent (as in Figure 1). As the skill is proceduralized, performance becomes resource-insensitive (see Figure 2).

Attentional demands associated with phases of skill acquisition provide a conceptual framework for describing the influence of individual differences in ability and motivation on task performance. The operation of motivational processes in this framework is described in the next section.

Motivation

Motivation refers to the direction of attentional effort, the proportion of total attentional effort directed to the task (intensity), and the extent to which attentional effort toward the task is maintained over time (persistence; e.g., Campbell & Pritchard, 1976; Humphreys & Revelle, 1984; R. Kanfer, 1987;

Kleinbeck, 1987; Naylor, Pritchard, & Ilgen, 1980). Some theories of motivation distinguish between determinants of choice and determinants of action (see Bandura, 1986; R. Kanfer, in press; and Kuhl, 1984, 1985, for discussion of this distinction). For example, Kuhl (1984) described two related types of motivation: choice motivation and control motivation. According to Kuhl (1984), behavior is determined not only by an individual's choice among action alternatives (choice motivation) but also by additional variables that affect action during attempts to accomplish the goal (control motivation). In an integrative review of the motivation literature, R. Kanfer (in press) has proposed that motivation affects choice, action, and ultimately performance through the operation of two cognitive resource allocation processes, termed *distal* and *proximal*. A brief review of this approach follows, but additional details can be found in R. Kanfer (in press).

Distal Motivational Processes

The choice to engage any, some, or all of one's resources for attainment of a goal is termed a *distal motivational process*. R. Kanfer (1986, 1987) has described three perceived functional relations that determine distal decisions: (a) perceived performance–utility, (b) perceived effort–utility, and (c) perceived performance–resource relation. For example, consider an individual faced with learning a new skill. The individual judges the utility of performing this new skill through a perceived performance–utility function. If the utility is positive, a decision to engage in the task must also be predicated on a judgment of the relation between the individual's effort and performance (i.e., the perceived performance–resource function). The perceived performance–resource function provides a mapping between effort and expected performance that allows an evaluation of the benefits of particular levels of performance relative to anticipated costs of expending effort. Optimization of effort–utility and performance–utility yields an intended level of effort to be devoted to the task.

The influence of these mechanisms on goal choice and intended task effort has been documented in the literature (e.g., reviews by Mitchell, 1982; Naylor et al., 1980). Distal motivational processes are initially antecedent to task engagement; that is, the operation of these processes does not draw attention away from the learning task. Specifically, distal decisions set the stage for resource availability during task engagement. A distal effort allocation does not univocally determine performance, because additional factors, such as objective information-processing demands of the task and self-regulatory processes, also influence performance.

When goals are readily attainable, distal effort allocation clearly influences subsequent performance (see, e.g., Mitchell, 1982; Vroom, 1964). Daily choices, such as what to wear or which work task to begin first in the morning, prompt effort allocations that typically permit the goal to be realized quickly and without difficulty. In contrast, when goals involve acquisition of complex or novel skills, goal attainment requires sustained attentional effort in the face of difficulties. Such situations require iterative proximal motivational activities to guide and sustain attentional effort (Bandura, 1986; F. H. Kanfer & Schefft, 1988; Kuhl, 1984).

Proximal Motivational Processes

Proximal motivational processes determine the distribution of effort across on-task and off-task activities during task engagement (i.e., effort previously devoted through distal decisions). These motivational processes comprise self-regulatory activities (i.e., self-monitoring, self-evaluation, and self-reaction). In contrast with distal motivational processing, a critical feature of proximal motivational processes is that their engagement requires attentional effort, effort that may compete with on-task and off-task demands.

Proximal motivational processes have been considered from two perspectives: clinical–experimental and action control. For example, clinical–experimental and social psychological self-regulation theories have focused on the processes involved in control of behavior in conflict situations (e.g., Bandura, 1977, 1982; Carver & Scheier, 1981, 1985; F. H. Kanfer, 1977; F. H. Kanfer & Schefft, 1988). Similarly, action control and achievement theories have considered interactions among proximal conative and affective processes and components of the information-processing system, such as memory and motor skills (e.g., Atkinson & Birch, 1970; Heckhausen, Schmalt, & Schneider, 1985; Kuhl, 1986). In both perspectives, self-regulatory processes are critical determinants of performance and, thus, of the development of competencies.

Self-Regulatory Activities

Self-regulatory activities are triggered when (a) the perceived difficulty of achieving the intention exceeds some threshold and (b) the individual is confident that he or she has the capability to successfully attain the goal (Bandura, 1986; F. H. Kanfer & Schefft, 1988; Kuhl, 1984). That is, activation of self-regulatory processes is expected when persons adopt difficult goals and correspondingly perceive themselves to possess adequate abilities or skills for accomplishing the goal.

Self-regulation subsumes three interdependent activities: *self-monitoring, self-evaluation,* and *self-reaction.* In the next section, we briefly describe these three self-regulatory activities in the context of the resource-allocation framework (for a more detailed discussion, see R. Kanfer, 1987).

Self-Monitoring

Self-monitoring refers to the individual's allocation of attention to specific aspects of his or her behavior as well as the consequences of the behavior. Factors that influence which facets of behavior are attended to include those, for example, that have functional significance for goal attainment or those associated with behavioral outcomes that are highly valued. Self-monitoring may occur in response to internal or external prompts. For example, when performance outcomes are deemed important, persons may allocate more attention to observing performance outcomes.

Successful self-monitoring requires that one attend to behaviors corresponding to one's goals. Note, however, that attention to one's performance is not synonymous with accurate assessment of one's capabilities. Persons often make erroneous judgments of competence that may lead to insufficient allocations

of effort and, consequently, deficient performance (R. Kanfer, 1986, 1987; see also Bandura, 1988).

Self-Evaluation

Self-evaluation involves a comparison of current performance with the desired goal state; individuals check their progress against a standard or referent. The size and direction of the goal–performance discrepancy interacts with self-reactions (see later) to influence subsequent decisions regarding allocation of effort (Bandura & Cervone, 1986).

Self-Reactions

There are two types of self-reactions. The first type involves self-satisfactions (an affective judgment), the other involves perceptions of task-specific capabilities (i.e., self-efficacy expectations). In the context of goal-directed behavior, Bandura (1988) proposed that evaluation of one's own performance affects both self-satisfaction and self-efficacy expectations.

The importance of these functions in the self-regulatory system and in the control of specific patterns of behavior has been demonstrated in numerous studies of learning and performance (see reviews by Bandura, 1977, 1986; F. H. Kanfer, 1977). For example, when goal–performance discrepancies are small or are positive, individuals are satisfied and self-regulatory processing may be disengaged. In contrast, when goal–performance discrepancies are negative (either moderate or large), dissatisfaction is high and motivation to reduce the discrepancy is maintained. If individuals perceive themselves to be sufficiently capable of attaining the goal, self-dissatisfaction may yield a decision to increase task effort and continue self-regulatory processing (Bandura & Cervone, 1986).

Individual differences in self-regulation may also be considered. Kuhl's action control framework (1984) has suggested that an individual's orientation toward action or state affects the efficiency of self-regulatory processing. Individuals with an action orientation are task-focused. In contrast, persons with a state orientation tend to focus on internal or emotional states. Kuhl and Koch (1984) found that action-oriented subjects performed a novel motor-tracking task better than state-oriented subjects. These authors suggested that the lower performance of state-oriented subjects was due to their performing a "hidden second task" (p. 151). State-oriented subjects allocated attentional effort toward emotional concerns. Essentially, attentional focus on emotional states disrupts the mapping of distal resource allocations (i.e., intended effort) to actual allocations of on-task effort.

Summary

R. Kanfer (1987, in press) has proposed a resource-allocation framework of motivation with two components. Motivational processes that affect decisions to engage effort constitute the first component (distal). These processes place a volitional limit on total resource availability. Determinants of effort allocations between on-task, off-task, and self-regulatory activities constitute the second component (proximal). Proximal resource allocation processes follow the establishment of a difficult goal that the individual believes he or she can enact, and occur during task engagement. As such, these processes reflect information-processing strategies used to build and sustain goal-directed behavior. Engagement of proximal motivational processes demands a cognitive resource overhead.

Implications of Motivation from a Resource Perspective

The engagement of proximal motivational processes differentially affects performance of novel and well-learned tasks. On the one hand, explicit training in self-regulation may enhance performance in well-learned tasks by strengthening goal commitment and increasing attentional effort toward goal attainment. Often, when individuals perceive their performance to be satisfactory, self-regulatory processes used during learning are disengaged (i.e., the result of a small goal–performance discrepancy). The use of goal setting to introduce a difficult standard can lead to enhanced performance (see Latham & Lee, 1986). These effects are presumably accomplished through distal allocations of increased effort and through the reengagement of self-regulation, thus increasing task effort (R. Kanfer, in press).

On the other hand, a frequent situation in which persons allocate, and tasks demand, almost full use of cognitive resources occurs when persons first encounter a difficult and novel, or complex task (see Figure 2). The attentional demands of novel tasks mediate (or obviate) the beneficial influence of self-regulatory activity. Persons generally commit substantial effort to the task during the initial stages of skill acquisition. Self-regulatory activities that would prompt greater allocation of attentional effort (a distal process) are limited because there is little additional effort available. Furthermore, attentional effort is required to develop new declarative knowledge for task performance. Attentional demands associated with proximal self-regulation must compete with attentional demands of the task (cf. F. H. Kanfer & Stevenson, 1985). Therefore, the beneficial consequences of self-regulation can only be obtained when there are sufficient cognitive resources available for engaging in self-regulatory activity itself. When the self-regulatory activities themselves demand resources that can only be provided through a reduction in resources allocated to the task, self-regulation may impair performance and also impair learning.

The notion that proximal motivational processes demand cognitive resources can be integrated with skill acquisition theory to generate the following two hypotheses:

1. When the task is resource-dependent (e.g., during the declarative phase of skill acquisition), the engagement of self-regulatory activities will deprive the task of needed resources. Unless the benefits of self-regulation are stronger than the costs of resource diversion, performance (and subsequent learning) will suffer.

2. Following development of a declarative representation of the task (i.e., in the knowledge compilation or procedural phases of skill acquisition), the engagement of self-regulatory activities will enhance performance. This benefit is due to the availability of attentional resources for self-regulatory activity *and due to the consequences of self-regulation that serve to increase resource allocations to on-task activity.*

Individual Differences in Intellectual Ability

The performance–resource function posited by Norman and Bobrow (1975) may also be used as a springboard for describing an individual-differences approach to abilities and task perfor-

mance. Norman & Bobrow described resources as portions of a subject's attentive capacity. Ackerman (1984, 1986a, 1987) has suggested that individual differences in general intellectual ability may be conceptualized as differences in individuals' total attentional–cognitive capacity. Thus, the performance–resource function designation may be translated into a *performance–ability function.*

The resource approach to individual differences in ability suggests that attentional–cognitive resources can be conceptualized as an undifferentiated pool, representing the limited capacity of the human's information-processing system.[2] Individual differences in general ability are reflected in differences in total resource capacity. Given a conceptual mapping from an individual's general intellectual ability to his or her level of attentional functioning (e.g., see Ackerman, 1986b; Zeaman, 1978), ability differences may be translated into individual differences in attentional resources. The resource demands of a task and the relations between resources and performance may thus be mapped onto the relations between abilities and performance. From this perspective, resource-dependent tasks are anticipated to be *general ability-dependent,* and resource-insensitive tasks are similarly expected to be *general ability-insensitive.*

From a general ability perspective, differences in task performance attributable to amount of attention allocated to the task are posited to be parallel to differences in performance attributable to individual differences in level of general cognitive ability–intelligence. In addition, there will be a correspondence between the attentional requirements of information-processing tasks and the degree of association between general intellectual abilities and task performance (e.g., as evidenced in Kyllonen, 1987).

Abilities and Skill Acquisition

On the basis of reviews of the literature and a series of empirical studies, Ackerman (1986a, 1987, 1988) has proposed that three major ability classes are critically important for predicting individual differences in performance during the three phases of skill acquisition. A brief review of this approach follows, but additional details are presented in Ackerman (1988).

Phase 1: General Intelligence

Definitions of general intelligence that encompass the individual's repertoire of knowledge and facility with "acquiring,

---

[2] Differential psychologists will recognize this proposition as consistent with the construct of *g,* some general intellectual ability. Interesting historical parallels of attention theory and ability theory have been noted (Ackerman, 1986b), for example, (a) the unitary theories of Spearman (1904) and Kahneman (1973) and (b) the independent primaries theories of Thurstone (1938) and Wickens (1984); but (c) there is no current compromise attention theory as there is a hierarchical approach to ability (such as Vernon, 1961). Although we do not explicitly address many of the various facets of cognitive abilities (e.g., Guilford, 1967) or particular information processes (e.g., Carroll, 1980; see also review by Fleishman & Quaintance, 1984), our approach to the issue is consistent with a hierarchical approach, in which some general ability accounts for approximately 50% of the variance in the universe of ability measures (Vernon, 1961). However, although consideration of subdivisions of attention will be of ultimate importance to the field, the current integrative investigation required a parsimonious, if somewhat narrow, approach to attention.

storing in memory, retrieving, combining, comparing, and using in new contexts information and conceptual skills" (Humphreys, 1979) are closely related to the information-processing construct of declarative knowledge. Numerous studies have indicated that general abilities (e.g., reasoning) and broad content abilities (such as verbal, numerical, and spatial) predict individual differences in task performance (e.g. see Ackerman, 1989; reviews by Cronbach & Snow, 1977; Fleishman, 1972).

General intellectual abilities appear to be involved in the aspects of task acquisition that make substantial demands on declarative knowledge (and, thus, the attentional system). When learners first confront a novel task, the attentional load on the learners is quite high. When these demands are high, correlations between general intellectual abilities and task performance are also high. As learners begin to understand the demands of the task (through instructions, for example) and derive plans of action for performance, the attentional demands decrease, and the correlations between general intellectual abilities and performance decline. That is, there appears to be a monotonically increasing association between the attentional demands of the task and performance correlations with some general intellectual ability factor (Ackerman, 1986a, 1988; Kyllonen, 1987; Sternberg, 1977). These attentional demand effects can also be seen in the changes of working memory capacity correlations with individual differences in task performance over practice (Kyllonen & Woltz, in press; Woltz, 1988).

Phase 2: Perceptual Speed

A second major component of the ability spectrum is a broad class of perceptual speed abilities. These abilities (which are typically measured by so-called clerical tests such as Proofreading, Number Checking, Cancelling As, Digit–Symbol) represent situations in which individuals must develop simple procedures for task accomplishment and build them into rapid, accurate, and efficient perceptual and motor programs. Abilities in this domain are most predictive of individual differences in task performance in which proceduralized knowledge is built and maintained by the learners.

As learners traverse the skill acquisition curve, moving from the declarative to procedural phases, correlations between perceptual speed abilities and task performance increase, even as the correlations between general abilities and performance decline. When learners already have a basic understanding of how to do the task but are seeking more efficient methods for accomplishing the task with minimal attentional effort, abilities demanded by the task are similar to those demanded by perceptual speed tests. From this perspective, perceptual speed measures seem to identify those persons who can proceduralize information the fastest, or most efficiently (Ackerman, 1989).

Phase 3: Psychomotor Abilities

Psychomotor abilities are typically measured in reaction time and accuracy of simple motor behaviors (such as simple reaction time, performance on Purdue Pegboard, Rotary Pursuit, Complex Coordination, and other tests that require little information processing or cognition) (e.g., Fleishman, 1954). Whereas the perceptual speed ability represents cognitive processing of generally simple (but still cognitively involving)

items, psychomotor ability represents processing speed (and accuracy to a certain degree), mostly independent of information processing per se.

As learners move into the final autonomous, or automatic, phase of skill acquisition, their performance is no longer limited by the speed of proceduralization, but rather by the learner's asymptotic psychomotor speed and accuracy. Thus, individual differences in final, skilled performance are not necessarily determined by the same abilities that affect the initial level of task performance or the speed of skill acquisition. Rather, psychomotor abilities that tap processes that only minimally depend on information processing reflect the processes that limit skilled performance after extensive practice. For the broad sphere of tasks that "importantly depend on motor behavior" (Adams, 1987), psychomotor abilities appear to be significant predictors of individual differences in asymptotic task performance (e.g., Ackerman, 1989; Fleishman & Hempel, 1954, 1955; although, see reanalysis by Ackerman, 1987).

An Integrated View

Toward a Unified Model

By mapping abilities and motivation to the performance–resource function, any subject's performance may be represented as a joint function of the subject's relative attentional capacity (i.e., cognitive ability) and the proportion of the subject's total capacity actually devoted to the task (motivation).

Figure 3 illustrates the integrated framework underlying the present research and previously stated hypotheses. As shown, the model elaborates on Kahneman's (1973) model of attentional capacity (Kahneman, 1973, p. 10, Figure 1-2). Attentional capacity is viewed as an interindividual differences attribute. Attentional resources are allocated across different activities; feedback loops are posited for adjustment of allocations, proportion of total capacity allocated, and for external influences at the level of allocation of capacity and allocation policy. In contrast with Kahneman, however, our representation explicitly distinguishes among three types of possible activities: (a) off-task activities, (b) on-task activities, and (c) self-regulatory activities.

A basic assumption underlying our model is that changes in the amount of capacity used and policies for allocation of attention are accomplished through motivational processes. The resource framework also provides a means of conceptualizing dynamic changes in performance as a function of abilities, motivation, and task characteristics. Over time, distal and proximal motivational processes influence the reallocation and mobilization of additional portions of capacity to various activities. When task resource demands are high, the individual may allocate more available attention to the task or adjust the proportion of capacity engaged. Conversely, when task demands are reduced, the individual may attend to off-task activities or may reduce the proportion of capacity engaged.

In this model, self-regulation is an essential mechanism for bringing about changes in allocation policy toward a task or total proportion of resource capacity actually engaged. Without activation of self-regulatory processes, an individual would be expected to continue to devote the same amount of resources originally committed to a task through the initial distal decision

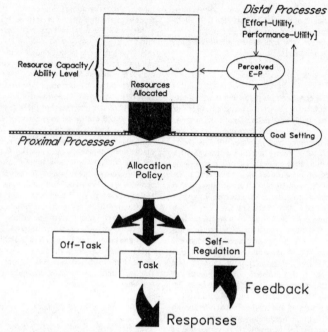

Figure 3. A model of ability–motivation interactions for attentional effort. (The model is derived from a model of attention proposed by Kahneman, 1973. See text for description of model components.)

processes. (Resource availability may also be affected by fluctuations of anxiety, fatigue [see Revelle, in press], or external stressors such as heat or noise.)

Individual differences in ability level and resource capacity will determine the total amount of resources that can be devoted to any set of activities. Consistent with Figure 1, low-ability individuals must devote a greater portion of their capacity than high-ability individuals to achieve similar levels of task performance.

Changes in the performance–resource function that occur during skill acquisition (i.e., changes from declarative to procedural knowledge) are not directly represented in Figure 3 but are addressed in the integrated framework. As noted previously, the potential drawback to activation of self-regulatory processes is that such processes may draw from resources needed to develop a declarative representation of the task. In this initial, resource-dependent phase of learning, self-regulatory activity itself represents a cognitive cost and the products of self-regulation cannot be readily realized.

Changes in the true performance–resource function are posited to be detected by self-regulatory processes (i.e., self-monitoring). As the task becomes less resource-dependent (over practice), individuals discover that fewer resources need to be devoted to the task to maintain performance. As such, resources might be diverted to other activities, including additional self-regulatory processing. Alternatively, the individual may choose

to reduce the proportion of attentional capacity currently engaged. To the degree that self-regulatory activities in tasks approaching resource-insensitivity not only enable motivational processing without cost but further increase, direct, and sustain on-task attentional effort, external influences that prompt self-regulation as task resource demands decrease may enhance performance. Taking into consideration individual differences in ability, the detrimental and beneficial effects of self-regulatory activity in the declarative and later phases of skill acquisition, respectively, are expected to be greater for low-ability individuals than for high-ability individuals.

Implications of the Model

Although there are numerous implications of this integrated framework of ability–motivation determinants of skill acquisition and performance (e.g., see R. Kanfer & Ackerman, 1989), the purpose of the three experiments reported in this article is to investigate the more salient features of the model that relate to interactions between abilities and motivation during learning.

In Experiment 1 we investigate the effects of abilities and motivation during the declarative, or early, phase of skill acquisition, when task resource demands are high. In Experiment 2 we investigate ability and motivation effects during the knowledge compilation, or intermediate, phase of skill acquisition, when task resource demands are reduced. In Experiment 3 we manipulate the resource demands of the task by part-task training to provide a simultaneous empirical test of the interactive influences of ability, motivation, and task information-processing demands during skill acquisition.

Experiment 1

In this experiment, we examined the performance of subjects by using an air traffic controller (ATC) task paradigm. Previous approaches to studying ability and motivational determinants of skill acquisition have tended to concentrate on relatively simple perceptual speed, memory, and psychomotor tasks (e.g., proofreading, addition tasks, rotary pursuit). Although such tasks are tractable from a distal motivational or a components of information-processing perspective, these tasks tend to be learned quickly so that the majority of skills are acquired within a brief period of practice. In these situations, the important components of learning take place in the first few trials of task practice, and sometimes before the learner even begins the task (on the basis of understanding the task instructions). In addition, the learner faced with a simple or discrete task has few degrees of freedom when it comes to strategy development, persistence in the face of failure, self-generation of feedback, and so forth. To examine ability and motivational determinants of skill acquisition, a task environment must be used in which there is (a) a gradual accretion of component skills, (b) flexibility to try out different strategies, and (c) the sharing of attention among task components and self-regulatory activities.

Several prerequisites exist for the productive investigation of ability–motivation interactions during skill acquisition. Specific requirements relate to the development of a task paradigm that (a) depends on cognitive processes (as opposed to essentially motor or perceptual/motor processes), (b) requires substantial allocation of cognitive resources during initial learning, and (c) is complex enough to allow for subject flexibility in re-

sponding to motivational interventions (e.g., through development of alternative strategies or through increases in attention to the task). We developed the ATC task with these needs in mind.

As implied by our model, a novel, complex task imposes high resource demands on persons of all ability levels (i.e., performance is resource-dependent throughout the ability range). As such, general ability–performance correlations are predicted to be moderately to highly positive for initial performance but to decline with task practice. (Similarly, as skills are acquired, perceptual speed ability–performance correlations are predicted to increase, then to decline.)

In Experiment 1 we also explored the impact of goal assignments made during the initial phase of skill acquisition, when the task is assumed to impose substantial demands on attentional resources. We examined the performance of subjects assigned a specific and difficult performance goal to that of subjects in a no-goal ("Do your best") condition. In addition, evidence addressing differential allocation of attention across activities (i.e., on-task activities, off-task activities, self-regulatory activities) was examined through use of behavioral and self-report measures. Finally, results obtained in this study provide baseline data for evaluation of later procedural manipulations of motivational variables (timing of goal setting) and task information-processing demands (e.g., through part-task training).

Method

The Air Traffic Control (ATC) Task

The ATC task is a rule-based, real-time, computer-driven task that simulates some of the activities performed by air traffic controllers. The overall objective for subjects performing this task was to land planes safely and efficiently. An example of the ATC task display is presented in Figure 4. As shown, the following task elements were displayed when performing the task: (a) four runways, (b) 12 hold pattern positions, and

FLT#	TYPE	FUEL	POS.
———	———	———	———
			3 n
			3 s
161	747	5	3 e
			3 w
403	747	6	2 n
889	727	6	2 s
			2 e
			2 w
631	727	6	1 n
144	prop	5	1 s
903	DC10	6	1 e
122	747	* 3	1 w

```
Score    :  150
Landing Pts: 150  Penalty Pts:    0
Runways  : DRY
Wind     : 40 - 50 knots from SOUTH

Flts in Queue: ···
        <F1> to accept

         Winds 40-50 knots
         Winds from South
         Runways dry
```

```
=============================== s   #1 <-

===========727=======          s   #2

||||||||||||||||||||||||||||   e   #3

|||||||||||||||||||            e   #4
```

```
     Can use short runways when:
747 - Never          Prop - Always
DC10 - Not Icy & not 40-50 knots
     727 - Dry or 0-20 knots
```

Figure 4. The Kanfer–Ackerman Air Traffic Controller Task. (The figure is a literal static representation of the real-time task display. See text for a description of task elements.)

(c) a queue stack with asterisks indicating planes requesting permission to enter the hold pattern. Two runways run north–south; two runways run east–west. One north–south and one east–west runway is short; one north–south and one east–west runway is long.

The hold pattern, located in the middle left section of Figure 4, contained 12 hold pattern positions, divided into three levels (analogous to three platters at different altitudes in the sky over the airport). Hold pattern position was indicated by number and letter in the Position (POS) column. Level 1 hold positions represent the lowest altitude and Level 3 hold positions represent the highest altitude. Four positions, corresponding to the points of the compass (i.e., N, S, E, W), were available in each level.

Planes are admitted to the hold pattern from the queue. The queue, located at the upper right of the screen, displayed the number of planes requesting permission to enter the hold pattern. Each plane request was represented by an asterisk. Planes entered the queue at the rate of one about every 7 s. Plane requests remained in the queue until the subject placed the plane in the hold pattern.

As shown in Figure 4, four types of planes entered the subject's hold pattern: 747s, 727s, DC10s, and props. Plane information was displayed in the hold pattern. When a plane was placed in the hold pattern, flight number (FLT#), plane type (TYPE), and number of minutes of fuel remaining (FUEL) were displayed. Within each trial an approximately equal number of plane types was randomly drawn from the queue. Fuel remaining, determined when the plane was brought into the hold pattern, was randomly varied from 4 to 6 min. Once the planes entered the hold pattern, fuel remaining decreased in real time, such that when 0 min of fuel remained, the plane crashed.

Subjects also received information on airport weather conditions. Weather information was used (in accordance with the rule set) to determine what planes were allowed to land on which runways. Three elements composed weather conditions: wind speed, wind direction, and ground condition. Wind speed and wind direction information were displayed on the *wind* line at the top right corner of the screen. Ground condition was displayed on the *runways* line. Updates to weather conditions were displayed throughout each task trial. Three types of wind speed were presented (0–20 knots, 25–35 knots, and 40–50 knots). Four types of wind direction were displayed (north, south, east, and west). Three levels of ground conditions were used (runways dry, wet, or icy). Changes in weather conditions (defined as a change in at least one of the three weather condition components) were varied randomly during a task trial. On average, these changes occurred about twice a minute (i.e., 20 weather changes were initiated during each 10-min task trial).

Feedback and knowledge of results. The first component of knowledge of results was a one-to-one mapping between keystrokes made by the subject, and operation of a cursor on the screen. As planes were selected, various parts of the display were highlighted. When a plane was moved from one hold position to another, or to a runway, the subject saw an analogous change to the display. Subjects also received three types of continuously updated performance information throughout each trial. Cumulative performance (score) for the current trial was based on a specified point scheme. Subjects received 50 points for each plane successfully landed. Ten points were deducted for each technical error made (violation of the rules). One hundred points were deducted from the performance score for each plane that ran out of fuel in the hold pattern (i.e., plane crashed). Performance scores could be negative

RULE		KEYWORD
RULE 1:	PLANES MUST LAND INTO THE WIND. (That is, if the wind is from the South, the plane must be landed on a n-s runway)	[DIRECTION]
RULE 2:	PLANES CAN ONLY LAND FROM LEVEL 1.	[LEVEL]
RULE 3:	PLANES IN THE HOLD PATTERN CAN ONLY MOVE 1 LEVEL AT A TIME, BUT TO ANY AVAILABLE POSITION IN THAT LEVEL.	[HOLD]
RULE 4:	GROUND CONDITIONS AND WIND SPEED DETERMINE THE RUNWAY LENGTH REQUIRED BY DIFFERENT PLANE TYPES. [ALL PLANES CAN USE LONG RUNWAYS.] IN PARTICULAR: 747's ALWAYS REQUIRE LONG RUNWAYS. DC10's CAN USE SHORT RUNWAYS ONLY WHEN RUNWAYS ARE DRY OR WET AND WIND SPEED IS LESS THAN 40 KNOTS. 727's CAN USE SHORT RUNWAYS ONLY WHEN THE RUNWAYS ARE DRY OR WIND SPEED IS 0 - 20 KNOTS. PROP's CAN ALWAYS USE SHORT RUNWAYS.	[LENGTH]
RULE 5:	PLANES WITH LESS THAN 3 MINUTES FUEL LEFT MUST BE LANDED IMMEDIATELY.	[FUEL]
RULE 6:	ONLY ONE PLANE AT A TIME CAN OCCUPY A RUNWAY.	[OCCUPIED]

Figure 5. A list of operational rules for the air traffic controller task. (Keywords [on the right side] are used to index rule pop-up keys during the task.)

or positive, depending on how many planes were landed relative to number of errors made and planes crashed. In addition, subjects received separate landing (landing points) and error (penalty points) information. Landing points, based on the number of planes landed, started at 0 and increased by 50 points for each plane landed. Penalty points, reflecting the number of rule violations and plane crashes, started at 0 and decreased for each error. All subjects were informed of the point scheme in the initial task instructions.

Task rules. For the experiments described here, six rules governed task performance (shown in Figure 5). These rules described the conditions required for successful manipulation of planes. When subjects performed actions that did not comply with a rule, the action command was ignored, an error message was presented on the screen indicating which rule was violated, and 10 points were deducted from the cumulative score and added to the penalty point score. Rules 1 and 4 described weather condition rules for landing planes on runways. Rule 2 required that plane landings must be initiated from one of the four hold pattern positions in Level 1. Rule 3 described the rule governing movement of planes within the hold pattern. Rule 5 required that planes with 3 or less min of fuel left must be landed immediately. A warning asterisk was displayed next to the FUEL value when remaining fuel fell below 4 min (e.g., see FLT# 122 in Figure 4). If the plane was not landed prior to a FUEL value of 3, a 10-point penalty was incurred for each minute that subjects failed to land the plane. Rule 6 required that only one plane occupy a runway at any time.

All rules, except Rule 4, described simple, noncontingent conditions governing task performance. In contrast, Rule 4 described a plane-contingent rule that involved both simple and complex elements (i.e., the specific ground and wind-speed conditions that must be met for landing each plane type on short and long runways). Simple, noncontingent elements of this rule addressed landing requirements for 747s and props (747s could never land on short runways; props could always land on short runways). For 727s, a disjunctive rule relating wind and ground conditions regulated when these plane types could land on short runways. For DC10s, a conjunctive wind and ground condition rule for short runway usage was imposed. Because positive task performance is based on the number of plane landings, it was to the subject's advantage to use both long and short runways simultaneously. Knowledge of the complex rules that govern when 727s and DC10s may use a short runway was thus an important determinant of skilled performance.

Subjects could call up brief descriptions of each rule throughout all task trials. To call up a rule, subjects were instructed to press a key corresponding to the rule they wished to view. The requested rule appeared on the lower right corner of the screen for 10 s. Subjects could call up any of the rules as many times as they wished during task trials. Note, however, that calling up a rule did not stop the simulation.

Figure 6 displays an example error message. Error messages, which were displayed in the lower right-hand section of the screen, appeared immediately following a rule error or plane crash. Error messages were displayed for 10 s.

Task requirements. Subjects performed the following three principal actions: (a) accepting planes into the hold pattern, (b) moving planes in the three-level hold pattern, and (c) landing planes on appropriate runways. Subjects manipulated planes by using only four keys on the computer keyboard (plus keys for rule call-ups). For example, planes were moved down the hold pattern by pressing the "down-arrow" (↓) key once for each position in the hold pattern. A one-to-one correspondence between keyboard and screen actions was maintained by linking each keyboard response to movement of a small cursor arrow on the screen (see the "<-" symbol in Figure 6). Specific keyboard actions taken to move a plane in the hold pattern and to place a plane on a runway resulted in highlighting of the target plane and real-time movement of the plane across the runway. Successful performance on this task required knowledge about how to make plane movements using the computer keyboard as well as knowledge of the rules governing plane movements and landings.

Apparatus

Instructions, stimulus presentation, and response collection were implemented with Xerox 1186 microcomputers under IBM PC emulation software and hardware, with standard keyboard (numeric keyboard on the right side of the keyboard) and white-on-black cathode-ray-tube monitors. A schematic keyboard diagram and a key function diagram, indicating which keys were to be used and the function of those keys, were placed on the right of the computer keyboard. A template, indicating rules associated with computer keys 1–6, was taped above the top number row of the keyboard to assist subjects in selecting the correct key for calling up specific ATC rule displays.

Each subject sat at an individual microcomputer workstation, within a carrel. The carrels provided visual restriction to the subject's own display. The carrels also provided moderate sound restriction, which was supplemented with a white-noise effect from computer cooling fans and central ventilation systems. The result was a generally undisturbed

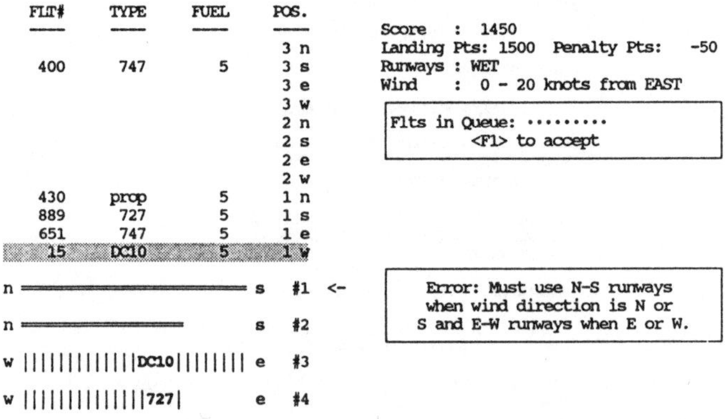

Figure 6. An illustration of error feedback in the air traffic controller task. (The error message is displayed in the lower right side of the figure.)

environment for the individual subjects. At the conclusion of the experiment, data were off-loaded from the Xerox microcomputers to diskettes for storage and data reduction. Data collected from each subject included all self-report and performance measures as well as all keystroke responses made during each performance trial.

Subjects

Participants in Experiment 1 were 322 U.S. Air Force enlisted personnel undergoing basic training at Lackland Air Force Base, near San Antonio, Texas (27 women). Subjects were tested in intact "flights," approximately 25–29 recruits at a time. Record-keeping difficulties precluded obtaining exact age information for the subjects. However, most subjects were between 18 and 22 years old at the time of testing. (Prior to data analysis, data from a few subjects were discarded, some for a lack of ability testing records [2], and others for failure to follow task instructions [4]. Finally, because a few subjects had incomplete data [e.g., computer failure, sickness], the degrees of freedom differ by as much as 2 or 3 df on some analyses). The final sample contained 316 subjects.

Procedure

General procedure—all subjects. Subjects began the experiment at individual workstation carrels. Subjects first received an introduction to the session, instructions on use of the keyboard, and instructions for the ATC task. The ATC task instructions were both narrative and interactive. For the most part, subjects read about the task components, commands, rules, and procedures. Interactive instruction was provided for such keyboard response procedures as (a) accepting planes from the queue, (b) moving planes in the hold pattern, (c) landing planes on a runway, and (d) initiating a rule call-up. Instructions were subject-paced, but most subjects completed the instructions in about 20 min.

Following instructions, subjects were told to "do your best" on the upcoming task trial, and then performed a single 10-min task trial. The trial was immediately followed by a brief questionnaire. The common first task trial (Trial 1) provided the baseline for assessment of pretreatment effects.

No-goal control condition. Following the first task trial, the no-goal control group received nine 10-min task trials (Trials 2–10). To minimize massed practice effects, subjects were given 10-min breaks following completion of each set of three trials (i.e., after Trial 4 and Trial 7). Subjects were not allowed to discuss the task with one another during the breaks. Subjects were instructed to "do your best" prior to each set of three trials. These subjects were told, "Your objective in the next three trials is to get the best performance score you can." Immediately following Trial 4 and Trial 10, subjects completed short computerized self-report questionnaires. After the final questionnaire, subjects were administered a rules/knowledge test. In this test, subjects were required to write out (with pencil and paper) the six rules governing performance on the ATC task in as much detail as possible. When subjects returned the forms, they were debriefed and excused.

Early-goal condition. The procedure described for the no-goal group was repeated for the early-goal group, with the following exceptions. Task-specific motivation was manipulated by assignment of a specific and difficult performance goal for three task trials (i.e., Trials 2–4). Subjects in the early-goal condition received the goal assignment prior to Trial 2. Subjects were assigned a cumulative performance score goal of 1,900 points (per trial) for Trials 2, 3, and 4. The 1,900-point goal was selected on the basis of results obtained in pilot experiments (no goal) with the ATC task. Pilot data indicated that 1,900 points represented a difficult performance goal (approximately 90th percentile) for Trials 2, 3, and 4. Subjects in the early-goal assignment condition were told the following:

For the next three trials, you have been assigned a specific performance goal. Your assignment is to achieve a performance score of 1,900 points by the end of the trial. That is, on EACH of the next three trials your goal is to achieve a performance score of 1,900 points.

In addition to the performance goal assignment, subjects in the early-goal condition were given periodic opportunities to check their progress relative to the goal during the three assigned goal trials. Subjects were told the following:

You can check on how well you are doing by "calling up" more performance information. Several times during the trial, a special signal (***F10***) will appear at the top right of your screen. When this signal appears, you may press the F10 key to get more information about how you are doing, relative to the performance goal assignment.

The F10 signal was displayed for 10 s for each minute of each trial (beginning 1:00 min into the trial). Subjects who pressed the F10 key during the signal received a message at the bottom right of their screen indicating the percentage of the goal they would obtain. This performance–goal feedback was calculated by extrapolating from the subject's current performance, divided by the assigned goal point total. An example of the message displayed is: "Based on your current performance, you will attain 80% of your goal."

Early-goal subjects also completed two brief questionnaires. The first questionnaire was administered immediately following the first goal assignment and prior to Trial 2. The second questionnaire was completed immediately following Trial 4. Following Trial 4, no further goal assignments were given. Beginning with Trial 5, all subjects in the early-goal condition were instructed to "do your best."

To simplify administration of the experiment, goal condition (no goal vs. early goal) was manipulated by flights of subjects who participated in the experiment at the same time (early goal $N = 149$; no goal $N = 167$).

Measured Variables

Ability measures. Estimates of cognitive-intellectual ability were derived from a composite based on the 10-test Armed Services Vocational Aptitude Battery (ASVAB). The ASVAB was completed by the subjects several months prior to the experiment, and test scores were obtained from personnel records. A global estimate of cognitive ability (general intellectual ability) was obtained using a unit-weighted composite based on all 10 subscales of the ASVAB.[3] Subjects were then divided into high-ability and low-ability groups by using a median split on the ability composite. This split was used as a two-level blocking factor in ANOVAS reported later.[4] For separate ability analyses (General and Perceptual

---

[3] The ASVAB is composed of the following subtests: General Science, Arithmetic Reasoning, Word Knowledge, Paragraph Comprehension, Numerical Operations, Code Speed, Auto Shop, Math Knowledge, Mechanical Comprehension, and Electronics Information.

[4] Use of median splits for a continuous variable often incur at the cost of discarding valuable information (e.g., see discussion by Cronbach & Snow, 1977). On the benefit side, though, a Treatment × Blocks design has the advantage of simplicity in discussion, through the use of group comparisons (e.g., high- vs. low-ability groups). In the following discussion, we present the results of analyses by using the simplified Treatment × Blocks approach, though we note the outcomes of full information regression analyses when they yield divergent results. One issue of great importance, however, is the possibility of nonlinear relations between ability measures and subjective measures of volition and affection (Snow, in press). For all of the ability–subjective measure analyses reported in this article (there are a total of 83 comparisons), only three (or 3.6%) were found to yield significant nonlinear trends (at the $\alpha = .05$ level). This pattern is in the acceptable range of those that

Speed factors), a hierarchical factor solution was derived from the ASVAB data.

Goal-related measures. Self-report questionnaire items for composite goal measures are shown in Table 1 (Section I). Subjects in the early-goal condition completed brief self-report questionnaires immediately following the goal instructions and again immediately following the last assigned goal trial. The first questionnaire contained five 8-point Likert-scale questions, assessing goal commitment and self-confidence in goal attainment. In addition, subjects were asked to predict the performance score they thought they would obtain on the next task trial (i.e., Trial 2).

To assess the impact of the goal manipulation on self-regulatory processing, six 8-point Likert-scale items (1 = *never;* 8 = *constantly*) were administered immediately following the final goal trial (i.e., Trial 4). Four items, assessing attention to the goal, were summed to form a composite goal-attention scale score. Two items, assessing frequency of performance monitoring, were summed to provide a composite performance-monitoring scale score.

Self-reports of volitional/conative activities: Trials 8–10. Subjects in the no-goal and early-goal conditions completed a self-report questionnaire following Trial 10. This questionnaire comprised items assessing spontaneous goal setting, the frequency of various types of thoughts during the final set of trials (Trials 8–10), and items pertaining to general perceptions of the ATC task. The occurrence of various types of thoughts during the final three trials of ATC performance was assessed by using a modification of Sarason's Cognitive Interference Questionnaire (CIQ; Sarason, 1978; for a description of the CIQ, see Sarason, Sarason, Keefe, Hayes, & Shearin, 1986). The CIQ is designed to assess the frequency of intruding thoughts during task performance and requires subjects to indicate, using a 5-point Likert rating scale (1 = *never;* 5 = *very often*), how frequently the thought described in each statement occurred to the subject while performing a just completed task. The CIQ includes 22 items pertaining to thoughts about the task (e.g., "I thought about how poorly I was doing") and off-task thoughts (e.g., "I thought about personal worries"). In our modified version, items were written to include thoughts about various aspects of the task (e.g., "During the last three trials, how often did you set a specific score goal for yourself?" "I focused my total attention on making fewer errors"). A subset of adapted CIQ items and new items (e.g., assessing specific on-task thoughts and positive self-reactions) were administered using an 8-point Likert rating scale (1 = *never;* 8 = *constantly*). In particular, items assessed attention to task components, thoughts pertaining to performance evaluation, negative and positive self-reactions, and off-task thoughts. Items comprising composite measures of attention are shown in Table 1 (Section II). Subjective task perceptions assessed possible attitudinal differences among subjects as a consequence of the goal manipulation. Subjects completed four Likert rating-scale items assessing perceived task difficulty and task pressure. Items for the composite task perception measures are listed in Table 1 (Section III).

Internal consistency reliability estimates of composite scales for different self-report variables are presented in Table 2. The low reliabilities obtained for some of the self-report composite scales (e.g., negative self-reactions) are only problematic to the degree that the null hypothesis is not rejected. Corrections for reliability would only serve to accentuate the size of significant effects found in the data.

Performance measures. Multiple measures of task performance were obtained at each trial, including number of planes landed (landings), number of rule violations (errors), cumulative performance score, mean

would be expected by chance, when the null hypothesis is true. (In fact, none of these significant nonlinear effects was found on the same variable across experiments.) Therefore, we believe that no nonlinear relations between this ability composite and our subjective measures exist to a meaningful degree.

reaction time to wind changes, and number of plane crashes. Number. of rule call-ups by all subjects and number of performance–goal feedback call-ups (by subjects in the early-goal condition) were also recorded for each (goal-present) task trial.

Performance in the ATC task is clearly multidimensional. For the subject, two components were added together to yield the cumulative score (on which assigned goals were based). These components were number of planes landed (landings) and number of errors committed (errors). Because it was possible for learners to improve cumulative scores by increasing number of landings or decreasing the number of errors, these variables were critical for performance assessment.[5] These two measures, landings and errors, were used in all analyses of performance. During the task, these two variables were displayed on the screen, as was the cumulative performance score. These measures had the additional advantage over cumulative performance score of being ratio scale measures of performance.

Results

One major purpose of this experiment was to review the basic skill acquisition parameters of the ATC task, including an examination of ability–performance relations. In addition, the goal-setting manipulation was implemented to evaluate the overall impact of goal setting in this complex task acquisition scenario. From the latter perspective, Experiment 1 was seen as exploratory.

Goal Manipulation Check

To examine the potential influence of ability on distal motivational mechanisms, one-way analyses of variance (ANOVAs) were conducted on predicted performance score, goal commitment, and self-confidence in goal attainment among subjects in the early-goal condition. As expected, ability exerted a significant effect on subjects' predicted performance score, $F(1, 106) = 8.01$, $p < .01$.[6] Subjects in the low-ability group predicted attainment of a lower performance score ($M = 1,484$) than subjects in the high-ability group ($M = 1,681$). Nonetheless, ability had no significant effect on commitment to attaining the assigned goal ($F < 1$) or on self-confidence ratings for goal attainment ($F < 1$). Overall, early-goal subjects reported a moderate commitment to goal attainment ($M = 4.57$). However, subjects generally reported relatively low confidence in their capability for goal attainment ($M = 6.71$; higher scores reflect lower self-confidence ratings) and predicted their perfor-

---

[5] We investigated the joint effects of these variables through multivariate procedures, which are not reported here for the sake of brevity. The landings and errors measures were relatively independent, though negatively correlated (average correlation between the two variables for any given trial was $r = -.208$, $p < .01$). That is, more landings were associated with somewhat fewer errors. Because individuals differed in ability, the total number of trials was small and, because learning was taking place with practice, it was not possible to map out speed–accuracy functions. The mean changes in error rates and landings for each experiment condition, however, do not suggest speed–accuracy tradeoffs as a general strategy for subjects.

[6] Thirty-seven subjects (18 low ability; 19 high ability) were designated as missing on this measure because of failure to understand instructions for how to enter predicted score on the computer. Unlike other measures requiring a 1–7 response, this question required subjects to enter their predicted score.

Table 1
Items Composing Self-Report Measures

Section I: Goal measures
    Commitment to assigned goal (1 = *extremely committed;* 24 = *extremely uncommitted*):
        How hard are you willing to work to achieve the assigned performance goal?
        I am willing to put in a great deal of effort to achieve my assigned goal.
        How committed are you to working as hard as possible to reach the assigned performance goal?
    Self-confidence for goal attainment (1 = *extremely certain;* 16 = *extremely uncertain*):
        How certain are you that you have the ability to achieve the assigned performance goal?
        How confident are you that you can fully achieve your assigned goal?
    Attention to the goal assignment (1 = *none;* 32 = *total attention*):
        How often did you
        . . . think about your assigned goal?
        . . . worry about not being able to reach your performance goal?
        How much attention did you pay to reaching your assigned performance goal?
        During the trials, I often forgot about trying to reach the assigned performance goal.
    Performance monitoring (1 = *none;* 16 = *constantly*):
        How often did you check your performance score?
        How often did you compare your performance to the assigned goal?
Section II: Attention measures
    Spontaneous goal setting (1 = *all trials;* 12 = *none of the trials*):
        During the last set of three trials, how often did you
        . . . set a specific score goal for yourself?
        . . . set a specific plane landing goal for yourself?
        . . . set a specific goal concerning errors (maximum penalty score)?
    On-task attention (1 = *never;* 48 = *constantly*):
        I focused my total attention on
        . . . making fewer errors.
        . . . learning a specific rule.
        . . . being ready for a change in the wind direction.
        . . . landing as many planes as I could.
        . . . responding more quickly to weather changes.
        . . . keeping as many planes on the runways as possible.
    Off-task attention (1 = *never;* 16 = *constantly*):
        I daydreamed while doing the task.
        I let my mind wander while doing the task.
    Attention to performance evaluation (1 = *never;* 24 = *constantly*):
        I thought about:
        . . . how I was doing compared to others.
        . . . how others have done on this task.
        I wondered about how my performance compared with others.
    Positive self-reactions (1 = *never;* 32 = *constantly*):
        I thought about
        . . . how much I was improving.
        . . . how well I was doing.
        . . . how enjoyable the task was.
        . . . outdoing my previous performance.
    Negative self-reactions (1 = *never;* 16 = *constantly*):
        I thought about
        . . . how poorly I was doing.
        . . . how dissatisfied I was with my performance.
Section III: Task perceptions
    Task difficulty (1 = *extremely difficult;* 16 = *extremely easy*):
        How difficult was this task?
        How much of your attention was required to perform this task?
    Task pressure (1 = *extremely demanding;* 16 = *extremely undemanding*):
        How pressured did you feel while performing this task?
        How fast-paced was this task?

Note. Measures of commitment to assigned goal and self-confidence for goal attainment were administered immediately following goal assignment. Measures of attention to the goal assignment and performance monitoring were administered immediately following final goal trial. Sections II and III were administered to all subjects immediately following final task trial (Trial 10 in Experiments 1 and 2, and Trial 6 in Experiment 3).

mance score to be substantially below the 1,900-point goal assignment (M = 1,604 points). Consistent with prior findings (e.g., Locke, Frederick, Lee, & Bobko, 1984; Wood & Bandura, 1988), the correlation between self-confidence ratings and predicted score was significant (r = −.54, $p < .01$). Both predicted score and self-confidence in goal attainment were also significantly correlated with Trial 1 performance (r = .27, $p < .01$; and r = −.15, $p < .05$, respectively). This pattern of findings

Table 2
Internal Consistency Reliabilities of Composite Self-Report Measures

	Experiment					
	1		2		3	
Scale	RE	*N*	RE	*N*	RE	*N*
Section I: Goal measures (goal conditions only)						
Commitment to Assigned Goal (3)	.61	149	.82	142	.81	275
Self-Confidence for Goal Attainment	.83	149	.81	142	.77	275
Attention to the Goal Assignment (4)	.76	148	.71	142	.72	275
Performance Monitoring	.37	148	.49	142	.30	275
Section II: Attention measures (final three trials)						
Spontaneous Goal Setting (3)	.67	312	.64	138	.72	547
On-Task Attention (6)	.77	312	.73	138	.76	547
Attention to Performance Evaluation (3)	.83	312	.84	138	.85	547
Positive Self-Reactions (4)	.70	312	.77	138	.73	547
Negative Self-Reactions	.57	312	.53	138	.67	547
Off-Task Attention	.62	312	.68	138	.53	547
Section III: Task perceptions						
Task Difficulty	.40	312	.41	138	.40	547
Task Pressure	.36	312	.27	138	.32	547

Note. Number of items in scales with more than two items are in parentheses. RE = reliability estimate. (For scales with two items, reliability estimate is correlation between the items; for scales with greater than two items, reliability estimate is coefficient alpha.) Section I contains measures administered only to subjects in goal conditions.

indicates that the generally low expectations about capability for goal attainment were more closely associated with the subject's past performance (i.e., Trial 1) than with intellectual abilities, as measured by the ASVAB.

The influence of ability on self-regulatory activities during the goal trials was examined with a set of one-way ANOVAs on measures taken during and following the goal trials. As expected, no significant effects for ability were obtained on reported attention to the goal ($F < 1$), extent of performance monitoring ($F < 1$), or number of feedback call-ups to check progress toward the goal during the goal trials ($F < 1$). Early-goal subjects reported thinking about the assigned goal "almost all the time" ($M = 21.1$). However, subjects only requested a mean of 4.64 goal feedback call-ups during the three goal trials (although there were 27 possibilities to call up the feedback). This latter finding raises the possibility that the goal manipulation may have been less effective than was desirable in stimulating self-regulatory processing during the goal trials.

Performance: Behavioral Measures

Ability–Performance Results

From the ability portion of our model, one major set of hypotheses pertains to initial correlations between general ability and performance and changes in these correlations during skill acquisition. Because the task was complex, novel, yet involved consistent information-processing demands, performance was expected to be determined initially by general intellectual abilities. However, these correlations were expected to attenuate as practice continued. In contrast, correlations between perceptual speed measures were predicted to increase in association with performance, then decrease with later practice.

To derive correlations between ability factors and perfor-

mance variables, a multiple-step analysis procedure was used. First, a common, factor-analytic structure representing abilities underlying the ASVAB was derived. The Air Force normed reference group of 2,620 applicants to the U.S. Armed Forces was chosen to provide this basic model of abilities (Ree, Mullins, Mathews, & Massey, 1982). Initial factoring was accomplished by using squared multiple correlations in the diagonal, with four factors resulting from the analysis (see Ree et al. for details). The reference factor matrix (from Ree et al.) was then rotated by using an orthogonalized hierarchical rotation procedure (Schmid & Leiman, 1957). This method allows for the derivation of higher order factors (in this case, a single General ability factor) and representation in a single orthogonal factor solution. The final factor solution contained the first-order factors identified as Verbal, Vocational–Technical Information, Math, and Perceptual Speed abilities, along with, and independent of, a second-order General ability factor.

These ability factors (especially the Perceptual Speed factor) are not estimated with as many reference tests as is normally desirable (i.e., greater than three tests per factor). However, in addition to the large norming sample data, there is substantial evidence that points to both the convergent and divergent validity of these factors (see, e.g., reviews in Technical Supplement to the Counselor's Manual for the Armed Services Vocational Aptitude Battery Form-14, 1985).

Each of the group ASVAB intercorrelation matrices (for this experiment and the later ones) was independently factored and then rotated (by a Procrustes procedure; see Schönemann, 1966) to the normed target solution. An example factor solution—from the no-goal group data—is presented in Table 3.

With the exception of the communality estimates, all of the sample matrices well-fitted the target solution after transformation. The differences in communality estimates between the current data and the normed data are attributable to the restric-

Table 3
ASVAB Hierarchical Solution for Experiment 1: No-Goal Condition

	Ability factor				
Test	General	Verbal	Vocational–Technical Information	Math	Perceptual Speed
1. General Science	*.552*	*.401*	.125	.120	−.225
2. Arithmetic Reasoning	*.547*	−.033	.021	*.385*	.141
3. Word Knowledge	*.540*	*.476*	−.043	.068	−.067
4. Paragraph Comprehension	*.536*	*.347*	−.003	−.001	.168
5. Numerical Operations	*.310*	−.150	−.247	.195	*.624*
6. Coding Speed	.263	−.095	−.221	.087	*.612*
7. Auto and Shop Information	*.304*	−.010	*.682*	−.144	−.233
8. Mathematics Knowledge	*.583*	.041	−.114	*.423*	.187
9. Mechanical Comprehension	*.532*	.108	*.453*	.066	−.151
10. Electronics Information	*.489*	.154	*.524*	−.010	−.244

Note. ASVAB = Armed Services Vocational Aptitude Battery. General = second-order ability factor. Loadings greater than .300 are given in italics.

tion of range of abilities found in the current samples; these subjects were all of high enough ability to pass the initial selection hurdles on the basis of the ASVAB test scores.[7] For our purposes, the use of Procrustes transformations does not encounter any of the common objections to the use of the Procrustes procedure in other situations.

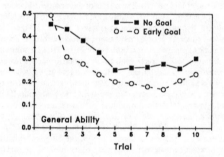

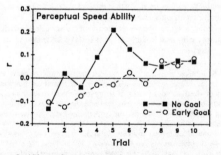

Figure 7. Ability–performance correlations by ability factor, condition, and air traffic controller task trial. (No-goal condition is in solid lines and filled squares; early-goal condition is in dashed lines and open circles.)

The final step in determining ability–performance correlations was use of the Dwyer extension procedure (Dwyer, 1937) for determining the factor loadings (i.e., correlations with the abilities, in this orthogonal factor space) of the individual task performance variables. For a detailed discussion of this procedure, see Humphreys (1960; see also Ackerman, 1986a, 1987). The results from this series of calculations are correlations between the five ASVAB abilities and task performance at each practice trial, for each experiment. From this set of ability factors, only two are of current theoretical interest: the General and Perceptual Speed factors (see Ackerman, 1988).

Correlations between the two key abilities (General and Perceptual Speed) and performance are presented in Figure 7 (these correlations were derived separately for the no-goal and early-goal conditions).

As can be seen from Figure 7, the data were generally consistent with the predictions. Initial performance was moderately associated with the General ability factor (*r*s = .45 and .49, for no-goal and early-goal conditions, respectively), and later performance showed decreasing correlations with the General ability. Also, at least in the no-goal condition, Perceptual Speed showed increasing, then decreasing correlations with performance (which are associated with transitions through the skill acquisition phases).

The first indication of an interaction between ability and motivation is revealed by the differences between the pattern of ability–performance correlations for the no-goal and early-goal groups. At Trial 1 (pretreatment), the general ability–performance correlations were equivalent for the two groups. However, when the goal manipulation was implemented, the correlation between general ability and performance (in the early-goal group) dropped to a greater degree than occurred in the control group (*r* = .45 to .42 in no goal, *r* = .49 to .31 in early goal; a test for the significance of the difference between Trial 1 and Trial 2 correlations for the early-goal group was significant, *z* = 3.79, *p* < .01; formulae for this test may be found in Glass &

---

[7] For the three experiments reported in this article, the mean level of subject ability was 0.4 $\hat{\sigma}$ units above the normative sample mean, with a sample standard deviation of 69% of that of the norm.

Stanley, 1970). This decline in association continued through the remaining task trials, *even after the goal was removed* (i.e., after Trial 4). That is, the goal-setting intervention appeared to reduce dependence of task performance on general intelligence; this is a divergent result from the one posed by Vroom (1964), who maintained that performance is a multiplicative function of ability and motivation. Although these two curves were not significantly different from one another by our conservative test, $\chi^2(10, N = 314) = 8.04, p > .05$, the declines in general ability-performance correlations within each curve clearly were significant.[8]

In addition, although less dramatic, there was an attenuated increase in Perceptual Speed ability-performance correlations in the early-goal condition (once again, the correlations were equivalent at Trial 1). No peak is seen in the early-goal correlations (at least in the amount of practice given), suggesting that the subjects did not reach the later stages of skill acquisition. These Perceptual Speed ability-performance patterns were indeed significantly different, $\chi^2(10, N = 314) = 29.88, p < .01$. Taken together, the two ability-performance correlation patterns indicate that the early-goal manipulation reduced the role of cognitive-intellectual abilities in determining individual differences in performance.

Means and ANOVA Results

Results of separate 2×2 (Goal $\times$ Ability) ANOVAs on landings and errors on Trial 1, prior to the goal assignment, indicated the expected significant main effects for ability on landings, $F(1, 309) = 64.05, p < .01$, but no significant effects for errors ($F < 1$). Low-ability subjects landed substantially fewer planes than high-ability subjects. No significant effects were obtained for the Goal factor, $F(1, 309) = 1.13, p > .05$, for landings; $F < 1$, for errors. Given the power associated with this sample size, such a result (along with random assignment to treatment), provides confidence in a lack of pretreatment differences between these groups.

Given little a priori knowledge about the task information-processing demands, two contrasting hypotheses can be examined with respect to the effects of the goal manipulation. If the task were pitched at an easy level (i.e., few resource demands), subjects would be expected to benefit from goal setting (although low-ability subjects would be expected to benefit the most). If the task were pitched at a too difficult level, subjects would be expected to show deficits associated with the competing resource demands of the task and self-regulation (with low-ability subjects expected to show the largest deficits). To test these possibilities, we conducted $2 \times 2 \times 9$ (Goal $\times$ Ability $\times$ Trial) repeated measures ANOVAs separately (for Trials 2-10) on landings and errors (after a test for homogeneity of regression between ability and performance was passed).

With respect to error scores, significant main effects were obtained for ability, $F(1, 2464) = 4.77, p < .05$; and trial, $F(1, 2464) = 19.12, p < .01$. High-ability subjects made fewer errors ($M_{high} = 9.32$) than low-ability subjects ($M_{low} = 10.82$). In addition, all subjects made significantly fewer errors with practice ($M_{T1} = 12.68; M_{T10} = 8.97$). No other significant main or interaction effects were obtained for errors.

For landings, significant main effects were obtained for ability, $F(1, 308) = 19.03, p < .01$ ($M_{high} = 34.07, M_{low} = 30.19$);

and trial, $F(8, 2464) = 593.80, p < .01$, as well as a significant Ability $\times$ Trial interaction effect, $F(8, 2464) = 6.67, p < .01$. The Ability $\times$ Trial interaction indicates that low- and high-ability subjects converged in performance during task practice (low-ability subjects improved more over trials). Among low-ability subjects, mean number of landings increased from 16.79 to 36.59 (Trial 2 to Trial 10). Among high-ability subjects, mean number of landings increased from 23.53 to 39.97. The Ability $\times$ Trial interaction was consistent with ability-performance theory expectations and with the ability-performance correlations reported previously (see also Ackerman, 1987, 1988, 1989).

Across the nine task trials, results obtained in both landing and error score analyses indicated no significant goal effect ($F < 1$) or Goal $\times$ Ability interaction effects, $F(8, 2464) = 1.08, p > .05$. These results indicate that the task was neither pitched too difficult nor too easy for the subject population under investigation.

However, because attentional demands imposed by the task were expected to decline over practice, and should have declined more quickly for high-ability subjects (see Figure 7), we expected a lagged, or emergent, effect of the goal manipulation on performance at later trials. That is, any benefit from the goal will be expected to accrue first to the high-ability subjects. To test this notion, we conducted a post hoc $2 \times 2 \times 3$ (Goal $\times$ Ability $\times$ Trial) ANOVA on landings obtained in the final set of three trials (Trials 8-10). The results of this analysis did indeed indicate a Trial $\times$ Goal $\times$ Ability interaction, $F(2, 616) = 5.99, p < .01$. Examination of the interaction, shown in Figure 8, indicates that at Trial 8, early-goal subjects performed about the same as the no-goal subjects. However, by Trial 10, subjects in the high-ability, early-goal group demonstrated increased performance in comparison with the no-goal group, whereas subjects in the low-ability, early-goal group continued to perform at a level equivalent to the low-ability, no-goal group. This finding strengthens the notion that goal assignments can exert a subtle, emergent effect on performance (Campbell, 1984; Wood, Locke, & Smith, 1986; Wood, Mento, & Locke, 1987).

Consistent with our proposed model, the late performance improvement among high-ability, early-goal subjects appears to be related to the declining attentional demands of the task. The lack of performance improvement during later trials among low-ability, early-goal subjects is consistent with the notion of resource constraints associated with intellectual ability. For the low-ability subjects, the slower decline of resource demands did not appear to enable these subjects to take advantage of self-regulatory activity.

---

[8] To put these cross-group comparisons into a statistical context, we tested the difference between the two intertrial correlation matrices, each of which included a vector of ability-performance correlations. A LISREL program was implemented in which the intertrial correlations were left free to vary, and the ability-performance correlations were fixed as equal. A χ^2 goodness-of-fit test was then applied to the model. The power of this procedure appears limited, but it is at least a yardstick by which these patterns may be compared. For example, the no-goal/early-goal general ability-performance comparisons in the top of Figure 7 are significantly different even by a simple nonparametric Sign test (9 of the 10 trials had lower correlations in the early-goal condition—which leads to a rejection of the null hypothesis at $\alpha = .05$—but were not significant by the LISREL procedure).

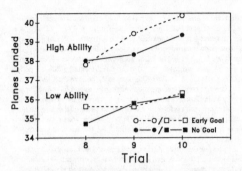

Figure 8. Planes landed as a function of air traffic controller task trial for final three trials, by condition and by ability group (median split). (No-goal condition is in solid lines; early-goal condition is in dashed lines. High-ability group is in circles; low-ability group is in squares.)

Attentional Measures

Results obtained on 2 × 2 (Goal × Ability) ANOVAs of attentional measures taken following Trial 10 are shown in Table 4. Significant main effects for ability were obtained on four of the nine variables. Low-ability subjects reported more spontaneous goal setting, spending more time thinking about their performance compared with others, and having more frequent negative self-reactive thoughts than high-ability subjects. Early-goal subjects reported checking their performance scores during the final task trials less frequently than no-goal subjects. Although the ANOVA did not indicate a significant ability effect, a full-information regression did indicate a small but significant ability effect; namely, high-ability subjects perceived the task to be more pressured than low-ability subjects (presumably this difference in significance levels is a result of the particularly modest reliability of the measure). This pattern of findings is consistent with the performance results that indicate a relatively more powerful effect of individual differences in ability relative to the motivational intervention. The less frequent performance checking by early-goal subjects (compared with no-goal subjects) during the final set of task trials supports the inference

that the initial goal assignment had an emergent effect on later attentional allocation policies. This explanation implies that early-goal subjects allocated few resources to self-regulatory activities because of high task demands on available attention or low self-confidence in goal attainability. Interestingly, high-ability subjects reported the ATC task to be significantly more difficult than did low-ability subjects.

Discussion

Results obtained in this experiment show that ability exerts a strong influence on early performance in complex skill acquisition. Consistent with the proposed model, the influence of general ability on performance attenuates as attentional demands of the task decline with practice. The pattern of declining general ability–performance correlations is consistent with previous findings in the literature, as discussed earlier (e.g., see Fleishman & Hempel, 1954, 1955). In our complex ATC task, characterized by consistent information-processing demands, this pattern is further reflected by greater performance improvement with practice of low-ability subjects, compared with that of high-ability subjects (i.e., the Ability × Trial interaction).

The pattern of ability–performance correlations obtained in the early-goal condition provides some evidence of a demand on cognitive resources associated with the goal assignment. Nonetheless, goal assignments made during the initial stage of skill acquisition appeared to exert no global effects on mean performance. Further examination of manipulation effects on self-regulatory activities may help explain this finding. During the early stage of skill acquisition, attentional demands imposed by the task were high and mean Trial 1 landing performance was generally quite low ($M = 9.08$). Given the high resource demands of the task and the strong positive correlation between Trial 1 performance and self-confidence ratings in capability for goal attainment, subjects may have opted to allocate fewer resources to self-regulatory activity in favor of greater allocations to on-task performance. The relatively low level of F10 goal–performance call-ups during the goal trials supports this explanation and suggests that the goal manipulation stimulated only minimal self-regulatory activity. Failure to trigger substantial self-regulatory activity among early-goal subjects, in turn,

Table 4

ANOVAs for Experiment 1: No-Goal and Early-Goal Conditions

	Factor			
Measure	Ability	Goal	Ability × Goal	MS_E
Spontaneous goal setting	4.17*	.00	.80	7.85
On-task attention	1.26	2.18	.44	74.16
Off-task attention	.02	2.39	.05	3.67
Attention to performance evaluation	7.39**	.18	.05	26.24
Positive self-reactions	2.57	.07	1.73	35.76
Negative self-reactions	10.64**	1.81	1.74	10.44
Task difficulty	4.89*	1.54	1.16	8.00
Task pressure	1.75	5.00*	.98	5.11
Performance checking	2.98	14.69**	3.26	5.66

Note. ANOVAs = analyses of variance. Degrees of freedom = (1, 308) for each measure.
* $p < .05$. ** $p < .01$.

would explain the absence of motivational effects on the performance measure.

Finally, the main effect of ability on self-report measures of attentional activity during the last three trials is particularly interesting. Low-ability subjects reported more frequent thoughts about performance compared with others, and more frequent negative self-reactions during the final three task trials compared with high-ability subjects. The presence of a main effect for ability on landings precludes determination of whether the more frequent self-evaluative thoughts and lower level of performance checking were a partial cause or consequence of performance. In either case, however, our model indicates that allocation of attentional resources to off-task activities will impair skill acquisition and task performance.

Experiment 2

Experiment 1 provided the baseline data for the ability–performance relations, along with some indications of the nature of goal-setting influences in this complex skill acquisition task. The next step was to further examine the facilitative effects of a goal-setting manipulation in the context of skill acquisition.

Two features of the integrated model were investigated in this study. First, the proposed model indicates that the products of self-regulatory processing may aid learning, depending on the extent to which self-regulation strategies ultimately increase on-task attentional effort (Bandura, 1986; F. H. Kanfer & Hagerman, 1987; Kuhl, 1986). To attain these benefits, however, persons must have sufficient available cognitive resources. Second, the model predicts a reduction in attentional resource demands with practice as persons make the transition from a declarative representation of the task to procedural knowledge. As task resource demands are reduced, additional cognitive resources become available for self-regulation. Although motivational interventions triggering self-regulatory activities demand cognitive resources, such resources are not required for adequate task performance, *subsequent to the declarative phase of skill acquisition*. Thus, an imposed goal is not expected to shift critical resources away from task performance during the intermediate phase of skill acquisition. Furthermore, because there are resources available during this stage of skill acquisition, the increased task effort product of self-regulation can be reallocated back into on-task activities. Thus, we predicted that self-regulatory activities engaged in during the intermediate phase of skill acquisition would enhance task performance.

Method

Subjects

In this experiment, 144 U.S. Air Force trainees (all men) were tested in a late-goal assignment condition. Subjects were tested in "flights," as described in Experiment 1. (Prior to data analysis, data from two subjects were discarded for failure to follow task instructions.) As in Experiment 1, because a few subjects had incomplete data (e.g., computer failure, sickness), the degrees of freedom differ by as much as 2 or 3 *df* on some analyses.) The final sample contained 142 subjects.

Procedure

The procedure used in this experiment was identical to that in Experiment 1, except that the motivational manipulation was introduced at a later stage of practice (i.e., at Trial 5). Subjects in the late-goal condition received "do your best" instructions for Trials 1–4. Prior to Trial 5, late-goal subjects received their first goal assignment. These subjects were assigned a cumulative performance score goal of 2,200 points (per trial) for Trials 5, 6, and 7. The 2,200-point goal was selected on the basis of prior research indicating that this score represented a difficult performance goal (approximately 90th percentile) for Trials 5, 6, and 7. Late-goal subjects completed questionnaires prior to and following the goal trials. As in Experiment 1, subjects were provided periodic opportunities to check their performance with respect to the goal during the three assigned goal trials, using the F10 key. Following Trial 7, late-goal subjects were instructed to "do your best" for the remaining three task trials.

Dependent measures. Ability, performance, and self-report measures were identical to those used in the previous experiment. Reliabilities of self-report measures for the late-goal condition are shown in Table 2.

Results

Manipulation Checks

Goal manipulations. Again, one-way ANOVAS on self-report measures of distal motivation were conducted to assess the impact of ability on these variables. A significant effect for ability was obtained on subjects' predicted performance scores, $F(1, 123) = 5.11, p < .05.$[9] As in Experiment 1, both low- and high-ability subjects predicted attainment of performance scores below the goal assignment ($M_{low} = 1,854; M_{high} = 2,013$). Nevertheless, ability had no significant effect on goal commitment ($F < 1$) or self-confidence ratings for goal attainment ($F < 1$).

To compare the relative influence of the early-goal and late-goal assignments, a series of 2 × 2 (Ability × Goal) ANOVAS were also conducted. No significant differences were obtained between level of goal commitment among early-goal and late-goal subjects ($F < 1$). However, subjects in the late-goal assignment condition reported significantly higher self-confidence in capability for goal attainment than did early-goal subjects, $F(1, 290) = 16.38, p < .01; M_{early} = 6.71, M_{late} = 5.33$. Corresponding to the correlational results obtained in Experiment 1, self-confidence ratings among late-goal subjects were not significantly correlated with intellectual ability ($r = -.04$) but were significantly correlated with predicted performance score ($r = -.59, p < .01$) and performance on Trial 4 (i.e., the trial immediately prior to the goal assignment; $r = -.34, p < .01$). The correlational patterns obtained in the late-goal condition are similar to those obtained in the early-goal condition and suggest that the higher self-confidence ratings of late-goal subjects are associated with self-observations of improvement over trials.

Late-goal subjects also reported significantly more frequent self-regulatory activity during the goal trials, compared with early-goal subjects. Late-goal subjects reported a higher frequency of performance monitoring, $F(1, 289) = 10.64, p < .01; M_{early} = 6.86, M_{late} = 8.20$, compared with early-goal subjects. Furthermore, early-goal subjects used the F10 key call-ups significantly fewer times than did late-goal subjects, $F(1, 290) = 11.90, p < .01; M_{early} = 4.63, M_{late} = 7.39$. These findings sup-

---

[9] Thirteen subjects (10 low ability, 3 high ability) were designated as missing because of failure to understand instructions for entering their predicted performance scores.

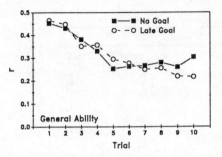

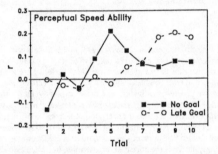

Figure 9. Ability–performance correlations by ability factor, condition, and air traffic controller task trial. (No-goal condition [from Experiment 1] is in solid lines and filled squares; late-goal condition is in dotted lines and open circles.)

port the inference that the early-goal assignment in Experiment 1 resulted in less self-regulatory activity than did the late-goal assignment.

Performance: Behavioral Measures

Tests of the Ability × Motivation interactions were conducted by comparing Trials 5–10 performance of late-goal subjects with corresponding trial performance of no-goal subjects in Experiment 1. A 2 × 2 × 6 (Goal × Ability × Task Trial) repeated measures ANOVA was conducted on landing and error scores (again, after a check was made for homogeneity of regression between ability and performance). The error score ANOVA indicated a significant main effect for trial, $F(5, 1515) = 6.08$, $p < .01$; all subjects made fewer errors with practice. No other significant effects or interactions were obtained on errors.

Results obtained in the ANOVA of landings demonstrated significant main effects for ability, $F(1, 303) = 14.38$, $p < .01$; and trial, $F(5, 1515) = 118.70$, $p < .01$. High-ability subjects landed more planes than low-ability subjects across all trials, although both high- and low-ability subjects improved with practice. Examination of the ability–performance correlations obtained in the late-goal condition provides additional evidence for these effects. As shown in Figure 9, the pattern of general ability–performance correlations across trials among late-goal subjects

is characterized by a gradual decline across task trials, essentially equivalent to the no-goal condition, $\chi^2(10, N = 309) = 4.10$, $p > .05$. The major difference between the no-goal and late-goal curves pertains to the perceptual speed ability–performance correlations, $\chi^2(10, N = 309) = 31.18$, $p < .01$. Similarly to the early-goal condition, the late-goal data show a slower rise in correlations (after Trial 4, when the goal is implemented), again indicating a disruption of the normal skill acquisition sequence.

In addition to significant main effects, a significant Goal × Trial interaction effect, $F(5, 1515) = 3.42$, $p < .01$, was also obtained on landing scores. As shown graphically in Figure 10, subjects in the late-goal condition showed greater performance improvement over trials, compared with subjects in the no-goal condition. This interaction effect provides support for the hypothesized beneficial effects of motivation when implemented during an intermediate phase of skill acquisition. These data support the hypothesis that the benefits of motivational manipulations occur as the resource demands of the task decline during skill acquisition (in contrast with Experiment 1). No significant Goal × Ability interaction was obtained, suggesting that the task was not yet general resource-insensitive for high-ability subjects. Taken together, these findings indicate that, during an intermediate stage of skill acquisition, low- and high-ability subjects derive parallel benefits from the motivation manipulation.

Attentional Measures

Results obtained on 2 × 2 (Goal × Ability) ANOVAs of attentional measures taken following Trial 10 are displayed in Table 5. Consistent with findings obtained in Experiment 1, low-ability subjects reported significantly more spontaneous goal setting than high-ability subjects ($M_{\text{low}} = 7.23$; $M_{\text{high}} = 8.05$). However, subjects in the late-goal condition reported significantly less spontaneous goal setting than subjects in the no-goal condition ($M_{\text{late goal}} = 8.12$; $M_{\text{no goal}} = 7.19$). Subjects in the late-goal condition also reported less attention to their performance

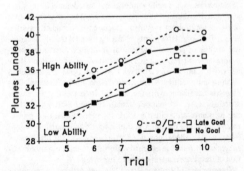

Figure 10. Planes landed as a function of air traffic controller task trial for final six trials, by condition and by ability group (median split). (No-goal condition [from Experiment 1] is in solid lines; late-goal condition is in dotted lines. High-ability group is in circles; low-ability group is in squares.)

Table 5

ANOVAs for Experiment 2: No-Goal and Late-Goal Conditions

	Factor			
Measure	Ability	Goal	Ability × Goal	MS_E
Spontaneous goal setting	5.05*	6.96**	.43	7.89
On-task attention	.37	.46	1.36	77.98
Off-task attention	1.21	.02	1.23	4.73
Attention to performance evaluation	.39	.53	3.98*	26.89
Positive self-reactions	3.21	.32	.85	40.60
Negative self-reactions	2.17	2.55	.30	10.98
Task difficulty	2.50	2.97	2.71	8.53
Task pressure	2.80	.66	.37	5.12
Performance checking	.00	22.48**	.02	5.42

Note. ANOVAs = analyses of variance. Degrees of freedom = (1, 301) for each measure.
* $p < .05$. ** $p < .01$.

score, compared with no-goal subjects ($M_{\text{late goal}} = 3.83$; $M_{\text{no goal}} = 5.11$).

A significant Ability × Goal interaction was obtained on frequency of thoughts about normative performance. In this crossover interaction, low-ability subjects reported more comparison thoughts than did high-ability subjects in the no-goal conditions ($M_{\text{no goal, low}} = 10.33$; $M_{\text{no goal, high}} = 8.86$), whereas the reverse pattern was obtained for the late-goal condition ($M_{\text{late goal, low}} = 8.76$; $M_{\text{late goal, high}} = 9.68$). No significant main or interaction effects were obtained on positive or negative self-reactions during task performance, perceived task difficulty, or perceived task pressure (although the full-information regression revealed an ability effect for perceived task pressure [and for task difficulty], similar to that in Experiment 1; i.e., high-ability subjects reported greater task pressure [and greater task difficulty]).

Discussion

The results obtained in Experiment 2 demonstrate that a motivational intervention during the intermediate stage of skill acquisition (i.e., when ability–attentional task demands are partly attenuated) enhanced task performance. The imposition of a late-goal assignment was also associated with higher reported levels of self-regulatory activity during the goal trials. The gradual decline of general intellectual ability–performance correlations across trials suggests that activation of self-regulatory activity did not drain resources from task performance but in fact may have redirected attentional effort toward the task. This result is consistent with the delayed increases in perceptual speed ability–performance correlations (see Figure 9). The failure to obtain an Ability × Goal interaction effect on performance indicates that high-ability subjects continued to benefit from on-task allocations of effort, suggesting that high-ability subjects continued to operate within the resource-limited portion of the performance–resource function.

Comparison of early-goal and late-goal groups on measures of reported self-regulatory activity indicates that early-goal subjects engaged in less self-regulatory activity than late-goal subjects. This finding cannot be readily explained in terms of differences in objective goal difficulty across the two conditions,

because the assigned performance goal of 1,900 points in the early-goal condition and 2,100 points in the late-goal condition represented the 87th and 88th percentile of performance scores obtained in each condition on Trials 4 and 7, respectively. However, we propose two further alternative explanations for this finding. First, an unspecified cognitive contingency mechanism might exist that controls the operation of self-regulatory activities, depending on the attentional demands of the task. For example, when task demands are high, this mechanism would automatically limit the allocation of attention, but when task demands are reduced, resource allocations to self-regulation would be placed under volitional control.

A second explanation is that the differential self-observations of performance made by subjects in the early-goal and late-goal conditions affected their willingness to engage in goal-directed self-regulatory activity. Lower confidence ratings on capability of goal attainment among early-goal subjects may have been due to observation of one trial of relatively poor performance. In contrast, late-goal subjects observed improvement in their performance over the four trials preceding the goal assignment.

A test of these explanations with respect to the demands and consequences of self-regulatory activities on task performance requires creating a situation in which subjects' observations of their past performance lead to similar perceptions of confidence in goal attainment, despite differences in the development of skills. If the cognitive, ability-based mechanism explanation is correct, then the provision of a goal assignment during the declarative phase of skill acquisition (when task demands are high) should markedly hinder the performance of low-ability persons but not affect the performance of high-ability persons (compared to a no-goal control condition). When attentional demands are reduced, however, the provision of a goal assignment during the intermediate phase of skill acquisition should enhance the performance of both groups as predicted by the model.

In contrast, if the self-confidence explanation is correct, then the provision of a goal assignment during the declarative phase of skill acquisition should exert the effects hypothesized by the integrated model. That is, high-ability persons should also demonstrate lower performance compared to a no-goal control condition. Goal assignments during the intermediate phase of skill acquisition would be expected to enhance task performance as predicted by the model. Experiment 3 was designed to further explore these hypotheses, by an explicit manipulation of the task information-processing demands in a part-task training paradigm.

Experiment 3

Experiments 1 and 2 provided data that address several issues outlined in the proposed motivation/ability/information-processing framework. The findings obtained in these two experiments are consistent with the changing ability–performance correlations expected within the proposed framework. Furthermore, the results of these experiments provide tentative support for the proposition that the impact of motivational interventions (e.g., goal setting) on performance depends on the dynamic changes in attention/information-processing demands of the task during skill acquisition.

The third, and final, experiment tested the hypothesized joint effects of ability differences, self-regulatory activities, and attentional demands within an experimental paradigm that explicitly altered the information-processing demands of the task with a set of two different part-task training procedures, denoted *declarative* and *procedural*. The declarative knowledge training part-task procedure was implemented to reduce the attentional demands of the full ATC task. Thus, when the task attention demands are reduced, goal setting (that triggers self-regulatory activities), is expected to lead to performance improvements. The second part-task procedure, procedural knowledge training, was also structured to facilitate full-task performance, but to do so without reducing cognitive–declarative resource demands of the full task. Goal setting that triggers self-regulatory activities, when the subjects are under high resource load, was expected to result in a decrement in performance.

In keeping with the concepts of the three phases of skill acquisition, the purpose of the declarative part-task training paradigm was to allow subjects to form a declarative knowledge foundation for performing the ATC task prior to full-task engagement. This declarative knowledge training was designed so that subjects would begin the full task at a point close to where the resource demands for performance begin to markedly diminish.

The procedural knowledge part-task training paradigm was also structured to facilitate full-task performance. However, procedural knowledge training only focused on development of the motor sequence skills that facilitate performance in the full task. As such, positive transfer from training to full-task transfer was expected, but the cognitive–declarative attentional resource demands of the task were not expected to be markedly reduced. Thus, subjects engaged in procedural part-task training were predicted to begin the full task at a point where resource demands for performance remained high.

Given that both declarative and procedural part-task training paradigms involve repetitive trials in which persons improve with practice, we expected subjects in both part-task conditions to demonstrate similar, high levels of self-confidence in goal attainment prior to starting the first full-task ATC trial.

The following three sets of general hypotheses were derived from the proposed model and from the nature of these part-task training procedures:

1. With declarative knowledge part-task training, goal setting will facilitate skill acquisition (with greater facilitation as the skills are acquired, i.e., an emergent effect).

2. With procedural knowledge part-task training, goal setting will impair skill acquisition.

3. Given that low-ability subjects are most likely to perform in a more resource-limited area of the performance–resource function, benefits and impediments from goal setting will have greater impact on the performance of low-ability subjects than on that of high-ability subjects.

Method

Subjects

Participants in this study were 568 U.S. Air Force recruits (166 women). Subjects were tested in "flights," as described in Experiment 1. (Prior to data analysis, data from some subjects were discarded, some for a lack of ability testing records [3], and others for failure to follow task instructions [13]. Finally, because a few subjects had incomplete data [e.g., computer failure, sickness], the degrees of freedom differ by as much as 2 or 3 *df* on some analyses.) The final sample size was 552 subjects.

Procedure

As in Experiments 1 and 2, all subjects received, by computer, an introduction to the session and instructions for performing the ATC task at the start of the experimental session. Following completion of the standard instructions, subjects were then assigned by "flight" to either a declarative ($N = 278$) or procedural ($N = 274$) part-task training condition.

Part-Task Training Manipulations

The part-task training manipulations were designed to result in different ATC task performance–resource functions by providing subjects with one of two types of part-task training prior to engaging in the full ATC task. Subjects performed 210 trials (over about a 40-min period) in either a declarative or procedural part-task training condition.

Declarative part-task training. In this condition, subjects were required to *learn the rules* of the ATC task. Subjects were told that the purpose of the part-task training procedure was to help prepare them for performing the full ATC task. Subjects were instructed to respond to the question in each scenario as quickly as possible, while maintaining an accuracy level of about 90% correct over each trial block.

Subjects were shown a series of static task scenarios. In each scenario, an ATC rule was shown and a question was asked that related to the proper operation of the task with respect to the given rule. An example scenario presented to subjects is displayed in Figure 11. In this scenario, the display indicates an attempt to land a DC10 plane from the hold pattern on a long runway. Rule 4 (which governs the plane type–runway type matching conditions) is also displayed on the screen along with an inquiry ("Is a ↵ [carriage return] a legal move [for this situation]?"). Subjects were required to indicate the correct answer to the question by pressing keys designated as *yes* or *no*. Immediately following the response, a feedback message was displayed for 1.5 s before a new scenario was presented. Feedback following each response indicated (a) the correctness of the response, (b) the cumulative accuracy of responses within the trial block, and (c) the cumulative mean reaction time of correct responses within the trial block. After each trial block, subjects received information on the average accuracy and reaction time of correct responses across trial blocks.

Scenarios were divided into seven trial blocks, consisting of 30 scenarios per block. All six ATC rules were covered in a comprehensive manner across trial blocks, although each trial only queried about a single rule. The simplest rules were included in early trial blocks, and complex rules were given in later trial blocks.

Procedural part-task training. In this condition, subjects received practice in *learning the keyboard response procedures* of the task. Subjects were shown a series of dynamic task scenarios (presented in real time) and subjects were instructed to complete the key sequence that was displayed on the screen. An example of a trial task scenario is shown in Figure 12.

Each trial/key sequence scenario represented logical moves (or series of moves) that would be followed by a skilled ATC task performer. As illustrated in Figure 12, a subject could be shown a scenario with a plane in Position 1n of the hold pattern. The instructions tell the subject to perform the specific key sequence that would select and get the plane, move it down through Level 1, and then to an appropriate runway. Subjects were instructed to press the keys rapidly but also to note the results of the keypresses that were displayed on the screen as the keys were pressed. If an incorrect key was pressed, the trial ended, and the subject was shown an *error* message. Otherwise, after completion of each correct key sequence, subjects were shown a *correct* message. In addition, accuracy information was presented at the end of each block of 30 trials. Subjects received seven blocks of trials. The length and complexity of key sequences increased within and across trial blocks.

Goal Manipulations

Following completion of part-task training, all subjects performed six 10-min trials of the full ATC task. Prior to beginning the full ATC task, half of the subjects in each part-task training condition were randomly assigned to a no-goal condition. Remaining subjects were assigned to the goal conditions. Thus, there were four between-subjects conditions in this experiment: (a) declarative–no goal, (b) declarative–goal, (c) procedural–no goal, and (d) procedural–goal conditions.

Subjects in the goal conditions were assigned a specific and difficult performance goal of 2,200 points for each of the first three full-task trials (Trials 1–3). The goal was identical to that assigned in Experiment 2. Also, as in Experiment 1 and 2, when the goal was activated, subjects were able to check their goal progress with the F10 key. Subjects in the

no-goal conditions were instructed to "do your best" on each trial. For Trials 4–6, all subjects were instructed to "do your best."

Dependent Measures

Ability, performance, and self-report measures described previously were used in this experiment. Distal motivational processes and self-regulatory activity among subjects in the goal conditions were assessed prior to beginning the first full ATC task trial and immediately following Trial 3, respectively. Reliabilities of all composite self-report measures are shown in Table 2.

Results

Manipulation Checks

Part-task training manipulations. To assess the extent to which the declarative part-task training procedure facilitated declarative knowledge representation, a 2 × 2 × 2 (Training × Goal × Ability) ANOVA was conducted on composite scores from the rules/knowledge test. The scoring scheme used for coding free-form responses to the rules/knowledge test was to assign one point for correct description of each rule (or subcomponent of a rule). A composite rules/knowledge test score was obtained for each subject by summing the points earned across all rules. Maximum score possible was 14 points.

ANOVA results support the contention that declarative part-task training improved declarative knowledge of the rules. Although the subjects did not yet have complete knowledge of all the rules, subjects in the declarative condition remembered an average of one rule more than subjects in the procedural condition, $F(1, 548) = 17.10$, $p < .01$; $M_{dec} = 5.74$, $M_{proc} = 4.78$. Furthermore, the mean score obtained in the procedural training condition is quite similar to the overall mean score obtained by no-goal subjects in Experiment 1 ($M = 4.66$), suggesting that the procedural training condition did not substantially affect declarative task knowledge in a manner different from task performance only. In accordance with the notion of ability as an

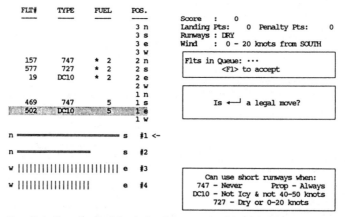

Figure 11. An illustration of a declarative knowledge part-task training trial. (The box in the lower right side of the figure shows Rule 4; the box above the rule shows the question asked of the subject.)

```
        FLT#    TYPE    FUEL    POS.
                                ────
                                3 n
                                3 s
                                3 e
                                3 w
                                2 n
                                2 s
                                2 e
                                2 w
        496     prop    5       1 n
  ->                            1 s
                                1 e
        286     DC10    5       1 w

  n ══════════════════ s  #1

  n ═══════════════════ s  #2

  w |||||||||||||||||||||||||| e  #3

  w ||||||||||||||||||| e  #4
```

```
Score    :    0
Landing Pts:    0   Penalty Pts:    0
Runways : WET
Wind     : 40 - 50 knots from SOUTH

┌─────────────────────────┐
│ Flts in Queue: ········  │
│       <F1> to accept     │
└─────────────────────────┘

┌─────────────────────────┐
│ Type the following keys: │
│   ↑ ←┘ ↓ ↓ ↓ ↓ ↓ ←┘     │
└─────────────────────────┘
```

Figure 12. An illustration of a procedural knowledge part-task training trial. (The box in the middle right side of the figure shows the instructions to the subject.)

important determinant of learning, a significant main effect for ability, $F(1, 548) = 79.34, p < .01$, was also obtained, with high-ability subjects remembering approximately two rules more than low-ability subjects ($M_{high} = 6.18, M_{low} = 4.33$). Of further note is the significant main effect for goal, $F(1, 548) = 6.11, p < .05$. Subjects in the goal conditions remembered an average of 0.5 fewer rules than subjects in the no-goal conditions ($M_{goal} = 5.04; M_{no\ goal} = 5.49$).

Goal manipulations. A fundamental issue in this experiment concerned the similarity among groups in initial self-confidence ratings of capability to attain the assigned goal (i.e., for declarative-goal and procedural-goal conditions). Results obtained in a 2 × 2 (Training × Ability) ANOVA on this measure indicated no significant main or interaction effects. Overall, subjects in Experiment 3 reported a relatively high level of self-confidence ($M = 5.61$), similar to the level of the late-goal subjects in Experiment 2 ($M = 5.33$). This finding permits testing of the cognitive/ability explanation and lends support for the notion that group differences in self-confidence ratings in Experiments 1 and 2 were related to systematic differences in self-observation of prior ATC task performance.

A similar 2 × 2 (Training × Ability) ANOVA on goal commitment scores indicated no significant main or interaction effects. Findings obtained on predicted performance score, however, revealed a significant main effect for ability, $F(1, 225) = 13.49, p < .01$.[10] High-ability subjects expected to attain higher performance scores than low-ability subjects ($M_{high} = 1,780; M_{low} = 1,298$).

Analyses conducted on measures of self-regulatory activities during the assigned goal trials provide partial support for the hypothesis of an association between operation of self-regulatory processes and general intellectual ability. A significant main effect for ability was obtained for self-reported attention to performance, $F(1, 274) = 4.75, p < .05$, but no significant ability effect was obtained for attention to the goal. High-ability subjects reported less frequent performance monitoring ($M_{high} = 6.63; M_{low} = 7.47$) than did low-ability subjects.

Performance: Behavioral Measures

Ability–performance data. As shown in the ability–performance correlation patterns displayed in Figure 13, correlations between general ability and performance start off moderate and decline with practice across all four conditions (initial average $r = .48$; final average $r = .26$).

Particularly noteworthy, though, are the differences between the no-goal and goal patterns for declarative and procedural conditions. Although the initial correlations between general ability and performance are essentially equivalent for the declarative–no-goal and goal groups, they are markedly larger in the procedural–no-goal group than in the procedural–goal group, though only for the first two trials. In comparison with the results from Experiments 1 and 2, the lower general ability–performance correlations in the procedural–goal condition mirror those in the early-goal condition. The similarity of no-goal and goal curves in the declarative conditions mirrors the equivalent curves found in the no-goal and late-goal comparison. Such findings support our earlier inferences about the conditions that reflect substantial resource demands associated with early phases of skill acquisition (the procedural and early-goal conditions) and similarly reflect attenuated resource demands associated with later phases of skill acquisition (the declarative and late-goal conditions).

Although there were only six trials of full ATC task practice, there is a general trend for Perceptual Speed ability–performance correlations to follow the expected pattern during skill acquisition. Correlations between perceptual speed and performance start off low at Trial 1 (average $r = .04$) and increase through the last full-task trial (Trial 6; average $r = .19$). Although not significantly different, the contrast between the no-goal condition of the declarative task and the declarative–goal condition is also consistent with the findings from Experiment

[10] Forty-six subjects (31 low ability, 15 high ability) were designated as missing on this measure because of failure to understand instructions for responding to this question.

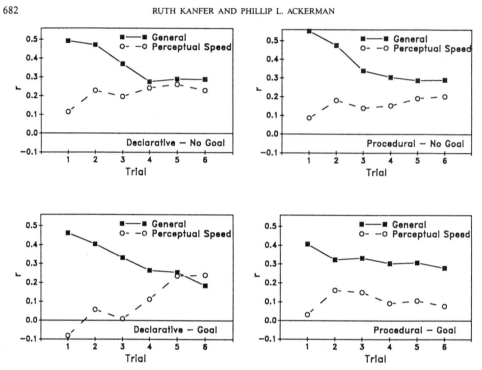

Figure 13. Ability–performance correlations by ability factor, condition, and full-task practice trial. (General ability–performance correlations are in solid lines and filled squares. Perceptual speed–performance correlations are in dashed lines and open circles.)

2, $\chi^2(6, N = 280) = 3.36$, $p > .05$. That is, the goal condition shows a smaller initial correlation between Perceptual Speed ability and performance and a steeper slope of increase over task trials. These data are consistent with the earlier inference that the goal condition leads to a delay in knowledge compilation (which would be associated with a greater reliance on Phase 1 information processing during the goal trials). The patterns of perceptual speed ability–performance correlations for the two procedural conditions do not address this issue in any definitive fashion, because it was quite possible that some proceduralization of skills took place during the part-task training (and thus, prior to the full ATC task trials). For the pairwise tests of ability–performance patterns, only the difference between the procedural–goal and declarative–goal conditions (Perceptual Speed ability) was significant, $\chi^2(6, N = 274) = 14.09$, $p < .05$.

Landings: Means and ANOVA results. A summary of the 2 × 2 × 2 × 6 (Training × Goal × Ability × Trial) ANOVA on landings is provided in Table 6 (as before, a test for homogeneity of regression between ability and performance was passed). As shown, a number of significant main and higher order interaction effects were present. To clarify these effects in the context of the predictions, we will concentrate on these results with respect to Trial 1 of the full ATC task and Trial 6, as well as performance effects across the entire set of trials.

Trial 1. The heaviest demands on the cognitive information-processing system occur when subjects first encounter the full ATC task. (This fact is reflected in the ability–performance correlations discussed previously). As shown in Figure 14, depicting the performance of declarative and procedural training groups across trials, initial performance differences in both part-task training conditions are clearly influenced by intellectual ability.

Although no significant main effect was obtained for training type, it is important to note that Trial 1 landing performance across both no-goal, part-task training conditions was significantly superior to Trial 1 performance in the no-goal condition in Experiment 1, $t(446) = 4.99$, $p < .01$; $M_{\text{no goal, dec & proc}} = 12.02$; $M_{\text{no goal}} = 8.48$. That is, part-task training raised performance an average of 42% above novice performance obtained in the no-goal (no part-task training) control condition. Error rates did not significantly differ across these conditions ($M_{\text{no goal, dec & proc}} = 11.75$; $M_{\text{no goal}} = 12.28$).

Under the high resource-load conditions, the self-regulatory demands of the goal manipulation were hypothesized to create a classic dual-task scenario (i.e., in the procedural–goal condition). That is, subjects needed to share resources between competing demands to perform the full ATC task *and* to engage in self-regulatory activities. An examination of this prediction was

Table 6

Repeated-Measures ANOVA for Experiment 3: Landings and Errors

Factor	Landings	Errors
Between-subjects		
Ability	74.82**	13.54**
Training	3.82	4.18*
Goal	1.52	6.67*
Ability × Training	.53	.98
Ability × Goal	.95	2.36
Training × Goal	11.91**	2.42
Ability × Training × Goal	1.29	1.48
MS_E	320.24	302.14
Within-subjects		
Trials	2,047.61**	18.33**
Ability × Trials	8.04**	6.39**
Training × Trials	3.42**	8.27**
Goal × Trials	1.83	2.11
Ability × Training × Trials	.03	.35
Ability × Goal × Trials	1.49	1.73
Training × Goal × Trials	1.38	.41
Ability × Training × Goal × Trials	3.30**	1.36
MS_E	19.90	31.35

Note. ANOVA = analysis of variance. For between-subjects factors, dfs = (1, 540). For within-subjects factors, dfs = (5, 2,700).
* $p < .05$. ** $p < .01$.

made with a post hoc ANOVA on Trial 1 performance. As expected, the goal manipulation resulted in a general decrement in performance at this early stage of full-task practice, $F(1, 544) = 5.77, p < .05$. On the basis of our proposed model, the negative effects of the goal assignment on performance were expected to be greater in the procedural conditions. At this stage of practice, the Goal × Training interaction was indeed significant, $F(1, 544) = 5.33, p < .05$, although it was not a large effect.

Across trials. Across the six trials of full ATC task practice, the various influences of part-task training type and goal manipulations became more pronounced. The significant Goal × Training interaction effect in Table 6 supports the hypothesis of a differential effect of motivational processes contingent on resource demands imposed by the task. Consistent with hypotheses derived from the model, the goal-setting manipulation was beneficial in the declarative condition (in which cognitive resource demands were reduced) but detrimental in the procedural condition (in which cognitive resource demands remained high).

However, the crux of the investigation is revealed in the significant Training × Goal × Ability × Trial interaction. Although four-way interactions are often difficult to interpret, this result is also consistent with the proposed model and the hypotheses presented previously. This interaction may be partially described by further examination of the two panels in Figure 14. As illustrated in Figure 14, the detrimental effect of the goal assignment in the procedural condition was greater for low-ability subjects than for high-ability subjects. In contrast, as shown, the beneficial effect of the goal assignment in the declarative condition exerted a greater effect on low-ability subjects than on high-ability subjects. When resource demands were high (procedural condition), performance of low-ability subjects was *hurt more* than that of high-ability subjects by the goal

assignment, but when resource demands were reduced (declarative condition), low-ability subjects *benefited more* from the goal assignment than did high-ability subjects.

Trial 6. The interaction between motivation and information-processing demands at the end of task training can be seen in Figure 15. Performance in the less resource-sensitive task condition (declarative training), under the assigned goal condition, was superior to performance in the no-goal condition. In contrast, performance in the resource-dependent (procedural training) task condition, under the assigned goal condition, was *inferior* to performance in the no-goal condition.

Additional ability interactions are seen at the end of the full ATC task trials in Figure 14. Low-ability subjects in the procedural condition with the assigned goal appeared to approach a performance asymptote at a much lower level of performance than was found in the other conditions. In contrast, as also illustrated in Figure 14, low-ability subjects in the declarative condition with the assigned goal ultimately performed as well as high-ability subjects in the goal and no-goal conditions; however, low-ability subjects in the declarative–no-goal condition clearly demonstrated suboptimal skill acquisition.

Errors. Results obtained in the ANOVA on error scores are presented in Table 6. The results of this analysis mirror the results of landings, with two notable exceptions. First, a significant main effect was obtained for training; subjects in the de-

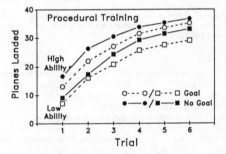

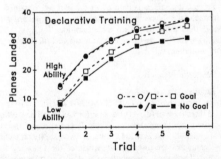

Figure 14. Planes landed as a function of full air traffic controller task trial, by condition and by ability group (median split). (No-goal conditions are in solid lines; goal conditions are in dotted lines. High-ability group is in circles; low-ability group is in squares.)

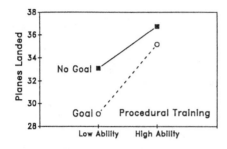

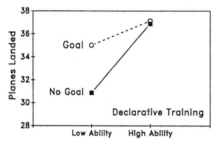

Figure 15. Planes landed in Trial 6, by condition and by ability group (median split). (No-goal conditions are in solid lines; goal conditions are in dotted lines.)

clarative conditions made fewer errors than those in the procedural conditions. As indicated by the Training × Trial interaction, this difference between training conditions attenuated with practice. At the beginning of the full ATC task, subjects in the declarative conditions made an average of 28% fewer errors than did subjects in the procedural conditions (M_{dec} = 9.97, M_{proc} = 13.81). In Trial 6, subjects in the declarative conditions made only 2% fewer errors than did subjects in the procedural conditions (M_{dec} = 10.42, M_{proc} = 10.66).

Second, a significant main effect for goal was obtained on error scores. Subjects in the goal conditions committed more errors than those in the no-goal conditions (M_{goal} = 12.28, $M_{no\,goal}$ = 10.77), even though no omnibus goal effect was found for the landings variable.

Attentional Measures

Results obtained in 2 × 2 × 2 (Training × Goal × Ability) ANOVAs on subjective reports of cognitive activities during the final three trials of full ATC task performance and perceptions of task difficulty are shown in Table 7. The effects of the task manipulations and individual differences in ability on subjective responses are discussed in terms of the following four classes of activity: (a) spontaneous goal setting, (b) attentional focus, (c) perceived task difficulty, and (d) affective self-reactions.

Spontaneous goal setting. The significant main effect for abil-

ity on this measure is consistent with the fact that high-ability subjects were less affected by the goal-setting manipulation than were low-ability subjects. The significant Training × Goal interaction indicated that subjects in the declarative–goal condition set goals more often during Trials 4–6 than did their no-goal counterparts. In contrast, subjects in the procedural–goal condition set goals less often than their no-goal counterparts. These results suggest that subjects' adoption of goal-setting procedures was influenced by their experience during the first three trials. When sufficient resources were available for goal setting (i.e. declarative condition), subjects continued to use the goal-setting procedure. However, when the demands caused by goal assignments drew resources away from task performance (i.e., procedural condition), subjects appeared to respond by reducing their use of the goal-setting procedure in later trials.

In addition, the significant Ability × Goal interaction indicates that subsequent goal-setting activity was also affected by the joint influence of goal assignments and resource availability. In the no-goal conditions, high- and low-ability subjects reported similar frequencies of spontaneous goal setting. In the goal conditions, however, low-ability subjects reported setting goals more frequently than did high-ability subjects. This finding is consistent with ability effects on self-report measures of self-regulatory activity during the assigned goal trials and suggests that high-ability subjects were more able to disregard nonoptimal learning strategies than were low-ability subjects.

Attentional focus. As shown in Table 7, a significant Training × Goal interaction effect was obtained for amount of attention directed to on-task activities. Consistent with the model and previously discussed performance findings, subjects in the procedural–goal condition reported devoting less attention to on-task elements than did subjects in other conditions. In addition, goal subjects reported significantly less performance checking during the final trials than did no-goal subjects.

Examination of measures assessing nontask activities revealed an interesting pattern of results. Specifically, a significant main effect for ability was obtained on attention to performance compared with others, with high-ability subjects reporting fewer of these thoughts than low-ability persons. Furthermore, a significant Training × Goal interaction effect was obtained for attention to off-task activities and for thoughts about performance compared with others. Subjects in the procedural–goal condition reported allocating a greater amount of attention to off-task activities and to normative standing than did subjects in other conditions, a finding that is consistent with the results for on-task activities. Finally, a significant Ability × Training × Goal interaction on the off-task variable indicated that low-ability subjects in the declarative–goal condition reported less off-task activity than did subjects in the other conditions.

Task perceptions. Results obtained on measures of perceived task difficulty and task pressure are consistent with the model and performance data. Significant main effects for goal on both measures indicate that subjects in the goal condition found the task to be more difficult and involve more pressure than no-goal subjects. In addition, low-ability subjects perceived the task as *less* demanding than did high-ability subjects.

Affective reactions. As expected (e.g., Tellegen, 1985), positive and negative self-reactions were essentially uncorrelated ($r = -.02$). Analyses of both self-reaction variables indicated that low-ability subjects reported more negative self-reactions

Table 7
ANOVAs for Experiment 3: Goal Setting, Attention to Task Facets, and Self-Reactions

				Factor				
Measure	Ability (A)	Training (T)	Goal (G)	A × G	A × T	T × G	A × T × G	MS_E
Spontaneous goal setting	4.33*	.15	.43	.30	4.97*	6.45*	.11	8.50
On-task attention	3.57	.00	1.19	.88	.02	4.40*	3.29	74.04
Off-task attention	.28	1.21	1.47	.16	1.71	10.65**	4.44*	2.52
Attention to performance evaluation	4.26*	.46	1.61	1.29	1.10	6.73**	.00	25.00
Positive self-reactions	10.30**	.21	.00	.12	.59	.75	3.51	40.86
Negative self-reactions	5.44*	2.61	39.68**	.02	1.47	8.91	.22	14.79
Task difficulty	2.63	.02	24.84**	.09	.17	1.65	.00	6.44
Task pressure	8.35**	2.44	11.31**	.40	.04	1.16	2.25	4.60
Performance checking	1.13	3.59	40.23**	.21	3.45	.07	.24	5.74

Note. ANOVAs = analyses of variance. Degrees of freedom = (1, 539) for each measure.
* $p < .05$. ** $p < .01$.

and fewer positive self-reactions than did high-ability subjects. Imposition of the goal also increased frequency of negative self-reactions for both high- and low-ability subjects. However, examination of the significant Training × Goal interaction effect on negative self-reactions indicated that subjects in the procedural condition with an assigned goal reported more frequent negative self-reactions than all other conditions. Thus, task and motivational manipulations in this study had significant effects on negative self-reactions but not on positive self-reactions.

Discussion

The results obtained in Experiment 3 support the integrated model. In the procedural training condition, goal assignments had a negative influence on performance, with a larger dysfunctional effect obtained for low-ability subjects than for high-ability subjects. In the declarative training condition, goal assignments had a positive influence on performance, with a larger beneficial effect on low-ability subjects than on high-ability subjects. Consistent with these performance results, procedural-goal subjects reported less attention to on-task activities, more attention to off-task activities, and more frequent negative self-reactions. Subjects assigned a goal reported that the full ATC task was more difficult and they felt more pressured than subjects in the no-goal condition. Finally, ability exerted significant effects on frequency of performance checking, perceptions of task pressure, and frequency of reports of negative and positive self-reactions.

The absence of part-task training effects on self-confidence ratings among subjects in the goal conditions reduces the likelihood that performance differences obtained were due to systematic differences in initial self-perceptions of performance capabilities. However, ability effects obtained on measures of self-regulatory activity during the assigned goal trials strengthen the possibility of ability-related differences in use of self-regulatory strategies.

General Discussion

The theoretical framework and the three experiments presented here addressed the operation of dynamic interactions between conative and cognitive ability determinants of skill acquisition. The following elements contribute to the external validity and potential generalizability of the results obtained: (a) the relatively large size of the samples, (b) the range of talent on cognitive ability measures and likely heterogeneity in strength of achievement-related motives afforded by use of this field sample, (c) the use of a complex and novel real-time task enabling assessment of effects over the course of learning, and (d) the similarity of findings across experiments. Although it is encouraging that the pattern of findings provides initial support for our model, it is also the case that the findings raise a number of yet unresolved issues that have implications for future research in disparate motivation and cognitive ability research domains. The relevance of findings for each of these areas is discussed in turn.

Ability–Motivation Interactions

The results from our experiments support theory-based predictions of ability–motivation interactions during complex skill acquisition. However, only partial support is provided for Vroom's (1964) description of motivation–ability interactions. Our findings indicate that goal assignments provided during the declarative stage of skill acquisition may produce a decrement in performance among both low- and high-ability groups. In Experiment 3, the goal assignment resulted in an overall detrimental effect on performance with greater impairment among low-ability subjects than among high-ability subjects.

The ability–motivation interactions demonstrated in Experiment 3 were predicted from our theoretical framework, though such results run counter to the traditional assumption that increasing motivation results in greater gain among high-ability subjects than among low-ability subjects. Our results indicate that low-ability subjects benefit more from the imposition of a goal assignment following declarative part-task training than do high-ability subjects. This effect is expected given the joint effects of individual differences in resource availability and changes in the performance resource function across stages of skill acquisition. From a pragmatic standpoint, the form of the ability–motivation interactions found in this research suggests that goal-setting interventions may be potentially more, rather than less, useful among low-aptitude individuals than high-aptitude individuals *when implemented after the initial phase of skill acquisition.*

Ability Considerations

Individual differences in cognitive abilities clearly exerted an effect on performance in all conditions. The influence of general ability on performance in the no-goal conditions reflects individual differences in resource availability and indicates the fundamental importance of this construct in complex skill acquisition. It is important to note, however, that the imposition of a goal assignment sometimes influences ability–performance correlations. In Experiment 1 (early goal) and Experiment 3 (procedural knowledge training condition), general ability–performance correlations declined when a goal was introduced. In Experiment 2 (late goal) and Experiment 3 (declarative knowledge training condition), the imposition of a goal was not associated with changes in general ability–performance correlations. These findings suggest that motivational interventions early in training may reduce the validity of ability predictors of performance. However, these results suggest methods for optimal tailored training programs for trainees of different ability levels. Furthermore, such findings may be used as a foundation to search for further intervening conative or affective constructs that may directly moderate ability–performance correlations.

Motivational Considerations

An important issue raised by this research concerns the effectiveness of goal assignments on the stimulation of self-regulatory activities. Our results indicate that the allocation of resources to self-regulation appears to depend on subjects' perceived confidence in capability for goal attainment. In Experiment 1, low self-confidence ratings were associated with low levels of self-regulatory activity. In Experiment 3, task-specific confidence in capability, induced through positive prior experiences in procedural part-task training was associated with higher levels of self-regulatory activity. Our findings support previous assertions by Bandura (1977, 1986) and Kuhl (1985) that perceived confidence in capability for goal attainment is closely related to the initiation of self-regulatory processing. In addition, it is interesting to note that self-confidence ratings for the full ATC task were significantly influenced by prior experiences with a part-task training procedure. Additional research to clarify the determinants of transfer of self-confidence expectations across tasks has important practical implications for training.

Although perceptions of performance capability may stimulate self-regulatory activity, our data also suggest that individual differences in intellectual ability affect the character of self-regulatory activity. For example, low-ability subjects reported more spontaneous goal setting than did high-ability subjects in all experiments. Research in metacognition (for reviews, see Brown, 1987; Campione, 1987; Kluwe, 1987) suggests that self-regulation processes may be viewed as comprising the following two components: (a) cognitions about one's abilities, effort, and functioning, and (b) strategies for control over one's cognitive activity. From this perspective, individual differences in intellectual ability may exert an important influence on the efficiency with which persons who perceive themselves as capable of goal attainment engage in self-regulatory activities. From a metacognitive approach, our results indicate that the influence of self-regulation on allocation policies depends on both knowledge about one's cognitive state and knowledge and use of self-regulatory strategies to enhance performance. In the context of well-practiced activities, self-regulation strategies are often known or acquired with training. For example, skilled computer programmers often develop specific strategies for writing elegant program code (e.g., taking a long-term, modular perspective), as opposed to use of brute-force methods of programming. Perceived capabilities for writing such code may determine whether these self-regulatory strategies are put to use, and the extent to which they are adhered to.

In learning contexts, however, deficits in performance may arise from either self-evaluation of incapability to attain the goal or ineffective self-regulatory strategies. Thus, acquisition of expert programming skills may be influenced by perceptions of lack of intellectual ability or deficits in the self-regulatory strategies used to generate program code. Although perceptions of intellectual incapability may accurately reflect knowledge about one's deficits in self-regulatory strategies for controlling cognitive activity, these conditions can impair further efforts and preclude opportunities for the development of successful strategies. Environmental interventions that enhance perceptions of capabilities may immunize persons from premature reductions of effort toward cognitive strategy development (Bandura, 1988; Frayne & Latham, 1987). Our findings suggest further research is needed in these three areas: (a) the relationship between general intellectual ability and self-regulatory strategies controlling cognitive activity, (b) the influence of self-evaluation of capabilities on self-regulatory skill use, and (c) the cues that persons use in developing perceptions of cognitive capabilities and initiating self-regulatory activities.

Our experiments focused on only a small portion of the proposed model. Specifically, we examined the effects of proximal motivational processes on complex skill acquisition. Numerous studies have indicated the importance of distal motivational processes on task performance (e.g., see Feather, 1982; Lee, Locke, & Latham, 1989). We did not explicitly examine the influence of distal motivational processes. However, our proposed model provides a theoretical foundation for extending previous work on distal processes to the complex skill acquisition domain. Specifically, distal variables such as goal commitment (e.g., Hollenbeck & Klein, 1987) and goals for task engagement (e.g., Dweck, 1986; Dweck & Leggett, 1988) may affect proximal allocation policies as well as mobilization of attentional resources. Similarly, our findings highlight how little is known about the characteristics of efficient self-regulatory strategies. Kuhl (1985) suggests a number of self-regulatory strategies that may be used to benefit performance. The influence of different motivational manipulations on the use of emotional control, motivation control, and other self-regulatory strategies represents another area of obvious importance.

Finally, our findings address conclusions drawn from recent meta-analytic studies of goal-setting research (Mento, Steel, & Karren, 1987; Tubbs, 1986; Wood, Mento, & Locke, 1987). In particular, Wood et al. (1987) concluded that task complexity moderates the goal–performance relation such that the effect of goal setting on performance is stronger on simple tasks than on complex tasks. Results obtained in our article are generally consistent with Wood et al.'s findings (see also Johnson & Kanfer, 1989) but suggest a more comprehensive, theoretically based account of the individual differences, task demands, and motivational processes underlying these observed effects. In the proposed framework, complex, novel tasks impose greater attentional demands and reduce the opportunity for benefits of self-regulatory activity. In simple tasks, resource demands are likely to be lower because of the prior development of a declarative representation of the task (or minimal demands on the attentional system). Goal setting in this context facilitates performance. The proposed framework and data presented in this article suggest, however, that goal setting may also facilitate complex task performance when presented in later phases of skill acquisition. Moreover, the beneficial effects of goal setting during the later phase are most likely to accrue to low-ability rather than to high-ability persons.

Our findings also suggest that future investigations of task characteristics in goal-setting research should focus on tasks in which more is known about the cognitive demands associated with performance at various stages of skill acquisition. The gradual decline of general ability–performance correlations demonstrated in Experiment 1 indicates that the ATC task is particularly well-suited for the study of aptitude–treatment interactions during learning of complex, consistent information-processing tasks. Results obtained by using the part-task training procedures in Experiment 3 demonstrate that information-processing demands of the task and motivational variables may be independently manipulated. Finally, the ATC task paradigm enables more refined analysis of the unique effects of distal and proximal motivational processes.

Summary

In summary, the findings provide initial support for our integrated model emphasizing the interrelationships of (a) ability constraints on attentional resource capacity, (b) dynamic cognitive resource demands imposed by tasks, (c) the effects of resource availability on self-regulatory processing, and (d) the influence of motivational processing on attentional task effort. Our findings indicate that interventions designed to engage motivational processes may impede task learning when presented prior to an understanding of what the task is about. In these instances, cognitive resources necessary for task understanding are diverted toward self-regulatory activities. Because persons have few spare resources at this phase of skill acquisition, these self-regulatory activities can provide little benefit for learning. In contrast, interventions designed to engage motivational processing following development of declarative knowledge may facilitate performance.

Previous studies indicate a positive effect for goal setting on task performance among tasks that are neither completely novel nor performed at asymptotic levels. The results obtained in Experiment 3 (declarative knowledge training) complement these studies and further indicate that the beneficial effects of goal assignments are more pronounced for low-ability persons than for high-ability persons. However, a great deal of additional research is needed to determine the precise effects of cognitive abilities and motivational interventions on knowledge and ac-

tion components of the self-regulatory system during various phases of skill acquisition. The proposed integrated–interactive model and findings presented here represent an initial step in this direction.

References

Ackerman, P. L. (1984). *A theoretical and empirical investigation of individual differences in learning: A synthesis of cognitive ability and information processing perspectives.* Unpublished doctoral dissertation, University of Illinois, Urbana.

Ackerman, P. L. (1986a). Individual differences in information processing: An investigation of intellectual abilities and task performance during practice. *Intelligence, 10,* 101–139.

Ackerman, P. L. (1986b, April). *Attention, automaticity and individual differences in performance during task practice.* Symposium paper presented at the annual meeting of the American Educational Research Association, San Francisco.

Ackerman, P. L. (1987). Individual differences in skill learning: An integration of psychometric and information processing perspectives. *Psychological Bulletin, 102,* 3–27.

Ackerman, P. L. (1988). Determinants of individual differences during skill acquisition: Cognitive abilities and information processing. *Journal of Experimental Psychology: General, 117,* 288–318.

Ackerman, P. L. (1989). Individual differences in skill acquisition. In P. L. Ackerman, R. J. Sternberg, & R. Glaser (Eds.), *Learning and individual differences: Advances in theory and research* (pp. 165–217). New York: Freeman.

Adams, J. A. (1987). Historical review and appraisal of research on the learning, retention, and transfer of human motor skills. *Psychological Bulletin, 101,* 41–74.

Anderson, J. R. (1982). Acquisition of cognitive skill. *Psychological Review, 89,* 369–406.

Anderson, J. R. (1983). *The architecture of cognition.* Cambridge, MA: Harvard University Press.

Anderson, J. R. (1985). *Cognitive psychology and its implications* (2nd ed.). New York: Freeman.

Arvey, R. D. (1972). Task performance as a function of perceived effort–performance and performance–reward contingencies. *Organizational Behavior and Human Performance, 8,* 423–433.

Atkinson, J. W. (1957). Motivational determinants of risk-taking behavior. *Psychological Review, 64,* 359–372.

Atkinson, J. W., & Birch, D. (1970). *The dynamics of action.* New York: Wiley.

Atkinson, J. W., & Feather, N. T. (Eds.). (1966). *A theory of achievement motivation.* New York: Wiley.

Bandura, A. (1977). *Social learning theory.* Englewood Cliffs, NJ: Prentice-Hall.

Bandura, A. (1982). The self and mechanisms of agency. In J. Suls (Ed.), *Psychological perspectives on the self* (Vol. 1, pp. 3–39). Hillsdale, NJ: Erlbaum.

Bandura, A. (1986). *Social foundations of thought and action: A social cognitive theory.* Englewood Cliffs, NJ: Prentice-Hall.

Bandura, A. (1988). Self-regulation of motivation and action through goal systems. In V. Hamilton, G. H. Bower, & N. H. Fryda (Eds.), *Cognitive perspectives on emotion and motivation* (pp. 37–61). Dordrecht, The Netherlands: Martinus Nijhoff.

Bandura, A., & Cervone, D. (1986). Differential engagement of self-reactive influences in cognitive motivation. *Organizational Behavior and Human Decision Processes, 38,* 92–113.

Brown, A. (1987). Metacognition, executive control, self-regulation and other more mysterious mechanisms. In F. E. Weinert & R. H. Kluwe (Eds.), *Metacognition, motivation, and understanding* (pp. 65–116). Hillsdale, NJ: Erlbaum.

Bryan, W. L., & Harter, N. (1899). Studies on the telegraphic language:

The acquisition of a hierarchy of habits. *Psychological Review, 6*, 345–375.

Campbell, D. J. (1984). The effects of goal contingent payment on the performance of a complex task. *Personnel Psychology, 37*, 23–40.

Campbell, J. P., & Pritchard, R. D. (1976). Motivation theory in industrial and organizational psychology. In M. D. Dunnette (Ed.), *Handbook of industrial and organizational psychology* (pp. 63–130). Chicago: Rand McNally.

Campione, J. C. (1987). Metacognitive components of instructional research with problem learners. In F. E. Weinert & R. H. Kluwe (Eds.), *Metacognition, motivation, and understanding* (pp. 117–140). Hillsdale, NJ: Erlbaum.

Carroll, J. B. (1980). *Individual difference relations in psychometric and experimental cognitive tasks* (Tech. Rep. No. 163). Chapel Hill: L. L. Thurstone Psychometric Laboratory, University of North Carolina. (NTIS No. AD-A 086057 and ERIC Document Reproduction Service No. ED 191 891)

Carver, C. S., & Scheier, M. F. (1981). *Attention and self-regulation: A control theory approach to human behavior.* New York: Springer-Verlag.

Carver, C. S., & Scheier, M. F. (1985). A control-systems approach to the self-regulation of action. In J. Kuhl and J. Beckmann (Eds.), *Action control: From cognition to behavior* (pp. 237–266). New York: Springer-Verlag.

Cronbach, L. J. (1957). The two disciplines of scientific psychology. *American Psychologist, 12*, 671–684.

Cronbach, L. J. (1975). Beyond the two disciplines of scientific psychology. *American Psychologist, 30*, 116–127.

Cronbach, L. J., & Snow, R. E. (1977). *Aptitudes and instructional methods.* New York: Irvington.

Dachler, H. P., & Mobley, W. H. (1973). Construct validation of an instrumentality-expectancy-task goal model of work motivation: Some theoretical boundary conditions. *Journal of Applied Psychology, 58*, 397–418.

Dunnette, M. D. (1976). Aptitudes, abilities, and skills. In M. D. Dunnette (Ed.), *Handbook of industrial and organizational psychology* (pp. 473–520). Chicago: Rand McNally.

Dweck, C. S. (1986). Motivational processes affecting learning. *American Psychologist, 41*, 1040–1048.

Dweck, C. S., & Leggett, E. L. (1988). A social–cognitive approach to motivation and personality. *Psychological Review, 95*, 256–273.

Dwyer, P. S. (1937). The determination of the factor loadings of a given test from the known factor loadings of other tests. *Psychometrika, 2*, 173–178.

Feather, N. T. (Ed.). (1982). *Expectations and actions: Expectancy-value models in psychology.* Hillsdale, NJ: Erlbaum.

Fisk, A. D., Ackerman, P. L., & Schneider, W. (1987). Automatic and controlled processing theory and its application to human factors problems. In P. A. Hancock (Ed.), *Human factors psychology* (pp. 159–197). New York: North Holland.

Fisk, A. D., & Schneider, W. (1983). Category and word search: Generalizing search principles to complex processing. *Journal of Experimental Psychology: Learning, Memory, & Cognition, 10*, 181–197.

Fitts, P., & Posner, M. I. (1967). *Human performance.* Belmont, CA: Brooks/Cole.

Fleishman, E. A. (1954). Dimensional analysis of psychomotor abilities. *Journal of Experimental Psychology, 48*, 437–454.

Fleishman, E. A. (1958). A relationship between incentive motivation and ability level in psychomotor performance. *Journal of Applied Psychology, 56*, 78–81.

Fleishman, E. A. (1972). On the relation between abilities, learning, and human performance. *American Psychologist, 27*, 1017–1032.

Fleishman, E. A. (1975). Toward a taxonomy of human performance. *American Psychologist, 30*, 1127–1149.

Fleishman, E. A., & Hempel, W. E., Jr. (1954). Changes in factor structure of a complex psychomotor test as a function of practice. *Psychometrika, 19*, 239–252.

Fleishman, E. A., & Hempel, W. E., Jr. (1955). The relation between abilities and improvement with practice in a visual discrimination reaction task. *Journal of Experimental Psychology, 49*, 301–312.

Fleishman, E. A., & Quaintance, M. K. (1984). *Taxonomies of human performance.* Orlando, FL: Academic Press.

Frayne, C. A., & Latham, G. P. (1987). Application of social learning theory to employee self-management of attendance. *Journal of Applied Psychology, 72*, 387–392.

French, E. G. (1957). Effects of interaction of achievement, motivation, and intelligence on problem-solving success. *American Psychologist, 12*, 399–400.

Gagné, R. M. (1989). Some reflections on learning and individual differences. In P. L. Ackerman, R. J. Sternberg, & R. Glaser (Eds.), *Learning and individual differences: Advances in theory and research* (pp. 1–11). New York: Freeman.

Gagné, R. M., & Fleishman, E. A. (1959). *Psychology and human performance.* New York: Holt.

Galbraith, J., & Cummings, L. L. (1967). An empirical investigation of the motivational determinants of task performance: Interactive effects between instrumentality–valence and motivation–ability. *Organizational Behavior and Human Performance, 2*, 237–257.

Gavin, J. F. (1970). Ability, effort, and role perceptions as antecedents of job performance. *Experimental Publication System, 5*, Manuscript No. 190A.

Ghiselli, E. E. (1966). *The validity of occupational aptitude tests.* New York: Wiley.

Glaser, R. (1967). Some implications of previous work on learning and individual differences. In R. M. Gagné (Ed.), *Learning and individual differences* (pp. 1–18). Columbus, OH: Charles E. Merrill.

Glass, G. V., & Stanley, J. C. (1970). *Statistical methods in education and psychology.* Englewood Cliffs, NJ: Prentice-Hall.

Graen, G. B. (1967). *Work motivation: The behavioral effects of job content and job context factors in an employment situation.* Unpublished doctoral dissertation, University of Minnesota, Minneapolis.

Guilford, J. P. (1967). *The nature of human intelligence.* New York: McGraw-Hill.

Hancock, P. A. (1986). Sustained attention under thermal stress. *Psychological Bulletin, 99*, 263–281.

Heckhausen, H., Schmalt, H. D., & Schneider, K. (1985). *Achievement motivation in perspective.* New York: Academic Press.

Hollenbeck, J. R., & Klein, H. J. (1987). Goal commitment and the goal-setting process: Problems, prospects, and proposals for future research. *Journal of Applied Psychology, 72*, 212–220.

Humphreys, L. G. (1960). Investigation of the simplex. *Psychometrika, 25*, 313–323.

Humphreys, L. G. (1979). The construct of general intelligence. *Intelligence, 3*, 105–120.

Humphreys, M. S., & Revelle, W. (1984). Personality, motivation, and performance: A theory of the relationship between individual differences and information processing. *Psychological Review, 91*, 153–184.

Hunter, J. E. (1986). Cognitive ability, cognitive aptitudes, job knowledge, and job performance. *Journal of Vocational Behavior, 29*, 340–362.

Ilgen, D. R., & Klein, H. J. (1988). Individual motivation and performance: Cognitive influences on effort and choice. In J. P. Campbell, R. J. Campbell, & Associates (Ed.), *Productivity in organizations: New perspectives from industrial and organizational psychology* (pp. 143–176). San Francisco: Jossey-Bass.

Johnson, D. S., & Kanfer, R. (1989). *Goal–performance relations: The effects of initial task complexity and task practice.* Unpublished manuscript, University of Houston, Houston, TX.

Kahneman, D. (1973). *Attention and effort.* Englewood Cliffs, NJ: Prentice-Hall.

Kanfer, F. H. (1977). The many faces of self-control, or behavior modification changes its focus. In R. B. Stuart (Ed.), *Behavioral self-management* (pp. 1–48). New York: Brunner/Mazel.

Kanfer, F. H., & Hagerman, S. (1987). A model of self-regulation. In F. Halisch & J. Kuhl (Eds.), *Motivation, intention, and volition* (pp. 293–307). New York: Springer-Verlag.

Kanfer, F. H., & Schefft, B. K. (1988). *Guiding the process of therapeutic change.* Champaign, IL: Research Press.

Kanfer, F. H., & Stevenson, M. K. (1985). The effects of self-regulation on concurrent cognitive processing. *Cognitive Therapy and Research, 9,* 667–684.

Kanfer, R. (1986, July). *Toward a unified theoretical framework of performance motivation: Situational and self-regulatory determinants.* Symposium paper presented at the 21st International Congress of Applied Psychology, Jerusalem, Israel.

Kanfer, R. (1987). Task-specific motivation: An integrative approach to issues of measurement, mechanisms, processes, and determinants. *Journal of Social and Clinical Psychology, 5,* 237–264.

Kanfer, R. (in press). Motivation theory and industrial/organizational psychology. In M. D. Dunnette (Ed.), *Handbook of industrial and organizational psychology: Vol. 1: Theory in industrial and organizational psychology.* Palo Alto, CA: Consulting Psychologists Press.

Kanfer, R., & Ackerman, P. L. (1989). Dynamics of skill acquisition: Building a bridge between abilities and motivation. In R. J. Sternberg (Ed.), *Advances in the psychology of human intelligence* (Vol. 5, pp. 83–134). Hillsdale, NJ: Erlbaum.

Kleinbeck, U. (1987). The effects of motivation on job performance. In F. Halisch and J. Kuhl (Eds.), *Motivation, intention, and volition* (pp. 261–271). New York: Springer-Verlag.

Kluwe, R. H. (1987). Executive decisions and regulation of problem-solving behavior. In F. E. Weinert & R. H. Kluwe (Eds.), *Metacognition, motivation, and understanding* (pp. 31–64). Hillsdale, NJ: Erlbaum.

Kuhl, J. (1984). Volitional aspects of achievement motivation and learned helplessness: Toward a comprehensive theory of action control. In B. A. Maher (Ed.), *Progress in experimental personality research* (Vol. 13, pp. 99–171). New York: Academic Press.

Kuhl, J. (1985). Volitional mediators of cognition-behavior consistency: Self-regulatory processes and action versus state orientation. In J. Kuhl & J. Beckmann (Eds.), *Action control: From cognition to behavior* (pp. 101–128). New York: Springer-Verlag.

Kuhl, J. (1986). Integrating cognitive and dynamic approaches: A prospectus for a unified motivational psychology. In J. Kuhl and J. W. Atkinson (Eds.), *Motivation, thought, and action* (pp. 307–336). New York: Praeger.

Kuhl, J., & Koch, B. (1984). Motivational determinants of motor performance: The hidden second task. *Psychological Research, 46,* 143–153.

Kyllonen, P. C. (1987). Theory-based cognitive assessment. In J. Zeidner (Ed.), *Human productivity enhancement: Vol. 2. Acquisition and development of personnel* (pp. 338–381). New York: Praeger.

Kyllonen, P. C., & Shute, V. J. (1989). A taxonomy of learning skills. In P. L. Ackerman, R. J. Sternberg, & R. Glaser (Eds.), *Learning and individual differences: Advances in theory and research* (pp. 117–163). New York: Freeman.

Kyllonen, P. C., & Woltz, D. J. (in press). Role of cognitive factors in the acquisition of cognitive skill. In R. Kanfer, P. L. Ackerman, & R. Cudeck (Eds.), *Abilities, motivation, and methodology: The Minnesota Symposium on Learning and Individual Differences.* Hillsdale, NJ: Erlbaum.

Latham, G. P., & Lee, T. W. (1986). Goal setting. In E. A. Locke (Ed.), *Generalizing from laboratory to field settings* (pp. 101–117). Lexington, MA: Lexington Books.

Lawler, E. E. (1966). Ability as a moderator of the relationship between job attitudes and job performance. *Personnel Psychology, 19,* 143–164.

Lawler, E. E. (1973). *Motivation in work organizations.* Monterey, CA: Brooks/Cole.

Lawler, E. E., & Porter, L. W. (1967). Antecedent attitudes of effective managerial performance. *Organizational Behavior and Human Performance, 2,* 122–142.

Lawler, E. E., & Suttle, J. L. (1973). Expectancy theory and job behavior. *Organizational Behavior and Human Performance, 9,* 482–503.

Lee, T. W., Locke, E. A., & Latham, G. P. (1989). Goal-setting theory and job performance. In L. A. Pervin (Ed.), *Goal concepts in personality and social psychology* (pp. 291–326). Hillsdale, NJ: Erlbaum.

Locke, E. A. (1965). The interaction of ability and motivation in performance. *Perceptual and Motor Skills, 21,* 719–725.

Locke, E. A. (1968). Toward a theory of task motivation and incentives. *Organizational Behavior and Human Performance, 3,* 157–189.

Locke, E. A., Frederick, E., Lee, C., & Bobko, P. (1984). Effect of self-efficacy, goals, and task strategies on task performance. *Journal of Applied Psychology, 69,* 241–251.

Locke, E. A., Shaw, K. N., Saari, L. M., & Latham, G. P. (1981). Goal setting and task performance: 1969–1980. *Psychological Bulletin, 90,* 125–152.

Maier, N. R. F. (1955). *Psychology in industry* (2nd ed.). Boston: Houghton-Mifflin.

Melton, A. W. (1964). The taxonomy of human learning: Overview. In A. W. Melton (Ed.), *Categories of human learning* (pp. 325–339). New York: Academic Press.

Mento, A. J., Steel, R. P., & Karren, R. J. (1987). A meta-analytic study of the effects of goal setting on task performance: 1966–1984. *Organizational Behavior and Human Decision Processes, 39,* 52–83.

Mitchell, T. R. (1974). Expectancy theory models of job satisfaction, occupational preference, and effort: A theoretical, methodological, and empirical appraisal. *Psychological Bulletin, 81,* 1053–1077.

Mitchell, T. R. (1982). Expectancy-value models in organizational psychology. In N. T. Feather (Ed.), *Expectations and actions: Expectancy-value models in psychology* (pp. 293–312). Hillsdale, NJ: Erlbaum.

Mitchell, T. R., & Nebeker, D. M. (1973). Expectancy theory predictions of academic effort and performance. *Journal of Applied Psychology, 57,* 61–67.

Naylor, J. C., Pritchard, R. D., & Ilgen, D. R. (1980). *A theory of behavior in organizations.* New York: Academic Press.

Newell, A., & Rosenbloom, P. S. (1981). Mechanisms of skill acquisition and the law of practice. In J. R. Anderson (Ed.), *Cognitive skills and their acquisition* (pp. 1–55). Hillsdale, NJ: Erlbaum.

Nissen, M. J., & Bullemer, P. (1987). Attentional requirements of learning: Evidence from performance measures. *Cognitive Psychology, 19,* 1–32.

Norman, D. A., & Bobrow, D. B. (1975). On data-limited and resource-limited processes. *Cognitive Psychology, 7,* 44–64.

Pinder, C. C. (1984). *Work motivation.* Glenview, IL: Scott Foresman.

Porter, L. W., & Lawler, E. E. (1968). *Managerial attitudes and performance.* Homewood, IL: Irwin.

Ree, M. J., Mullins, C. J., Mathews, J. J., & Massey, R. H. (1982). Armed services vocational aptitude battery, item and factor analyses of Forms 8, 9, and 10 (AFHRL-TR-8155). Brooks Air Force Base, TX: Manpower and Personnel Division, U.S. Air Force.

Revelle, W. (in press). Personality, motivation, and cognitive performance. In R. Kanfer, P. L. Ackerman, & R. Cudeck (Eds.), *Abilities, motivation, and methodology: The Minnesota Symposium on Learning and Individual Differences.* Hillsdale, NJ: Erlbaum.

Sarason, I. G. (1978). The Test Anxiety Scale: Concept and research. In I. G. Sarason & C. D. Spielberger (Eds.), *Stress and anxiety* (Vol. 2, pp. 27–44). Washington, DC: Hemisphere.

Sarason, I. G., Sarason, B. R., Keefe, D. E., Hayes, B. E., & Shearin, E. N. (1986). Cognitive interference: Situational determinants and traitlike characteristics. *Journal of Personality and Social Psychology, 51,* 215–226.

Schmid, J., & Leiman, J. M. (1957). The development of hierarchical factor solutions. *Psychometrika, 22,* 53–61.

Schneider, W., & Fisk, A. D. (1982). Dual task automatic and control processing: Can it be done without cost? *Journal of Experimental Psychology: Learning, Memory, and Cognition, 8,* 261–278.

Schönemann, P. H. (1966). A generalized solution of the orthogonal procrustes problem. *Psychometrika, 31,* 1–10.

Snow, R. E. (1986). Individual differences and the design of educational programs. *American Psychologist, 41,* 1029–1039.

Snow, R. E. (1989). Aptitude–treatment interaction as a framework for research on individual differences in learning. In P. L. Ackerman, R. J. Sternberg, & R. Glaser (Eds.), *Learning and individual differences: Advances in theory and research* (pp. 13–58). New York: Freeman.

Snow, R. E. (in press). Cognitive-conative aptitude interactions in learning. In R. Kanfer, P. L. Ackerman, & R. Cudeck (Eds.), *Abilities, motivation, and methodology: The Minnesota Symposium on Learning and Individual Differences.* Hillsdale, NJ: Erlbaum.

Snow, R. E., Kyllonen, P. C., & Marshalek, B. (1984). The topography of ability and learning correlations. In R. J. Sternberg (Ed.), *Advances in the psychology of human intelligence* (Vol. 2, pp. 47–103). Hillsdale, NJ: Erlbaum.

Spearman, C. (1904). "General intelligence," objectively determined and measured. *American Journal of Psychology, 15,* 201–293.

Sternberg, R. J. (1977). *Intelligence, information processing, and analogical reasoning: The componential analysis of human abilities.* Hillsdale, NJ: Erlbaum.

Technical Supplement to the Counselor's Manual for the Armed Services Vocational Aptitude Battery Form-14. Chicago, IL: U.S. Military Entrance Processing Command.

Tellegen, A. (1985). Structures of mood and personality and their relevance to assessing anxiety, with an emphasis on self-report. In A. H. Tuma & J. D. Maser (Eds.), *Anxiety and the anxiety disorders* (pp. 681–706). Hillsdale, NJ: Erlbaum.

Terborg, J. R. (1977). Validation and extension of an individual differences model of work performance. *Organizational Behavior and Human Performance, 18,* 188–216.

Thurstone, L. L. (1938). Primary mental abilities. *Psychometric Monographs, 1,* ix, 1–121.

Tubbs, M. E. (1986). Goal setting: A meta-analytic examination of the empirical evidence. *Journal of Applied Psychology, 71,* 474–483.

Vernon, P. E. (1961). *The structure of human abilities.* New York: Wiley.

Vroom, V. H. (1960). *Some personality determinants of the effects of participation.* Englewood Cliffs, NJ: Prentice-Hall.

Vroom, V. H. (1964). *Work and motivation.* New York: Wiley.

Weiner, B. (1986). *An attributional theory of motivation and emotion.* New York: Springer-Verlag.

Wickens, C. D. (1984). Processing resources in attention. In R. Parasuraman & D. R. Davies (Eds.), *Varieties of attention* (pp. 63–102). New York: Academic Press.

Woltz, D. J. (1988). An investigation of the role of working memory in procedural skill acquisition. *Journal of Experimental Psychology: General, 117,* 319–331.

Wood, R., & Bandura, A. (1989). Impact of conceptions of ability on self-regulatory mechanisms and complex decision making. *Journal of Personality and Social Psychology, 56,* 407–415.

Wood, R. E., Locke, E. A., & Smith, K. G. (1986). *Goal setting and strategy effects on complex tasks: A theoretical analysis.* Unpublished manuscript, Australian Graduate School of Management, Sydney, New South Wales, Australia.

Wood, R., Mento, A. J., & Locke, E. A. (1987). Task complexity as a moderator of goal effects: A meta-analysis. *Journal of Applied Psychology, 72,* 416–425.

Yeh, Y.-Y., & Schneider, W. (1985, August). *Designing a part-task training strategy for complex skills.* Paper presented at the 93rd Annual Convention of the American Psychological Association, Los Angeles, CA.

Zeaman, D. (1978). Some relations of general intelligence and selective attention. *Intelligence, 2,* 55–73.

Received March 2, 1988
Revision received November 2, 1988
Accepted November 4, 1988 ∎

Part IV
What Training Methods Work Best?

[10]

PERSONNEL PSYCHOLOGY
1989, 42

THE INFLUENCE OF TRAINING METHOD ON SELF-EFFICACY AND IDEA GENERATION AMONG MANAGERS

MARILYN E. GIST
University of Washington

This field experiment examined the influence of two training methods on self-efficacy and performance during training for innovative problem solving. A training method composed of cognitive modeling with practice and reinforcement generated significantly higher participant self-efficacy than a method involving lecture and practice alone. Participants in modeling training significantly outperformed those in the lecture condition on measures of the quantity and divergence of ideas generated. Findings are discussed in terms of training designs for innovative problem solving.

Human resource managers are challenged with designing training programs to yield the highest performance results possible. A sizeable portion of training dollars is spent on training and development for managers, yet few empirical studies exist to guide the selection of training design.

Management Training

Wexley and Baldwin (1986) defined management training as "those activities designed to impart specific skills (e.g., time management, delegation) which would be immediately applicable in a particular organizational setting" (p. 280). Early reviews of management training found that case reports dominated the literature, with very few empirical studies to guide effective training design (Campbell, 1971; Campbell, Dunnette, Lawler, & Weick, 1970; I. L. Goldstein, 1980). Recent reviews have suggested the need for greater theoretical rigor in training studies and for an exploration of the effectiveness of various training methods when matched with different types of training content (Keys & Wolfe, 1988; Wexley & Baldwin, 1986).

The author extends special thanks to Edwin A. Locke, M. Susan Taylor, Benson Rosen, and Terence Mitchell for their valuable comments on this study. Also, the helpful guidance of the anonymous reviewers is appreciated.

Correspondence and requests for reprints should be addressed to Marilyn E. Gist, Department of Management and Organization, Graduate School of Business Administration, Mackenzie Hall, DJ-10, University of Washington, Seattle, WA 98195.

In an effort to clarify the effectiveness of management training, Burke and Day (1986) conducted a meta-analysis of 70 studies. The training methods of (1) modeling, and (2) lecture/discussion with role play or practice were reported as superior to either lecture or lecture and discussion alone. This analysis was based on the relatively small number of studies that were available for each methodology. No data were provided on the relative effectiveness of training methodologies for different content areas.

In the context of training, most research on modeling has involved *behavioral* modeling: the demonstration of behaviors or behavioral strategies that lead to effective performance. While live modeling is possible, video-based modeling typically has been used in behavioral modeling studies (Decker, 1982; Dillon, Graham, & Aidells, 1972; Gist, Rosen, & Schwoerer, 1988; A. P. Goldstein & Sorcher, 1974).

Despite its overall effectiveness as a training method, several disadvantages have mitigated the ubiquitous application of behavioral modeling. First, Keys and Wolfe (1988) noted that it can be quite expensive. Organizations with limited training resources may be able to use behavioral modeling for only a fraction of their training programs. Second, behavioral modeling may be difficult or impossible to adapt for some tasks (i.e., those lacking in observable behaviors). Examples might include tasks that are performed primarily through cognitive processing (e.g., those drawing heavily on memory, judgment). Finally, Dillon et al., (1972) found that behavioral modeling may not be effective for certain tasks, even when behaviors can be observed (e.g., brainstorming).

Because of these limitations, alternatives to behavioral modeling training sometimes may be preferred. Thus, the practical and theoretical significance of alternative methods should be examined, with attention to specific training content.

Behavioral modeling involves a visual observation of the behaviors of a model performing a task. An alternative form of modeling is based on a process of attending (or "listening") to one's *thoughts* as one performs an activity and utilizing self-instructional thoughts (or "statements") to guide performance. Sentences that are appropriate for cognitive, self-instructional use may be initiated and orally "modeled" by a trainer; later, these sentences may be practiced silently by the training participants. This form of modeling, *cognitive* modeling, has received promising, though limited, application in a training context (i.e., improving the creativity of college students—Meichenbaum, 1975). Thus, the first objective of this study was to examine a training pedagogy (1) that was based on cognitive modeling, (2) for its *practical* significance in a specific content area, (3) when training managers in a work context.

The second objective of this study was to assess the theoretical significance of cognitive modeling as a training pedagogy. The findings for management training that involved modeling were found to be "consistent with the impressive empirical support for social learning theory (cf. Bandura, 1977)" (Burke & Day, 1986, p. 242). However, few studies have analyzed management training methods in light of Bandura's model. Among those available, the focus has been on video-based behavioral modeling (cf. Burke & Day, 1986; Decker, 1984; Gist, Schwoerer, & Rosen, in press; Latham & Saari, 1979). Empirical evidence is needed to guide management training designs that are based on pedagogies other than behavioral modeling. Thus, this study examined a cognitive modeling design from the perspective of social learning theory.

Social Learning Theory and Training

Bandura (1977) identified four component processes that govern observational learning (i.e., learning from modeling): attention, retention, motor reproduction, and motivation. According to Bandura, the level of observational learning is determined partially by the use of appropriate cues for these processes. For example, attentional processes may be enhanced by the presence of relevant modeling stimuli, while retention could be enhanced through cognitive organization and rehearsal. Motor reproduction may occur through self-observation of reproduced activities and through accuracy feedback. Motivation may increase as a result of vicarious or external reinforcement (such as positive feedback or praise). Thus, modeling designs that incorporate appropriate cues for attention, retention, motor reproduction, and motivation might be considered anchored in social learning theory.

Having addressed the component processes of modeling, the question may arise as to just *how* modeling works to improve performance. When exposed to models, individuals "acquire mainly symbolic representations of the modeled activities which serve as guides for appropriate performances" (Bandura, 1977, p. 24). This has been demonstrated in training settings that utilized behavioral modeling methods. Decker (1980, 1984) has identified two types of symbolic codes that led to enhanced performance when participants were exposed to behavioral modeling: descriptive codes (a summary of the model's key *verbal* behaviors) and rule codes (*stated* principles underlying the model's performance). Since the effectiveness of behavioral modeling was influenced at least partially by the use of verbal, symbolic codes, it is plausible that the use of similar descriptive and rule codes in a cognitive modeling format also might lead to enhanced training performance for some content areas.

A related theoretical issue concerns the effect of modeling training on self-efficacy (a belief in one's capability of performing a specific task). Bandura (1977) suggested that live and symbolic modeling influence self-efficacy. This has been demonstrated for behavioral modeling in a training context involving managers (Gist, et al., in press). However, no direct test has been made of the influence of cognitive modeling training on self-efficacy. This issue is theoretically relevant because (1) vicarious influences constitute a known *antecedent* of self-efficacy (Bandura, 1982) and this study is exploring the effectiveness of cognitive modeling as a vicarious influence, and (2) positive correlations between self-efficacy and task performance have been found for several work-related tasks and settings (Barling & Beattie, 1983; Stumpf, Brief, & Hartman, 1987; Taylor, Locke, Lee, & Gist, 1984).

Thus, social learning theory may provide a theoretical framework through which we can understand the relative effectiveness of certain training methods over others. One measure of the effective utilization of social learning theory in a modeling training design (whether behavioral or cognitive modeling) would be to examine the design for its inclusion of process cues deemed to enhance attention, retention, motor reproduction, and motivation. A second measure of the effective use of social learning theory would be to examine self-efficacy as a training outcome.

> *Hypothesis 1*: Participants receiving cognitive modeling training will develop higher self-efficacy than participants who receive lecture training.

Training for Innovative Problem Solving

Innovation has become increasingly important to managers in both the public and private sectors. Evidence for this can be found in the practitioner literature, which suggests that "excellent" organizations encourage risk taking: the development and testing of new ideas (Peters & Waterman, 1982). Another manifestation of this interest in innovation is the proliferation of quality circles (QCs). Lawler and Mohrman (1985) estimated that more than 90% of Fortune 500 firms utilize quality circles. Organizations may prefer to generate ideas in-house because their own managers and employees typically have the greatest knowledge of the problem context and organizational culture.

While QCs have a number of reported organizational benefits, they are primarily problem-solving groups (Barrick & Alexander, 1987). Lawler (1986) estimated that over 200,000 workers in the United States have been involved in QCs. Since QC members are typically provided with training (Barrick & Alexander, 1987), they are major consumers of training technology for structured and innovative problem solving. However, Campbell et al. (1970) expressed concern over the lack of research on teaching problem-solving skills. I. L. Goldstein's (1980) review suggested that the situation had remained largely unchanged. Barrick and Alexander (1987) noted that while QCs were often effective, most studies of their effectiveness failed to specify a theoretical model. Thus, the final objective of this study was to explore innovative problem-solving (IPS) training from a theoretical perspective.

The *content* of IPS training (often synonymous with creativity training) in organizational settings is often on the associative thinking process, and some support for this can be found in the literature. Several studies of group brainstorming found it to be an effective technique for generating ideas (e.g., Dillon et al., 1972; Parnes & Meadow, 1960). However, other studies showed that individuals working alone and later pooling their ideas typically outperform those who work in interacting groups (e.g., Bouchard, Barsaloux, & Drauden, 1974; Bouchard & Hare, 1970; Graham & Dillon, 1974; Street, 1974). One explanation for the equivocal findings on the effectiveness of group brainstorming might be that the group process may inhibit the spontaneity of some group members. This rationale is consistent with the brainstorming guidelines proposed by Osborn (1963). These guidelines encourage the free associative thinking process. No criticism of any idea is allowed; individuals are encouraged to build on the ideas of others and to neither evaluate nor censor their own ideas.

When attention is turned to effective *methods* for teaching IPS, training researchers have less theoretical guidance. The promising findings for behavioral modeling that are reported in other contexts (cf. Burke & Day, 1986) may not generalize to creativity training. Dillon et al. (1972) found that a video tape of "correct" brainstorming performance did not lead to higher performance among those who watched the tape. They suggested that the tape may have left the subjects feeling helpless.

In contrast, Meichenbaum (1975) reported that cognitive modeling led to higher creativity performance among college students. Many of the self-instructional statements utilized in Meichenbaum's work are similar to the symbolic codes reported by Decker. For example, self-statements like "release controls; let your mind wander" resemble descriptive codes, while self-statements like "quantity helps breed quality" resemble rule codes (cf. Meichenbaum, 1977, p. 63).

Further, many of these self-statements appear to limit self-censorship (a cognitive process of self-judgments, such as "This idea is no good"). It is possible that self-censorship may stifle creativity by inhibiting free association. Thus, cognitive modeling may be effective in IPS training while behavioral modeling may not be, because cognitive modeling may correct the more appropriate determinants of performance: thoughts and cognitions as opposed to observable behaviors. Thus, empirical studies of cognitive modeling training in work organizations may find it to be effective for tasks that are based primarily on cognitive processing.

Hypothesis 2: Participants who receive cognitive modeling training will perform better on idea-generation tasks than will those who receive lecture training.

Methods

Subjects

Participants were managers in a major federal agency whose primary mission is scientific research and development. The agency has an administrative subdivision that provides support services in the following areas: resource management (i.e., financial management, procurement, and human resource management), facility operations (i.e., logistics, security, and facilities engineering and maintenance), and policy advising (i.e., public affairs, legal and patent counsel). This administrative subdivision contains 148 managers, 60 of whom were selected at random to attend a four-hour training course in innovative problem solving. The group of 60 was then randomly assigned to one of two training sections of 30 participants each. Because one of the participants left halfway through the training in order to attend another meeting, data analyses were conducted for the 59 who completed the entire training. Once the assignment was complete, the two training sections were found to be comparable in terms of gender (approximately 27% female, 73% male) and skill mix (approximately 46% from resource management divisions, 43% from facility operations divisions, and 11% from policy advising offices). The average level of management, as determined by the pay grade system used in the federal government, also was comparable between the groups: GS-13, Step 4.

Experimental Design

A field experiment was developed and conducted to test the hypotheses. The dependent variables were self-efficacy and performance in the generation of ideas. Training method was the sole independent variable in the design.

Training Approaches

A training program for innovative problem solving was designed to include three primary components. The first was an hour lecture that described the innovative problem-solving process as consisting of two stages: idea generation and idea evaluation. Participants were told that the analytical skills frequently used by managers made them adept at idea evaluation, but that different skills should be employed first in order to generate as many options to a problem as possible before beginning idea evaluation. Thus, it was explained that the objective of this training seminar was to enhance their skills at idea generation. The trainer provided conceptual background and a number of practical examples, which illustrated the importance of divergent thinking (generating ideas that can be categorized differently—a broadening of cognitive focus) as opposed to convergent thinking (seeking the one "best" solution to a problem—a narrowing of cognitive focus) during the idea-generation stage of IPS. In addition to placing an emphasis on divergent thinking, the trainer discussed other cognitive, intrapersonal factors that may inhibit IPS (such as inhibiting spontaneity out of fear that one's ideas may not be good or relying on habitual ways of viewing a problem).

The second component of the training involved a half hour of instruction in two techniques that can be used to enhance idea generation and promote IPS. The first technique was group brainstorming. Participants were told that, while the term was widely used, in practice, brainstorming sessions often combined idea generation and idea evaluation when the sessions actually should consist of idea generation only. Trainees were advised that effective brainstorming would be enhanced by following certain guidelines (Osborn, 1963). Four guidelines were advised: (1) No self-censorship is allowed as ideas come to mind; (2) build on the ideas of others when possible, but do not criticize their ideas. (3) freewheeling—the generation of wild ideas—is acceptable during idea generation; and (4) quantity is more important than quality in generating ideas.

The second technique, brainwriting (cf. Gryskiewicz, 1988), was developed in response to findings that individuals working individually and pooling their ideas often perform better than interacting groups (e.g., Bouchard et al., 1974; Graham & Dillon, 1974). For the period of brainwriting, participants worked silently in small groups for several rounds of idea generation. During each round, each participant wrote on paper several ideas for solving a problem and then passed the paper to a neighbor (also receiving one from another neighbor). Thus, participants were able to build again on the ideas of others—although they were told that this technique could be adapted for individual (solo) brainwriting. This process was repeated for five rounds. Brainwriting also relied on the guidelines of brainstorming (e.g., no self-censorship, building on ideas of others).

The final component of the IPS training consisted of two hours of practice activities (including positive feedback) that corresponded with the techniques of brainstorming and brainwriting. Practice consisted of having participants generate ideas to solve problems similar in nature to those used in the pre- and posttest performance tasks. Practice time was divided equally between the techniques of brainstorming and brainwriting. Participants were frequently reminded of the guidelines (e.g., no censorship) to be used with these techniques. During the practice sessions, positive feedback was given to indicate when the techniques were being used correctly and that the ideas generated were appropriate. For example, the trainer would comment that no criticism was observed during the last round of brainstorming or cite several ideas generated through brainwriting as examples of good results for their efforts.

Two versions of the training program were created; one served as the experimental treatment and the other as the control. The first two components (lecture and techniques) of each version were identical. Both groups had equal time to practice the techniques of brainstorming and brainwriting. However, the practice sessions were systematically varied to employ different training pedagogies.

In the control group, a method of lecture/discussion with practice was employed in accord with Burke and Day's (1986) report of the effectiveness of this method over lecture and discussion alone. Training began with lecture and discussion of the techniques described above. Participants were then allowed time for practice, and periodic, positive feedback was given by the trainer to the participants when the techniques were used correctly. Also, the trainer periodically told the participants that the ideas being developed with these techniques were considered good.

In the experimental group, the practice was structured to provide for cognitive modeling experiences. The *content* of the cognitive modeling paralleled the guidelines for brainstorming, which the participants had received earlier, so that no additional information about the task was being introduced. Participants were provided two types of cognitive models and asked to employ them in their practice. The first type of model involved patterns for lateral thinking (adapted from DeBono, 1971). These patterns supported the lecture material on divergent thinking by emphasizing the brainstorming guidelines for freewheeling and building on others' ideas. They provided self-instructive models that encouraged participants to feel comfortable with generating ideas through unusual cognitive associations. Participants were encouraged to monitor their performance periodically against patterns such as, "I deliberately search for alternative ways of looking at things" and "I separate the generation of ideas from their judgment and evaluation." These patterns are suggestive of rule codes used in symbolic modeling. After demonstrating these patterns, the trainer allowed participants to practice brainstorming while applying these modeled patterns to their thoughts during practice.

The second type of cognitive model involved "thought–counterthought" patterns. These patterns were designed to counteract inhibition of quantity and self-censorship during idea generation. Participants were encouraged to monitor their thought processes and to substitute counterthoughts (corrections) when they noticed thoughts that were "illegal" according to brainstorming guidelines. For example, an "illegal" thought would be "I might make a fool of myself" which could be countered with "I'm not worried about what others think." These patterns were adapted from Meichenbaum (1975), who found that cognitive modeling led to an increase in flexibility and originality on tests of divergent thinking. Thought–counterthought patterns are suggestive of descriptive codes used in symbolic behavioral modeling; the patterns and codes both articulate the differences between correct and incorrect "behavior." The trainer "modeled" several of these patterns for the participants. Participants were then given an opportunity to practice brainwriting while making note of their own cognitions as they worked.

The combined presentation time for the cognitive models was fairly short, and written hand-outs of the models were used. Thus, the experimental group had only slightly less time to practice the techniques of brainstorming and brainwriting than did the control group (two hours). In the experimental group, the trainer provided positive feedback consistent with the manner utilized with the control group.

When examining the modeling activity from the perspective of social learning theory, attention and retention cues are clearly evident in the *presence* and cognitive *rehearsal* of the modeled stimuli (thought patterns). Motor reproduction cues were provided through self-monitoring (*self-observation*) and positive *feedback about the accurate use* of the techniques and the acceptability of the ideas resulting from them. To enhance motivation cues (and to provide for greater reproduction through accuracy feedback), *external reinforcement* was utilized with the modeling group. The head of the agency's administrative subdivision presented one of the practice problems to be worked by the participants via anonymous, individual brainstorming. The ideas were collected and reviewed by him. Serving as a confederate, he selected approximately 30 ideas that appeared promising (reflecting about one idea per person), read them aloud to the group, and provided only positive feedback to the group on these ideas. He expressed his pleasure with the progress of the group as a whole and encouraged their continued use of the techniques. While the feedback provided was no more specific than that provided in the control group, the high status of the source was expected to enhance its external reinforcement (praise) effects. Thus, motivation cues were provided for the experimental group.

The cognitive modeling activity can be summarized as a demonstration of thought patterns that corresponded to the guidelines for brainstorming. While the control group practiced the brainstorming and brainwriting techniques using the guidelines alone, the experimental group practiced the techniques with cognitive models of the guidelines. In addition, while both groups received general, positive feedback, the experimental group received it from a higher status source. This external reinforcement was designed to *enhance* the motivation process component of observational learning (Bandura, 1977) for participants in the modeling training condition.

Since lecture/discussion with role play or practice is relatively effective as a management training pedagogy (Burke & Day, 1986), it was selected as the framework for training the control group. Thus, the overall design was established to contrast the effectiveness of two methodologies (cognitive modeling vs. lecture) rather than to determine which process component of modeling (i.e., attention, retention, motor reproduction, or motivation) contributed most to the training outcomes.

Procedure

All trainees were given an introduction to the course, along with a brief presentation by a high-ranking official of the agency on the need for innovative problem solving.

Next, trainees were given a brief practice exercise for individual brainstorming. Immediately following this, they completed a self-efficacy pretest and a pretest performance task. Training was then conducted, with the control group receiving training in the morning and the experimental group receiving training in the afternoon. The sessions ended with each group completing posttests for self-efficacy and performance. In addition, brief measures were taken of cognitive retention and course satisfaction. These measures served as a manipulation check on the similarity of course content and overall course presentation.

Measures

Performance tasks. Performance task 1 involved the generation of ideas to improve quality in the organization, and performance task 2 required the generation of ideas for improving customer service. These represented alternate forms of the same individual brainstorming task.

They were pilot tested on a similar population, and each was found to yield a mean number of eight ideas in ten minutes. Participants were allowed 15 minutes to complete each task. Two scores were assigned to each performance task: the total number of ideas generated (a quantity score, corrected for redundancies) and the number of different categories of ideas generated (idea divergence). Performance tasks were scored by two raters, blind to the purpose of the experiment, who worked independently. Interrater agreement was high: .96 for idea quantity and .94 for idea divergence; thus, the scores that were utilized reflect an average of those assigned by each rater.

Self-efficacy. Self-efficacy measures of magnitude and strength were tailored for the idea generation tasks. The instrument assessed efficacy over a range of increasing task difficulty following Bandura's (1977) structure. Each efficacy statement was phrased, "I am capable of generating at least x ideas in 10 minutes for improving an aspect of this organization." The format of the items was as follows:

	Yes/No	If yes, confidence (1–100)
...at least 2 ideas ...	_____	_____
...at least 4 ideas ...	_____	_____
.	_____	_____
.	_____	_____
.	_____	_____
...at least 20 ideas ...	_____	_____

Self-efficacy strength is calculated by summing the number of "yes" responses. Self-efficacy magnitude is derived from summing the points allocated for confidence (the participants were told that the confidence points ranged from 1 to 100—a range corresponding with extremely low to total confidence). Because the scales were highly correlated and yielded consistent results on separate analyses, they were combined for reporting purposes. The combined scale of efficacy strength and magnitude was found to have an internal consistency reliability coefficient of .73 with an item intercorrelation of .64.

Cognitive retention and course satisfaction. A ten-item quiz was given at posttest to assess retention of the learning points (training content) presented in the course. This measure was used to determine if any differential learning retention occurred between groups. If participants in the experimental group had a higher mean retention of learning points than those in the control group, then differences in presentation of the content might be an explanatory variable behind higher performance. A true/false scale was used to assess the participants' retention. Sample items from this measure included:

1. Innovative problem solving relies heavily on analytical thinking.
2. Personal spontaneity should be controlled to ensure that one's ideas are well-developed before they are suggested in innovative problem solving.
3. It is the quality rather than the quantity of ideas that is important in brainstorming.

Similarly, a reactive measure was administered to assess course satisfaction. The measure consisted of seven items whose internal consistency reliability (coefficient alpha) was found to be .83 with an item intercorrelation of .63. A 5-point scale (1 = Strongly disagree, 3 = Neither agree nor disagree, 5 = Strongly agree) was used to assess participants' reactions to the course. Sample items included

1. The course material was well presented.
2. I gained a strong understanding of the techniques.
3. Reasonable time was given to practicing the techniques.

Analysis and Results

Data collected from the field experiment were analyzed to assess the effects of cognitive modeling versus lecture training on self-efficacy and idea-generation performance. Table 1 shows the means, standard deviations, and correlations for the variables measured in this study.

Effects of Training Method on Self-efficacy

It was predicted that the training involving cognitive modeling would be superior to that involving lecture for enhancing self-efficacy. Table 1 shows that modeling participants did have higher posttest self-efficacy than lecture participants. Examination of the posttest self-efficacy magnitude scores reveals that trainees in the modeling condition averaged 8.24 while those in the lecture condition averaged 5.23. Similarly, posttest self-efficacy strength scores averaged 666.55 for participants receiving the modeling training and 503.67 for those who received the lecture training. Both groups showed increases in self-efficacy from pre- to posttest, and increases for the modeling group were particularly impressive. When the maximum range of self-efficacy scores is divided into thirds (high, moderate, and low), the mean pretest scores for both training groups and posttest scores for the lecture group indicate moderate levels of self-efficacy. However, mean scores on posttest magnitude

TABLE 1

Means, Standard Deviations, and Correlations of Study Variables

Variable	Modeling[a] M	SD	Lecture[b] M	SD	1	2	3	4	5	6	7	8	9	10
1. Pretest self-efficacy magnitude	4.72	1.71	4.47	2.30	—	.68***	.60***	.62***	.73***	.62***	.27	.42**	-.17	.21
2. Pretest self-efficacy strength	461.55	169.30	459.47	221.14	.60***	—	.53***	.54***	.63***	.71***	.53***	.61***	-.13	.13
3. Pretest idea quantity	6.79	3.25	6.17	3.40	.67***	.53**	—	.89***	.65***	.59***	.50**	.44**	.31*	.02
4. Pretest idea divergence	5.38	2.23	4.83	2.35	.63***	.51***	.95***	—	.64***	.55***	.44**	.54***	.23	.17
5. Posttest self-efficacy magnitude	8.24	2.22	5.23	2.51	.46**	.47**	.41**	.34*	—	.68***	.45***	.56***	.03	.35*
6. Posttest self-efficacy strength	666.55	192.42	503.67	232.84	.43**	.53***	.37*	.36*	.61***	—	.53***	.51**	-.03	.19
7. Posttest idea quantity	12.45	4.54	5.80	2.34	.41**	.49**	.57***	.53***	.73***	.73***	—	.82***	.17	.05
8. Posttest idea divergence	10.03	3.58	5.33	2.63	.31*	.48**	.55***	.53***	.60***	.52**	.92***	—	.01	.22
9. Cognitive retention	8.28	2.14	8.47	1.94	-.46**	-.46**	-.10	-.12	-.27	-.30	-.07	-.01	—	-.10
10. Course satisfaction	25.38	4.95	27.03	3.97	-.08	.10	-.16	-.29	-.15	-.15	-.02	-.01	-.03	—

Note: Correlations above the diagonal are from the lecture training; those below the diagonal are from the cognitive modeling training.
[a] $n = 29$; [b] $n = 30$
*$p < .05$; **$p < .01$; ***$p < .001$

TABLE 2

Analysis of Covariance of
Standardized and Combined Self-Efficacy Scores

Source of Variation	SS	df	MS	F*
Covariate, pretest self-efficacy	83.03	1	83.03	64.19
Main effect, training group	42.65	1	42.65	32.97
Explained	125.68	2	62.84	48.58
Residual	72.44	56	1.29	
Total	198.11	58	3.42	

*All F statistics are significant at $p < .001$

and strength for the modeling group can be considered as high levels of self-efficacy.

Significant correlations were found between self-efficacy magnitude and strength at pretest and at posttest for each treatment condition. Because separate analyses of self-efficacy magnitude and strength yielded consistent results, these measures were standardized and combined into one measure of self-efficacy. Table 2 reports the results of an analysis of covariance in which the combined self-efficacy measure was the dependent variable (while holding constant for the effects of pretest self-efficacy) and training approach was the sole independent variable. A significant covariate effect was noted for pretest self-efficacy ($F = 64.19$, $p < .001$). However, after controlling for this, training method still demonstrated a significant main effect on self-efficacy ($F = 32.97$, $p < .001$). Thus, Hypothesis 1 was supported.

Effects of Training Method on Idea Generation Performance

The cognitive modeling method was predicted to be superior to the lecture method for enhancing idea generation. Table 1 shows that participants in the modeling condition demonstrated superior performance when idea quantity was measured. Modeling participants generated an average of 12.45 ideas at posttest, compared with 5.80 ideas for those in the lecture condition. When idea divergence was measured, participants in the modeling condition also outperformed those in the lecture condition, generating an average of 10.03 categories (of ideas) and 5.33 categories respectively.

Because idea quantity and idea divergence were highly correlated at pretest and at posttest for participants in both the modeling and the lecture conditions, these indices were standardized and combined for subsequent analyses. An analysis of covariance was conducted using the

TABLE 3

Analysis of Covariance of
Standardized and Combined Performance Scores

Source of Variation	SS	df	MS	F*
Covariate, pretest performance	49.19	1	49.19	29.89
Main effect, training group	82.16	1	82.16	49.93
Explained	131.35	2	65.67	39.91
Residual	92.14	56	1.65	
Total	223.50	58	3.85	

*All F statistics are significant at $p < .001$

combined index of idea generation as a dependent variable and training approach as the sole independent variable, while holding constant
for pretest performance on the combined idea generation index. Table 3
shows the results of this analysis. Pretest idea generation was a significant covariate ($F = 29.89$, $p < .001$). However, after accounting for the
effects of the covariate, a significant main effect was demonstrated for
training method ($F = 49.93$, $p < .001$). Thus, Hypothesis 2 was fully
supported.

Cognitive Retention and Course Satisfaction

Supplemental analyses were performed on the measures of cognitive
retention and course satisfaction. The mean scores of the experimental
and control groups were compared, and no significant difference was
found for retention of course learning points ($t = .51$, $p < .615$) or for
satisfaction with the training ($t = 1.24$, $p < .221$). Thus, neither differences in content retention nor differences in reaction to the training
course accounted for the main effects found in this study.

Discussion

The generation and testing of innovative ideas has become increasingly important to organizations. This study explored several key issues
pertaining to the design of training programs for innovative problem
solving.

The superiority of a training method based on cognitive modeling
was impressive. While both training conditions covered identical lecture
content and offered very similar practice opportunities with the associative techniques of brainstorming and brainwriting, the cognitive modeling method significantly enhanced performance. A number of practical implications arise from these findings. First, this study partially

replicates Meichenbaum's (1975) findings on the value of cognitive self-instruction for idea generation during innovative problem solving. However, it extends Meichenbaum's findings to managers in a work organization. Future studies might explore whether these techniques would generalize to other types of employees and work settings (such as manufacturing employees who participate in quality circles or technical personnel engaged in design activities). A related issue is that the performance measures used in this study were measures of training task performance. More knowledge is needed about whether cognitive modeling would lead to superior training transfer (from the classroom to the job situation). Longitudinal studies might address the comparative retention rates (i.e., how long the effects last) of the alternative training methods. Also, the method of cognitive modeling should be assessed for its effectiveness in other training content areas (such as, interpersonal skills or decision making). To the extent that cognitive modeling pedagogy generalizes to other types of employees and training content, and that it leads to high transfer and retention, it may provide a low cost alternative to behavioral modeling. The present study was limited to demonstrating its effectiveness with managers during creativity training.

A number of theoretical implications arise from this study. First, the generalizability of cognitive modeling to other content areas should be assessed in a theory-driven manner. Recall that cognitive modeling was selected for this design because of the apparent unsuitability of behavioral modeling (Dillon et al., 1972). While a visual model of brainstorming performance might demonstrate observable behaviors, it is likely that these behaviors are the by-products of an underlying cognitive (nonbehavioral) process. This cognitive process, in turn, may be the important antecedent to effective performance. Thus, the IPS cognitive models may have been effective because they modeled a restructuring of the cognitive process. The similarity between the cognitive models used in this study and the typical rule and descriptive encoding that occurs when watching a behavioral model suggests that *the capacity of a modeling training design to produce relevant, symbolic, verbal coding* might be a more important theoretical concern than whether the modeling is behavioral or cognitive per se. Thus, the extension of cognitive modeling to other training content areas should be guided by the need for a restructuring of symbolic codes that pertain to cognitions guiding performance in those content areas. For example, on judgment tasks (i.e., decision-making tasks) and those that deal with storage and retrieval of information (memory-based tasks), performance might be improved through training that uses cognitive modeling alone or in conjunction with other methods. Future studies might explore these issues.

A second theoretical implication of this study arises from the finding that cognitive modeling training enhanced self-efficacy. This finding provides support for the notion that social learning theory was a basis of the training design. Additionally, the training design did include cues for each of the component processes of observational learning (attention, retention, motor reproduction, and motivation). However, no study has yet been made of the relative effects of each component process of modeling on performance outcomes during training. This study utilized external reinforcement as a cue for the motivation process component (Bandura, 1977). However, the contribution of this reinforcement to the overall effectiveness of the design cannot be determined. Perhaps some components of this design should be emphasized over others, or perhaps cognitive modeling may not require the same set of process components as behavioral modeling. The efficiency of vicarious learning might be improved through studies of the comparative effectiveness of each component.

Manipulation checks on the similarity of course content and presentation yielded no alternative explanation for these results. Measures of cognitive retention of the lecture material (course learning points) and of course satisfaction showed no significant difference between training conditions. It is possible that these measures may not have been sensitive enough to register differences. However, in this training, the information learned was not complex or particularly difficult, and the differences in the training methods were intended to be subtle enough to have little effect on participant satisfaction. It appears that the cognitive modeling was a more effective method because it provided superior symbolic coding to guide the participants as they applied the learning principles to task performance and, perhaps, because it provided additional reinforcement for that application.

Finally, self-efficacy was observed to correlate positively with performance as it has in several studies cited earlier. The first-order partial correlation between training method and the combined idea generation measure was found to be significant ($r = .50, p < .001$). This suggests that self-efficacy may serve as an intervening variable between training and task performance. Future research might explore this further.

Behavioral modeling is of questionable value in creativity training (Dillon et al., 1972), yet the cognitive modeling activity appears to be effective. Thus, this study offers an alternative to behavioral modeling training that may prove valuable for other training content areas as well. While these results are preliminary and should be validated before being generalized to different areas, they suggest a need for the development and testing of other, alternative modeling interventions. Collaborative efforts between trainers and researchers may accomplish this end. A significant challenge remains for the wider exploration of the effectiveness of training methods when coupled with training for different content and skills.

REFERENCES

Bandura A. (1977). *Social learning theory*. Englewood Cliffs, NJ: Prentice-Hall, Inc.

Bandura A. (1982). Self-efficacy: Mechanism in human agency. *American Psychologist, 37*, 122–147.

Barling J, Beattie R. (1983). Self-efficacy beliefs and sales performance. *Journal of Organizational Behavior Management, 5*, 41–51.

Barrick MR, Alexander RA. (1987). A review of quality circle efficacy and the existence of positive-findings bias. PERSONNEL PSYCHOLOGY, *40*, 579–592.

Bouchard T, Barsaloux J, Drauden G. (1974). Brainstorming procedure, group size, and sex as determinants of the problem-solving effectiveness of groups and individuals. *Journal of Applied Psychology, 59*, 135–138.

Bouchard T, Hare M. (1970). Size, performance, and potential in brainstorming groups. *Journal of Applied Psychology, 54*, 51–55.

Burke MJ, Day RR. (1986). A cumulative study of the effectiveness of management training. *Journal of Applied Psychology, 71*, 232–245.

Campbell JP. (1971). Personnel training and development. *Annual Review of Psychology, 22*, 565–602.

Campbell JP, Dunnette MD, Lawler EE, Weick KE Jr. (1970). *Managerial behavior, performance, and effectiveness*. New York: McGraw-Hill.

DeBono E. (1971). *Lateral thinking for management*. New York: American Management Association.

Decker PJ. (1980). Effects of symbolic coding and rehearsal in behavior-modeling training. *Journal of Applied Psychology, 65*, 627–634.

Decker PJ. (1982). The enhancement of behavior modeling training of supervisory skills by the inclusion of retention processes. PERSONNEL PSYCHOLOGY, *35*, 323–332.

Decker PJ. (1984). Effects of different symbolic coding stimuli in behavior modeling training. PERSONNEL PSYCHOLOGY, *37*, 711–720.

Dillon P, Graham W, Aidells A. (1972). Brainstorming on a "hot" Problem: Effects of training and practice on individual and group performance. *Journal of Applied Psychology, 56*, 487–490.

Gist ME, Rosen B, Schwoerer C. (1988). The influence of training method and trainee age on the acquisition of computer skills. PERSONNEL PSYCHOLOGY, *41*, 255–265.

Gist ME, Schwoerer C, Rosen B. (In press). Effects of alternative training methods on self-efficacy and performance in computer software training. *Journal of Applied Psychology*.

Goldstein AP, Sorcher M. (1974). *Changing supervisor behavior*. New York: Pergammon Press, Inc.

Goldstein IL. (1980). *Training in organizations: Needs assessment, development, and evaluation*. Monterey, CA: Brooks/Cole Publishing Co.

Graham W, Dillon P. (1974). Creative supergroups: Group performance as a function of individual performance on brainstorming tasks. *Journal of Social Psychology, 93*, 101–105.

Gryskiewicz SS. (1988). Trial by fire in an industrial setting: A practical evaluation of three creative problem solving techniques. In Kaufman G, Gronhaug K (Eds.), *Innovation: A cross-disciplinary perspective*. London: Oxford University Press.

MARILYN E. GIST 805

Keys B, Wolfe J. (1988). Management education and development: Current issues and emerging trends. *Journal of Management, 14*, 205–229.

Latham GP, Saari LM. (1979). The application of social learning theory to training supervisors through behavior modeling. *Journal of Applied Psychology, 64*, 239–246.

Lawler EE. (1986). *High-involvement management*. San Francisco: Jossey-Bass Publishers.

Lawler EE, Mohrman SA. (1985). Quality circles after the fad. *Harvard Business Review, 63*(1), 65–71.

Meichenbaum D. (1975) Enhancing creativity by modifying what subjects say to themselves. *American Educational Research Journal, 12*, 129–145.

Meichenbaum D. (1977). *Cognitive behavior modification*. New York: Plenum Press.

Osborn A. (1963). *Applied imagination*. New York: Charles Schribner's Sons.

Parnes S, Meadow A. (1960). Evaluation of persistence of effects produced by a creative problem-solving course. *Psychological Reports, 7*, 357–361.

Peters TJ, Waterman RH Jr. (1982). *In search of excellence*. New York: Harper Row.

Street W. (1974). Brainstorming by individuals, coacting and interacting groups. *Journal of Applied Psychology, 59*, 433–436.

Stumpf SA, Brief AP, Hartman K. (1987). Self-efficacy expectations and coping with career-related events. *Journal of Vocational Behavior, 31*, 91–108.

Taylor MS, Locke EA, Lee C, Gist ME. (1984). Type A behavior and faculty research productivity: What are the mechanisms? *Organizational Behavior and Performance, 34*, 402–418.

Wexley KN, Baldwin TT. (1986). Management development. *Journal of Management, 12*, 277–294.

Journal of Applied Psychology
1989, Vol. 74, No. 3, 411–416

Self-Management Training for Increasing Job Attendance: A Follow-Up and a Replication

Gary P. Latham
Graduate School of Business Administration
University of Washington

Colette A. Frayne
School of Business Administration
University of Western Ontario

Determined the long-term effects of self-management training given to 20 unionized state government employees to increase their job attendance in a 6-month and a 9-month follow-up study. A repeated measures analysis of variance revealed that enhanced self-efficacy and increased job attendance were effectively maintained over time. Perceived self-efficacy at the end of training predicted subsequent job attendance. The control group ($n = 20$) was then given the same training in self-management by a different trainer. Three months later, this group showed the same positive improvement as the original training group with regard to increased self-efficacy and job attendance. These findings lend support to a self-efficacy based theory of job attendance.

In 1962, Äs argued that employee absenteeism was a social fact in need of a theory. Twenty years later, Johns and Nicholson (1982) found that despite a heavy investment of research effort, no major breakthrough in the prediction, understanding, and control of absenteeism had occurred.

There are at least two explanations for this impasse. The first is the measurement problem. Latham and his colleagues (Latham & Frayne, 1987; Latham & Napier, 1984; Latham & Pursell, 1975, 1977) have maintained that the primary interest of researchers should be to find a reliable measure on which to build theory and on which to evaluate the validity of predictors and the effectiveness of interventions. For this reason, they argued for the necessity of measuring job attendance in addition to, if not in place of, absenteeism. This argument was based on findings from four samples of employees that test–retest reliability coefficients of job attendance are significantly higher than typical measures of absenteeism (Latham & Frayne, 1987; Latham & Pursell, 1975). This occurs because absenteeism measures are almost always contaminated heavily by human judgment. The measures reflect the categorization behavior (e.g., jury duty, illness, injury, bereavement, vacation) of the recorder rather than the measurements of the researcher. Conversely, the recording of job attendance is relatively straightforward. The measurement is based on observations of employee presence at the work site.

For reasons that are not altogether clear, Nicholson and his colleagues (Chadwick-Jones, Nicholson, & Brown, 1982; Johns, 1984; Johns & Nicholson, 1982) have argued against relying on traditional test–theory concepts such as test–retest reli-

ability when studying a low base rate construct such as absenteeism. Arguments similar to Nicholson's have been put forth by Ilgen (1977) in explaining why interobserver reliability coefficients should be calculated in the place of test–retest reliability. This de-emphasis of the importance of stable measures (test–retest reliability) because of the difficulty in obtaining them is one possible explanation of why prediction, let alone control of absenteeism, has often proven to be elusive. Lack of stability in measurement can increase the likelihood of Type II measurement error.

Nicholson and his colleagues (Chadwick-Jones et al., 1982; Johns, 1984; Johns & Nicholson, 1982) have suggested a second explanation for the lack of progress in research on absenteeism, namely, a focus on the individual employee to the exclusion of the social dynamics affecting employee absences. Nicholson and Johns (1982) interpreted their data as indicating the existence of absence cultures within organizations that result in group norms, which in turn affect attendance behavior. In reviewing this research, Johns (1984) concluded that it is unlikely that cost-effective interventions exist for solving absenteeism at the level of the individual employee. Moreover, where such an intervention is used, symptom substitution is likely. It would appear, however, that his conclusions are unduly pessimistic.

Frayne and Latham (1987) evaluated training in self-management (Kanfer, 1970, 1975, 1980) in terms of its effects on job attendance. This mode of training was selected for three reasons. First, the training is cost-effective in that it requires minimal trainer time. Second, evidence from clinical psychology shows that this form of training is effective in the treatment of substance abuse behavior (Kanfer, 1986) that often occurs within a culture that maintains and strengthens it. Thus, it was hypothesized that training in self-management should also be effective in increasing job attendance despite a culture that may reinforce absenteeism. Third, the implicit theory underlying the study was that people who come to work judge themselves as efficacious (Bandura, 1977, 1986) in coping with environmental demands (e.g., supervisory conflict, peer pressure, family obligations, transportation issues, illness), whereas those

Preparation of this article was supported in part by the Ford Motor Company Affiliate Fund to Gary P. Latham.

We wish to thank Albert Bandura and Fred Kanfer for their helpful comments on a preliminary draft of this article, and Dawn Winters for her editorial assistance.

Correspondence concerning this article should be addressed to Gary P. Latham, Graduate School of Business Administration, DJ-10, University of Washington, Seattle, Washington 98195.

who do not come to work perceive themselves as inefficacious. It was hypothesized that training in self-management would increase one's perceived self-efficacy with regard to responding effectively to those demands, which in turn would increase one's job attendance.

The training was conducted with unionized state government employees. Data collected 3 months later showed that, compared with a control group, training in self-regulatory skills taught employees how to manage personal and social obstacles to job attendance, and it raised their perceived self-efficacy, that is, they could exercise influence over their behavior. There was no evidence of symptom substitution as measured by tardiness, turnover, and supervisory or employee self-report (Frayne, 1986). However, if employee attendance had not been measured and only a measure of absenteeism had been used, a Type II error would have been made. The results would have shown that the intervention was only marginally significant.

The purpose of this research was twofold. First, a follow-up study was conducted to determine the extent to which relapse occurred 6 months and 9 months subsequent to the training in self-management. Relapse can be problematic in self-management training because the emphasis is on the individual rather than the people in one's environment reinforcing the newly acquired coping skills (Brownell, Marlatt, Lichtenstein, & Wilson, 1986). It can be especially problematic when the culture in which the trainee is functioning does not support these behaviors.

The second purpose of this study was to test the hypothesis that perceived self-efficacy explains why people come or do not come to work by studying a second sample of employees. This was done by training the control group and comparing its performance with that of the original experimental group, and by correlating a measure of self-efficacy with subsequent job attendance.

Method

Sample

The employees in this study were those who were described by Frayne and Latham (1987). No turnover had occurred. These people ($n = 40$) were unionized state government employees employed as carpenters, electricians, and painters.

Procedure

As described by Frayne and Latham (1987), 20 of the 40 employees had been randomly assigned to a training condition in which they had been taught self-regulatory skills for job attendance. In brief, the trainees had received eight weekly 1-hr group sessions in which they had been taught to (a) set proximal and distal goals for job attendance, (b) write a behavioral contract with themselves for administering self-chosen reinforcers and punishers, (c) self-monitor their attendance behavior, (d) administer these incentives, and (e) brainstorm potential problems and solutions for things that might interfere with adherence to the training program. In addition, during the 8-week training period, weekly 30-min meetings were held one-on-one between the trainer and each trainee to discuss issues that the trainee was reluctant to discuss in the group setting.

Six months and 9 months subsequent to the training, reaction, learning, cognitive, and behavioral measures were taken to evaluate the

effects of the training over time. The purpose of the reaction measures was to assess whether employee liking of the training diminished over time. In addition, the employees were interviewed to determine whether the reasons given for absenteeism had changed.

The learning measures were collected to determine whether the employees retained the knowledge disseminated in the training program. If the knowledge was not retained, it could explain a return to pretraining levels of job attendance that might occur. The cognitive measure, perceived self-efficacy, was measured to determine its importance as a psychological variable affecting job attendance. A decrease in the trainees' self-efficacy would also explain any decrease in job attendance that may have occurred, given no change in affective reaction or knowledge retention. Finally, both job attendance and employee sick leave were measured. Sick leave was measured because it accounted for 49.8% of the organization's categorized reasons for absenteeism (Frayne & Latham, 1987). Measuring both job attendance and categorized sick leave permitted multiple operationalism of the dependent variable of primary interest, namely, employee presence at the work site.

Subsequent to the 9-month follow-up assessment, the employees in the control group received the identical training in self-management described by Frayne and Latham (1987). The only difference between the two studies was the trainer. Frayne conducted the first training program; a person in the organization's personnel department, trained by Frayne, was the trainer in the replication study. The data for this second experiment were collected 3 months subsequent to the training. The results were compared with those collected from the original experimental group 3 months after it had been trained.

Results

Manipulation Checks

Goal commitment: The coefficient alpha of a four-item commitment measure (e.g., "To what extent will you strive to attain the goal?" "How important is it to you to at least attain the goal that was set?") administered during the final week of training in the Frayne and Latham study was .81; in the subsequent training of the replication group 1 year later, it was .84. The means of the responses to the 5-point Likert type items ($M = 4.73$, $SD = .22$; and $M = 4.81$, $SD = .25$) in the two samples were high and not significantly different.

Criterion Measures

Reaction measures. Assessing the long-term reactions to the training was especially important because many trainees in the Frayne and Latham study had asserted during the first week of training that sick leave was a privilege that belonged to them. Thus, it was important to determine whether the trainee's subsequent positive affect toward the program 3 months after the training was maintained. The 5-point five-item questionnaire (e.g., "The training I received helped me overcome obstacles preventing me from coming to work") used by Frayne and Latham was completed anonymously 6 months and 9 months after the training had been completed. The coefficient alphas were .78 and .75, respectively. The test–retest reliability coefficient between Month 3 and Month 9 was .83.

In the replication sample, the alpha was .74, three months after the training had occurred. This is comparable with the alpha of .73 obtained in the original 3-months study. The test–retest reliability of the reaction measures over the 3-month

Table 1
Means and Standard Deviations of Learning Measure by Training and Control Group

Group	Pretraining		3 months		6 months		9 months		12 months	
	M	*SD*	*M*	*SD*	*M*	*SD*	*M*	*SD*	*M*	*SD*
Training	15.60	4.2	29.95	7.0	28.65	6.1	28.92	10.1	27.90	8.6
Control	16.20	4.3	15.70	4.6	16.10	3.8	15.40	5.6	28.90	7.3

Note. The 12-months score is a 1-year follow-up for the training group and a 3-months follow-up for the newly trained control group.

period in the original study was .81; in the replication study it was .84.

The employee reactions in the original training group assessed 3 months after the training had taken place ($M = 4.46$, $SD = .41$) remained highly positive 6 months ($M = 4.48$, $SD = .46$) and 9 months later ($M = 4.47$, $SD = .43$). The difference among these values is not statistically significant. Thus, employee affect toward the training program remained highly positive.

The employee reactions in the replication sample 3 months after receiving the training from a different trainer was also high ($M = 4.45$, $SD = .43$). A *t* test revealed no significant difference between their highly positive attitude and that exhibited by the original training group ($M = 4.43$, $SD = .49$) 3 months after their training had taken place.

Learning measures. To determine whether people learned and retained the knowledge disseminated in the training program, the learning test used by Frayne and Latham was administered and scored 6 months and 9 months subsequent to the training. The coefficient alphas of the 12 situational items were .74 and .80, respectively. The trainees were not informed as to the scoring of their answers. The alpha for the replication sample calculated 3 months subsequent to training was .78. This compares favorably with the alpha of .82 obtained in the original 3-months study. The alpha calculated for the original training group 12 months later was .84. The test–retest reliability of the questionnaire between Months 3 and 9 was .81. The test–retest reliability between the premeasure and Month 3 for the replication sample was .80. This too compares favorably with the reliability estimate of .85 obtained in the original study. The respective means and standard deviations are shown in Table 1.

A repeated measures analysis of variance (ANOVA) revealed no significant difference among Months 3 through 9. Thus, the knowledge acquired in the training did not decrease over time. Moreover, an ANOVA revealed no significant difference between

the replication sample's 3-months scores and the original training group's 3-months scores.

Job Attendance. The test–retest reliability (stability) of the attendance measure from Month 3 until Month 12 (36 weekly measures) for the 40 employees in this study was .91. This was assessed by employee time cards. This is in sharp contrast with the stability of the sick leave categorization, namely .39. The correlation between these two measures was −.62. Tables 2 and 3 show the respective means and standard deviations of the attendance and sick leave measures.

A repeated measures multivariate analysis of variance on these two dependent variables revealed a significant difference between the training and the control group on the basis of data collected in Months 3, 6, and 9, $T(2, 37) = 9.84$, $p < .05$). A univariate repeated measures ANOVA revealed a significant difference between the training and the control group for the attendance measure. Thus, the increase in job attendance as a result of training in self-management did not diminish significantly over time. However, as was the case in the Frayne and Latham study, the *F* test was only marginally significant at the .10 level for the measure of sick leave. This latter finding undoubtedly reflects its low test–retest reliability. A univariate *F* test for the replication sample 3 months subsequent to training, and the original training group 3 months subsequent to training, revealed no significant differences.

To understand from the employees' perspective why the training increased job attendance, employees in the original training group were assured confidentiality and were then asked to state candidly their reasons for using sick leave. This occurred during Week 2 of the training and in Months 3, 6, and 9. The procedure was not used with the replication sample because the trainer was an employee of the organization. The reasons given for sick leave were classified into the nine categories shown in Table 4. Of these nine, family problems (e.g., "my relationship with my spouse is on the rocks, so I need to get away") were initially

Table 2
Means and Standard Deviations of Attendance Measure by Training and Control Groups

Group	Pretraining		3 months		6 months		9 months		12 months	
	M	*SD*	*M*	*SD*	*M*	*SD*	*M*	*SD*	*M*	*SD*
Training	33.1	5.6	35.7	4.2	38.6	1.4	38.2	2.4	38.4	3.8
Control	32.3	7.6	30.0	4.9	31.6	4.3	30.9	3.3	34.9	4.3

Note. Attendance is number of hours present per 40-hr scheduled work week. The 12-months score is a 1-year follow-up for the training group and a 3-months follow-up for the newly trained control group.

Table 3
Means and Standard Deviations of Sick Leave Absenteeism by Training and Control Groups

Group	Pretraining		3 months		6 months		9 months		12 months	
	M	SD	M	SD	M	SD	M	SD	M	SD
Training	5.26	3.6	4.12	2.4	3.68	1.4	3.58	2.6	3.72	2.2
Control	4.96	2.2	5.03	3.6	5.14	2.8	5.11	3.9	4.01	2.4

Note. The 12-months score is a 1-year follow-up for the training group and a 3-months follow-up for the newly trained control group.

listed most frequently. The interviews with these individuals, subsequent to the training, indicated that most absences occurred for what they stated were truly medically related, that is, illness or a medical appointment.

Self-Efficacy

The coefficient alphas of the measure of self-efficacy for 3, 6, and 9 months subsequent to the training of the original training group were satisfactory (.89, .89, and .87, respectively). The test–retest reliability of this measure between Months 3 and 9 was .88. In the replication sample, the alpha was .87 for the measure reported 3 months after the training. The test–retest reliability over 3 months was .89; in the original 3-months study it was .92.

The means and standard deviations for the measure of the trainees' self-efficacy is shown in Table 5. A repeated measures ANOVA revealed a significant difference, $F(1, 119) = 27.22$, $p < .01$, $\omega^2 = .18$, $p < .05$, across Months 3, 6, and 9. Thus, perceived self-efficacy increased significantly. Moreover, an ANOVA revealed no significant difference between the original experimental and control groups 3 months after the training of the control group had been conducted.

The correlations between self-efficacy measured 3 months after the training, and job attendance 3, 6, and 9 months subsequent to the training, were .45, .48, and .46, respectively. All of these values were significant at the .05 level. Thus, the self-efficacy measure predicts job attendance at several points in time. Self-efficacy has been found to be at the root of relapse prevention (Marlatt & Gordon, 1985).

Tardiness/Turnover/Generalizability

Data were collected on tardiness and voluntary and involuntary turnover to determine if the training program affected either of these behaviors adversely. No significant differences were found between the training and control groups throughout the study. Thus, there was no evidence of symptom substitution.

Interviews with supervisors ($n = 12$) revealed that they observed positive changes on the part of the trainees. They reported that the training taught the individuals effective strategies for maintaining schedules of job shop work orders as well as job completion. Several trainees were observed sharing viewpoints regarding effective ways of completing their work on time. One supervisor reported that his personal satisfaction with two of the trainees' job performance was so high that he had recommended both of them for leadership positions.

Another trainee, who had come to each session in a slovenly fashion, began taking interest in good grooming habits and appearance. This trainee stated that he had begun to feel better about himself as a result of his performance during the training and on the job. Three individuals reported using the self-management techniques for problems other than sick leave, namely, weight loss, smoking, and stress reduction. They stated that they had members of their family (e.g., wife, son) serve as external verifiers of their progress in the program. In the 6-month follow-up interviews, one individual reported a 30-lb reduction in weight, another a reduction in smoking from 2.5 packs per week to .5 packs per week, and a third a significant improvement in a personal relationship as a result of effectively managing stressful situations. Two other individuals reported using the self-management techniques for implementing a body-building program and managing financial expenses. This anecdotal information is supportive of data on the generalizability of self-management techniques to other behaviors (Bandura, 1986).

Discussion

With few exceptions (e.g., Saari & Latham, 1982), the long-term use and effectiveness of behavioral science interventions

Table 4
Self-Reported Reasons for Absenteeism for Training Group (%)

Classification	Pretraining	3 months	6 months	9 months
Family problems	25	12	6	5
Coworker problems	20	10	4	5
Transportation	15	8	5	5
Perceived employee privilege	12	5	5	4
Medical appointments	10	28	30	32
Legitimate illness	5	36	45	42
Alcohol/drug issues	8	—	—	—
Job boredom	5	—	—	—

Table 5
Means and Standard Deviations of Self-Efficacy Measure by Training and Control Groups

	Pretraining		3 months		6 months		9 months		12 months	
Group	M	SD	M	SD	M	SD	M	SD	M	SD
Training	45.0	14.3	60.2	15.1	86.6	11.3	87.5	10.2	85.9	8.6
Control	46.4	13.2	45.8	14.3	46.0	12.7	44.9	13.8	63.6	12.3

Note. The 12-months score is a 1-year follow-up for the training group and a 3-months follow-up for the newly trained control group.

are not measured (Hinrichs, 1978). The 6- and 9-months follow-up studies reported in this article are another exception. The significance of these follow-up studies and the replication is fourfold. First, training in self-management skills has been shown to be an effective way to strengthen self-efficacy in employees who have difficulties in coming to work. This finding replicates the study by Frayne and Latham (1987). That the training was conducted by a different trainer attests to the generality of the procedure.

Second, the effectiveness of this training does not appear to extinguish with time. The people who had the benefit of training in self-management continued to adhere to their self-prepared behavioral contract by reinforcing goal attainments and punishing failure to do so. This methodology appears to be highly effective in ensuring and maintaining goal commitment. In contrast, the job attendance of the control group did not increase until it also received the training in self-management.

Third, there continues to be no evidence of symptom substitution on the part of those who practice self-management techniques. This fact, plus the cost-effectiveness of this training, casts significant doubt on the assertion of Nicholson and his colleagues (e.g., Chadwick-Jones et al., 1982) that the utility of behavioral interventions that focus on the individual are of questionable value.

Fourth, and most important, both the correlational data and the replication of the Frayne and Latham (1987) experiment provide suggestive evidence for a theory of job attendance. This theory, *self-efficacy* (Bandura, 1977, 1982), states that people who have a high sense of coping efficacy will display higher job attendance than those who have a lower sense of efficacy that they can manage problem situations. Consistent with this conceptualization, perceived self-efficacy at the end of training predicted job attendance 9 months later.

A self-efficacy based theory of job attendance should not be viewed as in conflict or in competition with Nicholson's social dynamics explanation of absenteeism. The discovery of group norms indigenous to absenteeism cultures within organizations that affect employee behavior was an important finding that furthered the understanding of absenteeism. However, it would be questionable ethically to inculcate in employees the belief that they are not responsible for their own behavior. Thus, the finding that job attendance can be increased by empowering employees with self-management skills is an equally important discovery.

A possible limitation of the present follow-up study and replication is that the work culture per se was not systematically studied, nor was an attempt made to directly change it. The samples of employees were chosen, however, because they were members of a strong union working in a governmental setting where previous management controls had proven ineffective in increasing job attendance. The focus of the training was on the individual employee. However, the theory on which the training is based is interactionist in that it explicitly advocates a model of reciprocal determinism among the person, behavior, and environment (Bandura, 1986). Moreover, a program that achieves widespread increases in job attendance is very likely to alter group norms. Whether direct efforts to alter group norms could achieve similar stable changes remains to be evaluated through systematic comparisons.

Another possible issue in this study is that contamination in the replication experiment could have occurred as a result of informal norms or expectations created from the knowledge of the positive results obtained in the initial study. This *demand effect* can occur in almost any applied experiment in which the rationale given to participants for conducting the study is based in part on results obtained in previous experiments. In this study, the subjects in the two experiments were from the same work setting. However, it must be remembered that no change in the control group's behavior occurred for 9 months, and the behavior changed only after the control group received the training from a different trainer. Although it is likely that favorable comments from people in the initial training program predisposed people in the replication experiment to enter the training with a positive attitude, this study produced results similar to the first experiment in which such a bias could not have occurred.

As noted by Frayne and Latham (1987), a problem indigenous to both an attendance and an absenteeism measure is that they do not reflect the distinction between voluntary and involuntary absenteeism. Taking sick leave because one is ill, and lying to, or negotiating with, a supervisor to record a vacation day as sick leave are distinctly different behaviors. To overcome this contamination in measurement, a researcher would have to observe each person who stayed away from work to determine whether illness was a valid reason. The practicality of involving medical experts and calculating subsequent interobserver reliability coefficients makes the likelihood of conducting this research relatively low.

As a small step toward this ethnographic stance, the second author, as noted previously, assured the trainees confidentiality in comments made to her. As was shown in Table 4, only 5% of the absenteeism prior to training was said to be due to legitimate illness. Thus, the significance of these self-reports is threefold. First, they explain why absenteeism measures are usually

416   GARY P. LATHAM AND COLETTE A. FRAYNE

highly confounded with socially approved justifications. Employees candidly admit that they often do not tell the truth as to why they do not come to work. This finding underscores the importance of measuring job attendance in addition to, if not in place of, organizationally categorized absences. Second, the relatively small percentage of people who reported that they missed work, prior to the Frayne and Latham (1987) study, because they were truly sick supports the notion of an absenteeism culture (Chadwick-Jones et al., 1982). Third, after the self-management training, the follow-up reports indicated that absenteeism was no longer masquerading under sickness labels. When sick leave was taken, it was actually due to illness.

References

Äs, D. (1962). Absenteeism: A social fact in need of a theory. *Acta Sociologica, 6,* 278–285.

Bandura, A. (1977). *Social learning theory.* Englewood Cliffs, NJ: Prentice-Hall.

Bandura, A. (1982). Self-efficacy mechanism in human agency. *American Psychologist, 37,* 122–147.

Bandura, A. (1986). *Social foundations of thought and action: A social cognitive theory.* Englewood Cliffs, NJ: Prentice-Hall.

Brownell, K., Marlatt, G., Lichtenstein, E., & Wilson, G. (1986). *American Psychologist, 41,* 765–782.

Chadwick-Jones, J. K., Nicholson, N., & Brown, C. A. (1982). *Social psychology of absenteeism.* New York: Praeger.

Frayne, C. A. (1986). *The application of social learning theory to employee self-management of attendance.* Unpublished doctoral dissertation, University of Washington.

Frayne, C. A., & Latham, G. P. (1987). The application of social learning theory to employee self-management of attendance. *Journal of Applied Psychology, 72,* 387–392.

Hinrichs, J. R. (1978). *Practical management of productivity.* New York: Van Nostrand Reinhold.

Ilgen, D. R. (1977). Attendance behavior: A reevaluation of Latham and Pursell's conclusions. *Journal of Applied Psychology, 62,* 230–233.

Johns, G. (1984). Unresolved issues in the study and management of absence from work. In P. S. Goodman & R. S. Atkin (Eds.), *Absenteeism: New approaches to understanding, measuring, and managing employee absence* (pp. 360–390). San Francisco: Jossey-Bass.

Johns, G., & Nicholson, N. (1982). The meanings of absence: New strategies for theory and research. In B. M. Staw & L. L. Cummings (Eds.), *Research in organizational behavior* (Vol. 1, pp. 127–172). Greenwich, CT: JAI Press.

Kanfer, F. H. (1970). Self-regulation: Research, issues, and speculations. In C. Neuringer & J. L. Michael (Eds.) *Behavior modification in clinical psychology* (pp. 178–220). New York: Appleton-Century-Crofts.

Kanfer, F. H. (1975). Self-management methods. In F. H. Kanfer & A. P. Goldstein (Eds.), *Helping people change* (pp. 309–355). New York: Pergamon Press.

Kanfer, F. H. (1980). Self-management methods. In F. H. Kanfer & A. P. Goldstein (Eds.), *Helping people change: A textbook of methods* (2nd ed.). New York: Pergamon Press.

Kanfer, F. H. (1986). Implications of a self-regulation model of therapy for treatment of addictive behaviors. In W. R. Miller & N. Heather (Eds.), *Treating addictive behaviors: Vol. II. Processes of change* (pp. 272–314). New York: Plenum Press.

Latham, G. P., & Frayne, C. A. (1987). *The stability of job attendance of unionized workers.* Paper presented at the annual meeting of the Academy of Management Association, New Orleans, LA.

Latham, G. P., & Napier, N. K. (1984). Practical ways to increase employee attendance. In P. S. Goodman & R. S. Atkin (Eds.), *Absenteeism: New approaches to understanding, measuring, and managing employee absence* (pp. 322–359). San Francisco: Jossey-Bass.

Latham, G. P., & Pursell, E. D. (1975). Measuring absenteeism from the opposite side of the coin. *Journal of Applied Psychology, 60,* 369–371.

Latham, G. P., & Pursell, E. D. (1977). Measuring attendance: A reply to Ilgen. *Journal of Applied Psychology, 62,* 239–246.

Marlatt, G., & Gordon, J. (Eds.). (1985). *Relapse prevention: Maintenance strategies in addictive behavior change.* New York: Guilford Press.

Nicholson, N., & Johns, G. (1982, August). *The absence culture and the psychological contract—Who's in control of absence?* Paper presented at the 20th International Congress of Applied Psychology, Edinburgh, Scotland.

Saari, L. M., & Latham, G. P. (1982). Employee reactions to continuous and variable ratio reinforcement schedules involving a monetary incentive. *Journal of Applied Psychology, 67,* 506–508.

Received November 12, 1987
Revision received May 25, 1988
Accepted May 25, 1988 ∎

[12]

Journal of Applied Psychology
1986, Vol. 71, No. 2, 232–245

A Cumulative Study of the Effectiveness of Managerial Training

Michael J. Burke
Department of Management
New York University

Russell R. Day
Illinois Institute of Technology and
Chicago and North Western Transportation Company

The published and unpublished literature on the effectiveness of managerial training has produced conflicting results and left more unanswered questions than definitive statements concerning the effectiveness of managerial training. In the present study, meta-analysis procedures were applied to the results of 70 managerial training studies to empirically integrate the findings of the studies. The meta-analysis results for 34 distributions of managerial training effects representing six training content areas, seven training methods, and four types of criteria (subjective learning, objective learning, subjective behavior, and objective results) indicated that managerial training is, on the average, moderately effective. For 12 of the 17 managerial training method distributions, the 90% lower bound credibility values were positive, and thus the effectiveness of these training methods, at least at a minimal level, can be generalized to new situations. It is stressed that although this meta-analysis assisted in clarifying what we have learned about managerial training, a great deal of empirical research on managerial training is needed before more conclusive statements can be made.

Every year, managerial training and development programs are implemented in most private and public organizations. The pervasiveness of managerial training is well recognized (cf. Lundberg, Dunbar, & Bayless, 1973; Wexley & Latham, 1981; Wikstrom, 1973). The objective of most managerial training and development programs is to teach or improve various managerial skills to improve on-the-job performance (Goldstein, 1980; Wexley & Latham, 1981). In particular, a great deal of managerial training is focused on improving job performance in the areas of human relations, self-awareness, problem solving and decision making, motivation/values, and general management. Many organizations, however, are unaware of the effectiveness of training programs in these areas. This lack of knowledge concerning the results of managerial training is primarily due to the lack of evaluative research on these programs. Four notable reviews (Campbell, 1971; Campbell, Dunnette, Lawler, & Weick, 1970; Goldstein, 1980; Wexley, 1984) attempted to integrate the available evaluative managerial training research. Campbell et al. (1970) concluded that the literature on the relation of training to management performance reveals little about what kind of knowledge and skills contribute to managerial effectiveness. According to Campbell (1971), "the training development literature is voluminous, nonempirical, nontheoretical, poorly written, and dull" (p. 565). Unfortunately, as in his review and the Campbell et al. (1970) review, Goldstein's (1980) review indicated that the vast majority of literature in the managerial training area, and training in general, was still not empirical or based on theory. A large proportion of the managerial training and development literature was dominated by low-utility anecdotal presentations (Goldstein, 1980). Wexley (1984) concluded that considerably more research is urgently needed in the area of management development. In general, these four reviews illustrated that the relation between managerial training and the acquisition of managerial skills is not clear.

Although noteworthy, these reviews left some important questions unanswered. First, How effective, in general, is managerial training with respect to different criteria? In addition, there are many different types (i.e., content areas) of managerial training. As noted above, these include human relations, general management functions, problem solving and decision making, self-awareness, motivation/values, and specialties. Which types of management training programs are effective and to what degree? Moreover, there are numerous managerial training methods (e.g., lecture, discussion, role playing). Important questions remain concerning the relative effectiveness of different methods or combinations of methods in improving learning or acquisition of skills. In order to obtain answers to these questions, the results of management training studies must be empirically integrated.

Integrating the results of managerial training studies, as well as studies for other organizational interventions, via meta-analytic techniques (cf. Glass, McGaw, & Smith, 1981; Hunter, Schmidt & Jackson, 1982) will assist in determining the effectiveness of interventions. The findings of such research are likely to be of theoretical import to researchers as well as practical import to organizational decision makers. The purpose of this study was to apply the process of meta-analysis (cf. Glass et al., 1981; Hunter et al., 1982) to the available managerial training and development literature to determine the effectiveness of managerial training.

We attempted to answer the following questions: (a) Across studies with respect to various criteria, how effective is managerial training? (b) For each type of criterion measure, what is the relative effectiveness of different types of managerial training (i.e., human relations, general management, self-awareness, problem solving and decision making, motivation/values, and specialties)?

The authors would like to thank Nambury Raju, Frank Schmidt, and two anonymous reviewers for helpful comments on an earlier draft of this article.

Correspondence concerning this article should be addressed to Michael J. Burke, 600 Tisch Hall, Department of Management, New York University, 40 West 4th Street, New York, New York 10003.

(c) For each type of criterion measure, what is the relative effectiveness of different managerial training methods and combinations of methods?

Method

Selection of Studies and Coding of Study Characteristics

Each study in the present analysis had to meet three criteria: (a) The study involved managerial or supervisory personnel, (b) it evaluated the effectiveness of one or more training programs, and (c) it included at least one control or comparison group. Studies were located by conducting computer searches of the ERIC and PsychINFO indexes and by scanning bibliographies of the published and unpublished sources. The degree of methodological rigor or quality of the research design was not a selection criterion. After all literature searches, the total number of nonredundant papers collected for analysis was 70. Subsequent to the identification and selection of studies was the task of coding each study for analysis.

Study characteristics such as sample size and criterion reliability were collected and coded in order to correct reported results for artifacts such as sampling error and attenuation. An attempt was also made to include all pertinent information related to managerial training research. The studies were coded for the content area of training (human relations, problem solving and decision making, and so forth), the type of training method (technique) used, the type of outcome (criterion) variable measured, the type of industry in which the study was performed, length of training time, time between training and evaluation, assignment of subjects, type of comparisons made, use of before and after measures, and whether the results reported were significant or not. Subject characteristics included in the coding were sex, level of management, and years of experience as a manager or supervisor. In addition, type of trainer (i.e., professional trainer, researcher, other) was included in the coding. Descriptions of all the studies are presented by training content area in Table 1.

In order to ensure the reliability of the coding scheme developed for this meta-analysis, two studies were randomly selected and independently read and coded by five judges. The judges were two doctoral-level industrial psychology students and three industrial/organizational psychologists. The pairwise interrater agreement ranged from 87% to 90%. The overall interrater agreement was 88%.

Definitions of Training Content Areas, Training Methods, and Criteria

In categorizing studies, the following definitions (descriptions) were used for training content. They are similar to those developed by Campbell et al. (1970).

General management programs. This is the broadest type of development effort and typically includes material on labor relations, management theory and practice, company policies and procedures, labor economics, and general management functions. The primary goal of these training programs is the teaching of facts, concepts, and skills.

Human relations/leadership programs. The content of these programs is narrower than that of the general management programs category in that the focus is on human relations problems of leadership, supervision, attitudes toward employees, and communication.

Self-awareness programs. The content of these programs is on understanding one's own behavior and how one's behavior is viewed by others, identifying the so-called games people play, and learning about one's strengths and weaknesses. Typical training methods are sensitivity training, laboratory training, T-groups, and transactional analysis.

Problem-solving/decision-making programs. The emphasis of these programs is on teaching generalized problem-solving and decision-making skills that would be applicable to a wide range of work problems that managers encounter.

Rater training programs. In these programs managers are trained to minimize errors when they are observing and evaluating their subordinates.

Motivation/values training programs. The content of these programs deals with increasing managers' motivation or modifying a manager's values or attitudes.

A set of definitions was also used for categorizing studies by training method. These training method definitions were as follows.

Lecture. This is the most traditional method for presenting information, usually involving a carefully prepared oral presentation on a subject by a qualified individual (Reith, 1976).

Lecture/group discussion. This category includes the lecture method described above, as well as group discussion. The discussion often focuses on specific problems or new areas of knowledge. Active participation by the trainee is encouraged. This type of training provides the opportunity for clarification, feedback, and considerable trainee involvement.

Leader Match. This is a method used in human relations/leadership training that incorporates self-paced workbooks and standardized problems (Fiedler, Chemers, & Mahar, 1976). The self-paced workbooks are designed to teach trainees how to apply the principles of Contingency Theory (Fiedler, 1964, 1967) to their leadership position. More specifically, the Leader Match training program is designed to teach individuals how to become aware of their leadership style through the self-paced workbook, how to diagnose the situation in which they work, and how to change the situation to fit their personality.

Sensitivity training. The classical model of sensitivity training is a group meeting without an agenda in which participants discuss topics dealing with the "here and now" of the group process (Hinrichs, 1976). Sensitivity training represents both a distinct training method and a specific content area (defined above as self-awareness). Laboratory education, a label applied to a more complete training program in which the main component is some form of sensitivity group, was considered sensitivity training for this study.

Behavioral modeling. This method of training is based on Bandura's (1977) social learning theory and emphasizes observation, modeling, and feedback in order to modify behavior.

Lecture/group discussion with role playing or practice. This category represents a common combination of methods using lecture/group discussion as well as role playing or practice. Role playing is designed such that trainees assume parts of specific personalities in a contrived situation. It typically involves modeling, practice, and feedback. Practice refers to providing the trainee with the opportunity to engage in the activity or skill which is being taught.

Multiple techniques. This category includes studies that employed three (excluding the Lecture/group discussion with role playing category) or more training methods. Most of these studies had a common method such as lecture or group discussion and more specific methods such as a case study, business game, or audiovisual presentation.

We developed four criterion-measure categories on the basis of two dimensions: (a) level of criterion and (b) subjectivity–objectivity. The level of criterion dimensions was determined according to Kirkpatrick (1976); three of Kirkpatrick's four levels were used: learning, behavior, and results.

Subjective learning. This category included measures that assessed what principles, facts, attitudes, and skills were learned during or by the end of training as communicated in statements of opinion, belief, or judgment completed by the trainee or trainer (observer).

Objective learning. Included in this category were measures that assessed what principles, facts, attitudes, and skills were learned during or by the end of training by objective means, such as number of errors made or number of solutions reached, or by standardized test (e.g., knowledge test).

Subjective behavior. This category included measures that evaluated changes in on-the-job behavior perceived by trainees, peers, or supervisor.

(text continues on page 237)

234   MICHAEL J. BURKE AND RUSSELL R. DAY

Table 1
Managerial Training Studies Used in Meta-Analysis

Author(s)	Sample description	Sample size	Type of training	Criteria
Human relations/leadership				
Baum, Sorensen, & Place (1970)	Insurance company middle managers	12-T[a] 12-C	Lecture, small group discussion, case studies	Perceptions of influence exercised by subordinates
Burnaska (1976)	General Electric middle managers	62-T 62-C	Behavioral modeling	Ratings of interpersonal skills
Byham, Adams, & Kiggins (1976)	Financial accounting supervisors	8-T 8-C	Behavioral modeling, practice, audiovisual aids	Ratings on interpersonal skills from subordinates
Canter (1951)	Insurance company supervisors	18-T 18-C	Lecture	Knowledge tests, questionnaires on human relations
Carron (1964)	Chemical company supervisors	23-T 12-C	Group discussion, role playing	Leadership Opinion Questionnaire, Authoritarianism Scale
Csoka & Bons (1978)	College ROTC military leaders	26-T1[b] 27-C1 38-T2 76-C2	Self-paced workbook, Leader Match	T1. Composite leadership ratings from superiors and peers T2. Rank orderings by superiors
Decker (1982)	First-line hospital supervisors	12-T 12-C	Behavioral modeling, audiovisual aids	Ratings by trained raters of ability to coach and handle employee complaints
DiVesta (1954)	Air Force medical administrative supervisors	94-T	Lecture	Knowledge tests, performance ratings
Fiedler & Mahar (1979a)				
Study 1	Public health volunteer leaders	9-T 27-C 11-T 33-C	Self-paced workbook, Leader Match	Performance ratings by superiors
Study 2	Same	18-T 12-C 16-T 10-C	Leader Match vs. alternative training program of similar format and length vs. control group	Same
Fiedler & Mahar (1979b)	College ROTC military leaders	190-T 215-C	Leader Match	Overall performance ratings by advisors and peers
Fiedler, Mahar, & Schmidt (1976)				
Study A	Urban county government middle managers	15-T 15-C	Leader Match, group discussion, audiovisual aids	Biyearly performance evaluations (ratings)
Study B	Police	7-T 10-C	Same	Performance ratings by immediate superior
Study C	Public works supervisors	14-T 13-C	Same	Performance ratings by two superiors
Fleishman (1953)	Industrial foremen	90-T 32-C	Lecture, group discussion, role playing	Supervisory Behavior Description Questionnaire, Foreman's Leadership Opinion Questionnaire
Goldstein & Sorcher (1974)	General Electric foremen	100-T 100-C	Behavioral modeling	Subordinate productivity
Hand & Slocum (1970)/ Hand, Richard, & Slocum (1973)[c]	Steel plant middle managers	21-T 21-C	Group discussion, case studies, practice	Leadership Opinion Questionnaire, Supervisory Behavior Description Questionnaire, knowledge test, sensitivity to others questionnaire, performance ratings, salary increases
Harris & Fleishman (1955)	First-level supervisors, truck manufacturing	39-T 59-C	Lecture, group discussion, visual aids	SBD ratings
Jennings (1954)	First-level supervisors	20-T 20-C	Case study, forced leadership method	Performance rankings
Latham & Saari (1979)	Paper company foremen	20-T 20-C	Behavioral modeling	Knowledge tests, ratings by superiors, ratings during role play
Lawshe, Bolda, & Brune (1959)				
Study 5	First-level supervisors	12-T 15-C	Role playing	Ratings in performance in skills test

Table 1 (*continued*)

Author(s)	Sample description	Sample size	Type of training	Criteria
Leister, Borden, & Fiedler (1977)	Naval officers	27-T 29-C	Leader Match, visual aids	Performance ratings by superiors
Maier (1953)	First-level supervisors	44 T groups 36 C groups	Role playing, group discussion	Ratings during role play, number of solutions reached
Mayo & DuBois (1963)	Military officers	211-T 211-C	Lecture	Ratings by superiors
Moon & Hariton (1958)	General Electric engineering managers	66-T 67-C	Lecture, group discussion, role playing, practice	Survey ratings by subordinates
Mosel & Tsacnaris (1954)	Air Force officers	83-T 44-C	Lecture	How Supervise
Moses & Ritchie (1976)	Telephone company supervisors	90-T 93-C	Behavioral modeling	Ratings during role play tests on interpersonal skill
Smith (1976)				
Study 1	IBM middle managers	18-T 13-C	Behavioral modeling	Subordinate ratings
Study 2	Same	36-T	Behavior modeling and team building vs. behavioral modeling vs. lecture–discussion	Skills test in communication, sales performance
Stroud (1959)	Telephone company supervisors	103-T 91-C	Lecture, group discussion, role playing	Superiors ratings of performance, Leader, Behavior Description Questionnaire
Trice & Belasco (1968)	First-level supervisors	55-T 55-C	Lecture, group discussion, role playing	Knowledge test, attitude scale
General management functions				
Alves & Hardy (1963)	Los Angeles County supervisors	46-T 46-C	Lecture, case studies	Attitude questionnaire from subordinates
Buchanan & Brunstetter (1959)	First-level supervisors	224-T	Laboratory education	Survey questionnaire
Couch & Strother (1971)	First-level manufacturing supervisors	30-T 30-C	Lecture	Self-reported critical incidents
Goodacre (1957)	B. F. Goodrich middle managers	400-T 400-C	Lecture, group discussion	Knowledge tests, attitude survey, performance ratings
Goodacre (1963)	General Electric middle managers	218-T 279-C	Lecture, practice	Questionnaires reported by subordinates
House & Tosi (1963)	Engineer managers	24-T 33-C	Lecture	Self-report questionnaire
Ivancevich & Smith (1981)	Sales managers	20-T 20-T 20-C	Videotaping, role play vs. role play, lecture vs. controls	Goal setting rating forms reported by subordinates
Kondrasuk (1972)	Public service middle managers	13-T 13-C	Lecture, case study, role play, group discussion, audiovisual aids	Knowledge test
Latham & Kinne (1974)	First-level logging supervisors	10-T 10-C	Lecture, practice	Worker productivity
Mahar (1981)	School curriculum supervisors	5-T 5-C	Behavioral modeling, practice	Ratings of developed educational programs
Mahoney, Jerdee, & Korman (1960)	Middle managers	46-T 13-C	Conference and case study methods	Management Practices Quiz, case analysis, attitude scale
McGehee & Gardner (1955)	Textile production foremen	10-T 11-C	Lecture, practice	Knowledge test, attitude scale, performance ratings
Miner (1965)	Research & development supervisors	52-T 49-C	Lecture	Advancement, motivation needs
Schwarz, Stilwell, & Scanlan (1968)	Insurance company middle managers	28-T 29-C	Lecture, group discussion, case study, role play, audiovisual aids	Leadership Behavior Description Questionnaire by subordinates, self-reported critical incidents
Wexley & Nemeroff (1975)	Medical center supervisors	9-T 9-T	Role playing, practice, goal setting, feedback	Leadership Behavior Description Questionnaire by subordinates, subordinates absenteeism
Wilburn (1979)	First-level manufacturing	75-T 75-C	Lecture, conference, & case study method; role playing; practice	How Supervise

(*table continued*)

236   MICHAEL J. BURKE AND RUSSELL R. DAY

Table 1 *(continued)*

Author(s)	Sample description	Sample size	Type of training	Criteria
Wolfe & Moe (1973)	Health care supervisors	17-T 17-C	Lecture, case study	How Supervise
Problem solving/decision making				
Moffie, Calhoon, & O'Brien (1964)	Papermill middle managers	32-T 28-C	Standardized work problems	Watson-Glaser Critical Thinking Appraisal
Roy & Dolke (1971)	First-level supervisors	12-T 12-C	Lecture, case study, practice, group discussion	Knowledge test
Smith & Kight (1959)	First-level supervisors	33-T 69-C	Lecture, group discussion, role play, practice	Number of problems solved during test
Wilson, Mullen, & Morton (1968)	Middle managers	21-T 28-C	Conference & case study method, practice on standardized problems	Self-reported questionnaire
Self-awareness				
Argyris (1965)	Business executives	15-T 15-C	T-groups	Observer ratings during training
Boyd & Ellis (1963)	Public utility middle managers	42-T 12-T 10-C	T-groups vs. lecture-group discussion vs. no-training group	On-the-job behavior changes observed by subordinates
Bunker (1965)	Middle managers from various industries	229-T 112-C	T-groups	Open-ended behavior change descriptions by co-workers and self
Hand & Slocum (1972)	Middle managers	21-T 21-C	Lecture, laboratory education	Leadership Opinion Questionnaire, Supervisory Behavior Description Questionnaire, performance ratings, attitude scale
Harrison (1962)	Business executives	8-T 12-C	T-groups	Self-reported description of others
Harrison & Lubin (1965)	Middle managers	23-T 46-C	Laboratory education	Peer ratings for self-expression and amount of learning
Katz & Schwebel (1976)	Data processing	12-T 13-C	Laboratory education	Problem Analysis Questionnaire, peer ratings, Crowne-Marlowe Social Desirability Scale
Miles (1960 & 1965)	Elementary school principals	34-T 34-C	Laboratory education	Leader Behavior Description Questionnaire, ratings for behavior changes
Rubin (1967)	Supervisors from various occupations	30-T 11-C	T-groups	Sentence completion test for self acceptance and reduction in prejudice
Schutz & Allen (1966)	Middle managers	71-T 30-C	T-groups	Self-report questionnaire on interpersonal behavior
Smith (1963)	Middle managers	108-T 44-C	T-groups	Attitude scale
Steele (1968)	Middle managers	72-T 39-C	Laboratory education	Managerial Behavior Questionnaire on interpersonal values
Underwood (1965)	First-level supervisors	15-T 15-C	Laboratory education	Ratings by co-workers
Valiquet (1968)	Middle managers	34-T 15-C	Laboratory education	Description on open-ended questionnaire by peers
Motivation/values				
Arnoff & Litwin (1971)	Manufacturing executives	11-T 11-C	Lecture, group discussion, business games	Rate of advancement in company
Durand (1975)	Owners and operators of businesses	11-T 9-C	Lecture, case study, group discussion	Achievement motivation scores on Thematic Apperception Test, locus of control, interview, business activity questionnaire
Gruenfeld (1966)	Business executives	69-T 46-C	Lecture	Allport Vernon Study of Values
Miner (1960)	Research & development supervisors	55-T 30-C	Lecture	Sentence Completion Questionnaire
Viteles (1959)	Business executives	17-T 16-C	Lecture, group discussion	Knowledge test, Allport Vernon Study of Values
Rater training				
Ivancevich (1979)	Engineering supervisors	22-T 22-T	Workshop training vs. discussion & lecture	Reduction in halo and leniency rating errors

Table 1 (*continued*)

Author(s)	Sample description	Sample size	Type of training	Criteria
Levine & Butler (1952)	Manufacturing supervisors	11-T 9-T 9-C	Lecture vs. conference method vs. no training	Ability to make less biased performance ratings
Warmke & Billings (1979)	Nursing supervisors	14-T 10-T 15-T 13-C	Lecture vs. discussion vs. scale construction vs. no training	Reduction in performance rating errors

[a] T = trained group, C = comparison group.
[b] Indicates specific training group.
[c] Initial evaluations were reported in the 1970 article; follow-up analyses of the same study were reported in the 1973 article.

Objective results. This category included measures that evaluated tangible results, such as reduced costs, improved quality or quantity, promotions, and reduced number of errors in making performance ratings.

Meta-Analysis Procedure

Effect sizes were used as the common metric in this meta-analysis. Effect size or magnitude of effect can be defined as the normalized difference between a trained group and a comparison group. This can be restated as

$$ES = (M_t - \bar{M}_c)/S_w,\qquad(1)$$

where ES is effect size, M_t is the treatment or trained group mean score on the dependent variable, M_c is the comparison or control group mean score on the dependent variable, and S_w is the within-group standard deviation on the dependent variable, given by the following formula:

$$S_w = \sqrt{\frac{(N_t - 1)S_t^2 + (N_c - 1)S_c^2}{N_t + N_c - 2}},\qquad(2)$$

where N_t is the number of subjects in the trained group, N_c is the number of subjects in the comparison group, S_t^2 is the variance for the trained group on the dependent variable, and S_c^2 is the variance for the comparison group on the dependent variable. Thus, an ES of +1 indicates that if a person at the mean of the comparison group were given the treatment (in this case training), he or she would be expected to rise to the 84th percentile of the comparison group.

An effect size was calculated on the outcome variable or variables reported in each study. If a study had more than one outcome variable, each variable was treated as independent and was entered separately into the overall analysis. For studies that reported only t, F, or other inferential statistics, ES was calculated by the appropriate conversion formulas (cf. Glass et al., 1981; Hunter et al., 1982; Schmidt, Hunter, & Pearlman, 1982). In addition, each ES was corrected for attenuation due to the unreliability of the criterion measure used in a particular study by the following equation:

$$ES_{ci} = \frac{ES_i}{\sqrt{r_{yy}}},\qquad(3)$$

where ES_{ci} is the effect size corrected for criterion unreliability, ES_i is the attenuated effect size, and r_{yy} is the criterion reliability. When a criterion reliability was not reported, the average value for the set of studies in an analysis was substituted.

Given that studies with larger sample sizes would provide more accurate estimates of the true or population effect size, each individual effect size was weighted on the basis of the specific sample size from which it came. The true mean effect size was thus calculated as

$$\bar{M}_t = \frac{\sum (N_i ES_{ci})}{\sum N_i},\qquad(4)$$

where $\bar{M}_t$ is the estimated true mean effect size, ES_{ci} is the unattenuated effect size for each outcome reported, and N_i is the total sample size used in calculating a specific ES_{ci} (cf. Hunter et al., 1982). In addition, the disattenuated effect size variance was calculated as

$$\hat{V}_{kc} = \frac{\sum N_i (ES_{ci} - \bar{M}_t)^2}{\sum N_i}\qquad(5)$$

where V_{kc} is the unattenuated effect size variance, ES_{ci} is the disattenuated effect size for each outcome reported, $\bar{M}_t$ is the mean population effect size, and N_i is the total sample size used in calculating a specific ES_{ci}.

In order to determine the true or population effect size variance, the sampling error across studies was calculated. The sampling error variance corrected for criterion unreliability was assessed by Hunter et al.'s (1982) formula:

$$V_e = \left(\frac{4(1 + \bar{M}_t^2/8)K}{\sum N_i}\right)\cdot\left(\frac{1}{K}\cdot\frac{1}{r_{yy}}\right),\qquad(6)$$

where V_e is the sampling error variance, r_{yy} is the particular criterion reliability for the outcome reported, N_i is the total sample size, and K is the number of effect sizes reported.

The formula for estimating the population (true) effect size variance then became:

$$\hat{V}_t = \hat{V}_{kc} - V_e,\qquad(7)$$

where $\hat{V}_t$ is the estimated true effect size variance, $\hat{V}_{kc}$ is the estimated disattenuated effect size variance, and V_e is the estimated sampling error variance.

The corrected variance term would be approximately zero if the effect size were constant across studies (i.e., homogeneous). If 75% or more of the observed effect size variance was accounted for by artifactual effects, then the hypothesis that the results were situation specific was rejected. Furthermore, when the difference was judged to be of practical significance (e.g., variance due to sampling error and criterion unreliability account for less than 75% of the observed variance), follow-up regression analyses were performed to determine what study characteristics other than sample size and criterion unreliability were contributing to the between-studies variance. In addition, after the unattenuated effect size variance was corrected for sampling error, lower bound credibility values were established for each estimated population effect size.

This procedure was followed in analyzing (a) training results for each of the four criterion-measure categories, (b) training results for each of the six training content areas with respect to the four criterion categories, and (c) training results for each of the seven training method categories, again with respect to the four criterion categories.

Results

Training Content

Subjective learning criteria. As shown in Table 2, only 12.4% of the observed variance over all studies using subjective learning

238   MICHAEL J. BURKE AND RUSSELL R. DAY

Table 2

Results for Content of Managerial Training on Subjective Learning Criteria

Training areas	No. of ESs	No. of studies	N	$\overline{ES}$	V_{obs}	V_e	% of variance accounted for	$\hat{M}_\delta$	$\hat{V}_\delta$	90% C.V.
Overall areas[a]	58	21	9,971	.31	.374	.028	12.4	.34	.199	-.23
Human relations	21	8	2,156	.69	.265	.051	31.9	.76	.108	.34
General management	20	4	6,878	.13	.378	.014	16.0	.14	.073	-.21
Self-awareness	15	7	832	.80	.524	.091	18.6	.86	.399	.06

Note. V_{obs} is the observed effect size variance. V_e is sampling error variance. $\overline{ES}$ is the observed weighted mean according to sample size.
[a] The content areas of problem solving, motivation/values and rater training were not included in separate breakdowns because only two or less studies in each area were found that used subjective learning criteria. However, they were included in the overall results for subjective learning criteria if data were available.

criteria was accounted for on the basis of artifactual effects. Human relations had the highest percentage of observed effect size variance accounted for (31.9%).

On the basis of 21 studies, the estimated true mean effect size for subjective learning criteria was .34. As Table 2 indicates, all of the true mean effect sizes for the training content areas were positive. Notably, the estimated true effect sizes for human relations and self-awareness were each more than three quarters of one standard deviation above the mean of the comparison groups. Moreover, the overall estimated true effect size variance for subjective learning criteria was .199 (see Table 2). For each of the training content areas, the estimated true effect size variances for subjective learning criteria were also substantially greater than zero.

Objective learning criteria. As indicated in Table 3, artifactual effects accounted for only 13.3% of the observed effect size variance over all studies for objective learning criteria. Likewise, artifactual sources of variance did not account for a substantial proportion of the observed effect size variance for three of the four content distributions (see Table 3). The results for the motivation/values content category should be treated with caution because only three studies, with a total of 12 effects, were found for this area.

The estimated true mean effect size and variance for objective learning criteria, over all studies, were .38 and .339, respectively. Consequently, a lower bound credibility value of -.37 was obtained. Similarly, negative lower bound credibility estimates were obtained for all other training content areas with the exception of motivation/values.

Subjective behavior criteria. The results for managerial training content distributions with studies that used subjective

behavior criteria are presented in Table 4. Over all studies, using subjective measures of behavior as criteria, artifactual sources of variance only accounted for 13.8% of the observed effect size variance. Corresponding small percentages of variance accounted for by artifacts were found for general management and self-awareness training. Human relations training, however, had a relatively large percentage (60.5%) of the observed effect size variance accounted for by artifactual sources.

The estimated true mean effect size and variance for subjective behavior criteria, over all studies, were .49 and .344, respectively. As a result of these findings, a negative lower bound credibility value of -.26 was obtained for this analysis. General management and self-awareness training also had relatively large estimated true effect size variances and negative lower bound credibility values. On the other hand, human relations training had some variability in estimated true effect sizes (.061), yet the lower bound credibility value was positive (.12).

Objective results criteria. Over all studies using objective results as criteria, 22% of observed effect size variance was accounted for by artifacts (see Table 5). For the three content distributions, the corresponding percentages were higher: 31%, 33%, and 100% for human relations, rater, and general management training, respectively.

The estimated true mean effect sizes were substantial (more than one half of one standard deviation) in all cases. For the overall analysis with objective results as criteria, as well as for the rater training content distribution, the estimated true effect size variances were also large. As a result of large estimated true variances, these latter two distributions had negative lower bound credibility values. Human relations training, however, had a sizeable positive lower bound credibility estimate (.63).

Table 3

Results for Content of Managerial Training on Objective Learning Criteria

Training areas	No. of ESs	No. of studies	N	$\overline{ES}$	V_{obs}	V_e	% of variance accounted for	$\hat{M}_\delta$	$\hat{V}_\delta$	90% C.V.
Overall areas[a]	77	22	8,280	.33	.517	.052	13.3	.38	.339	-.37
Human relations	33	8	2,281	.33	.208	.090	35.8	.41	.161	-.10
General management	17	6	4,530	.18	.447	.019	25.1	.21	.057	-.10
Problem solving	11	3	605	.16	1.005	.094	14.4	.17	.573	-.80
Motivation/values	12	3	450	.74	.141	.153	100.0	.85	0	.85

Note. V_{obs} is the observed effect size variance. V_e is sampling error variance. $\overline{ES}$ is the observed weighted mean according to sample size.
[a] The content areas of self-awareness and rater training were not included in separate breakdowns because only two or less studies in each area were found that used objective learning criteria. However, they were included in the overall results for objective learning criteria if data were available.

Table 4
Results for Content of Managerial Training on Subjective Behavior Criteria

Training areas	No. of ESs	No. of studies	N	$\overline{ES}$	V_{obs}	V_e	% of variance accounted for	$\hat{M}_\delta$	$\hat{V}_\delta$	90% C.V.
Overall areas[a]	277	39	26,025	.44	.384	.055	13.8	.49	.344	−.26
Human relations	118	17	6,537	.39	.158	.094	60.5	.44	.061	.12
General management	88	11	11,707	.36	.476	.039	7.1	.40	.506	−.51
Self-awareness	52	7	6,944	.61	.837	.038	10.1	.65	.342	−.09

Note. V_{obs} is the observed effect size variance. V_e is sampling error variance. $\overline{ES}$ is the observed weighted mean according to sample size.
[a] The content areas of problem solving, motivation/values and rater training were not included in separate breakdowns because only two or less studies in each area were found that used subjective behavior criteria. However, they were included in the overall results for subjective behavior criteria if data were available.

Training Method

Subjective learning criteria. For the four training method distributions that had subjective learning criteria (see Table 6), artifactual sources of variance did not account for a large proportion of the observed effect size variance. The largest percentage of observed effect size variance accounted for was 39% for behavioral modeling. The estimated true mean effect sizes for the four training method distributions were relatively large in all cases. Also, although there was a fair degree of variation in the estimated true effects for these four distributions, all lower bound credibility value estimates were positive. Furthermore, behavioral modeling had a sizeable (.76) lower bound credibility value.

Objective learning criteria. As seen in Table 7, criterion unreliability and sampling error variance did not account for a large percentage of the observed effect size variances for the four training method distributions that had objective learning criteria. A majority of the observed effect size variance (56%) was accounted for by artifactual sources for the category of lecture with discussion and either role playing or practice.

The magnitude of the estimated true mean effect sizes for the four training method distributions varied considerably. Particularly notable was the size of the estimated true mean effect size of .93 for lecture with discussion and either role playing or practice. Moreover, the latter method category had a lower bound credibility value of .46. On the other hand, the lower bound credibility values for the remaining three training method categories were negative or approximately equal to zero.

Subjective behavior criteria. The managerial training method results for studies employing subjective measures of behavior as

criteria are presented in Table 8. For three managerial training method categories—Leader Match, behavioral modeling, and lecture with discussion and either role playing or practice—a substantial percentage (70% or greater) of the observed effect size variance was accounted for by artifactual sources. In addition, the training method distributions for lecture and lecture with discussion had 47% and 51% of the observed effect size variance accounted for by artifacts, respectively. Sensitivity training and the multiple techniques distribution had small percentages of observed effect size variance accounted for by artifacts.

The estimated true mean effect sizes were positive and greater than or equal to .4 for five of the seven training method distributions. In particular, sensitivity training and behavioral modeling had estimated true mean effect sizes of .73 and .78, respectively. Sensitivity training, however, as well as the multiple techniques distribution had negative lower bound credibility values. The lower bound credibility values for lecture, lecture with discussion, and lecture with discussion and either role playing or practice were positive.

Objective results criteria. Two distributions of training method effects with objective results as criteria were analyzed and are reported in Table 9. The multiple techniques category had 100% of the observed effect size variance accounted for by artifactual sources of variance. The lecture method only had approximately 22% of the observed effect size variance accounted for by artifacts. In addition, the estimated true mean effect sizes were relatively large for both training method distributions. However, because of the large estimated true effect size variance for the lecture method, this method had a negative lower bound credibility value.

Table 5
Results for Content of Managerial Training on Objective Results Criteria

Training areas	No. of ESs	No. of studies	N	$\overline{ES}$	V_{obs}	V_e	% of variance accounted for	$\hat{M}_\delta$	$\hat{V}_\delta$	90% C.V.
Overall areas[a]	60	11	2,298	.57	.407	.110	22.0	.67	.323	−.06
Human relations	3	3	314	1.01	.349	.045	30.8	1.04	.102	.63
General management	10	4	606	.49	.110	.075	100.0	.53	0	.53
Rater training	46	3	1,326	.50	.478	.256	33.4	.64	.510	−.27

Note. V_{obs} is the observed effect size variance. V_e is sampling error variance. $\overline{ES}$ is the observed weighted mean according to sample size.
[a] The content area of Self-Awareness, Problem Solving and Motivation/Values were not included in separate breakdowns since only two or less studies in each area were found that used objective results criteria. However, they were included in the overall results for objective results criteria if data were available.

Table 6
Results for Training Methods on Subjective Learning Criteria

Method[a]	No. of ESs	No. of studies	N	$\overline{ES}$	V_{obs}	V_e	% of variance accounted for	$\hat{M}_\delta$	$\hat{V}_\delta$	90% C.V.
Sensitivity training	15	7	832	.80	.524	.091	18.6	.86	.399	.06
Behavioral modeling	7	3	657	.92	.305	.053	39.3	.99	.081	.76
Lecture/discussion plus role play or practice	10	3	1,058	.60	.218	.048	25.0	.66	.146	.17
Multitechnique (3 or more)	15	4	1,258	.70	.286	.060	24.4	.76	.185	.21

Note. V_{obs} is the observed effect size variance. V_e is sampling error variance. $\overline{ES}$ is the observed weighted mean according to sample size.
[a] The training methods of lecture, lecture/discussion and Leader Match were not included in separate breakdowns because only two or less studies for each method were found that used subjective learning criteria.

Discussion

Training Content

For subjective learning criteria, over all studies and for the specific content breakdowns (i.e., human relations, general management functions, and self-awareness), it was found that controllable statistical artifacts account for small to moderate percentages of the observed effect size variances. It is highly unlikely that additional, uncontrolled statistical artifacts would have substantially increased the percentages of observed variance accounted for. Relatively larger amounts of unaccounted-for variance in these distributions may well be explained by other substantive variables (e.g., training method) that we were not able to simultaneously control in this study. Furthermore, although care should be exercised in the selection and implementation of a human relations training program because the degree of its effectiveness is likely to vary with other substantive variables, the trainer (and organization) can be fairly confident that this type of training will be effective in improving subjective learning.

The results for objective learning criteria, over all training studies, indicated that controlled-for statistical artifacts accounted for only a small percentage of the observed effect size variance. In addition, the breakdowns for three of the four training content areas (i.e., human relations, general management, and problem solving) did not provide plausible explanations for this large unaccounted-for variation in effect sizes.

The highly negative results for problem-solving and decision-making training were based on three studies with a total of 11 effects. As early as 1970, Campbell et al. stated disappointment with the results and number of studies evaluating problem-solving and decision-making training. Because of the lack of studies for this analysis, as well as the incompleteness of the reported results, the effectiveness of problem-solving and decision-making training programs is still difficult to estimate.

In addition, the small true mean effect size for general management involving objective learning criteria was probably due to a study in which a large sample was used, and few significant changes were found on the knowledge tests (Goodacre, 1957). In another study evaluating learning criteria in general management training (Mahoney, Jerdee, & Korman, 1960), the trained group actually had lower scores than did the control group on the knowledge tests. To explain these results, the authors claimed that the criterion measure used was not relevant to the training program and that instructors were not adequately prepared. Because there have been few well-designed studies within this area, no definite conclusions can be reached as to the effectiveness of general management functions training.

It was found, however, that training programs that focused on increasing motivation or improving values as measured by objective learning criteria were quite effective. That is, managers who received training were moved to the 79th percentile of the untrained group. For this analysis, the situational specificity hy-

Table 7
Results for Training Methods on Objective Learning Criteria

Method[a]	No. of ESs	No. of studies	N	$\overline{ES}$	V_{obs}	V_e	% of variance accounted for	$\hat{M}_\delta$	$\hat{V}_\delta$	90% C.V.
Lecture	20	5	1,708	.28	.134	.078	43.6	.37	.101	−.03
Lecture/discussion	24	4	4,782	.20	.202	.027	34.1	.23	.051	−.06
Lecture/discussion plus role play or practice	8	3	267	.82	.345	.172	55.8	.93	.136	.46
Multitechnique (3 or more)	13	6	607	.73	.609	.117	23.3	.81	.385	.01

Note. V_{obs} is the observed effect size variance. V_e is sampling error variance. $\overline{ES}$ is the observed weighted mean according to sample size.
[a] The training methods of Leader Match, sensitivity training and behavioral modeling were not included in separate breakdowns because only two or less studies for each method were found that used objective learning criteria.

Table 8
Results for Training Methods on Subjective Behavior Criteria

Method	No. of ES's	No. of studies	N	$\overline{ES}$	V_{obs}	V_e	% of variance accounted for	$\hat{M}_\delta$	$\hat{V}_\delta$	90% C.V.
Lecture	12	3	1,055	.41	.076	.059	47.4	.46	.065	.13
Lecture/discussion	11	4	5,102	.10	.115	.012	50.9	.11	.012	.03
Leader Match	69	5	3,081	.36	.137	.117	100.0	.40	0	.40
Sensitivity training	49	8	7,153	.67	.712	.035	7.8	.73	.453	−.13
Behavioral modeling	17	5	446	.70	.275	.201	100.0	.78	0	.78
Lecture/discussion plus role play or practice	21	4	1,117	.30	.169	.096	70.0	.34	.042	.07
Multitechnique (3 or more)	76	11	5,169	.45	.419	.078	11.7	.51	.597	−.48

Note. V_{obs} is the observed effect size variance. V_e is sampling error variance. $\overline{ES}$ is the observed weighted mean according to sample size.

pothesis can be rejected because 100% of the observed effect size variance was accounted for by artifactual effects. Therefore, managerial training for change in motivation and values does appear to lead to increased motivation and appropriate value changes as measured by objective learning criteria. However, these results should be interpreted with some caution, considering that only three studies with a total of 12 effects were found in this area. Although the effectiveness of managerial training as measured by learning criteria is important, the effects of training on job performance and behavior is of considerable importance to the individual manager and to the organization.

As with learning criteria, after correcting for the artifactual effects of sampling error and criterion reliability in the distributions with subjective behavior criteria, a substantial amount of observed effect size variance remained unaccounted for in the overall analysis, as well as in the specific content breakdowns. A primary factor influencing this overall result was the 11 studies for general management training that had a lower bound credibility estimate of −.51. If other artifacts had been removed, such as range restriction, the resulting true variance would have been even smaller. It is highly unlikely, however, that accounting for other statistical artifactual sources would have altered this result. As noted above, a more likely explanation is that other substantive variables moderate the effectiveness of different types (i.e., content) of managerial training.

In contrast to the results based on subjective and objective learning criteria, the magnitudes of the true mean effect sizes based on subjective behavior criteria were similar for the training content areas. That is, the range of true mean effect size was .40

to .65. In particular, self-awareness training, which typically uses some form of laboratory education/sensitivity training, was also shown to be fairly effective, on the average, in changing managerial behavior on the job. Although self-awareness training yielded the highest true mean effect size, the criterion measures typically used for evaluating self-awareness training were of questionable utility. In many instances, observers were asked to report changes in on-the-job behavior, or individual self-reports of behavior change were used as an index of training effectiveness. These criterion measures may not necessarily reflect changes in actual job performance. Therefore, it is suggested that in the future, evaluations of self-awareness training use actual job performance criteria.

The results of the overall analysis for objective results criteria indicated that a majority of the observed variation in effect sizes was not explained by statistical artifacts. The results for the content area of human relations training, however, revealed this type of training to be on the average very effective and likely to produce some improvement in managerial performance regardless of the situation. It should be noted that only three studies were involved in this analysis and thus the power of this analysis is suspect.

Similarly, some caution is warranted in the interpretation of the rater training results because only three studies were examined. More research using management personnel as subjects is needed before more definitive conclusions can be drawn regarding the effectiveness of rater training with respect to job performance for these individuals.

In contrast to the results based on learning criteria and subjective behavior, general management training was shown to be

Table 9
Results for Training Methods on Objective Results Criteria

Method[a]	No. of ES's	No. of studies	N	$\overline{ES}$	V_{obs}	V_e	% of variance accounted for	$\hat{M}_\delta$	$\hat{V}_\delta$	90% C.V.
Lecture	15	3	520	.64	.394	.125	21.5	.82	.456	−.04
Multitechnique (3 or more)	13	5	634	.49	.099	.096	100.0	.52	0	.52

Note. V_{obs} is the observed effect size variance. V_e is sampling error variance. $\overline{ES}$ is the observed weighted mean according to sample size.
[a] The training methods of Lecture/Discussion, Leader Match, Sensitivity Training, Behavioral Modeling and Lecture/Discussion plus Role Play or Practice were not included in separate breakdowns since only two or less studies for each method were found that used objective results criteria.

very effective, on the average, in improving performance as measured by objective results. Based on the finding that this training was shown to generalize across settings for objective results criteria, the potential for general management training's having an impact on organization's bottom line in a new setting may be high. More research in this area would be enlightening, especially from the viewpoint of evaluating the influence of general management training on organizational economic gains. Although training content such as general management is an important factor in choosing a training program for a particular application and in providing a means of organizing evaluations of training programs, another important factor is the method of training.

Training Method

The results for the four training method categories with respect to subjective learning criteria indicated that these assisted to a moderate degree in explaining the unaccounted-for observed effect size variance for subjective learning criteria. It is important to note that the methods of behavioral modeling, sensitivity training, lecture with discussion and either role playing or practice, and multiple techniques are highly likely to lead to positive training results in a new situation at least at a minimal level. In particular, the results suggested that behavioral modeling is a sound method for improving learning across situations as measured by subjective learning criteria. Overall, these are encouraging results for the aforementioned training methods in regard to subjective learning criteria.

For studies using objective learning criteria, the results indicated that the training methods of lecture, lecture with discussion, and lecture with discussion and either role playing or practice did assist in accounting for some of the unexplained variance for the overall analysis with objective learning criteria. An important finding was that a majority (56%) of the observed effect size variance for the category of lecture with discussion and either role playing or practice was accounted for by criterion unreliability and sampling error. Furthermore, this latter category had a sizeable lower bound credibility value, indicating that this method of training is very likely to generalize across situations using objective learning criteria.

The results for studies using subjective behavior criteria indicated that unaccounted-for variance in the overall analysis can partially be explained by training method. That is, the lecture, lecture with discussion, lecture with discussion and either role playing or practice, Leader Match, and behavioral modeling methods were helpful in explaining the large amount of unaccounted-for variance in the overall analysis for subjective behavior criteria. Noteworthy were the positive lower bound credibility values obtained for the three distributions of studies using the lecture method. These results indicate that training that employs the lecture method is likely to generalize across situations to some degree. These positive results for the lecture method are encouraging in light of authors (Bass & Vaughn, 1966; Korman, 1977; McGehee & Thayer, 1961) who have questioned the usefulness of this method and training directors who have expressed low opinions of the lecture method (cf. Caroll, Paine, & Ivancevich, 1972).

The results suggest that the effectiveness of the Leader Match training method with respect to subjective behavior criteria generalizes across situations. The results for the Leader Match training method are consistent with the findings of Rice (1978, 1979) and Fiedler and Mahar (1979a, 1979b). On the basis of these results, as well as the cost-effectiveness of Leader Match training compared with that of other leadership training programs, this method of leadership training is encouraged.

The effectiveness of managerial behavioral modeling training with respect to subjective behavior criteria was also shown to generalize across situations. This finding is consistent with the impressive empirical support for social learning theory obtained from well-controlled studies in experimental situations (cf. Bandura, 1977), as well as previous findings in organizational settings (cf. Burnaska, 1976; Byham, Adams, & Kiggins, 1976; Latham & Saari, 1979; Smith, 1976). The magnitude of the estimated true mean effect for behavioral modeling provides an indication of how useful this method of managerial training is likely to be in improving managerial behaviors.

Another interesting finding for studies using subjective behavior criteria was that managerial sensitivity training had a relatively high true mean effect size. This result is by definition consistent with the breakdown of training content for self-awareness training. That is, sensitivity training was always categorized as self-awareness training for training content and likewise for training method. Consequently, when one of these variables (i.e., content or method) was controlled, the other, of necessity, was also controlled. These results, however, do not necessarily point to situational specificity of sensitivity training. As with other breakdowns, other substantive variables (e.g., qualifications of the trainer) may help explain some of the large unaccounted-for variance in observed effect sizes. It is unlikely that substantive variables would assist in explaining most of this large unaccounted-for variation. These results are not encouraging for the generalizability of sensitivity training with respect to subject behavior criteria; future research will be necessary to make such determinations. Furthermore, these findings are in contrast to Smith's (1975) conclusions regarding the effectiveness of sensitivity training. The typical criterion measures used for evaluating sensitivity training were also of questionable utility. In many instances, either observers were asked to report changes in on-the-job behavior, or individual self-reports of behavior changes were used as an index of training effectiveness. These criterion measures may not necessarily reflect changes in actual job performance. For a discussion of some of the potential problems with sensitivity training, the reader is referred to Wexley and Latham (1981).

The results for one of the two distributions analyzed for objective results criteria, the multiple training techniques distribution, tended to generalize across settings. The theoretical and practical soundness of this latter result is questionable because a variety of different techniques were included in each study. In addition, the statistical power of this latter finding is suspect considering that the analogous finding for subjective behavior criteria had twice as many studies and that approximately six times the number of effects and different results were obtained. Overall, too few studies, for all methods of managerial training, used objective results criteria necessary to conduct meaningful analyses and derive sound conclusions with respect to these types of dependent variables.

Limitations

Some limitations of the present meta-analysis should be noted. The number of studies was relatively small. Although an attempt was made to locate all relevant studies, it is likely that some pertinent studies were not included. The relatively small number of studies, however, is more a reflection of the lack of empirical research on managerial training than of the thoroughness of the present literature search. Another limitation is that only two artifactual sources, criteron reliability and sampling error, were taken into account. Other potentially important artifactual sources of variance (e.g., range restriction, typographical errors) could not be controlled or corrected for. By not correcting for other sources of artifactual variance, the variance due to situational specificity was slightly inflated. The degree of inflation was not evaluated. A third limitation is that criterion reliability data was not available in many instances and had to be estimated. The degree to which the estimated reliabilities reflected the actual values was undeterminable. This study also suffered from the inability to conduct some potentially useful follow-up analyses because many studies did not report necessary information.

Conclusions

One conclusion is that researchers need to improve their reports evaluating organizational interventions such as providing information on the degree of range restriction, criterion and predictor reliabilities, sample characteristics, and a thorough description of their methodology. Such information will equip investigators with the necessary data to perform cumulative analyses of the effectiveness of managerial training, as well as that of other organizational interventions.

Another conclusion, based on the results for the training content distributions, is that trainers and organizational decision makers should not rely heavily on training program content descriptions and labels when choosing and judging the probable utility of a managerial training program. More important, the results from the training method analyses point toward the choice of a particular method that might be most effective in improving results related to a certain type of criterion measure. To aid in such decision making, further research aimed at determining the effectiveness of different training methods with respect to different types of dependent variables appears worthwhile. In particular, the breakdowns in Tables 6 through 9 with relatively few studies (i.e., five or less), as well as the breakdowns that could not be reported because of insufficient number of studies (e.g., lecture method on subjective learning criteria), suggest areas where there is a pressing need for sound empirical research.

In addition, the level of experience of the trainer may be a significant factor influencing the effectiveness of training programs. Future research aimed at assessing the influence of the trainer's experience and qualifications on the effectiveness of training would be enlightening.

Moreover, the results of this meta-analysis indicate that different managerial training methods do not necessarily lead to increased knowledge and improved job performance. These findings are consistent with previous reviews of the managerial training literature (Campbell, 1971; Campbell et al., 1970; Goldstein, 1980). The results from this meta-analysis go beyond these reviews by quantitatively evaluating the degree to which the effectiveness of managerial training generalizes across settings for various training content areas, training methods, and outcome measures. Overall, different methods of managerial training are on the average moderately effective in improving learning and job performance. Furthermore, in most instances, positive lower bound credibility values were obtained, and these effects do indicate gains in knowledge and improved performance. Even small effects of less than one half of one standard deviation have been shown through utility analysis to lead to a substantial economic impact on the organization (Hunter & Schmidt, 1983). It is hoped that this study will aid researchers and practitioners in judging the probable utility of different managerial training programs, as well as alert them to the need to empirically evaluate and thoroughly report the effectiveness of organizational interventions.

In conclusion, this meta-analysis can be viewed as an initial step in clarifying what we have learned about managerial training and highlighting areas where future research is needed. The completion of well-designed, thoroughly reported empirical studies in the areas noted above will provide the necessary data for more refined meta-analysis of managerial training and training in general.

References

Alves, E., & Hardy, W. R. (1963). Evaluating supervisory training in Los Angeles County. *Training Directors, 17,* 36–40.

Argyris, C. (1965). Explorations in interpersonal competence—II. *Journal of Applied Behavioral Science, 1,* 255–269.

Arnoff, J., & Litwin, G. H. (1971). Achievement motivation training and executive advancement. *Journal of Applied Behavioral Science, 7,* 215–229.

Bandura, S. (1977). *Social learning theory.* Englewood Cliffs, NJ: Prentice-Hall.

Bass, B. M., & Vaughn, J. A. (1966). *Training in industry: The management of learning.* Belmont, CA: Wadsworth.

Baum, B. H., Sorensen, P. F., Jr., & Place, W. S. (1970). The effect of managerial training on organizational control: An experimental study. *Organizational Behavior and Human Performance, 5,* 170–182.

Boyd, J. B., & Ellis, J. D. (1962). *Findings of research into senior management seminars.* Toronto: Hydro-Electric Power Commission of Ontario.

Buchanan, P. C., & Brunstetter, P. H. (1959). A research approach to management improvement. *Journal of the American Society of Training Directors, 13,* 18–28.

Bunker, D. R. (1965). Individual applications of laboratory training. *Journal of Applied Behavioral Science. 1,* 131–147.

Burnaska, R. F. (1976). The effects of behavior modeling and training upon managers' behaviors and employees' perceptions. *Personnel Psychology, 29,* 329–335.

Byham, W. C., Adams, D., & Kiggins, A. (1976). Transfer of modeling training to the job. *Personnel Psychology, 29,* 345–349.

Campbell, J. P. (1971). Personnel training and development. *Annual Review of Psychology, 22,* 565–602.

Campbell, J. P., Dunnette, M. D., Lawler, E. E., & Weick, K. E., Jr.

244   MICHAEL J. BURKE AND RUSSELL R. DAY

(1970). *Managerial behavior, performance, and effectiveness.* New York: McGraw-Hill.

Canter, R. R., Jr. (1951). A human relations training program. *Journal of Applied Psychology, 35,* 38–45.

Caroll, S. J., Paine, E. T., & Ivancevich, J. J. (1972). The relative effectiveness of training methods—expert opinion and research. *Personnel Psychology, 25,* 495–510.

Carron, T. J. (1964). Human relations training and attitude change: A vector analysis. *Personnel Psychology, 17,* 403–424.

Couch, P. D., & Strother, G. B. (1971). A critical incident evaluation of supervisory training. *Training and Development Journal, 25,* 6–11.

Csoka, L. S., & Bons, P. M. (1978). Manipulating the situation to fit the leader's style: Two validation studies of Leader Match. *Journal of Applied Psychology, 63,* 295–300.

Decker, P. (1982). The enhancement of behavior modeling training of supervisory skills by the inclusion of retention processes. *Personnel Psychology, 35,* 323–331.

DiVesta, F. J. (1954). Instruction-centered and student-centered approaches in teaching a human relations course. *Journal of Applied Psychology, 38,* 329–335.

Durand, D. E. (1975). Effects of achievement motivation and skill training on the entrepreneurial behavior of black businessmen. *Organizational Behavior and Human Performance, 14,* 76–90.

Fiedler, F. E. (1964). A contingency model of leadership effectiveness. In Berkowitz, L. (Ed.), *Advances in experimental psychology* (pp. 149–190). New York: Academic Press.

Fiedler, F. E. (1967). *A theory of leadership effectiveness.* New York: McGraw-Hill.

Fiedler, F. E., Chemers, M. M., & Mahar, L. (1976). *Improving leadership effectiveness: The Leader Match concept.* New York: Wiley.

Fiedler, F. E., & Mahar, L. (1979a). The effectiveness of contingency model training: A review of the validation of Leader Match. *Personnel Psychology, 32,* 45–62.

Fiedler, F. E., & Mahar, L. (1979b). A field experiment validating contingency model leadership training. *Journal of Applied Psychology, 64,* 247–254.

Fiedler, F. E., Mahar, L. & Schmidt, D. (1976). *Four validation studies of contingency model training* (Tech. Rep. No. 75–70). Seattle, WA: Organizational Research, University of Washington.

Fleishman, E. A. (1953). Leadership climate, human relations training, and supervisory behavior. *Personnel Psychology, 6,* 205–222.

Glass, G. V., McGaw, B., & Smith, M. L. (1981). *Meta-analysis in social research.* Beverly Hills, CA: Sage.

Goldstein, A. P., & Sorcher, M. (1974). *Changing supervisor behavior.* New York: Pergamon Press.

Goldstein, I. L. (1980). Training in work organizations. *Annual Review of Psychology, 31,* 229–272.

Goodacre, D. M. (1957). The experimental evaluation of management training principles and practice. *Personnel, 33,* 534–538.

Goodacre, D. M. (1963). Stimulating improved man management. *Personnel Psychology, 16,* 133–143.

Gruenfeld, L. W. (1966). Management development effect on changes in values. *Training and Development Journal, 20,* 18–26.

Hand, H. H., Richard, M. D., & Slocum, J. W., Jr. (1973). Organizational climate and the effectiveness of a human relations training program. *Academy of Management Journal, 16,* 185–195.

Hand, H. H., & Slocum, J. W., Jr. (1970). Human relations training for middle management: A field experiment. *Academy of Management Journal, 13,* 403–410.

Hand, H. H., & Slocum, J. W., Jr. (1972). A longitudinal study of the effects of a human relations training program on managerial effectiveness. *Journal of Applied Psychology, 56,* 412–417.

Harris, E. F., & Fleishman, E. A. (1955). Human relations training and the stability of leadership patterns. *Journal of Applied Psychology, 39,* 20–25.

Harrison, R. (1962). Impact of the laboratory on perceptions of others by the experimental group. In C. Argyris (Ed.), *Interpersonal competence and organizational effectiveness* (pp. 261–271). Homewood, IL: Dorsey-Irwin.

Harrison, R., & Lubin, B. (1965). Personal style, group composition, and learning. *Journal of Applied Behavioral Science, 1,* 286–301.

Hinrichs, J. R. (1976). Personnel training. In M. D. Dunnette, (Ed.), *Handbook of industrial and organizational psychology* (pp. 829–860). Chicago: Rand McNally.

House, R. J., & Tosi, H. (1963). An experimental evaluation of a management training program. *Academy of Management Journal, 6,* 303–315.

Hunter, J. E., & Schmidt, F. L. (1983). Quantifying the effects of psychological interventions on employee job performance and work-force productivity. *American Psychologist, 38,* 473–478.

Hunter, J. E., Schmidt, F. L., & Jackson, G. B. (1982). *Meta-Analysis.* Beverly Hills, CA: Sage.

Ivancevich, J. M. (1979). Longitudinal study of the effects of rater training on psychometric error in ratings. *Journal of Applied Psychology, 64,* 502–508.

Ivancevich, J. M., & Smith, S. V. (1981). Goal setting interview skills training: Simulated and on-the-job analyses. *Journal of Applied Psychology, 66,* 697–705.

Jennings, E. E. (1954). The dynamics of forced leadership training. *Journal of Personnel Administration and Industrial Relations, 1,* 110–118.

Katz, S. I., & Schwebel, A. I. (1976). The transfer of laboratory training. *Small Group Behavior, 7,* 271–285.

Kirkpatrick, D. L. (1976). Evaluation of training. In R. L. Craig (Ed.), *Training and Development Handbook* (2nd ed., Chapter 18). New York: McGraw-Hill.

Kondrasuk, J. N. (1972). *Evaluation of management-by-objectives training.* Unpublished doctoral dissertation, University of Minnesota.

Korman, A. K. (1977). *Organizational behavior.* Englewood Cliffs, NJ: Prentice-Hall.

Latham, G. P., & Kinne, S. B. III. (1974). Improving job performance through training in goal setting. *Journal of Applied Psychology, 59,* 187–191.

Latham, G. P., & Saari, L. M. (1979). The application of social learning theory to training supervisors through behavior modeling. *Journal of Applied Psychology, 64,* 239–246.

Lawshe, C. H., Bolda, R. A., & Brune, R. L. (1959). Studies in management training evaluation: II. The effects of exposures to role playing. *Journal of Applied Psychology, 43,* 287–292.

Leister, A., Borden, D., & Fiedler, F. E. (1977). Validation of contingency model leadership training: Leader Match. *Academy of Management Journal, 20,* 464–470.

Levine, J., & Butler, J. (1952). Lecture versus group decision in changing behavior. *Journal of Applied Psychology, 36,* 29–33.

Lundberg, C., Dunbar, R., & Bayless, T. L. (1973). Contemporary management training in large corporations. *Training and Development Journal, 27,* 34–38.

Mahar, C. A. (1981). Training of managers in program planning and evaluation: Comparison of two approaches. *Journal of Organizational Behavior Management, 3,* 45–56.

Mahoney, T. A., Jerdee, T. H., & Korman, A. (1960). An experimental evaluation of management development. *Personnel Psychology, 13,* 147–163.

Maier, N. R. F. (1953). An experimental test of the effect of training on discussion leadership. *Human Relations, 6,* 161–173.

Mayo, G. D., & DuBois, P. H. (1963). Measurement of gain in leadership training. *Educational and Psychological Measurement, 23,* 23–31.

McGehee, W., & Gardner, J. E. (1955). Supervisory training and attitude change. *Personnel Psychology, 8,* 449–460.

McGehee, W., & Thayer, P. W. (1961). *Training in business and industry.* New York: Wiley.

Miles, M. B. (1960). Human relations training: Processes and outcomes. *Journal of Counseling Psychology, 7,* 301–306.

Miles, M. B. (1965). Changes during and following laboratory training: A clinical-experimental study. *Journal of Applied Behavioral Science, 1,* 215–242.

Miner, J. B. (1960). The effect of a course in psychology on the attitudes of research and development supervisors. *Journal of Applied Psychology, 44,* 224–232.

Miner, J. B. (1965). *Studies in management education.* New York: Springer.

Moffie, D. J., Calhoon, R., & O'Brien, J. K. (1964). Evaluation of a management development program. *Personnel Psychology, 17,* 431–440.

Moon, G. G., & Hariton, T. (1958). Evaluating an appraisal and feedback training program. *Personnel, 35,* 36–41.

Mosel, J. N., & Tsacnaris, H. J. (1954). Evaluating the supervisor training program. *Journal of Personnel Administration and Industrial Relations, 1,* 99–104.

Moses, J. L., & Ritchie, R. J. (1976). Supervisory relationships training: A behavioral evaluation of a behavior modeling program. *Personnel Psychology, 29,* 337–343.

Reith, J. (1976). Group methods: Conferences, meetings, workshops, seminars. In Craig, R. L. (Ed.), *Training and development handbook* (2nd ed., Chapter 34). New York: McGraw-Hill.

Rice, R. W. (1978). Construct validity of the Least Preferred Co-Worker (LPC) score. *Psychological Bulletin, 82,* 597–622.

Rice, R. W. (1979). Reliability and validity of the LPC scale: A reply. *Academy of Management, 4,* 291–294.

Roy, S. K., & Dolke, A. M. (1971). Evaluation of a supervisory training program. *Training and Development Journal, 25,* 35–39.

Rubin, I. (1967). Increased self-acceptance: A means of reducing social prejudice. *Journal of Personality and Social Psychology, 5,* 233–239.

Schmidt, F. L., Hunter, J. E., & Pearlman, K. (1982). Assessing the economic impact of personnel programs on workforce productivity. *Personnel Psychology, 35,* 333–347.

Schutz, W. C., & Allen, V. L. (1966). The effects of a T-group laboratory on interpersonal behavior. *Journal of Applied Behavioral Science, 3,* 265–286.

Schwarz, F. D., Stilwell, W. P., & Scanlan, B. K. (1968). Effects of management development on manager behavior and subordinate perception: Part I. *Training and Development Journal, 22,* 38–50.

Smith, E. E., & Kight, S. S. (1959). Effects of feedback on insight and problem solving efficiency in training groups. *Journal of Applied Psychology, 43,* 209–211.

Smith, P. B. (1963). Attitude changes associated with training in human relations. *British Journal of Social and Clinical Psychology, 2,* 104–112.

Smith, P. B. (1975). Controlled studies of the outcomes of sensitivity training. *Psychological Bulletin, 82,* 597–622.

Smith, P. E. (1976). Management modeling training to improve morale and customer satisfaction. *Personnel Psychology, 29,* 351–359.

Steele, F. I. (1968). Personality and the "laboratory style." *Journal of Applied Behavioral Science, 4,* 25–45.

Stroud, P. V. (1959). Evaluating a human relations training program. *Personnel, 36,* 52–60.

Trice, H. M., & Belasco, J. A. (1968). Supervisory training about alcoholics and other problem employees. *Quarterly Journal of Studies on Alcohol, 29,* 382–398.

Underwood, W. J. (1965). Evaluation of laboratory-method training. *Training Directors Journal, 19,* 34–40.

Valiquet, M. I. (1968). Individual change in a management development program. *Journal of Applied Behavioral Science, 4,* 313–326.

Viteles, M. S. (1959). Human relations and the humanities in the education of business leaders: Evaluation of a program of humanistic studies for executives. *Personnel Psychology, 12,* 1–28.

Warmke, D. L., & Billings, R. S. (1979). Comparison of training methods for improving the psychometric quality of experimental and administrative performance ratings. *Journal of Applied Psychology, 64,* 124–131.

Wexley, K. N. (1984). Personnel training. *Annual Review of Psychology, 35,* 519–551.

Wexley, G. P., & Latham, K. N. (1981). *Developing and training human resources in organizations.* New York: Scott, Foresman and Company.

Wexley, K. N., & Nemeroff, W. F. (1975). Effectiveness of positive reinforcement and goal setting as methods of management development. *Journal of Applied Psychology, 60,* 446–450.

Wikstrom, W. S. (1973). *Supervisory training* (Rep. No. 612). New York Conference Board.

Wilburn, J. M. III. (1979). *An evaluation study: The relationship of cognitive and affective perceptions to participation in a management development program.* Unpublished doctoral dissertation, North Carolina State University.

Wilson, J. E., Mullen, D. P., & Morton, R. B. (1968). Sensitivity training for individual growth-team training for organization development. *Training and Development Journal, 22,* 47–53.

Wolfe, J., & Moe, B. L. (1973). An experimental evaluation of a hospital supervisory training program. *Hospital Administration, 18,* 65–77.

Received November 26, 1984
Revision received June 10, 1985 ∎

Part V
What Conditions Support Training?

[13]

PERSONNEL PSYCHOLOGY
1988, 41

TRANSFER OF TRAINING: A REVIEW AND DIRECTIONS FOR FUTURE RESEARCH

TIMOTHY T. BALDWIN
Indiana University

J. KEVIN FORD
Michigan State University

Transfer of training is of paramount concern for training researchers and practitioners. Despite research efforts, there is a growing concern over the "transfer problem." The purpose of this paper is to provide a critique of the existing transfer research and to suggest directions for future research investigations. The conditions of transfer include both the generalization of learned material to the job and the maintenance of trained skills over a period of time on the job. The existing research examining the effects of training design, trainee, and work-environment factors on conditions of transfer is reviewed and critiqued. Research gaps identified from the review include the need to (1) test various operationalizations of training design and work-environment factors that have been posited as having an impact on transfer and (2) develop a framework for conducting research on the effects of trainee characteristics on transfer. Needed advancements in the conceptualization and operationalization of the criterion of transfer are also discussed.

Positive transfer of training is defined as the degree to which trainees effectively apply the knowledge, skills, and attitudes gained in a training context to the job (Newstrom, 1984; Wexley & Latham, 1981). Transfer of training, therefore, is more than a function of original learning in a training program (Atkinson, 1972; Fleishman, 1953). For transfer to have occurred, learned behavior must be generalized to the job context and maintained over a period of time on the job.

There is growing recognition of a "transfer problem" in organizational training today (Michalak, 1981). It is estimated that while American industries annually spend up to $100 billion on training and development, not more than 10% of these expenditures actually result in transfer to the job (Georgenson, 1982). While researchers have similarly concluded that much of the training conducted in organizations fails to transfer to the work

---

A previous draft of this manuscript was presented at the 47th annual meeting of the National Academy of Management, New Orleans, August, 1987.

Authors contributed equally and are listed alphabetically.

The authors wish to thank Ray Noe and two anonymous reviewers for their helpful comments.

Correspondence and requests for reprints should be addressed to Timothy T. Baldwin, 939 Woodbridge Drive, Bloomington, IN 47401.

setting (e.g., I. Goldstein, 1986; Mosel, 1957; Wexley & Latham, 1981), a comprehensive review and critique of the empirical research on transfer has not appeared.

Several researchers have stated that the existing literature on transfer offers little of value to trainers concerned with maximizing positive transfer (Gagne, 1962; Wexley, 1984). On the other hand, Hinrichs (1976) has suggested that trainers often fail to apply the scientific knowledge that does exist. Rather than argue for one viewpoint or the other, it is our belief that it is more beneficial to investigate systematically what we do know about transfer of training and to consider how we can proceed to learn more. Rather than continue to bemoan what is a widely recognized concern, we must begin to specify the type of investigations needed to generate the knowledge base for improving our understanding of transfer issues.

The purpose of this paper is to provide a critique of the existing transfer research and to suggest directions for future research investigations. First, we will provide an organizing framework outlining the factors we believe affect transfer of training. Second, we will review the existing research on factors affecting transfer. Third, we will present a critique of the research and highlight critical research gaps. Finally, we will specify the types of research needed to improve our understanding of the transfer process.

A Framework for Examining Training Transfer

Examination of transfer issues requires a clear understanding of what is meant by transfer as well as the identification of factors that affect transfer. Figure 1 presents a framework for understanding the transfer process. In Figure 1, the transfer process is described in terms of training-input factors, training outcomes, and conditions of transfer. The conditions of transfer include both the (1) generalization of material learned in training to the job context and (2) maintenance of the learned material over a period of time on the job. Training outcomes are defined as the amount of original learning that occurs during the training program and the retention of that material after the program is completed. Training-input factors include training design, trainee characteristics, and work-environment characteristics. The major training-design factors are the incorporation of learning principles (Bass & Vaughan, 1966), the sequencing of training material (Gagne, 1962; Tracy, 1984), and the job relevance of the training content (Campbell, 1971; Ford & Wroten, 1984). Trainee characteristics consist of ability or skill, motivation, and personality factors. Work-environment characteristics include climatic factors such as supervisory or peer support as well as constraints and opportunities to perform learned behaviors on the job.

BALDWIN AND FORD 65

Training Inputs   **Training Outputs**   **Conditions of Transfer**

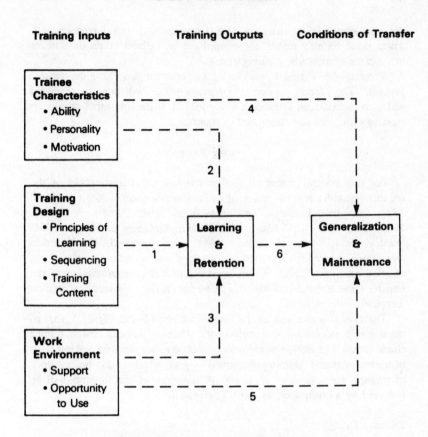

Figure 1: **A Model of the Transfer Process**

As the model indicates, training outcomes and training-input factors are posited to have both direct and indirect effects on conditions of transfer. These effects are specified in terms of six linkages, which are critical for understanding the transfer process. Working backwards in the model, training outcomes of learning and retention are seen as having direct effects on conditions of transfer (Linkage 6). That is, for trained skills to transfer, training material must be learned and retained (Kirkpatrick, 1967). Trainee characteristics and work-environment characteristics are also hypothesized to have direct effects on transfer regardless of initial learning during the training program or retention of the training material (Linkages 4 and 5, respectively). For example, well-learned skills may not be maintained on the job due to lack of motivation or lack of supervisory support. Finally, training outcomes (learning and retention) are viewed as directly affected by the three training inputs of training design, trainee characteristics, and the work-environment characteristics (Linkages 1, 2, and 3 respectively). These three training inputs, therefore, have an indirect effect on transfer through their impact on training outcomes.

The model in Figure 1 provides a framework for describing the transfer process. The literature examining transfer issues will now be reviewed and then be critiqued in relation to the impact of training-input factors on training outcomes and conditions of transfer.

Literature Review

For this review, empirical studies cited in the major works of the organizational-training literature (e.g., Bass & Vaughan, 1966; Campbell, 1971; Campbell, Dunnette, Lawler & Weick, 1970; Decker & Nathan, 1985; Ellis, 1965; I. Goldstein, 1980, 1986; McGehee & Thayer, 1961; Wexley, 1984; Wexley & Latham, 1981) were examined. Other studies were identified through an extensive literature search and cross-referencing of cited studies. Therefore, this review provides an examination of the transfer-issue research that has been referenced in the organizational-training literature.

The review was based on the framework provided in Figure 1; that is, the research was reviewed in terms of the effects of training design, trainee characteristics, or work-environment factors on either learning and retention of trained material (training outcomes) or generalization and maintenance of training (conditions of transfer). A summary of the findings will be followed by a critique of the existing research.

Training Design

A large proportion of the empirical research on transfer has concentrated on improving the design of training programs through the incorporation of learning principles. Research has centered on four basic principles: (1) identical elements, (2) teaching of general principles, (3) stimulus variability, and (4) various conditions of practice.

Identical elements. The notion of identical elements was originally proposed by Thorndike and Woodworth (1901). They hypothesized that transfer is maximized to the degree that there are identical stimulus and response elements in the training and transfer settings. Empirical research supports the use of identical elements as a means of increasing the retention of both motor (Crafts, 1935; Gagne, Baker, & Foster, 1950) and verbal behaviors (Duncan & Underwood, 1953; Underwood, 1951).

General principles. Teaching through general principles maintains that transfer is facilitated when trainees are taught, not just applicable skills, but also the general rules and theoretical principles that underlie the training content (McGehee & Thayer, 1961). For example, Judd (1908) and Hendrickson and Schroeder (1941) demonstrated the usefulness of teaching through general principles by using rules of light infraction to improve proficiency in underwater shooting. Crannell (1956), in a series of three studies, showed the value of teaching general principles for problem solving by improving subjects' ability to learn card-sorting tricks. Goldbeck, Bernstein, Hillix, and Marx (1957) found that individuals instructed in the principles of analyzing problems were better able to locate problems with malfunctioning electronic equipment.

Stimulus variability. Stimulus variability is the notion that positive transfer is maximized when a variety of relevant training stimuli are employed (Ellis, 1965). Proponents state that several examples of a concept to be learned strengthen the trainee's understanding so that he/she is more likely to see the applicability of a concept in a new situation (Duncan, 1958; Ellis, 1965). The principle of stimulus variability has received empirical support with respect to training outcomes. For example, Shore and Sechrest (1961) found that using a moderate number of different examples that were repeated a few times each was more effective in enhancing learning than using one example repeatedly.

Conditions of practice. Conditions of practice include a number of specific design issues, including massed or distributed training, whole or part training, feedback, and overlearning. Massed versus distributed training is the issue of whether or not to divide training into segments. Research evidence suggests that material learned under distributed practice is generally retained longer than material learned by massed practice (Briggs & Naylor, 1962; Naylor & Briggs, 1963). There is also evidence that difficult and complex tasks result in higher performance when massed practice sessions are given first, followed by briefer sessions with more frequent rest intervals (Holding, 1965).

Whole versus part training concerns the relative efficiency of practice with all the material as opposed to practice on one part at a time. Evidence suggests that the whole method is advantageous for enhancing training outcomes when (1) the intelligence of the learner is high, (2) practice is distributed rather than massed, and (3) the training material is high in task organization but low in task complexity (Naylor & Briggs, 1963).

Feedback, or knowledge of results, refers to information provided to trainees about their performance. Evidence shows that feedback is a critical element in achieving learning and that timing and specificity are critical variables in determining its effects (e.g., Wexley & Thornton, 1972). Some authors have suggested that the optimal specificity of feedback may be dependent on the trainee and the stage of learning (Blum & Naylor, 1968), although empirical evidence is lacking.

Overlearning refers to the process of providing trainees with continued practice far beyond the point when the task has been performed successfully (McGehee & Thayer, 1961). Research indicates that the greater the amount of overlearning, the greater the subsequent retention of the trained material (Atwater, 1953; Gagne & Foster, 1949; Mandler, 1954). More recently, Hagman and Rose (1983) reported the results of several studies sponsored by the Army Research Institute that provide empirical support for the value of overlearning on retention in military training contexts.

While researchers have also stressed the importance of design issues such as sequencing and the relevance of training content, (e.g., Gagne, 1962), empirical research is lacking. One exception is the work of Decker (1980, 1982), who has explored the effects of different types of learning points on the reproduction and generalization of skills taught in behavior-modeling programs.

Trainee Characteristics

A wide variety of trainee characteristics thought to affect transfer have been suggested in the practitioner literature (e.g., Robinson, 1984; Trost, 1982); however, empirical investigations of ability, personality, and motivational effects on training and transfer outcomes are quite limited.

Existing research evidence shows that trainee success in early stages of training or on training samples predicts transfer on some training tasks (Downs, 1970; L. Gordon, 1955; M. Gordon & Cohen, 1973; McGehee, 1948). And investigations of a variety of ability and aptitude tests also show moderate success for such measures as predictors of trainability (e.g., M. Gordon & Kleiman, 1976; Neel & Dunn, 1960; Robertson & Downs, 1979; Ryman & Biersner, 1975; M. Smith & Downs, 1975; C. Taylor, 1952; E. Taylor & Tajen, 1948; Tubiana & Ben-Shakhar, 1982). But Ghiselli's (1966) review of the literature in the area characterized the typical predictive power of aptitude tests for the prediction of trainability as "far from impressive" (p. 125).

With respect to personality variables, Noe and Schmitt (1986) found limited support for the effects of locus of control on pretraining motivation and learning. Baumgartel, Reynolds, and Pathan (1984) found that managers high in need for achievement and having an internal locus of control were more likely to apply new knowledge gained in training to work settings. On the other hand, Miles (1965), in a study of a sensitivity program, concluded that personality factors had no direct effect on transfer.

Several studies have investigated the effects of motivational factors on transfer. Ryman and Biersner (1975) found a significant relation between trainee confidence in the successful completion of a Navy diving training program and subsequent class success and dropout rate. Tubiana and Ben-Shakhar (1982) found a significant relation between motivation to succeed in training and a composite criterion of training performance, a probability assessment of promotion potential, and a sociometric measure of the trainee's popularity with peers. Results from a study by Hicks and Klimoski (1987) show that a trainee's perception that he/she had a choice to attend (or not attend) a managerial-skills training program influenced motivation to learn and subsequent learning in the program. Noe and Schmitt (1986) found that trainees with high job involvement were more motivated to learn and transfer skills to the work setting. Baumgartel et al. (1984) showed that managers who believed in the value of training were more likely to apply skills learned in training. Finally, Eden and colleagues (Eden & Ravid, 1982; Eden & Shani, 1982) found that higher self-expectancies led to higher training performance in two studies of military personnel.

Post-training interventions such as goal setting and feedback have been used to increase the motivation of the trainee to transfer skills learned in training. For example, Wexley and Nemeroff (1975) found that trainees assigned goals after a management development program were significantly better at applying their learning than were members of a control group. Reber and Wallin (1984) showed that both feedback and goal setting produced higher levels of skill transfer to the work setting than did either approach separately.

Work-environment Characteristics

While the practitioner literature on training (e.g., Eddy, Glad, & Wilkins, 1967) stresses that positive transfer is highly contingent on factors in the trainee's work environment, empirical evidence is sparse. Baumgartel and his associates (Baumgartel & Jeanpierre, 1972; Baumgartel et al., 1984; Baumgartel, Sullivan, & Dunn, 1978) have conducted a line of research indicating that managers in favorable organizational climates (with freedom to set goals and a supportive environment) are more likely to apply new knowledge to work settings. And Hand, Richards, and Slocum (1973) concluded that positive changes in human-relations skills 18 months after training were due to organizational decisions such as salary and promotions that reinforced the attitudes learned in training. Huczynski and Lewis (1980) found that a management style that included pre-course discussion with one's boss and subsequent boss sponsorship contributed most to the transfer of skills.

Critique of the Existing Literature

Tables 1, 2, and 3 present outlines of the research on the effects of training design, trainee characteristics, and work-environment characteristics, respectively. The next section provides a critique of the research to identify what is known about transfer and to aid in the specification of the type of research needed to improve our understanding of the transfer process.

Training-input Factors

Table 1 presents the studies referenced by training researchers (e.g., I. Goldstein, 1986; Wexley & Latham, 1981) as the empirical basis for what is known with respect to training design and learning principles. An examination of the table reveals that the research on learning principles was typically completed before 1970. The sample used for most of the studies was composed of college students completing relatively straight-forward memory and psychomotor-skills tasks. For example, to examine the impact of identical elements, Underwood (1951) used a sample of 54 college students, whose task was to pair adjectives. In a more recent study, Schendel and Hagman (1982) had 38 soldiers disassemble machine guns under various conditions of overlearning.

The criterion measure of interest for all the studies was oriented toward training outcome. Typically, measures of retention were taken immediately after completion of the training task. Mandler and Heinemann (1956), for example, used the number of correct trials immediately after training to examine the effects of overlearning on retention. The research indicates that learning principles have an effect on learning and immediate retention of training material. Nevertheless, attempts to examine retention over time or the effects of retention on the generalization and maintenance of skills have been rare.

To summarize, Table 1 shows that studies examining training-design factors have used college students working on simple memory and motor tasks, with immediate learning or retention as the criterion of interest (Linkage 1 of the transfer model in Figure 1). From an examination of these study characteristics, two basic limitations of the existing research become evident.

First, the tasks used limit generalizability of the results to short-term, simple motor tasks and memory-skills training. The use of such tasks is problematic, given that organizational training is often conducted to enhance individual competence on long-term, complex skills such as interpersonal communication and managerial problem solving. The effect of

TABLE 1

Empirical Studies of Transfer of Training—Training Input Factors: Design of Training

Author(s)	Sample	Task or training content	Variables	Design[a]	Criteria
Adams (1955)	127 Military trainees	Distinguishing spatial arrangements of a stimulus pair	Stimulus variability	E	Immediate[b] proficiency on an arrangement task
Atwater (1953)	32 College students	Pairing words	Conditions of practice (overlearning)	E	Immediate proficiency in pairing words correctly
Baldwin (1987)	72 College students	Behavior modeling of assertive skills	Stimulus variability	E	Immediate measure of learning; immediate reproduction of skills; generalization of skills to a novel context four weeks later; unobtrusive measure of skill use four weeks later
Briggs & Naylor (1962)	144 College Students	Maintaining control of a compensatory tracking system	Conditions of practice (whole vs. part)	E	Immediate measure of tracking proficiency
Briggs & Waters (1958)	160 ROTC college students	Pilot training; simulator tracking task	Conditions of practice (whole vs. part)	E	Immediate measure of total number of errors in sorting cards to illustrate understanding
Callentine & Warren (1955)	120 College students	Concept attainment with geometric figures	Stimulus variability	E	Immediate measure of total number of errors in sorting cards to illustrate understanding
Cominsky (1982)	34 Graduate students	Teaching reflection of feeling	General principles and stimulus variability	Q-E	Taped role plays, immediately after program completion
Crafts (1935)	64 College students	Card sorting	Identical elements	E	Immediate ability on test card sorting task
Crannel (1956) reports results of three experiments	248 College students	Card trick problems	General principles	E	Immediate measure of number of problems completed in one hour (Experiments 1 & 2); 6-week measure of whether two problems could be completed in 10 minutes (Experiment 3)

[a]E=Experimental; Q–E = Quasi-experimental.
[b]In this context, the term immediate denotes a period directly after the training took place; that is, no significant time elapsed between training and measurement of trained skills

TABLE 1 (continued)

Author(s)	Sample	Task or training content	Variables	Design[a]	Criteria
Decker (1980)	90 College students	Behavioral modeling of assertive skills	Type of learning points	E	Immediate reproduction of skills; immediate generalization of skills
Decker (1982)	24 First-line supervisors	Coaching and handling employee complaints	Type of learning points	Q-E	Immediate reproduction of skills; immediate generalization of skills
Digman (1959)	41 College students	Hitting a target button with rotor	Conditions of practice (massed vs. spaced)	E	Immediate task proficiency
Duncan (1958)	600 College students	Movement of a lever into one of 13 slots	Stimulus variability	E	Two proficiency tests given: (1) 24 hours after training, (2) 48 hours after training
Duncan & Underwood (1953)	186 College students	Moving a lever into slots in response to color-light stimuli	Identical elements	E	Retention of learning 24 hours and 14 months after acquisition
Forgus & Schwartz (1957)	39 Female college students	Learning a new alphabet	General principles	E	Immediate recall, simple transposition, and a measure of problem solving proficiency
Fryer & Edgerton (1950)	334 Military trainees	Gunnery training	Conditions of practice (massed vs. spaced) (instruction methods)	E	Immediate test of learning and retention of learning after 2 months
Gagne & Foster (1949)	145 Enlisted navy men	Reaction to light by pressing control panel switch	Conditions of practice (overlearning)	E	Immediate measures of (1) amount of time to complete trials, (2) no. of errors
Goldbeck, Bernstein, Hillix, & Marx (1957)	40 Male college students	Troubleshooting problems with electronic equipment	General principles	E	Immediate test of troubleshooting proficiency

Study	Sample	Variety of military tasks	Conditions of practice	Q-E/E	Criterion
Hagman & Rose (1983) results of 13 experiments	Military personnel	Variety of military tasks			Both immediate proficiency and retention over time
Haselrud & Meyers (1958)	76 College students	Deciphering word codes (taught coding rules)	General principles	E	Immediate number of correct codings
Hendrickson & Schroeder (1941)	90 Eighth grade boys	Shooting an air gun at submerged underwater targets (taught principle of light infraction)	General principles	E	Immediate measure of accuracy on hitting underwater targets
Hilgard, Irvine, & Whipple (1953)	60 High-school students	Card trick problems	General principles	E	(1) Overnight measure of retention; (2) proficiency on simple transposition task; (3) proficiency on three problem-solving tasks
Hilgard, Edren, & Irvine (1954)	150 High-school students	Card trick problems	General principles	E	Overnight retention, number and type of errors made
Judd (1908)	Unspecified number of fifth and sixth grade boys	Shooting darts at submerged underwater targets (taught principle of light infraction)	General principles	E	Immediate accuracy on hitting underwater target with depth charge
Macpherson, Dees, & Grindley (1948)	200 College students	Line drawing, pushing a lever, pressing a Morse key	Feedback	E	Immediate task proficiency
Mandler (1954)	60 College students	Operating hand switches in sequences on a switchboard having six switches arranged in a hexagon; stimuli were letters of the alphabet	Conditions of practice (overlearning)	E	Immediate errorless trials
Mandler & Heinemann (1956)	60 College students	Assembly of verbal units from nonsense syllables	Conditions of practice (overlearning)	E	Immediate number of correct trials

TABLE 1 (continued)

Author(s)	Sample	Task or training content	Variables	Design[a]	Criteria
Morrisett & Hovland (1959)	63 High-school students	Discriminating pairs of geometric figures	Stimulus variability	E	Immediate ability to discriminate between pairs
Naylor & Briggs (1963)	112 Female college students	Markov prediction task	Conditions of practice (whole vs. part)	E	Immediate number of correct predictions
Reynolds & Bilodeau (1952)	612 Basic trainee airmen	(1) Rudder control, (2) complex coordination, (3) rotary pursuit	Conditions of practice (massed vs. spaced)	E	Immediate proficiency and retention after 10 weeks
Schendel & Hagman (1982)	38 Reserve soldiers	Disassembly/assembly of M60 machine gun	Conditions of practice (overlearning)	E	8-week Retention interval
Shore & Sechrest (1961)	64 College students	Concept attainment	Stimulus variability	E	Immediate number of correct tests of concept attainment
Thorndike (1927)	24 People varying in age from 20 to 42+	Estimating length of paper strips blindfolded	Feedback	E	Immediate accuracy of length estimates
Thorndike & Woodworth (1901)	5 College students	Observing words for certain characteristics	Identical elements	E	Immediate speed and accuracy in word recognition
Trowbridge & Cason (1932)	60 College students	Drawing lines blindfolded	Feedback	E	Immediate proficiency of line drawing
Underwood (1951)	54 College students	Pairing adjectives	Identical elements	E	Immediate number of correct responses
Wexley & Thornton (1972)	261 College students	Introductory psychology course	Feedback	E	Course exams
Woodrow (1927)	76 College students	Memorization tasks (taught memory rules)	General Principles	E	Immediate memory scores

these learning principles on training outcomes for more complex and interrelated tasks is unknown. While it is relatively straightforward to operationalize principles such as overlearning in controlled experimental settings with motor or memory tasks, the appropriate operationalization of learning principles in more complex organizational-training programs is problematic. For example, there is no empirical data regarding how much and in what ways a trainer should incorporate learning principles such as stimulus variability into a behavior-modeling program to enhance the transfer of managerial skills. In addition, W. Schneider (1985) suggests that several training-design maxims (e.g., practice makes perfect) are fallacious when training for "high performance" skills.

Second, the criterion measures of interest in these studies have been learning and short-term retention. While these measures are certainly appropriate, given the goals of the original research, any claims by training researchers regarding the implications of these "robust" findings for enhancing transfer of training must be made with caution. Training outcomes of learning and retention constitute necessary but not sufficient conditions for generalization and maintenance of skills. Therefore, we need research that explicitly examines the direct effects of training-design factors on training outcomes (Linkage 1) and then examines the effects of training outcomes on conditions of transfer (Linkage 6).

Trainee Characteristics

Table 2 presents the studies that have examined the relation of trainee characteristics to transfer of training. There are fewer such studies, but they are more recent than those focusing on training-design characteristics. Examination of the table reveals a variety of different samples, training tasks, and designs used. The sample includes managers, college students, and line personnel. The training tasks range from general interpersonal skills such as human-relations training to specific skills programs such as time management.

The criterion measure typically used in these studies was retention of the learned material (Linkage 2). Retention was commonly measured through written tests, which asked trainees to recall trained material immediately or shortly after completion of the training program (see, for example, Wexley & Baldwin, 1986). In some studies, information on generalization and maintenance of trained skills to the job (Linkage 5) was also gathered. The major source of information about behavioral change was the trainee him/herself, with such information being gathered soon after completion of the training program. For example, upon completion of a network-analysis training program, Huczynski and Lewis (1980) asked trainees about their intentions to transfer skills learned. Four months later they asked them for

TABLE 2

Empirical Studies of Transfer of Training—Training Input Factors: Trainee Characteristics

Author(s)	Sample	Training content	Variables	Source & (timing)	Criteria — Measures & Results
Baumgartel & Jean-pierre (1972)	240 Indian managers	Management development program	Demographic (educ., age, job-income level); motivation (value & relevance of training); personality (composite scale)	Self (immediate)[a]	*Effort to apply*—41% of respondents indicated some intended effort to apply. Significantly related to job income but no other significant relationship with trainee characteristics.
				Self (unknown)	*Perceived success in transferring*—Of those indicating effort to apply, 47% indicated high success, 38% medium, and 15% low or no success. No *r*'s with trainee characteristics reported.
				Supervisor (unknown)	*Attempt to Use*—21% of bosses indicated some subordinate attempt to use. No *r*'s with trainee characteristics reported.
Baumgartel, Reynolds, & Pathan (1984) Study 1	260 American managers	Human relations	Demographic (rank-job level); Motivation (value of training); personality (locus of control)	Self (immediate)	*Effort to apply*—Significantly related to locus of control. Relation with other trainee characteristics measured was n.s.[b]
				Self (unknown)	*Perceived success in transferring*—Significantly related to belief in the value of training. Relation with other trainee charasteristics measured was n.s.
Baumgartel, Reynolds, & Pathan (1984) Study 2	246 Indian managers	Management development program	Personality (locus of control, need to achieve)	Self (immediate)	*Effort to apply*—Significantly related to locus of control and need achievement. Others were n.s.

Study	Sample	Training	Trainee characteristics	Criterion measure (timing)[a]	Results
Downs (1970)	82 Sewing machinists	Sewing machine training	Ability (training sample)	Instructor (immediate)	*Final instructor rating*—Significantly related ($r = .50$) to score on training sample.
Eden & Ravid (1982)	60 Military personnel	Clerical skills	Motivation (self & instructor expectancy)	Instructor (immediate)	*Learning exams*—Significant main effect for self-expectancy. High expectancy conditions had greater exam score average than controls. 27–30% of variance explained by self-expectancy.
Eden & Shani (1982)	105 Military personnel	Military combat command course	Motivation (instructor expectancy)	Instructor (immediate)	*Learning exams*—Significant main effect for instructor expectancy. High expectancy conditions had greater exam score average than controls. Instructor expectancy explained 73% of variance in learning exam performance.
Fleishman (1953)	122 Manufacturing foremen	Leadership training	Demographic (age, educ., tenure, number of subordinates)	Self (before training & varied from 2–24 after training)	*Leader behaviors (LBDQ)*—All relationships with trainee characteristics were n.s.[b]
Gordon (1955)	400 Military recruits	Radio code training	Ability (early training time required)	Instructor (immediate)	*Radio code test score*—Significantly related to early training time required for three separate groups varying in previous radio code exposure.
Gordon & Cohen (1973)	58 Welding program trainees	Plate welding	Ability (early training performance)	Instructor (immediate)	*Time required to complete training*—Significantly related to early training performance on each of the first four tasks in training.
Gordon & Kleiman (1976)	101 Police trainees	Fundamentals of police work	Ability (training sample, IQ)	Instructor (immediate)	*Sum of graded exercises*—Significantly related to both work sample tests and IQ tests but the work sample tests yielded significantly higher r's in most cases.

[a] Immediate denotes that no significant time elapsed between training and measurement of trained skills.
[b] n.s. denotes statistically nonsignificant.

TABLE 2 (continued)

Author(s)	Sample	Training content	Variables	Source & (timing)	Criteria — Measures & Results
Hicks & Klimoski (1987)	85 Managers	Two-day performance review training	Motivation (degree of choice to select training, realistic preview)	Self (immediate)	*Appropriateness of training*—Main effects for degree of choice and type of prior info.
				Self (immediate)	*Profit from training*—Main effects for degree of choice and type of prior info.
				Self (immediate)	*Satisfaction w/ training*—Main effects for degree of choice.
				Self (immediate)	*Learning*—Main effects for degree of choice.
				Instructor (immediate)	*Achievement test*—Main effects for degree of choice.
				Trained observers (immediate)	*Role play*—No significant effects.
Huczynski & Lewis (1980)	48 Electronic managers	Three-day network analysis training program	Motivation (attend on own, value of training, prior course discussion)	Self (4 months after training	*Attempt to transfer*—35% of respondents made some attempt to transfer. Those who attempted transfer were more likely to have (1) attended the course on their own initiative, (2) believed the course would be beneficial, and (3) had prior discussions of the course.
Komacki, Heinzemann, & Lawson (1980)	55 Vehicle maintenance personnel	One-hour safety training	Motivation (reinforcing feedback)	Trained observers (weekly up to 40 weeks)	*Safety behaviors exhibited*—Significant increases in safety performance occurred when training was combined with feedback (15% over training only and 26% over baseline).

Study	Sample	Training	Trainee characteristics	Criterion (source/timing)	Results
McGehee (1948)	21 Rug-mill trainees	Preparation of rug-spools	Ability (initial effectiveness in OJT training)	Instructor (immediate)	*Time required to attain acceptable average production*—Significantly related to time required to complete early training periods. Most significant increase in prediction was from 1st to 2nd period.
Miles (1965)	34 Elementary school principals	Two-week human relations	Demographic (tenure, no. of subs); personality (ego strength, flexibility, need affiliation)	Self (immediate)	*Perceived change from training*—Significantly related to feedback received. Relation with all other personality and motivation variables was n.s.
			motivation (desire for change, feedback received, involvement, unfreezing)	Peer (immediate)	*Perceived change from training*—Significantly related to unfreezing, involvement, and feedback received. Relation with desire for change and other variables was n.s.
				Self (8 months after training)	*On-the-job change*—Significantly related to unfreezing. Relation with other variables was n.s.
Neel & Dunn (1960)	32 Supervisory trainees	10-week supervisory skills training	Ability (IQ-Wonderlic); personality ("How Supervise", authoritarianism)	Instructor (immediate)	*Course examinations*—Significantly related to Wonderlic (r = 25), "How Supervise" scale (r = .69), and authoritarianism (r = .39).
Noe & Schmitt (1986)	60 School educators	Managerial skills	Motivation (expectancies, motive to learn, exploratory behavior, job involvement); personality (locus of control)	Trained Raters (immediate)	*Learning (in-basket exercises)*—Relation with all trainee characteristics n.s. Rresidual value for job involvement = (.41).
				Self (varied 1-3-4 mos. after training)	*Motivation to transfer*—Relation with all trainee characteristics n.s.
				Supervisor (3 mos. after training)	*Behavior*—Relation with all trainee characteristics n.s.

TABLE 2 (continued)

Author(s)	Sample	Training content	Variables	Source & (timing)	Criteria Measures & Results
Reber & Wallin (1984)	105 Farm machinery workers	Safety procedures	Motivation (reinforcing feedback and goals)	Peers (3 mos. after training)	*Behavior (peer)* Relation with all trainee characteristics n.s.
				Trained observers (weekly up to 40 weeks)	*Safety behaviors exhibited*—Main effects for each of three interventions: (1) safety rule training alone, (2) goal setting, (3) feedback and goal setting. Percentage of safety behaviors exhibited varied such that (control) 62.80%, (1) 70.85%, (2) 77.54%, (3) 95.39%.
Ryman & Biersner (1975)	548 Military personnel	Technical (diving & underwater) skills	Motivation (course expectations, confidence, leadership efficacy, concern); personality (conformity)	File data (immediate)	*Program graduation*—Across 3 programs, successful graduation had a significant positive relationship with training motivation, leadership, and conformity and was negatively related to training concerns.
Smith & Downs (1975)	236 Ship-building apprentices	Variety of ship-building skills	Ability (trainability assessment)	Instructor (3–12 months after trainability assessment)	*Performance test*—Trainability assessments were successful in predicting performance after a 3-month period in the skill for which they were designed. They were less successful after a 12-month period and no single assessment predicted performance for all skills.
Taylor (1952)	120 Automotive mechanic trainees	Mechanic skills	Ability (aptitude test battery)	Instructor (immediate)	*Performance test*—Aptitude test battery was effective in identifying trainees who had the necessary knowledge and skills to skip the first four weeks to training and still do approximately as well as those who took the whole course.
Taylor & Tajen (1948)	313 Clerical trainees	Clerical, record-keeping skills	Ability (numeric score on test battery)	Instructor (immediate)	*Performance test*—Individuals' performance test scores on IBM punch card equipment were predicted with a one-hour pretraining test battery such that 70% of the selected trainees did better than the average unselected trainee.

Study	Sample	Training	Variables	Measurement	Results
Tubiana & Shakhar (1982)	459 Israeli military	Basic military training	Demographic (education); ability (language test, 2 IQ tests); motivation (motive to serve in combat; personality (activeness, sociability, responsibility, independence, & promptness)	Superior officer (immediate)	*Performance potential*—Officer rating of potential had a significant positive relationship to education ($r = .21$), language test scores ($r = .24$), intelligence ($r = .32$) and composite of personality & motivation ($r = .33$).
Wexley & Baldwin (1986)	256 College students	Time management	Motivation (goal setting, relapse prevention)	Instructor (immediate); Self (8 weeks after training); Observer (8 weeks after training); *Behavior*—No significant effects observed.	*Learning*—Main effect for assigned goal setting. *Behavior*—Main effects for assigned & participative goal setting.
Wexley & Nemeroff (1975)	27 Health care managers	Two-day supervisory skills program	Motivation (goal setting)	Self (60 days after training); Subordinate (60 days after training)	*Behavior*—Goal setting treatments were significantly more effective than a control group in improving the leader behavior of managers. *Behavior*—Assigned goal-setting group was most effective in increasing subordinate work satisfaction.

their perceptions of their success in transferring skills from the training program. Few studies used behavioral ratings (Noe & Schmitt, 1986) or observed and recorded actual behaviors (e.g., Komacki, Heinzemann, & Lawson, 1980; Reber & Wallin, 1984) to evaluate the extent of transfer.

The research on trainee characteristics has two critical problems, which reduce its usefulness for understanding the factors affecting the transfer process. The first problem is the lack of theoretical frameworks to guide research. A number of individual-difference factors have been examined, including job involvement (Noe & Schmitt, 1986), need for achievement (Baumgartel & Jeanpierre, 1972; Baumgartel et al., 1984), belief in the value of training (Baumgartel et al. 1984; Ryman & Biersner, 1975), and intelligence level (Tubiana & Ben-Shakhar, 1982). Some motivational strategies have also been examined for their impact on transfer; they include goal setting (Reber & Wallin, 1984; Wexley & Baldwin, 1986; Wexley & Nemeroff, 1975), feedback (Komaki et al., 1980; Reber & Wallin, 1984), choice in attending training (Hicks & Klimoski, 1987; Huczynski & Lewis, 1980), realistic information about the training program (Hicks & Klimoski, 1987), and relapse prevention (Wexley & Baldwin, 1986). Despite these efforts, the lack of a systematic approach to this area has resulted in minimal improvements in our understanding of the transfer process. Systematic research is needed in which models would be developed, tested, and revised on the basis of empirical research. Noe (1986) has provided an initial attempt to identify key personality and motivational factors that affect transfer and to hypothesize expected linkages and relationships among these factors and transfer. More efforts at model development are needed.

A second critical issue is the lack of adequate criterion measures of transfer in the studies examining the effects of trainee characteristics. Self-report measures of transfer are not adequate for developing a data base regarding the relation of trainee characteristics to transfer or for determining which interventions have the greatest effect on transfer. For example, Wexley and Baldwin's (1986) conclusion that a post-training goal-setting intervention was more effective than a relapse-prevention intervention must be tempered by the fact that the conclusion was based solely on self-reported generalization of skills and not on actual behavioral changes.

Environmental Characteristics

Table 3 presents information about the seven studies that have examined the relation of environmental characteristics to transfer of training. We located no studies in which an intervention was made to change the work environment and the effects of those changes on the extent of transfer was examined. Instead, studies used large-scale surveys to examine the relationships of correlates such as work climate (Baumgartel et al., 1984),

TABLE 3

Empirical Studies of Transfer of Training—Environmental Factors

				Criteria	
Author(s)	Sample	Training content	Variables	Source & (timing)	Measures & Results
Baumgartel & Jean-pierre (1972)	240 Indian managers	Management development program	Perceptions of transfer climate	Self (immediate)[a]	*Effort to apply*—Favorable organization climate perceptions were significantly and positively related to effort to apply.
Baumgartel, Reynolds, & Pathan (1984) (Study 1)	260 American managers	Human relations	Perceptions of transfer climate	Self (immediate)	*Effort to apply*—Favorable organization climate perceptions were significantly and positively related to effort to apply; the most favorable organization climate was characterized by high appreciation for performance and innovation, encouragement of risk taking and freedom to set own performance goals.
Baumgartel, Reynolds, & Pathan (1984) (Study 2)	246 Indian managers	Management development program	Perceptions of transfer climate	Self (immediate)	*Effort to apply*—Favorable organization climate perceptions were significantly and positively related to effort to apply. The most favorable organization climate was characterized by high appreciation for performance and innovation, a climate of freedom, a rational reward system, and openness in relationships among managers.
Fleishman (1953)	122 Manufacturing foremen	Leadership training	Perceptions of leadership climate	Self (varied 2–24 mos. after training)	*Leader behavior (LBDQ)*—Leader behavior was significantly affected by the leadership climate in the trainee's work environment. Trainees who returned to supervisors high in consideration exhibited more consideration. No such change occurred for those returning to supervisors lower in consideration.

[a]Immediate denotes that no significant time elapsed between training and measurement of trained skills.

Continued overleaf

Table 3 (continued)

Author(s)	Sample	Training content	Variables	Source & (timing)	Criteria
					Measures & Results
Hand, Richards & Slocum (1973)	21 Middle managers	Human relations training	Perceptions of transfer climate	Self (3 & 18 mos. after training)	*3-Month evaluation*—No significant changes in attitudes or behaviors of trainees were observed. *18-Month evaluation*—Significant positive changes in attitudes were observed in the experimental group; negative changes existed in the control group. Three climate perceptions (whether the organization favors participation by subordinates, innovative behavior, and independence of thought), moderated the findings.
Huczynski & Lewis (1980)	48 Electronic managers	Three-day network analysis training program	Supervisor support & perceptions of transfer climate	Self (4 mos. after training)	*Attempt to transfer*—Transfer attempts were more likely when the trainees had pre-training discussions with boss and where the boss "sponsored" the new idea. The management style and attitudes of the trainee's boss were found to be the most important factor in attempt to transfer.
Miles (1965)	34 Elementary school principals	Two-week human relations program	Perceptions of transfer climate	Self (8 mos. after training)	*Perceived on-the-job change*—Organizational factors (security, autonomy, power, & problem-solving adequacy) mediated the perceived change associated with laboratory training.

leadership climate (Fleishman, 1953) and supervisory support (Huczynski & Lewis, 1980) to transfer criteria.

Most of the training programs studied were interpersonal-skills (human-relations) programs. Given that behavioral changes in interpersonal relations are difficult to operationalize, it is not surprising that the transfer criterion measure frequently used was a self-reported measure of effort to transfer (e.g., Baumgartel & Jeanpierre, 1972, Baumgartel et al., 1984). Many of the measures were gathered immediately or soon after the training program was completed. A few studies, such as Hand et al., (1973), collected self- and supervisor reports of behavior change at more than one point in time after completion of the training program.

There are two major problems with the research examining work-environment characteristics and transfer. The first issue is the static nature of the research in relation to the dynamic nature of the transfer process. The "strong" support for the importance of environmental characteristics to transfer is based solely on correlational studies in which causality can not be inferred. What is needed is the identification of key work-environment variables and the operationalization of these variables. For example, while research suggests that supervisory support is an important component affecting transfer, there is little attempt to understand the supervisory behaviors that lead to perceptions of support by trainees. Only by clearly operationalizing work characteristics such as support can interventions be developed and their effects on generalization and maintenance of training be examined.

A second issue is the criterion problem. The studies on environmental characteristics have typically used self-reports of behavioral change as the major measure of transfer. In fact, Baumgartel and his associates have often used an "intention to transfer" measure, which is actually a "motivation to transfer" measure rather than a measure of the extent of generalization and maintenance of trained skills. Only one study, Hand et al. (1973), examined maintenance of trained behaviors across time as they measured self-reports and supervisory reports of behavior 3 months and 18 months after completion of the training program. The results indicated no change in behavior at 3 months but changes in behavior after 18 months. Given only two data points in time and the fact that process measures were not taken, it is impossible to determine why these results were found. Research is needed in which measures are taken at multiple intervals to examine the interactive effects of work characteristics and time on skill utilization and skill decrements after completion of a training program.

Overall Critique of the Research

While the limited number and the fragmented nature of the studies examining transfer are disturbing by themselves, a critical review of the existing research reveals that the samples, tasks, designs, and criteria used limit even further our ability to understand the transfer process. This review and critique of the research brings to mind a quote by Campbell (1971) that "we know a few things but not very much" (p. 593). Yet the review and critique has also led to the identification of specific problems with research conducted in this area. The next section provides a more specific and detailed discussion of needed future directions for research into the transfer process.

Future Research Directions

The critique of the transfer literature indicates that there are a number of research gaps that need to be addressed. The following section suggests needed future research directions regarding training design, trainee characteristics, work environment, and criterion issues relevant to transfer.

Training Design

Of the transfer research completed, it is clear that the experimental work on improving the training process is the most developed and rigorously researched. The results of research on the effects of the learning principles of identical elements, general principles, conditions of practice, and stimulus variability on retention has been quite robust. Nevertheless, we are still confronted with the problem of generalizing from these results to actual organizational-training settings.

In this section, several salient operational questions associated with the learning principles will be identified and illustrated with the use of a common organizational-training example. For this purpose, the case of training a new sales representative to sell computer equipment will be used. The salient operational questions will lead to a discussion of needed research questions. For illustrative purposes, operational issues relevant to principles of identical elements and stimulus variability will be highlighted.

Identical elements. The principle of identical elements predicts that transfer will be maximized to the degree that there are identical stimulus and response elements in the training and transfer settings. The critical operational problem is: "What, specifically, in the training program must be made identical to the actual work environment to facilitate learning, retention, and transfer?" One aspect of similarity is the degree to which the actual conditions of the training program (surroundings, tasks, equip-ment) match the work environment (physical fidelity). A second aspect of similarity is the degree to which trainees attach similar meanings in the training and organizational context (psychological fidelity). While there is some evidence that physical fidelity is less important than psychological fidelity (Berkowitz & Donnerstein, 1982), the concepts and their relative importance for different training content and skills have been neglected in the industrial-training literature.

To use the example of the new sales representative, one training tac-tic might be to replicate the relevant physical characteristics of the sales context exactly, including products, types of clients, office surroundings, and common distractions. Or, the training could focus on creating accurate reproduction of behavioral and cognitive processes that are necessary for performing the sales job. One could create training stimuli that necessitate the same responses and decision-making processes that the trainee should use in real sales situations. Research is needed to explore the type and level of fidelity needed to maximize transfer, given time and resource con-straints. Unfortunately, the industrial-training literature does not provide specifications for what constitutes optimal levels of physical and psycholog-ical fidelity in various types of industrial-training programs. It is necessary to understand the type of learning involved and the instructional events being considered before it is possible to choose the most effective learning procedures, or operationalization of principles.

Stimulus variability. Maximizing stimulus variability is based on the notion that transfer is maximized when a variety of relevant training stimuli are employed (e.g., Ellis, 1965). Kazdin (1975) has noted that transfer is enhanced by developing a variety of situations or by using differentially reinforced stimuli to avoid the problem of training becoming attached to a narrow range of stimuli and responses. In this way, variability can serve to strengthen understanding of the applicability of the training to new situa-tions (Duncan, 1958) and to foster innovation and generalization of skills (Bandura, 1977).

Operationalization of stimulus variability in organizational-training pro-grams is problematic. Consider the example of developing models for a behavior-modeling program on building interpersonal skills for a new sales representative. Modeling is intended to provide the majority of the cog-nitive aspects of the training, including attention to a modeling display, mental coding, and mental rehearsal (Decker & Nathan, 1985; A. Gold-stein & Sorcher, 1974). Yet, in behavior-modeling training, models are typically very simple and often redundant, and trainees are conditioned to think that the specific behaviors modeled and reinforced are universally applicable in handling problem situations on the job (Parry & Reich, 1984).

Three options for increasing stimulus variability in the modeling component of behavior-modeling training are character, situational, and model-competence variability. With character variability, a variety of different model characteristics (age, sex, organizational level) can be displayed. A second direction is to vary the situations modeled. For example, if one modeling tape entitled "assertive communication" portrays a salesperson assertively requesting a customer to reconsider a product, a second model could be shown that portrays a salesperson assertively requesting that the order department fill his/her order as soon as possible. A third way to increase variability is to vary the competence of the models. Models might be varied in terms of the extent to which they correctly demonstrate the key behaviors (high to low competence). Current behavior-modeling programs typically use effective models that are repeatedly shown. Yet, concept formation and problem-solving research suggest that negative models, in addition to positive models, can improve the process of retention and generalizability of skills (e.g., Bourne, 1970; Bourne & Guy, 1968; Craik & Lockhart, 1972).

Consequently, in the sales example, variability can be increased via different models, situations, and/or levels of model effectiveness. Also, while the focus in this section has been on the model displays, it should be noted that behavior modeling is a multi-stage process that should also include instructor input, role playing, and feedback. Thus, stimulus variability might also be introduced by the instructor (e.g., by providing varied examples or experiences) or by participants themselves in the role-playing scenarios. Unfortunately, at the present time, decisions regarding the focus and extent of stimulus variability in organizational-training programs such as behavior modeling must be based on intuition and conjecture rather than empirical support.

Baldwin (1987) has begun applied work examining the impact of stimulus variability within a behavior-modeling program. Variability has been operationalized in terms of the inclusion of different situations and different levels of effectiveness (effective or ineffective modeling) for assertive behaviors displayed by a videotaped model. Results suggest that increases in the variability of model competence enhance trainee generalization of learned skills. Similarly, in a counseling setting, Cominsky (1982) used different therapists (character variability) for the same patient rather than continuous work with one therapist and found that the increased stimulus variability led to enhanced treatment gains.

It is evident that there is much to be learned about the operationalization of training-design principles. Extending beyond the domain of organizational-training literature, recent research in the areas of information processing and instructional theory holds promise for furthering our understanding of training-design issues.

Cormier (1984) contends that an information-processing perspective has implications for training design. He points out that the principle of identical elements can be reconceptualized by using what we know about encoding and retrieval processes. More specifically, a training stimulus is conceptualized as a collection of attributes or elements (E. Smith, Shoben, & Rips, 1974; Underwood, 1969) that vary in terms of redintegrative capacity (Flexser & Tulving, 1978). Redintegration refers to the capacity of one part of a stimulus complex to re-evoke or cue the entire complex (Cormier, 1984). The redintegrative value of the available retrieval information is the critical determinant of its effectiveness. Applying this notion to transfer of training suggests that transfer should be the highest when the stimulus attributes with the highest redintegrative capacity are present in the task. In this view, it is not fidelity (either physical or psychological) per se that contributes to high positive transfer, but rather, the presence of retrieval information that has a high redintegrative capacity. Even low-fidelity training stimuli can be effective in producing transfer by providing the trainee with the essential cuing relationships between the stimulus attributes of the task environment and the appropriate responses.

While the task of identifying which attributes in training environments have high or low redintegrative value remains, the value of this conceptualization and framework for training is relatively straightforward. The fidelity of a training stimulus to the actual stimuli can be based on those attributes with high redintegrative value for correct responses. Those attributes with lower redintegrative value can be modified or eliminated without substantial loss of transfer (Cormier, 1984). These suggestions have considerable practical implications since high fidelity is often very difficult and expensive to create.

Research on information processing also suggests new avenues for better understanding the design principle of stimulus variability. An information-processing perspective suggests that when individuals are exposed to a variety of related or similar material across different presentations, they can more easily integrate new material with that already in memory into a common representation. From this perspective, stimulus variability is thought to aid transfer by providing a means by which an individual distinguishes relevant from irrelevant attributes (abstraction) and by enhancing the probability that additional relevant attributes are encoded into the functional representation of the to-be-remembered item. Therefore, research on the extent to which variability induces the formation of higher-order concepts or facilitates the abstraction of critical dimensions of task performance and stimulus recognition is needed.

The work of instructional theorists such as Gagne and Briggs (1979) is also relevant for transfer researchers interested in training-design issues. Gagne and Briggs developed a set of learning categories that permits them to analyze tasks and code behavior into one of several learning outcomes (e.g. intellectual skills, motor skills, cognitive strategies). Further, they have begun to examine each of the outcomes and determine the conditions of learning and instructional events that best support that learning outcome. While Gagne and Briggs (1979) focus on learning outcomes, a logical extension of the model would be the inclusion of the transfer outcomes of generalization and maintenance discussed earlier.

To further illustrate this point, consider that much of the conduct being modeled in training programs designed to teach motor skills is exactly prescribed. Therefore, it is desirable for trainees to adopt the modeled behaviors in essentially the same form as they are portrayed (Bandura, 1977). For example, there is little leeway permitted in the proper way to safely operate a power tool or perform a surgical operation. Consequently, the objective is to have trainees mimic behavior as closely as possible. In the case of interpersonal or supervisory skills, however, the objective is more to inculcate generalizable rules or concepts (specifying a class of behaviors to be used, given certain stimuli) and not simply to enable the trainee to reproduce only those behaviors specifically modeled. In fact, in the training of interpersonal and supervisory skills, the title "behavior" modeling is perhaps a misnomer. The training objective is to have observers extract the common attributes exemplified in modeled responses and formulate the rules for generating behavior with similar structural characteristics. Stated simply, the ultimate goal in complex skill-modeling training is to teach the trainee one or more principles (not strictly a list of behaviors) that will allow him/her to learn, generalize, and apply behaviors different from those modeled. It is clear that investigation directed at building a contingency model of transfer-oriented instructional design would provide information important for developing training environments more conducive to positive transfer.

Trainee Characteristics

A limited amount of research has examined ability, motivational, and personality characteristics for their effects on transfer. We need research that more clearly identifies the important trainee characteristics and applies them in organizational settings. An interactive approach to research is also needed to begin testing for optimal matches between trainee characteristics and training-program design and content.

The research on ability and personality characteristics has failed to identify those factors that are most critical in a training context. In addition, the focus of this research has been on distinguishing between individuals who are successful and those who are unsuccessful in transferring skills rather than on placing individuals into programs that optimally match their characteristics.

Empirical evidence suggests that need for achievement (Baumgartel & Jeanpierre, 1972; Baumgartel et al., 1984), locus of control (Noe & Schmitt, 1986), and general intelligence (Neel & Dunn, 1960; Robertson & Downs, 1979) can be factors in learning and transferring skills. While further identification of key individual-difference variables is needed, there is a critical need for the development of a research perspective that attempts to understand the relationships of trainee characteristics and training-program design to transfer. The major application of the existing research on stable indivdual differences is that transfer can be facilitated by carefully selecting individuals who have certain personality and/or ability characteristics for the training program.

Given that in many organizations selection of trainees is not a viable option (everyone must be trained), researchers must begin a program of research on placement, rather than selection, of individuals into the type of program that is optimal (in terms of transfer), given certain trainee characteristics. The existing research does not speak to the issue of placement because the instructional methodology (e.g., lecture, case study, discussion) of specific types of training programs (e.g., assertiveness, human relations, time management) have been held constant in the studies completed. Studies are needed in which personality/ability factors are measured and individuals placed into training programs under different conditions of instructional methodology to determine which "types" of individuals best match which types of programs for effective transfer of skills to the job.

Cronbach and Snow (1977) have labelled this concern for providing each trainee with the appropriate model of instruction the "aptitude–treatment interaction." When an aptitude–treatment interaction is found, trainees should be assigned differentially to alternative training methods to maximize the probability of transfer. Similarly, we posit that a "personality–treatment interaction" would call for assigning trainees with external locus of control, for example, to a different method of instruction than trainees with an internal locus of control. As noted by I. Goldstein (1986), the examination of how individual differences moderate the effectiveness of different training methods requires refinement of individual-difference measures and the development of a typology of instructional methodology of the sort proposed by Gagne and Briggs (1979) discussed earlier.

Research examining motivational issues of transfer lacks a coherent framework for understanding factors affecting the transfer process. We propose that the expectancy model (Lawler, 1973; Vroom, 1964) provides just such a useful heuristic for integrating research on transfer motivation and for leading to new directions for transfer research.

The expectancy model provides a useful heuristic for understanding transfer because of its interactive perspective on motivation. Perceptions—and therefore motivation—are affected by both individual and work-environment factors, which must be interpreted by an individual and translated into choices among various behavioral options. This perspective has not been adequately acknowledged in the transfer literature: few studies have attempted to examine multiple influences on motivation to learn or motivation to transfer skills. From the expectancy framework (Lawler, 1973), it can be seen that there are numerous factors (locus of control, self esteem, past experience, communications from others) that need to be examined for their relevance to the transfer process. For example, social interaction regarding the usefulness of a training program may affect an individual's expectancies regarding the relationship between doing well in the program and attaining valued outcomes.

Second, the expectancy framework stresses the importance of a dynamic perspective on motivation. Individuals are seen as active information processors who adapt their attitudes, behaviors, and beliefs to their social context and to their own past experiences. Organizational procedures and reward systems, as well as information obtained from interactions with peers and superiors in the work environment, affect an individual's construction of the reality within the work setting, including perceptions of expectancies (Daft & Weick, 1984). This implies that new experiences, once integrated into a person's construction of reality, can result in changes in these expectancies. Unfortunately, most studies examining motivational factors and transfer have examined motivation from a static perspective, gathering information at one period of time. Similarly, all the research on motivational effects on transfer has focused on the effects within a single training program. Given that expectancies can change over time, important issues that have not been researched are the cumulative effects of past training experiences on an individual's expectancies and subsequent motivation to transfer currently trained skills to the job.

Environmental Characteristics

Progress in the research on environmental characteristics requires the operationalization of key variables such as climate and supervisory support at a level of specificity that allows for the development of interventions for changing environmental characteristics and testing their effects on transfer of training. I. Goldstein (1985) has discussed environmental characteristics as either facilitating or inhibiting the transfer of training, and more research is needed to identify and operationalize variables that significantly facilitate or inhibit transfer. Also needed is research that examines the effects of environmental characteristics from a levels-of-analysis perspective. Such a perspective would lead to the examination of the effects of differences in climate or support across workgroups, and even across organizations.

Supervisory support. Supervisory support for training has been cited as a key work-environment variable affecting the transfer process (e.g., see Fleishman, 1953; House, 1968). Employees look towards their supervisor for important information regarding how to work successfully within the social environment of the organization. As Huczynski & Lewis (1980), state, employees who perceive that a training program is important to the supervisor will be more motivated to attend, learn, and transfer trained skills to the job. While support is critical, development of a concept of what is meant by support has lagged far behind anecdotal evidence of the importance of support. In addition, those trained skills and behaviors most affected by supervisory support have not been examined.

Supervisory support is clearly a multidimensional construct, which could include encouragement to attend, goal-setting activities, reinforcement activities, and modeling of behaviors (Baumgartel et al., 1984; Eddy, Glad, & Wilkins, 1967; Huczynski & Lewis, 1980; Maddox, 1987). A supervisor can demonstrate encouragement to attend through both verbal and nonverbal cues. For example, a supervisor may demonstrate a lack of knowledge about the content of the training program or show his/her reluctance to allow subordinates to attend by rescheduling training when minor crises arise in the department. In relation to goal setting, supervisors can discuss the content and benefits of the program and set goals prior to (focus on improving these skills) and subsequent to (action plans for applying skills) attendance in the program (Wexley & Baldwin, 1986). Reinforcement refers to the provision of rewards for using behaviors developed in the training program. Supervisors can first insure that trainees have the opportunity to use the new skills in which they are trained. Then, the supervisor can provide praise, better assignments, and other extrinsic rewards for trainees who utilize their new skills. Reinforcement processes can also work in reverse; for example, a supervisor who ignores the use of a new skill or actively attacks the use of new skills can cause the trained behaviors to "extinguish." Finally, modeling has been shown to be a powerful force in affecting behavioral change (Sims & Manz, 1982). Employees tend to imitate supervisors who have power over them in order to gain rewards. Therefore, the extent to which the supervisor behaves in ways congruent with the training objectives will have a major impact on transfer of trained skills by subordinates.

Empirical work is needed so that the supervisory-support factors that have the greatest impact on transfer can be identified. With this information, interventions can be developed to change managerial behaviors to increase supervisory support prior to subordinate attendance in a specific training program.

Levels-of-analysis issues. The existing research on influences of the work environment on transfer has been correlational in nature. Perceptions of supervisory support by individual trainees are correlated with self- or other reports of transfer of trained skills to the job. Such measures, which are often collected soon after completion of the training program, are clearly inadequate for developing a base of knowledge about the transfer process. In addition to serious criterion problems, this type of study is problematic as it focuses solely on the individual level of analysis.

The literature describing research into climate (B. Schneider, 1983) indicates that there are often reliable differences in level of support and other climate factors across workgroups within an organization as well as across different organizations. Organizations and departments within organizations can be differentiated in terms of goal orientation, time orientation, formality of structure, and interpersonal orientation (Lawrence & Lorsch, 1969). For example, an organization's philosophy about its people (interpersonal orientation) can have important implications for the transferring of skills from a human-relations training program. This perspective calls for research at the organizational level of analysis in which the same training program is offered across multiple organizations. Similarly, from a group level of analysis, a research and development department with a long time perspective may be more supportive of interpersonal-skills training programs that do not have immediate, objective payoffs while production departments under time pressures would be less supportive of such programs.

Consequently, an organization-wide training program for improving interpersonal skills will most likely lead to different amounts of transfer across departments, depending on the support or congruence of the training program with the climate or philosophy of the various departments within the organization. An examination of the transfer literature reveals no existing attempts to empirically examine the effects of work environmental characteristics on transfer from a levels-of-analysis perspective.

Criterion Issues

The conditions of transfer include generalization of skills or behaviors learned in the training program and the maintenance of those skills and behaviors over a specified period of time. The review of the transfer literature reveals that research has concentrated on the training-input factors that might affect transfer rather than focusing on the appropriate measurement of the conditions of transfer. This neglect of criterion issues is surprising, given the long-standing concern of applied psychologists over the "criterion problem" (Cascio, 1982; Wallace, 1965). The usefulness of the empirical research on transfer is severely limited by the use of criterion measures that are deficient and contaminated. Advancement in criterion measurement requires a greater appreciation of the issues relevant to measuring generalization and maintenance of skills and behaviors.

Generalization. To examine the successful generalization of trained skills or behaviors, a clear identification of the knowledge, skills, and behaviors expected to be transferred to the job is needed. Then a systematic collection of the appropriate information is needed to make effective training decisions related to the value of various training programs (I. Goldstein, 1986) and to systematically reassess training needs for possible redesign of the training program (Ford & Wroten, 1984).

To develop appropriate measures of generalization requires a linkage of needs-assessment information, the specification of training objectives, and the determination of criteria to use to determine how much of the knowledge, skills, and behaviors learned in training are transferred to the actual job. In addition, the relevance of the skills learned for effective job performance must be determined. While these suggested linkages are certainly not new, few attempts have been made in the transfer literature to list the criteria of success that one should expect on the basis of training objectives and training evaluation criteria. Such an approach is critical to the development of an empirical base regarding transfer.

Once the knowledge, skills, and behaviors that should be exhibited on the job are specified, the next step is to determine baselines that describe how often we can expect trainees to exhibit those knowledges, skills, and behaviors on the job. A task analysis is needed to detail the importance and frequency of the tasks performed on the job. The tasks that are affected by the trained behaviors and skills can then be identified. Other analysis techniques, such as the collection of critical incidents, can help provide a taxonomy of situations that call for the use of the trained skills or behaviors. The combination of task importance and frequency and a taxonomy of situations can provide a baseline for determining how often one should expect trained behaviors to be exhibited on the job. This would force the explicit recognition that an important component in developing transfer measures of generalization is the identification of how often and in what situations a trainee could reasonably be expected to demonstrate the trained behaviors or skills.

Maintenance. While generalization refers to the extent to which trained skills and behaviors are exhibited in the transfer setting, maintenance concerns the length of time that trained skills and behaviors continue to be used on the job. Decreases in the use of trained skills on the job could be a result of skill decrements over time. Or, the decrease in use could be a result of decreased motivation to use the skills due to constraints in the work environment or a lack of rewards for using the skills. Regardless, this perspective requires a highly dynamic approach to the study of transfer that is lacking in the literature.

Such a dynamic perspective has been taken in research examining the amount of learning that occurs in training or educational settings over time. Researchers in the learning field have represented the dynamic process of learning in the form of "learning curves" (e.g., see Bass & Vaughan, 1966). Learning curves represent how well a certain skill is learned and the speed with which an individual acquires that skill. The kind of task being trained, the design of the training program, and the characteristics of the trainee have been found to have major impacts on how quickly an individual attains the level of performance that meets established standards (Blum & Naylor, 1968).

Similarly, we posit that a useful way to think about maintenance of trained knowledge, skills, and behaviors is through the use of "maintenance curves," which represent the changes that occur in the level of knowledge, skills, or behaviors exhibited in the transfer setting as a function of time elapsed from completion of the training program. The development of a maintenance curve requires the consideration of three issues. First, a baseline of the level of knowledge, skill, or behavior that a trainee exhibits prior to and at the end of the training program must be established. The amount of differentiation between pre- and post-training levels indicates the decrement that must occur to return to the pre-training baseline. Second, an adequate time interval that allows for the determination of overall trends or variations in skill or behavior levels must be established. Third, at multiple time intervals, measurements must be taken to examine changes in the shape and slope of the maintenance curve over time.

The five types of maintenance curve presented in Figure 2 illustrate the points made above. Type A demonstrates a curve in which there is a slow tapering off of a trained skill over time towards the pre-training baseline. This indicates the successful transfer of skills that is maintained over time but is in need of a "booster" session at some point to return to post-training baseline conditions. Type B indicates a failure in transfer as the post-training level drops immediately upon returning to the work site. In this case the person has demonstrated an ability to use the skill appropriately (based on performance in the training) but immediately reverts back to old ways of doing things on the job, for whatever reason. The third example, Type C, demonstrates an attempt by the trainee to use the skills trained on the job for a period of time, which is followed by a sharp decline in the use of a skill towards the pre-training baseline. This decline could occur due to the lack of success in using a trained skill on the job, perceived lack of support for using the skill, or some combination. Type D highlights the situation in which a trainee's learning and retention of trained material was minimal. In this case, there is little chance for the skills to generalize

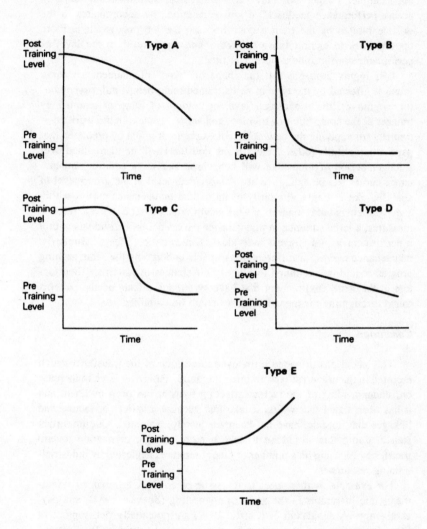

Figure 2: **Types of Transfer Maintenance Curves**

and be exhibited on the job. Finally, Type E demonstrates a situation in which the skill level actually increases over time once back on the job. For example, a supervisor may learn some behavioral modeling skills in giving performance feedback. Positive reactions by subordinates to the skills exhibited by the trainee once back on the job may result in more opportunities to exhibit those behaviors and an increase in the level of performance of those behaviors over time.

It is highly probable that the shape or "type" of maintenance curve found is affected by the type of skills trained (e.g., behavioral, psychomotor, cognitive), the proficiency level or amount of material retained by trainees at the completion of training, and supportiveness in the work environment for applying the new skill. For example, it might be predicted that psychomotor skills (other factors being constant) will be maintained over a longer period of time than will behavioral skills. In addition, maintenance curves can be examined at the individual level or the group level of analysis. For example, similarity of individual maintenance curves within a department would suggest a work-environment effect. Given reliable measures, a large variance in maintenance curves across individuals within a department would suggest individual-characteristics effects. Similarly, maintenance curves for different departments undergoing the same training program could be examined to identify differences in patterns. Then factors in the work environment that have systematic effects on the patterns found through the maintenance curves could be identified.

Conclusion

This paper has provided a review and critique of the transfer research reported in the organizational-training literature. Future research to increase our understanding of the factors affecting transfer has been outlined, and it has been stated that we must take into account a variety of factors and linkages that, to date, have not been adequately examined. One important step in doing this would be to take a more eclectic orientation toward transfer by focusing on a number of other literatures neglected by industrial-training researchers.

For example, with respect to the issue of conducive transfer environments, the literatures in the areas of counseling (Spevak, 1981), and psychotherapy (A. Goldstein & Kanfer, 1979) are potentially rich sources of ideas for testing and application to organizational settings. To illustrate, researchers in those areas have investigated the value of "buddy systems" for facilitating transfer (Barrett, 1978; Karol & Richards, 1978). A buddy system refers to two trainees being paired to reinforce each other in order to maintain learning, provide advice, and be alert for signs of relapse in themselves and the buddy. In a study of habitual smoking reduction,

Karol and Richards (1978) found that the buddy system condition exhibited substantially less relapse to smoking than did a control condition.

Another strategy investigated in a counseling context has been that of "booster sessions" (Ashby & Wilson, 1977; Kingsley & Wilson, 1977). A booster session is an extension of training and usually involves periodic face-to-face contact of either a planned or unplanned nature between trainee and trainer. An obesity study by Kingsley and Wilson (1977) found that the inclusion of booster sessions at 2-, 3-, 4-, and 5-week intervals induced a significantly greater percentage of maintained weight loss than did the absence of boosters.

Marx (1982) has begun a program of research adapting a transfer strategy termed "relapse prevention," which was originally designed and successfully implemented in the treatment of addictive behaviors (Marlatt & J. Gordon, 1980; Perri, Shapiro, Ludwig, Twentyman, & McAdoo, 1984) to industrial settings. As Marx has noted, this approach seems particularly applicable as a post-training transfer strategy for industrial training. The relapse prevention model consists of both cognitive and behavioral components designed to facilitate the long-term maintenance of learned behaviors by teaching individuals to understand and cope with the problem of relapse.

In the area of educational psychology, Wlodkowski (1985) recently presented a comprehensive list of strategies for enhancing adult motivation to learn. While the author's focus was primarily on learning (not transfer) outcomes, and empirical evidence presented was quite limited, such work could serve as a departure point for empirical investigations aimed at investigating transfer in organizational contexts.

Aside from exploring other literatures, it is also readily apparent that we need to begin research that takes a more interactive perspective. Most of the existing research has focused exclusively on one input factor (design, trainee, work environment) rather than attempting to develop and test a framework that incorporates the more complex interactions among these training inputs. Consequently, we have a quite limited knowledge base about which input factors have the greatest impact on transfer under various conditions (such as type of organization and type of training program). A recent paper by I. Goldstein and Musicante (1985) is one of the first attempts to bring together several of the different factors usually examined independently (principles of learning, environment characteristics) and apply them together to an organizationally relevant (rater training) context.

In addition, training research cannot continue to ignore the job relevance of the training content as a critical factor affecting what is learned, retained, and transferred to the work setting. Transfer research has implicitly assumed the job relevance of the training content without attempting to specify what the desired skills or behaviors are or what the training content should be to insure skill acquisition. When training content is not valid,

100   PERSONNEL PSYCHOLOGY

trainees may actually be successful in learning and transferring knowledge and skills that are inappropriate for effective job performance. Ford and Wroten (1984) and I. Goldstein (1986) have developed techniques for examining the content validity of training programs. Information from these analyses can then be used to refine training content and to increase the job relevance of the training program. In future studies on transfer, researchers should provide evidence of the job relevance of the training material before examining the effects of other input factors on generalization and maintenance of trained skills.

Perhaps most importantly for the present, there is a critical need to conduct research on transfer with more relevent criterion measures of generalization and maintenance. Conclusions from the existing research are problematic, given the relatively short-term, single-source, perceptual data base that has been created. It is hoped that the model presented, the review conducted, and the suggestions given in this paper will help spur further efforts at examining transfer from a broader and more dynamic perspective.

REFERENCES

Adams JA. (1955). Multiple vs. single problem training in human problem solving. *Journal of Experimental Psychology, 48*, 15–18.

Ashby WA, Wilson GT. (1977). Behavior therapy for obesity: Booster sessions and long-term maintenance of weight loss. *Behavior Research and Theory, 15*, 451–463.

Atkinson RC. (1972). Ingredients for a theory of instruction. *American Psychologist, 27*, 921–931.

Atwater SK. (1953). Proactive inhibition and associative facilitation as affected by degree of prior learning. *Journal of Experimental Psychology, 46*, 400–404.

Baldwin TT. (1987, August). *The effect of negative models on learning and transfer from behavior modeling: A test of stimulus variability.* Presented at the 47th annual meeting of the Academy of Management, New Orleans, LA.

Bandura A. (1977). *Social learning theory.* Englewood Cliffs, NJ: Prentice-Hall.

Barrett CJ. (1978). Effectiveness of widow's groups in facilitating change. *Journal of Consulting and Clinical Psychology, 46*, 20–31.

Bass BM, Vaughan JA. (1966). *Training in industry: The management of learning.* Belmont, CA: Wadsworth.

Baumgartel H., Jeanpierre F. (1972). Applying new knowledge in the back-home setting: A study of Indian managers' adoptive efforts. *Journal of Applied Behavioral Science, 8*(6), 674–694.

Baumgartel H, Reynolds M, Pathan R. (1984). How personality and organizational-climate variables moderate the effectiveness of management development programmes: A review and some recent research findings. *Management and Labour Studies, 9*, 1–16.

Baumgartel H, Sullivan GJ, Dunn LE. (1978). How organizational climate and personality affect the pay-off from advanced management training sessions. *Kansas Business Review, 5*, 1–10.

Berkowitz L, Donnerstein E. (1982). External validity is more than skin deep: Some answers to criticisms of laboratory experiments. *American Psychologist, 37*, 245–257.

Blum ML, Naylor JC. (1968). *Industrial psychology: Its theoretical and social foundations.* New York: Harper Row.

Bourne LE. (1970). Knowing and using concepts. *Psychological Review, 77*, 546–556.

Bourne LE, Guy DE. (1968). Learning conceptual rules: The role of positive and negative instances. *Journal of Experimental Psychology, 77*, 488–494.

Briggs GE, Naylor JC. (1962). The relative efficiency of several training methods as a function of transfer task complexity. *Journal of Experimental Psychology, 64*, 505–512.

Briggs GE, Waters LK. (1958). Training and transfer as a function of component interaction. *Journal of Experimental Psychology, 56*, 492–500.

Callentine MF, Warren JM. (1955). Learning sets in human concept formation. *Psychological Reports, 1*, 363–367.

Campbell JP. (1971). Personnel training and development. *Annual Review of Psychology, 22*, 565–602.

Campbell JP, Dunnette MD, Lawler EE, Weick KE. (1970). *Managerial behavior, performance and effectiveness.* New York: McGraw-Hill.

Cascio WF. (1982). *Costing human resources: The financial impact of behavior in organizations.* Boston: Kent Publishing.

Cominsky IJ. (1982). Transfer of training in counselor education programs: A study of the use of stimulus variability and the provision of general principles to enhance the transfer of the skill of reflection of feeling. *Dissertation Abstracts International, 43*(1–A), 76.

Cormier S. (1984). *Transfer of training: An interpretive review.* (Technical Report No. 608). Alexandria, VA: Army Research Institute for the Behavioral and Social Sciences.

Crafts LW. (1935). Transfer as related to number of common elements. *Journal of General Psychology, 13*, 147–158.

Craik FIM, Lockhart RS. (1972). Levels of processing: A framework for memory research. *Journal of Verbal Learning and Verbal Behavior, 11*, 671–684.

Crannell CW. (1956). Transfer in problem solution as related to the type of training. The *Journal of General Psychology, 54*, 3–14.

Cronbach LJ, Snow RE. (1977). *Aptitudes and instructional methods.* New York: Irvington.

Daft RL, Weick KE. (1984). Toward a model of organizations as interpretation systems. *Academy of Management Review, 9*, 284–295.

Decker PJ. (1980). Effects of symbolic coding and rehearsal in behavior modeling training. *Journal of Applied Psychology, 65*, 627–634.

Decker PJ. (1982). The enhancement of behavior modeling training of supervisory skills by the inclusion of retention processes. PERSONNEL PSYCHOLOGY, *32*, 323–332.

Decker PJ, Nathan BR. (1985). *Behavior modeling training.* New York: Praeger Publishers.

Digman JM. (1959). Growth of a motor skill as a function of distribution of practice. *Journal of Experimental Psychology, 57*, 310–316.

Downs S. (1970). Predicting training potential. *Personnel Management, 2*, 26–28.

Duncan CP. (1958). Transfer after training with single versus multiple tasks. *Journal of Experimental Psychology, 55*, 63–72.

Duncan CP, Underwood BJ. (1953). Transfer in motor learning as a function of degree of first task learning and inter-task similarity. *Journal of Experimental Psychology, 46*, 445–452.

Eddy WB, Glad DD, Wilkins DD. (1967). Organizational effects on training. *Training and Development Journal, 22*(2), 36–43.

Eden D, Ravid G. (1982). Pygmalion versus self-expectancy: Effects of instructor and self-expectancy on trainee performance. *Organizational Behavior and Human Performance, 30*, 351–364.

Eden D, Shani AB. (1982). Pygmalion goes to boot camp: Expectancy leadership and trainee performance. *Journal of Applied Psychology, 67*, 194–199.

Ellis HC. (1965). *The transfer of learning.* New York: Macmillan.

Fleishman E. (1953). Leadership climate, human relations training, and supervisory behavior. PERSONNEL PSYCHOLOGY, *6*, 205–222.

Flexser AJ, Tulving E. (1978). Retrieval independence in recognition and recall. *Psychological Review, 85,* 153–171.

Ford JK, Wroten SP. (1984). Introducing new methods for conducting training evaluation to program redesign. PERSONNEL PSYCHOLOGY, *37,* 651–666.

Forgus RH, Schwartz RJ. (1957). Efficient retention and transfer as affected by learning method. *Journal of Psychology, 43,* 135–139.

Fryer DH, Edgerton HA. (1950). Research concerning off-the-job training. PERSONNEL PSYCHOLOGY, *3,* 262–284.

Gagne RM. (1962). Miltary training and principles of learning. *American Psychologist, 17,* 83–91.

Gagne RM, Baker K, Foster H. (1950). On the relation between similarity and transfer of training in the learning of discriminative motor tasks. *Psychological Review, 57,* 67–79.

Gagne RM, Briggs LJ. (1979). Principles of instructional design. New York: Holt, Rinehart Winston.

Gagne RM, Foster H. (1949). Transfer to a motor skill from practice on a pictured representation. *Journal of Experimental Psychology, 39,* 342–54.

Ghiselli EE. (1966). *The validity of occupational aptitude tests.* New York: John Wiley & Sons.

Georgenson DL. (1982). The problem of transfer calls for partnership. *Training and Development Journal, 36*(10), 75–78.

Goldbeck RA, Bernstein BB, Hillix WA, Marx MH. (1957). Application of the half split technique to problem solving tasks. *Journal of Experimental Psychology, 53,* 330–338.

Goldstein AP, Kanfer FH. (1979). *Maximizing treatment gains: Transfer enhancement in psychotherapy.* New York: Academic Press.

Goldstein AP, Sorcher M. (1974). *Changing supervisory behavior.* New York: Pergamon Press.

Goldstein IL. (1980). Training in work organizations. *Annual Review of Psychology, 31,* 229–272.

Goldstein IL. (1985, August). *Organization analysis and evaluation models.* Presented at the 1985 meeting of the American Psychological Association, Los Angeles, CA.

Goldstein IL. (1986). *Training in Organizations: Needs assessment, development and evaluation.* Monterey, CA: Brooks/Cole.

Goldstein IL, Musicante GA. (1985). The applicability of a training transfer model to issues concerning rater training. In Locke E (Ed.), *Generalizing from laboratory to field settings* (pp. 83–98). Lexington, MA: Lexington Books.

Gordon LV. (1955). Time in training as a criterion of success in radio code. *Journal of Applied Psychology, 39,* 311–313.

Gordon ME, Cohen SL. (1973). Training behavior as a predictor of trainability. PERSONNEL PSYCHOLOGY, *26,* 261–272.

Gordon ME, Kleiman LS. (1976). The prediction of trainability using a work sample test and an aptitude test: A direct comparison. PERSONNEL PSYCHOLOGY, *29,* 243–253.

Hagman JD, Rose AM. (1983). Retention of military tasks: A review. *Human Factors, 25*(2), 199–213.

Hand HH, Richards MD, Slocum JM. (1973). Organization climate and the effectiveness of a human relations program. *Academy of Management Journal, 16,* 185–195.

Haselrud GM, Meyers S. (1958). The transfer value of given and individually derived principles. *Journal of Educational Psychology, 49,* 293–298.

Hendrickson G, Schroeder W. (1941). Transfer of training in learning to hit a submerged target. *Journal of Educational Psychology, 32,* 206–213.

Hicks WD, Klimoski RJ. (1987). Entry into training programs and its effects on training outcomes: A field experiment. *Academy of Management Journal, 30,* 542–552.

Hilgard ER, Edren RD, Irvine RP. (1954). Errors in transfer following learning with understanding: Further studies with Katona's card-trick experiments. *Journal of Experimental Psychology, 47,* 457–464.

Hilgard ER, Irvine RP, Whipple JE. (1953). Rote memorization, understanding and transfer: An extension of Katona's card-trick experiments. *Journal of Experimental Psychology, 46,* 288–292.

Hinrichs JR. (1976). Personnel Training. In, Dunnette MD (Ed.), *Handbook of Industrial and Organizational Psychology* (pp. 861–88). Chicago: Rand McNally.

Holding DH. (1965). *Principles of training.* London: Pergamon Press.

House RJ. (1968). Leadership training: Some dysfunctional consequences. *Administrative Science Quarterly, 12,* 556–571.

Huczynski AA, Lewis JW. (1980). An empirical study into the learning transfer process in management training. *Journal of Management Studies, 17,* 227–240.

Judd CH. (1908). The relation of special training and general intelligence. *Educational Review, 36,* 42–48.

Karol RL, Richards CS. (1978, November). Making treatment effects last: *An investigation of maintenance strategies for smoking reduction.* Presented at the meeting of the Association for Advancement of Behavior Therapy, Chicago, IL.

Kazdin AE. (1975). *Behavior modification in applied settings.* Homewood, IL: Dorsey Press.

Kingsley RG, Wilson GT. (1977). Behavior therapy for obesity: A comparative investigation of long-term efficacy. *Journal of Consulting and Clinical Psychology, 45,* 288–298.

Kirkpatrick DL. (1967). Evaluation of training. In Craig RL, Bittel LR (Eds.), *Training and development handbook* (pp. 87–112). New York: McGraw-Hill.

Komacki J, Heinzemann AT, Lawson L. (1980). Effects of training and feedback: Component analysis of a behavioral safety program. *Journal of Applied Psychology, 65,* 261–70.

Lawler EE III. (1973). *Motivation in work organizations.* Monterey, CA: Brooks/Cole.

Lawrence PR, Lorsch JW. (1969). *Organization and environment: Managing differentiation and integration.* Homewood, IL: Irwin.

MacPherson SJ, Dees V, Grindley GC. (1948). The effect of knowledge of results on performance: II. Some characteristics of very simple skills. *Quarterly Journal of Experimental Psychology, 1,* 68–78.

Maddox M. (1987). *Environmental and supervisory influences on the transfer of training.* Unpublished manuscript, Michigan State University, E. Lansing, MI.

Mandler G. (1954). Transfer of training as a function of response overlearning. *Journal of Experimental Psychology, 47,* 411–417.

Mandler G, Heinemann SH. (1956). Effects of overlearning of a verbal response on transfer of training. *Journal of Experimental Psychology, 52,* 39–46.

Marlatt GA, Gordon JR. (1980). Determinants of relapse: Implications for the maintenance of behavior change. In Davidson PO, Davidson SM (Eds.), *Behavioral medicine: Changing health lifestyles* (pp. 410–452). New York: Brunner/Mazel.

Marx RD. (1982). Relapse prevention for managerial training: A model for maintenance of behavioral change. *Academy of Management Review, 7,* 433–441.

McGehee W. (1948). Cutting training waste. PERSONNEL PSYCHOLOGY, *1,* 331–340.

McGehee W, Thayer PW. (1961). *Training in Business and Industry.* New York: Wiley.

Michalak DF. (1981). The neglected half of training. *Training and Development Journal, 35*(5), 22–28.

Miles MB. (1965). Changes during and following laboratory training: A clinical-experimental study. *Journal of Applied Behavioral Science, 1,* 215–242.

Morrisett L, Hovland CI. (1959). A comparison of three varieties of training in human problem solving. *Journal of Experimental Psychology, 58,* 52–55.

Mosel JN. (1957). Why training programs fail to carry over. *Personnel, 4*, 56–64.

Naylor JC, Briggs GE. (1963). The effect of task complexity and task organization on the relative efficiency of part and whole training methods. *Journal of Experimental Psychology, 65*, 217–224.

Neel RG, Dunn RE. (1960). Predicting success in supervisory training programs by the use of psychological tests. *Journal of Applied Psychology, 44*, 358–360.

Newstrom JW. (1984, August). *A role-taker/ time differentiated integration of transfer strategies.* Presented at the 1984 meeting of the American Psychological Association, Toronto, Ontario.

Noe R. (1986). Trainees' attributes and attitudes: Neglected influences on training effectiveness. *Academy of Management Review, 11*, 736–749.

Noe RA, Schmitt N. (1986). The influence of trainee attitudes on training effectiveness: Test of a model. PERSONNEL PSYCHOLOGY, *39*, 497–523.

Parry SB, Reich LR. (1984). An uneasy look at behavior modeling. *Training and Development Journal, 30*(3), 57–62.

Perri MG, Shapiro RM, Ludwig WW, Twentyman CT, McAdoo WG. (1984). Maintenance strategies for the treatment of obesity: An evaluation of relapse prevention training and post treatment contact by mail and telephone. *Journal of Consulting and Clinical Psychology, 52*, 404–413.

Reber RA, Wallin JA. (1984). The effects of training, goal setting, and knowledge of results on safe behavior: A component analysis. *Academy of Management Journal, 27*, 544–560.

Reynolds B, Bilodeau IM. (1952). Acquisition and retention of three psychomotor tests as a function of distribution of practice during acquisition. *Journal of Experimental Psychology, 44*, 19–26.

Robertson I, Downs S. (1979). Learning and the prediction of performance: Development of trainability testing in the United Kingdom. *Journal of Applied Psychology, 64*, 42–50.

Robinson JC. (1984). You should have sent my boss. *Training, 21*(2), 45–47.

Ryman DH, Biersner RJ. (1975). Attitudes predictive of diving training success. PERSONNEL PSYCHOLOGY, *28*, 181–188.

Schendel JD, Hagman JD. (1982). On sustaining procedural skills over a prolonged retention interval. *Journal of Applied Psychology, 67*, 605–610.

Schneider B. (1983). Interactional psychology and organizational behavior. In Cummings LL, Staw BM (Eds.), *Research in Organizational Behavior* (Vol. 5, pp. 1–31). Greenwich, CT: JAI Press.

Schneider W. (1985). Training high performance skills: Fallacies and guidelines. *Human Factors, 27*(3), 285–300.

Sims HP, Manz CC. (1982, January). Modeling influences on employee behavior. *Personnel Journal*, pp. 45–51.

Shore E, Sechrest L. (1961). Concept attainment as a function of positive instances presented. *Journal of Educational Psychology, 52*, 303–307

Smith EE, Shoben EJ, Rips LJ. (1974). Structure and process in semantic memory: A feature model for semantic decisions. *Psychological Review, 81*, 214–241.

Smith MC, Downs S. (1975). Trainability assessments for apprentice selection in shipbuilding. *Journal of Occupational Psychology, 48*, 39–43.

Spevak PA. (1981). Maintenance of therapy gains: Strategies, problems and promise. *JSAS Catalog of Selected Documents in Psychology, 11*, 35. (MS. No. 2255).

Taylor CW. (1952). Pretesting saves training costs. PERSONNEL PSYCHOLOGY, *5*, 213–239.

Taylor EK, Tajen C. (1948). Selection for training: Tabulating equipment operators. PERSONNEL PSYCHOLOGY, *1*, 341–348.

Thorndike EL. (1927). The law of effect. *American Journal of Psychology, 39*, 212–222.

Thorndike EL, Woodworth RS. (1901). The influence of improvement in one mental function upon the efficiency of other functions. *Psychological Review, 8*, 247–261.

Tracy WR. (1984). *Designing training and development systems.* New York: Amacom.

Trost A. (1982). They may love it but will they use it? *Training and Development Journal. 36*(1), 78–81.

Trowbridge MH, Cason H. (1932). An experimental study of Thorndike's theory of learning. *Journal of General Psychology, 7*, 245–260.

Tubiana JH, Ben-Shakhar G. (1982). An objective group questionnaire as a substitute for a personal interview in the prediction of success in military training in Israel. PERSONNEL PSYCHOLOGY, *35*, 349–357.

Underwood BJ. (1951). Associative transfer in verbal learning as a function of response similarity and degree of first-line learning. *Journal of Experimental Psychology, 42*, 44–53.

Underwood BJ. (1969). Attributes of memory. *Psychological Review, 76*, 559–573.

Vroom VH. (1964). *Work and motivation.* New York: Wiley.

Wallace SR. (1965). Criteria for what? *American Psychologist, 20*, 411–417.

Wexley KN. (1984). Personnel training. *Annual Review of Psychology, 35*, 519–551.

Wexley KN, Baldwin TT. (1986). Post-training strategies for facilitating positive transfer: An empirical exploration. *Academy of Management Journal, 29*, 503–520.

Wexley KN, Latham GP. (1981). *Developing and Training Human Resources in Organizations.* Glenview, IL: Scott Foresman.

Wexley KN, Nemeroff W. (1975). Effectiveness of positive reinforcement and goal setting as methods of management development. *Journal of Applied Psychology, 64*, 239–246.

Wexley KN, Thornton CL. (1972). Effect of verbal feedback of test results upon learning. *Journal of Educational Research, 66*, 119–121.

Wlodkowski RJ. (1985). *Enhancing adult motivation to learn.* San Francisco: Jossey-Bass.

Woodrow H. (1927). The effect of type of training upon transference. *Journal of Educational Psychology, 18*, 159–172.

[14]

PERSONNEL PSYCHOLOGY
1991, 44

THE PERILS OF PARTICIPATION: EFFECTS OF CHOICE OF TRAINING ON TRAINEE MOTIVATION AND LEARNING

TIMOTHY T. BALDWIN, RICHARD J. MAGJUKA
School of Business, Department of Management
Indiana University

BRIAN T. LOHER
Mansfield University

This study presents an empirical test of the effects of trainee choice of training on subsequent motivation and learning. 207 trainees were randomly assigned to one of three conditions: (a) no choice of training; (b) choice of training—but choice not received; (c) choice of training—with choice received. A pilot study was used to create a unique training context whereby trainees could be differentiated on the three conditions of choice, while all ultimately received the identical training module. Results indicated that, after controlling for cognitive ability, those trainees having a choice of training did have greater motivation to learn, provided they were ultimately given the training of their choice. On the other hand, trainees allowed to choose but whose choice was not the training module subsequently delivered were less motivated and learned less than those not asked to participate in the choice of training at all. These findings suggest that, in an organizational training context, there may be some "perils of participation." Implications for future research and practice are discussed.

Considerable evidence in the behavioral sciences literature suggests that both ability and motivation are important influences on individual performance (Porter & Lawler, 1968). Consistent with this, the notion that "trainability" is a function of an individual's ability and motivation to learn is widely accepted among researchers and practitioners in education and training (Goldstein, 1986). Although the exact nature of the relationship between ability and motivation has not been firmly established (Dunnette. 1972), few would question Maier's (1973) assertion that even if individuals possess the prerequisite ability to learn the content of a course, performance will likely be poor if motivation is low or

---

A previous draft of this manuscript was presented at the Fifth Annual Conference of the Society for Industrial & Organizational Psychology, Miami Beach Florida, April 20–22, 1990.

All authors contributed equally.

Correspondence and requests for reprints should be addressed to Timothy T. Baldwin, Indiana University, School of Business, Department of Management, 2729 Glen Ellen Drive. Bloomington, IN 47404.

absent. Consequently, researchers and program designers alike have a vested interest in understanding motivation in training contexts.

As Noe (1986) points out, the ability component of trainability has received the vast majority of literature attention. Most investigators concerned with the trainability issue have focused on trainee ability levels as the primary variable of interest (Gordon & Cohen, 1973; Siegel & Ruh, 1973). This focus on ability has evolved despite a recurring lament of management trainers that their trainees generally have ample ability to learn course content, but often lack sufficient motivation to learn. Such perceptions would seem to be a strong stimulus for more concerted research attention and the development and evaluation of motivation enhancing interventions.

One recurring prescription for enhancing motivation to learn is to have trainees participate in the assessment stage of the training process (Newstrom & Lilyquist, 1979; Oppenheimer, 1982; Wlodkowski, 1985). Adult learning theorists (Knowles, 1984; Scheer, 1979) posit that because adults will learn only what they feel a desire to learn, involvement in the selection of training is potentially a potent motivator. Unfortunately, empirical evidence in support of the notion that trainee involvement enhances motivation and learning is sparse. In fact, the prescription to involve trainees in the assessment process is nearly always based on insufficient evidence, ranging from anecdotes derived from personal experiences to results of opinion surveys. Nonetheless, the notion that trainee participation in the needs assessment phase may lead to positive training outcomes is an intriguing one. Participation has been shown to be an effective strategy for enhancing commitment to decisions in other human resource activities (e.g., Schweiger & Leana, 1986; Silverman & Wexley, 1984; Vroom & Jago, 1988), although the results are by no means unequivocal (Locke & Schweiger, 1979).

In one of the only empirical research investigations of participatory processes in the training literature, Hicks and Klimoski (1987) found that those trainees who perceived they had a high degree of freedom to attend training reported more favorable post-training reactions and had higher achievement scores than those who perceived they had little freedom in their choice to attend. As the authors note, those findings are consistent with the work of Salancik (1977) and others, suggesting that increased commitment occurs under conditions of participation and choice.

However, because participation represents a multidimensional construct, considerably more research is needed before we can conclude that it invariably works as a strategy to improve training outcomes. As several authors have recently noted, participation can take a variety of different forms and could take place at any of several points in the training assessment process (Cotton, Vollrath, Froggatt, Lengnick-Hall, & Jennings,

1988; Schweiger & Leana, 1986). Further, aside from variance regarding the provision of choice, it is also clear that the trainer or organizational response to trainee choice may vary. We contend that the organizational response to provisions of choice, as much as the provision itself, will have significant effects on training outcomes.

Because a common training needs assessment strategy is to solicit trainee input on the training programs they would like to attend (Wexley & Latham, 1981), the form of participation explored here was the nature of the choice that trainees have regarding the training they receive. That is, the "choice" of interest in the present study concerns the selection of training content, rather than simply the choice to attend training in general. Figure 1 presents a straightforward conception of how trainee choice may be linked to motivation to learn and to subsequent training outcomes, such as reactions and learning.

As the figure illustrates, provisions for trainee choice may or may not be present. This varies across organizations and even across training programs within an organization. Further, in organizational settings, the provision of choice does not imply that everyone receives their choice. In fact, organizations differ widely on the degree to which trainee choice is ultimately reflected in the training programs provided (Wexley & Latham, 1981). While the existing literature has generally treated *choice* and *choice-accepted* as synonymous conditions, we posit that they are distinctly different and are likely to lead to different pre-training attitudes and training outcomes.

The notion that differences in the nature of trainee choice and subsequent reception (or rejection) of that choice may lead to different outcomes is consistent with the conceptual and empirical work on procedural justice (Folger & Greenberg, 1985; Greenberg & Folger, 1983). One central premise of the procedural justice literature is known as the "fair process effect." That is, people are more apt to accept decisions and their consequences if they have participated in making them (Folger, Rosenfield, Grove, & Corkran, 1979). However, authors in the area of procedural justice have also discussed the limiting conditions of the fair process effect and have concluded that the provision of choice will *not* always enhance satisfaction with decision outcomes.

One particular case where a participatory process (choice) may not lead to favorable outcomes is what Folger et al. (1979) labeled the "frustration effect." The frustration effect refers to the possibility that the provision of choice may raise expectations; expectations which, if the choice is not accepted, will be dashed. The result is that individuals whose choice is not accepted may be potentially less satisfied with subsequent outcomes than those not even given a choice at all (a mute group).

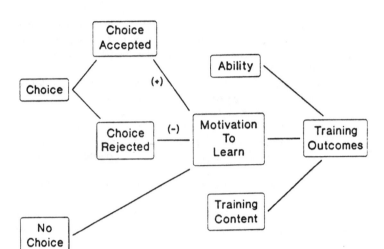

Figure 1: **A Model of Trainee Choice in the Training Process**

From an organizational training perspective, this possibility has significant implications. For example, if alternative training choices are offered and are viewed by trainees as viable, then surely there will be trainees who do not receive what they choose. In a given situation, it is even possible that a majority of trainees will not receive what they choose. The result might be lower trainee motivation than if an administrator had not provided a choice at all. Empirical research is needed that directly tests whether the frustration effect does, in fact, extend to outcomes associated with participation in training needs assessment and, most importantly, to objective training measures, such as program learning.

The purpose of the present investigation was to empirically examine the effects of trainee choice and the response (or lack thereof) to that choice on pre-training attitudes and training outcomes. Specifically, we were interested in exploring whether being given a choice of training content and actually getting that choice would enhance pre-training motivation and post-training attitudes and learning. Based on the previous literature, which has consistently associated participation with higher levels of motivation (Wagner & Gooding, 1987), it was anticipated that trainees receiving their choice of training would have higher pre-training motivation to learn.

TIMOTHY T. BALDWIN ET AL.   55

On the other hand, based on the conceptual work in support of the frustration effect, it was expected that trainees given a choice but not receiving that choice would have lower levels of pre-training motivation. Furthermore, based on recent research that has found a significant relationship between pre-training motivation and positive post-training outcomes (Baldwin & Karl, 1987), it was expected that trainees receiving their choice of training would have more positive reactions to training and higher levels of learning.

Method

Training Program and Participants

Given the increasing demand for skills-based training and managerial competencies, a practical, skills-based training program on performance appraisal and feedback was created and served as the setting for this research. The program was adapted from a major corporate training provider and was offered as an opportunity for participants to attend a professional seminar (at no cost) that would focus on practical business skills. Trainees enrolled with the knowledge that the training would be an approximately 2-hour, skill-based module and would be similar to the type of managerial training typically conducted for employees in major corporations. No specific content was identified in order to allow for the manipulation of choice described below. The program was delivered on the campuses of Indiana University on nine different occasions. The number of trainees who subsequently completed the training was 242. The trainee pool was quite diverse and included traditional full-time students, full-time working people attending class part-time, and adult education participants. The age of trainees ranged from 20 to 42 and 119 of the trainees were female. Measures of cognitive aptitude and socioeconomic status indicated considerable variance in the ability and backgrounds of the trainees.

Design and Procedure

To examine the impact of trainee choice on pre-training motivation and training outcomes, a controlled experiment was created where (a) trainee ability could be measured and statistically controlled and (b) the trainees would differ on the type of choice they had prior to training, but would ultimately receive an identical training stimulus. This was done to avoid confounds associated with different training stimuli and/or different levels of ability, which would make the isolation of participation effects impossible. Results of a pilot study were used to create such a controlled experimental situation in the manner described below.

At the beginning of the experimental session, one group of trainees (*choice-not-received*) was given a list of titles and descriptions of four modules they might choose to attend. The trainees were asked to rank-order the topics, beginning with the training module that they most preferred. Based on a pilot study where individuals (similar to those participating in the study in all respects) rank-ordered 30 potential training modules, the list of four modules included three modules that were highly ranked by pilot participants and one average-ranked module. The average-ranked module was entitled "performance appraisal" and was the training program actually developed and administered in the study. Given their options, it was our a priori expectation that the majority of trainees in the first condition would *not* choose performance appraisal as their most desired topic and would therefore represent a condition of having choice but not receiving that choice. In fact, consistent with our pilot data, only 11% ($n = 6$) of this group chose performance appraisal as their most preferred training module.

A second group of trainees (*choice-received*) was given a different list and description of four possible training modules. The second group's list consisted of three modules that were ranked very low by pilot participants and the same average-rated module, performance appraisal. The ranking procedure was identical and it was our a priori expectation that the majority of trainees *would* choose performance appraisal as the most desirable module. In fact, again consistent with the pilot data, 86% ($n = 73$) of this group did choose performance appraisal. The fact that most, but clearly not all, chose performance appraisal indicates that the choice was a reasonable one and that the alternative modules were not so undesirable as to make the choice artificial. Finally, a third group (*no-choice*) was simply told that they would be attending a training module on performance appraisal.

While the conditions of choice are described independently above, assignment to condition was random and both choice-received and choice-not-received conditions were always manipulated within the same training session. This was accomplished by using identical looking forms for both choice-received and choice-not-received, but then randomly distributing them in the stack handed out prior to the session. This was done in order to eliminate any concern regarding potential differences in the training stimulus used in different sessions. Hence, even had randomness not been maintained in the session assignment, trainees would have been divided into the two groups within the session.

The dissimilar sample sizes in the conditions (most prominently a lower number in choice-not-received) were created as a consequence of our procedure for realistically simulating the choice-not-received condition. First, majority vote was used as our mechanism for creating choice-not-received. This was supported by evidence from a similar group of trainees who indicated that majority rule would be the fairest and most appropriate way to select training content, given a number of different preferences. Using a majority rule procedure, in conjunction with our pilot data predictive of how people would choose, allowed us to structure the sessions in a way that insured more choice-received people would be in each session than choice-not-received. This allowed us to legitimately convey that the majority of people in each training session got what they most preferred (remember that both conditions were represented in each training session). Therefore, at no time were any trainees given false feedback; that is, those who did not receive their choice were in the minority and were truly outvoted. What they did not know was that their list of options differed from the majority group. It was our judgment that this created a realistic, normatively consistent, and also minimally deceptive way to create the controlled conditions required to test propositions regarding the effects of choice on training outcomes.

To summarize, three conditions were created to which trainees were randomly assigned: (a) no choice; (b) choice—but choice not received; and (c) choice—with choice received. Trainees in the no-choice condition represented those who were simply given training with no participative input. In the choice-not-received condition, trainees were asked to evaluate some modules and make a choice, but were not given the training module they requested. Finally, trainees in the choice-received condition were provided the opportunity to evaluate some modules and make a choice, and then actually did receive their choice preference. Because no distinction was made on the magnitude of the distance from top rank (e.g., between those who put performance appraisal second vs. those who put it third), the manipulation represented a particularly conservative test of the effects of choice on training outcomes.

To control for ability, all trainees completed a measure of general cognitive ability. The topic for the training was then presented. In the two choice conditions, the announcement was portrayed as the result of a tabulation of trainee rankings. The trainees completed the pre-training motivation measure and then attended the instructional module on performance appraisal. At the end of the module, several outcome measures were administered.

58   PERSONNEL PSYCHOLOGY

Measures

Cognitive ability. General cognitive ability was assessed with the revised form of the Wonderlic personnel test (Wonderlic, 1985). The Wonderlic is a 12-minute timed test, with items of increasing difficulty.

Pre-training motivation. A 7-item scale adapted from previous research (Baldwin & Karl, 1987; Noe, 1986; Ryman & Biersner, 1982) was used to measure trainee motivation prior to the start of training. Trainees were asked to indicate on a 5-point scale the extent to which they agreed or disagreed with each of the seven items. Example items included "I am willing to exert considerable effort in learning this module" and "I will try to learn as much as I can in this module."

Post-training motivation. Post-training motivation was measured by repeating the items from the pre-training motivation scale. The items were rephrased slightly to assess trainees' perceptions following the training (e.g., "I exerted considerable effort in learning this module" and "I tried to learn as much as I could in this module"). Response scales were identical to those used on the pre-training motivation measure.

Learning measures. Trainee learning was evaluated through the use of two learning measures. The instructional videotape presented 12 key points and several other issues that pertained to the effective conduct of performance appraisals. For the first learning measure, denoted *open-ended learning*, trainees were asked to identify and describe as many of the 12 learning points as possible. Responses were scored as 0 (incorrect), 1 (partially correct), or 2 (fully correct). The open-ended measure was designed to assess trainee ability to recall and reiterate the program learning points.

The second learning measure, denoted *short-answer learning*, asked trainees to provide responses to more general information presented in the module (e.g., "Explain the importance of asking for employee input on past performance and future goals"). The four short-answer items were scored in the same manner as the open-ended items, but were designed to assess a greater level of trainee understanding of the program content.

Both learning measures were adapted from the manual accompanying the training module provided by the training firm. Scoring of both the open-ended and short-answer measures was done by a trained graduate student using a detailed key that included examples of typical trainee responses and appropriate scoring. To allow for the assessment of reliability, a subset ($n = 60$, approximately 25%) of both learning measures was scored by a second trained graduate student. Percentage of interrater agreement was 90% for the open-ended measure and 89% for the short-answer.

Results

Results presented are for those trainees who met the a priori criteria established for each of the three conditions: (a) all trainees in the no-choice condition, (b) those trainees in the choice-not-received condition who did not rank performance appraisal as their top choice, and (c) those trainees in the choice-received condition who did rank performance appraisal as their training module of choice. Trainees who did not meet the required conditions ($n = 18$) and some incomplete data dropped the sample size to 207 for the comparative analyses.

Means, standard deviations, and zero-order correlations among the variables across choice conditions are presented in Table 1. Scores on the cognitive ability measure were significantly correlated with performance on the learning measures. This made it appropriate to control for cognitive ability across trainees when evaluating training outcomes. Pre-training motivation was positively associated with the number of key learning points recalled on the open-ended measure ($r = .20, p < .01$). Appropriate responses on the open-ended measure correlated with the number of correct responses on the short-answer outcome measure ($r = .36, p < .01$).

Table 2 presents the adjusted cell means and standard deviations for pre-training motivation and the two learning measures, after controlling for cognitive ability. Inspection of the adjusted means suggests that average pre-training motivation was highest within the choice-received condition and lowest among those whose choice was not received. Mean performance on the learning measures appeared to favor the no-choice condition.

MANCOVA (Multivariate Analysis of CoVariance) was used to examine the significance of the apparent differences across conditions. The independent variable was the condition of choice (i.e., choice-received, choice-not-received, no-choice). Cognitive ability scores were treated as a covariate. Due to their redundancy with other measures, post-training motivation and the outcome composite are not included in the description of the MANCOVA results.

The overall multivariate test was significant [Pillais $F(6, 404) = 2.80$, $p < .01$]. The overall univariate tests are reported in the first portion of Table 3. The results indicate that the condition of choice had an impact on pre-training motivation and performance on one of the learning measures. Orthogonal contrasts between the choice conditions were conducted to further explore the nature of the observed differences. The first contrast compared the no-choice and choice-received conditions. The second contrast compared the choice-not-received group with the

TABLE 1

Means, Standard Deviations, and Zero-Order Correlations

Variable	M	SD	1	2	3	4	5
1. Cognitive ability	25.76	4.66	—				
2. Pre-training motivation	3.36	0.57	00	(81)			
3. Post-training motivation	3.33	0.69	07	51**	(86)		
4. Open-ended learning	14.21	4.38	13*	20**	24**	(90)	
5. Short-answer learning	3.57	1.58	18**	01	15*	36**	(89)

Note: Correlation matrix decimals ommitted to conserve space. Reliability coefficients for measures presented in diagonals.

*p<.05;   **p<.01

TABLE 2

Adjusted Cell Means and Standard Deviations

Condition	N	Pre-training motivation	Open-ended learning	Short-answer learning
No-choice	84	3.31 (0.52)	14.69 (4.43)	3.90 (1.46)
Choice-received	73	3.51 (0.64)	14.28 (4.45)	3.45 (1.71)
Choice-not-received	50	3.23 (0.53)	13.74 (4.27)	3.12 (1.55)

Note: Standard deviations presented in parentheses.

TABLE 3

Univariate ANCOVA Results Controlling for Cognitive Ability

Dependent variable	F	df	p
Overall			
Pre-training motivation	4.21	2/203	.02
Open-ended learning	0.73	2/203	ns
Short-answer learning	4.12	2/203	.02
Contrast 1 (No-choice vs. Choice-received)			
Pre-training motivation	4.42	1/203	.04
Open-ended learning	0.39	1/203	ns
Short-answer learning	3.45	1/203	.07
Contrast 2 (Choice-not-received vs. No-choice and Choice-received)			
Pre-training motivation	4.01	1/203	.05
Open-ended learning	1.08	1/203	ns
Short-answer learning	4.78	1/203	.03

Note: df = degrees of freedom.

average of the other conditions. The objective was to isolate any dysfunctional effects of allowing a choice but not subsequently responding to that choice. Results are presented in Table 3. Pre-training motivation was significantly higher among individuals who were allowed to choose and whose choice was accepted compared with the no-choice condition $[F(1, 203) = 4.42, p < .05]$. On one of the outcome measures, learning was marginally higher within the no-choice condition versus those whose choice was accepted $[F(1, 203) = 3.45, p < .07]$. Learning was significantly lower on the same outcome measure when the chosen training topic was not received $[F(1, 203) = 4.78, p < .03]$.

Discussion

What stands out most from the results of the present study are the significant effects of the provision of choice and subsequent reception or rejection of that choice on trainee motivation to learn and learning outcomes. More specifically, trainees who received their choice had a higher level of motivation to learn prior to entering the training session than those who were not provided a choice or made a choice which they did not receive. On the other hand, not receiving one's choice was associated with a significantly lower motivation to learn and learning outcomes. Therefore, this study lends empirical support to the notion that motivation to learn can be enhanced by providing trainees with choices of training content, but only under the condition that they ultimately receive the training they choose. Interestingly, while the higher motivation in the choice-received condition was expected to be a precursor to higher learning, in this study, there were no significant differences in learning between those who received their choice and those not given any choice.

The positive effect found for the choice-received condition is consistent with previous theoretical and empirical work (Deci, 1980; Hicks & Klimoski, 1987; Salancik, 1977). Intrinsic motivation theory, for example, suggests that offering a choice among alternative outcomes is a crucial mechanism for increasing feelings of mastery and self-determination (Deci, 1980). In fact, the notion that choice is inherently a "good" thing is a pervasive one and the results of the present study suggest that it can be good in training contexts as well.

Given the widespread acceptance of choice as a positive element, however, perhaps the most provocative finding of the present study is that which suggests that there is a potential risk involved in affording choice in a training context. That is, when trainees made a choice but did not receive their choice, there was a significant decline in their motivation to learn and in their subsequent learning. This finding is consistent with Folger et al.'s (1979) notion of a frustration effect and also with Brehm's (1972) notion of psychological reactance. It may also be attributed to trainees' perception that their own preferences were out of line with others, which subsequently detracted from their performance in the training. In any event, this finding is consistent with results of research on organizational development interventions. Researchers have found that individuals who are asked to participate in the data gathering stage of an intervention, but whose information and suggestions are not incorporated into the final product, are subsequently less committed to the program (Huse & Cummings, 1985). It should be noted, however, that the findings of the present study suggest that the impact of frustration and reactance effects may go beyond attitudinal change and also influence more objective measures of program learning and training achievement.

The discussion above highlights what we think is a crucial issue regarding the use of choice as a motivational strategy in training contexts. As Folger & Greenberg (1985) point out, asking people what they want and then letting them have their desired choice is closely related to having people choose their own outcomes in the first place. When participation comes in the form of choice, the key question is whether the act of providing a choice produces any *incremental* motivation or learning over and above that produced by the desired outcome itself. While many writers and researchers have implicitly or explicitly endorsed the act of providing choice as an effective strategy in a variety of contexts, the present results suggest that positive outcomes of choice in training are contingent on reception of that choice.

From an organizational training perspective, then, choice may be a good thing only when trainee choice is ultimately reflected in the training received. As discussed earlier, in organizational settings, the provision of choice in no way implies that everyone receives their choice. This reflects a sharp distinction between the conception of choice embedded in the research literature and the daily practice of organizational training. In the research literature, choice is almost universally treated synonymously with choice-received. In practice, however, constraints on organization resources and competitive necessities often result in organizations not guaranteeing to their membership that they will receive whatever option is selected. Instead, when members are allowed to participate, a key stage is that they analyze alternatives and in some way communicate their preferences to others. Once preferences are known, someone who is responsible for a final decision adopts a decision rule and selects an alternative.

Perhaps the most important implication of this study is that it highlights what might be called the "perils of participation." As noted earlier, if alternative training choices are offered and are viewed by trainees as viable, then surely there will be trainees (perhaps even a majority) who do not receive what they choose. The present results suggest that such a scenario could perhaps result in lower motivation and poorer training outcomes than if an administrator had not provided a choice at all. It therefore appears that the relationship of choice to training outcomes is a complex one and contingent on the level of analysis; that is, providing choice of training may be a functional strategy at the individual level (where reception of choice can be insured), but may be a potentially dysfunctional strategy at the organizational level (where multiple choices and resource constraints prohibit universal choice reception).

Therefore, when administrators provide trainees a choice and ensure that they receive their choice, then affording choice may increase trainee motivation to learn and, perhaps, subsequent learning. This strategy would seem to be especially appropriate for those administering management development programs where there is not a clear organizational preference for trainees to learn one particular training module versus another (e.g., effective writing skills vs. effective listening skills). However, in this study, when trainees had no choice their learning scores were linked, not surprisingly, to the degree to which the training session motivated them to learn. This suggests that when the provision of choice is bypassed, an administrator can still induce learning, but that learning will be significantly more dependent on the effectiveness of the training session itself. Of course, this finding leaves unanswered for training administrators difficult questions concerning how to identify, develop, and select effective instructional programs that will motivate trainees to learn desired skills.

While the controlled experimental design was required here to allow isolation of choice effects and the elimination of confounds, as with any controlled experiment, some caution is warranted in generalizing these results to other training contexts. For example, many organizations offer a range of voluntary training opportunities, which presumably vary in attractiveness among employees. In such a case, it might be unlikely that trainees would be confronted with the type of choice rejection situation confronted here. In addition, it may be that individuals develop expectations based on their position. For example, managers may be given discretion in course selection, while nonmanagers may have few opportunities to exercise choice. This might mean that for those employees who are quite accustomed to not getting what they request, there would be a less pronounced frustration effect than that observed here.

On the other hand, the effects for choice may be more dramatic in other organizational training contexts. For example, while the training program in this study directly simulated organizational practice, the choice stimulus was relatively modest. Future research should examine the effects of choice when the professional and organizational stakes are greater and, therefore, the consequences of receiving or not receiving one's choice are heightened. Examples include studying the aggregate effects of choice on pre-training motivation and subsequent performance when (a) participants are required to exert greater effort and spend considerably more time prior to making a choice, (b) participants receive their training via varying conditions of procedural justice, and (c) trainees are accountable to others for ensuring successful performance in a program once selected. In terms of the results reported in this paper, we believe that by increasing the stakes, the effects of choice (particularly not receiving one's choice) may be even stronger. In addition, the contribution of trainee choice in relation to other training enhancement strategies, such as goal setting and accountability (cf., Wexley & Baldwin, 1986), warrants further investigation.

REFERENCES

Baldwin TT, Karl K. (1987, August). *The development and empirical test of a measure for assessing motivation to learn in management education*. Paper presented at the 47th Annual Meeting of the National Academy of Management, New Orleans, LA.

Brehm J. (1972). *Responses to loss of freedom: A theory of psychological reactance*. New York: General Learning Press.

Cotton JL, Vollrath DA, Froggatt DA, Lengnick-Hall ML, Jennings KR. (1988). Employee participation: Diverse forms and different outcomes. *Academy of Management Review, 13*, 8–22.

Deci EL. (1980). *The psychology of self-determination*. Lexington, MA: Heath Publishers.

Dunnette MD. (1972). *Performance equals ability and what?* (Technical Report 4009; ONR Contract # N00014-68-A-0141). Minneapolis: University of Minnesota, Center for the Study of Organizational Performance and Human Effectiveness.

Folger R, Greenberg J. (1985). Procedural justice: An interpretive analysis of personnel systems. In Rowland K, Ferris G (Eds.), *Research in Personnel & Human Resource Management* (Vol. 3, pp. 141–183). Greenwich, CT: JAI Press.

Folger R, Rosenfield D, Grove J, Corkran L. (1979). Effects of voice and peer opinions on responses to inequity. *Journal of Personality and Social Psychology, 37*, 2253–2261.

Goldstein IL. (1986). *Training in organizations: Needs assessment, development, and evaluation* (2nd edition). Monterey, CA: Brooks/Cole.

Gordon ME, Cohen SL. (1973). Training behavior as a predictor of trainability. PERSONNEL PSYCHOLOGY, *26*, 261–272.

Greenberg J, Folger R. (1983). Procedural justice, participation, and the fair process effect in groups and organizations. In Paulas PB, *Basic Group Processes* (pp. 235–256). New York: Springer-Verlag.

Hicks WD, Klimoski RJ. (1987). Entry into training programs and its effects on training outcomes: A field experiment. *Academy of Management Journal, 30*, 542–552.

Huse EF, Cummings TG. (1985). *Organization development and change*. St. Paul, MN: West Publishing Company.

Knowles M. (1984). *The adult learner: A neglected species*. Houston: Gulf Publishing.

Locke EA, Schweiger DM. (1979). Participation in decision-making: One more look. In Staw BM (Ed.), *Research in Organizational Behavior* (Vol. 1, pp. 265–339). Greenwich, CT: JAI Press.

Maier NRF. (1973). *Psychology in industrial organizations*. Boston: Houghton-Mifflin.

Newstrom JW, Lilyquist JM. (1979). Selecting needs analysis methods. *Training and Development Journal, 33*(10), 52–56.

Noe RA. (1986). Trainees' attributes and attitudes: Neglected influences on training effectiveness. *Academy of Management Review, 11*, 736–749.

Oppenheimer RJ. (1982). An alternative approach to assessing management development needs. *Training and Development Journal, 36*(3), 72–76.

Porter LW, Lawler EE. (1968). *Managerial attitudes and performance*. Homewood, IL: Irwin.

Ryman DH, Biersner RJ. (1975). Attitudes predictive of diving training success. PERSONNEL PSYCHOLOGY, *28*, 181–188.

Salancik GR. (1977). Commitment and the control of organizational behavior and belief. In Staw BM, Salancik GR (Eds.), *New directions in organizational behavior* (pp. 1–54). Chicago: St. Clair Press.

Scheer W. (1979). *Personnel Administration Handbook* (2nd ed.). Chicago: The Dartness Corp.

Schweiger DM, Leana CR. (1986). Participation in decision making. In Locke EA (Ed.), *Generalizing from laboratory to field settings* (pp. 147–166). Lexington, MA: Lexington Books.

Siegel AL, Ruh RA. (1973). Job involvement, participation in decision making, personal background and job behavior. *Organizational Behavior and Human Performance, 9*, 318–327.

Silverman SB, Wexley KN. (1984). Reaction of employees to performance appraisal interviews as a function of their participation in rating scale development. PERSONNEL PSYCHOLOGY, *37*, 703–710.

Vroom VH, Jago AG. (1988). *The new leadership: Managing participation in organizations*. Englewood Cliffs, NJ: Prentice-Hall.

Wagner JA III, Gooding RZ. (1987). Shared influence and organizational behavior: A meta-analysis of situational variables expected to moderate participation-outcome relationships. *Academy of Management Journal, 30*, 524–541.

Wexley KN, Baldwin TT. (1986). Post-training strategies for facilitating positive transfer: An empirical exploration. *Academy of Management Journal, 29*, 503–520.

Wexley KN, Latham GP. (1981). *Developing and training human resources in organizations*. Glenview, IL: Scott-Foresman & Co.

Wlodkowski RJ. (1985). *Enhancing adult motivation to learn*. San Francisco: Jossey-Bass.

Wonderlic CF. (1985). *Revised form of the Wonderlic Personnel Test*. Northfield, IL: E.F. Wonderlic, Inc.

Part VI
The Effects of Training

Part VI
The Effect of Training

[15]

Why Do Wages Increase with Tenure? On-the-Job Training and Life-Cycle Wage Growth Observed Within Firms

By JAMES N. BROWN*

Empirical results in this paper indicate that firm-specific wage growth occurs almost exclusively during periods of on-the-job training. This finding suggests that within-firm wage growth is mainly determined by contemporaneous productivity growth. The results provide no evidence that contractual considerations are an important source of firm-specific wage growth.

When an expensive machine is erected, the extraordinary work to be performed by it before it is worn out, it must be expected, will replace the capital laid out upon it, with at least the ordinary profits. A man educated at the expense of much labor and time to any of those employments which require extraordinary dexterity and skill, may be compared to one of those expensive machines. The work which he learns to perform, it must be expected, over and above the usual wages of common labor, will replace to him the whole expense of his education, with at least the ordinary profits of an equally valuable capital. [Adam Smith, 1776]

Nearly 200 years after Adam Smith's original statement, the "human capital" model of earnings was extended in the work of Milton Friedman and Simon Kuznets (1945), Jacob Mincer (1958, 1962, 1974), Theodore W. Schultz (1960, 1961), and Gary S. Becker 1962, 1964). This work views "point-in-time" earnings differences within the broader context of life-cycle earnings and wage profiles. It explains the concave pattern of life-cycle earnings and wages as reflecting a similar pattern in life-cycle productivity, deriving from optimal investments that diminish

gradually over the life cycle. Much of this work, especially that dealing with firm-specific skills and labor turnover, emphasizes factors other than contemporaneous productivity in explaining earnings and wage profiles. In all this work, however, an understanding of life-cycle productivity profiles is essential to an understanding of life-cycle earnings and wage growth.

In contrast, more recent theoretical work has sought to explain life-cycle wage growth without appealing to contemporaneous life-cycle productivity growth. In an initial paper, Becker and George J. Stigler (1974) showed why it might be sensible for firms to separate the payment of workers from their output as a way to keep workers from shirking, and this theme has since been developed by several authors. A related explanation was developed by Joanne Salop and Steven Salop (1976), who showed that rising wage profiles may serve as a self-selection device to discourage potential "movers" from seeking employment. Another explanation was developed by Boyan Jovanovic (1979), who demonstrated that elementary models of job-matching under imperfect information can also generate the upward-sloping concave wage profiles implied by simple human capital models.[1]

Despite the growing number of theories, however, the body of empirical work aimed

*Department of Economics, State University of New York, Stony Brook, NY 11794. I have benefited from comments made by participants in seminars at the University of Chicago, Princeton University, MIT, Columbia University, the University of Western Ontario, McMaster University, and SUNY Stony Brook. I thank Jacob Mincer for many stimulating discussions and helpful suggestions. Any errors are mine.

[1] These citations are by no means exhaustive. Other early work in this area includes that of S. J. Nickell (1976), Smith Freeman (1977), Michael Rothschild and Joseph E. Stiglitz (1976), Edward P. Lazear (1979, 1981), Milton Harris and Bengt Holmstrom (1982), and Louis Guasch and Andrew Weiss (1982).

at testing the human capital model against these alternatives is still quite limited.[2] The relative paucity of such work is somewhat surprising, given the potential for simple tests based on (partial) correlations between wages, tenure, and some indicator of productivity. Indeed, Mincer suggested such a test as early as 1974, when he observed that the human capital model might be contradicted by the data, if it could be shown that earnings growth was largely independent of productivity growth.

Such a test was implemented by James L. Medoff and Abraham (1980, 1981), who found no statistically significant correlation between wage growth and ordinal performance rankings among professional and managerial workers in a small number of U.S. corporations. From this finding, Medoff and Abraham concluded that human capital may play only a minor role in explaining the generally observed positive relation between earnings and labor market experience:

> Despite the straightforward nature of the test required to establish the superiority of the human capital explanation of the experience-earnings profile over alternative models in which factors other than productivity growth determine earnings growth, no one has ever provided evidence which demonstrates that experience-earnings differentials can in fact be explained by experience-productivity differentials (Medoff and Abraham, 1981, p. 187).

Given the limited empirical work that has addressed this issue, it is reasonable to look for additional evidence bearing on the importance of productivity versus other factors in explaining wage growth. This paper examines some additional evidence contained in the Panel Survey of Income Dynamics, which in Waves 9 (1976) and 11 (1978) asked respondents the following question:

($Q1$) "On a job like yours, how long would it take the average new person to become fully trained and qualified?"[3]

Using answers to this question with corresponding information on job tenure, it is possible to estimate the contemporaneous effect of training on wages, as distinct from the effects of tenure or experience. Although these estimates do not provide a direct test of productivity versus other factors in explaining wage growth, they do allow an indirect test that can be of value in judging the potential importance of alternative models in explaining the data.

To elaborate, if contemporaneous productivity growth is important in shaping wage profiles, some extra wage growth should be observed during periods when the "average new person" is becoming fully trained and qualified. Without some correlation between wage growth and training, it would be difficult to argue that productivity growth is an important determinant of contemporaneous wage growth, and there would certainly be no compelling empirical reason to make this case.[4] Similarly, if purely "contractual" factors are essential in explaining wage profiles, the data should display some firm-specific

---

[2] Recent papers by Robert C. Marshall and Gary A. Zarkin (1987), Joseph G. Altonji and Robert A. Shakotko (1987), Katharine G. Abraham and Henry S. Farber (1987), and Robert Topel (1986) find that firm-specific tenure accounts for only a small component of life-cycle wage growth. This finding suggests that "contractual" factors, which are inherently firm-specific, may be unimportant in explaining within-firm wage profiles. More recent work by Topel (1987) finds substantial effects of tenure, however. In addition, as noted by Topel in his more recent work, "Tenure only measures time in a particular job, and may be only remotely related to the relevant concept of human capital." Thus, the role of productivity versus other factors in determining wage growth remains at issue.

[3] This question was also included in Wave 18 (1985) of the PSID, which became available after this work was completed. For other work based on this question, see Greg J. Duncan and Saul Hoffman (1979), Harvey S. Rosen (1982), James N. Brown (1983), and Mincer (1988).

[4] Wages could still be tied to productivity in a longer-run sense, of course, and models that emphasize productivity could still be of value in understanding cross-sectional differences in lifetime wealth.

VOL. 79 NO. 5   *BROWN: WHY DO WAGES INCREASE WITH TENURE?*   973

wage growth that occurs independently of training. Without such wage growth, it would be difficult to argue that purely contractual factors are important in shaping wage profiles, and there would be no great empirical payoff from modeling such effects.

The following sections apply this reasoning in evaluating the relative importance of productivity and other factors in explaining wage growth. Section I develops the estimating framework used in the empirical analysis. Section II describes the data. Section III presents the estimates and discusses their implications. Section IV concludes with a brief summary of the major findings.

I. A Framework for Measurement

Suppose that skills grow continuously at a constant proportional rate during each year of on-the-job training, and that wages rise in proportion to skills.[5] Ignoring error terms, these assumptions imply that at time t, for an individual with H_{it} years of training in a given job,

$$(1) \qquad W_{it} = wS_{i0}e^{rH_{it}}$$

or, equivalently, that

$$(2) \qquad \log(W_{it}) = \log(wS_{i0}) + rH_{it},$$

where W_{it} denotes the ith individual's wage, S_{i0} denotes the individual's (unobservable) stock of skills upon entry into the current job, w denotes the proportionality factor between wages and skills, H_{it} denotes years of training in the current job, and r denotes the proportional rate by which skills (and wages) increase with additional years of training in the current job.

Assuming that training occurs at a full-time rate during the first R_i years of tenure in a given job and becomes zero thereafter,

---

[5] This formulation assumes that general and specific skills are rewarded equally within the firm. This framework could easily be extended to allow for a distinction between general and specific skills, but the data studied here allow no such distinction to be made empirically.

the variable H_{it} will be equal to tenure in the current job whenever training is in progress, and will be equal to R_i when training is complete. In this case, letting τ_{it} denote tenure and D_{it} denote an indicator equal to unity when τ_{it} is less than R_i, equation (2) becomes:

$$(3) \quad \log(W_{it}) = \log(wS_{i0}) \\ + r\left[D_{it}\tau_{it} + (1 - D_{it})R_i\right],$$

which implies that (log) wages will increase within jobs according to a linear spline function, with a kink at R_i years of tenure in the current job.

The assumptions embodied in (3) are likely to be more restrictive than the data warrant, but these assumptions can be easily relaxed. If skills grow at a variable rate during training, or if wages grow at a variable rate with skills, a nonlinear relation between $\log(W_{it})$ and H_{it} can be substituted for the linear version in (3). If the returns to training occur in a lump-sum fashion, the last term in (3) can be estimated in an unrestricted fashion to allow a discrete jump in wages when training is complete. If aggregate effects are present in the data, measures that control for these effects can be added to (3). Finally, if wage growth depends on tenure for reasons other than skill acquisition, or if skills acquired in previous jobs affect current wages through more than just the additive term S_{i0}, some additional function of tenure or labor market experience can be added to (3) to allow for such effects.

Incorporating these additional considerations, equation (3) becomes:

$$(4) \quad \log(W_{it}) = \log(wS_{i0}) + D_{it}f_1(\tau_{it}) \\ + (1 - D_{it})f_2(R_i) \\ + f_3(\tau_{it}, X_{it}) + \beta Y_t,$$

where the $f_i(\cdot)$ denote as yet unspecified functions, X_{it} denotes total labor market experience, and Y_t denotes a control for aggregate effects. Treating $\log(wS_{i0})$ as an unobserved individual fixed effect, and augmenting (4) with an additive error term that is assumed to be i.i.d. over time and across individuals, equation (4) provides the basic framework for the empirical work that follows.[6]

II. The Data

The estimates that follow are based on a sample of 5,056 observations for 995 heads of households surveyed in waves 9–17 (1976–1984) of the *Michigan Panel Survey of Income Dynamics* (PSID). Observations for this sample were selected primarily on the basis of availability and internal consistency of the data. Respondents in this sample were questioned about the length of time required to complete training in the current position only in the 1976 and 1978 interviews. For other interview years, this information on job training is available only for those respondents who hold the same position as that held during either the 1976 or 1978 interview years. This fact limits the sample available for study, but a sufficient number of respondents remain in their 1976 and 1978 positions long enough to allow construction of a reasonably large, multiyear sample.

Various samples can be constructed, depending on the interview year that serves as the reference point and the manner in which the sample is extended to include additional years. The primary sample used in this study includes the years 1976 through 1984 and contains all available observations from this period that correspond to the respondent's 1976 position. The sample is limited to respondents who remained with their 1976 position during at least 2 interviews, and for whom other relevant information is available. The maximum panel length for any sample member is thus 9 years, while the minimum panel length is 2 years. Table 1 presents summary statistics for this sample, along with definitions of variables used in the following empirical analysis.[7]

As of 1976, the average age for respondents in this sample was 34.5 years. Respondents averaged roughly 11.5 years of schooling, with roughly 15 years of labor force experience. Of this experience, an average of about 9.5 years had been spent with previous employers. Respondents in 1976 averaged slightly more than 5 years of tenure with their current employer, of which they had spent about 3 years in their current position.

The average job in this sample required only a little more than 1 year of training.[8] About 60 percent of respondents in this sample reported values of required training less than or equal to one-half year. Roughly 15 percent of respondents reported values of required training between one-half year and 1 year, 11 percent between 1 and 2 years, and 15 percent in excess of 2 years. Two percent of respondents in this sample reported values of required training in excess of 5 years. As of 1976, one-fourth of respondents held positions for which their current tenure was less than their reported level of required training.

III. Empirical Results

A. *Does Training Generate Wage Growth?*

Table 2 presents estimates from alternative specifications of equation (4). In Table 2, as in all subsequent tables, the dependent variable is the logarithm of the real hourly wage (deflated by the CPI-U). The term wS_{i0} is treated as an individual fixed effect. The $f_i(\cdot)$ functions are assumed to be quadratic, with $f_3(\cdot)$ a general quadratic form in the three components of labor market experience: tenure in the current position, tenure

---

[6]All estimates in this paper are based on a fixed-effect specification. For cross-section estimates based on the same general model, see Brown (1983).

[7]The Appendix to this paper (available from the author upon request) contains an extensive discussion of issues related to the construction of this sample. The Appendix also verifies the robustness of findings discussed below to alternative sampling schemes and econometric specifications.

[8]In the 1976 interview, all respondents who reported training requirements in excess of 8 years were assigned the same code. A few respondents affected by this censoring were excluded from the sample. The following statements regarding required levels of training are conditioned on this restriction.

TABLE 1—SAMPLE MEAN VALUES FOR SELECTED CATEGORICAL VARIABLES

(995) Heads of Households)			
DEMOGRAPHIC:		**1976 JOB:**	
White	0.587	Supervise Others	0.305
Male	0.784	Union Contract	0.358
SEO Subsample	0.450	Required Training <1/2 Year	0.586
OCCUPATION:	Required Training	0.164 >1.2 Year and <1 Year	
Professional and Managerial	0.157	Required Training >1 Year and < 2 Years	0.107
Sales and Clerical	0.173	Required Training > 2 Years and < 5 Years	0.123
Craftsmen and Foreman	0.206	Required Training > 5 Years	0.021
Transport Equipment Operatives	0.063	Required Training >1976 Tenure in Current Position	0.249
Operatives and Nonfarm Labor	0.303	Required Training >1976 Tenure with Current Employer	0.154
Service	0.098		
INDUSTRY[a]		Training Other Than Education Required to get 1976 Job	0.568
Manufacturing	0.411	Learning New Skills on Job (in 1976)	0.752
Construction	0.077	That Could Lead to Better Job or Promotion	
Transportation, Communication, and Public Utilities	0.113	Current Position is First Position with Employer	0.591
Wholesale and Retail Trade	0.155		
Financial, Business, and Personal Service	0.101		
Publishing, Medical, and Education	0.138		
Recreation	0.006		

SUMMARY STATISTICS FOR SELECTED NON-CATEGORICAL VARIABLES
(995 HEADS OF HOUSEHOLDS)

VARIABLE:	MEAN	STD. DEV.	MIN.	MAX.
Age in 1976	34.50	11.28	18.00	64.00
Years of Schooling (as of 1976 Interview)	11.66	2.73	0.00	17.00*
Years of Work Experience Since Age 18 (as of 1976 Interview)	14.81	10.59	1.00*	45.00

Continued overleaf

TABLE 1—CONTINUED

VARIABLE:	MEAN	STD. DEV.	MIN.	MAX.
Years with Previous Employers Since Age 18 (as of 1976 Interview)	9.51	9.29	0.00[b]	42.75
Years with Current Employer (as of 1976 Interview)	5.21	5.61	0.08*	41.00
Years with Current Employer Prior to 1976 Position	2.33	5.08	0.00[b]	37.00
Years in 1976 Position (as of 1976 Interview)	2.87	2.35	0.08*	8.00*
Years Required to Complete Training in 1976 Position	1.10	1.56	0.08*	8.17*
Real 1976 Wage (1967 Dollars)	2.85	1.05	1.10	5.79
Length of Individual Panel	5.09	2.60	2.00[b]	9.00[b]

DEFINITIONS OF VARIABLES APPEARING IN SUBSEQUENT TABLES

DEPENDENT VARIABLE:

W: Natural logarithm of real hourly wage, deflated by the CPI-U

INDEPENDENT VARIABLES:

INDEX: BLS index of real average hourly earnings in total private nonagricultural employment, adjusted for overtime (in manufacturing only) and interindustry shifts

POS: Years of tenure in 1976 position

PREMP: Years with previous employers since age 18

PRPOS: Years with current employer prior to 1976 position

R: Years of tenure required to become fully trained and qualified in the 1976 "job." (See question (Q1) in text). In Tables 2 and 3, the work "job" is taken to mean the current position. In Table 4, the word "job" is taken to mean the current firm

D: Indicator for tenure in the current "job" less than or equal to the level required to become fully trained and qualified (R). In Tables 2 and 3, the word "job" is taken to mean the current position. In Table 4, the word "job" is taken to mean the current firm

H: Cumulative training to date in the current position, equal to position-specific tenure for tenure less than or equal to R, and equal to R otherwise. This measure interprets question (Q1) as describing position-specific training intervals

H':   Cumulative training to date in the current firm, equal to firm-specific tenure for tenure less than or equal to R, and equal to R otherwise. This measure interprets question (Q1) as describing position-specific training intervals

TABLE 1—CONTINUED

INDEPENDENT VARIABLES:

ENTREQ:	Indicator for other training required to enter 1976 job. (See question (Q2) in text)
PRIOR:	Indicator for respondents reporting tenure with the 1976 firm (*TEN*) greater than tenure in the 1976 position (*POS*)
TEN1–TEN4:	Indicators for first four years of tenure with 1976 employer
OTHRSKL:	Indicator for learning other skills that could lead to better job or promotion. (See question (Q3) in text)
SUMPROM:	Cumulative promotions within the 1976 firm, beyond the 1976 position

Source: Panel Survey of Income Dynamics, Wave 9–17. Data for consumer prices and aggregate wages were taken from the 1988 Economic Report of the President, Tables B-44 and B-58. See Appendix for further discussion of data.
*Denotes a point of truncation induced by survey coding.
[a]Household, Mining, Farm, and Government workers are excluded.
[b]Respondents with negative values for these variables are excluded.

in previous positions with the current employer, and tenure with previous employers.[9] Required levels of training, taken from question (Q1), are assumed to describe incremental training in the 1976 position. Aggregate effects that might obscure the *ceteris paribus* relation between wages, tenure, and training are controlled for by inclusion of a real wage index for total private nonagricultural employment.

Columns (i)–(iv) present estimates that restrict the $f_1(\cdot)$ and $f_2(\cdot)$ functions to be the same, as in equation (3). Effectively, this restriction requires that there be no discrete change in wages upon completion of training, and allows the wage profile to be written in terms of cumulative training to date, H. For reference, columns (i')–(iv') in panel b present estimated training coefficients from equations in which this restriction is relaxed.[10]

From the similarity between the estimates involving $D * POS$ and those involving $(1-D) * R$ in columns (i')–(iv'), it appears that the data are adequately described by the restricted estimates in columns (i)–(iv). Given this fact, the following discussion focuses only on equations in which this restriction has been imposed. In no case do these restrictions influence the results that follow.[11]

The coefficient estimates for H and H^2 in column (i) imply a maximum of only 3 percent cumulative wage growth over 3 years of training. Taken at face value, these estimates seem to show that wages and productivity are not contemporaneously correlated. However, these low estimates may simply reflect

[9]Tenure data in the PSID often show inconsistencies over time. To minimize the consequences of these inconsistencies, this study uses reported tenure from the 1976 interview (the interview from which training measures are taken) to impute tenure in later years, with later values incremented by elapsed time between interviews. This imputation continues until a change in position is subsequently reported. See the Appendix for further discussion of this issue.

[10]Other parameter estimates from the unrestricted equations are quite similar to those in columns (i)–(iv), and so are omitted from panel b.

[11]Test statistics for the equality of the $f_1(\cdot)$ and $f_2(\cdot)$ functions are listed as Test no. 1 in Table 2. Although strict equality is rejected at conventional significance levels in columns (i) and (ii), and is nearly rejected in column (iii), the assumption of equality nevertheless provides an adequate description of the data for present purposes. When additional interaction terms involving required training are introduced in column (iv), equality is no longer rejected. Also, as seen below in Table 3, equality of these functions is not rejected if dummy variables for early tenure are included in the specification.

978 THE AMERICAN ECONOMIC REVIEW DECEMBER 1989

TABLE 2—PANEL A, FIXED-EFFECT ESTIMATES OF WITHIN-POSITION WAGE PROFILES*

VARIABLE:	(i)	(ii)	(iii)	(iv)
LOG OF AGGREGATE	0.97010	0.97407	0.95687	0.93817
WAGE INDEX	(0.9742)	(0.09738)	(0.09698)	(0.09690)
TENURE IN CURRENT	0.03211	0.03192	0.03165	0.03115
POSITION (POS)	(0.00274)	(0.00274)	(0.00273)	(0.00274)
POS²	−0.00088	−0.00088	−0.00087	−0.00084
	(0.00015)	(0.00015)	(0.00015)	(0.00015)
POS • COMPLETED TENURE	−0.00085	−0.00084	−0.00086	−0.00086
IN PREVIOUS FIRMS (PREMP)	(0.00009)	(0.00009)	(0.00009)	(0.00009)
POS • COMPLETED TENURE IN	−0.00082	−0.00082	−0.00078	−0.00076
PREVIOUS POSITIONS WITH	(0.00014)	(0.00015)	(0.00014)	(0.00014)
CURRENT FIRM (PRPOS)				
CUMULATIVE TRAINING	0.02166	0.09530	0.18188	0.27240
TO DATE IN CURRENT	(0.01341)	(0.03014)	(0.03307)	(0.04284)
POSITION (H)				
H²	−0.00346	−0.01249	−0.02377	−0.04953
	(0.00184)	(0.00373)	(0.00433)	(0.00739)
H•DUMMY FOR OTHER	−	−0.9161	−0.07301	−0.08478
TRAINING REQUIRED TO	−	(0.03310)	(0.03338)	(0.03343)
GET CURRENT JOB (ENTREQ)				
H² • ENTREQ	−	0.01161	0.00880	0.01123
	−	(0.00425)	(0.00431)	(0.00434)
H•DUMMY FOR SECOND OR	−	−	−0.16453	−0.14737
SUBSEQUENT POSITION WITH	−	−	(0.02264)	(0.02715)
CURRENT FIRM (PRIOR)				
H²•PRIOR	−	−	0.02111	0.01878
	−	−	(0.00480)	(0.00405)
H•REQUIRED TRAINING	−	−	−	−0.01105
IN CURRENT POSITION (R)	−	−	−	(0.00628)
H² • R	−	−	−	0.00339
	−	−	−	(0.00089)
SSE:	56.826	56.753	56.214	55.956
DFE:	4054	4052	4050	4048
MODEL F:	50.26	50.24	50.63	50.76

*Within-position estimates, based on 5,056 observations for 995 respondents. Standard errors are in parentheses. Variables are defined in Table 1.

errors in measuring respondents' skills. Such measurement error appears likely for two reasons.

First, column (i) includes no control for skills accumulated in previous positions. The estimates in column (i) implicitly assume that all respondents began the 1976 position with the same initial stock of skills and at the same point on the wage-skills profile. If, as seems likely, this assumption is invalid,

the estimates in column (i) will be biased by the omission of an interaction term involving current and prior levels of training.[12] If the

[12] If log wages are quadratic in the sum of training in the current position (H) and prior training (h), the omitted term is given by $2a_2 \cdot \bar{H} \cdot \bar{h}$, where a_2 denotes the second-order coefficient in the quadratic relation between log wages and total training, and where s's denote deviations from within-position means.

TABLE 2—PANEL B, TRAINING COEFFICIENTS FROM UNRESTRICTED VERSIONS OF COLUMNS (I)–(IV)*

	(i′)	(ii′)	(iii′)	(iv′)
EFFECTS OF TRAINING IN PROGRESS ($D=1$)				
VARIABLE:				
$D * POS$	0.02472	0.09757	0.18600	0.27751
	(0.01438)	(0.03461)	(0.03825)	(0.05395)
$D * POS^2$	−0.00279	−0.01285	−0.02459	−0.04817
	(0.00195)	(0.00416)	(0.00474)	(0.01000)
$D * POS * ENTREQ$	–	−0.09059	−0.08084	−0.09441
	–	(0.03789)	(0.03835)	(0.03854)
$D * POS^2 * ENTREQ$	–	0.01313	0.01098	0.01379
	–	(0.00471)	(0.00479)	(0.00486)
$D * POS * PRIOR$	–	–	−0.15210	−0.13533
	–	–	(0.02900)	(0.02955)
$D * POS^2 * PRIOR$	–	–	0.02038	0.01740
	–	–	(0.00421)	(0.00430)
$D * POS * R$	–	–	–	−0.01299
	–	–	–	(0.00722)
$D * POS^2 * R$	–	–	–	0.00323
	–	–	–	(0.00118)
EFFECTS OF COMPLETED TRAINING ($D=0$):				
VARIABLE:				
$(1-D) * R$	0.02350	0.09185	0.17340	0.25699
	(0.01445)	(0.03241)	(0.03551)	(0.04444)
$(1-D) * R^2$	−0.00452	−0.01163	−0.02171	−0.05690[a]
	(0.00232)	(0.00541)	(0.00625)	(0.01250)
$(1-D) * R * ENTREQ$	–	−0.08936	−0.06325	−0.06359
	–	(0.03544)	(0.03595)	(0.03609)
$(1-D) * R^2 * ENTREQ$	–	0.01013	0.00550	0.00467
	–	(0.00593)	(0.00601)	(0.00607)
$(1-D) * R * PRIOR$	–	–	−0.16849	−0.15092
	–	–	(0.02858)	(0.02913)
$(1-D) * R^2 * PRIOR$	–	–	0.02235	0.01994
	–	–	(0.00498)	(0.00504)
$(1-D) * R^2 * R$	–	–	–	−.00357
	–	–	–	(0.00110)
F-STATISTIC FOR TEST no. 1:	$F(2,4052)$ = 4.214	$F(4,4048)$ = 3.084	$F(6,4044)$ = 2.102	$F(8,4040)$ = 0.749
PROBABILITY VALUE FOR TEST no. 1:	0.015	0.015	0.061	0.630

*In place of a single quadratic in H, these equations estimate separate quadratics in $D * POS$ and $(1-D) * R$, the two additive components of H. The quadratic in $D * POS$ measures the effects of training when training is in progress and corresponds to the $f_1(\cdot)$ function in equation (4). The quadratic in $(1-D) * R$ measures the effects of training after training is complete and corresponds to the $f_2(\cdot)$ function in equation (4). Tests for the equality of these two quadratics are listed as test no. 1 in this and subsequent tables.

[a] The quadratic effect of completed training, $(1-D) * R^2$, is not equivalent to an interaction between the level of required training, R, and the linear effect of completed training, $(1-D) * R$. The estimated coefficient for $(1-D) * R^2$ thus represents the sum of these two effects. Equality of the $f_1(\cdot)$ and $f_2(\cdot)$ functions requires this combined effect to equal the sum of those for $D * POS^2$ and $D * POS * R$.

wage-skills profile is concave, this omission will cause training effects to be underestimated as respondents with high levels of prior training (whose wage growth reflects flatter segments of the profile) are wrongly assumed to reflect marginal returns to training along steeper segments of the profile.

Second, the training period for the 1976 position may itself be measured with error, due to the ambiguous wording of question (Q1). Because the word "job" was not precisely defined in this question, it is not clear whether respondents referred to the current position (as assumed here), the current firm, or perhaps the current occupation in answering this question. If some respondent's answers to question (Q1) described training periods that began upon entry to the firm or occupation, rather than upon entry to the current position, these respondents could be wrongly classified as undergoing training in the 1976 position when their training was actually complete. If so, measured training effects would be understated, as the absence of training-related wage growth over some part of the measured training interval for these respondents would be mistaken for a lower return to training over the entire interval.

To provide some control for unobserved prior training and for measurement error caused by the inclusion of prior training in answers to question (Q1), column (ii) introduces linear and quadratic interaction terms between cumulative training (H) and a dummy variable ($ENTREQ$) indicating respondent's affirmative answers to the following question:

(Q2)   "Do you also have to get some work experience or special training to get a job like yours?,"[13]

If respondents who answered "yes" to this question began their 1976 position on a flatter segment of the wage-skills profile, or if

these respondents included prior training in their answers to question (Q1), the interaction terms in column (ii) should indicate a smaller (and perhaps zero) contemporaneous wage effect for such respondents.

The estimated coefficients involving H and $ENTREQ$ in column (ii) fit this pattern. For respondents reporting some entry-related training requirements, the estimated contemporaneous return to training is negligible. For respondents answering "no" to the above question, however, a substantial contemporaneous return to training becomes evident. For these "no" respondents, the estimates in column (ii) imply a maximum of roughly 18 percent cumulative wage growth over 4 years of training.

As a further control for unobserved prior training and for measurement error in current training status, column (iii) introduces an additional pair of interaction terms involving H and a dummy variable ($PRIOR$) that identifies respondents who had held prior positions with their 1976 employer. If some of these respondents answered question (Q1) by describing total training in the current firm, rather than incremental training in the current position alone, estimated training effects would be smaller for this group, because "measured" training intervals for these respondents would incorrectly extend beyond the actual completion of training in the 1976 position. Smaller effects also would be found if skills learned in prior positions were more substitutable within firms than across firms, in which case the effects of omitted prior training would (*ceteris paribus*) be larger for respondents who had held prior positions within their current firm.

The estimates in column (iii) fit this pattern also. While the contemporaneous return to training is estimated to be zero or slightly negative for respondents with prior firm experience and other training requirements, respondents with no other training requirements and no prior firm experience show even larger contemporaneous training effects than those estimated in column (ii). For members of this latter group (who are more likely to be observed near the origin of the wage-skills profile, and for whom answers

---

[13]As seen in Table 1, about 57 percent of respondents answered "yes" to this question.

VOL. 79 NO. 5 *BROWN: WHY DO WAGES INCREASE WITH TENURE?* 981

about training requirements are more likely to apply to the current position), the estimates in column (iii) imply a maximum of roughly 35 percent cumulative wage growth over 4 years of training.

As a final control for unobserved prior training and measurement error in current training status, column (iii) introduces a pair of interactions between cumulative training (H) and reported levels of required training (R). If training in prior positions were positively correlated with training in the 1976 position, or if respondents with especially large values for required training were more likely to have included prior training in their answers to question (Q1), estimated training effects should be smaller for these respondents.[14]

Of course, this interpretation assumes that all respondents share a common profile relating productivity to cumulative training regardless of the training requirements reported for any given job. It is possible, however, that the relation between productivity and training might vary by levels of R. If so, the additional interaction terms in column (iv) could simply reflect this heterogeneity.

The estimated interactions involving H and R in column (iv) suggest that both measurement error and heterogeneity may be present in the data. Consistent with the presence of heterogeneity, these estimates imply wage profiles that reach maxima at higher levels of training for respondents reporting greater training requirements. For some respondents, however, these implied maxima occur prior to the completion of training, and for a small fraction of the sample, the last few years of training are implied to have a substantial negative effect on wages.

Evaluated at the required levels reported by respondents (and referring to respondents with no prior firm experience and no other training required for entry to the current job), the estimates in column (iv) imply cumulative training-related wage growth of 12

percent for those reporting one-half year of required training, 22 percent for those reporting 1 year, roughly 30 to 35 percent for those reporting 2 to 5 years, 18 percent for those reporting 6 years, 10 percent for those reporting 7 years, and 4 percent for those reporting 8 years of required training. This pattern of negative marginal training effects for the few respondents (2 percent of the sample) reporting more than 5 years of required training appears to reflect measurement errors caused by the inclusion of prior training in answers to question (Q1). For other respondents, column (iv) indicates a strong contemporaneous link between wage growth and training.

B. *Do "Contracts" Generate Wage Growth?*

Early-Tenure Wage Growth. The estimates in Table 2 suggest a strong contemporaneous link between productivity and wages. These estimates assume, however, that the effects of purely tenure-related factors are adequately captured by a quadratic specification. If this assumption is invalid, the training effects measured in Table 2 may be biased. In particular, if factors unrelated to training cause wage profiles to be initially steeper and subsequently flatter than a quadratic profile can allow, the poor fit of the quadratic profile could generate training effects such as those in Table 2, simply because training occurs primarily in the early stages of employees' tenure.

To explore this possibility, equation (iv) of Table 2 was reestimated with dummy variables (*TEN*1-*TEN*4) included to indicate each of an employee's first 4 years with a firm. If the training effects in Table 2 merely reflect the failure of the quadratic profile to capture early-tenure wage growth, these effects should be absorbed by the early-tenure dummies. The results are presented in column (i) of Table 3.

The estimates in column (i) indicate reasonably large early-tenure effects that are not captured by quadratic functions of tenure and training. These effects amount to roughly 8 percent over the first 4 years of tenure in the firm, with the bulk occurring in the first

---

[14]For evidence that current and prior training requirements are positively correlated, see Mincer (1988).

TABLE 3—FIXED-EFFECT ESTIMATES OF WITHIN-POSITION AND WITHIN-FIRM WAGE PROFILES, EARLY-TENURE EFFECTS INCLUDED[*]

VARIABLE:	(i)[a]	(ii)[a]	(iii)[b]	(iv)[b]
LOG OF AGGREGATE	0.85471	0.85557	0.86985	0.88660
WAGE INDEX	(0.09820)	(0.09816)	(0.09703)	(0.09627)
TENURE IN CURRENT	0.02363	0.02337	0.02669	0.02291
POSITION (POS)	(0.00368)	(0.00368)	(0.00358)	(0.00358)
POS^2	−0.00048	−0.00048	−0.00045	−0.00037
	(0.00019)	(0.00019)	(0.00019)	(0.00019)
POS • COMPLETED TENURE	−0.00085	−0.00083	−0.00100	−0.00093
IN PREVIOUS FIRMS (PREMP)	(0.00009)	(0.00009)	(0.00009)	(0.00009)
POS • COMPLETED TENURE IN	−0.00067	−0.00066	−0.00063	−0.00063
PREVIOUS POSITIONS WITH	(0.00015)	(0.00015)	(0.00014)	(0.00014)
CURRENT FIRM (PRPOS)				
CUMULATIVE TRAINING	0.20962	0.19865	0.22600	0.21000
TO DATE IN CURRENT	(0.04468)	(0.04486)	(0.04353)	(0.047323)
POSITION (H)				
H^2	−0.04040	−0.03898	−0.04228	−0.3983
	(0.00762)	(0.00764)	(0.00727)	(0.00722)
H • DUMMY FOR OTHER	−0.08542	−0.08227	−0.08850	−0.08349
TRAINING REQUIRED TO	(0.03338)	(0.03337)	(0.03300)	(0.03175)
GET CURRENT JOB (ENTREQ)				
H^2 • ENTREQ	0.01148	0.01111	0.01193	0.01117
	(0.00433)	(0.00433)	(0.00391)	(0.00388)
H • DUMMY FOR SECOND OR	−0.09750	−0.09518	−0.10677	−0.10339
SUBSEQUENT POSITION WITH	(0.02889)	(0.02890)	(0.02740)	(0.02718)
CURRENT FIRM (PRIOR)				
H^2 • PRIOR	0.01308	0.01284	0.01437	0.01420
	(0.00422)	(0.00422)	(0.00371)	(0.00368)
H • REQUIRED TRAINING	−0.00789	−0.00689	−0.00715	−0.00544
IN CURRENT POSITION (R)	(0.00633)	(0.00634)	(0.00610)	(0.00606)
H^2 • R	0.00277	0.00263	0.00257	0.00231
	(0.00090)	(0.00090)	(0.00085)	(0.00084)
DUMMY FOR FIRST YEAR	−0.08357	−0.01843	−0.02274	−0.03227
WITH FIRM (TEN1)	(0.01914)	(0.03108)	(0.03165)	(0.03142)
DUMMY FOR SECOND YEAR	−0.03075	−0.01587	−0.02957	−0.03334
WITH FIRM (TEN2)	(0.01423)	(0.02461)	(0.02473)	(0.02454)
DUMMY FOR THIRD YEAR	0.01386	0.02481	0.00779	0.00704
WITH FIRM (TEN3)	(0.01090)	(0.02013)	(0.02015)	(0.01998)
DUMMY FOR FOURTH YEAR	0.00660	0.02272	0.01081	0.00966
WITH FIRM (TEN4)	(0.00859)	(0.01566)	(0.01570)	(0.01557)
TEN1 • DUMMY FOR LEARNING	−	−0.08536	−0.07409	−0.07381
OTHER SKILLS (OTHRSKL)	−	(0.03200)	(0.03275)	(0.03249)
TEN2 • OTHRSKL	−	−0.01951	−0.00363	−0.00430
	−	(0.02571)	(0.02595)	(0.02575)
TEN3 • OTHRSKL	−	−0.04902	−0.03301	−0.03357
	−	(0.02123)	(0.02128)	(0.02111)

TABLE 3—CONTINUED

VARIABLE:	(i)[a]	(ii)[a]	(iii)[b]	(iv)[b]
TEN4 • OTHRSKL	–	– 0.02043	– 0.00868	– 0.00877
	–	(0.01717)	(0.01724)	(0.01710)
CUMULATIVE PROMOTIONS	–	–	–	0.08195
BEYOND 1976 POSITION	–	–	–	(0.00946)
(SUMPROM)				
SSE:	55.75	55.430	63.892	62.856
DFE:	4044	4040	4362	4361
MODEL F:	50.88	50.78	51.09	51.94
F-STATISTIC	$F(8,4036)$	$F(8,4032)$	$F(8,4354)$	$F(8,4353)$
FOR TEST no. 1[c]	= 0.821	= 0.842	= 1.014	= 1.253
PROBABILITY VALUE	0.570	0.552	0.419	0.270
FOR TEST no. 1				
F-STATISTIC	$F(2,4042)$	$F(2,4038)$	$F(2,4360)$	$F(2,4359)$
FOR TEST no. 2[d]	= 0.748	= 0.658	= 2.540	= 1.819
PROBABILITY VALUE	0.473	0.518	0.079	0.162
FOR TEST no. 2:				

*Variables are defined in Table 1. Standard errors are in parentheses.
[a] Within-position estimates, based on 5,056 observations from 1976 position.
[b] Within-firm estimates, based on 5,378 observations from 1976 firm.
[c] Test no. 1 restricts the $f_1(\cdot)$ and $f_2(\cdot)$ functions in equation (4) to be equal.
[d] Test no. 2 imposes the parameter restrictions shown in equation (6).

year.[15] With these early-tenure effects included, the effect of training (as measured by cumulative wage growth at the maximum of the "baseline" wage-training profile) is reduced by about 8 percentage points; the difference now appearing in the early-tenure dummies, particularly that for the first year. Despite this reduction, however, the estimated effects of training remain substantial, reaching a maximum of about 27 percent over 3 years of training.

The interpretation of the early-tenure dummies in column (i) is unclear. These effects could represent purely contractual arrangements (such as those modeled by Salop and Salop, 1976), but they could also represent training effects that do not fit a quadratic profile. Column (ii) presents evidence supporting the latter interpretation. This col-umn introduces interaction terms between the early-tenure dummies and a dummy variable (OTHRSKL) indicating respondents' affirmative answers to the following question:

(Q3)   "Do you feel you are learning things in your job that could lead to a better job or to a promotion?,"[16]

If factors unrelated to skill acquisition are important in determining early-tenure wage growth, the early-tenure effects previously observed should be present regardless of employees' answers to this question. As columns (iv)–(vi) show, however, these effects are present only for respondents who claim that they are learning new skills. Once skill acquisition is controlled for in this manner, there remains no significant firm-specific

[15] When dummy variables for position-specific tenure are included, these dummies are numerically small and statistically insignificant.

[16] As seen in Table 1, about 75 percent of respondents answered "yes" to this question.

wage growth that one might attribute to other factors.[17]

Long-Term Wage Growth Within Positions. Column (ii) of Table 3 shows two major components of within-position wage growth. One component is concentrated in the first few years of tenure with the firm and, depending on the level of required training, can amount to roughly 35 percent wage growth. Of this component, all but about 10 percentage points can be described as a quadratic function of cumulative training. The remaining 10 percentage points occur mainly upon completion of the first year with an employer, and occur only for respondents who report that they are learning new skills during that year.

The second component is reflected in the quadratic function of tenure in column (ii). This component appears to reflect factors other than skill acquisition, for it occurs mainly after employees claim to be fully qualified in their current job. As measured in column (ii), this component accounts for roughly 30 percent wage growth over a 25-year period.

Does this second component measure the effect of tenure on wages? In general, the answer is no. As others have noted, tenure and experience are perfectly collinear within jobs, so that fixed-effect methods cannot separate the effects of tenure from those of general labor market experience (or a simple time trend, for that matter).[18]

Despite this limitation, however, the estimates in column (ii) do allow a test of the hypothesis that this long-term component contains no factors that are firm-specific. This test is relevant to the question of long-term "contractual" wage growth, because if such wage growth is present in the data, the long-term component of wages should display some firm-specificity. In the absence of such specificity, it seems unlikely that contractual factors, which are inherently firm-specific, could explain this component.

To develop this test for firm-specificity, consider the case in which this long-term component depends only on total labor force experience:

$$(5) \quad \log(W_{it}) = a_0 + a_1 X_{it}$$
$$+ a_2 X_{it}^2 + \text{other terms.}$$

Treating this component as a function of total experience alone imposes several restrictions on the relation between log wages and the elements of which total experience is composed. In particular, if total experience is written as the sum of tenure in the current position (*POS*), tenure in previous positions with the current employer (*PRPOS*), and

---

[17]The early-tenure effects estimated in column (ii) appear consistent with estimates in Marshall and Zarkin (1987), Altonji and Shakotko (1987), and Topel (1987), all of which indicate "first year with employer" effects ranging from 5 to 10 percent. These previous estimates cannot be interpreted as pure tenure effects, however, because they are based on annual earnings data that may combine earnings on the current job with earnings from prior jobs when tenure on the current job is less than one year. As a result, the earlier findings reflect some combination of mobility effects and pure tenure effects. The estimates in Table 2 avoid this problem by using (post-1976) wage data that refer only to the job held at the time of the interview. The similarity between these and the earlier findings provides some confirmation that the earlier findings were not greatly influenced by mobility effects. In addition, these estimates provide an interpretation for the earlier findings, as the interaction terms involving *OTHRSKL* indicate a strong connection between early-tenure wage growth and skill acquisition.

This problem does not arise in estimating training effects, because the training spline function is not perfectly collinear with time within positions. For various methods of dealing with this problem when information on training intervals is not exploited, see Altonji and Shakotko (1987), Abraham and Farber (1987), and Topel (1987).

[18]Due to the perfect collinearity of tenure and time within jobs, the cumulative magnitude of the second component is sensitive to manner in which aggregate effects are modeled. If aggregate controls are excluded, the magnitude of this component is reduced by roughly 50 percent. If year dummies are introduced, the magnitude of this component is increased, as are the standard errors for the variables included in this component. Other properties of this component (discussed below) are not sensitive to the choice of aggregate controls, however, and the conclusions of this section do not depend on the choice of these controls.

VOL. 79 NO. 5 BROWN: WHY DO WAGES INCREASE WITH TENURE? 985

tenure with previous employers ($PREMP$), equation (5) implies:

$$
(6) \quad \log(W_{it})
$$

$$
= \big(a_0 + a_1 PREMP_i + a_2 PREMP_i^2
$$

$$
+ a_1 PRPOS_i + a_2 PRPOS_i^2
$$

$$
+ 2 a_2 PREMP_i * PRPOS_i \big)
$$

$$
+ a_1 POS_{it} + a_2 POS_{it}^2
$$

$$
+ 2 a_2 PREMP_i * POS_{it}
$$

$$
+ 2 a_2 PRPOS_i * POS_{it}
$$

$$
+ \text{other terms},
$$

where the term in parentheses is fixed within a given position, and where the remainder (except for "other terms") is simply the long-term component estimated in column (ii).

Intuitively, if this component depends only on total experience, all elements of experience should affect wages equally, and wages should be independent of the distribution of past experience across jobs and positions. In equation (6), this independence requires equality among the linear and quadratic effects of $PREMP$, $PRPOS$, and POS. It also requires that the interaction effects of $PREMP*PRPOS$, $PREMP*POS$, and $PRPOS*POS$ each be twice the effect of POS^2.

Not all of these restrictions can be tested with the fixed-effect framework employed in this paper. Because $PREMP$ and $PRPOS$ are fixed within a given position for each sample member, effects involving only these variables are indistinguishable from the person-specific intercept a_0.[19] Nevertheless, it is possible to test the restriction that the interaction effects of $PREMP*POS$ and $PRPOS*POS$ are each twice the effect of POS^2.

As seen in columns (i) and (ii) of Table 3, this restriction fits the data well. The estimated coefficients for $PREMP*POS$ and $PRPOS*POS$ are each roughly twice the corresponding estimate for POS^2. The F-statistics for these restrictions (listed in Table 3 as Test no. 2) are each less than 0.75, with probability values of about 0.50.

If firm-specific factors are an important source of long-term wage growth, current wage growth should be influenced by the distribution of past experience across positions and employers. Columns (i) and (ii) show no such influence. On the basis of these estimates, therefore, firm-specific factors appear unimportant in determining the long-term component of wage growth within positions.[20]

Long-Term Wage Growth Across Positions. The preceding analysis has focused only on wage growth within a single position. It has ignored any wage growth that might occur across positions within the firm. If "contractual" wage growth occurs primarily through promotions, however, this omission could understate the importance of contracts in generating wage growth. To allow for this possibility, columns (iii) and (iv) of Table 3 present estimates based on an extended data set that includes "post-promotion" observations for respondents who were promoted beyond their 1976 position within their 1976 firm.[21]

Because these data contain information about required training only for positions held in 1976 and 1978, information about post-promotion training is not generally available. As a result, columns (iii) and (iv) simply assume that no additional training occurs after the 1976 position, attributing any training-related wage growth that might occur after promotion to factors other than

---

[19] This is equivalent to saying that experience, tenure in the firm, and tenure in the position are all perfectly collinear within positions. As a result, their separate linear effects cannot be distinguished.

[20] This result parallels the findings of Abraham and Farber (1987), Altonji and Shakotko (1987), and Marshall and Zarkin (1987).

[21] Of the 995 respondents included in the current sample, 99 respondents were promoted beyond their 1976 position during the sample period. For these respondents, an additional 322 observations corresponding to "post-promotion" positions with the 1976 employer are available.

training. By ignoring any additional training that respondents might undertake subsequent to promotion, columns (iii) and (iv) are likely to understate the role of training in accounting for wage growth across positions, and correspondingly overstate the potential role of other factors in accounting for this wage growth.

For a point of reference, column (iii) reestimates column (ii) using these extended data. The resulting estimates are quite similar to those in column (ii), except for a larger long-run component, which now reaches a maximum of roughly 40 percent over a 30-year period. This increase reflects the contribution of promotion-related wage growth to the overall wage growth observed within firms.[22]

Column (iv) measures this contribution more directly by introducing a step function in cumulative promotions beyond the 1976 position (*SUMPROM*).[23] With this addition, the remaining long-run component is now quite similar to that estimated in column (ii), implying roughly 30 percent wage growth over a 30-year period. All other estimates in column (iv) are close to their counterparts in column (ii).[24] Except for the presence of an 8 percent wage gain associated with promotion, column (iv) tells the same basic story as that told by column (ii).

Are promotions an important overlooked source of "contractual" wage growth in these data? The answer appears to be no. Although the wage gain associated with promotion is substantial (equivalent to completion of the first year with an employer), promotions occur too infrequently in these data to account for a major component of observed wage profiles.

In this sample, only 99 of 995 respondents experienced a promotion within the sample period. For those respondents who were promoted beyond their 1976 position, the mean waiting time to promotion was 6.6 years. Among those not promoted, the mean incomplete waiting time was 6.2 years for the 532 respondents who separated from their 1976 employer prior to any promotion, and was 11.3 years for the 364 respondents who remained in their 1976 position throughout the sample period. Even if promotions occurred at the average intervals observed for those actually promoted, and even if promotions always resulted in an 8 percent wage gain, promotions in these data could at most account for an average annual rate of growth equal to 1.2 percent for only one-tenth of the sample.

Given the infrequency of promotions in these data, as well as the likelihood that promotions are accompanied by additional training, the basic message of the data appears unchanged when wage growth across positions is included in the analysis: little firm-specific wage growth in these data can be attributed unambiguously to factors other than productivity growth.

C. Do "Contracts" Lessen Wage Growth?

Tables 2 and 3 indicate large training effects for respondents who are in their first position with a firm, who report no other training requirements for entry to the current job, and who do not report "extreme" values for required training on the current job. Respondents who report prior training requirements, prior firm experience, or unusually high (for this sample) levels of required training show much smaller training effects. This pattern may reflect unobserved prior training and measurement error in current training status, but it could also reflect contractual smoothing of wages in matches that have greater levels of specific capital or greater expected duration.

Although incentive and selection considerations appear not to generate wage growth in the absence of productivity growth, these considerations may still be important in determining the degree to which wage profiles

[22] Promotion-related wage growth is also reflected in the larger *F*-statistic for Test no. 2 in column (iii).

[23] Promotions do not represent exogenous "treatments" in these data, and so the estimated coefficients for cumulative promotions in Table 3 cannot be interpreted as the effect that would follow from a randomly assigned promotion. These coefficients should instead be interpreted simply as rough measures of the potential role for promotion-related wage growth in accounting for the overall wage growth observed within firms.

[24] Also, the *F*-statistic for Test no. 2 is reduced when cumulative promotions are included.

follow productivity profiles. If the incentive and selection effects of upward-sloping wage profiles are reduced when match-specific information and rents are already present, reliance on any contemporaneous link between wages and productivity may also be reduced in such circumstances. If so, the interaction terms in Tables 2 and 3 may be capturing such an effect.[25]

The data provide only a limited basis on which to distinguish between these alternatives, but the available evidence suggests that the interaction effects in Tables 2 and 3 do not reflect contractual wage smoothing. One piece of evidence is provided by the fact that when the early-tenure dummies are interacted with *ENTREQ* and *PRIOR*, the estimated interaction terms are numerically small and statistically insignificant, while other parameter estimates are virtually unchanged. If the interaction terms in Tables 2 and 3 primarily reflect contractual wage smoothing, it seems unlikely that similar interactions would be unimportant for the early-tenure dummies. Because the interactions involving *ENTREQ* and *PRIOR* matter only for *H* and not for the early-tenure dummies, it seems reasonable to interpret these interactions as reflecting something about the variable *H*, rather than something more general about labor contracts.

Table 4 provides additional evidence regarding the interaction terms involving prior tenure. This table presents estimates based on a redefined measure of training (*H'*) that interprets question (Q1) as referring to the firm rather than to the current position.[26] If the interaction terms involving *PRIOR* in Tables 2 and 3 primarily reflect the effects of prior training on the marginal return to current training, or if these interactions reflect the inclusion of prior training in answers to question (Q1), these interaction terms should become less pronounced in Table 4.

As seen in columns (i) and (ii) (which correspond to columns (ii) and (iv) of Table 3), the use of this redefined training measure causes the interaction terms involving *PRIOR* to become much smaller, while leaving the "baseline" effects of training essentially unchanged. Once training is redefined in this manner, no evidence remains that training effects differ across positions within the firm. The interaction terms involving prior firm tenure in Tables 2 and 3 thus appear to reflect factors associated with prior training, rather than "contractual" differences related to tenure.[27]

The interaction terms involving required training (*R*) also become insignificant in these equations. (This result would follow if respondents who reported extreme values for required training mainly interpreted question (Q1) as referring to the firm). It appears that a common profile relating wages to cumulative training (as now defined) describes the data adequately, without further reference to reported training requirements.[28] In light of this fact, columns (iii) and (iv) of Table 4 provide a more concise summary of the data by omitting the interaction terms involving prior firm tenure and required levels of training.[29]

---

[25]These terms could also reflect either diminishing intensity of investment per year spent in training, increasing specificity of acquired skills, or a diminishing share of investments financed by workers as tenure increased.

[26]More precisely, this measure is defined as $D' \cdot TEN + (1 - D') \cdot R$, where *TEN* denotes tenure with the current firm and *D'* denotes a dummy variable equal to unity when tenure with the firm is less than or equal to *R*, and zero otherwise.

[27]Smaller interaction terms involving *PRIOR* and *H'* could also result if some workers with prior firm tenure were wrongly interpreted as having completed training when their training was still in progress. (This misinterpretation could occur if respondents actually described position-specific training in answering question (Q1)). This alternative explanation can be tested with unrestricted estimates of training effects, however, and the data reject this alternative.

[28]The *F*-statistics for Test no. 1 in Table 4 are larger than those in Table 3. Nevertheless, unrestricted estimates of these equations are not substantively different from those in Table 4. It should be noted that these higher *F*-statistics derive mainly from the interaction terms included to control for measurement errors in training. If Test no. 1 is applied only to the "baseline" wage profile, the null hypothesis in Test no. 1 is not rejected.

[29]A joint *F*-test for these interaction terms yields a value of 1.136 for column (iii) and 1.030 for column (iv). The probability values for these statistics are 0.338 and 0.390, respectively.

TABLE 4—FIXED-EFFECT ESTIMATES OF WITHIN-POSITION AND WITHIN-FIRM WAGE PROFILES, "FIRM-SPECIFIC" INTERPRETATION OF TRAINING QUESTIONS[*]

VARIABLE:	(i)[a]	(ii)[b]	(iii)[a]	(iv)[b]
LOG OF AGGREGATE	0.84238	0.87899	0.83835	0.87638
WAGE INDEX	(0.09795)	(0.09606)	(0.09781)	(0.09593)
TENURE IN CURRENT	0.02124	0.02142	0.02123	0.02139
POSITION (POS)	(0.00354)	(0.00344)	(0.00353)	(0.00344)
POS^2	−0.00037	−0.00030	−0.00037	−0.00030
	(0.00019)	(0.00018)	(0.00019)	(0.00018)
POS • COMPLETED TENURE	−0.00082	−0.00093	−0.00082	−0.00093
IN PREVIOUS FIRMS (PREMP)	(0.00009)	(0.00009)	(0.00009)	(0.00009)
POS • COMPLETED TENURE IN	−0.00069	−0.00065	−0.00068	−0.00065
PREVIOUS POSITIONS WITH	(0.00015)	(0.00014)	(0.00015)	(0.00014)
CURRENT FIRM (PRPOS)				
CUMULATIVE TRAINING	0.21766	0.21504	0.16710	0.18183
TO DATE IN CURRENT	(0.06513)	(0.06355)	(0.04332)	(0.04102)
FIRM (H')				
H'^{2}	−0.03874	−0.03827	−0.02145	−0.02425
	(0.01221)	(0.01156)	(0.00546)	(0.00448)
H' • DUMMY FOR OTHER	−0.14591	−0.15262	−0.13845	−0.14261
TRAINING REQUIRED TO	(0.04976)	(0.04716)	(0.04699)	(0.04489)
GET CURRENT JOB (ENTREQ)				
H'^{2} • ENTREQ	0.01721	0.01861	0.01724	0.01864
	(0.00702)	(0.00603)	(0.00611)	(0.00520)
H' • DUMMY FOR SECOND OR	−0.03373	−0.04416	−	−
SUBSEQUENT POSITION WITH	(0.07795)	(0.07431)	−	−
CURRENT FIRM (PRIOR)				
H'^{2} • PRIOR	0.00425	0.00498	−	−
	(0.00938)	(0.00859)	−	−
H' • REQUIRED TRAINING	−0.00049	−0.00481	−	−
IN CURRENT POSITION(R)	(0.01142)	(0.01123)	−	−
H'^{2} • R	0.00166	0.00105	−	−
	(0.00160)	(0.00151)	−	−
DUMMY FOR FIRST YEAR	−0.02680	−0.03970	−0.02934	−0.04214
WITH FIRM (TEN1)	(0.03098)	(0.03131)	(0.03094)	(0.03126)
DUMMY FOR SECOND YEAR	−0.02020	−0.03620	−0.01782	−0.03428
WITH FIRM (TEN2)	(0.02457)	(0.02449)	(0.02453)	(0.02445)
DUMMY FOR THIRD YEAR	−0.02196	0.00540	0.02506	0.00815
WITH FIRM (TEN3)	(0.02017)	(0.02001)	(0.02011)	(0.01996)
DUMMY FOR FOURTH YEAR	0.02101	0.00890	0.02310	0.01067
WITH FIRM (TEN4)	(0.01568)	(0.01559)	(0.01564)	(0.01555)
TEN1 • DUMMY FOR LEARNING	−0.08587	−0.07597	−0.08812	−0.07659
OTHER SKILLS (OTHRSKL)	(0.03213)	(0.03260)	(0.03197)	(0.03245)
TEN2 • OTHRSKL	−0.01888	−0.00421	−0.02052	−0.00559
	(0.02576)	(0.02577)	(0.02574)	(0.02576)
TEN3 • OTHRSKL	−0.04868	−0.03357	−0.04951	−0.03423
	(0.02127)	(0.02113)	(0.02126)	(0.02113)

TABLE 4—CONTINUED

VARIABLE:	(i)[a]	(ii)[b]	(iii)[a]	(iv)[b]
TEN4 • OTHRSKL	−0.02096	−0.00975	−0.02159	−0.01004
	(0.01720)	(0.01712)	(0.01719)	(0.01711)
CUMULATIVE PROMOTIONS	−	0.08188	−	0.08191
BEYOND 1976 POSITIONS		(0.00946)		(0.00945)
(SUMPROM)				
SSE:	55.592	62.958	55.654	63.018
DFE:	4040	4361	4044	4365
MODEL F:	50.62	51.85	50.81	52.05
F-STATISTIC	F(8,4032)	F(8,4353)	F(4,4040)	F(4,4361)
FOR TEST no. 1[c]	= 2.521	= 2.172	= 2.102	= 2.144
PROBABILITY VALUE:	0.014	0.034	0.040	0.036
FOR TEST no. 1:				
F-STATISTIC	F(2,4038)	F(2,4159)	F(2,4042)	F(2,4363)
FOR TEST no. 2:[d]	= 0.328	= 1.945	= 0.346	= 1.650
PROBABILITY VALUE:	0.720	0.143	0.708	0.192
FOR TEST no. 2:				

*Variables are defined in Table 1. Standard errors are in parentheses. All estimates assume that training intervals described in question (Q1) began upon entry to the current firm, rather than upon entry to the current position.
[a] Within-position estimates, based on 5,056 observations from 1976 position.
[b] Within-firm estimates, based on 5,378 observations from 1976 firm.
[c] Test no. 1 restricts the $f_1(\cdot)$ and $f_2(\cdot)$ functions in equation (4) to be equal.
[d] Test no. 2 imposes the parameter restrictions shown in equation (6).

The estimates in columns (iii) and (iv) imply "baseline" training effects that reach a maximum of roughly 30 percent after 3 to 4 years of training. As before, the estimates in these columns show no evidence of purely contractual wage growth. Also as before, these estimates show smaller training effects for jobs requiring prior skills or training upon entry.[30]

It remains unclear whether this last result reflects unmeasured prior training, measurement error in current training status, or some relation between job-entry requirements and contractual wage smoothing.[31] Because the data show little evidence of wage smoothing related to prior tenure, however, the importance of wage smoothing related to entry

[30] These results are robust to alternative sampling schemes based on race, sex, SEO subsample membership, and completed job duration. The data show somewhat greater training-related wage growth among white males and nonsupervisory workers, but the differences are small relative to sampling error. The data also show some mixed evidence that contemporaneous training effects are smaller for union workers. When equations for union workers are separately estimated, the data show only negligible effects of H (similar comments apply for the variable H'). However, the early tenure effects associated with skill acquisition (measured by the interactions between OTHRSKL and the early-tenure dummies) are quite large for union workers. These effects amount to roughly 17 percent over the first 4

years of tenure in the firm, and are about equal in magnitude to the estimated effects of H for nonunion workers.
[31] The interaction effects involving ENTREQ are equivalent to the effects of about 1.5 years of training along the baseline profile, but similar interactions could also result if entry-related training requirements led to increased mobility costs for workers, or if workers' willingness to meet these requirements signaled lower anticipated mobility. In these latter cases, contracts for workers having met such requirements might have had less reason to employ deferred payment schemes to discourage mobility, and might therefore have had less reason to link wages with contemporaneous productivity.

990   THE AMERICAN ECONOMIC REVIEW   DECEMBER 1989

requirements seems doubtful. This view is reinforced by the fact that respondents typically describe entry-related training as being general in nature.[32] Although the evidence is not conclusive, it appears most reasonable to interpret the interaction terms involving entry-related training as reflecting factors other than contractual wage smoothing. Purely "contractual" factors do not appear to be an important determinant of wage profiles in these data.

IV. Summary and Conclusions

This paper has examined the comparative roles played by training and contractual factors in determining within-firm wage growth. Focusing on those respondents for whom training effects are least likely to be observed with error, the data indicate a strong contemporaneous link between training and wage growth, even when dummy variables for early tenure and promotions are allowed to capture any non-quadratic wage growth that occurs in the data. Using the "baseline" wage profile in column (iv) of Table 4 to calculate cumulative wage growth at each respondent's reported level of required training, column (iv) implies an average cumulative training effect equal to about 11 percent.[33] Combined with estimated early-tenure effects that are present only for those acquiring skills, the training-related wage growth implied by Table 4 averages roughly 20 percent for members of the sample studied here.[34]

[32]Among respondents answering "yes" to question (Q2), the model description of prior training involves (to paraphrase PSID coding) no mention of specific skills, but rather mentions only broad types of work, such as "mechanical knowledge," "knowledge of finance," or "public relations background."

[33]This figure falls below the 20–30 percent range of maximum effects cited earlier, because most respondents report training intervals that end before the estimated wage-training profile reaches its maximum. The lower figure also reflects concavity of the wage-training profile. While the average effect of training implied by column (iv) is only 11 percent, the effect implied at the average level of training exceeds 20 percent.

[34]These findings also bear on the more basic question of whether wages contain any firm-specific compo-

The data indicate no major role for purely contractual factors that might cause wages to increase in the absence of productivity growth. Once training is held constant, virtually no firm-specific wage growth remains to be attributed to these other factors. The most reasonable inference from these data, therefore, is that wages increase with tenure primarily because productivity increases with tenure.

nent at all (see references cited in fn. 1). Although the data studied here provide no direct measure of the specificity of skills, these data clearly indicate that firm-specific intervals of training are important in understanding individuals' wage histories. Unless training is perfectly general, and unless the incidence of training is independent of firm-specific factors (in which case the estimates in this paper merely identify the mechanism through which experience affects wages), the training effects estimated here indicate that wages contain a sizable firm-specific component.

REFERENCES

Abraham, Katharine G., and Farber, Henry S., "Job Duration, Seniority, and Earnings," *American Economic Review*, June 1987, 77, 278–97.

Altonji, Joseph G. and Shakotko, Robert A., "Do Wages Rise with Job Seniority?," *Review of Economic Studies*, July 1987, 54, 437–59.

Becker, Gary S., "Investment in Human Capital: A Theoretical Analysis," *Journal of Political Economy*, October 1962, 70, no. 5, part 2, 9–49.

_____, "*Human Capital: A Theoretical and Empirical Analysis with Special Reference to Education*, New York: National Bureau of Economic Research, 1964.

_____, and Stigler, George J., "Law Enforcement, Malfeasance, and Compensation of Enforcers," *Journal of Legal Studies*, January 1974, 3, no. 1, 1–18.

Brown, James N., "Are Those Paid More Really No More Productive?," Measuring the Relative Importance of Tenure versus On-the-Job Training in Explaining Wage Growth," Working Paper no. 169, Industrial Relations Section, Princeton University, October 1983.

Duncan, Greg J. and Hoffman, Saul, "On-the-Job Training and Earnings Differences by Race and Sex," *Review of Economics and Statistics*, November 1979, *61*, 594–603.

Freeman, Smith, "Wage Trends as Performance Displays Productivity: A Model and Application to Academic Early Retirement," *Bell Journal of Economics*, Autumn 1977, *8*, 419–43.

Friedman, Milton and Kuznets, Simon, *Income from Independent Professional Practice*, New York: National Bureau of Economic Research, 1945.

Guasch, J. Louis and Weiss, Andrew, "An Equilibrium Analysis of Wage-Productivity Gaps," *Review of Economic Studies*, July 1979, *49*, 485–97.

Harris, Milton and Holmstrom, Bengt, "Ability, Performance, and Wage Differentials," *Review of Economic Studies*, July 1982, *49*, no. 3, 315–33.

Jovanovic, Boyan, "Job Matching and the Theory of Turnover," *Journal of Political Economy*, October 1979, *87*, no. 5, part 1, 972–90.

Lazear, Edward P., "Why Is There Mandatory Retirement?," *Journal of Political Economy*, December 1979, *87*, no. 6, 1261–84.

_____, "Agency, Earnings Profiles, Productivity and Hours Restrictions," *American Economic Review*, September 1981, *71*, 606–20.

Marshall, Robert C. and Zarkin, Gary A., "The Effect of Tenure on Wage Offers," *Journal of Labor Economics*, July 1987, *5*, no. 3, 308–30.

Medoff, James L. and Abraham, Katharine G., "Experience, Performance, and Earnings," *Quarterly Journal of Economics*, December 1980, *95*, 703–36.

_____ and _____, "Are Those Paid More Really More Productive?, The Case of Experience," *Journal of Human Resources*, Spring 1981, *16*, no. 2, 186–216.

Mincer, Jacob, "Investment in Human Capital and the Personal Income Distribution," *Journal of Political Economy*, August 1958, *66*, no. 4, 281–302.

_____, "On-the-Job Training: Costs, Returns, and Some Implications," *Journal of Political Economy*, October 1962, *70*, no. 5, part 2, 50–79.

_____, *Schooling, Experience, and Earnings*, New York: National Bureau of Economic Research, 1974.

_____, "Job Training, Wage Growth, and Labor Turnover," Columbia University Working Paper, May 1988.

Nickell, Steven J., "Wage Structures and Quit Rates," *International Economic Review*, February 1976, *17*, 191–203.

Rosen, Harvey, S., "Taxation and On-the-Job Training Decisions," *Review of Economics and Statistics*, August 1982, *64*, no. 3, 442–49.

Rothschild, Michael and Stiglitz, Joseph E., "Equilibrium in Competitive Insurance Markets: An Essay on the Economics of Imperfect Information," *Quarterly Journal of Economics*, November 1976, *90*, no. 4, 630–49.

Salop, Joanne and Salop, Steven, "Self-Selection and Turnover in the Labor Market," *Quarterly Journal of Economics*, November 1976, *90*, no. 4, 619–28.

Schultz, Theodore W., "Capital Formation by Education," *Journal of Political Economy*, December 1960, *68*, no. 6, 571–83.

_____, "Investment in Human Capital," *American Economic Review*, March 1961, *51*, 1–17.

Smith, Adam, *An Inquiry into the Nature and Causes of the Wealth of Nations*, New York: Penguin, 1986.

Stiglitz, Joseph E., "Incentives, Risk and Information: Notes toward a Theory of Hierarchy," *Bell Journal of Economics*, Autumn 1975, *6*, no. 2, 552–79.

Topel, Robert, "Job Mobility, Search, and Earnings Growth: A Reinterpretation of Human Capital Earnings Functions," in Ronald G. Ehrenberg, ed., *Research in Labor Economics*, 1986, *8*, Greenwich, CT: JAI Press, 199–223.

_____, "Wages Rise with Job Seniority," University of Chicago Working Paper, November 1987.

[16]

ᶜAcademy of Management Journal
1987. Vol. 30, No. 2. 316-335.

APPLYING UTILITY CONCEPTS TO A TRAINING PROGRAM IN SUPERVISORY SKILLS: A TIME-BASED APPROACH

JOHN E. MATHIEU
Pennsylvania State University
RUSSELL L. LEONARD, JR.
Signet Banking Corporation

An application of utility analysis concepts, this study employed a quasi-experimental design to demonstrate the effects of a training program in supervisory skills on the performance ratings of 65 bank supervisors. We expanded the utility formula presented by Schmidt, Hunter, and Pearlman, incorporating economic considerations suggested by Boudreau in a time-based framework. Results indicated considerable dollar benefit to the organization from training supervisors. The utility formula was modified to permit examination of influences of adjusting various parameters of the model and of training additional groups on overall utility benefits.

Applied research in the behavioral sciences has shown an increased awareness of utility concepts in recent years (Boudreau & Berger, 1985; Cascio, 1982; Landy, Farr, & Jacobs, 1982; Schmidt, Hunter, & Pearlman, 1982). Those studies have suggested that the dollar value of various personnel programs has gone largely unnoticed or has been considerably underestimated in the past. Schmidt, Hunter, McKenzie, and Muldrow (1979) demonstrated the cost-effectiveness of using valid selection procedures. Several papers have presented examples of the potential benefits of employee training programs in dollar values (Boudreau, 1983b; Landy et al., 1982; Schmidt et al., 1982), but empirical data from actual applications in organizational settings are lacking.

The purpose of this study was to apply utility analysis to a training program in supervisory skills conducted in a bank. Further, we expanded the utility formula presented by Schmidt and his colleagues (1982) to include parameters suggested by Boudreau (1983a, 1983b) in order to calculate utility benefits over time.

The authors are grateful to Terry Dickinson, Scott Tannenbaum, and three anonymous reviewers for their many helpful comments and suggestions on an earlier version of this paper. We would also like to thank Charles Woodworth for his effort and contributions on the cost accounting portion of the study.

A Utility Formula

Schmidt, Hunter, and Pearlman (1982: 335) derived the following formula for assessing the dollar value of a training program:

$$\Delta U = T N d_t SDy - NC, \qquad (1)$$

where

ΔU = the dollar value of a training program,

T = the duration, in number of years, of a training program's effect on performance,

N = the number of individuals trained,

d_t = the true difference in job performance between the average trained and the average untrained employee in units of standard deviation,

SDy = the standard deviation of job performance in dollars of the untrained group,

and

C = the cost of training per individual.

This formula essentially embodies a static, single-group design that assesses the utility of conducting a training program on a single group of individuals and does not take into account the influence of employee flows or the effects of adding training groups. Boudreau (1983b) noted that these deficiencies could lead to considerable underestimation of the utility of a training program but alternatively demonstrated (1983a) how previous applications of the formula may have overestimated marginal utilities because they failed to incorporate economic considerations into the derivations of overall utility gains. He suggested the addition of three economic parameters to the model: (1) *variable costs*—costs that covary with productivity increases, such as bonuses or commissions; (2) *organizational marginal tax rates*—the tax rate applicable to changes in reported profits attributable to a training program; and (3) *discounting*—adjusting for the fact that revenue gained in later years is worth less than revenue gained at the time of training, since present money can at least be invested at prevailing interest rates. Boudreau (1983b) derived a utility formula that takes into account the influence of both employee flows and economic parameters on marginal utility estimates. We slightly modified Boudreau's formula in order to derive ongoing marginal utility estimates and to assess better the utility of conducting a training program in supervisory skills in a time-based framework.

A Time-based Utility Model

Schmidt and his coauthors (1982) suggested that the effects of a training program on performance (d_t) may diminish over time. To account for this phenomenon, they proposed that estimates of marginal utility be multiplied by a value representing the midpoint of the period over which training is expected to last. However, since organizations only gain utility benefits from

trained individuals who remain with them, the effect of turnover on the size
of a trained group of individuals must be taken into account (Boudreau &
Berger, 1985). Previous applications of concept of utility analysis have multiplied projected benefits by the mean tenure of individuals in a given job
class. For training interventions, the number of trained individuals should
be adjusted downward by the mean percentage of turnover in a job class over
the period of time that utility benefits are computed. The utility benefits
from training additional groups of employees also need to be taken into
account in order to assess fully the impact of a training program.

McKeon (1981) and Cascio (1982) described detailed procedures for estimating the cost of conducting training. However, their procedures should be
modified to provide cost estimates that distinguish nonrecurring from recurring costs. Organizations absorb nonrecurring costs during the development
of a program; they include equipment purchases and trainers' salaries during
the period. Recurring costs are absorbed each time a program is presented;
they include session expenses like the cost of facilities and trainers' salaries,
and costs corresponding to the number of participants in a program, such as
training materials and trainees' salaries. Separating costs in this fashion
permits the incorporation of each into utility calculations for the time periods in which an organization actually incurs each expense. Thus, a program's
high initial expenses may indicate that costs exceed benefits for the first few
training groups or first few years of operation. However, at a certain point an
organization may actually derive benefit from a program; this point represents the beginning of the payback period. This approach will clarify information for decision makers regarding the utility of personnel programs in a
return-on-investment framework (Cronshaw & Alexander, 1985).

Equation 2 expands Schmidt and colleagues' formula to allow calculation of utility estimates that take into account the influences of turnover,
diminishing effects of training, and estimated costs over one-year periods.
We chose the one-year metric because it coincides with the typical period of
organizational budget decisions and with the publication of information
pertaining to several parameters of the formula, such as yearly reports on
turnover and applicable tax rates.

$$\Delta U_k = \sum_{g=1}^{G_k} (N_{gk} \, SDy \, d_{t_{gk}} - C_k), \qquad (2)$$

where

k = the number of years over which utility estimates are calculated,
ΔU_k = the marginal utility gained in year k,
G_k = the total number of groups trained through year k,
N_{gk} = the number of trainees in group g in year k adjusted for turnover,[1]

---

[1] If the average percentage of yearly turnover for a job class is set at M, the following
computation adjusts for the first-year value: $N_{g1} = N_{g0} (1 - M/2)$. Subsequent yearly values are
computed as follows: $N_{gk} = N_{gk-1} (1 - M)$.

SDy = the standard deviation of performance in dollar units,

$d_{t_{gk}}$ = the effect size estimate for training group g in year k,[2]

and

C_k = the costs incurred in year k.

For training interventions, Equation 2 calculates the cost value for the groups trained in year k. Naturally, the first-year cost value would also include the costs of program development. Use of Equation 2 permits estimation of utility gains in any given period or over any specified length of time after training occurs. However, as Boudreau (1983a) noted, these estimates must be adjusted for economic considerations for them to reflect accurately the organizational benefits of increased productivity. Equation 3, which expands Equation 2, includes the influences of discounting, tax rate, and variable costs:

$$\Delta U_k = \sum_{g=1}^{G_k} \frac{1}{(1+i)^k} [N_{gk} SDy (1+V)(1-TAX_k) d_{t_{gk}}]$$

$$- [C_k \frac{1}{(1+i)^k} (1-TAX_k)], \tag{3}$$

where

i = the discount rate,

V = the variable costs,

and

TAX_k = the organizational tax rate for year k.

Several features of this formula should be highlighted. As does Boudreau's (1983b) application, Equation 3 provides a more complete and precise definition of utility than earlier utility models did, as well as a method for projecting costs and benefits over time. It is algebraically the same as Boudreau's (1983b) Equation 5, with one major difference: whereas Boudreau's equation sums the number of treated employees in a workforce in each future time period and multiplies by a constant effect size, Equation 3 allows both the number of treated employees in a workforce and the effect size to vary according to the time of treatment. When the effect size parameter is held constant, Equation 3 is algebraically equivalent to Boudreau's Equation 5.

---

[2] Assuming there is some reduction in the effectiveness of training over time, the most representative estimate of first-year size (d_t) is that which exists six months after training. In the present case, we obtained our criterion measure approximately six months after employees had completed training. Effect size estimates obtained at other times would require adjustment in order to align them with the six-month period. Setting the average percentage of yearly decrease in effectiveness of training at P, we computed subsequent yearly values as follows: $d_{t_{gk}} = d_{t_{gk-1}}$ (1 − P).

Two other minor differences between the two equations should be noted. First, we replaced the terms $(r_{x, sv})(\bar{Z}_x)$ with d_t, the appropriate effect size estimate for a training intervention. Second, we discounted the costs associated with training in the same period when benefits would begin to accrue; the exponent for the discount factor for costs is k rather than $k - 1$. The basis for this decision was the fact that there was no appreciable time lapse between development and implementation of the particular training program we studied (cf. Boudreau, 1983b: 399, footnote 1).

METHODS

Participants

All participants worked at a bank in the Southeast that employs approximately 3,000 people. Personnel records indicated that 65 individuals had completed a training program in supervisory skills in the previous year. The bank had solicited participants through general company announcements and memos sent directly to each branch and department; employees either nominated themselves to participate or were nominated by their supervisors. No systematic data were available regarding how well the trainees represented all eligible employees. However, as discussed below, we assessed several variables other than training that can influence employees' performance and used them to compare trainees to a control group constructed post hoc.

Training Procedures

The training program in supervisory skills that the bank used is a commercially available system; it is designed to be presented by trained in-house employees and utilizes a modular, behavior modeling format. The bank ran five training programs, each of which met for four full-day sessions, one a week for four weeks. During each session, a trainer led the group in a discussion of common work situations requiring supervisory action, such as improving subordinates' performance or giving recognition; participants viewed a film depicting a supervisor effectively handling an appropriate situation, received a list of three to six learning points or "key actions," discussed the effectiveness of the model in demonstrating the key actions, and then role-played the desired behaviors either in small groups or in front of the entire group. Other participants gave feedback on their performance to those who took roles. The sequence was repeated over three or four modules during each session. Trainers advised participants to keep the handouts listing the key actions and other training materials at hand in their work settings.

Quasi-experimental Design

The 65 trained individuals represented three job classes at the bank; there were 10 head tellers, 36 branch managers, and 19 operations managers. Head tellers supervised other tellers working at their branches in addition to themselves performing teller duties. Branch managers supervised all of a branch's employees in addition to performing duties like handling loan transactions. Operations managers held an assortment of positions, such as security officers, accountants, and group leaders in computer programming.

A post hoc, quasi-experimental design was constructed to examine the effects of training on individuals' performance (Cook & Campbell, 1979). Because individuals had not been randomly assigned for training, we made an effort to match a control group ($N = 65$) to trainees on all performance-relevant variables retrievable from personnel records. Using a complete listing of the company's personnel, we selected individuals for the control group from the same job classes and geographical locations and matched them to trainees on the bases of salary, tenure, gender, and age.

Comparisons between the trained and control groups on the matching variables revealed no significant differences: salary $\bar{x} = \$19,652$ vs. $\$20,408$; tenure, $\bar{x} = 10.32$ vs. 11.43 years; gender, 29 vs. 34 percent men; and age, 39.39 vs. 39.41 years.

In addition to the matching information, for a proxy pretest measure (Cook & Campbell, 1979: 112–115) we obtained from personnel records the most recent performance appraisals completed prior to training for trained individuals and appraisals from the corresponding time period for members of the control group. The performance appraisals consisted of a 30-item scale on which supervisors rated each subordinate, with 1 = performance is well below expected levels to 5 = performance consistently exceeds superior levels in performance goals and quality. Some representative rating dimensions were volume of work, ability to learn new duties, and delegating duties and authority. The coefficient alpha for a unit-weighted composite of these ratings was .93.

Although the bank uses such appraisals primarily for administrative and compensational purposes, it is reasonable to expect them to correlate with other performance indicators, and therefore they may be used to help to equate the training and control groups statistically. The training group and the control group did not differ significantly on the performance appraisal measure ($t_{128} = .37$, $p > .10$).

Research Procedures

Supervisors ($N = 62$) of employees in the trained and the control groups were asked to participate in an evaluation study that the Human Resource Planning and Development Department of the bank conducted approximately six months after employees completed training. Each supervisor received a packet containing a cover letter and two parts. The cover letter explained that the purpose of the study was to evaluate the effectiveness of several training programs and related activities currently being conducted and to determine the need for various types of additional programs.

For the first part of the evaluation study, supervisors estimated the dollar value to the bank of three levels of performance on the part of employees. They assigned dollar values to performance in the 15th, 50th, and 85th percentiles. We used these estimates to compute values of SDy for the three job classes: head tellers (N = 19), operations managers (N = 25), and branch managers (N = 18). The instructions and wording for estimating each of the three percentiles of performance were essentially the same as those described by Schmidt and his colleagues (1979) and by Bobko, Karren, and Parkington (1983).

The second part of the evaluation study asked supervisors to evaluate from one to nine subordinates on an 18-item rating scale; the number depended on how many of the individuals in the trained and control groups reported directly to them. We took care not to identify which Human Resource Planning and Development program was being examined or which of the employees being rated had been trained. Since people in both the trained and the control groups had participated in various programs presented by the department, we felt the potential biasing effect of knowledge of the treatment was minimal.

Measurements

Performance measure. The rating scale contained two items for each of nine performance dimensions that the bank had identified during a redesign of its performance appraisal system for supervisors shortly before the present study. These items appear in the Appendix. Since the estimates of SDy and the utility of the training program pertain to overall job performance (Schmidt et al., 1979), we used a single unit-weighted composite of the items as the criterion measure (α = .90).

Training costs. An internal audit conducted by the Human Resource Planning and Development Department provided data on costs. Following the outlines and formulas presented in McKeon (1981) and Cascio (1982), we identified these nonrecurring or program development costs: (1) trainers' materials and video tapes, $10,000; and (2) salaries, benefits, and travel for trainers for five days, $2,800, for a total one-time cost of $12,800.

Recurring costs break down into the fixed and variable costs associated with conducting each training program. Fixed costs per program included: (1) trainer's salary and benefits for four days, $670; (2) equipment and materials for four days, $155; and (3) facilities for four days, $116, for a total of $941. Five training programs were conducted during the year, three for branch managers and one each for head tellers and operations managers. Costs corresponding to the number of trainees in each program included (1) work books and handouts provided to each trainee, $84; and (2) the average salary and benefits for four days per trainee, $283 for head tellers, $323 for operations managers, and $517 for branch managers. Therefore, the variable training costs per trainee for the three job classes were $367, $407, and $601, respectively.

Estimates of turnover. The bank's personnel records were examined for the five years prior to the training in order to estimate the average yearly rate of turnover for each job class. This examination resulted in the following mean values: head tellers, 12.17 percent (s.d. = 3.71); operations managers,

16.90 percent (s.d. = 6.25); and branch managers, 10.48 percent (s.d. = 3.62).

Economic factors. After consulting experts in bank finance, we determined the appropriate discount rate to be 15 percent and the applicable organizational tax rate to be 46 percent. These values seem conservative as compared to those Boudreau (1983a) suggested. 0–15 percent for the discount rate and 45 percent for the tax rate.

Discussions with bank employees revealed salary to be the only variable cost clearly and consistently associated with improvements in performance. Employees' salaries and benefits would rise to the extent that appraisals were sensitive to improvements in performance following training. We therefore reduced utility gains from training by a percentage calculated by dividing each job's variable costs by its *SDy* value. The Appendix presents the procedure for estimating variable costs as a percentage of *SDy*.

RESULTS

Effect of Training

Cook and Campbell defined the quasi-experimental design that we employed to assess the effect of training on employees' overall performance as an untreated control group design with proxy pretest measures (1979: 112–115). We used performance appraisals conducted prior to training as the proxy pretest measure in order to help reduce spurious effects of prior performance on the criterion measure represented by the 18-item supervisory rating composite. A hierarchical multiple regression analysis was performed using the correlations presented in Table 1 to determine the influence of training on performance. We regressed the criterion measure first on the pretest measure to control for any spurious pretraining differences in performance. Entered next, a dichotomous variable identifying group (control = 0, trained = 1) accounted for significant additional variance ($t_{127} = 1.77$, $p < .05$, one-tailed test). The overall equation accounted for over 24 percent

TABLE 1
Correlations, Means, Standard Deviations, and Reliabilities
for Performance Measures[a]

Variables	Means	Standard Deviations	1	2	3
1. Group[b]	0.50	.50			
2. Pretest	3.49	.47	.0329	(.93)	
3. Criterion	3.66	.53	.1523*	.4751**	(.90)

[a] Diagonal entries represent internal consistency estimates (α).

[b] Groups were coded as follows: control = 0, trained = 1.

* $p < .05$, one-sided tests.

** $p < .01$

of variance in the criterion ratings $(F_{2,127} = 20.54, p < .001)$.[3] The partial correlation associated with the group variable $(r = .16, p < .05)$ represents the independent effect of training on performance. Applying the conversion formulas that Schmidt and his colleagues (1982: 337) presented translates that value to a score for d_t of .3146. This value should be considered as a conservative estimate of the true effect of training on employees' performance since we did not correct the measures for attenuation (Schmidt et al., 1982).

Estimates of SDy

Two *SDy* distributions were computed from supervisors' percentile estimates: one by subtracting the 15th percentile from the 50th, the second by subtracting the 50th from the 85th. As in previous investigations (Bobko et al., 1983; Schmidt et al., 1979), the estimates for *SDy* that we found varied widely within each job class. Close inspection of the raw distributions for the dollar estimates of the value of performance in the three percentiles and the two *SDy* distributions produced through application of Schmidt and colleagues' procedure revealed the reasons for the large discrepancies.

For the operations managers, both of the two estimates for *SDy* from three supervisors exceeded $86,000, and the remaining estimates for this job class were all less than $8,000. The discrepant values may represent either outliers or actual differences attributable to different jobs. Regardless, the elimination of the three extreme estimates reduces the variance of the *SDy* distributions and produces more a conservative, lower value for *SDy*.

Additional large variances observed in the two remaining job classes were traceable to a different cause. Inspection of the raw distributions revealed that the estimated value of performance in the 15th percentile was $0 in three cases each for head tellers and branch managers. In fact, in another instance, a supervisor estimated the utility of a branch manager's performance in the 15th percentile to be –$35,000. Burke and Frederick (1984) and Weekley, Frank, O'Connor, and Peters (1985) also obtained zero and negative estimates for 15th percentile performers. These peculiar estimates may result from supervisors' failing to comprehend the nature of percentiles; however, they may be accurate assessments of the utility of 15th percentile performance—excessive loan losses could result in a branch manager's performance costing $35,000. Eliminating estimates with zero or negative values reduced the variance in the two *SDy* distributions and yielded more conservative *SDy* values.

Paired *t*-tests were computed to examine whether the two trimmed *SDy* distributions differed significantly for each job class. No significant differences emerged: for head tellers, $t_{15} = .63, p > .50$; for operations managers,

---

[3] Other analyses not reported here tested for differences attributable to job class, training session attended, influences of the matching variables on the performance rating criterion, and potential interactions. No significant relationships emerged; further details are available from the first author.

1987   *Mathieu and Leonard*   325

TABLE 2
Parameters of Utility Analysis Formula Varying with Job Class

Parameters	Head Tellers	Operations Managers	Branch Managers
Training costs per individual[a]	$367	$407	$601
Numbers trained[b]	10	19	36
Average turnover[c]	12.17	10.48	16.90
SDy	$2,369	$3,123	$10,064
Variable costs[a]	−6.68%	−7.29%	−2.87%

[a] See text for computations; variable costs are expressed as percentage of SDy.
[b] Figures represent actual numbers of trainees.
[c] These are mean percentages computed over previous five years.

$t_{21} = .17, p > .80$; and for branch managers, $t_{13} = -.49, p > .60$. Thus, we averaged the two distributions for each job class to provide the final values of SDy for use in the utility computations: for head tellers, $SDy = \$2,369$ (s.d. = 837); for operations managers, $SDy = \$3,122$ (s.d. = 1,496); and for branch managers, $SDy = \$10,064$ (s.d. = 4,932).[4]

Utility Analysis

Inserting the mean SDy values computed above into Equation 5, which appears in the Appendix, yielded estimates of variable costs as a percentage of SDy as follows: for head tellers, 6.68; for operations managers, 7.29; and for branch managers, 2.87. Estimates for all of the parameters necessary for the utility analysis computations were thus available. For illustrative purposes, the following parameters remained fixed for estimates of the utility of training individuals in each job class: $d_t = .3146$, session costs = $941, tax rate = 46 percent, and discount rate = 15 percent. Table 2 presents values for parameters that vary with each job class.

Table 3 presents projected raw and adjusted utility estimates over 20 years for individuals who were trained in the first year; estimates exclude program development costs. The second column in Table 3 presents the appropriate discount values used in computations for the adjusted utility estimates. The first column under each job class contains the projected number of trainees remaining in the organization for each year. As illustrated, this number drops below 1.00 beginning in year 19 for head tellers and does so in year 20 for branch managers. Utility benefits from training operations managers would actually continue to accrue until year 27.

The upper portion of Table 4 presents the summed total utility estimates including program development costs for some selected time periods. The

---

[4] An alternative strategy to trimming the extreme estimates is to use nonparametric statistics to test the assumption that the two SDy distributions do not differ significantly (Bobko et al., 1983). Wilcoxon matched-pairs, signed-rank tests (two-sided) computed on the full distributions failed to discredit the hypothesis that the two SDy estimates were drawn from the same population ($p > .05$) within each job class. Nevertheless, we chose to use the mean SDy values from the trimmed distributions in order to remain conservative.

summed total of the raw estimates of the utility of training 65 employees is $78,493 at the end of the first year alone. The benefits continue to rise to $421,427 by year 5 and $750,883 by year 20. Adjusting the raw utility estimates for economic considerations results in drastic reductions in these figures. The summed adjusted total utility estimates from training the same 65 employees drops to $34,627 at the end of year 1, to $148,465 by year 5, and to $194,885 by year 20. Although still compelling, the adjusted utility estimates are substantially lower than those suggested by the raw utility formula.

The estimates entail some assumptions about the stability of several of the model's parameters. Perhaps the most tenuous assumption is that the effect of training on performance (d_t) remains constant over time; the alternative argument is that the effects of training on performance dissipate over time. In order to examine the influence of the first assumption, we recomputed raw and adjusted utility estimates for each job class with a 25 percent reduction in d_t each year. The lower portion of Table 4 shows these values. It is clear that if the effectiveness of training declines over time the apparent utility of a program is severely reduced, particularly in the later years. In this

TABLE 3
Utility Estimates for Trainees by Job Class[a]

Years	Discount Values	Head Tellers			Operations Managers			Branch Managers		
		N	Raw	Adjusted	N	Raw	Adjusted	N	Raw	Adjusted
1	.870	9.39	$2,388	$ 902	18.00	$ 9,015	$3,628	32.96	$79,890	$36,107
2	.756	8.25	6,147	2,342	16.12	15,835	5,994	27.39	86,714	34,391
3	.658	7.24	5,399	1,789	14.43	14,176	4,666	22.76	72,060	24,851
4	.572	6.36	4,742	1,366	12.92	12,690	3,632	18.91	59,882	17,958
5	.497	5.59	4,165	1,043	11.56	11,360	2,828	15.72	49,762	12,976
6	.432	4.91	3,658	797	10.35	10,170	2,201	13.06	41,352	9,377
7	.376	4.31	3,213	609	9.27	9,104	1,713	10.85	34,363	6,776
8	.327	3.79	2,822	465	8.30	8,150	1,334	9.02	28,556	4,896
9	.284	3.33	2,478	355	7.43	7,296	1,038	7.49	23,730	3,538
10	.247	2.92	2,176	271	6.65	6,531	808	6.23	19,720	2,557
11	.215	2.57	1,912	207	5.95	5,847	629	5.17	16,387	1,847
12	.187	2.25	1,679	158	5.33	5,234	490	4.30	13,618	1,335
13	.163	1.98	1,475	121	4.77	4,685	381	3.57	11,316	965
14	.141	1.74	1,295	92	4.27	4,194	297	2.97	9,404	697
15	.123	1.53	1,138	70	3.82	3,755	231	2.47	7,814	504
16	.107	1.34	999	54	3.42	3,361	180	2.05	6,494	364
17	.093	1.18	878	41	3.06	3,009	140	1.70	5,396	263
18	.081	1.03	771	31	2.74	2,694	109	1.42	4,484	190
19	.070	<1.00			2.45	2,411	85	1.18	3,726	137
20	.061	<1.00			2.20	2,159	66	<1.00		
Totals			$47,339	$10,715		$141,676	$30,451		$574,668	$159,729

[a] Raw estimates were computed with Equation 2; adjusted estimates used Equation 3. N = projected number of trainees remaining in the organization for each year. Dollar values exclude program development cost of $12,800.

TABLE 4
Summed Utility Estimates for All Trainees by Job Class[a]

(a) Utility Estimates Holding Training's Effectiveness Constant

Years	Head Tellers		Operations Managers		Branch Managers		Totals	
	Raw	Adjusted	Raw	Adjusted	Raw	Adjusted	Raw	Adjusted
1	$ 2,388	$ 902	$ 9,015	$ 3,628	$ 79,890	$ 36,107	$ 78,493	$ 34,627
3	13,935	5,033	39,026	14,289	238,664	95,349	278,825	108,661
5	22,843	7,443	63,077	20,749	348,307	126,283	421,427	148,465
10	37,191	9,940	104,327	27,843	496,028	153,427	624,746	185,200
15	44,691	10,589	128,042	29,871	554,567	158,774	714,500	193,224
20	47,339	10,715	141,676	30,451	574,668	159,729	750,883	194,885

(b) Utility Estimates with 25 Percent Yearly Decrease in Training's Effectiveness[b]

Years	Head Tellers		Operations Managers		Branch Managers		Totals	
	Raw	Adjusted	Raw	Adjusted	Raw	Adjusted	Raw	Adjusted
1	$ 2,388	$ 902	$ 9,015	$ 3,628	$ 79,890	$36,107	$ 78,493	$ 34,627
3	10,036	3,665	28,866	10,748	185,459	75,879	211,561	84,282
5	13,355	4,572	37,814	13,175	226,467	87,561	264,836	99,298
10	15,583	4,987	44,156	14,345	250,064	92,192	297,003	105,514
15	15,859	5,013	45,021	14,425	252,283	92,408	300,363	105,836
20	15,887	5,014	45,139	14,430	252,478	92,418	300,704	105,852

[a] Raw estimates were computed with Equation 2; adjusted estimates were computed with Equation 3; totals include program development costs of $12,800.

[b] Applicable effect size estimates for years given are 1 = .315, 3 = .177, 5 = .100, 10 = .024, 15 = .006, and 20 = .001.

case, the estimated adjusted utility falls to $99,298 by year 5 and to $105,852 by year 20. However, equally worthy of attention are the utility gains that remain, even in this conservative example.

DISCUSSION

The purpose of this study was to develop a time-based utility model for personnel programs and to illustrate its application to a training program in supervisory skills. We modified the utility formula developed by Schmidt and his colleagues (1982) to incorporate the influence of employee flows (Boudreau, 1983b) and economic factors (Boudreau, 1983a) over time. Procedures for estimating the costs associated with training presented by McKeon (1981) and by Cascio (1982) were modified to differentiate nonrecurring from recurring costs. This time-based approach provided clearer and more realistic information than has previously been available regarding the utility of training programs in terms of return on investment. To our knowledge, it is the first application of such techniques to assess the utility of a training program conducted in an actual organizational setting.

The results were compelling, not only in terms of dollar values, but also from the standpoint of the information they provided for managerial decisions regarding future human resource programs in our particular setting. Recent years have seen an increased concern with the costs associated with training (Gilbert, 1976; McKeon, 1981). In this case, the cost of training 65 employees exceeded $50,500. However, results of the utility analysis suggest that the cost of *not training* employees may be even higher.

Adjusted for economic factors, the net utility to the organization of training this single group of employees was over $34,600 in the first year alone. This figure rose dramatically to over $108,600 by year 3 and to over $148,400 by year 5. Even if the effectiveness of training should decrease by 25 percent a year, the benefit of conducting the program is still impressive: $84,282 by year 3 and $99,298 by year 5. Naturally, practitioners and researchers alike may be a bit skeptical of these results. As Schmidt and his colleagues (1982) noted, we are simply not accustomed to thinking about the impact of personnel programs in economic terms. Also, since the values for SDy and d_t were based on subjective ratings, some concern regarding the influence of measurement error on these parameters seems warranted. Boudreau (1984) developed a technique called break-even analysis to address the influence of measurement error on results of utility analysis.

Break-even Analysis

Break-even analysis is a method to determine the minimum value for SDy that is necessary, given the other parameters of the utility model, for a personnel program to yield positive utility. Break-even values can be compared to the actual estimates of SDy used in this study. To the extent that the break-even values approach the SDy values used to compute the results of the utility analysis, error of measurement in obtaining values for SDy leads to greater uncertainty regarding the utility of a program. To the extent that the break-even values are far below the actual values for SDy used in the utility analysis, error of measurement in SDy should have little or no influence on a decision whether or not to adopt a program. In the present context, the equation for computing break-even values using the adjusted utility analysis results presented in the top half of Table 4 is as follows:

$$U = (INC)(SDy) - COSTS , \qquad (4)$$

where

U = the summed utility gained in any particular time period adjusted for economic factors,

INC = the increase in utility for each increase in SDy for that period of analysis and that particular group of employees,

SDy = the estimated SDy for that group of employees, and

$COSTS$ = the program costs for that group of employees adjusted for economic factors.

For this analysis, costs include a portion of the program development costs of $12,800 determined on the basis of the number of employees in the particular group.

Break-even SDy is equal to $COSTS$ divided by INC. For example, utility gained in year 1 from training ten head tellers is $3,067. This value exceeds the $902 value reported in Table 4 because the latter compensated for session and individual costs that the value for $COSTS$ includes in this equation. The total cost of training ten tellers—including costs per session, per individual, and 15 percent of program development, adjusted for economic factors—is $3,089. Applying Equation 4 yields a value for INC of 2.60 and a break-even SDy value of $1,189, which is 50 percent of the SDy value used in the utility analysis. Break-even SDy values for year 1 are $1,346 for the operations managers and $2,389 for the branch managers, which are 43 and 24 percent of the values used in the utility computations. These break-even values for the first year are all below the lower boundary of the 95 percent confidence intervals of the SDy distributions generated from the Schmidt et al. (1979) procedure we used. Naturally, the break-even values would continue to decrease over time as utility benefits continued to accumulate. For instance, break-even values for SDy in year 5 would be $576 (24%) for the head tellers, $594 (19%) for the operations managers, and $977 (10%) for the branch managers. It is also possible to estimate the break-even value for d_t by substituting d_t for SDy in Equation 4. In year 1, break-even values for d_t were .1579 for the head tellers, .1356 for the operations managers, and .0747 for the branch managers.

A break-even analysis using the conservative utility values based on a 25 percent yearly reduction in the effectiveness of training (Table 4, lower portion) produces similar results. All break-even SDy values are still less than 50 percent of the values used in the utility analysis. The values for year 5 are $745 (31%), $789 (25%), and $1,309 (13%) for the head tellers, operations managers, and branch managers, respectively. These results suggest that although measurement error in SDy or d_t may alter the magnitude of projected utility benefits, a decision whether or not to introduce a training program should be unaffected. The training program we assessed appeared to be warranted, even given large amounts of measurement error.

Employee Flow Analysis

The utility analysis presented thus far investigated only the benefit from training 65 supervisors. However, these findings underestimate the true value of the program since the analysis did not include the influence of training additional groups (Boudreau, 1983b). The utility gained from additional training must be taken into account in order to project a realistic estimate of the benefit of the training program. Equation 3 is designed to accommodate employee flows and to permit organizational decision makers to ask "what if" types of questions.

For example, a decision maker might ask what the summed overall utility of the program would be if training were conducted with additional groups for five years. Given the turnover rates used in the analysis and the fact that the bank operates more than 120 branches, at least 15 openings in each job class should occur each year. The results in the upper portion of Table 5 incorporate the influence of projected employee flows and are based on the training of 15 new employees in each job class each year for five years.

Computed on the basis of 45 employees, the summed adjusted utility of the program in year 1 with the first group is $13,490. The figure rises to $104,120 by year 3 and to $219,577 by year 5, when the last group will have been trained. The organization would continue to derive benefit from the program in later years from employees that remain in the organization. The figures in Table 5 demonstrate vividly the effects of training additional groups on overall utility estimates. The estimate for the tenth year of the utility of training 225 employees in the first five years is over $364,300, even after adjustments for economic considerations. Equally dramatic are the differences between the raw and adjusted utility estimates. Not only is there a substantial difference in the magnitude of the two estimates, but the ratio between the two increases the further in time they are projected. The ad-

TABLE 5
Summed Utility Estimates for Training 15 Employees in Each Job Class for Five Years[a]

(a) Utility Estimates Holding Training's Effectiveness Constant

Years	Head Tellers Raw	Head Tellers Adjusted	Operations Managers Raw	Operations Managers Adjusted	Branch Managers Raw	Branch Managers Adjusted	Totals Raw	Totals Adjusted
1	$ 4,053	$ 1,574	$ 6,919	$ 2,771	$ 33,523	$ 15,155	$ 31,695	$ 13,490
3	38,701	13,385	56,952	19,807	202,855	76,938	285,708	104,120
5	101,922	30,046	147,183	43,487	472,848	152,054	709,153	219,577
10	243,788	54,732	352,868	78,863	933,925	236,776	1,517,781	364,361
15	317,934	61,147	471,119	88,975	1,116,640	253,468	1,892,893	397,580
20	356,687	62,813	539,103	91,865	1,156,522	255,456	2,039,512	404,124

(b) Utility Estimates with 25 Percent Yearly Decrease in Training's Effectiveness[b]

Years	Head Tellers Raw	Head Tellers Adjusted	Operations Managers Raw	Operations Managers Adjusted	Branch Managers Raw	Branch Managers Adjusted	Totals Raw	Totals Adjusted
1	$ 4,053	$ 1,574	$ 6,919	$ 2,771	$ 33,523	$ 15,155	$ 31,695	$ 13,490
3	30,547	10,569	45,805	15,983	171,654	65,710	235,206	86,252
5	69,575	20,795	102,277	30,745	354,287	116,614	513,339	162,144
10	115,139	29,289	167,034	42,690	510,981	147,365	780,354	213,334
15	120,790	29,813	175,869	43,501	525,716	148,802	809,575	216,106
20	121,491	29,846	177,074	43,555	526,765	148,856	812,530	216,247

[a] Raw estimates were computed with Equation 2; adjusted estimates were computed with Equation 3; totals include program development costs of $12,800.

[b] Applicable effect size estimates for years given are 1 = .315, 3 = .177, 5 = .100, 10 = .024, 15 = .006, and 20 = .001.

justed estimate is 43 percent of the raw estimate in year 1 and it successively decreases to 20 percent of the raw estimate by year 20.

The figures in Table 5 also demonstrate that the utility of a training program depends in part on the types of employees trained. Clearly, the utility of training branch managers exceeds that of training operations managers—for whom there is a 5.47 to 1 ratio in year 1—or head tellers, with a 9.63 to 1 ratio in year 1. The difference is mainly attributable to the higher *SDy* estimate for branch managers. Other parameters that vary by job class, such as training costs, turnover, and variable costs, also affect utility estimates but do so in the present case to a lesser extent than *SDy*.

The summed utility estimates presented in the upper portion of Table 5 were recomputed under the assumption that the effectiveness of training diminishes 25 percent each year. The lower half of Table 5 presents the results of these analyses. Not surprisingly, the utility estimates drop considerably, but continue to demonstrate substantial economic benefit from conducting supervisory skills training; estimates are $86,252 by year 3, $162,144 by year 5, and $213,334 by year 10.

Issues and Implications for Future Research

The effectiveness of training in improving overall performance obviously affects the utility of a program. Anything that influences this effectiveness has an impact on the utility derived. Similarly, any factor that may contaminate an evaluation of the effectiveness of training will bias utility estimates. The degree of confidence we can have in the validity of a value for d_t is a function of the research design employed. The quasi-experimental design we used rules out several, but not all, threats to validity (Cook & Campbell, 1979). Unfortunately, we did not have the luxury of a true experimental design. Random assignment of supervisors to training, multiple measures of the internal validity of the training, and a longitudinal assessment of the effectiveness of training could lend further support to the present findings. For purposes of comparison, however, a recent meta-analysis (Burke & Day, 1986) of 17 effect size estimates from five managerial training studies using behavioral modeling techniques and subjective behavior criteria found an average effect size estimate of .70 (s.d. = .52). After correcting the observed findings for statistical artifacts, the average effect size was estimated to be .78 (s.d. = 0.0). Thus, the present value for d_t of .3146 does not appear to be particularly atypical; yet the paucity of well-controlled empirical studies[5] precludes a definitive statement at this time as to the effectiveness of modular, behavioral modeling training programs in supervisor skills.

As demonstrated, the duration of the effect of training on performance plays an important role in the utility computations. Schmidt and his colleagues (1982) suggested that the effect of training may decline over time. Applying utility analysis could help to identify when it would be most profitable to conduct retraining or to present refresher seminars. Alternatively,

---

[5] Latham and Saari (1979), however, is a particularly good exception.

Burnaska (1976) indicated that it may take time for managers to practice the skills they have learned and for perceptions of their performance to improve. To the extent that the second position is correct, scores for d_t would increase over time as managers honed the skills that they have learned. Clearly, there is a need for longitudinal studies in organizational settings in order to begin to address the effect of time on d_t scores.

As in earlier investigations (Bobko et al., 1983; Schmidt et al., 1979; Weekley et al., 1985), the estimates for *SDy* we used varied greatly within each job class. The heterogeneity of jobs within the group of operations managers and some zero—and one negative—estimates of the utility of 15th percentile performance for the head tellers and branch managers accounted for this variation. We chose to eliminate widely discrepant estimates in order to remain conservative. Future research efforts should examine the reasons for this large variation and explore methodological refinements to reduce it.

The number of employees trained has a direct relationship to the overall utility of a program. Similarly, the percentage of turnover among trained employees affects utility since an organization only derives benefits from trained employees who remain in it. We assumed that the likelihood of turnover among trained and untrained employees in a given job class was essentially equal. The utility formula will need adjustment to the extent that receiving training leads to a higher or lower likelihood of termination of employment.

The present utility model could be expanded to include the influence of training on several additional parameters. These might include the influence of training on the attitudes of trainees and their subordinates and absenteeism among them. Since the specific factors that supervisors consider when estimating *SDy* are unknown at the present time, it is not clear whether or not the model takes these additional factors into account. It is clear that both employees' attitudes and absenteeism have significant bottom-line implications for organizations (Cascio, 1982).

Finally, this study used an omnibus unit-weighted supervisory rating as a performance criterion. Alternatively, examination of the specific aspects of overall performance that training affects and their relationships to *SDy* may provide a clearer understanding of how training employees relates to utility.

Implications for Decision Making

The findings of this study should not be viewed as simply a thinly veiled attempt to justify a training program. The results of the utility and break-even analyses indicate clearly that the program was cost-effective. Organizational decision makers could use such information to determine the allocation of resources between personnel programs and other organizational efforts to improve productivity. Alternatively, given a limited budget, a personnel department could determine which employees should be trained first on the basis of the projected utility of training different groups of employees. Our results suggested that the utility of training branch managers far exceeds that of training operations managers or head tellers, although training the second two groups also generated positive utility. However, the information and formulas presented here may also apply to several other types of decisions.

For example, by using the present information and altering various parameters of the utility model, a decision maker could determine the smallest number of supervisors needed to warrant presenting a program. Similarly, someone could estimate the cost-effectiveness of investing more in training—perhaps by training more supervisors or by training them sooner—relative to the utility of their performance levels. Utility analysis formulas may also be of use for organizations wondering which type of supervisory skills training would be best for their own situation. Most of the information required for the utility computations, such as turnover percentages, values for SDy, and economic factors, may be available or may be estimated before firms choose a program. Then, for example, a decision maker could project the relative utility of various forms of managerial training using the effect size estimates reported by Burke and Day (1986) and cost surveys or estimates for the different programs. Thus, the usefulness of this study's findings goes far beyond their ability to justify the cost of a training program.

Finally, we have concentrated on the organizational benefits of training. Naturally, the participants in a program also benefit, typically in terms of self-enhancement or career development. Although they are difficult to quantify, employees and their organizations may value these benefits all the same. Thus, decisions on introducing training programs may be based on what training provides for employees rather than what it gains for the organization, or such decisions may take both beneficiaries into account.

In summary, this study demonstrated the utility of a training program in supervisory skills in a bank. In addition, we sought to identify several areas for future research and how utility theory and its applications can be used for making organizational decisions. We hope that this and other applications will help to promote greater use of utility theory and its techniques in the future.

REFERENCES

Bobko, P., Karren, R., & Parkington, J. J. 1983. Estimation of standard deviations in utility analyses: An empirical test. *Journal of Applied Psychology*, 68: 170–176.

Boudreau, J. W. 1983a. Economic considerations in estimating the utility of human resource productivity improvement programs. *Personnel Psychology*, 36: 551–576.

Boudreau, J. W. 1983b. Effects of employee flows on utility analysis of human resource productivity improvement programs. *Journal of Applied Psychology*, 67: 396–406.

Boudreau, J. W. 1984. Decision theory contributions to HRM research and practice. *Industrial Relations*, 23: 198–217.

Boudreau, J. W., & Berger, C. J. 1985. Decision-theoretic utility analysis applied to employee separations and acquisitions. *Journal of Applied Psychology Monograph*, 70: 581–612.

Burke, M. J., & Day, R. R. 1986. A cumulative study of the effectiveness of managerial training. *Journal of Applied Psychology*, 71: 232–245.

Burke, M. J., & Frederick, J. T. 1984. Two modified procedures for estimating standard deviations in utility analysis. *Journal of Applied Psychology*, 69: 482–489.

Burnaska, R. F. 1976. The effects of behavior modeling training upon managers' behaviors and
  employees' perceptions. *Personnel Psychology*, 29: 329–335.

Cascio, W. F. 1982. *Costing human resources: The financial impact of behavior in organizations.* Boston, Mass.: Kent Publishing Co.

Cook, T. D., & Campbell, D. T. 1979. *Quasi-experimentation: Design and analysis issues for
  field settings.* Boston, Mass.: Houghton Mifflin Co.

Cronshaw, S. F., & Alexander, R. A. 1985. One answer to the demand for accountability: Selection utility as an investment decision. *Organizational Behavior and Human Decision
  Processes*, 35: 102–118.

Gilbert, T. F. 1976. Training: The $100 billion opportunity. *Training and Development Journal*,
  30 (11): 3–8.

Landy, F. J., Farr, J. L., & Jacobs, R. R. 1982. Utility concepts in performance measurements.
  Organizational Behavior and Human Performance, 30: 15–40.

Latham, G. P., & Saari, L. M. 1979. Application of social-learning theory to training supervisors
  through behavioral modeling. *Journal of Applied Psychology*, 64: 239–246.

McKeon, W. J. 1981. How to determine off-site meeting costs. *Training and Development
  Journal*, 35(5): 116–122.

Schmidt, F. L., Hunter, J. E., McKenzie, R. C., & Muldrow, T. W. 1979. Impact of valid selection
  procedures on work-force productivity. *Journal of Applied Psychology*, 64: 609–626.

Schmidt, F. L., Hunter, J. E., & Pearlman, K. 1982. Assessing the economic impact of personnel
  programs on workforce productivity. *Personnel Psychology*, 35: 333–347.

Weekley, J. A., Frank, B., O'Connor, E. J., & Peters, L. H. 1985. A comparison of three methods of
  estimating the standard deviation of performance in dollars. *Journal of Applied Psychology*,
  70: 122–126.

APPENDIX

Performance Measurement Scale

Feminine pronouns were used for ratings of women. For questions beginning with "to what
extent," response alternatives ranged from 1 = not at all to 5 = to a very great extent. For other
questions, responses ranged from 1 = strongly disagree to 5 = strongly agree. R indicates reverse
coding prior to analysis.

Job knowledge:

To what extent is his technical/managerial knowledge and proficiency in need of further
development? (R)

He keeps himself informed of events happening outside of the department that impact the
function of the work unit.

Planning and organization:

To what extent does he logically group job activities to best accomplish action plans and
objectives?

He seems to deal with each work-related problem as it arises and fails to anticipate future
needs.

Decision making:

To what extent does he gather relevant information in order to thoroughly develop alternative solutions when making important decisions?

He displays indecisiveness when making recommendations or when taking actions, and
inspires little confidence in his decisions. (R)

Communication:
   To what extent does he keep subordinates, peers, and supervisors "in the dark" and fail to communicate important work-related information? (R)
   He conveys an attitude or willingness to discuss ideas, problems, and concerns in a candid yet supportive manner.

Leadership:
   To what extent is he effective at delegating duties and responsibilities?
   He provides little guidance or direction for his subordinates. (R)

Personnel management:
   To what extent does he fail to recognize, or to take action to alleviate work-related problems between employees? (R)
   He compliments good subordinate performance, and takes appropriate disciplinary action with subordinates whose performance is unacceptable.

Expense management:
   To what extent does he tend to exceed budget allocations or neglect the cost considerations of work? (R)
   He attempts to utilize internal resources prior to tapping external sources.

Creativity and initiative:
   To what extent does he fail to consider new or innovative procedures to accomplish assignments? (R)
   He is always developing new and unique approaches to accomplish goals and to solve problems.

Interpersonal relations:
   To what extent is he aware of the personal concerns of others?
   He is not able to disagree with others without producing conflict. (R)

Calculation of variable costs:
   The bank's performance appraisal system rates employees on a scale ranging from 1 to 5. Employees who receive a 3 are entitled to a set percentage of salary increase. This amount increases an additional 2 percent for employees who receive a 4 and another 2 percent for individuals who receive a 5. Since all employees in the present study received 3 or better, it follows that performance improvements would result in higher performance appraisals and subsequently higher salaries and benefits.
   Given that rationale, we computed the percentage of utility benefits paid back to employees in the present case using the following equation:

$$V = \frac{[SD_p(S + B).02]}{SDy} \tag{5}$$

where V = variable costs, SD_p = the standard deviation of employees' performance appraisals, S = average employee salary, and B = average employee benefits computed as 33 percent of annual salary, as calculated from bank records.

John E. Mathieu is an assistant professor of psychology at Pennsylvania State University. He received his Ph.D. degree in industrial/organizational psychology from Old Dominion University in 1985. His current research interests include the application of utility concepts and multilevel theories of organizational behavior.

Russell L. Leonard, Jr. received his Ph.D. degree from Ohio State University; he is Vice-President, Human Resources Planning & Development, at Signet Banking Corporation in Richmond, Virginia and oversees all training and organizational development work within the 9.2 billion bank holding company. He is also an adjunct professor of management at Virginia Commonwealth University.

The Review *of* Economics *and* Statistics

Vol. LXIX   February 1987   Number 1

THE COMPARATIVE ADVANTAGE OF EDUCATED WORKERS IN IMPLEMENTING NEW TECHNOLOGY

Ann P. Bartel and Frank R. Lichtenberg*

Abstract—We estimate labor demand equations derived from a (restricted variable) cost function in which "experience" on a technology (proxied by the mean age of the capital stock) enters "non-neutrally." Our specification of the underlying cost function is based on the hypothesis that highly educated workers have a comparative advantage with respect to the adjustment to and implementation of new technologies. Our empirical results are consistent with the implication of this hypothesis, that the relative demand for educated workers declines as the ages of plant and (particularly) of equipment increase, especially in R & D-intensive industries.

I. Introduction

THE notion of the "learning curve," which was evidently first formalized about half a century ago, has turned out to be a useful and widely applicable concept in the analysis of production behavior.[1] The general acceptance of the learning curve hypothesis reflects a consensus, as expressed by Kaplan (1982, p. 98), that "the cost of doing most tasks of a repetitive nature decrease[s] as experience at doing these tasks accumulate[s]." According to the standard learning curve model, costs decline with accumulated experience, but at a diminishing rate. In his seminal article on "learning by doing," Arrow noted that

A...generalization that can be gleaned from many of the classic learning experiments is that learning associated with repetition of essentially the same problem is subject to sharply diminishing returns. There is an equilibrium response pattern for any given stimulus, towards which the behavior of the learner tends with repetition. To have steadily increasing performance, then, implies that the stimulus situations must themselves be steady evolving rather than merely repeating. (1962, pp. 155–156)

The hypothesis that there is a learning curve associated with a production activity implies that the duration of experience with the technology is

Received for publication August 26, 1985. Revision accepted for publication March 31, 1986.

* Columbia University.

[1] For example, see Dudley (1972), Preston and Keachie (1964) and Rapping (1965).

an argument of the cost and production functions, and that the first and second partial derivatives of cost (output) with respect to experience are negative (positive) and positive (negative), respectively.

Despite the recognition that experience "matters" in cost functions, it has, virtually without exception, been ignored in modern econometric analysis of cost and production. Although most such models include a "technology" variable as an argument, that variable is supposed to represent the "level" or "state" of technology (and changes in it the extent of technical progress) rather than experience with technology.

The primary objective of most econometric studies of cost and production is to analyze the structure and determinants of factor demand. Factor demand equations are obtained by partially differentiating the cost function with respect to factor prices, and setting the derivatives equal to zero, to satisfy the necessary conditions of producer equilibrium. For this reason, whether or not experience is included in the cost function will affect the specification of factor demand equations only if experience affects costs "non-neutrally," that is, only if it has other than a purely first-order effect on costs.

The major hypothesis to be developed and tested in this paper is that experience does *not* enter the cost function "neutrally," and thus (from a geometric perspective), that ceteris paribus increases in experience do not result in "parallel" shifts in the cost function. Consequently, equilibrium shares of factors in production costs are a function of the amount of experience with the technology, as well as of the conventional determinants (e.g., relative factor prices).

More specifically, we postulate that highly-educated workers have a comparative advantage with respect to learning and implementing new technologies, and hence that the demand for these workers relative to the demand for less-educated workers is a declining function of experience.[2] Nelson and Phelps (1966) incorporated a similar proposition as an assumption in a simple neoclassical model of economic growth; Nelson, Peck, and Kalachek (1967) provided some interesting anecdotal evidence; in the only econometric study of the subject, Welch (1970) estimated a model of relative earnings of workers by education category on cross-sectional U.S. farm data. His analysis refers only to agriculture, and evidence from other sectors is clearly needed to determine the validity and applicability of the hypothesis. The purpose of our paper is to provide such evidence, using what we believe are superior measures of experience on a technology.

In the next section of the paper the previous literature is reviewed. In section III we formulate an econometric model of the demand for highly-educated workers, derived from a cost function in which experience enters non-neutrally. The model is estimated on a panel of 61 U.S. manufacturing industries observed in 1960, 1970, and 1980; the results are given in section IV. A brief summary and conclusions follow.

II. Theoretical Perspectives and Literature Review

This section has three main objectives. We begin by attempting to provide a theoretical justification for the hypothesis that the demand for educated, relative to uneducated, workers declines with experience on a technology. We then distinguish this proposition from others concerning the relationship between education and technical change. Finally, we review existing evidence apposite to our hypothesis.

A. Hypotheses Regarding Education and Technology

Two premises—one about the impact of the introduction of new technology on the production environment, the second about differences in the way educated and uneducated workers function in

that environment—are sufficient to justify our hypothesis about the effect of experience on a technology on the structure of labor demand. The first premise is that the degree of uncertainty as to what constitutes effective task performance declines with experience on a technology. The replacement or modification of an existing technology by a new one represents a major "shock" to the production environment, and workers (and perhaps management as well) initially are very uncertain as to how they should modify their behavior. The transition from old to new technology results in job tasks and operating procedures which are not only *different* but, in the short run at least, less well-defined. Wells (1972, pp. 8-9) has argued, in the context of the "product life-cycle" model, that in its infancy "the manufacturing process is not broken down into simple tasks to the extent it will be later in the product's life."

The second premise underlying our hypothesis is that the productivity of highly-educated relative to less-educated workers is greater, the more uncertainty characterizing the production environment. Nelson and Phelps (1966, p. 69) argue that "education enhances one's ability to receive, decode, and understand information." Presumably this is why, according to Welch (1970, p. 47), "educated persons ... can distinguish more quickly between the systematic and random elements of productivity responses." When a new product or process has recently been introduced, there is "more (remaining) to be learned" about the technology, and there is a greater premium on the superior "signal-extraction" capability of educated labor.

Before considering the existing empirical evidence and our own new results, it behooves us to contrast the hypothesis developed above to two other propositions about the relationship between education and the introduction of new technology, or technical change. These contrasts involve two distinctions, one between the *adoption* and the *implementation* of new technology, and the other between the *short-run* and *long-run* impact of technical change on skill or educational requirements.

There is abundant evidence, from studies of both consumer and producer (entrepreneur) behavior, that more highly-educated individuals tend to adopt innovations sooner than less-educated

---

[2] We are agnostic as to the extent to which this advantage derives from skills conferred by education as opposed to an alternative (selection) function of education—in other words, how much school *produces* "learning ability," versus how much (exogenously) better learners choose to attend school.

individuals.[3] Our hypothesis, however, is that educated workers have a comparative advantage with respect to the *implementation* of innovations, which occurs following, and conditional on, adoption. (The learning curve depicts the improvement in performance following adoption of a new technology.) Under the hypothesis about the relationships between education and adoption, on the one hand, and education and implementation, on the other hand, the directions of causality between education and innovation are opposite. Education "causes" individuals to adopt (earlier); the adoption of an innovation (which requires implementation for full realization of benefits) "causes" increased relative demand for educated workers. While there is, then, a kind of "simultaneity" with respect to the relationship between education and innovation, we argue below that the (single) equation we estimate is part of a *recursive* simultaneous equations system that can be consistently estimated by ordinary least squares (OLS).

The second hypothesis from which we wish to distinguish our story might be referred to as the "biased technical change hypothesis." If technical change is biased or nonneutral, the transition from an old to a new technology will result in *permanent* changes in equilibrium factor shares, holding output and relative factor prices constant.[4] Models incorporating biased technical change abstract from the process of implementing new technologies (which is precisely our concern); the implicit assumption is that the structure of factor demand does not vary after adoption. Our hypothesis is that the process of *adjustment* to (implementation of) the new technology is educated-labor-using. We do not venture to speculate as to whether in long-run equilibrium, new technologies are more educated-labor using than the technologies which they replace.[5] It *is* an implication of our hypothesis, however, that sectors or industries characterized by high rates of innovation, which are, as a result, continuously implementing new technologies, will tend to create the most opportunities (demand) for highly-educated workers.

B. Previous Work on "Experience on a Technology" and Labor Demand

We turn now to a brief summary of the existing evidence concerning the relationship between "experience" on a technology and the education-structure of labor demand. Bright (1961) observed that the skill requirements of jobs in several industries first increased and then decreased sharply as the degree of mechanization grew. This finding is consistent with the hypothesis that the process of adjustment to new technology is skilled-labor-using, and that technical change is biased in favor of unskilled labor.

Nelson et al. provide some anecdotal evidence on the tendency of the average educational attainment of workers to decline as a technology matures:

> The early ranks of computer programmers included a high proportion of Ph.D. mathematicians; today, high school graduates are being hired. During the early stage of transistors chemical engineers were required to constantly supervise the vats where crystals were grown. As processes were perfected, they were replaced by workers with less education. (1967, p. 144–145)

Welch (1970) investigated the relationship between the demand for labor by education category and an indicator of experience (actually, an indicator of the "newness" of inputs, or of the *lack* of experience) using 1959 cross-sectional (state) farm data. Welch implicitly assumed that workers (at least in some educational categories) were immobile across states, so that wages were not equalized across states. In his model relative wages by education class are endogenous, determined by (exogenous) *quantities* of labor by education class, nonlabor inputs, and the "newness" indicator, in addition to other variables. The measure that he uses to proxy the rate of flow of new inputs (hence the degree of *in*experience with the technology) is a weighted average of expenditures per farm for research over the past nine years. Welch found that the wage rate of college graduates relative to

---

[3] See Wells (1972), p. 9, and Nelson and Phelps (1966), pp. 70 and 72. Wozniak (1984) found that farm operators with more education are more likely to be adopters of innovations than operators with less education, but that education did not affect the utilization of an innovative input several periods after its introduction.

[4] A general framework for analyzing technical change biases was developed by Binswanger (1974). Examples of studies that tested the biased technical change hypothesis are Levy et al. (1983) and Denny and Fuss (1983).

[5] We agree with Binswanger (1974) p. 975, however, that long-run technical change biases may be endogenous, determined by relative factor prices, although his evidence suggests that "it takes very substantial changes in factor prices in order to perceptibly influence the biases."

that of "laborers with conventional skill" was positively and significantly related to research expenditures. But because, as he argues, "agriculture is probably atypical inasmuch as a larger share of the productive value of education may refer to allocative ability than in most industries" (1970, p. 47), evidence from other sectors (and perhaps based on different assumptions and methodology) is needed to determine the validity and applicability of the hypothesis.

III. Econometric Specification

In this section we specify a cost function in which the age of the technology enters non-neutrally with respect to labor input classified by education, and derive from it a labor demand equation to be estimated below.

In view of the issues we wish to explore, it is convenient and, we think, reasonable to specify a model of *total labor cost* rather than a model of total cost of production (the sum of labor, capital, and materials costs). Abstracting from materials cost is acceptable if raw materials are separable from primary inputs in the total-cost function. Although there is evidence against such separability, the failure of this assumption to hold is unlikely to affect our estimates or hypothesis tests regarding the effect of "age" on the structure of labor demand. If one hypothesizes that capital is a "quasi-fixed" input that producers cannot adjust freely in response to relative price changes, it is appropriate to specify a *restricted variable* cost function, according to which minimum variable-input cost is determined by variable input prices, the stock of capital, output, and perhaps other variables.[6] Since we are excluding materials inputs from consideration, total variable cost reduces to total labor cost.

To keep the model as simple as possible, we postulate there to be only two categories of labor ("highly educated" and "less educated"), and specify the following general form for the restricted variable or total labor cost function:

$$TLC = f(W_1, W_2, AGE, K, Q, T) \qquad (1)$$

[6] See Mohnen et al. (1986) for a detailed discussion of restricted variable cost functions.

where

TLC = total labor cost

W_1 = wage rate of highly-educated workers

W_2 = wage rate of less-educated workers

AGE = age of the technology

K = stock of quasi-fixed capital (plant and equipment)

Q = real output

T = index of the state of technology.

The minimum total labor cost of producing a level of output Q using a capital stock K and a technology of state T and age AGE, given wage rates W_1 and W_2, is determined by equation (1). It is convenient to define a four-element (row) vector Z, where

$Z_1 = AGE$
$Z_2 = \ln K$
$Z_3 = \ln Q$
$Z_4 = T$,

so that we can rewrite (1) as

$$TLC = f(W_1, W_2, Z). \qquad (2)$$

We assume that equation (2) can be approximated by the translog function

$$\ln TLC = \alpha_0 + \alpha_1 \ln W_1 + \alpha_2 \ln W_2$$
$$+ \tfrac{1}{2} \big[\alpha_{11}(\ln W_1)^2 + \alpha_{12}(\ln W_1)(\ln W_2)$$
$$+ \alpha_{21}(\ln W_2)(\ln W_1) + \alpha_{22}(\ln W_2)^2 \big]$$
$$+ \sum_{j=1}^{4} \big[\beta_j Z_j + \beta_{1j}(\ln W_1)(Z_j)$$
$$+ \beta_{2j}(\ln W_2)(Z_j) \big]. \qquad (3)$$

(We suppress quadratic and interaction terms among the Z_j which would vanish in the first-order conditions.) Shephard's lemma implies the following necessary condition for cost-minimization:

$$\frac{\partial \ln TLC}{\partial \ln W_i} = S_i \qquad (i = 1, 2) \qquad (4)$$

where S_i = share of ith labor category in total labor cost. Differentiating equation (3) with respect to $\ln W_1$, imposing the usual symmetry and homogeneity restrictions, and using the equi-

EDUCATED WORKERS AND NEW TECHNOLOGY 5

librium condition (4), we obtain

$$S_1 = \alpha_1 + \alpha_{11}\ln(W_1/W_2) + \sum_j \beta_{1j}Z_j \qquad (5)$$

where S_1 = share of cost of highly-educated labor in total labor cost. Equation (5) implies that, in general, the equilibrium share of educated-labor's cost in TLC is determined by relative wages and by AGE, K, Q, and T. The central hypothesis we wish to test is that $\beta_{11} < 0$, i.e., that increases in experience with, or in the age of, the technology lead to reductions in S_1. We allow for nonzero β_{1j} ($j = 2, 3, 4$) because it is plausible that K, Q, and T also determine S_1 and because (as we discuss in detail below) these variables are potentially correlated with AGE. According to the "capital-skill complementarity" hypothesis, for example, $\beta_{12} > 0$, and if the TLC function is nonhomothetic and characterized by nonneutral technical change, β_{13} and β_{14} will also be nonzero.

Factor-share equations are conventionally estimated on time-series data for a given industry or sector, which is reasonable under the hypothesis that cost-function parameters are invariant over time (but not necessarily across industries). In our empirical work, however, we estimate S_1-equations on a *panel* of 61 industries each observed in the (Census of Population) years 1960, 1970, and 1980. There are several reasons for taking this approach. First, reasonably good estimates of the distribution of employment and labor cost by education and industry are available only in Census years. One could, of course, estimate equation (5) on *aggregate* time-series data, but even at the aggregate level, *annual* data on S_1 would be subject to substantial measurement error. Moreover, it is much less reasonable to maintain the convenient assumption that (relative) wage rates are exogenous at the aggregate level than it is at the industry level.

The equations which we actually estimate on our panel are variants of the following "fixed effects" or "analysis of covariance" model:

$$S_{1kt} = \gamma_k + \zeta_t + \beta_{11}AGE_{kt} + \beta_{12}\ln K_{kt} \\ + \beta_{13}\ln Q_{kt} + \epsilon_{kt} \qquad (6)$$

where the double kt-subscript refers to the value of the variable for industry k in year t, and ϵ is a disturbance term. By including the industry effects γ_k we control for the effects of any permanent

differences across industries in unmeasured determinants of S_1; the time dummies, ζ_t, control for the effects of changes over time in unmeasured determinants which are common to all industries. Within this econometric framework the coefficients on the covariates AGE, K and Q capture the partial relationships between *deviations* of these variables from their respective industry means and deviations of S_{1kt} from its respective industry mean. A heuristic interpretation of our estimation procedure is that it reveals whether an industry which experienced an increase in AGE above the average experienced by all industries between, say, 1960 and 1970, had a (significantly) below-average increase in S_1 during that period.

The reader will note that whereas equation (5) includes the relative-wage variable and the technology index T on the right hand side, these variables are absent from equation (6).[7] We can at least partially justify the omission of these variables from our estimating equations on the following grounds. In contrast to Welch, we assume that both types of labor are mobile across industries in the long run, so that (relative) wages are both equalized across industries and exogenous to any given industry in any particular year. Under this assumption all of the relative-wage variation in our sample is in the time-dimension, and this variation is controlled for by the presence of time dummies.[8]

T, the index of the state of technology, is excluded from equation (6) because we lack industry- and year-specific data on this variable. To the extent that the total sample variation in T is accounted for by permanent interindustry differences and by changes common to all industries, T is controlled for by the industry- and year-

---

[7] Data on relative wages are not available by industry. Even if such data were available, under the hypothesis of interindustry labor mobility, the observed variation in relative wages across industries would reflect variation in (relative) "labor quality" and other measurement error, rather than variation in the true user cost of labor.

[8] It is true that the effect on S_1 of a given change in relative wages will be different in industries with different elasticities of substitution between the two types of labor (and hence different values of α_{11}); we might think of the time dummies as capturing, inter alia, the product of the year-specific relative wage and the *mean* across industries of α_{11}. Indeed under suitable assumptions we can interpret all of our parameter estimates (e.g., β_{11}) as means of the respective distributions of parameters across industries.

effects.[9] We recognize, however, that industries experience different rates of technical change, so that not all of the variation in T will be captured by the fixed effects. Of course, if technical progress is, in reality, neutral with respect to the structure of labor demand, then we do not commit a specification error by omitting T from the share equation.

We turn now to an issue of obviously critical importance in our research design—the measurement of "age of the technology." The age or "newness" of the technology is for us, as it was for Welch, not directly observable. As noted above, Welch used R & D expenditure as a proxy for "newness" of inputs. We also find industries' R & D spending to contribute to the explanation of the observed variation in S_1, but in a way different from that hypothesized or investigated by Welch. Our proxy for the age of an industry's technology is the age of its capital stock (or the ages of its two components, plant and equipment).

If one accepts the notion of embodied technological change, then the age of the capital stock is identical to the age of the technology.[10] Even if technological change is not completely embodied, we expect there to be a strong relationship between the age of the capital stock and the age of the technology. The link between the age of capital and the age of technology results from the assumption that the introduction of new technology increases equilibrium industry output, due to both demand increases arising from product innovations and cost reductions arising from process innovations. Output increases in turn lead to a higher rate of investment and a younger capital stock.[11] The link can also be interpreted as consistent with the product life cycle approach (Wells,

1972), according to which early in a product's life, a low capital to labor ratio is used because of frequent design changes. Once a stable production technique is established, intense capital investment occurs, thereby producing a correlation between age of the capital stock and age of the technology in a cross section of industries.

Before turning to our empirical analysis, we wish to make several econometric points. First, two comments regarding our proxy for AGE. The mean age of the capital stock is, like (the quantity of) the capital stock itself, determined by the past history of investment. Thus one can view an equation including the mean age variable as a specification including a very restricted distributed lag on past investment. In principle, it might be desirable to relax this restriction, and to include an unconstrained distributed lag, but this would be likely to introduce severe multicollinearity and render the interpretation of our estimates difficult. Second, we recognize that a significant fraction of investment may involve simply replacing old capital with capital of similar design, as opposed to the installation of capital embodying new technology. We try to take account of this by allowing the effect of changes in capital age on S_1 to depend on an industry's own and "embodied" R & D-intensity. In any case, however, the fact that some or even most investment is merely "replacement" investment implies that the mean age of capital is a "noisy" (error-ridden) indicator of the age of the technology, which should render our hypothesis tests on β_{11} strong tests (i.e., biased towards acceptance of the hypothesis that $\beta_{11} = 0$).[12]

Finally, a comment regarding "simultaneity." While we noted above that there is a sense in which the relationship between AGE and education is "simultaneous," we submit that equation (6) can be viewed as part of the following *recursive* two-equation system:

$$relative\ employment = f(AGE, relative\ wages, Z)$$
$$AGE = f(relative\ wages, X)$$

where X represents such factors as technological opportunities and growth in product demand, and

---

[9] In fact, specifying time dummies is somewhat less restrictive than specifying a time trend, the proxy for T frequently employed in previous econometric factor-demand studies, such as Binswanger (1974) and Levy, Bowes, and Jondrow (1983).

[10] Much of the neoclassical growth literature on embodied technical change is predicated on the assumption that "technological progress must be embodied in design changes built into new machines alone." (See Burmeister and Dobell (1970), p. 90.) We do not need to assume that machines purchased at time t embody technology of vintage t. We require only the weaker assumption that the technology embodied in new machines is newer, on average, than the technology embodied in existing machines.

[11] Jorgenson's 1971 survey of the literature on investment concluded that output was clearly the major determinant of investment in fixed capital.

[12] Griliches (1984) has shown that the well-known measurement-error-induced bias-towards-zero result of the bivariate regression model generalizes, under suitable conditions, to the multivariate case.

EDUCATED WORKERS AND NEW TECHNOLOGY 7

Z reflects determinants of relative employment. Because, under our assumptions, labor is perfectly mobile across industries, there is no reason for decisions by producers in an industry to introduce new technology to be based on relative *quantities* of labor employed in the industry; as we suggest in the conclusion, however, they *will* be based on relative *wages*. Labor mobility, as observed above, implies that relative wages would be equalized across industries, and thus controlled for by the time dummies. Since the above system is recursive, the first equation can be consistently estimated by OLS.

IV. Empirical Analysis

A. Data

Variants of equation (6) are estimated on a pooled cross-section time-series data set containing 61 manufacturing industries in each of the years 1960, 1970 and 1980.[13] Data on the demographic characteristics of the workers in these industries were obtained from the Labor Demographics Matrices of the Bureau of Industrial Economics (BIE). Information on the age and the quantity of the industry's capital stock is taken from the Bureau of Industrial Economics' Capital

---

[13] The 61 industries are the industry sectors used by the BIE for their labor demographic matrices.

Stocks Data Base. Data on real output are from the Census/SRI/Penn Data Base which is derived primarily from the Annual Survey of Manufactures and the Census of Manufactures,[14] and finally, information on the R & D intensity of each industry is obtained from the technology matrix constructed by Scherer (1984).

B. Basic Results

The results of estimating variants of equation (6) by OLS are shown in table 1.[15] The dependent variable is the share of labor cost attributed to highly educated workers, defined as those with greater than a high school education. Since our data set does not report labor cost, we approxi-

---

[14] See Griliches and Lichtenberg (1984b) for a complete description.

[15] We tested for first-order serial correlation of the residuals by estimating a version of equation (6) that included lagged dependent and independent variables; the coefficient on the lagged dependent variable may be interpreted as an estimate of ρ, the autocorrelation coefficient. The point estimate and t-ratio of ρ were, respectively, 0.044 and 0.33, so we could not reject the null hypothesis of serially uncorrelated residuals. Since the frequency of our data is decennial, the low estimated value of ρ is not surprising. (The *quarterly* autocorrelation coefficient implied by our estimate, $\hat{\rho}^{1/40} = .044^{.025} = .925$, is, however, quite high.) Because $\hat{\rho}$ was estimated to be very small and insignificant, and also because, as Brown (1985) observes, GLS (generalized least squares) does not necessarily yield smaller true standard errors than OLS when ρ is estimated, we did not pursue estimation by GLS.

TABLE 1.—DEPENDENT VARIABLE: LABOR COST SHARE OF EMPLOYEES WITH 13 + YEARS OF EDUCATION
(*t*-statistics in parentheses)

Independent Variable	(1)	(2)	(3)	(4)	(5)	(6)	(7)	(8)
AGECAP	−0.0074 (−2.66)							
AGEEQ		−0.0086 (−2.60)		−0.0078 (−2.42)	−0.0063 (−1.90)	−0.0065 (−1.93)		
AGEPL			−0.0017 (−0.88)					
AGEEQ • OWNRD							−0.4821 (−2.86)	
AGEEQ • IMPRTRD								−0.6954 (−1.71)
Log (REAL CAPITAL STOCK)				0.0321 (2.67)		0.0069 (0.38)	0.0161 (0.87)	0.0143 (0.73)
Log (REAL OUTPUT)					0.0360 (3.24)	0.0315 (1.94)	0.0227 (1.38)	0.0325 (2.00)
R^2	0.962	0.962	0.961	0.964	0.964	0.964	0.966	0.964
N	183	183	183	183	174	174	174	174

Note: All equations include year and industry dummies, which are in all cases jointly highly statistically significant. The independent variables are defined in the text. The employment share of workers with 13+ years of education was 0.158 in 1960, 0.190 in 1970 and 0.271 in 1980. The mean age of the capital stock was 9.25 years in 1960, 9.18 in 1970 and 9.45 in 1980.

mate it by using the information on employment in the following way. We have two classes of workers: highly educated (L_1) and less educated (L_2). Define $(l = L_1/(L_1 + L_2))$ which is L_1's share in total employment; and $\omega = W_2/W_1$, the ratio of less educated to highly educated wages. Then it can be shown that L_1's share in labor cost is given by[16]

$$S_1 = \left(1 + \omega(l^{-1} - 1)\right)^{-1}. \tag{7}$$

We have information on l from the BIE and we can obtain an estimate of ω in each of the years 1960, 1970 and 1980 from the Current Population Reports.[17] Since we assume ω is constant across industries for any given year, the cost share is simply a nonlinear transformation of the employment share.[18]

Columns (1), (2) and (3) of table 1 report regressions using alternative measures of the age of the capital stock and omitting $\ln K$ and $\ln Q$; the first column uses the average age of the plant and equipment combined $(AGECAP)$ while the second column uses the average age of equipment only $(AGEEQ)$ and the third uses the average age of plant only $(AGEPL)$.[19] While $AGECAP$ and $AGEEQ$ both have the hypothesized signs and are significant, $AGEPL$ does not have a significant effect. This is not surprising since technology is more likely to be embodied in the industry's equipment. The insignificance of $AGEPL$ is also important because it casts doubt upon an alternative interpretation of the negative effect of $AGECAP$. The alternative argument is that industries that are relocating their plants to developing

regions such as the South are more likely to increase their share of educated workers because they will be hiring new labor force entrants who, on average, have more education. If this argument were correct, $AGEPL$ would have a negative and significant coefficient. In the remainder of table 1, we use equipment age to measure the age of the technology in the industry.

While the negative and significant effect of $AGEEQ$ in column (2) strongly supports our hypothesis regarding the superior ability of educated workers to adapt to new technology, it is likely that changes in $AGEEQ$ are highly correlated with the growth rates of the capital stock and of output in the industry; i.e., growing industries have newer equipment. In order to control for this, columns (4), (5) and (6) in table 1 add the logarithms of the real capital stock and real output to the cost share equation. When only the log capital stock is added to the equation, its coefficient is positive and significant (and the coefficient on $AGEEQ$ remains negative and significant), a finding consistent with the "capital-skill complementarity" hypothesis. Because growth in the capital stock and in real output tend to be highly correlated across industries, the output term in column (5) has a coefficient similar to the capital term in column (4) and a similar effect on the $AGEEQ$ coefficient, although it reduces its significance somewhat more. When both the capital and output variables are included (column (6)), only the output variable is significant, and $AGEEQ$ remains significant.

These estimates appear to provide rather strong support for our hypothesis about the effect of the introduction of new technology on the relative demand for educated workers. We can gauge the magnitude of this impact in the following way. Consider the two industries with maximum and minimum sample values of $AGEEQ$: (1) Wood Containers, in which, in 1980, the mean age of the equipment is 8.66 years and the labor cost share of highly educated workers is 0.307 and (2) Electronic Components and Accessories in which, 1980, the mean age of equipment is 5.19 years and the labor cost share of highly educated workers is 0.433. According to the estimated parameter on $AGEEQ$ in column 6, 18% of the observed difference in the labor cost share of highly educated workers between these two industries is due to the difference in the ages of their equipment.

---

[16] Since
$$S_1 = W_1 L_1/(W_1 L_1 + W_2 L_2) = 1/(1 + \omega(L_2/L_1)).$$
[17] From the Current Population Reports, we calculate the ratio of mean total earnings of year-round full-time workers with 13+ years of education to the comparable mean for workers with less than 13 years of education. The values of the ratio are 0.59 in 1960, 0.62 in 1970 and 0.68 in 1980.
[18] The results we present below are virtually identical to those that use the employment share.
[19] According to Arrow (see quote in introduction), we should expect diminishing returns to learning. This implies that a nonlinear specification of the age variable is appropriate. In regressions not reported here, we tried the logarithm of AGE and the inverse of AGE and found that the t-statistics on these variables were virtually identical to the t-statistics on AGE reported in table 1. Since the linear version fits equally well and is considerably easier to interpret, we only report the linear results in this paper.

EDUCATED WORKERS AND NEW TECHNOLOGY 9

TABLE 2.—EFFECTS OF AGE OF TECHNOLOGY ON EMPLOYMENT SHARES OF WORKERS
WITH 13 + YEARS OF EDUCATION, WITHIN SPECIFIED AGE GROUPS

Age Group*	(1) AGEEQ		(2) AGEEQ • OWNRD	
	b	t	b	t
1. 14–17	− 0.0021	(− 1.08)	− 0.0189	(− 1.94)
2. 18–24	− 0.0071	(− 1.72)	− 0.0400	(− 1.90)
3. 25–34	− 0.0074	(− 1.85)	− 0.0781	(− 4.06)
4. 35–44	− 0.0024	(− 0.66)	− 0.0352	(− 1.88)
5. 45–54	− 0.0033	(− 0.74)	− 0.0241	(− 1.07)
6. 55 +	− 0.0030	(− 0.71)	− 0.0024	(− 0.11)

Note: Each parameter shown here comes from a separate regression equation. Every equation also includes the log
of the real capital stock, the log of real output, a vector of industry dummy variables and a set of time dummy
variables.
*The means of the employment shares of workers with 13+ years of education are as follows:

	1960	1970	1980
1. 14–17	0.004	0.005	0.009
2. 18–24	0.149	0.190	0.218
3. 25–34	0.214	0.236	0.354
4. 35–44	0.166	0.210	0.290
5. 45–54	0.127	0.170	0.235
6. 55 +	0.107	0.132	0.204

C. The Role of R & D

Up to this point, we have been assuming that
the effect of *AGE* on the distribution of labor cost
is constant across industries. It is reasonable to
hypothesize, however, that the impact on S_1 of a
change in *AGE* will be greater in more R & D-
intensive industries. This is because new capital is
most likely to embody new technology in
R & D-intensive industries. In order to test this
hypothesis, we replaced *AGEEQ* by the interaction of *AGEEQ* with the industry's 1974 R & D-
intensity.[20] We use two different measures of R &
D-intensity. The first is *OWNRD* which equals the
ratio of the industry's 1974 R & D expenditures
to its 1974 nominal output. The second is
IMPRTRD which is the ratio of 1974 R & D
"imported" from other industries, i.e., embodied
in products purchased from other industries, to
1974 nominal output. In principle, we might expect $\partial S_i/\partial AGE$ to depend more on *IMPRTRD*
than on *OWNRD* because *IMPRTRD* measures
the R & D that is embodied in the industry's capital
stock. However, as can be seen in columns (7) and
(8), the effect of *AGEEQ* is more significant when
we use *OWNRD* rather than *IMPRTRD*, probably because of the large amount of error in

[20] Time-series data on R & D-intensity by industry are not
available for our industry classification. However, industries'
relative R & D-intensities are generally thought to be very
stable over time.

measuring *IMPRTRD*.[21] Further, when *AGEEQ*
and *AGEEQ • OWNRD* are used together, the
coefficient on *AGEEQ* is not significant, while the
interaction term is.[22] These findings demonstrate
that the effect of the age of technology on the
labor cost share of highly educated workers depends upon the R & D intensity of the industry.

D. Controlling for the Age of Employees

Although the significant negative effects of
AGEEQ in table 1 lend strong support to our
guiding hypothesis, there is potentially an alternative interpretation of the results. The industries
that have been most innovative are also likely to
be hiring many new employees, and these new
hires will be younger, on average, than the experienced workers in the industry. Since average
educational attainment has been increasing over
the period we are studying,[23] it is possible that the
coefficients observed in table 1 are simply due to

[21] See Scherer's (1984) discussion of the complicated al-
gorithm in constructing imported R & D. Griliches and
Lichtenberg (1984a) also found that the imported R & D variable had an insignificant effect on productivity growth, holding
OWNRD constant, again suggesting the existence of substantial measurement error in this variable.
[22] The *t*-value on *AGEEQ* is − 0.37 and the *t*-value on
*AGEEQ*OWNRD* is − 2.11.
[23] The percentage of the civilian labor force aged 16 and over
that had completed at least one year of college was 18.9 in
1960, 26.2 in 1970 and 35.1 in 1980.

the entrance of young educated workers into the labor market. We can address this problem by estimating the employment share equation separately for different age groups.[24] If the adjustment hypothesis is correct, then we should still observe a negative effect of the age of technology on the employment share of educated workers within age groups. The results are shown in table 2, where we tried two specifications. In column (1) we assumed that the effect of *AGEEQ* does not vary across industries and in column (2), we assumed that *AGEEQ's* effect is a function of the R & D intensity of the industry. Recall from table 1 that the latter specification produced much stronger results. In column (2) of table 2, we see that four out of the six parameters are negative and significant. The hypothesis regarding the superior ability of educated workers to adjust to new technology is borne out for employees under age 45. The insignificance of the parameters for workers over age 45 can be explained in one of two ways. First, firms may be unable to adjust the composition of their senior workers because of seniority rights regarding layoff and discharge. A second explanation is that the value of education depreciates such that individuals educated more than twenty-five years ago are no better able to adjust to new technology than their less educated peers. The estimates presented in table 2 show that our finding of a significant ceteris paribus relationship between the educated labor share and the average age of equipment is not merely reflecting a relationship between changes in the *age-structure* of an industry's workforce and of its capital stock.

V. Conclusions

In this paper we have estimated variants of a labor demand equation derived from a (restricted variable) cost function in which "experience" on a technology (proxied by the mean age of the capital stock) enters "non-neutrally." Our specification of the underlying cost function was based on the hypothesis that highly educated workers have a comparative advantage with respect to the adjustment to and implementation of new technologies. Our empirical results are consistent with the im-

plication of this hypothesis, that the relative demand for educated workers declines as the capital stock (and presumably the technology embodied therein) ages. According to our estimates, the education-distribution of employment depends more strongly on the age of equipment than on the age of plant, and the effect of changes in equipment age on labor demand is magnified in R & D-intensive industries.

The evidence we have provided has several important policy implications. First, it suggests that macroeconomic policies which affect rates of innovation and investment (particularly in equipment) will affect the relative demand for workers classified by education, and hence the aggregate skill distribution of employment and earnings. Thus, policies such as the investment tax credit, accelerated depreciation, and liberalization of antitrust restraints on R & D joint ventures, will be expected to increase highly-educated workers' share in labor income. Our results may also have a bearing on the role of government education policy in promoting economic growth. In particular, government subsides and other policies which tend to encourage the acquisition of education and increase the relative supply of highly-educated workers, will be expected to accelerate the rate of diffusion of new industrial technologies by lowering the costs of adjustment and implementation.

REFERENCES

Arrow, Kenneth, "The Economic Implications of Learning by Doing," *The Review of Economic Studies* (1962), 155–157.
Binswanger, H., "The Measurement of Technical Change Biases with Many Factors of Production," *American Economic Review* 64 (Dec. 1974), 964–976.
Bright, James R., "Does Automation Raise Skill Requirements?" *Harvard Business Review*, 1961.
Brown, Charles, "Military Enlistments: What Can We Learn from Geographic Variation?" *American Economic Review* 75 (Mar. 1985), 228–234.
Burmeister, Edwin, and A. Rodney Dobell, *Mathematical Theories of Economic Growth* (New York: Macmillan, 1970).
Denny, M., and M. Fuss, "The Effects of Factor Prices and Technological Change on the Occupational Demand for Labor: Evidence from Canadian Telecommunications," *Journal of Human Resources* 17 (2) (1983), 161–176.
Dudley, Leonard, "Learning and Productivity Change in Metal Products," *American Economic Review* 62 (Sept. 1972), 662–669.
Griliches, Zvi, "Data Problems in Econometrics," NBER Technical Working Paper No. 39. July 1984 (forthcoming as chapter 25 in *Handbook of Econometrics*, Vol. 3, edited by Z. Griliches and M. Intriligator.
Griliches, Zvi, and Frank Lichtenberg, "Interindustry Technology Flows and Productivity Growth: A Re-examination," this REVIEW 66 (May 1984a), 324–328.

[24] It is quite likely, however, that the employment share of educated workers by age group is subject to substantially greater measurement error than the overall educated employment share.

EDUCATED WORKERS AND NEW TECHNOLOGY 11

——, "R & D and Productivity at the Industry Level: Is There Still a Relationship?," in Zvi Griliches (ed.), *R & D, Patents, and Productivity* (Chicago: University of Chicago Press, 1984b).

Jorgenson, Dale W., "Econometric Studies of Investment Behavior: A Survey," *Journal of Economic Literature* 10 (Dec. 1971), 1111–1147.

Kaplan, Robert S., *Advanced Management Accounting* (Englewoods Cliffs: Prentice-Hall, 1982).

Levy, Robert, Marianne Bowes, and James Jondrow, "Technical Change and Employment in Five Industries: Steel, Autos, Aluminum, Coal, and Iron Ore," The Public Research Institute, June 1983 (xerox).

Mohnen, Pierre, M. Ishaq Nadiri, and Ingmar Prucha, "R & D, Production Structure, and Productivity Growth in the U.S., Japanese and German Manufacturing Sectors," *European Economic Review* 30 (Aug. 1986).

Nelson, Richard, Merton Peck, and Edward Kalachek, *Technology, Economic Growth, and Public Policy* (Washington, D.C.: Brookings, 1967).

Nelson, R., and E. Phelps, "Investment in Humans, Technological Diffusion, and Economic Growth," *American Economic Review* 56 (2) (1966).

Preston, Lee E., and E. C. Keachie, "Cost Functions and Progress Functions: An Integration," *American Economic Review* 54 (Mar. 1964, Part I), 100–106.

Rapping, Leonard, "Learning and World War II Production Functions," this REVIEW 47 (Feb. 1965), 81–86.

Scherer, Fredric M., "Using Linked Patent and R & D Data to Measure Interindustry Technology Flows," in Zvi Griliches (ed.), *R & D, Patents, and Productivity* (Chicago: University of Chicago Press, 1984).

Welch, Finis, "Education in Production," *Journal of Political Economy* 78 (Jan. 1970), 35–59.

Wells, Louis T., Jr. (ed.), *The Product Life Cycle and International Trade* (Boston: Harvard Business School Division of Research, 1972).

Wozniak, Gregory, "The Adoption of Interrelated Innovations: A Human Capital Approach," this REVIEW 66 (Feb. 1984), 70–79.

[18]

INTERMEDIATE SKILLS IN THE WORKPLACE: DEPLOYMENT, STANDARDS AND SUPPLY IN BRITAIN, FRANCE AND GERMANY*

by Hilary Steedman, Geoff Mason and Karin Wagner

Previous international comparisons of workforce skills by the National Institute have focussed on the relative shortage of craft skills in Britain. The present study is concerned with the next higher level of supervisory and technician skills; on the basis of visits to factories and technical colleges in Britain, France and Germany, and analysis of labour force statistics, it compares and contrasts the provision and deployment of these intermediate skills in manufacturing industry in the three countries. At supervisory level only Germany undertakes a significant amount of training and to standards adequate to the increased complexity and technical demands of modern manufacturing. At technician (Higher National) level, the numbers acquiring comparable qualifications in Britain and France are substantially higher than in Germany: in part this reflects the allocation of a large proportion of technical support functions in German industry to craft-trained personnel. After examining the relative distribution of training costs between employers, individuals and the public authorities in the three countries, the paper makes proposals for a more cost-effective mix of craft- and technician-level skills in British manufacturing which might, in the process, reduce the need for over-qualified personnel to 'plug the gaps' in skills among shopfloor workers and supervisors.

Introduction

This paper presents evidence on differences in the mix of skills employed in manufacturing in Britain and two other European countries and charts in particular the effects of national differences in the supply of intermediate skills on the organisation of production. Explanations for these differences in skill mix are sought by examining the way in which intermediate skills training is provided and financed in the three countries and the rewards accruing to individuals in the form of skill-related wage differentials.

Previous studies of manufacturing industry carried out by the National Institute (metalworking, wood-working and clothing production in Britain and Germany) have found that in these sectors the typical British firm tends to concentrate on the mass production of standardised products while its German counterpart produces a highly differentiated product range which allows the German firm to compete more effectively in international markets. These differences have been held to arise in part from firms adapting to different supplies of shopfloor skills, in particular craft-level skills.[1]

However, craft-trained workers constitute only one part of a larger group of trained middle-level employees in manufacturing who are collectively important to its successful prosecution. This group we designate as of 'intermediate skill level': it is bounded at the lower limit by the unskilled labourer and semi-skilled operator (normally without lengthy formal training or certification in the countries studied) and at the upper limit by university and polytechnic graduates, normally engaged either in management or in high-level research, design and development. A logical next step in our comparative study of European manufacturing was to investigate,

first, the way in which the whole range of intermediate skills—in particular, supervisory and technical skills—deployed both on and off the shopfloor; secondly, national differences in the supplies of skills available; and thirdly, the possible policy implications. At the same time our comparisons were extended to a second European country, France, which was expected to be of interest in terms of recent policy measures designed to raise intermediate skill levels.[2]

Flows at intermediate skill level

Collectively, those at intermediate skill level are responsible for the efficient day-to-day organisation, management and execution of production including the provision of all the necessary technical services required for its smooth running. In our cross-country studies we identified three types of intermediate skill in production distinguished by function—craft/execution, foreman/management, technician/technical support. Table 1 shows that when flows are adjusted for the size of the total labour force in each country, Britain produces only a quarter as many skilled craft employees of execution as either France or Germany. At higher technician level, both British and French flows are substantially higher than in Germany. However, neither Britain nor France engages in systematic training of foremen to the equivalent of the *Meister* qualification in Germany. The skill mix available to German employers is clearly more biased towards supervisory and practical shopfloor skills than that available in either Britain or France.

In Section 1 we investigate for the three countries chosen, Britain, France and Germany, the way in which employees working at intermediate skill level

* Financial support for this study was provided by the Economic and Social Research Council, the Employment Department (formerly the Training Agency) and the Scottish Council Development and Industry: they are not responsible in any way for the views expressed in this article.

Table 1. Numbers obtaining engineering and technology qualifications at intermediate level in UK, France and Germany 1986

standardised for size of total labour force in each country, 000s

	UK	France	Germany
Higher intermediate			
Higher technicians[a]	23	22	13
Meister-qualified	–	–	31
Total	23	22	**44**
Lower intermediate			
Lower technicians[b]	14	19	–
Craftsmen[c]	27	107	107
Total	41	126	107

Source.   Derived from S J Prais. *Qualified Manpower in Engineering. Britain and other industrially advanced countries. National Institute Economic Review*, February 1989 Table 1 and text. Numbers adjusted to avoid double-counting of qualifications. In addition, all French numbers have been increased by 16·7 per cent and rounded in order to standardise for the size of the total labour force in each country in 1986.

Notes.
a   In Britain. HNC, HND. In France BTS. DUT; in Germany. Techniker qualifications.
b   In Britain. BTEC National Certificate and National Diploma. SCOTVEC National Certificate. In France, Brevet Professionnel. Bac Technologique. Brevet de technicien (netted out totals to allow for those continuing to higher levels)
c   In Britain. City and Guilds Part II passes in a relevant subject. In France. CAP. BEP in a relevant area. In Germany. *Berufsabschluss* in a relevant area. For further details see S J Prais (op. cit.)

are deployed in production and identify systematic differences which can be explained in terms of differing supplies of trained and qualified individuals at intermediate skill level. In Section 2 we examine the flows and standards reached in supervisory and technician-level qualifications in the three countries and in Section 3 we analyse ways in which the supply is ensured. Section 4 provides a summary and points to conclusions for policy in this area.

Methodology

The investigation reported here aims to cast light on these complex issues with the help of (a) visits to manufacturing plants in the three countries (approximately ten in each country) to examine the tasks on which technicians, foremen and other skilled labour are employed; (b) visits to colleges offering courses leading to higher technician qualifications to compare standards in the three countries; (c) additional analysis of Labour Force Survey data in the three countries (German *Mikrozensus*, French *Enquête-Emploi*. British Labour Force Survey) and (d) comparisons of relative earnings by occupational category in the three countries.

Fieldwork was carried out in· 1988–90.[3] Visits were made to thirty manufacturing companies in the three countries, roughly two thirds of them engaged in engineering (automotive components. small pumps and motors) and one third in textile spinning (cotton. worsted woollen mixtures and acrylic fibres). The former industry is based on batch production and final assembly of components; the latter is based on

runs of variable length but is akin to 'process plants' usually working on continuous shifts in which massive banks of automated or semi-automated machinery are fed and supervised by a limited number of shopfloor personnel. The variation in organisation between the two industries was intended to provide a firmer basis for analysing the changing roles of both foremen and technicians in consequence of technological developments.

The plants visited in each country were chosen to be as similar as possible with respect to type of product and employment size. In view of our limited resources it was not possible to aim at a sample which was representative of plant-sizes in each of these industries; but the process of matching products and keeping within a broad band of employment sizes (mostly within the range of 100–900 employees) would, we hoped, be sufficient to highlight any important differences between the countries. In any case, 100 employees usually proved to be the minimum size for gathering useful information about technician employment. Firms below this size often employed only one or no technicians and bought in technical services needed. Researchers—two or more for each visit—collected data on the size of the total and direct work-force, system of shopfloor supervision, vocational qualifications and updating. provision of technical services and on earnings. In addition, visits were made to the production area. and discussions were held with foremen and technicians on the nature of their responsibilities.

1. Deployment in the workplace

1·1 Changes in manufacturing technology and intermediate skills

Two important sets of developments have transformed manufacturing in the three countries examined in the course of the last 30 years. In Germany, the effects had been felt by the beginning of the 1970s; in France and Britain, a decade later. The first set was technological: the use of miniaturised electronic circuits enabled large amounts of data to be processed swiftly in the office; similarly, on the shopfloor microprocessor control systems allowed a far wider range of machining operations to be carried out on a single machine and with much reduced changeover times between operations. The majority of German manufacturers introduced information-processing technology into production-planning and integrated microprocessor-controlled machinery into production lines in advance of those in Britain and France.[4] The second set of developments were economic and were brought about by the intensification of competition in global trade during the last two decades. Successful manufacturers were obliged by international competitive pressures to offer a wider range of higher quality goods and more reliable delivery deadlines. Again, as our previous comparisons of matched plants have revealed, many German firms responded with great promptness to these market forces and, indeed, in many cases led them.

Pressures on shopfloor foremen from these two factors have greatly enlarged and in part transformed their function. Foremen must now not only 'get the goods out of the door' but get the right goods out of the door and within more tightly-specified time schedules. Competitive pressure to minimise stocks of components and work-in-progress and respond quickly to customer orders requires the planning of component supplies to be carried out on a longer time-scale, greater liaison with other departments and/or outside suppliers, and careful prioritising of work to ensure that equipment and skills are combined as effectively as possible.

New computer-controlled (CNC) capital equipment has a number of important implications for the foreman's function. Most obviously, he is required to plan and supervise the use of complex machines which he may himself never have operated. To some extent built-in monitoring functions—whereby machines monitor, for example, toolwear and operator performance—reduce the need for detailed supervision of work-in-progress. At the same time, however, the need for rapid decision-making concerning the overall flow of production at shopfloor level is greatly increased.[5]

For foremen the switch has been from a reactive role, restricted to the immediate area supervised, to a proactive role, looking ahead, making judgements, liaising with technical support departments and planning to meet output and delivery targets.[6] He consequently needs to be more than just 'an experienced operative who can also read and write' or 'the man with the whip' which are the ways older-style foremen were characterised in British factories visited.

While foremen in modern manufacturing plants are now required to take a broader view of the production process as a whole, the technician's tasks, especially in engineering, have become more specialised during the last thirty years.[7] Technician occupations responded earlier than supervisory occupations to technical innovation. Many technical activities such as drawing and design and production engineering have been transformed by the introduction of microprocessor-controlled equipment. At the same time new occupations, e.g. in CNC programming and quality control have emerged.

1·2 Supervisors and technicians: complementary, not interchangeable

In modern manufacturing the roles of foreman and technician are complementary, the foreman coping with a wide variety of problems arising from the need to manage ever-changing combinations of labour, materials and equipment and the technician providing specialised technical services which contribute to the smoother and more efficient exploitation of the means of production.

In all three countries foremen work on the shopfloor and the management of people and materials is their primary concern. Technical staff are mainly based in offices or in laboratories and are engaged in activities such as research and design, sales, work planning and scheduling, machine programming, costing and materials procurement and quality testing. Except in the smallest companies, the foreman's task is to recognise when it is appropriate to call on these specialist support services and to be able to follow their advice if so required.[8]

It became clear to us in the course of our visits that provision of the right mix of supervisory skills and technical support is crucial to the smooth running of production. Indeed, the ability of both foremen and technicians to carry out their tasks properly depends to a very large extent upon the complementary services provided by the other. This was illustrated by the spinning plants visited in Britain. In these plants, specialised maintenance services were provided by staff permanently sited on the shopfloor because of the overriding need to keep machinery in continuous operation. One of the management's complaints was that, notwithstanding the provision of technical services, foremen spent too much time 'under the frame' i.e. carrying out emergency repairs (a situation which appeared to have arisen from a combination of ageing equipment, shortages of skilled mechanics and insufficient planned maintenance); the supervision of production was suffering as a consequence.

When, as in this case, technical support skills are inadequate or insufficient, foremen are prevented from managing by the need to supplement the maintenance service. Where, on the other hand, foremen have insufficient technical expertise—as in the case of some British engineering plants visited—technician-programmers may be obliged to by-pass the foreman (who cannot programme) and liaise directly with shopfloor craftsmen resulting in confusion of lines of command. These imbalances are not easily resolved. Skills and expertise cannot always be upgraded quickly enough—particularly where older workers are concerned—to allow foremen to acquire the level of technical knowledge necessary to cope with new technology.[9]

The technical competence required of trained *Meister* in Germany leads to a more effective partnership between foremen and technicians, even though responsibilities and tasks are clearly separated.[10] The additional technical study undertaken in Germany in order to obtain the *Meister* certificate is intended to enable a foreman to discuss the automation requirements for his production line with management as well as production engineers and skilled workers i.e. to have an informed appreciation of technical matters and to be able to communicate appropriately with colleagues at all levels.[11]

Visits undertaken for this study confirm the value of the *Meister* courses in Germany in ensuring that most foremen have the understanding required to cope with the logistics of the production process and to handle cost control. In addition, the breadth of technical knowledge coupled with the formal training in instructional skills and the organisation of training programmes received by qualified *Meister* ensures that they are well-equipped to meet their responsibilities for on-the-job training of shopfloor workers and apprentices.

1·3   The deployment of foremen and technicians

Important differences between the three countries arose in the range of functions undertaken by supervisors. In Germany, in contrast to Britain and France, foremen were routinely required to be aware of a section's production costs, and production schedules were delivered to them several days in advance to assist forward planning. In Britain, foremen in both spinning and engineering frequently mentioned that 'crisis management'—chasing missing materials,

rescheduling to cope with machine breakdowns or training new staff where turnover was very high and new employees were normally untrained—occupied the greater part of their time. In France, 'crisis management' was not mentioned, but foremen were concerned as to whether their (craft) training was adequate to cope with the rapidly-increasing technical demands of their work where new technology was being introduced very rapidly. Most of the French plants' older foremen with craft (CAP) qualifications were working alongside newly-recruited younger foremen with higher-technician (BTS) qualifications and the obvious difference in levels of formal technical knowledge helped to fuel their anxieties.

We also observed marked differences between France and Britain on the one hand and Germany on the other in the use of technician-level skills. In British and French plants we normally found that a number of those working in production on the shopfloor held technician-level qualifications; in Germany we never encountered anyone holding *Techniker* qualifications in shopfloor (i.e. skilled/semi-skilled) positions. In Britain the special expertise of those holding 'shopfloor technician' positions was usually recognised (by wage differentials) and their knowledge was put to use in, for example, providing advice and guidance to semi-skilled production workers (interpreting drawings, advising on assembly problems).

In France, a position of 'shopfloor technician' (*technicien d'atelier*) was formally established and recognised for collective-bargaining purposes in the late 1970s and we saw and/or spoke with *techniciens d'atelier* in most of the French engineering plants visited. These shopfloor technicians would have programming and first-line maintenance responsibilities in addition to production work, usually on the more sophisticated CNC machinery. Although formally recognised and institutionalised as a separate hierarchy between skilled 'craft' workers and higher-level technicians, this group's function was similar to that of the British shopfloor workers who held technician qualifications, namely to supply technical expertise to compensate for low skill levels on the shopfloor and in first-line supervision.[12] In Germany, where adequate supplies of craft and supervisory skills are available, we saw no cases of technicians employed on the shopfloor, nor is there a category designated as 'shopfloor technician'.

1·4   The 'match' between employment and qualification

In carrying out this investigation it has been necessary to distinguish between the person *employed* as a foreman or technician and the person *holding* qualifications normally recognised as 'foreman' and 'technician' qualifications. In our visits in the three countries we asked two sets of questions, the first related to those employed and known as technicians, *techniciens* or *Techniker* (sometimes complicated by the fact that in some British companies all technicians were called 'engineers') or foremen. *agents de maîtrise* or *Meister*.[13] For the first group ie. those *designated* foremen or technicians we asked about qualifications held and departments in which they worked or tasks assigned to them. We then enquired whether significant numbers of employees not employed as technicians or foremen nevertheless held technician and foreman qualifications. Inevitably, nowhere were the two groups—those employed as foremen/technicians and those holding foreman/technician qualifications—identical.

Indeed, in the provision of certain specialised technical services, the three countries studied had put into practice very different solutions. For instance, the plentiful supply of trained craft workers in Germany meant that in all but small firms craft-qualified personnel could be deployed full-time on machine (parts) programming away from the shopfloor. In Britain and France it was more common to employ those with higher technician qualifications for this task. In Britain, many trained craftsmen did have the expertise to take responsibility for programming but were normally too scarce a resource to be removed from direct production and a different solution (use of technicians) had to be found. Where technical skills were

in short supply (usually smaller firms with 100 employees or less) craftsmen programmed their own machines at the cost of lost production while the machines were idle. In France, technical services of this nature were rarely performed by craftsmen on the shopfloor.

Table 2 shows the qualifications structure of those groups designated as technicians in the Labour Force Surveys of the three countries. One striking point of contrast is that in Germany nearly all individuals designated as technicians (92 per cent) have at least a craft qualification whereas in Britain and France the comparable figure is only about 70 per cent and the remainder do not possess any vocational qualifications at all. As mentioned above, not all technical support activities *require* technician-level skills. Most technical tasks which directly service shopfloor production (such as machine-loading schedules, inventory control, machine programming and maintenance) are, with some additional training, best carried out by experienced craftsmen and the large pool of craft skills created over a long period in Germany has facilitated the allocation of these tasks to apprentice-trained personnel.

At higher levels of qualification important differences arise between Britain and France as well as Britain and Germany. As table 2 shows, only some 14 per cent of designated technicians in Britain possess higher intermediate qualifications, compared to

Table 2. Qualifications of technicians and foremen in all manufacturing, Britain, France 1988, Germany 1987.

Qualification	Britain %		France %		Germany %	
	Technicians	Foremen	Technicians	Foremen	Technicians	Foremen
No vocational qualification	31[a]	55	27[e]	44[e]	8[i]	7[m]
Lower intermediate	43[b]	39[b]	49[f]	51[f]	49[j]	29[j]
Higher intermediate	14[c]	3[c]	21[g]	4[g]	36[k]	64[k]
Degree or equivalent	12[d]	3[d]	3[h]	1[h]	7[l]	–
Total	100	100	100	100	100	100

Notes:
[a] No stated qualification, 0-70 'other qualification'. CSE only. GCE,GCSE O level or Scottish O level/Standard grade only, A level or Scottish Higher grade only.
[b] Apprenticeship completed, 0-13 'other qualifications'. City and Guilds. BTEC or SCOTVEC Ordinary National level.
[c] HNC, HND, (higher technician level) other higher education below degree level.
[d] All degree-level qualifications and above, 0-17 of 'other qualifications'.
[e] No stated qualification. Primary or secondary school leaving certificate only (CEP, BEPC), General Baccalaureat only.
[f] CAP, BEP (craft qualifications), Technical Baccalaureat.
[g] BTS/DUT (higher technician level) other higher education below degree level.
[h] All degree-level qualifications and above.
[i] School qualifications only.
[j] Completed apprenticeship, (Berufsabschluss) equivalent full-time vocational qualifications (Berufsfachschulabschluss).
[k] Technician (Techniker) and Meister qualification.
[l] Degree level qualifications from Fachhochschule and University.

Note: Occupational groups classified to the technician category in Britain and France are as described in Hilary Steedman, Improvements in workforce qualifications: Britain and France 1979–88, NIER, August 1990. Appendix B. Germany: Category 62 *Techniker* except 629 *Industriemeister, Werkmeister* plus 635 *Technische Zeichner*.

Sources: Britain: Labour Force Survey 1988, unpublished tabulations. France: Enquête-Emploi 1988, Table 05 Form. Germany: Statistisches Bundesamt, Bevölkerung und Erwerbstätigkeit, Fachserie 1, Reihe 4. 1-2. Beruf, Ausbildung und Arbeitsbedingungen der Erwerbstätigen 1987. Table 6.2. For foremen in Germany, own calculations on the basis of Stat. Bundesamt, Fachserie 11, Reihe 3, 1988 Clauß, T Zur beruflichen Situation von Meister and Technikern, Berichte zur beruflichen Bildung, Heft 113, 1990.

21 per cent in France and 36 per cent in Germany. At the same time the proportion of British technicians with degree-level qualifications is at 12 per cent some four times higher than in France and almost twice as high as in Germany. As shown in table 1, there is no evidence of a relative deficiency in the numbers acquiring higher technician qualifications in Britain which might account for the comparatively low proportion of British technicians with such qualifications and thus the apparent need to deploy large numbers of graduates at technician level. On the contrary, this mismatch between employment and qualifications appears to result from a 'drawing-down' process in British industry whereby substantial proportions of both higher technicians and graduates are deployed at levels which do not fully utilise their qualifications in order to compensate for the relatively low proportion of craft-skilled workers on the shopfloor in Britain and the absence of an intermediate category of *Meister*-trained employees.

1·5 'Drawing-down' in British plants

During our British plant visits we observed several instances of such 'drawing-down' in action. In some cases, as mentioned above, qualified technical staff had been formally designated to lower-level occupations but more commonly a situation had arisen where, even though they had been appointed to management and technical support positions appropriate to their qualifications, they were liable to find themselves caught up on a day-to-day basis with shopfloor production problems and were thus unable to devote themselves fully to their 'real' jobs.

In British spinning plants, for example, we encountered heads of technical departments qualified to Higher National level who were involved in a daily welter of 'trouble-shooting' and 'checking-up' activities all over their factories as a direct result of the limited competences of untrained foremen and shopfloor workers. This scenario had few parallels in French or German plants visited where, even if a significant proportion of shopfloor workers lacked vocational qualifications, the majority of foremen were qualified at least to craft level.

In several British engineering plants we observed similar (if less extreme) situations where the demands of implementing new technology apparently required graduate engineers to take responsibility for day to day supervisory tasks which, in German plants, would be the sole preserve of *Meister*-qualified foremen; and where production engineers with higher technician qualifications were obliged to spend a lot of their time dealing with equipment breakdowns arising from lack of preventive maintenance and shortages of craft-skilled maintenance and shopfloor workers.

In describing the ways in which highly qualified staff are frequently 'under'-employed in British factories, we would not wish to suggest that graduates and higher technicians have nothing to gain from shopfloor experience. On the contrary, we would argue that practical experience and regular access to the shopfloor are important requirements for all technical support staff if they are to carry out their duties effectively. However, the considerable evidence of mismatch between employment and high-level qualifications in British manufacturing does raise important questions about whether perceived shortages of highly qualified technical staff frequently reported by employers could be tackled, at least in part, by increased investment in shopfloor worker training. These issues are discussed further in Section 3 below.

1·6 Recruitment and qualifications of foremen and technicians

In all three countries only a small minority of foremen, some 20 per cent, reach that position before their mid-thirties i.e. before they have spent some 16–18 years in a less senior position.[14] Promotion to foreman positions continues to be primarily from the shopfloor.[15] From table 2 we see that in Germany more than 90 per cent of foremen hold craft qualifications and indeed almost two thirds of them are qualified *Meister*. By contrast, in Britain some 55 per cent of all foremen hold no vocational or higher-level qualifications and in France the equivalent proportion is 44 per cent.[16] Only in France did we find signs of a break with the tradition of recruitment from the shopfloor where some young graduates from higher technician schools (holding a BTS or DUT) had been appointed to foreman positions in the larger engineering and spinning plants visited.

In summary, all three countries continue to consider solid shopfloor experience an essential prerequisite for the recruitment of foremen. However, only in Germany does the large pool of skilled workers created by the well-established apprenticeship system ensure that virtually all foremen are qualified at least to craft level or above. At the same time the German *Meister* qualification makes a strong contribution to shopfloor supervisors' ability to maximise the benefits of new organisational methods and technology. This contrasts markedly with both Britain and France where no similar qualification is available to the vast majority of supervisors. In the short term, however, many French employers are responding to the increased organisational and technical demands made upon supervisors by using higher-level technicians for supervision and in the longer term they should achieve a higher proportion of foremen with craft qualifications as a result of the current policy of

66 *National Institute Economic Review May 1991*

upgrading shopfloor skill levels through greater investment in initial education and training to craft level. No similar strategies for development of supervisors appear to have been widely adopted in Britain and no alternatives were forthcoming from the British firms we visited.

In contrast to foremen, those occupying technician positions in the three countries are recruited in part from experienced shopfloor workers, and in part from those without previous shopfloor experience but having education with degree-level and sub-degree level technical qualifications.

In Britain and France, as shown in detail in table 2, around three quarters of all designated technicians have either no vocational qualifications or hold craft or lower level technical qualifications; those without qualifications usually work in a subsidiary role to a qualified person. It can be assumed that most of the 75 per cent of those engaged on technician work in Britain and France and holding no higher technician qualifications have been recruited internally from the shopfloor. In both Britain and France, the remaining quarter hold degree or higher technician qualifications. In the case of both countries this group would not normally have first acquired practical shopfloor experience as a qualified craftsman.[17]

In Germany, the vast majority of technicians have first completed a full craft training, passed the relevant craft examinations and then completed a period of work in the skilled occupation for which they have been trained. In contrast to both the other countries, skilled craft workers in Germany then train full-time off the job for two years in order to obtain a technician qualification. Only a small proportion of German technicians (at most about 7 per cent) have entered their posts without extensive shopfloor experience; these are typically graduates from *Fachhochschule* and university degree courses in engineering and related subjects.

Several British engineering firms that we visited complained that technicians who held higher-technician qualifications or degrees produced designs which required much modification before they could be put into production, and that technicians 'needed to get out onto the shopfloor'. In British engineering plants with a strong union presence, demarcation based on 'custom and practice' prevented technicians from machining test pieces themselves on the shopfloor and they were handicapped for the same reasons in design work. Such restrictions were unknown in France and Germany.

The strong craft background of German technicians, and unrestricted access to the shopfloor space, help to explain why German engineering firms reacted differently from their British and French counterparts to the question of whether skilled operators modified CNC machining programmes prepared by technicians. In Britain and France the response was usually that they did modify programmes—either with official permission or without since it was not normal for the technician to test his programme extensively or at all. In larger engineering plants in Germany we were told that no modification was necessary after the technician had prepared the programme and that machinists were required to concentrate on production.[18]

The next section of this paper compares the numbers obtaining foreman- and technician-level qualifications in all three countries in more detail and assesses the levels of technical competence reached in each case.

2. Standards of intermediate qualifications

2.1 Foremen: flows and standards

In Britain, specially-designed qualifications for foremen and supervisors, the NEBSS (National Examinations Board for Supervisory Studies) Certificate and Diploma, were instituted in 1964 (for details of courses and examinations and a comparison of British and German standards see Prais and Wagner *op. cit.*). Around 5000 obtained a NEBSS Certificate in 1985; applying 1985 pass-rates to published enrolments between 1979–89 it appears that some 50,000 certificates were obtained in the ten-year period, most commonly by those already in foreman posts studying principally during working hours and at the employer's expense.

Some 40 per cent on average of all foremen in British plants visited held craft qualifications (close to the figure derived from LFS analyses) and in almost all plants visited a majority of foremen had been sent on short courses to learn basic management skills. In only one British plant did we find a systematic attempt to equip all foremen with full NEBSS training: there all foremen had been sent on NEBSS courses with a success rate estimated at around 80 per cent.

In France a national Certificate for Supervisors, validated by professional trade associations in an industrial branch in association with ANFOPPE (Association Nationale pour la Formation et le Perfectionnement du Personnel d'Entreprise) is slowly establishing itself. In engineering, 2500 certificates have been awarded since the inception of the scheme in 1980. The length of the French courses (approximately 360 hours) often spread over a period of two years part-time study is similar to the British, as is the subject matter which covers issues relating to the organisation of work including statistical process control, motivation of individuals, health and safety and computer applications; as in Britain, a technical module is available but not compulsory. In contrast to

Britain, there is no final written examination of this certificate in France; assessment is conducted internally combined with a written project on which the candidate is orally examined by a nationally selected board of examiners.

Only in Germany do we find a well-established and widely-held 'supervisory qualification' the *Meister* certificate, open to all skilled workers and obtained during two years of self-financed part-time evening study. The obtaining of the *Meister* certificate—usually before promotion to a foreman position—does not guarantee such promotion. A large German engineering firm told us that several skilled workers had obtained the certificate but would not be promoted by the company because they did not have the right 'personal attributes'. They might decide to move elsewhere and the *Meister* certificate would facilitate promotion within another company. In other companies visited, those who had obtained the *Meister* certificate would continue as craftsmen until a position as foreman 'came up'. Some 40,000 passed the Meister examinations in Germany in 1985; in 1988 the figure was 46,000—similar to the number of NEBSS certificates awarded in Britain over a ten-year period.[19]

In all three countries, provision of training in supervisory skills is not confined to National or *Meister* Certificates but is also provided by a wide variety of courses, some short (as little as two days) and intensive, some involving part-time or distance-learning study from a multitude of providers, often originating from regional associations of employers or from local training groups. In quantitative terms at least, the supply of such courses in Britain was felt to be adequate in the companies visited and experiments with distance learning study (whereby supervisors study in their own time) by correspondence course seem to be providing the flexibility required by smaller firms where foremen cannot normally be spared for courses during working hours.

In the German plants visited all foremen held at least a *Berufsabschluss* qualification i.e. had completed a three year apprenticeship and the appropriate examinations. On average around two thirds of all foremen in German plants visited held a Meister qualification and the remaining one third held a craft qualification (these were mainly in older age groups). It was rare to find foremen in Germany who held *Techniker* qualifications and quite unknown to find any who held degrees.

British and French national qualifications for foremen appear to be of a similar standard (as far as can be judged). The British qualification is older and better-established than its French counterpart and the numbers qualifying in Britain are therefore higher than in France but still only one tenth of the numbers

in Germany. The quality of the German *Meister* course, soundly built on a thorough craft training, is still far in advance of both the British and the French qualifications. Plant visits which reveal the far wider range of foreman responsibilities in Germany only confirm this view.

2·2 Technicians: flows and standards

The British higher-technician qualification is known as the Higher National Certificate (HNC) or Higher National Diploma (HND) awarded by the Business and Technician Education Council (BTEC) in England and Wales and the Scottish Vocational Education Council (SCOTVEC) in Scotland. As shown in Table 1, the number of awards at this level in Britain is much the same as in France and substantially higher than in Germany.

Most British students entering courses for Higher National Certificates and Diplomas have previously taken an Ordinary National qualification in the same area, and almost all of those on HNC courses are in apprenticeship arrangements studying one day a week and receiving on-the-job training for the remainder of the week. Most complete their course by the age of 20–21. In engineering and technology areas in Britain most students follow the part-time route leading to an HNC; they outnumber the HND students who would normally be studying full time by 3:1. Access to the British courses is also open to students with GCE Advanced level or Scottish equivalent qualifications in suitable subjects.

In France the equivalent qualification is the *Brevet de technicien supérieur* (BTS) or *Diplôme universitaire de technologie* (DUT). Access to BTS courses is normally conditional on obtaining a *Baccalauréat* qualification, usually a technical *Baccalauréat*. They are mainly full-time courses. A very small number in France now take the BTS qualification while working on an apprenticeship contract four days a week and attending one day a week at an apprenticeship centre. However, this is a new development and numbers are at present very small: the overwhelming majority of those taking the French technician qualification enter the course straight from school without any previous experience except that provided by workshop training in the practical part of their technical *Bac* course. They will normally complete the two-year course at around the age of 21 or 22, depending on the age at which they obtained the *Baccalauréat*.

In Germany, study for a technician qualification leads to the award of a State examined technician certificate (*Staatlich geprüfte Techniker*). In marked contrast to higher technician courses in both Britain and France, the German *Techniker* course stipulates, as a condition of access, that trainees must have completed a three year craft apprenticeship in

National Institute Economic Review May 1991

the area which they intend to study at technician level and have at least two years prior experience on the shopfloor working in production. The highest qualification from the general education system needed by entrants to *Techniker* courses is only the *Hauptschulabschluss*, the leaving certificate equivalent to six or eight GCSE passes at grades D or E in Britain; however, the majority of *Techniker* candidates hold school-leaving qualifications above this level. The ages at which German employees gain *Techniker* qualifications vary considerably: the aspiring technician in Germany is unlikely to be in a position to start on the two-year full-time technician course before the age of 20–21. Earliest completion ages are likely to be 22 or 23 and the average age of those completing the qualification is 28.[20]

Under the auspices of the Engineering Council in Britain, it is now possible for holders of Higher National qualifications to study part-time over a 2–3 year period for a qualification equivalent to an honours degree which leads to 'chartered engineer' status. Those holding Higher National awards can also obtain the title 'incorporated engineer' (previously known as 'technician engineer') following two years 'responsible experience'. Some 2500 to 3000 holders of HNC/HND go on to obtain this title every year. A further 1500 people holding ONC/OND qualifications apply for the title of 'engineering technician' each year after fulfilling similar conditions.

While these schemes provide an additional professional status, they in some ways typify the split which exists in British industry between, on the one hand, engineering graduates and technicians with little or no experience of shopfloor production and, on the other hand, craft-skilled workers with limited possibilities of gaining further qualifications and progressing to higher levels of responsibility. This is the converse of the German system which values craft training and experience in direct production as the foundation for technician training. The German system also attaches importance to providing craft-trained workers with routes for vertical mobility within their professional field. Technician positions constitute an important means (in addition to supervisory positions) whereby craft workers in Germany can become upwardly mobile and gain access to management positions.[21]

Comparisons of examination papers suggest that British HNC qualifications (taken by 80 per cent of students at this level) are of a similar degree of difficulty but much less geared to specific applications than either French BTS or German *Techniker* qualifications. These comparisons are discussed in detail in Appendix 1. In summary, it seems reasonable to consider those holding higher technician qualifications in all three countries to be at broadly

equivalent levels of competence and technical expertise.

3. Ensuring the supply of intermediate skills

3·1 Financing of training at intermediate skill level

In this section we analyse the distribution of training costs and examine economic incentives to individuals to invest in training at intermediate skill level.

3·1·1 Craft In Britain employers bear nearly all the costs of craft training (including trainee wages and the costs of off-the-job-training and further education) with only a small contribution forthcoming in recent years from the public authorities in the form of wage subsidies for the first two years of training under the former YTS scheme.[22]

In France, a means-tested state grant may make a contribution to but does not cover the whole cost of a CAP trainee's living costs, otherwise subsistence while training is the responsibility of the trainee and his/her parents. All costs of training tuition are met by public authorities through the provision of training facilities free at point of use. All employers are subject to a remissible apprentice training tax of 0·02 per cent of payroll. It is debatable whether French employers should be considered as directly bearing any costs of off-the-job training or further education since cash payment of this tax to the exchequer is not earmarked in any way for training expenditure and it can therefore be considered as part of corporate taxation to which all firms are subject in each country.

In Germany, off-the-job tuition costs at FE colleges are met by the public authorities. As in Britain, German firms are responsible for a large proportion of training costs in the form of trainee wages and other payroll costs as well as the costs of on-the-job training and supervision. In comparison with Britain, however, trainee wages represent a relatively small proportion of adult wages and this has undoubtedly encouraged the much higher levels of craft training that have taken place in Germany compared to Britain.[23] By contrast, as we go on to show, in the case of supervisory and technician training the main differences between all three countries concern the relative distribution of training costs between employers, individuals and the public authorities.

3·1·2 Foremen In Britain and France, foremen who obtain a further qualification specifically related to foreman responsibilities normally do so in paid working hours with the cost of college and wages during training borne by the employer. In Germany, *Meister* training courses are followed in the employee's own time, so that no wage costs fall on the employer—at most, the employer may cooperate to the extent of rescheduling the employee's working hours to enable him/her to attend the required course. In contrast to France and Britain, where both publicly provided and private institutions charge users for adult training course costs, most courses leading to *Techniker* qualifications are financed by public authorities. *Meister* courses are provided by *Industrie und Handelskammern* (Chambers of Industry and Commerce) which charge fees to users.

The contrast between France and Britain on the one hand and Germany on the other is therefore striking: in France and Britain employers directly bear almost the whole cost of supervisory training while in Germany employers directly bear none of the cost; instead, it is shared between individuals and public authorities. The consequences in terms of the numbers and standard of supervisory qualifications obtained in each country display the same degree of contrast.

In the British and French firms visited, most foremen had received some additional training consisting in the overwhelming majority of cases of short courses up to a week; these did not lead or even contribute to a full foreman award of the standard of the German *Meister*, or even in most cases to the level of a NEBSS certificate or the French *Certificat National de Maîtrise*.

A small start has been made in Britain in courses comparable to the German *Meister*; these relate to tool-making and to the metal-working industries. So far under a hundred trainees a year are involved. There do not appear to be any similar schemes in France. It seems unlikely that with present financing arrangements British employers will invest the sums required to raise existing foreman training to German *Meister* standards.

3·1·3 Technicians The financing of training leading to the technician-level qualifications described in Section 2 also presents a contrast but, in this case, between Britain on the one hand and France and Germany on the other. Britain stands alone in that the bulk of training leading to Higher National qualifications is provided on-the-job with day-release for college courses and is financed almost entirely by employers with the aspiring technician receiving a trainee wage from the employer. The training period in Britain starts at age 16 and leads, through (Ordinary) National Certificate, to Higher National Certificate at age 21 or 22. The employer bears all tuition costs and the proportion of the trainee technician's wages that is not recouped through productive work. The first year is entirely 'off the job' with no productive work. The trainee foregoes higher wages in the interests of obtaining a qualification.

An earlier study carried out at the National Institute suggested that the average gross cost of technician training in a sample of engineering plants was some £26,000 per trainee (1984 earnings levels). The productive contribution of the trainee was estimated to be worth an average £11,500 leaving a net cost to the employer of approximately £14,500. This was about 60 per cent higher than the estimated net cost of craft apprentice training, reflecting both higher rates of technician trainee pay and the slower development of the productive contribution made by technician trainees compared to that made by trainee craft workers[24].

It is at first sight difficult to understand the British employer's willingness to finance technician training between the ages of 16 to 18 as well as post-18 as the earlier period is the most cost-intensive stage of the technician's training and, particularly in the first year, devotes much time to general skills of the sort that employers are not normally willing to finance. As the bulk of firm-specific on-the-job training takes place in the later stages of a technician apprenticeship, it would seem reasonable for the majority of Ordinary National qualifications to be obtained in full-time education before entering employment at age 18-plus, thus approximately halving the employer's costs. Although 18-plus recruitment to technician training programmes is not unknown in British industry, it remains exceptional and none of the firms that we visited had seriously considered such an option.

In our view, it would be wrong to characterise employers' recruitment of 16 year-old technician trainees as irrational. Some employers in heavily unionised plants and industries are 'locked-in' to this pattern of provision as a result of collective work place agreements. More importantly, however, employers compete with universities and polytechnics for the scarce resource of 16 year-olds with 'good' GCSE (grades A–C) maths and science (approximately 25 per cent of the age cohort). British employers, unlike their French counterparts, cannot rely on a high status technical route to attract able young people in sixth forms to technical careers and away from academic A-level studies which offer the prospect of a higher education place at the end. In order to attract a certain proportion of able youngsters to a career as a technician, employers must 'catch them young' and offer them in the work place the technical qualification route that the school sixth-form does not provide. If employers waited to try to recruit A-level students to technician traineeships, the fear at present is that many would reject the pay and prospects in favour of a higher education course. Britain's failure to construct and nurture a high quality technical track within the school system thus places an additional burden on British industry.

In both France and Germany. the costs of technician training are shared between the individual and the public authorities and do not fall on the employer. In France, BTS and DUT students enter from full-time schooling at 18 and cover their own maintenance costs either completely, or partially with the help of a State bursary. In Germany, aspiring technicians enter training after completing a craft apprenticeship and a period of full-time work in their chosen trade. As in France, tuition in publicly-provided institutions leading to technician-level courses is free of charge to the student. The allocation of maintenance costs while studying on full-time courses is variable as between the public authorities (Federal Labour Office) and the individual. For unemployed individuals and those threatened by unemployment, financial support which amounts to around 50 per cent of last gross earnings is available for the two-year period of full-time study, subject to certain conditions being met both by the course providers and the candidate. Since 1982. however, the majority of those undertaking technician training have received *loans* from the Federal Labour Office amounting to some 58 per cent of average net income. Loans are interest-free and must be repaid over a maximum ten year period, starting two years after the qualifications have been obtained. In all these cases, however, the employer bears no direct costs. Technician training in Germany contrasts with *Meister* training in that most qualify through full-time study and must thus run the risk of taking on a loan and covering subsequent repayment; numbers qualifying annually as *Techniker* are less than half those qualifying (predominantly through part-time study) as *Meister* (see table 1 above).

It is also instructive to compare the British situation. where individual firms make decisions about numbers of technicians trained. with Germany where the Federal Labour Office can (and does) 'steer' the supply of individuals for *Techniker* training. If there is unemployment or under-employment in certain types of technical occupation then the Federal Labour Office will withdraw financial support of the type mentioned above. This form of government intervention to influence the supply of skills at this level appears more effective in producing a cost-effective mix of skills than reliance on employer training decisions as in Britain.

As noted above, the numbers of those qualifying as higher technicians in Britain are already substantially higher than those obtaining *Techniker* qualifications in Germany in related fields. Yet. where craft-level skills are in short supply, as in Britain. even an increased supply at technician level will appear inadequate because many of these are required to 'plug gaps' at lower levels or to resolve technical

problems which elsewhere would be solved by foremen and craftsmen. In Germany, by contrast, the well-established system of craft training ensures that many trained to this level can be used in technician-level work; in this way, technical functions are (and are seen to be) more than adequately fulfilled by the smaller numbers of German *Techniker* available supplemented by those holding *Meister* and craft qualifications and employed in technician positions (see table 2 above).

In the light of the evidence cited above on the relative costs to British employers of technician and craft training, the ratio of craftsmen to technicians in British manufacturing appears to represent a much less efficient mix of skills than that employed in Germany. The next section investigates the ways in which the different patterns of earnings differentials in each country affect the willingness of individuals to share the costs of acquiring intermediate-level qualifications.

3·2 *Economic incentives to acquire qualifications*

There are clear and characteristic differences between Britain, France and Germany in the extent to which the earnings of technicians and foremen exceed those of craftsmen and unskilled employees; and these differentials in pay are related to—but not solely determined by—differences in the processes and financing of training. A broad picture of average differentials in the three countries is set out in table 3 (the estimates for France rely on a special, unpublished, tabulation for 1986; data for Germany have also been shown for that year; British figures are for 1989). It will be understood that the actual earnings of a particular individual depend not simply on his qualifications, but also on his experience and responsibilities; and also on whether his particular industry is expanding and looking for additional staff (as often in mechanical engineering in Germany), or is contracting (as fairly generally in textiles). The range of variation in the earnings of technicians quoted to us on our visits was considerable in all three countries, and depended strongly on responsibility and seniority in the management structure; but average earnings of technicians and of section foremen were very similar. In what follows we concentrate solely on the difference between countries in average differentials.

It is clear from table 3, and as has previously been noted. that skill-differentials for craftsmen in France are considerably greater than in both Britain and Germany. As between Britain and Germany. the differences are small up to craftsman-level. but above that—for foremen and technicians—differentials in Britain are much lower than in Germany.

To understand these differences it is necessary to remind ourselves of the differences in the provision of

Table 3. Earnings differentials of employees in manufacturing in Britain, 1989 and France and Germany, 1986, by degree of skill and responsibility

average earnings per week of unskilled employees in each country = 100

	Britain[a]	France	Germany
Unskilled	100	100	100
Semi-skilled	113	124	115
Skilled craftsman	126	154	121
Section foreman	139	171	169
Technician	140[b]	179[c]	169[d]

Sources: Britain, New Earnings Survey 1989; France, Enquête structure des salaires en 1986, INSEE, unpublished tabulation; Germany, Statistisches Jahrbuch 1986, pp 465 et seq (further details for Britain and Germany are in Prais and Wagner, 1988, Appendix, p 48).

Notes:
[a] Male employees only.
[b] Average of engineering technician, engineering and other draughtsmen, and laboratory technicians.
[c] Average of *technicien premier* and *superieur*.
[d] *Angestellte, Leistungsgruppe III* (as for *Meister*).

training to craft level. The long-standing system of quasi-obligatory vocational training in Germany for 15–18 year-olds who have left full-time schooling ensures a greater supply of qualified craftsmen than does the French system which relies to a greater extent on market incentives. In France training starts for some pupils at secondary vocational schools (*Lycées professionnels*) during the period of compulsory schooling; for others it starts at these schools after 16 and is largely self-financed; a minority enter apprenticeships at 16 after compulsory schooling. Securing an adequate number of qualified craftsmen with market incentives in France evidently requires a higher wage differential—in the region of 50 per cent over an unskilled employee—than the compulsory system of Germany which requires a differential of only about 20 per cent.

When we come to the next higher level of qualification represented by foremen Britain and France are closer in their differentials—earning about 10 per cent more than skilled employees; the similarity is perhaps not surprising since, at this level, both countries recruit foremen from among shopfloor workers without any requirement for additional training. Differentials at this qualification-level are higher (40 per cent) in Germany than in France and Britain, and this can be attributed to the need in Germany, to provide adequate economic incentives to qualified craftsmen to undertake, at their own expense, the training leading to *Meister* certification. When we come to the higher level of qualification represented by technicians, Germany and France are closer in their differentials—earning about 70–80 per cent more than unskilled employees; the similarity is explained by the fact that, at this level, *both* countries rely on market incentives for adequate recruitment.

The present-day much lower skill-differentials in Britain—only 40 per cent for a technician above an unskilled employee—thus seem anomalous in

contrast with France and Germany. As shown in an earlier study, skill-differentials in Britain thirty years ago were as high as, and perhaps even higher than in Germany;[26] the 1960s saw a very sharp contraction of differentials, and only in the 1980s has there been a widening of differentials but which, so far, has been very modest. Incentives to undertake training have been provided in Britain by employers paying for trainees' time while at college and paying for their college instruction and on-the-job training; in the 1980s government subsidies, under YTS and associated schemes, have helped to support the early years of a technician's training (but not the later years). In comparison with both France and Germany, an adequate supply of qualified technicians appears to have been provided in Britain but at the cost of failure to invest in training at lower levels of skill. In the other two countries, by contrast, the large shares of training costs borne by government and by individuals (with associated economic incentives in the form of wage differentials) appear to be maintaining a better balance of supplies at both craft and technician level.

Summary and conclusions

Summary

This investigation has been concerned with the adequacy of Britain's supply of skills at the intermediate level, comprising craft workers, foremen and technicians, in comparison with France and Germany. Organisational and technological changes in manufacturing have transformed the functions of foremen and technicians, and the requirement for foremen today is for more sophisticated skills of planning, communication and organisation within an advanced technological framework. Technical skills need to be broad and flexible and based upon practical shop-floor experience.

In the manufacturing plants visited, the first-line supervisor on the shopfloor, in charge of people and materials and responsible for output remains an important and essential pivot of the production process. Because demands have changed and new priorities (control of inventory, 'right first time' production, meeting deadlines and delivery dates) have emerged, foremen need, in addition to the more traditional supervisory skills, the ability to plan ahead, prioritise carefully and communicate with customers. They must achieve higher levels of technical understanding in order to liaise with programmers and maintenance staff. All this requires longer periods of both initial and continuing training—both on- and off-the-job—to higher levels and the challenge to firms is either to ensure that trained individuals are appointed or provide adequate training.

The comparison with France reveals that Britain is not alone in neglecting the further professional development of foremen; the present-day situation in France is broadly similar to that in Britain although in some respects it is improving more rapidly. Germany stands out as benefiting from its tradition of *Meister* training: German foremen take on logistical tasks and responsibilities in relation to, for example, cost control which are not tackled by the great majority of foremen in Britain and France. The latter often require an additional tier of intermediate management for these tasks. The additional technical and organisational training acquired by the German *Meister* enables them to work closely and effectively with technical support services such as work-scheduling, machine-programming and liaison with customers.

Although short training courses for those promoted to foremen are frequently provided in Britain and France, what is presently offered by most firms is not adequate to fulfill the needs set out above and not in any way comparable to the depth and breadth of the *Meister* course. We concluded that very few British firms had developed a feasible strategy for upgrading foremen capacities. In France, innovative strategies to upgrade skills at this level were noted in half of all firms visited; the French strategy is to solve the immediate problem by appointing highly-qualified technicians to supervisor positions, and to hope that the current rapid upgrading of work-force qualifications (as analysed in a recent Institute study)[27] will provide a satisfactory source for foreman recruitment in the future. Other strategies encountered include the introduction of cell-structures and team-working. Changes in French firms appear to have been facilitated by substantially greater foreman/unskilled pay-differentials than in Britain, and greater flexibility in redefining structures of responsibility and providing rewards appropriate for more highly-qualified staff.

In Britain, fear of disturbing the hierarchy of differential payments appears to be holding back medium-sized and larger firms from paying technically-qualified staff sufficiently to attract them to supervisory positions. Not surprisingly, we frequently heard that newly-trained technically-qualified staff in large firms had left for smaller firms which were more flexible in their approach.

Employer-financing of foreman training in Britain has not produced skills at the appropriate level, in contrast to the very adequate supply of *Meister* in Germany where public authorities and the individual share the direct costs. Understandable fears of poaching of highly-trained staff have held many British and French firms back from investing heavily in their own staff. French firms seem often to have decided that it is more cost-effective to appoint those who have qualified with the equivalent of a Higher National Diploma (their BTS) to foreman posts, than to bear the heavy costs of upgrading existing foremen to similar levels. The options in Britain seem to be either for firms to pay more for high levels of skill and encourage individuals to make their own investment as in Germany, or for greater government subsidies to firms to finance the continuing training of some of their employees to higher levels. The first of these options is more likely to lead to a response in accord with market pressures for skills as is demonstrated by the case of Germany. However, the much lower numbers of British foremen with craft qualifications must also be borne in mind. The pool of likely candidates who might put themselves forward for self-financed further training is consequently much smaller in Britain than in Germany and the second solution (public subsidies for employer financing of foreman training) might be necessary for some time to ensure an adequate supply.

In the case of technicians, the situation on standards and supply looks very different from that of foremen. British standards of training stand up well in comparison to France and Germany, and the current annual supply of higher-technician skills is somewhat greater in Britain. Of concern to Britain is the lengthy training process and the proportion of costs carried by employers in comparison to France and Germany. Germany appears to satisfy the needs of a technologically advanced economy at technician level by using craft-trained employees on many technician-level tasks and providing for a small proportion of skilled craft workers to receive an additional technical training on top of that undertaken during their initial apprenticeship; their system produces a very different and more practically-oriented mix of skills than exists in Britain.

In Britain, almost all the training at the levels considered in this investigation is carried out as a result of decisions made by individual firms to invest in their employees' skills. Our analysis and visits for this investigation confirm that, with few exceptions, the present arrangement provides an inappropriate mix of skills at intermediate level in Britain when the outcomes are compared, in particular, with Germany but also, to a lesser extent, with France. The greatest deficiencies in Britain are at craft and foreman level. This deficiency not only has serious consequences for shopfloor skills but also lowers standards of first-line supervision and inhibits the efficient provision of technical services. Our study makes clear that good craft skills make an important contribution to the competence of foremen and can form the basis for carrying out a range of technical tasks and for technician training.

Signalling of skill-needs to individuals by the adjustment of wage differentials together with public support for training courses and the trainee's investment of his own time in the financing of intermediate skills training as in Germany appear to result in closer matching of training to skill needs.

Conclusions

British employers bear a higher proportion of the costs of technician training than do employers in France and Germany. Even so, Britain produces proportionally as many technicians as France and considerably more than Germany while neglecting the cheaper craft training. Lack of sufficient craft skills increases the demand for technicians to 'plug the gaps'. Our study suggests that British employers could easily shift part of the cost of technician and craft training to colleges of Further Education and to the individual by recruiting trainee technicians and craft workers at 18 (instead of at 16) after they have obtained a BTEC or SCOTVEC (Ordinary) National qualification by full-time study in a FE college. Employer funds at present devoted to training 16 to 18 year olds could be switched to the (cheaper) craft-training area to provide flexible training and upgrading to craft level to employees of all ages where the deficiency in Britain is particularly acute. Increased supplies of craft-level employees would, in turn, allow the more effective deployment of technicians on technical support functions instead of (as at present) on shopfloor 'trouble-shooting'.

The implication for government policy in Britain seems to be that the current exclusive reliance on employers to diagnose and meet skill needs in a cost-effective manner needs to be reconsidered. Current arrangements result in an underproduction by firms of much-needed craft skills relative to the production of more costly technician skills. A strategy for creating a more appropriate mix is urgently needed; the evidence from this comparative study is that the sum of employers' training efforts will do no more than provide the skills to 'plug the gaps' in British manufacturing. Deep-rooted, nationwide deficiencies require a strategic response formulated and applied nationally. Training and Enterprise Councils are well-equipped to respond to local deficiencies but not to national ones. Government and individuals should bear a larger share of the cost and reap larger returns to training in order to achieve the training effort which can lead to the comprehensive upgrading of skills required for economic survival.

ACKNOWLEDGEMENTS

We would like to acknowledge first the companies in all three countries whose managers and other employees gave so generously of their time to assist us in our enquiries. In addition. we are grateful for advice from: M Bailey, Watford College; A Richards, Bolton Institute of Higher Education; T Wilson-Hooper. N Burgess. Bromley College of Technology; R Whittaker, B Peerless, Middlesex Polytechnic; H Ringhandt. Staatliche Technikerschule Berlin; H Strey, Techniker Fachschule, München; I Drexel, Institut für Sozialwissenschaftliche Forschung. München; J P Henri. Centre de Perfectionnement des Cadres, Roubaix; M Lemoine, Mécagim, Paris; J L Lépinay Centre AFORP–Drancy, Paris; B Vandeputte Comité Intertextile d'Apprentissage, Roubaix.

J-C Rabier, Laboratoire de Recherche en Economie Appliquee. Universite de Paris X and U Adler, IFO. München acted as consultants to the project. Their help in arranging visits and providing guidance and advice was invaluable. We have greatly benefited from the advice and encouragement of colleagues. in particular S J Prais, Ray Barrell and other colleagues at the National Institute. We also gratefully acknowledge the comments and suggestions from two referees and of the Training Agency. Two seminars organised by the European Centre for the Development of Vocational Training (CEDEFOP) provided valuable opportunities for discussion with European colleagues engaged in similar work.

NOTES

(1) A Daly, DMWN Hitchens and K Wagner, 'Productivity, machinery and skills in a sample of British and German manufacturing plants: results of a pilot enquiry', *National Institute Economic Review*, no. 111 February 1985. H Steedman, K Wagner, 'A second look at productivity, machinery and skills in Britain and Germany'. *National Institute Economic Review*, no. 122 November 1987. H Steedman, K Wagner, 'Productivity, machinery and skills: clothing manufacture in Britain and Germany', *National Institute Economic Review*, no. 128 May 1989.

(2) This report constitutes the third in a series of studies of intermediate skills in Britain, France and Germany. The first study dealt mainly with quantitative comparisons of flows of technically-qualified manpower and the international matching of qualifications. SJ Prais. 'Qualified manpower in engineering: Britain and other industrially advanced countries', *National Institute Economic Review*, February 1989. The second reported on special analyses of the French and British Labour Force Surveys in terms of the stocks of different categories of intermediate skill and different qualification levels—foremen, technicians and shop-floor workers. H. Steedman, 'Improvements in workforce qualifications: Britain and France 1979–88', *National Institute Economic Review*, August 1990.

(3) The field-work for this study was carried out between November 1988 and November 1990. Throughout this report 'Germany' should be taken as referring to the former 'Federal Republic of Germany'.

(4) For survey evidence of the extent of use of microelectronics-based technology in British, German and French manufacturing industry in 1983, see J Northcott et. al., *Microelectronics in Industry*, Policy Studies Institute. London, 1985, pp 53, 67, 68. The German lead over both Britain and France appears to be greatest in the use of CNC machine tools and the implementation of advanced machine and process control systems. For a detailed appraisal of survey evidence relating to the age and technical sophistication of machinery in the metal-working industries of the leading industrial nations, see SJ Prais 'Some international comparisons of the age of the machine-stock', *The Journal of Industrial Economics*, Vol XXXIV, No. 3, March 1986. More recently the Amdahl Executive Institute claims that 'West German companies have the advantage over their British, French and Italian competitors in using information technology (IT) for competitive advantage', 'Clues to success: Information Technology Strategies for Tomorrow', 1990.

(5) In all the spinning plants we visited where CNC automated machinery had been installed, supervisors were required to make very quick decisions about orders of priority when several machines required attention or adjustment at once. Similarly, in many engineering shops the very different production speeds of CNC and conventional machines coupled with moves towards greater product variety and smaller batch sizes clearly made substantial demands upon the organisational capacities of shopfloor supervisors.

(6) This change is confirmed by a recent British survey of supervisors in 16 industrial and commercial organisations. The level of skill required of supervisors was found to be increasing in (i) checking, assessing, discriminating (ii) complex procedures (iii) ordering, prioritising planning (iv) diagnosing, analysing, solving (v) adapting to new ideas. systems. R S Kandola, N A Banerji, M A Greene of Pearn Kandola Downs, 'The Role of Supervisors in Human Resource Development' Training Agency 1989.

(7) C Smith, *Technical workers: Class, labour and trade unionism*, Macmillan 1987 p.91. It is related there that in the decade 1963–73 the 'typical occupations' occupied by TASS (technicians union) members expanded from around 50 to some 400. However, Smith also documents the impact of technical change on engineering technicians, the decline of occupations such as tracers, rate-fixers and the rise of part-programmers and CAD/CAM designers.

(8) During our visits we observed this distinction between supervisory and technical roles everywhere except in a small number of French plants where some programming and first-line maintenance functions had been explicitly merged with shopfloor supervisory responsibilities. In some German plants *Meister*-qualified foremen worked closely with specialist programmers and work planners but did not themselves carry out these tasks; even this level of technical involvement depended on the more routine supervisory tasks being delegated to charge-hands (*Vorarbeiter*).

(9) The consequences of low levels of technical knowledge and skills for foremen's performance in a high-technology environment were highlighted in the French spinning plants we visited. Considerable efforts had been made to help the foremen acquire the level of technical expertise necessary to 'speak the same language' as the maintenance technician in charge of the 'state of the art' CNC machinery then being installed. Despite updating courses, some foremen in the French plants had been unable to cope and alternative (to shopfloor) recruitment to foreman posts from those with higher technician qualifications had been introduced by the management as a consequence. In the German spinning plants the very thorough training of the *Meister*-qualified foreman resulted in his having the technical background necessary to remedy machinery faults. However, it was considered inefficient to require him to carry out maintenance tasks which would have interfered with effective supervision; his training equipped him to localise faults correctly, to call the appropriate maintenance team, to estimate the time of repair and plan and change the production schedule accordingly.

(10) The apprenticeship training for maintenance workers in Germany in spinning (textile) starts with training as a machine operator (e.g. *Textilmaschinenfuhrer-Spinnerei*) for two years. They can then continue with a third year to become *Textilmechaniker* (eg. *Spinnerei*) so that all skilled mechanics have worked as skilled operators. Consequently, the *Meister* who have gone through the three year apprenticeship have a strong background in both maintenance and machine operation even before they undertake further technical training at *Meisterschule*.

(11) See SJ Prais, K Wagner, 'Productivity and Management: the Training of Formen in Britain and Germany'. *National Institute Economic Review*, no. 123. February 1988.

(12) In H Steedman. 1990, op cit. it was pointed out that the proportion of workers and foremen qualified to craft level was higher in France than in Britain and that the supply of such skills was increasing faster in France than in Britain. However, both France and Britain can be seen to have lower levels of skill in the manufacturing labour-force relative to Germany.

[13]   In Germany, it is important to distinguish further between those employed as foremen (*Meister*) and those holding *Meister* certificates ie. who have taken and passed *Meister* certificate examinations.

[14]   In both Britain and France the age structure of foremen engaged in manufacturing is similar: only 23 per cent are under 35 (compared to 40 per cent under 35 for total over 15 population in France, and 36 per cent under 35 for total over 16 population in Great Britain). The corresponding figure for Germany is 20 per cent. The mean age of foremen as recorded in the censuses is 43 for France, 44 for Britain and 47 for Germany. Census 1981, *Economic activity in Great Britain* Table 13, 4A, OPCS 1984. Recensement general 1982, Formation, Table 07 INSEE, 1984. *Statistisches Bundesamt*, Fachserie 1, Reihe 4 1.2, 1987.

[15]   In the two British case-study firms analysed by Thurley and Wirdenius, all foremen had been internally promoted from the shop-floor. K Thurley, H Wirdenius, *Supervision: A Reappraisal*, Heinemann 1973. Similar patterns for the recruitment of foremen in manufacturing industries have been reported for France. A study carried out in 1986–7 of 26 plants drawn from engineering, chemical, pharmaceutical and construction industries noted that an average of 70 per cent of all foremen in the plants investigated had been promoted from the shopfloor. F Eyraud, A Jobert, P Rozenblatt, M Tallard, *Les classifications dans l'Entreprise. Centre d'Etudes de l'Emploi/IRIS–Travail et Société*/LEST, October 1988. p.94. In a study of French, British and German foremen carried out between 1977 and 1979 in 9 plants in the three countries, 'In all countries, practically all the personnel in supervision have come up through the works'. M Maurice, A Sorge, M Warner, 'Societal Differences in Organising Manufacturing Units: A comparison of France, West Germany and Great Britain' in *Organization Studies* 1980 p.76.

[16]   This finding for France and Germany is confirmed by the contrast identified by König and Müller 'It is also characteristic of the category of foreman that in France it can be reached not only from the skilled worker category as in Germany, but also from that of semi-skilled workers'. W König and W Müller 'Educational systems and labour markets as determinants of worklife mobility in France and West Germany: a comparison of men's career mobility, 1965–1970', *European Sociological Review* Vol. 2, No. 2. September 1986 p.87.

[17]   In France, all those undertaking higher technician (BTS, DUT) training spend a three-month period in a work placement, but are unlikely to acquire craft skills. A very small number follow BTS or DUT courses on day release. In Britain, most of those obtaining an HNC qualification study on day release while in employment as technician trainees. However, their training route is differentiated from that of craft trainees and most practical work is likely to be in technical support departments rather than in direct production.

[18]   This finding is consistent with Sorge et. al. who found a greater tendency in large German plants to promote craft operators to staff status as programming technicians to avoid machine downtime because of lengthy programming. A Sorge, G Hartmann, M Warner, I Nicholas *Microelectronics and manpower in manufacturing*, Gower 1983 chs.5 and 8.

[19]   For a detailed analysis see S J Prais and K Wagner, 1988, op cit.

[20]   T Clauss, 'Zur beruflichen Situation von Meister und Technikern', *Berichte zur beruflichen Bildung*, Heft 113, 1990.

[21]   The contrast between France and Germany with respect to access to technician posts in the two countries has been analysed by Drexel in terms of a pattern of vertical access in Germany (from the shop-floor) and horizontal access in France (from full-time education). The analysis sought to determine whether access to German technician positions was moving towards the French model thus restricting the career prospects of craft workers in Germany. Drexel concludes that there is very little evidence that this change is taking place in Germany. I Drexel, Der Schwierige Weg zu einem neuen gesellschaftlichen Qualifikationstyp, in *Journal fur Sozialforschung*, Heft 3. Campus Verlag 1989.

[22]   Recent government initiatives have modified this situation in some limited respects. The Youth Training Scheme (YTS) subsidy was allowed to offset first and second year apprentice wages in industries such as engineering until its abolition in 1991. Reduced amounts are now available to TECs (Training and Enterprise Councils) to subsidise employer training of young people and vouchers made available to young people to cover off-the-job training costs are being piloted.

[23]   See I Jones, 'Skill Formation and Pay Relativities' in GDN Worswick, *Education and Economic Performance*, Gower, 1985.

[24]   Estimates of average technician training costs derived from I Jones, 'Apprentice Training Costs in British Manufacturing Establishments: Some New Evidence', *British Journal of Industrial Relations* Vol. xxiv. No. 3 1986, pp. 349–350. The finding of a large differential in net costs between technician and craft training programmes is broadly in line with surveys of training costs carried out by the Engineering Industry Training Board in the 1970s (Jones, 1986, pp. 354–5). More extensive and up-to-date work in this field is urgently needed.

[25]   For earlier analyses see L Needleman. 'The Structure of industrial earnings in seven Western European countries', in *Controlling Industrial Economies: Essays in Honour of C T Saunders* (ed. S F Frowen, Macmillan), 1983; C Saunders and D Marsden, *Pay inequalities in the European Communities* (Butterworth), 1981; and S J Prais, K Wagner, op. cit.

[26]   S J Prais, K Wagner (1988). op, cit. p.40.

[27]   H Steedman (1990) op. cit.

APPENDIX I   COMPARISON OF TECHNICIAN QUALIFICATIONS: BRITAIN, FRANCE AND GERMANY

Full-time technician courses in all three countries last for a period of two years. In all cases part-time study can also lead to a technician qualification. In Germany, part-time study for a *Techniker* qualification extends over a period of four years, double that of the full-time qualification. In France, the very small numbers who take the qualifications with part-time study still manage to take the same examinations as the full-time students while studying only part-time; however, they work throughout the year without the benefit of academic vacations. In Britain the part-time HNC qualification has the same time duration as the full-time HND (two years); however, it is recognised in Britain that the HNC does not cover as much ground as the HND whereas in both France and Germany the full-time and part-time routes lead to identical qualifications.[a]

In all three countries all formal instruction for technician qualification is college-based, in France and Britain in institutions of higher education and in Germany in institutions which operate within the vocational field. All three countries insist on a number of written examinations as a condition for the award of a technician qualification. Although all courses include elements of general education, requirements vary markedly: in Germany, 400 out of 2400 hours are spent on English, German and economic and social issues, in France, 4 out of 34 weekly study hours are spent on French and a foreign language. In Britain, courses in English and a foreign language are offered in many colleges but are not compulsory for the HNC qualification. Although these subjects are examined in France, it is possible to obtain the BTS while not reaching pass marks in the general subjects. The same is not true of Germany where passes in general subjects are included among the requirements for the award of *Techniker* qualifications.

Final examination papers from the three main qualifications described above, the French (*BTS*), the German (*Techniker*) and the British Higher National Certificate and Higher National Diploma were obtained from colleges in the three countries. These were then translated as necessary and discussed with lecturers in engineering in colleges in the three countries. In each case lecturers were asked to give an opinion as to whether their own students either would be able to tackle a paper from the two other countries as it stood, or alternatively whether their students would be able to answer such questions if their course had covered that ground. One of the difficulties of comparing qualifications at this level is that the three courses vary in the degree of specialisation that is required in particular technologies. In particular, lecturers in both Britain and France considered that the British HNC and HND qualifications were more general and theoretical, that is, were less narrowly specialised on particular technologies and less practically orientated than the respective French and German qualifications. In the three countries all discussants felt that the level of technical competence aimed at in technician courses was fairly similar. None of the three qualifications considered was felt to be 'out of line' with those in other countries although, inevitably, there was no exact correspondence between papers. For example a control technology theory paper from a Munich technical college, forming part of their examinations for the *Techniker* qualification, contained some questions which British lecturers considered could be answered by students on the lower level Ordinary National Diploma courses, whereas other questions were definitely at the Higher National level. Some rather specific questions on this paper were considered to be the sort of topic that would be studied at first or second year degree level; German and British experts commented that the German papers concentrated on a narrower range of technical competence and consequently went more deeply into certain topics than did similar British courses which were broader and less geared to a single set of technical applications.

On French BTS courses most examination papers tended to be narrowly focussed on practical applications in the same way as the German papers were. However, the BTS mathematics papers were of a more general nature and were universally agreed to be making somewhat greater demands than the equivalent British and German papers. Those British students who had taken mathematics courses over and above the bare minimum required for a Higher National award might be able to cope with the French papers. However, the mathematics taught for the German *Techniker* qualification is very much geared to practical applications (algebra, exponential functions, geometry and trigonometry) and German experts were of the opinion that French mathematics papers would be too theoretical for the German students.

Several points need to be borne in mind when considering the contrast between the greater German specialisation on practical applications and the greater British breadth and theoretical content at higher technician level. Firstly it was pointed out to us that the mathematics content in Britain (as in France) took account of the fact that some students aim to continue their studies at degree level; consequently much of the mathematics was of the sort that would be required if they were to be able to follow a degree course. German students would not normally be able to go straight onto a degree course after completing a *Techniker* qualification but would be required to follow additional bridging courses; for this reason it is not necessary for the mathematics to be so geared towards further study at degree level. Another difficulty put to us by lecturers in British colleges concerning specialisation on specific applications was related to the number of different industries from which HNC and HND students in one British college might be drawn. An expert from a German technical college considered that those completing the German technician courses were likely to be quicker in adapting themselves to their tasks in the workplace than the British Higher National students i.e. would require a shorter initial training period in the company. However, the broader theoretical grounding received by higher technicians in Britain should benefit them when they were subsequently required to adapt to changes in technology and in the range of tasks that they performed.

All the technician-level qualifications mentioned are recognised as being at sub-degree level in all three countries. In Britain and France the courses are recognised as falling within the general field of higher education; in Germany they are recognised as part of vocational (Fach) training rather than as part of higher education. For a number of students in both Britain and France, technician level study is used as a stepping stone to degree level study. In Germany, progression from technician-level courses to higher levels of study, e.g. degree-level engineering courses, requires a bridging course of between four and six months additional study of German, English, maths and social science; examinations must be passed in all these subjects as a condition of entry.

In summary, the balance struck between general and specific technical knowledge in higher technician qualifications differs between the three countries. The German qualification concentrates on specific and practical applications within a general framework laid down nationally. The French qualification, although following a fairly detailed nationally laid-down syllabus, also contains a great deal of practical application; mathematics tends to be more theoretical in the French BTS and of a higher degree of difficulty than the science and physics required. In both France and Britain higher technician courses are much more oriented towards subsequent degree-level study than in Germany where the emphasis is on progression from craft to technician levels.

NOTE

[a] For a detailed comparison of formal qualifications at this level in five European countries see G. Rothe, *Berufsbildungsstufen in mittleren Bereich, Materialen der Berufs-und Arbeitspädagogik,* Band 9, Villingen, 1989.

Part VII
Development

[19]

The Structure of Oppor-
tunity: How Promotion
Ladders Vary within and
among Organizations

James N. Baron
Stanford University
Alison Davis-Blake
Carnegie-Mellon University
William T. Bielby
*University of California, Santa
Barbara*

This paper analyzes data describing jobs in 100 establishments in order to test hypotheses about the characteristics
of jobs and organizations associated with the structure of
internal promotion ladders. The diversity of labor market
arrangements found within the organizations indicates
only weak support for hypotheses linking internal labor
markets to organizational or sectoral imperatives. At the
job level, however, there is support for hypotheses linking
job ladders to firm-specific skills, organizational structure,
gender distinctions, technology, occupational differentiation, the institutional environment, and the interests of
unions. The paper concludes with an examination of how
promotion ladders are formed from clusters of jobs associated with each other by occupation, skill, or gender
composition.•

There has been increasing interest in understanding the origins
and consequences of internal labor markets (ILMs), personnel
systems within organizations having internal job ladders and
other arrangements conducive to long-term employment.
Many researchers have assumed that ILMs are widespread in
the U.S. economy (but see Granovetter, 1984; Osterman,
1984) and have therefore devoted more attention to the interplay between ILMs and career mobility (see Baron, 1984). Managers and human resource planners have also been interested
in how ILMs work, since human resource management is
clearly very different in ILMs than in perfectly competitive labor
markets. Moreover, the efficiency benefits of ILMs have recently been touted in discussions of why Japanese organizations have out-performed their American counterparts (Ouchi
and Jaeger, 1978). However, much more has been written
about how ILMs function in theory than about what they are actually like in practice. There has been considerable theorizing
about why organizations differ in their reliance on ILMs, but
there have been fewer efforts to determine how well theorists'
descriptions correspond to actual organizations. This paper
focuses on ILMs in specific work organizations, concentrating
on the one facet that has received the most attention in past research: the existence of clearly and formally defined job ladders that provide promotion opportunities within a particular organization. Data describing job hierarchies in 100 diverse work
organizations are analyzed to examine various hypotheses
about why organizations have different opportunity structures.

BACKGROUND AND HYPOTHESES

Most authors define ILMs as having the following: few ports of
entry at the bottom of the hierarchy; promotion from within;
low turnover, due to strong worker identification with the firm;
firm-specific skills acquired on the job, giving rise to skill gradients that demarcate career paths; seniority-based rewards;
and formal grievance procedures (Doeringer and Piore, 1971;
Kalleberg and Sorenson, 1979). Some investigators view ILMs
as a response to organizational imperatives tending to encompass most or all jobs in a firm. Instead, we suggest below that
ILMs develop in response to characteristics of particular transactions or jobs, encompassing only some types of positions
within an organization.

•

A previous version of this paper was presented at the 1984 Academy of Management annual meeting. The authors gratefully acknowledge research support from
the National Science Foundation (SES 79-
24905), the Center for Advanced Study in
the Behavioral Sciences (BNS 76–22943).
and the Stanford Graduate School of Business. Teri Bush, Kelsa Duffy, and Jill
Fukuhara provided splendid technical support. Howard Aldrich, Robert Althauser,
Yinon Cohen, Frank Dobbin, Paul Osterman, and the ASQ reviewers and editors
offered helpful comments on earlier versions of this paper

Promotion Ladders

ILMs as a Response to Organizational Imperatives

Recent research has examined differences in attainment processes across economic and labor market sectors. Some authors have suggested that monopolistic or core firms and industries provide most of the privileged or "primary" jobs,
which exist within ILMs, whereas workers in small, periphery
firms and industries are typically unprotected from market
competition. These dualist formulations assume a basic distinction between one economic sector in which workers have access to career mobility through ILMs and another sector in
which they do not. However, there is still considerable debate
about whether the very notion of economic sectors or segments is empirically tenable (Hodson and Kaufman, 1982;
Baron and Bielby, 1984), much less whether economic sectors
correspond to segments of the labor market. Moreover, recent
typologies of labor markets (Kalleberg and Sorenson, 1979;
Althauser and Kalleberg, 1981) have noted that even organizations with little or no opportunity for internal advancement may
provide access to professional or craft labor markets, in which
workers can advance by moving interorganizationally. Thus, the
distinction between one sector of (large, bureaucratic, monopolistic, unionized) organizations having formally structured
ILMs with ample opportunities for internal career advancement
and another sector of organizations lacking formal ILMs and
providing few opportunities for internal advancement may
obscure more than it reveals.

To date, there has been little effort to determine whether work
organizations can in fact be so differentiated, although there is
a growing body of empirical research aimed at identifying sectors or industries of high and low opportunity (see Hodson and
Kaufman, 1982). However, if work organizations cannot be
characterized as having either many or few opportunities for internal mobility, then attempts to identify sectors or segments
of high and low opportunity seem fruitless. The previous dualist
work on economic segmentation and labor markets implies the
following hypothesis:

Hypothesis 1: Establishments can be classified into two distinct
groups or sectors based on their employment and promotion arrangements, one having formalized and highly structured ILMs and the
other lacking them.

The second set of five hypotheses is related to specific characteristics of establishments that have been claimed by theorists
to make the ILM an efficient organizational arrangement. First,
Weber (1947) emphasized lifetime employment and graded career ladders as an efficient response to the specialization that is
inevitable in large bureaucratic organizations, which implies
that size is a pre-eminent determinant of ILMs. Moreover,
since small firms supposedly lack the resources and skill specialization that are preconditions for promotion ladders (Oi,
1983), we hypothesize:

Hypothesis 2a: The larger the establishment, the more likely it is to
have an ILM.

The notion that job ladders in ILMs are defined by gradients of
firm-specific skill (and therefore sealed off to outsiders above
the entry level) implies that ILMs emerge principally because
they reduce the potential costs of turnover and opportunism
that employers face when workers' skills are firm-specific

(Doeringer and Piore, 1971; Williamson, 1975). This view has some limited empirical support in studies linking internal promotion to firm-specific skill requirements (Pfeffer and Cohen, 1984; Wholey, 1985). ILMs also ostensibly encourage employees with valuable firm-specific skills and abilities to remain with the organization and encourage senior workers to train new employees by protecting seniority rights. Thus,

Hypothesis 2b: The greater an establishment's dependence on firm-specific skills and on-the-job training, the more likely the establishment is to have an ILM.[1]

The interdependence of tasks associated with continuous process technologies makes it particularly important that senior workers transmit skills to junior workers and also imposes "nonseparabilities" among tasks and workers (Blauner, 1964; Alchian and Demsetz, 1972). ILMs ostensibly mitigate the conflicts and perceptions of inequity that often arise in such interdependent settings, where it is difficult to determine precisely who deserves praise or blame for any particular outcome. In contrast, craft production is thought to involve general human capital, giving rise to mobility systems that span firms (Caplow, 1954: 164–169; Piore, 1975). Thus, we predict:

Hypothesis 2c: Within the manufacturing sector, ILMs should be more prevalent in establishments using process technologies than in those using other technologies, especially craft production.

Because managers and production workers are linked more closely to the establishment's core technology, they are likelier to monopolize firm-specific skills and internal promotions than workers whose skills are more general and easily transferable across establishments (professional, technical, clerical, and service workers). Thus,

Hypothesis 2d: The greater the percentage of workers in managerial and production occupations, the more likely it is that the establishment will have ILMs: the greater the percentage of workers in professional, technical, clerical, and service occupations, the less likely that it will have ILMs.

Establishments that are part of a larger organizational entity, e.g., plants or branch offices, are more likely to develop the bureaucratic procedures and specialized subunits (e.g., personnel departments) that accompany the emergence of ILMs, due to the coordination difficulties such establishments confront. In addition, the need to shift workers across production sites within a multilocational organization may prompt more formalized promotion and transfer arrangements. Furthermore, as Pfeffer and Cohen (1984: 559) noted, being one of many sites may also be a proxy for total firm size, implying an effect similar to the one postulated above for establishment size. Pfeffer and Cohen found that branch establishments were more likely to have ILMs than either autonomous firms or headquarter establishments. Therefore, we hypothesize:

Hypothesis 2e: Establishments that are linked to a larger organizational entity are likelier to have ILMs than autonomous firms.

Some researchers have also traced the development of ILMs to union demands, arguing that unions bargain for job ladders, internal bidding systems, company-sponsored training programs, and seniority rights (Kahn, 1976; Rubery, 1978; Elbaum, 1984). Pfeffer and Cohen (1984: 568), however, who found a significant negative effect of unionization on their mea-

1
The units studied in this research were establishments, not all of which were independent firms. Nonetheless, we have used the more standard term "firm-specific" (rather than "establishment-specific") skills throughout.

Promotion Ladders

sure of ILM practices, argued that "unionization provides both
an alternative source of control . . . and a competing interest
that is less likely to be sympathetic to bureaucratic control strategies." They suggested that unions may champion some aspects of ILMs, such as seniority rights, while rejecting mobility
systems that reward loyalty to the firm. However, we believe
the interest of a union in ILMs depends on the nature of its
members' skills. When workers have been trained in a craft
that is transferable across organizations, they may strive to retain control over the conditions of their work, opposing personnel practices aimed at restricting worker mobility. In contrast,
union members are more likely to favor ILM systems when
workers' skills are firm-specific (see Williamson, 1981: 567;
Finlay, 1983). Therefore, we predict that

Hypothesis 2f: Unionized establishments are more likely than nonunionized ones to adopt ILMs if workers possess firm-specific skills.

Institutionalization perspectives suggest that bureaucratic personnel practices, including the use of job pathing to create career ladders, are especially prevalent in organizations that are
highly regulated by the government or that do not produce
easily measurable products, e.g., public organizations and
those in what Averitt (1968) termed the "social-overhead-
capital" sector (transportation, communication, finance, education, health care, culture, etc.). Because the outputs of these
organizations are often intangible, establishments are judged
by external constituents largely on the basis of the procedures
they adopt; consequently, organizations in "institutional" sectors strive to appear legitimate in the eyes of their publics, particularly the state, by adhering to established organizational
models, including those governing the employment relation
(Meyer and Rowan, 1977; DiMaggio and Powell, 1983; Meyer,
Scott, and Deal, 1983; Tolbert and Zucker, 1983). Moreover,
since workers' tasks in these organizations are usually highly
interdependent, ILMs provide incentive and governance arrangements that reduce the likelihood of shirking and increase
perceptions of internal equity (Alchian and Demsetz, 1972;
Williamson, 1981; Jacobs, 1981). Thus, we predict that

Hypothesis 2g: Establishments in "institutional" sectors or having
less tangible outputs are more likely to adopt ILMs.

Finally, neo-Marxists such as Edwards (1979) argue that core
bureaucracies use ILMs primarily to control workers by imposing race and sex divisions. Similarly, others (Kerr, 1954;
Doeringer and Piore, 1971) have suggested that it is customary
to arrange certain jobs in promotion ladders, even if no technical rationale exists for linking the roles. Gender is one key element of "customary law" in the workplace. Research has documented the sex segregation of career ladders in organizations
and the tendency for men to dominate promotion opportunities, even when gender differences in job assignments and
tenure are controlled (Grimm and Stern, 1974; Mennerick,
1975; Kanter, 1977; Talbert and Bose, 1977; Blau, 1977; Baron
and Bielby, 1985b). Consequently, we expect that

Hypothesis 2h: Establishments employing mainly women will be less
likely to adopt ILMs than establishments employing mainly men.

ILMs as a Response to Job Characteristics

Recent structural approaches to the labor market have suggested that differential career outcomes arise because some

individuals work in firms, industries, or sectors where ILMs provide various benefits, whereas other individuals do not (for a review, see Hodson and Kaufman, 1982). However, within a given establishment, there is typically substantial variation in the promotion structures for different jobs and workers. Particular jobs have their own imperatives and subenvironments, in addition to the general environment facing the organization as a whole. Whether based on technological requirements or the dictates of custom, establishments are likely to set up different promotion structures for particular types of jobs. This idea is not new, of course. For example, Dunlop (1957: 16) linked wage determination to the existence of job clusters, which he defined as "a stable group of job classifications or work assignments within a firm (wage determining unit) which are so linked (a) by technology, (b) by the administrative organization of the production process, including policies of transfer and promotion, or (c) by social custom that they have common wage-making characteristics." Similarly, Osterman (1984) has noted that there is not *one* ILM in an establishment, but usually a number of different ones; he describes how craft, industrial (firm-specific), and secondary employment systems often occur in the same organization, subjecting different groups of workers to different career opportunities and industrial relations rules (see also Althauser and Kalleberg, 1981). Therefore, it is just as important to avoid homogenizing organizations as industries or sectors where labor market arrangements are concerned.

Williamson's (1981) transaction cost framework suggests the same conclusion, namely, that establishment-level analyses of ILMs may be too aggregated. Williamson has argued that the relevant unit governing the internalization of exchanges is the transaction and that appropriate contractual arrangements and governance structures must be implemented to regulate each transaction. In the context of employment contracts, it seems reasonable to posit that each *job* reflects a distinct transaction, that is, where "one stage of activity terminates and another begins" (Williamson, 1981: 552). His approach thus implies an analysis of the characteristics of a given job that affect its likelihood of being in an ILM, rather than conducting establishment-level analyses that aggregate across diverse jobs involving different transactional properties.

Accordingly, we reformulated the establishment-level hypotheses about the determinants of ILMs in order to examine characteristics of jobs that account for their positions in promotion ladders. Each hypothesis below makes predictions only about the probability that a particular type of job is in an ILM. However, in the discussion accompanying many of these hypotheses, predictions are also made about where in the promotion ladder a given type of job is likely to be located (e.g., near the top, at the entry level, etc.).

Based on our earlier discussion, we predict that

Hypothesis 3a: Jobs that require large amounts of firm-specific training are more likely to be located in ILMs than jobs that require little or no such training.

Hypothesis 3b: Managerial and production jobs are more likely to be located in ILMs than professional, clerical, sales, and service jobs.

Promotion Ladders

When professional, clerical, sales, and service jobs *are* in ILMs, we expect them to be concentrated at the bottom of shorter ladders and more open to external entry, since they tend to involve general skills that are more transferable from firm to firm.

Dunlop (1957) noted that positions in which many individuals are employed often serve as "key jobs" that define promotion and wage ladders. Moreover, establishments presumably realize greater scale economies by creating formal promotion lines for these jobs than for positions with very few incumbents. Therefore, we expect that

Hypothesis 3c: Jobs with many incumbents are more likely to be in ILMs than jobs with few incumbents.

Given the pyramidal nature of organizations and mobility ladders, jobs with many incumbents are expected to be clustered at the bottom of promotion ladders. These are typically entry-level jobs, whereas farther up the ladder, jobs are more likely to have a smaller number of incumbents.

The customary use of gender as a basis for job assignment suggests that

Hypothesis 3d: Jobs held exclusively by women are less likely to be in formal promotion ladders than jobs held exclusively by men.

Also, since opportunities are generally more limited for women, women's jobs can be expected to be concentrated more at the bottom of those ladders to which women do have access.

We expect that jobs dealing primarily with information (data) have fewer firm-specific assets than jobs dealing with things, which often involve physical capital or workplace arrangements that are idiosyncratic. Even when jobs oriented toward information require considerable on-the-job training and experience, we expect that the skills involved are more transferable than in manual jobs with the same level of training time. Consequently, we predict that

Hypothesis 3e: Jobs oriented principally toward information are less likely to be structured within ILMs than jobs oriented toward things.

Among such jobs that *are* in ladders, those requiring complex informational tasks should be situated nearer the top. Performance in information-intensive jobs is likely to be especially difficult for the organization to monitor. Under these circumstances, establishments ostensibly guard against judgmental errors that may result from subjective performance criteria by developing their own rating language and by evaluating employees over longer periods (Williamson, Wachter, and Harris, 1975). Therefore, by the time workers have mastered complex informational tasks, they should be less likely to advance further, since the relevant screening will have already taken place.

The relationship between unionization and the development of ILMs is predicted to depend on the nature of the job. In particular, the interest of a union in internalizing the employment relationship is likely to depend on whether or not its members' jobs involve firm-specific skills (Williamson, 1981). Therefore, we predict:

Hypothesis 3f: Jobs in unionized establishments are most likely to be in promotion ladders when incumbents possess firm-specific skills.

Where unions and ILMs do coexist, we expect ladders to be longer and more tightly closed to external entrants, since such arrangements serve the interests of the union's membership. With an ILM in a unionized setting, one can also expect workers with fewer firm-specific skills to benefit dispropor-tionately, compared to employees who would "naturally" have leverage by virtue of their skill monopolies.

It has been argued that unions sometimes perpetuate male ad-vantage (e.g., Aronowitz, 1973; Deaux and Ullman, 1983). If so, then we should find that

Hypothesis 3g: The chances of mobility in all-male jobs are greater in unionized work settings than in nonunionized work settings.

Finally, some promotion policies may apply to all jobs within an establishment. For instance, Althauser and Kallebeger (1981) argued that some firms with ILMs have jobs that are outside promotion ladders but that still exist within what they call "firm labor markets," enjoying many of the same rights and priv-ileges. Organizing at least some rewards in common throughout an establishment not only realizes administrative economies and an increased sense of internal equity, but may also confer greater legitimacy on the organization from external constituents, such as the state, who expect or require a ra-tional, coherent, and consistent personnel system (Meyer and Rowan, 1977). Therefore, some organizational characteristics should affect the probability that a given job is part of an ILM. In particular, we expect that

Hypothesis 3h: Jobs in large, bureaucratic organizations, and in man-ufacturing, state, or social-overhead-capital sectors, are more likely to be in ILMs than jobs in other types of settings.

METHODS

Sample

These hypotheses were tested with data describing 1,883 jobs in 100 single-site California establishments studied between 1965 and 1979 by the U.S. Employment Service. The Employ-ment Service collected extensive information about job charac-teristics, including skills, gender composition, training, and the arrangement of jobs within promotion hierarchies (U.S. Depart-ment of Labor, 1972). These raw data (called "job analyses") were eventually used by the Employment Service in compiling the published *Dictionary of Occupational Titles* (*DOT*), but we were given access to the original source documents, which we photocopied and coded for our own research purposes. This job analysis information enabled us to diagram promotion lad-ders for each establishment studied. Employment Service ana-lysts also compiled information about the structure, technol-ogy, and environment of establishments, producing a "narrative report" and other archival materials for most of the organizations they visited. We obtained copies of these mate-rials as well, which were used to operationalize the various characteristics of establishments that were hypothesized to be associated with ILMs. The present analyses pertained to formal promotion ladders among jobs, as described by employers and U.S. government job analysts who studied the organizations in the sample; they do not necessarily describe the career move-ments of individuals. In our view, this focus is consistent with most definitions of ILMs, which emphasize the existence of job

Promotion Ladders

ladders and a set of personnel policies that exist independent of and prior to individual job incumbents.

Because the Employment Service did not always conduct detailed job analyses for all jobs in an establishment — for instance, when they judged administrative jobs to be identical to descriptions already contained in the *DOT* — comprehensive data on promotion paths were available for only 100 establishments. For these, information on promotion hierarchies was available for an average of 63 percent of the jobs and 72 percent of the workers (and for 88 percent of the line jobs and 90 percent of the line workers) in each establishment. Logistic regression analyses predicting whether or not an establishment was in the sample (i.e., had relatively complete promotion data) indicated that this group was generally representative of the larger sample of California establishments studied by the U.S. Employment Service. (In other words, the logistic regressions did not predict the presence or absence of missing data very faithfully.) Although the establishments we examined do not represent a probability sample from a distinct organizational population, they capture the diversity of industrial and organizational settings in California's economy. The sample overrepresented manufacturing and did not include observations in several major California industries (e.g., the construction and trucking industries and department stores and miscellaneous business services). However, reweighting observations to reflect the actual size distribution of establishments across California industries did not alter our findings appreciably (see Baron and Bielby, 1984: fn. 3).

Independent Variables

Establishment size was measured as the natural logarithm of the total number of workers in the establishment. The reliance of each establishment on *firm-specific skills* was measured as the average within-establishment training and experience required for its jobs. This was determined by adding the required orientation time, in-plant training time, on-the-job training time, and time required in other positions in the establishment for each job, as estimated by the Employment Service analyst. This sum was then converted into the metric by which "specific vocational preparation" (SVP) is measured in the *DOT* (ranging from 1 to 9) and then averaged across all jobs in the establishment (U.S. Department of Labor, 1972: 220–229). In some instances, there may have been ambiguity about whether skills learned in other jobs within the organization were entirely firm-specific or whether experience gathered in other organizations could be substituted for training within the establishment. Consequently, the variable was measured imperfectly.

Occupational composition was measured by the percentage in each establishment of each of the following categories, based on three-digit *DOT* codes: professional, technical, managerial, clerical, sales, business services, personal services, transportation, extraction, and production. Some categories with very small percentages of jobs were combined in the analyses (see Tables 2 and 3 below). *Linkages to a larger organization*, a crude proxy for bureaucratization, were measured by a binary variable coded zero if the establishment was an independent firm, and one otherwise. *Unionization* was measured by a binary variable coded one if any portion of the line workforce was unionized, and zero otherwise. The *industry sector* in which the establishment was located was used as a proxy measure for the tangibleness of the organization's outputs. Industry was coded as a series of six (nonexclusive) binary variables based on SIC codes: manufacturing; government; agriculture; wholesale or retail trade; services; and social-overhead-capital. *Gender composition* was measured as the percentage of women working in the jobs analyzed by the Employment Service in each establishment. The *modal technology* was represented by a series of (nonexclusive) binary variables adapted from Woodward (1965): unit-craft technology only; unit-craft technology in conjunction with another technology; batch or mass production; process technology only; and process technology in conjunction with another technology (Baron and Bielby, 1985a).

To test the job-level hypotheses, these establishment-level measures were supplemented with job-level indicators of job size, occupational type, gender composition, and training and skill requirements, drawn from Employment Service staffing schedules and job analyses. The complexity of workers' informational and technical duties was operationalized by job ratings on the *DOT* measures of "data" and "things," respectively. Because of gender biases in the third edition of the *DOT,* values were truncated at 6 for "data" and 7 for the "things" item (Cain and Treiman, 1981). For this research, the original scales were inverted, so that large-scale values denote complex involvements by workers.

Dependent Variables

Establishment level. Based on past theory and research, promotion ladders in the ideal-typical ILM can be characterized as follows:

1. Ladders should be fairly long, with few jobs "dead ended" at the top. This allows establishments to promote employees over an extended period of time and so retain employees with firm-specific skills.

2. Jobs should not be concentrated at the bottom of ladders, because this limits the number of promotions that establishments can offer. It also decreases the extent to which they can separate workers with various amounts of seniority, which supposedly encourages on-the-job training by protecting the seniority rights of more experienced workers who train junior employees.

3. Most jobs above the bottom of ladders should be closed to external entrants in order to retain skilled workers by insulating them from outside competition for promotions. Moreover, establishments that depend heavily on specific skills may not even be able to find qualified outsiders to staff high-level jobs.

4. Links between jobs should be clearly specified (i.e., a given job or set of jobs should promote to a clearly specified destination at a higher level). Vague promotional patterns decrease the ability of the ILM to facilitate training of neophytes by senior workers. When workers are not in specific ladders, it is more difficult to determine the skills a given worker will need next and to train junior workers in those skills. Moreover, since ILMs are thought to "effectuate standards of equity" (Doeringer and Piore, 1971: 29), promotion links can be expected to be specific

Promotion Ladders

and rationalized if they are to be perceived as legitimate by employees.

Accordingly, each establishment's promotion system was characterized on the following dimensions:

1. Percentage of jobs in promotion ladders (the number of jobs in promotion ladders divided by the total number of jobs analyzed in the establishment).

2. Natural logarithm of the average length (i.e., number of levels) of a promotion ladder. Jobs not in ladders were assigned a ladder length of one.

3. Percentage of jobs with promotion prospects (the number of jobs in a promotion ladder, but not at the top level, divided by the total number of jobs).

4. Percentage of "bottom-level" jobs (bottom-level jobs in ladders plus jobs not in promotion ladders, divided by the total number of jobs).

5. Percentage of jobs that could not be entered from outside the establishment. A job was considered open to outsiders if it was at the bottom of a promotion ladder or, for jobs above the bottom, if the employer stated that outsiders could be hired.

6. Percentage of jobs in "structured" promotional ladders. Structured ladders were defined as those in which each job promoted to no more than two specific jobs at a higher level, based on clearly specified criteria. In unstructured ladders, such as those found in a number of open bidding systems within the sample, any job at a given level could promote to any job at one or more higher levels. In a few cases, job analysts described certain specific promotion paths that were often used but not formally recognized by the employer and that might not be used in the future; these were coded as unstructured ladders.

These percentage measures were calculated across jobs rather than workers, because in an ILM the structure of jobs is presumed to exist prior to and independent of incumbents (Granovetter, 1981). Moreover, the structure of jobs was assumed to be more stable over time than the staffing patterns of workers observed in these cross-sectional data. (Nonetheless, the results are unchanged if the percentage measures are calculated across workers rather than jobs.)

To summarize how well each establishment's employment and promotion system approximated the ideal-type ILM, a factor analysis of these six variables was performed. All six measures loaded highly on a single principal component that captured 70.1 percent of the total multivariate association. Factor scores on this principal component were assigned to each establishment, representing the prevalence of ILM practices. High scores denoted establishments with proportionately more jobs in ladders; longer average ladders; a higher percentage of nonentry jobs; and proportionately more jobs above the bottom level, in structured ladders, and not "dead-ended."

Job level. To test the job-level hypotheses, four binary variables were created for each job. The first variable was coded "1" if the job was in a promotion ladder and "0" otherwise. For jobs in ladders, three other binary variables were created, each coded "1" if the job had the attribute in question (and "0" otherwise): (a) the job was on the bottom level of the ladder; (b) the job could be entered from outside the establishment; and (c) the job had additional mobility opportunities (i.e., was not dead-ended at the top of a ladder). These last three binary variables were defined as missing for jobs not in promotion ladders.

RESULTS

Organization Level: Hypothesis 1

The factor scores indicated that 16 of the 100 establishments had no promotion paths between jobs. Archival Employment Service data revealed that five of these establishments seemed to be in craft labor markets, where workers often advance by moving between establishments (e.g., a radio station and a small manufacturer of fine embroidery). For instance, narrative materials for the radio station noted that

The broadcasting industry has established informal, but definite promotional patterns and this station follows these patterns rather than promoting from within. In the broadcasting industry, a person usually begins a career in a small station in a minor market. After succeeding and achieving experience, the individual moves to a larger station in a bigger market, eventually arriving at a large station in a major marketing area. (Narrative report #1784, AM/FM radio station, 1971)

The other 11 establishments seemed to rely on secondary labor markets (e.g., a short-order restaurant and a pet store). Workers might move to other establishments of the same type, but they would probably gain little income or status by doing so.

To some extent, these results appear consistent with hypothesis 1, based on dualist notions of a division between one economic sector providing internal upward mobility and another providing either no mobility or mobility across organizations. As hypothesized, most of the establishments lacking internal promotion ladders were small and in "peripheral" industries. Also, many were owner-operated and, as Edwards (1979) predicted, owners seemed to exercise substantial personal control over the selection of workers.

However, other aspects of the results are harder to reconcile with simple dualist schemes. First, among the 84 establishments having at least one promotion ladder, there was great diversity in the amount of opportunity and the way it was structured. That is, there was a very continuous distribution of factor scores on the ILM measure. Mobility structures in these 84 establishments ranged from a single promotion ladder with two jobs (in a large establishment) to a few cases where one or two long promotion ladders included all the jobs in the establishment. This diversity was present even among establishments in the same detailed industry employing roughly the same number of people.

The results therefore corroborate Pfeffer and Cohen's (1984) idea that the amount of opportunity available within in an establishment has a continuous (rather than bimodal) distribution across organizations. Even establishments in the same detailed industry and size range varied from having no formal promotion structure, to elementary structures applying only to select jobs, to well-developed ILMs covering almost all workers, and nearly any amount of structure between these extremes. Conse-

Promotion Ladders

quently, attempts to identify sectors, industries, and perhaps even organizations of high-versus-low career opportunity may be fruitless.

For instance, restaurants have invariably been classified as part of the industrial periphery (see Zucker and Rosenstein, 1981: 882), and indeed, restaurants in the sample were represented in the group of establishments having no ILM. Yet one restaurant (19 workers) provided structured promotion ladders for all of its workers, while a larger one (87 workers) had only two promotion ladders, which included only 6 of 22 jobs. The smaller restaurant was a cafeteria operating in a government building and was legally required to hire and train handicapped workers. The promotion ladders in this restaurant allowed workers to move between jobs requiring diverse skills (e.g., chef, cashier) and thus provided training opportunities for workers. The larger restaurant, featuring haute cuisine, generally hired both inexperienced and experienced workers (e.g., dishwashers and chefs, respectively) from outside but provided no internal promotion opportunities for them. However, it did have promotion ladders and on-the-job training to train waiters, bus boys, and banquet captains, who were provided completion certificates attesting to their skills, "accepted by the most demanding employers in the country" (Narrative report #1523, 1966).

This diversity in labor market structures was also evidenced within other industries in our sample. These results thus support Baron and Bielby's (1980: 758) suggestion that researchers need to "move beyond simple, mechanistic notions of 'dualism' or 'segmentation' [by] focusing [instead] on the concrete organizational and suborganizational determinants of promotion."

Organization Level: Hypotheses 2a–2h

Table 1 presents descriptive statistics and pairwise-present correlations for the establishment characteristics and for factor scores on the ILM variable. (The correlation coefficients are reported in the upper triangle of Table 1 and the number of cases on which each correlation is based is shown in the lower triangle.) On first glance, these correlations appear to provide preliminary support for our predictions. For instance, establishment size, firm-specific training, process technologies, linkages to larger organizations, and unionization are all positively correlated with the ILM measure. Conversely, organizations with unit technologies, a high percentage of sales and service jobs, or a high percentage of women employees had lower factor scores, indicating a smaller fraction of jobs in well-defined promotion ladders.

Table 2 reports regressions of the ILM measure on establishment characteristics. For the 86 cases having complete data (56 in manufacturing), metric coefficients from an OLS regression are shown (column 1). Although several variables (size, craft technology, firm-specific training, and links to larger organizations) had significant net effects in the predicted direction, the other hypothesized net effects were very small. Column 2 of Table 2 shows essentially the same results within manufacturing. There is also a small tendency in manufacturing for organizations having many professional, technical, and managerial jobs to have less developed internal ladders. (Although we hypothesized a positive effect of managerial versus profes-

Table 1

Zero-Order Correlations and Descriptive Statistics for ILM Measure and Establishment Characteristics Variables (Correlations Shown above Diagonal, Number of Cases Shown below Diagonal)

Variable	1	2	3	4	5	6	7	8	9	10	11	12	13	14	15	16	Mean	SD[•]
1. ILM measure	100	.39***	-.29***	.11	.12	.23**	.07	.32***	.36***	-.00	.18	-.29***	.22**	.11	-.30***	.23**	0.00	1.00
2. Log establishment size	93	100	-.22	-.03	.22	.19	.20	.02	.34	-.01	-.27	-.06	.34	-.13	-.19	.54	3.91	1.44
3. Unit technology only	93	93	100	-.10	-.23	-.06	-.08	.20	-.10	-.01	-.04	.05	.05	-.09	.17	-.13	0.04	
4. Unit technology with other technology	100	93	93	100	.06		-.10						-.12				0.19	
5. Batch or mass technology	93	93	93	93	100	-.13	-.19	.38	-.15	-.15	-.09	-.19	.09	.08	-.03	.17	0.55	
6. Process technology only	93	93	93	93	93	100	-.29	.00	.14	-.47	-.10	-.43	.61	-.42	.04	.01	0.06	
7. Process technology with other technology	93	93	93	93	93	93	100	.10	.27	-.02	-.05	-.12	.20	-.12	-.18	.43	0.13	
8. Firm-specific training	93	93	93	93	93	93	93	100	-.02	-.17	.06	-.13	.29	.17	-.14	.20	3.41	1.33
9. Linked to larger organization	100	100	93	93	93	93	93	100	100	-.03	-.00	-.44	.15	-.30	-.18	.07	0.47	
10. Percent professional, technical, managerial jobs	100	100	93	93	93	93	93	100	100	100	.27	-.02	-.39	.56	-.20	.28	0.13	
11. Percent clerical jobs	100	100	93	93	93	93	93	100	100	100	100	.07	-.10	.05	-.12	.13	0.05	
12. Percent sales and service jobs	100	100	93	93	93	93	93	100	100	100	100	100	-.48	-.12	.25	-.09	0.11	
13. Manufacturing sector	100	100	93	93	93	93	93	100	100	100	100	100	100	-.56	.02	-.22	0.64	
14. State or social-overhead-capital sector	100	100	93	93	93	93	93	100	100	100	100	100	100	100	-.23	-.13	0.15	
15. Percent women	93	93	86	86	86	86	86	93	93	93	93	93	93	93	100	.15	0.23	0.26
16. Establishment unionized	100	93	93	93	93	93	93	100	100	100	100	100	100	100	93	100	0.27	

*p ≤ .10; **p ≤ .05; ***p ≤ .01; ****p ≤ .001 (two-tailed test). Significance levels reported only for correlations involving ILM measure.
[•]Standard deviation not shown for dichotomous variables.

Table 2

Regression of Internal Labor Market Variables on Establishment Characteristics

| | Dependent Variable | | | |
| | Factor scores | | Dichotomy | |
Independent Variable	All (N = 86)[a]	Mfg. (N = 56)[a]	All (N = 86)[a]	Mfg. (N = 56)[a]
Intercept	−1.33**	−1.69*	.51**	.49**
Establishment size	.18**	.21**	.09***	.10***
Unit technology only	−1.32**	−2.05***	−.72****	−.96****
Unit technology with other technology	.04	−.50*	−.05	−.17**
Batch or mass technology	−.28	−.53	−.31**	−.37**
Process technology only	−.05	−.66	−.42**	−.46**
Process technology with other technology	−.19	−.54*	−.21**	−.23**
Firm-specific training	.16**	.44****	.03	.10**
Linked to larger organization	.40**	.55**	.17**	.18**
Percent professional technical, managerial jobs	−.48	−1.97*	−.45**	−.65**
Percent clerical jobs	−.59	.01	.26	.56
Percent sales or service jobs	−.25	.49	−.29	−.33
Manufacturing sector	.39	−	.24*	−
State or social-overhead-capital sector	.25	−	.15	−
Percent women	−.41	−.18	−.10	.14
Establishment unionized	.02	.13	−.00	−.04
R^2	.43	.51	.48	.55
Adjusted R^2	.30	.36	.37	.41

*$p \leq .10$; **$p \leq .05$; ***$p \leq .01$; ****$p \leq .001$ (all tests one-tailed, except for intercept).
[a] Number of cases with complete data.

sional and technical jobs, both categories had almost identical effects when estimated separately. Given the scant variation across establishments in the sample in the percentage of both types of jobs, especially in manufacturing, we combined the two categories.) Apparently, within manufacturing, professional, technical, and managerial jobs (at least the ones studied by the Employment Service) tend to be in labor markets in which mobility spans establishments rather than occurring via organization-specific promotion ladders. Manufacturing establishments combining continuous processing with another technology were also lower on the ILM measure. In some of these large firms (e.g., several bakeries and a manufacturer of chewing gum), many of the jobs were not directly associated with the process technology (e.g., inspecting, wrapping, shipping), and therefore were either not in ladders or were in short, unstructured ladders. Thus, although jobs directly associated with the process technology tended to be in longer, relatively structured ladders, as hypothesized, the overall ILM scores for some of these establishments were low.

However, there is reason to conclude that the establishment characteristics in Table 2 actually distinguish establishments with any ladders from those with none, rather than distinguishing how much internal promotion opportunity exists or how structured it is. Columns 3 and 4 report counterpart OLS regressions for a dummy variable simply coded zero if the organization had no jobs in promotion ladders and one otherwise. In general, the establishment characteristics in Table 2 distinguish establishments with and without promotion ladders (columns 3 and 4) better than they explain the extent of ILM practices (columns 1 and 2). The results were generally consistent with the hypotheses proposed, except for the effect of process technology: contrary to expectation, its use is apparently associated with a somewhat lower net likelihood of ILM practices. (This statistical result is somewhat anomalous, however, inasmuch as almost every establishment in the sample that used process technologies also had ILMs.) As predicted, however, the likelihood of ILM practices was clearly lower among establishments using craft technologies. As in columns 1 and 2, some of the other variables, including occupational mix, industry sector, gender composition, and unionization, had only trivial effects on the dichotomous variable in columns 3 and 4.

In short, the hypotheses were largely substantiated in distinguishing those establishments (typically smaller and less bureaucratic) that rely extensively on professional, craft, or secondary labor markets from those that have ILMs. However, the same establishment characteristics bear surprisingly little relationship to the extensiveness of ILMs among establishments having them. This conclusion was buttressed by supplemental regression analyses of the ILM factor scores among establishments having one or more promotion ladders; although there were a few small effects in the predicted direction, the regression equations did not even account for a statistically significant fraction of the variation across establishments. The same general results also obtained when the six separate dimensions of job ladders were analyzed separately, rather than as composite factor scores, and when the dichotomous ILM measure was analyzed by logistic regression rather than OLS.

These weak results may reflect limitations of the measures used and the relatively small sample of establishments for which complete job-hierarchy information was available. We believe, however, that they reflect a more fundamental conceptual problem with studies that link work arrangements and labor market structures to their industry- and firm-level determinants; that is, that such studies obscure the diversity of labor market arrangements within organizations.

Job Level: Hypotheses 3a–3h

Table 3 reports logistic regression coefficients for the four discrete job-level outcomes described earlier. Among jobs that are in ladders, the probability of a job being enterable from the outside and of its not being a "dead end" is obviously much higher among jobs on the bottom of ladders. Consequently, Table 3 also separately reports results for those two outcomes among jobs that are *not* at the bottom of ladders (see columns 4 and 6).[2]

Hypothesis 3a. The logit results dramatically illustrate the diversity of ILM practices in specific organizations, insofar as they provide much stronger support for many of the hypotheses than was observed at the establishment level. In particular, jobs requiring substantial firm-specific training were much more likely to be in internal promotion ladders and, if so, to be above the bottom, in jobs shielded from external entry. The results in columns 4 and 6 indicate that, even above the bottom of ladders, jobs requiring firm-specific skills were more likely to afford future promotion prospects, as expected from the idea that job ladders help employers recoup training investments and encourage skill transmission from senior to junior workers.

Hypothesis 3b. Table 3 indicates some support for the hypotheses about occupational differences in job ladders. Professional and technical jobs were somewhat less likely than line

---

2

The 1,748 jobs analyzed in column 1 of Table 3 reflect staffing patterns in 100 establishments; the other regressions are based on the 84 establishments having some promotion ladder(s). These regressions do not include establishment-specific error terms to control for unmeasured organizational attributes that might affect the promotion prospects of all jobs in each establishment. Thus, errors may be correlated among jobs within an organization, and the "true" number of cases in Table 3 is less than the sheer number of jobs analyzed; consequently, significance levels should be interpreted cautiously. We thus re-estimated the logit models in Table 3, including a variable in each equation denoting the percentage of jobs in each establishment having the characteristic in question (e.g., jobs in ladders). There were only minor changes in the job-level results presented in Table 3 when unmeasured establishment-level effects were controlled in this way, and little weight has been given to any result that changed. The same was true when OLS results were compared to OLS models that explicitly incorporated a separate error term for each establishment.

Promotion Ladders

Table 3

Logistic Regression for Job-Level ILM Variables

Independent Variable (min., max.)	Whether in ladder	On bottom of ladder	Dependent Variable Can enter from outside		Has mobility prospects (not dead-end)	
			All jobs in ladders	Jobs above bottom	All jobs in ladders	Jobs above bottom
Intercept	−1.01(•••)	.80	1.61(•••)	−.75	−.52	2.01(•••)
Sales or service job (0, 1)	.17	.12	.09	.31	−.18	−.13
Managerial job (0, 1)	.25	.08	−.77 ••	−.64•	−.05	−.17
Professional or technical job (0, 1)	−.47 ••	1.22••••	.36	.01	1.45••••	1.11 •••
Clerical job (0, 1)	−.22	.42•	.53 ••	.89•••	.28	.12
Log$_e$ number of people in job (−1.39, 6.40)	.09 •	.34••••	.20 •••	.03	.54••••	.44 ••••
Whether job held exclusively by men (0, 1)	−.08	.34	.99 ••••	1.28••••	.49•	.35
Whether job held exclusively by women (0, 1)	−.44 ••	.31	.37 •	.36	−.02	−.51
Firm-specific training (1, 9)	.35 ••••	−.69••••	−.28 ••••	.10••	−.18••••	.06
Level of complexity: data (0, 6)	−.12 •••	−.25••••	−.03	.06	−.45••••	−.41 ••••
Level of complexity: things (0, 7)	.04 •	.01	.07 ••	.16••••	.02	.02
Log$_e$ establishment size (.69, 7.95)	.10 ••	.02	−.02	−.04	.03	.02
Whether establishment linked to larger organization (0, 1)	.21 •	.08	−.14	−.40••	.42•••	−.34 ••
Whether establishment unionized (0, 1)	−.64(•)	−1.57••••	−.33	−.87•	−.63	−.11
Union-firm-specific training (0, 9)	.07	.37••••	.22 ••••	.11•	.03	−.08
Union-male job (0, 1)	.18	−.61•	−1.64 ••••	−1.96••••	.02	.13
In state or social-overhead-capital sector (0, 1)	−.00	.62••	.71 •••	.61••	.49••	.42 •
In trade, service, or agricultural sector (0, 1)	−.64 •••	−1.15••••	.28	1.36••••	−.43	.04
Mean of dependent variable	.71	.43	.68	.43	.78	.61
Number of jobs	1748	1236	1228	699	1236	707
Jobs correctly classified (%)	72.8	84.0	68.9	72.9	80.9	74.8

•$p \leq .10$; ••$p \leq .05$; •••$p \leq .01$; ••••$p \leq .001$ (all tests one-tailed, except for those with significance levels shown in parentheses).

production jobs (the omitted category) to be in ladders. Professionals and technicians who were in ladders tended to be at the bottom rung, as were clerical workers (though less significantly). The logit results support the supposition that clerical jobs in ladders (even those above the bottom) are more easily entered from outside the organization, due to the transferability of skills. However, the clerical positions analyzed by the Employment Service were often production-related, male-dominated jobs, such as stock and shipping clerks, which are more likely to be organized into ladders than traditional female secretarial and clerical jobs. Therefore, the results reported here are probably somewhat weaker than they would be in a sample including a greater proportion of female clerical jobs. Managerial jobs in ILMs, in contrast to clerical roles, were apparently more difficult to enter from outside the enterprise; supplemental analyses suggested that this is due to the informational complexity of such jobs.

When the task and training requirements of different occupations were controlled for, professionals in ladders actually appeared more likely than workers in other jobs to have future mobility prospects (columns 5 and 6, Table 3), though supplemental analyses revealed that this is true only outside manufacturing. Particularly in nonmanufacturing organizations, professionals may be able to define job titles and career paths to their own advantage, given the widespread norm that professionals are the sole arbiters of their work. The fact that this effect manifested itself after controlling for training and task requirements suggests that the mobility benefits of professional jobs reflect the power to which their incumbents have access, rather than the functional importance of their work (see Scott, 1981: 153–156).

Hypotheses 3c and 3h. Table 3 refines the earlier findings linking organizational size to ILMs. Total establishment size had an independent positive effect on the likelihood of jobs being in ladders, suggesting that in designing promotion ladders to reduce turnover, large establishments may generalize the ILM to include most jobs in the organization (see hypothesis 3h). Not surprisingly, however, once a job is in a ladder, it is the size of the job, reflecting its position among the "rungs" of a ladder, that affects how mobility is structured, as predicted by hypothesis 3c. (Note that if an organization or job ladder has a constant span of control, then our measure of job size is perfectly correlated with level in the hierarchy. For example, in a ladder with a constant span of control of 10, there would be 1 person at the top level, 10 at level 2, 100 at level 3, and so on, and the common logarithm of job size would be 0 at level 1, 1 at level 2, 2 at level 3, etc. Thus, the size of the job should indicate its level within the promotion hierarchy.) The more people there are in a job within a ladder, obviously the more likely that job is to be toward the bottom level; thus it can be entered from outside more easily and has greater future mobility prospects (see Table 3). The results also support the hypothesis (3c) that key jobs with many incumbents are more likely to be in ladders than jobs with few occupants. Presumably, there are economies of scale in establishing formalized promotion paths out of those jobs. In contrast, promotions out of job classifications with few incumbents may not only be rarer, given the narrowing of the pyramid toward the top of ladders, but also governed more by informal and idiosyncratic criteria (Kanter, 1977).

The other measure of bureaucratic structure — whether the establishment is linked to a larger organization — also displayed the expected relationship with the dependent variables in most cases: jobs in linked establishments were more likely to be in ILMs and, if so, were more insulated from external competition and offered greater mobility prospects than comparable jobs in similar (but autonomous) establishments (see hypothesis 3h). These results are consistent with Pfeffer and Cohen's (1984) findings and their suggestion that being part of a larger entity fosters bureaucratization and organizational complexity beyond that resulting from scale imperatives.

Table 3 also supports the predictions about differences across industry sectors in mobility structures (hypothesis 3h). Even when other organizational and job attributes were controlled for, positions in trade, service, or agricultural industries (i.e., the so-called periphery) were considerably less likely to be in job ladders than comparable positions in the manufacturing, state, or social-overhead-capital sectors. Moreover, since ladders in the periphery tend to be shorter and to include fewer jobs (often only two or three positions), they are less likely to be pyramidally shaped, and jobs are therefore less likely to be concen-

Promotion Ladders

trated at the bottom of ladders than they are in other settings. Consequently, workers in the periphery are likely to exhaust the promotional benefits of ILMs more quickly than workers in the longer, more pyramidally shaped ladders often found in manufacturing. As expected, jobs in nonmanufacturing sectors (state, social-overhead-capital, trade, service, and agriculture), even jobs in ladders, were more easily entered from other organizations than in manufacturing (the omitted industry sector in Table 3). Although the models controlled for firm-specific training, these sectoral effects may partly reflect unmeasured differences between manufacturing and nonmanufacturing establishments in the nature of skills, with skills being more general and careers more frequently spanning organizations outside manufacturing. The finding that the net probability of a job being in an ILM was higher in "institutional" (state or social-overhead-capital) sectors also suggests that a given job is more likely to be part of a vertically differentiated division of labor there. In fact, establishments in institutional sectors have elsewhere been shown to proliferate more detailed job titles as a mechanism for sustaining internal status hierarchies (Baron and Bielby, 1986).

Hypothesis 3d. The job-level analyses provide evidence of segregated career opportunities by sex, which was not evident at the establishment level. Women's jobs were significantly less likely to be in job ladders. Moreover, among jobs in ladders, men's jobs were more open to the outside and somewhat less likely to be dead-ended, indicating that jobs limited to men are in ladders that are longer and that allow establishments to circumvent more easily procedures that limit promotions to internal candidates.

Hypothesis 3e. As expected, jobs with complex informational skills were less likely to be in ladders. However, jobs with complex informational skills that *were* in ladders were more likely to be at the top of those ladders (i.e., incumbents have exhausted their mobility prospects). Jobs with complex informational skills tended to fall into two categories. The first category consisted of managerial or technical jobs that were fairly unique to their establishment (e.g., a ceramic engineer in a tile manufacturing company) or for which no training was provided within the organization (e.g., a racetrack supervisor, a news director at a TV station, a chef). These jobs were not in ladders and appeared to be part of professional or technical labor markets that spanned organizations. This finding confirms the hypothesis that many informational skills are fungible, so organizations have less incentive to organize into ladders jobs requiring such skills. The second category consisted of such jobs as foreman, forewoman, or other supervisory positions at the top of ladders. This result is consistent with the notion that problems in monitoring informational work that has an establishment-specific dimension (as in the case of supervisors) favors the creation of job ladders in which worker performance can be monitored in less information-intensive jobs before promotion to informationally complex jobs.

Table 3 also shows that technically complex jobs were slightly more likely to be in ladders but were also more easily entered from outside. Closer examination of several of these jobs revealed that they tended to be either foreman positions or production jobs associated with precision equipment or instruments. Many of the jobs were in ladders used as a training ground for the pertinent skills. However, due to the technical nature of the jobs, establishments often also relied on external sources of workers, either to deal with increased demand, to take advantage of favorable local labor market conditions, or to offset difficulties associated with long internal training times. For example, one aircraft instrument manufacturer preferred to train workers in establishment-specific skills but also hired from outside the plant when necessary to meet production commitments (Narrative report #1642, 1968). Thus, in many instances, external and internal labor markets may co-exist in a given line of work, with particular employers' "make or buy" decisions being shaped by conditions in local product and labor markets (Osterman, 1984).

Hypotheses 3f and 3g. Table 3 shows that, consistent with establishment-level findings of Pfeffer and Cohen (1984), the net effect of unionization is to decrease slightly the likelihood of jobs being in promotion ladders. Supplemental analyses showed that this effect was even stronger within manufacturing, where there was also a significant interaction with specific training: as expected, unionism in manufacturing increased the likelihood of jobs that required firm-specific training being in ILMs, whereas unions resisted ILMs more when workers' skills were general (also see Finlay, 1983). Table 3 also indicates that among unionized workers in job ladders, workers in jobs lacking firm-specific skills were considerably *less* likely to be at the bottom of ladders and in positions open to outsiders when the establishment was unionized. Thus, unions, especially in manufacturing, do appear to favor ILMs when members have specific assets to protect. However, in unionized settings, jobs requiring little firm-specific skill appear to afford greater mobility chances and protection from external competition than one would otherwise expect, suggesting that once an ILM exists, a union may for political reasons extend its benefits to jobs occupied by its weaker or less skilled members (see Elbaum, 1984; Fried, 1984: 1035).

Open bidding systems are one mechanism that unions may use to protect workers with few firm-specific skills. In this sample, these systems usually consisted of a few entry-level positions (often only one or two), which could be entered from outside the firm. After a short probationary period in an entry position, workers are free to bid on various jobs in the plant. The relatively short time that workers are required to occupy entry-level jobs means that workers with limited firm-specific skills can readily advance to jobs above the lowest level. Another feature of open bidding systems that favors less skilled workers is the provision in many union contracts that outsiders can only be hired above the bottom if no qualified applicants can be found inside the organization through the bidding system. Of the 27 unionized enterprises in the sample, 16 (59.3 percent) had open bidding systems, and 5 more establishments (18.5 percent) had informal arrangements similar to bidding systems that emphasized promotion from within.

Consistent with hypothesis 3g, all-male jobs in unionized enterprises were considerably less likely to be on the bottom of promotion ladders than comparable all-male jobs elsewhere. Thus, even controlling for skills, unions appear to provide more job titles and promotion paths to advance mobility in "men's" work.

Promotion Ladders

Furthermore, unions apparently counteract the possibility of entry from outside that is otherwise available in all-male jobs, thus preserving mobility benefits for current male members of the establishment. These results suggest that when unions accept or foster ILMs, the benefits accrue disproportionately to males. Separate analyses for manufacturing jobs (not reported) revealed the same pattern of results as in Table 3, although the effects of occupation and gender composition were even stronger.

Job Cluster Formation

The fact that the job-level results were so much stronger and more consistent than the establishment-level results highlights the diversity of ILMs in a given organization. The present results imply that researchers should return to the concerns of early institutionalists interested in understanding the evolution of clusters of jobs that are linked by mobility and wages. As an aid to future theory and research, we briefly consider some evidence from the sample about several important bases of job cluster formation deserving future study.

Occupation. Doeringer and Piore (1971) suggested that job ladders develop around work roles having common technical skills or customs, and occupational distinctions clearly capture both. Indeed, at the level of three-digit *DOT* occupational codes (somewhat more detailed than the Census three-digit scheme), about one-third of the 290 distinct job ladders in the sample consisted of jobs within a single, three-digit *DOT* occupation. (At the level of two-digit *DOT* titles, the corresponding figure was 52 percent.) Another 37 percent of the ladders comprised two three-digit occupations, the second category typically representing a related supervisory role (e.g., foreman or forewoman). In general, our exploratory analyses of ladders substantiated Collins's (1979:45) conclusion that "employers thought of manual and nonmanual (and clerical) categories as hermetically sealed off from each other."

This division between blue- and white-collar jobs, which has been observed in aggregate studies of intragenerational mobility (Featherman and Hauser, 1978:173–176; Tolbert, 1982), seems deeply ingrained in most organizations. On the other hand, at least some organizations in the sample apparently lack strong technical or normative barriers that prevent grouping quite disparate occupations within a single mobility ladder. Just under half of the ladders in the sample contained jobs drawn from different one-digit *DOT* occupations, and 15 percent of the ladders contained jobs from three or more major occupational groups. There were examples of ladders spanning virtually every combination of the major occupational categories.

Within the sample, ladders that spanned major occupational groups seemed to fall into three basic types. The most common consisted of production or clerical jobs linked to managerial jobs. Most of these ladders consisted exclusively of male workers in production-related clerical jobs that led to lower-level management. In ladders containing both sexes, lines of progression often seemed to limit mobility prospects for women (e.g., integrated or all-female production jobs were linked to all-male managerial jobs). Thus, these ladders allowed movement across major occupational boundaries into higher status, white-collar roles for men much more than for women.

The second most common type of ladder consisted of one or two clerical, service, or technical jobs (e.g., shipping or inventory control clerks, janitors, or machine technicians) linked to production jobs. This usually occurred when the clerical, service, or technical jobs involved were a very small part of the organization's total workforce and the organization had a policy or philosophy of promotion from within; linking these jobs to production roles was the only way to provide mobility opportunities for incumbents. In some cases, these linkages were facilitated by open job bidding systems, which allowed clerical, service, and technical workers to bid for certain production jobs. Such bidding systems were observed in both union and nonunion enterprises. DiPrete and Soule (1986) have documented how EEO pressures in a Federal agency have led to a similar erosion of occupational boundaries in civil service job ladders.

The final type of cross-occupational ladder was one in which an open bidding system or an employer's insistence on cross-training workers created linkages among almost all jobs in an establishment. One tile manufacturing company, for example, used both of these practices, because "new employees seldom have previous experience in tile manufacturing" (Narrative report #774, 1978).

These results on the occupational composition of promotion ladders have several implications. They highlight how much career advancement may be obscured by studies measuring status attainment at the occupational level, since many well-developed promotion ladders only comprise job titles within a single detailed occupation. More importantly, they indicate that while there are mobility barriers between manual work and other jobs, there is also substantial diversity across organizations in how stringently promotion ladders are structured along occupational lines.

Skills. In some firms, commonalities of firm-specific skills may cut across occupations, thereby favoring more broadly defined job ladders. The notion that job ladders are designed to include jobs with related (but graded) training requirements is taken for granted by many analysts and practitioners; indeed, skill gradients are often treated as a defining characteristic of ILMs (Althauser and Kalleberg, 1981). To determine how closely job ladders in our sample correspond to gradients of skill and training, we examined the amount of training (both establishment-specific and general) required for each job in the 288 ladders having complete information. In 15 (5.2 percent) of these ladders, all jobs in the ladder required the same amount of training — that is, there was no gradient. In another 33 ladders (11.5 percent), requisite skills actually decreased for some potential moves up the ladder. Finally, the vast majority of the ladders (240, or 83.3 percent) corresponded to the ideal type, requiring increases in knowledge and skills for potential moves up the promotion ladder. The results thus confirm that jobs are frequently clustered in promotion hierarchies to facilitate on-the-job training.

The presence of a substantial number of job ladders with decreasing (or no) skill gradients, however, suggests that non-technical criteria can also be important in the creation of ILMs; an example is union bargaining agreements. Rungs of job lad-

Promotion Ladders

ders may correspond simply to wage differentials, as one analyst noted of two jobs linked in a ladder: "the two [job] titles are used in union contracts to distinguish the type of pipe being machined, which affects the piece rate, but not the base rate [or duties] of the job" (Job analysis #2911565, asbestos and cement pipe manufacturer, 1968). Open job bidding systems, which create job ladders with multiple jobs at each level, can also create decreasing skill levels. First, the bidding system may act merely as a vehicle for wage increases that are not closely tied to the degree of skill or amount of training required. For example, the Employment Service job analysis for the job of refinery and waste water operator in a plant processing organic fatty acids stated that "any worker in the plant may bid for this job (by union agreement). The usual promotion, however, is from 'Flaking Operator,' although experience in this occupation is not specifically qualifying for 'Refinery and Waste Water Operator'" (Job analysis #2912822, 1968). Second, because under open bidding systems there are multiple jobs at each level in a ladder, with complex paths among jobs, some jobs at higher levels can require less training than some (but not all) jobs at lower levels.

Labor shortages may also lead to inverted skill gradients in job ladders where workers are normally recruited from outside the establishment. Since establishments sometimes create ILMs to fill the vacant positions when shortages occur, positions requiring substantial firm-specific training may lead to positions requiring less firm-specific (but more general) skills. One bakery facing labor shortages, for example, often promoted workers from jobs in lower, unrelated classifications and then provided on-the-job training (Job analysis #2911944, 1967).

Gender. The data in this study suggest that within ILMs, jobs monopolized by men provided incumbents with greater opportunities to enter from the outside by capitalizing on some alternative skills, experience, or training. In a pen and pencil manufacturing company, for instance, mechanics for the molding machine were all men, usually hired from outside, while the molding machine operators were all women. However, promotion from operator to mechanic was not considered "normal" because the operators were women (Job analysis #2909975, 1965).

Jobs were pervasively segregated by sex in the sample. Among the 100 establishments, there were 1,999 jobs with data on sex composition, of which 1,071 had two or more workers (i.e., could be integrated). Of these 1,071 jobs, only 73 had both male and female incumbents. Consequently, it is not surprising that promotion ladders were also highly segregated by sex. This is frequently the case even when an organization hires men and women to perform the same specific occupational role, since distinct job titles are often used to separate women's jobs and promotion tracks from men's (Baron and Bielby, 1985b). Of the 268 promotion ladders in the sample with adequate information about gender composition, 191 (71.3 percent) were occupied exclusively by men, 17 (6.3 percent) exclusively by women, and 60 (22.4 percent) by both men and women. Thus, nearly 80 percent of the promotion ladders were completely segregated by sex. Furthermore, gender even played an important role in the placement of jobs within the 60 gender-integrated ladders. These promotion ladders fell into three categories. In the first type, subordinate jobs including women, men, or both promoted to superordinate jobs that included only men. This pattern of job structuring, which essentially provides promotion opportunities only to men, was found in 44 (73.3 percent) of these gender-integrated ladders. The second pattern was one in which lower-level jobs promoted to positions containing only women. This pattern, providing opportunity only to women, was found in only 6 (10.0 percent) of the promotion ladders in the sample. Although there were numerous ladders in which only women worked in the origin position(s) and only men occupied the destination slot(s), there was only one ladder in which the reverse was true. The third type of ladder was truly gender-integrated — that is, both men and women occupied jobs at all levels. This pattern occurred in 10 (16.7 percent) of the 60 ladders that contained male and female incumbents.

Employment Service analysts frequently noted that women were excluded from job ladders for reasons unrelated to skills and requirements; yet we found no cases of an employer who expressed a desire to increase hiring or promotion of women or minorities but was unable to locate qualified individuals. There were, however, numerous comments illustrating that, even fairly recently, considerable discretion remained in the general labeling of career lines and in access to them. For instance, in a brick and tile plant with 187 employees, the analyst noted in 1978 that "Women are beginning to fill nontraditional classifications such as Press Operator. The employer is *considering trying women* as Prouty Kiln Operator, a job always held by men" (Narrative report #774, 1978, emphasis added).

Sex segregation of jobs and career lines may be less pervasive today than when many of the establishments in the sample were analyzed. However, the results imply that gender is a powerful independent basis of clustering jobs in promotion ladders and of the position of jobs within those ladders. To be sure, men's jobs are more likely than women's to involve firm-specific skills and to be in large, unionized enterprises, where ILMs are more prevalent. However, the regression analyses documented net effects of gender composition on labor market structure, suggesting that segregated opportunities cannot be explained exclusively by differences in the technical characteristics of jobs and firms in which males versus females invest (cf., Polachek, 1979; Becker, 1985).

DISCUSSION

The analyses have several important theoretical implications. First, while they lend considerable support (at the job level, at least) to perspectives viewing ILMs as a response to exigencies of firm-specific human capital, they also indicate that opportunity structures are shaped in no small measure by political and institutional forces inside and outside organizations, for example, by gender differentiation, the presence of professional groups, unions, and the institutional environment. Second, the results highlight the diversity of labor market practices within organizations, providing support for approaches that view ILMs as a response to characteristics of particular transactions or jobs within an organization. Much theory and research has ignored the obvious but essential fact that jobs exist in their own subenvironments, just as firms and industries do. Although there are establishment-level differences in how opportunities and rewards are structured, some of which

Promotion Ladders

are documented by our analyses, investigators who fault neo-classical economics for assuming an overly homogeneous labor market should not themselves simply transfer that assumption of homogeneity to the organization.

The data also revealed a tremendous diversity in how broadly or narrowly mobility clusters were defined. Understanding the reasons for this diversity within and between firms should not only improve our ability to predict individuals' mobility and incomes but should also be of considerable practical interest. There has recently been much discussion about the benefits of less specialized career paths, such as those often employed in Japanese organizations (Ouchi and Jaeger, 1978), and about the factors that favor defining career ladders more broadly (e.g., Kanter, 1984). Research pinpointing the determinants and consequences of broad versus specialized promotion ladders would be of tremendous value.

It would be of considerable interest to know more about how organizations manage the internal diversity of labor market arrangements documented by this research. While technical and customary features of work may promote ILMs only within specific parts of an organization, diversifying employment and reward practices in this way presumably entails some costs. Though it is often argued that some benefits of ILMs "spill over" to workers in the organization whose jobs are not shielded from external competition, relatively little is known about how firms and unions balance the benefits of maintaining distinct employment subsystems against the benefits of incorporating all employees within a single personnel system. Practitioners might profitably contemplate the benefits and liabilities associated with having mobility clusters that balkanize workers, jobs, and rewards.

Researchers and practitioners might also consider the bases of those job clusters in the first place — a concern that preoccupied early institutional economists but which has received less attention lately. The analyses suggest that some job ladders cannot easily be ascribed to imperatives of firm-specific skills. Admittedly, many establishments in this sample were studied before vigorous enforcement of antidiscrimination laws motivated organizations to justify promotion ladders carefully and explicitly (see Arvey and Mossholder, 1977; Pearlman, 1980). Nevertheless, many job ladders in existence today may reflect technical constraints and customary practices from an earlier era better than they reflect current conditions. Understanding how job clusters emerge in the first place may aid scholars and practitioners in analyzing how ILMs become institutionalized and how (or whether) they are modified in response to changing circumstances. We examined only three interrelated bases of job clustering in ILMs: occupation, skill, and gender. Clearly, there are many other attributes of workers, jobs, and organizations that potentially affect whether and how specific roles become clustered together within promotion ladders (Piore, 1975).

Implementing this research agenda will require methodological pluralism. Researchers interested in the employment relationship and its career consequences address a set of concerns that cuts across diverse units of analysis and that demands historical analyses, comparative studies, and fine-grained ethnographies. Given the variety of analytic techniques, units of analysis, and types of samples employed in contemporary research on ILMs, it is encouraging that the results of this study are consistent in many respects with studies employing very different data or procedures. Hopefully, this paper will serve as a catalyst for future studies using diverse data and methods to examine the determinants and consequences of promotion hierarchies.

REFERENCES

Alchian, Armen A., and Harold Demsetz
1972 "Production, information costs, and economic organization" American Economic Review, 62: 777–795.

Althauser, Robert P., and Arne L. Kalleberg
1981 "Firms, occupations, and the structure of labor markets. In Ivar Berg (ed.), Sociological Perspectives on Labor Markets: 119–149. New York: Academic Press.

Aronowitz, Stanley
1973 False Promises. New York: McGraw-Hill.

Averitt, Robert T.
1968 The Dual Economy: The Dynamics of American Industry Structure. New York: Norton.

Arvey, Richard D., and K. M. Mossholder
1977 "A proposed methodology for determining similarities and differences among jobs." Personnel Psychology, 30: 363–374.

Baron, James N.
1984 "Organizational perspectives on stratification." Annual Review of Sociology, 10: 37–69.

Baron, James N., and William T. Bielby
1980 "Bringing the firms back in: Stratification, segmentation, and the organization of work." American Sociological Review, 45: 737–765.
1984 "The organization of work in a segmented economy." American Sociological Review, 49 454–473.
1985a "Technology and the division of labor." Unpublished manuscript, Graduate School of Business, Stanford University.
1985b "Organizational barriers to gender equality: Sex segregation of jobs and opportunities." In Alice Rossi (ed.), Gender and the Life Course, 233–251. New York: Aldine.
1986 "The proliferation of job titles in organizations." Administrative Science Quarterly, vol. 31 (in press).

Becker, Gary S.
1985 "Human capital, effort, and the sexual division of labor." Journal of Labor Economics, 3: S33–S58.

Blau, Francine M.
1977 Equal Pay in the Office. Lexington, MA: Lexington Books.

Blauner, Robert
1964 Alienation and Freedom. Chicago: University of Chicago Press.

Cain, Pamela S., and Donald J. Treiman
1981 "The *Dictionary of Occupational Titles* as a source of occupational data." American Sociological Review, 46: 253–278.

Caplow, Theodore
1954 The Sociology of Work. New York: McGraw-Hill.

Collins, Randall
1979 The Credential Society. New York: Academic Press.

Deaux, Kay, and J. C. Ullman
1983 Women of Steel: Female Blue-Collar Workers in the Basic Steel Industry. New York: Praeger.

DiMaggio, Paul J., and Walter W. Powell
1983 "The iron cage revisited: Institutional isomorphism and collective rationality in organizational fields." American Sociological Review, 48: 147–160.

DiPrete, Thomas A., and Whitman Soule
1986 "The organization of career lines: Equal employment opportunity and status advancement in a federal bureaucracy." American Sociological Review, 51: 295–309.

Doeringer, Peter B., and Michael J. Piore
1971 Internal Labor Markets and Manpower Analysis. Lexington, MA: D.C. Heath.

Dunlop, John T.
1957 "The task of contemporary wage theory." In John T. Dunlop (ed.), The Theory of Wage Determination: 3–27. London: Macmillan.

Edwards, Richard C.
1979 Contested Terrain. New York: Basic Books.

Elbaum, Bernard
1984 "The making and shaping of job and pay structures in the iron and steel industry." In Paul Osterman (ed.), Internal Labor Markets: 71–108. Cambridge, MA: MIT Press.

Featherman, David L., and Robert M. Hauser
1978 Opportunity and Change. New York: Academic Press.

Finlay, William
1983 "One occupation, two labor markets: The case of longshore crane operators." American Sociological Review, 48: 306–315.

Fried, Charles
1984 "Individual and collective rights in work relations: Reflections on the current state of labor law and its prospects." University of Chicago Law Review, 51: 1012–1040.

Granovetter, Mark S.
1981 "Toward a sociological theory of income differences." In Ivar Berg (ed.), Sociological Perspectives on Labor Markets: 11–47. New York: Academic Press.
1984 "Small is bountiful: Labor markets and establishment size." American Sociological Review, 49: 323–334.

Grimm, James W., and Robert N. Stern
1974 "Sex roles and internal labor market structures: The 'female' semi-professions." Social Problems, 21: 690–705.

Hodson, Randy, and Robert L. Kaufman
1982 "Economic dualism: A critical review." American Sociological Review, 43: 534–541.

Jacobs, David
1981 "Towards a theory of mobility and behavior in organizations An inquiry into the consequences of some relationships between individual performance and organizational success." American Journal of Sociology, 87: 684–707

Promotion Ladders

Kahn, Lawrence M.
1976 "Internal labor markets: San Francisco longshoremen." Industrial Relations, 15: 333–337.

Kalleberg, Arne, and Aage B. Sorenson
1979 "The sociology of labor markets." Annual Review of Sociology, 5: 351–379.

Kanter, Rosabeth M.
1977 Men and Women of the Corporation. New York: Basic Books.
1984 "Variations in managerial career structures in high-technology firms: The impact of organizational characteristics on internal labor market patterns." In Paul Osterman (ed.) Internal Labor Markets: 109–131. Cambridge, MA: MIT Press.

Kerr, Clark
1954 "The balkanization of labor markets." In E. Wight Bakke, Philip M. Hauser, Gladys L. Palmer, Charles A. Myers, Dale Yoder, and Clark Kerr (eds.), Labor Mobility and Economic Opportunity: 92–110. Cambridge, MA: MIT Press.

Mennerick, Lewis A.
1975 "Organizational structuring of sex roles in a nonstereotyped industry." Administrative Science Quarterly, 20: 570–586.

Meyer, John W., and Brian Rowan
1977 "Institutionalized organizations: Formal structure as myth and ceremony." American Journal of Sociology, 83: 340–363.

Meyer, John W., W. Richard Scott, and Terrence E. Deal
1983 "Institutional and technical sources of organizational structure: Explaining the structure of educational organizations." In John W. Meyer and W. Richard Scott (eds.), Organizational Environments: Ritual and Rationality: 45–67. Beverly Hills, CA: Sage.

Oi, Walter Y.
1983 "Heterogeneous firms and the organization of production." Economic Inquiry, 21: 147–171.

Osterman, Paul
1984 "White-collar internal labor markets." In Paul Osterman (ed.), Internal Labor Markets: 163–189. Cambridge, MA: MIT Press.

Ouchi, William G., and Alfred M. Jaeger
1978 "Type Z organization: Stability in the midst of mobility." Academy of Management Review, 3: 305–314.

Pearlman, Kenneth
1980 "Job families: A review and discussion of their implications for personnel selection." Psychological Bulletin, 87: 1–28.

Pfeffer, Jeffrey, and Yinon Cohen
1984 "Determinants of internal labor markets in organizations." Administrative Science Quarterly, 29: 550–572.

Piore, Michael J.
1975 "Notes for a theory of labor market stratification." In Richard C. Edwards, Michael Reich, and David M. Gordon (eds.), Labor Market Segmentation: 125–150. Lexington, MA: D.C. Heath.

Polachek, Solomon
1979 "Occupational segregation among women: Theory, evidence, and a prognosis." In Cynthia B. Lloyd, Emily S. Andrews, and Curtis L. Gilroy (eds.), Women in the Labor Market: 137–157. New York: Columbia University Press.

Rubery, Jill
1978 "Structured labor markets, worker organization and low pay." Cambridge Journal of Economics, 2: 17–36.

Scott, W. Richard
1981 Organizations: Rational, Natural, and Open Systems. Englewood Cliffs, NJ: Prentice-Hall.

Talbert, Joan, and Christine Bose
1977 "Wage attainment processes: The retail clerk case." American Journal of Sociology, 83: 403–424.

Tolbert, Charles M.
1982 "Industrial segmentation and men's career mobility." American Sociological Review, 47: 457–477.

Tolbert, Pamela, and Lynne G. Zucker
1983 "Institutional sources of change in the formal structure of organizations: The diffusion of civil service reform, 1880–1935." Administrative Science Quarterly, 28: 22–39.

U.S. Department of Labor
1972 Handbook for Analyzing Jobs. Manpower Administration. Washington, DC: U.S. Government Printing Office.

Weber, Max
1947 "Bureaucracy." (Originally published in 1922.) In H. H. Gerth and C. Wright Mills (eds.), From Max Weber: Essays in Sociology: 196–244. New York: Oxford University Press.

Wholey, Douglas R.
1985 "Determinants of firm internal labor markets in large law firms." Administrative Science Quarterly, 30: 318–335.

Williamson, Oliver E.
1975 Markets and Hierarchies. New York: Free Press.
1981 "The economics of organization: The transaction cost approach." American Journal of Sociology, 87: 548–577.

Williamson, Oliver E., Michael L. Wachter, and J. E. Harris
1975 "Understanding the employment relation: The analysis of idiosyncratic exchange." Bell Journal of Economics, 6: 250–280.

Woodward, Joan
1965 Industrial Organization: Theory and Practice. London: Oxford University Press.

Zucker, Lynne G., and Carolyn Rosenstein
1981 "Taxonomies of institutional structure: Dual economy reconsidered." American Sociological Review, 46: 869–884.

[20]

A Conception of Adult Development

Daniel J. Levinson   *Yale University*

ABSTRACT: Adult development is becoming an important field of study for psychology and other disciplines. Little has been done, however, to conceptualize the nature of adult development and to define the major issues in this field. The author summarizes his own formulations of life course, life cycle, life structure, and the adult development of the life structure in early and middle adulthood. He then discusses six major issues that must be dealt with by every structural approach to adult development: What are the alternative ways of defining a structural stage or period? What relative emphasis is given to the structures as compared to the transitional periods? How can we make best use of the distinction between hierarchical levels and seasons of development? Are there age-linked developmental periods in adulthood? What are the relative merits and limitations of various research methods? How can we bring together the developmental perspective and the socialization perspective?

The study of adult development is, one might say, in its infancy. It has been taken seriously in the human sciences for only the past 30 years or so, largely under the impact of Erikson's (1950, 1958, 1969) germinal writings. Erikson's most obvious contribution was his theory of stages in ego development. What is less obvious is that his view of development is deeply grounded in his conceptions of the life cycle and the life course. Each ego stage has its primacy at a particular age level or segment of the life cycle, from infancy to old age. The sequence of age segments and ego stages thus provides a representation of the life cycle as a whole; the meaning of a stage is defined in part by its place in the total sequence. In addition, his developmental concepts arose out of his primary concern with the individual life course: the process of living, the idea of life history rather than case history, the use of biography rather than therapy or testing as his chief research method. Without abandoning the distinction between self (psyche, personality, inner world) and external world (society, culture, institutions, history), he gave first consideration to the life course—the engagement of self with world.

Although a good deal has been learned since the 1950s about specific features of adult life, very little has been done to advance the general theory of adult development. At the same time, various fields of psychology (such as child development, gerontology, personality, social, clinical, and counseling psychology), as well as the social sciences and humanities, are becoming more aware that they need—and lack—an adult development perspective. Adult development is, in short, a significant

problem for psychology as a discipline and an important link between psychology and other disciplines, including sociology, biology, and history.

I have two primary aims here. First, I will present my conception of adulthood and of a developmental process within it. My intention is to explicate a theoretical position, not to prove it nor to argue for its superiority over others. The theory originated in my initial study of men's lives (Levinson, 1977, 1978). It has evolved over the last few years, particularly through my current research on women's lives (Levinson, in press). It is supported by a number of other studies (e.g., Gooden, 1980; Holt, 1980; Kellerman, 1975; Levinson, 1984; Stewart, 1976), but a great deal must yet be done to test and modify it. The theory includes the following elements: (a) The concepts of *life course* and *life cycle*, which provide an essential framework for the field of adult development; within this framework, studies of one process or age level can be connected to others, but without it, we have a miscellany of findings and no integrated domain of inquiry; (b) the concept of the *individual life structure*, which includes many aspects of personality and of the external world but is not identical with any of these and evolves in its own distinctive way; and (c) *a conception of adult development*—the evolution of the life structure in early and middle adulthood. Life structure development is different from, and should not be confused with, the development of personality, social roles, or other commonly studied processes.

Second, I will discuss adult development as a field of study. I will consider six major issues that help to define what the field is about and what work must be done to establish it more securely. The list is not complete, but it provides a useful starting point. Reference will be made to the work of others, but the main goal is to clarify my own position. Let it be clear that my aim is not to give a comprehensive review of the work in this field nor to seek consensus among the disparate approaches. I hope that others will be stimulated to present contrasting views.

The Life Course

Life course is one of the most important yet least examined terms in the human sciences. It is a descriptive term, not a high-level abstraction, and it refers to the concrete character of a life in its evolution from beginning to end. Both words in this term require careful attention.

The word *course* indicates sequence, temporal flow, the need to study a life as it unfolds over the years. To study the course of a life, one must take account of stability and change, continuity and discontinuity, orderly progression as well as stasis and chaotic fluctuation. It is

Copyright 1986 by the American Psychological Association, Inc. 0003-066X/86/$00.75
Vol. 41, No. 1, 3-13

not enough to focus solely on a single moment; nor is it enough to study a series of three or four moments widely separated in time, as is ordinarily done in longitudinal research. It is necessary, in Robert White's (1952) felicitous phrase, to examine "lives in progress" and to follow the temporal sequence in detail over a span of years.

The word *life* is also of crucial importance. Research on the life course must include all aspects of living: inner wishes and fantasies; love relationships; participation in family, work, and other social systems; bodily changes; good times and bad—everything that has significance in a life. To study the life course, it is necessary first to look at a life in all its complexity at a given time, to include all its components and their interweaving into a partially integrated pattern. Second, one must delineate the evolution of this pattern over time.

The study of the life course has presented almost insuperable problems to the human sciences as they are now constituted. Each discipline has claimed as its special domain one aspect of life, such as personality, social role, or biological functioning, and has neglected the others. Every discipline has split the life course into disparate segments, such as childhood or old age. Research has been done from such diverse theoretical perspectives as biological aging, moral development, career development, adult socialization, enculturation, and adaptation to loss or stress, with minimal recognition of their interconnections. The resulting fragmentation is so great that no discipline or viewpoint conveys the sense of an individual life and its temporal course.

The recognition is slowly dawning that the many specialties and theoretical approaches are not isolated entities but aspects of a single field: the study of the individual life course. During the next decade, this study will emerge as a new multidisciplinary field in the human sciences, linking the various disciplines. With the formation of a more comprehensive, systematic conception of the life course, the parts will become less isolated and each part will enrich the others.

The Life Cycle

The idea of the life cycle goes beyond that of the life course. In its origin this idea is metaphorical, not descriptive or conceptual. It is useful to keep the primary imagery while moving toward more precise conceptualization and study. The imagery of "cycle" suggests that there is an underlying order in the human life course; although each individual life is unique, everyone goes through the same basic sequence. The course of a life is not a simple, continuous process. There are qualitatively different phases or seasons. The metaphor of seasons appears in many contexts. There are seasons in the year. Spring is a time of blossoming, and poets allude to youth

as the springtime of the life cycle. Summer is the season of greatest passion and ripeness. An elderly ruler is "the lion in winter." There are seasons within a single day— dawn, noon, twilight, the full dark of night—each having its counterpart in the life cycle. There are seasons in love, war, politics, artistic creation, and illness.

The imagery of the life cycle thus suggests that the life course evolves through a sequence of definable forms. A season is a major segment of the total cycle. Change goes on within each season, and a transition is required for the shift from one to the next. Every season has its own time, although it is part of and colored by the whole. No season is better or more important than any other. Each has its necessary place and contributes its special character to the whole.

What are the major seasons in the life cycle? Neither popular culture nor the human sciences provide a clear answer to this question. The modern world has no established conception—scientific, philosophical, religious, or literary—of the life cycle as a whole and of its component phases. There is no standard language that demarcates and identifies several gross segments of the life cycle. The predominant view, rarely stated explicitly, divides it into three parts: (a) an initial segment of about 20 years, including childhood and adolescence (preadulthood); (b) a final segment starting at around 65 (old age); and (c) between these segments, an amorphous time vaguely known as adulthood.

A good deal is known about the preadult years, which for a century have been the main province of the field of human development. The developmental perspective has been of crucial importance here. The idea is now accepted that in the first 20 years or so all human beings go through an underlying sequence of periods— prenatal, infancy, early childhood, middle childhood, pubescence, and adolescence. Although all children go through common developmental periods, they grow in infinitely varied ways as a result of differences in biological, psychological, and social conditions. In its concrete form, each individual life course is unique. The study of preadult development seeks to determine the universal order and the general developmental principles that govern the process by which human lives become increasingly individualized.

Historically, the great figures in the study of child development, such as Freud and Piaget, have assumed that development is largely completed at the end of adolescence. Given these assumptions, they had no basis for concerning themselves with the possibilities of adult development or with the nature of the life cycle as a whole. An impetus to change came in the 1950s when geriatrics and gerontology were established as fields of human service and research. Unfortunately, gerontology has not gone far in developing a conception of the life cycle. One reason, perhaps, is that it skipped from childhood to old age without examining the intervening adult years. Present understanding of old age will be enhanced when more is known about adulthood; thus, old age can be connected more organically to the earlier seasons.

I would like to thank my wife, Judy D. Levinson, for her contributions to the substance and spirit of this article and my colleague, Boris M. Astrachan, for his intellectual, moral, and administrative support.

Correspondence concerning this article should be addressed to Daniel J. Levinson, Department of Psychiatry, Yale University School of Medicine, 34 Park St., New Haven, CT 06519.

There is now very little theory, research, or cultural wisdom about adulthood as a season (or seasons) of the life cycle. We have no popular language to describe a series of age levels after adolescence. Words such as *youth, maturity,* and *middle age* are ambiguous in their age linkages and meanings. The ambiguity of language stems from the lack of any cultural definition of adulthood and how people's lives evolve within it. In the human sciences, too, we have no adequate conception of the nature of adulthood. We have a detailed picture of many trees but no view of the forest and no map to guide our journey through it.

I turn now to my own view of the life cycle. It derives from my research and draws upon the work of earlier investigators such as Erikson (1950, 1969), Jung, von Franz, Henderson, Jacobi, and Jaffe (1964), Neugarten (1968), Ortega y Gasset (1958), and van Gennep (1960). (For a fuller review, see Levinson & Gooden, 1985.)

Eras: The Macrostructure of the Life Cycle

I conceive of the life cycle as a sequence of *eras.* Each era has its own biopsychosocial character, and each makes its distinctive contribution to the whole. There are major changes in the nature of our lives from one era to the next, and lesser, though still crucially important, changes within eras. They are partially overlapping: A new era begins as the previous one is approaching its end. A *cross-era transition,* which generally lasts about five years, terminates the outgoing era and initiates the next. The eras and the cross-era transitional periods form the macrostructure of the life cycle, providing an underlying order in the flow of all human lives yet permitting exquisite variations in the individual life course.

Each era and developmental period begins and ends at a well-defined modal age, with a range of about two years above and below this average. The idea of age-linked phases in adult life goes against conventional wisdom. Nevertheless, these age findings have been consistently obtained in the initial research and in subsequent studies. The idea of age-linked eras and periods now has the status of an empirically grounded hypothesis that needs further testing in various cultures.

The first era, *Preadulthood,* extends from conception to roughly age 22. During these "formative years" the individual grows from highly dependent, undifferentiated infancy through childhood and adolescence to the beginnings of a more independent, responsible adult life. It is the era of most rapid biopsychosocial growth. The first few years of life provide a transition into childhood. During this time, the neonate becomes biologically and psychologically separate from the mother and establishes the initial distinction between the "me" and the "not me"— the first step in a continuing process of individuation.

The years from about 17 to 22 constitute the *Early Adult Transition,* a developmental period in which preadulthood draws to a close and the era of early adulthood gets underway. It is thus part of both eras, and not fully a part of either. A new step in individuation is taken as the budding adult modifies her or his relationships with family and other components of the preadult world and begins to form a place as an adult in the adult world. From a childhood-centered perspective, one can say that development is now largely completed and the child has gained maturity as an adult. The field of developmental (i.e., child) psychology has traditionally taken this view. Taking the perspective of the life cycle as a whole, however, we recognize that the developmental attainments of the first era provide only a base, a starting point from which to begin the next. The Early Adult Transition represents, so to speak, both the full maturity of preadulthood and the infancy of a new era. One is at best off to a shaky start, and new kinds of development are required in the next era.

The second era, *early adulthood,* lasts from about age 17 to 45 and begins with the Early Adult Transition. It is the adult era of greatest energy and abundance and of greatest contradiction and stress. Biologically, the 20s and 30s are the peak years of the life cycle. In social and psychological terms, early adulthood is the season for forming and pursuing youthful aspirations, establishing a niche in society, raising a family, and as the era ends, reaching a more "senior" position in the adult world. This can be a time of rich satisfaction in terms of love, sexuality, family life, occupational advancement, creativity, and realization of major life goals. But there can also be crushing stresses. Most of us simultaneously undertake the burdens of parenthood and of forming an occupation. We incur heavy financial obligations when our earning power is still relatively low. We must make crucially important choices regarding marriage, family, work, and life-style before we have the maturity or life experience to choose wisely. Early adulthood is the era in which we are most buffeted by our own passions and ambitions from within and by the demands of family, community, and society from without. Under reasonably favorable conditions, the rewards of living in this era are enormous, but the costs often equal or even exceed the benefits.

The *Midlife Transition,* from roughly age 40 to 45, brings about the termination of early adulthood and the start of middle adulthood. The distinction between these two eras, and the concept of Midlife Transition as a developmental period that separates and connects them, are among the most controversial aspects of this schema. The research indicates, however, that the character of living always changes appreciably between early and middle adulthood (Holt, 1980; Gooden, 1980; Levinson, 1978, 1984, in press). Similar observations, based on different methods and evidence, are given in the work of Jung, Ortega, Erikson and others, noted earlier. The process of change begins in the Midlife Transition (though the forms and degree of change vary enormously) and continues throughout the era. One developmental task of this transition is to begin a new step in individuation. To the extent that this occurs, we can become more compassionate, more reflective and judicious, less tyrannized by inner conflicts and external demands, and more genuinely loving of ourselves and others. Without it, our lives become increasingly trivial or stagnant.

The third era, *middle adulthood*, lasts from about age 40 to 65. During this era our biological capacities are below those of early adulthood but are normally still sufficient for an energetic, personally satisfying and socially valuable life. Unless our lives are hampered in some special way, most of us during our 40s and 50s become "senior members" in our own particular worlds, however grand or modest they may be. We are responsible not only for our own work and perhaps the work of others, but also for the development of the current generation of young adults who will soon enter the dominant generation.

The next era, *late adulthood*, starts at about age 60. The *Late Adult Transition*, from 60 to 65, links middle and late adulthood and is part of both. I will not discuss late adulthood here. My speculations regarding this era (and a subsequent one, late late adulthood) are given in Levinson (1978).

The Life Structure and Its Development in Adulthood

My approach to adult development grows out of, and is shaped by, the foregoing views regarding the life course and the life cycle. I am primarily interested in apprehending the nature of a person's life at a particular time and the course of that life over the years. Personality attributes, social roles, and biological characteristics are aspects of a life; they should be regarded as aspects and placed within the context of the life.

The key concept to emerge from my research is the *life structure*: the underlying pattern or design of a person's life at a given time. It is the pillar of my conception of adult development. When I speak of periods in adult development, I am referring to periods in the evolution of the life structure. I will first introduce the concept of life structure and then describe my theory and findings about its evolution in adulthood.

The meaning of this term can be clarified by a comparison of life structure and personality structure. A theory of personality structure is a way of conceptualizing answers to a concrete question: "What kind of person am I?" Different theories offer numerous ways of thinking about this question and of characterizing oneself or others; for example, in terms of traits, skills, wishes, conflicts, defenses, or values.

A theory of life structure is a way of conceptualizing answers to a different question: "What is my life like now?" As we begin reflecting on this question, many others come to mind. What are the most important parts of my life, and how are they interrelated? Where do I invest most of my time and energy? Are there some relationships—to spouse, lover, family, occupation, religion, leisure, or whatever—that I would like to make more satisfying or meaningful? Are there some things not in my life that I would like to include? Are there interests and relationships, which now occupy a minor place, that I would like to make more central?

In pondering these questions, we begin to identify those aspects of the external world that have the greatest

significance to us. We characterize our relationship with each of them and examine the interweaving of the various relationships. We find that our relationships are imperfectly integrated within a single pattern or structure.

The primary components of a life structure are the person's *relationships* with various others in the external world. The other may be a person, a group, institution or culture, or a particular object or place. A significant relationship involves an investment of self (desires, values, commitment, energy, skill), a reciprocal investment by the other person or entity, and one or more social contexts that contain the relationship, shaping it and becoming part of it. Every relationship shows both stability and change as it evolves over time, and it has different functions in the person's life as the life structure itself changes.

An individual may have significant relationships with many kinds of others. A significant other might be an actual person in the individual's current life. We need to study interpersonal relationships between friends, lovers, and spouses; between parents and their adult offspring at different ages; between bosses and subordinates, teachers and students, and mentors and protégés. A significant other might be a person from the past (e.g., Ezra Pound's vital relationship with the figure of Dante) or a symbolic or imagined figure from religion, myth, fiction, or private fantasy. The other might not be an individual but might be a collective entity such as a group, institution, or social movement; nature as a whole, or a part of nature such as the ocean, mountains, wildlife, whales in general, or Moby Dick in particular; or an object or place such as a farm, a city or country, "a room of one's own," or a book or painting.

The concept of life structure requires us to examine the nature and patterning of an adult's relationships with all significant others and the evolution of these relationships over the years. These relationships are the stuff our lives are made of. They give shape and substance to the life course. They are the vehicle by which we live out— or bury—various aspects of our selves and by which we participate, for better or worse, in the world around us. Students of the life course seek to determine the character of each relationship, its place within the person's evolving life, and the meaning of this life for the person and his or her world.

At any given time, a life structure may have many and diverse components. We found, however, that only one or two components—rarely as many as three—occupy a central place in the structure. Most often, marriage–family and occupation are the central components of a person's life, although wide variations occur in their relative weight and in the importance of other components. The central components are those that have the greatest significance for the self and the evolving life course. They receive the largest share of the individual's time and energy, and they strongly influence the character of the other components. The peripheral components are easier to change or detach; they involve less investment of self and can be modified with less effect on the fabric of the person's life.

In terms of open systems theory, life structure forms a boundary between personality structure and social structure and governs the transactions between them. A boundary structure is part of the two adjacent systems it connects, yet is partially separate or autonomous. It can be understood only if we see it as a link between them. The life structure mediates the relationship between the individual and the environment. It is in part the cause, the vehicle, and the effect of that relationship. The life structure grows out of the engagement of the self and the world. Its intrinsic ingredients are aspects of the self and aspects of the world, and its evolution is shaped by factors in the self and in the world. It requires us to think conjointly about the self and the world rather than making one primary and the other secondary or derivative. A theory of life structure must draw equally upon psychology and the social sciences.

Developmental Periods in Early and Middle Adulthood

In tracing the evolution of the life structure in the lives of men and women, I have found an invariant basic pattern (with infinite manifest variations): The life structure develops through a relatively orderly sequence of age-linked periods during the adult years. I want to emphasize that this is a finding, not an a priori hypothesis. It was as surprising to me as to others that the life structure should show such regularity in its adult development, given the absence of similar regularity in ego development, moral development, career development, and other specific aspects of the life.

The sequence consists of an alternating series of *structure-building* and *structure-changing* (transitional) periods. Our primary task in a structure-building period is to form a life structure and enhance our life within it: We must make certain key choices, form a structure around them, and pursue our values and goals within this structure. Even when we succeed in creating a structure, life is not necessarily tranquil. The task of building a structure is often stressful indeed, and we may discover that it is not as satisfactory as we had hoped. A structure-building period ordinarily lasts 5 to 7 years, 10 at the most. Then the life structure that has formed the basis for stability comes into question and must be modified.

A *transitional* period terminates the existing life structure and creates the possibility for a new one. The primary tasks of every transitional period are to reappraise the existing structure, to explore possibilities for change in the self and the world, and to move toward commitment to the crucial choices that form the basis for a new life structure in the ensuing period. Transitional periods ordinarily last about five years. Almost half our adult lives is spent in developmental transitions. No life structure is permanent—periodic change is given in the nature of our existence.

As a transition comes to an end, one starts making crucial choices, giving them meaning and commitment, and building a life structure around them. The choices are, in a sense, the major product of the transition. When all the efforts of the transition are done—the struggles to

improve work or marriage, to explore alternative possibilities of living, to come more to terms with the self—choices must be made and bets must be placed. One must decide "This I will settle for," and start creating a life structure that will serve as a vehicle for the next step in the journey.

Within early and middle adulthood, the developmental periods unfold as follows (see Figure 1). We have found that each period begins and ends at a well-defined average age; there is a variation of plus or minus two years around the mean. (For a discussion of the age-linkages, see Issue 4 below.)

1. The *Early Adult Transition,* from age 17 to 22, is a developmental bridge between preadulthood and early adulthood.

2. The *Entry Life Structure for Early Adulthood* (22 to 28) is the time for building and maintaining an initial mode of adult living.

3. The *Age 30 Transition* (28 to 33) is an opportunity to reappraise and modify the entry structure and to create the basis for the next life structure.

4. The *Culminating Life Structure for Early Adulthood* (33 to 40) is the vehicle for completing this era and realizing our youthful aspirations.

5. The *Midlife Transition* (40 to 45) is another of the great cross-era shifts, serving both to terminate early adulthood and to initiate middle adulthood.

6. The *Entry Life Structure for Middle Adulthood* (45 to 50), like its counterpart above, provides an initial basis for life in a new era.

7. The *Age 50 Transition* (50 to 55) offers a mid-era opportunity for modifying and perhaps improving the entry life structure.

8. The *Culminating Life Structure for Middle Adulthood* (55 to 60) is the framework in which we conclude this era.

9. The *Late Adult Transition* (60 to 65) is a boundary period between middle and late adulthood, separating and linking the two eras.

The first three periods of early adulthood, from roughly 17 to 33, constitute its "novice phase." They provide an opportunity to move beyond adolescence, to build a provisional but necessarily flawed entry life structure, and to learn the limitations of that structure. The two final periods, from 33 to 45, form the "culminating phase," which brings to fruition the efforts of this era.

A similar sequence exists in middle adulthood. It, too, begins with a novice phase of three periods, from 40 to 55. The Midlife Transition is both an ending and a beginning. In our early 40s we are in the full maturity of early adulthood and are completing its final chapter; we are also in the infancy of middle adulthood, just beginning to learn about its promise and its dangers. We remain novices in every era until we have had a chance to try out an entry life structure and then to question and modify it in the mid-era transition. Only in the period of the Culminating Life Structure, and the cross-era transition that follows, do we reach the conclusion of that season and begin the shift to the next. During the novice phase

Figure 1
Developmental Periods in the Eras of Early and Middle Adulthood

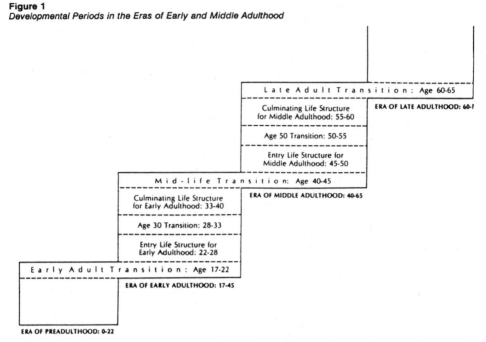

Note. This is an expanded adaptation of an earlier version that appeared in *The Seasons of a Man's Life* (p. 57) by D. J. Levinson with C. N. Darrow, E. B. Klein, M. H. Levinson, and B. McKee, 1978, New York: Alfred A. Knopf, Inc. Copyright 1978 by Alfred A. Knopf, Inc. Adapted by permission.

we are, to varying degrees, both excited and terrified by the prospects for living in that era. To varying degrees, likewise, we experience the culminating phase as a time of rich satisfactions and of bitter disappointments, discovering as we so often do that the era ultimately gives us much more and much less than we had envisioned.

This sequence of eras and periods holds for men and women of different cultures, classes, and historical epochs. There are, of course, wide variations in the kinds of life structures people build, the developmental work they do in transitional periods, and the concrete sequence of social roles, events, and personality change. The theory thus provides a general framework of human development within which we can study the profound differences that often exist between classes, genders, and cultures.

The Field of Adult Development: Six Major Issues

Like Pirandello's (1964) play, "Six Characters in Search of an Author," the study of adult development might be titled *Dozens of Fragments in Search of an Animating Source and a Unifying Plot*. The fragments have to do with personality change and development (cognitive,

moral, ego, and the like), occupational career development, marriage and family development, adult socialization, biological development, adaptation to stress, and more. Diverse studies deal with one or another of these topics, but they have no evident connection with each other and no clear place in a larger scheme of things.

It is time we asked more seriously, What do we mean by "adult development"? What are the main tasks confronting us as we attempt to define and establish it as a field of study? I have attempted to pursue these questions by identifying six fundamental issues. These issues are important to anyone entering this field, whatever the approach. In dealing with the issues, one is taking a position, explicit or implicit, regarding the nature of the field. No position, my own included, has as yet been more than minimally conceptualized and subjected to empirical test.

I will discuss each issue primarily from the vantage point of my own theory and research. To exemplify the diversity of approaches, comparisons will be drawn between life structure theory and other, more or less structural theories of development. These include the structural stage theories of Kegan (1982), Kohlberg (1969, 1973), Loevinger (1976), Piaget (1970) and Werner (1940). Also relevant are personality theories in which the idea of structure is important but is less fully articulated, such as Freud's theory of psychosexual stages, Jung's (Jung, von Franz, Henderson, Jacobi, & Jaffe, 1964) theory of adult individuation, and Erikson's (1950) theory of ego stages.

I will not deal here with other, nonstructural approaches. The most common of these is to look for age-linked changes in specific variables. A set of "age curves" showing regular increase or decrease in certain variables with age may be interpreted as evidence for an underlying developmental sequence. This approach tends to be quantitative and variable centered and to portray development as a continuous, incremental process. The structuralists, in contrast, emphasize patterns rather than single variables, and they look for a series of qualitatively (structurally) different stages rather than continuous, quantitative change. The two approaches are not mutually exclusive but are rarely held conjointly. Coming to a more balanced view of their relative merits is one of the important issues in the field, but it is beyond the scope of this article.

The basic structural model, most clearly articulated by Piaget (1970) and held with variations by many developmental theorists, is that development in any domain involves the evolution of a structure (cognitive, moral, ego, or whatever). The structure develops through a series of stages or periods. Structural theorists generally use the term *stage.* I use the term *period,* partly to avoid the connotation of hierarchical progression so common in the other theories. When I need a very general term referring to a segment (stage, period, era, or whatever) within a developmental sequence, I speak of *phase.* In every structural theory, a phase of building and maintaining a structure is followed by a phase of transformation or transition, which leads to the formation of a qualitatively different structure. One research problem is to identify a sequence of structures. Another is to understand what happens in a transition: the process by which one structure is transformed into another and the factors that shape this process.

It is not my goal here to examine and evaluate the various theories. All of them have been useful, and all reflect the rather primitive stage of psychology as a discipline. All of us are groping our way in the dark, working with imperfect concepts, methods, and evidence. Our chief task at this time is not to make exaggerated claims but to further the growth of an infantile discipline. My intent in identifying the following issues is to provide an analytic basis on which we can compare various approaches, clarify the similarities and differences among them, and consider the state of this field as a whole.

In question form, the six issues may be stated as follows:

1. What are the alternative ways of defining a structural stage or period?
2. What relative emphasis is given to the structures and structure-building periods or stages, as compared to the transitional, structure-changing periods?

3. How can we make best use of the distinction between hierarchical levels and seasons of development?
4. Are there age-linked developmental periods in adulthood?
5. What are the relative merits and limitations of various research methods?
6. How can we bring together the developmental perspective and the socialization perspective?

Issue 1. What are the alternative ways of defining a structural stage or period? In the Piagetian tradition, development is a sequence of stages. Each stage is defined in terms of the *structure* that characterizes it. A stage, in this view, *is* a structure; or to put it another way, a stage is a time of building and maintaining a structure. Other developmental theorists, such as Erikson and Freud, defined a stage in terms of its *developmental tasks.* Thus, Erikson identified each ego stage in terms of a polarity (trust vs. mistrust, generativity vs. stagnation or exclusivity). A person is in a stage when that polarity is of central importance in experiencing the self and relating to the world. The primary developmental tasks of a stage are to come to terms with both of its polar opposites and to arrive at some balance or integration of the poles, so that they are no longer entirely antithetical. One positive outcome of the developmental work is the formation of a stage-specific virtue, such as fidelity or caring. However, Erikson did not posit a single optimal ego *structure* as the defining characteristic of an ego stage. Rather, he described various kinds of developmental work on the tasks and various kinds of developmental achievement or impairment that may be the products of the stage.

Like Erikson and Freud, I define each period primarily in terms of its developmental tasks. I am also concerned with the kinds of life structures that are formed in every structure-building period, and in that sense I am perhaps more of a "structuralist" than they. Unlike Piaget, however, I do not identify a particular structure as the predominant or optimal one for a given period; the life structures generated in any period are infinitely varied.

Issue 2. What relative emphasis is given to the structures and structure-building periods or stages as compared to the transitional, structure-changing periods? Piaget tended to focus mainly on the sequence of structures. When he spoke of a stage, he meant a structure. His successive stages in cognitive development form a hierarchical series of cognitive levels or structures. Although recognizing that transitions are required for the shift from one structure to another, he did not study the transitional process. He treated the transitions as lacunae or zones of ambiguity between the structures, rather than as stages in their own right, possessing a distinctive character of their own. By and large, Piaget studied the structures rather than the course of development as a continuing evolution.

In contrast, there is now a growing body of research on transitions; for example, periods of change and readjustment following a major life event such as marriage, divorce, the birth of a child, retirement, or the loss of a loved one (Hareven & Adams, 1982; Lowenthal, Thurnher, & Chiriboga, 1975). In this work, the focus on the process of change is often so strong that little attention is given to the states (structures) that precede and follow it. A transition is a shift from state A to state B; it is as important to study A and B as it is to study the intervening process of change. Much of the recent theory and research on transitions is centered narrowly on adaptation and change stemming from a single event. This work contributes to our knowledge of events and adaptations, but it is generally not based on a theory of adult development, and it cannot, in itself, generate a theory of adult development (Levinson, 1980).

In studying the development of the life structure, I give equal weight to the structure-building periods and the structure-changing periods. Adults spend almost as much time in the latter as in the former, and both play a crucial part in adult development. To those who focus chiefly on structures, I would emphasize the importance of the transitional, structure-changing periods. And to those who deal primarily with transitions, I would emphasize that a crucially important feature of any transition is the new structure emerging from it. I am equally concerned with the life structures people form at different ages and with the transitions that lead from one life structure to another. I study the sequence by which individuals build, live within, modify, and rebuild the life structure over a span of many years. The standard methods of cross-sectional and longitudinal research are not adequate for this task. We must develop biographical methods that more fully capture the flow of the life course (see Issue 5, below).

Issue 3. How can we make best use of the distinction between hierarchical levels and seasons of development? In the Piagetian approach, the successive stages form a hierarchical progression from lower to higher on a developmental scale. Stage 3 is developmentally more advanced than stage 2, and less advanced than stage 4. In other theories, such as Freud's, Erikson's, and mine, the phases have more of the character of seasons. Phase 3 comes after phase 2 and to some extent builds upon it, but phase 3 is not necessarily more "advanced." Each phase has its own intrinsic value, appropriate to its place in the life cycle. The sequence of phases is seen within the framework of the life cycle rather than as a temporal order governed solely by its own internal logic.

This issue is of fundamental importance in the study of adult development. The imagery of a hierarchy of developmental stages is prevalent in the study of childhood, where development takes primarily the form of positive growth. There are generally agreed-upon criteria for judging that one stage represents a "higher level" than another in preadulthood, where we make such dramatic advances in body shape and size, cognitive complexity, adaptive capability, and character formation. The variables that show such rapid growth until age 20 or so tend to stabilize in early adulthood and then gradually decline over the course of middle and late adulthood. At the same time, other psychosocial qualities may develop to greater maturity in middle and late adulthood.

It is essential to keep in mind that development is not synonymous with growth. Rather, it has the twin aspects of "growing up" and "growing down." Perhaps the best term for the former is *adolescing,* which means moving toward adulthood, and for the latter, *senescing,* which means moving toward old age and dissolution. The balance of the two varies from era to era.

In preadulthood we are mostly, though not only, adolescing. In late adulthood we are mostly senescing, though there is some vitally important adolescing to be done as we come to the culmination of the entire life cycle and attempt to give fuller meaning to our own lives, to life and death as ultimate states, and to the condition of being human. At the end of the life cycle, as we engage in the final process of biological senescing, we are also engaged in the final work of psychosocial adolescing, of growing up to our full adulthood. It is a costly oversimplification to equate childhood with growth and old age with decline.

In early and middle adulthood, adolescing and senescing coexist in an uneasy balance. Biologically, the forces of senescence come to equal and then gradually to exceed those of adolescence. Psychosocially, there are possibilities for further growth, but they are by no means assured of realization and they are jeopardized by external constraints as well as inner vulnerabilities. We must deal with this coexistence of growth and decline in our own lives and in our research on adult development. Simple models of growth do not hold in adulthood. It is inappropriate to study adult development with childhood-centered models. Adulthood has its own distinctive character and must be studied in its own right, not merely as an extrapolation from childhood. Erikson warned us of this long ago, and Jung even earlier, but it is a hard lesson to learn.

In studying the development of the life structure, we are not yet wise enough about life to say with precision that one life structure is developmentally higher, or more advanced, than another. We still know very little about the complexities and contradictions of the human life course. When we have learned much more about the kinds of life structures people build at different ages, under different conditions, we may be more able to evaluate, conceptualize, and measure the variations in developmental level among life structures.

It is clearly unrealistic to assume that a person's culminating life structure for early adulthood (in the 30s) will necessarily be more advanced developmentally than the preceding entry life structure (in the 20s). And when we compare the culminating life structure for early adulthood with the entry life structure for middle adulthood, we have to take account of the change in eras, which presents new possibilities and new burdens. The great challenge now, as we go about establishing this field, is to observe and describe the individual life course as richly as possible and to generate concepts that represent its underlying complexity, order, and chaos.

Taking a small step toward evaluation, I have been developing the concept of the *satisfactoriness* of the life structure (Levinson, 1978). Like many of my concepts, this one has both an external and an internal reference. Externally, it refers to the *viability* of the life structure in the external world—how well it works and what it provides in the way of advantages and disadvantages, successes and failures, rewards and deprivations. Internally, it refers to the *suitability* of the life structure for the self. The key questions here are the following: What aspects of the self can be lived out within this structure? What aspects must be neglected or suppressed? What are the benefits and costs of this structure for the self?

Satisfactoriness of the life structure is not the same as "level of adjustment," "sense of well being," or "life satisfaction" as these are usually assessed in questionnaire or brief interview studies. Some people feel quite satisfied with lives that are reasonably comfortable and orderly but in which they have minimal engagement or sense of purpose. Their lives have much viability in the world but little suitability for the self. When the self is so little invested in the life, the life in turn can offer little to the self—though many adults settle for this condition. Likewise, people who are passionately engaged in living, and who invest the self freely in the life structure, may experience much turmoil and suffering. They ask more of life than it can readily provide. The intense engagement in life yields more abundant fruits but exacts a different and in some ways greater toll.

Assessing the satisfactoriness of the life structure is thus a complex matter. We cannot do it by means of a few behavioral criteria or questionnaire items. Moreover, the basis for assessment must be different in different seasons of life. The range of possibilities in building an entry life structure for early adulthood is much different from that in, say, the culminating life structure for middle adulthood.

It is important also to distinguish between the development of the life structure and the development of the self during the adult years. Psychologists who have strong intellectual origins in the study of childhood tend to think of development as growth in various aspects of the self, such as cognition, morality, and ego functions. The study of adulthood, and especially of life structure development, takes us beyond the focus on the self: It requires us to examine the life course in its complexity, to take into account the external world as well as the self, to study the engagement of the self in the world, and to move beyond an encapsulated view of the self. As we learn more about the lived life and the evolution of the life structure, we will have a sounder basis for studying the adult development of the self.

Issue 4. Are there age-linked developmental periods in adulthood? The discovery of age-linked periods in the adult development of the life structure is one of the most controversial findings of my research. The most common response among psychologists and social scientists is incredulity. It is simply not possible, they aver, that development should unfold in so orderly a sequence during adulthood—a standard series of periods, each beginning at a well-defined modal age with a range of only four or

five years around it. They note that the available evidence goes against the hypothesis of age-linked stages in adult personality development. Moreover, social roles and careers evolve in accord with institutionally defined timetables that vary widely among institutions and cultures. Those who regard adulthood as a series of major life events (such as marriage, loss, and retirement) that may bring about changes in individual adaptation or personality, and who have no conception of adult development as a source of order in the life course, maintain that these life events occur at widely varying ages and thus make impossible the kind of temporal order I have found.

I have replied (1978, 1980, 1981) to these objections on both theoretical and empirical grounds. I agree that neither individual personality nor social roles evolve through a standard sequence of age-linked stages in adulthood. The only investigator who posited such a sequence of personality stages was Gould (1978), but his hypothesis awaits further testing. Erikson (1950) and Vaillant (1977) proposed a sequence of ego stages but were less specific about the age linkages. I agree, further, that major life events occur at varying ages. The study of events does not in itself provide a basis for a theory of adult development. It is abundantly evident that, at the level of events, roles, or personality, individual lives unfold in myriad ways. I make no claim for order in the concrete individual life course; indeed, I believe that there is much more diversity and disorder than most researchers have been able to see, through their narrow theoretical lenses and methodological constraints.

I do propose, however, that there is an *underlying* order in the human life course, an order shaped by the eras and by the periods in life structure development. Personality, social structure, culture, social roles, major life events, biology—these and other influences exert a powerful effect on the actual character of the individual life structure at a given time and on its development during adulthood. It is my hypothesis, however, that the basic nature and timing of life structure development are given in the life cycle at this time in human evolution.

As I have emphasized from the start, I offer this viewpoint as a tentative, empirically grounded hypothesis, not as a fully demonstrated truth. I did not have it in mind when I started my research on the adult development of men. The concept of life structure emerged slowly during the first years of that research. The discovery of a sequence of alternating, age-linked structure-building and transitional periods came even more slowly. That sequence has been found in the intensive study of many lives: the accounts of the 40 men interviewed in my first study (1978) and the 45 women interviewed in my current study (Levinson, in press); the accounts of over 100 men and women, from different countries and historical periods, whose lives have been sufficiently portrayed in biographies, autobiographies, novels, and plays; a study of women's lives into their 30s by Stewart (1976); a study of Black men by Gooden (1980); biographical studies of Jung (Holt, 1980) and of Willi Brandt (Kellerman, 1975); a pilot sample of 30 to 40 men and women interviewed for my forthcoming project on middle adulthood; and accounts of the life cycle written over 2,000 years ago by Confucius, Solon, and the authors of the Talmud (Levinson, 1978). I know of no systematic evidence disconfirming the hypothesis. As new evidence comes in, the theory will, no doubt, be modified, amplified, and made more complex.

The hypothesis of age-linked periods in life structure development is thus well grounded in empirical evidence, though not in quantitative, large-sample research. To say that it "must" be wrong, that it "doesn't make sense," is simply to say that it violates the conventional wisdom or the assumptions of other theories. We cannot confirm or disconfirm a theory of life structure by studying changes in personality, social role, moral functioning, or the like. Such a theory can be tested adequately only by intensive studies of the individual life course, through which we follow the evolution of the life structure over a span of years.

Issue 5. What are the relative merits and limitations of various research methods? The favored methods in developmental research have traditionally been the cross-sectional and the longitudinal. *Cross-sectional* research is the most efficient and manageable, but it has severe limitations as a means of exploring the process of development.

Longitudinal research has the great advantage of enabling us to study a sample over a span of years, but it has major disadvantages as well. The initial concepts and methods may become outmoded after a few years, but the method requires administration of the same measures at periodic intervals over the course of at least several adult years. The measures may have different meanings and validities at one point in history than at others. This is a particular difficulty in research on adult development. Longitudinal research ordinarily involves massive testing and interviewing at intervals of 1 to 10 or more years. The sample means are then used to plot continuous age curves, which may represent developmental sequences. This method is at its best when we have well-identified variables that stem directly from developmentally important concepts and for which we have measures of established reliability and validity. We are far from this ideal in the field of adult development. Even when interesting age curves are found, we are often uncertain about the validity of the measures, the significance of the variables, and the theory of development for which the findings are relevant. A premature emphasis on quantification often keeps us from exploring the phenomena under study and from generating powerful concepts from which appropriate measures can be derived.

The *biographical* method is an effort to reconstruct the life course by interviewing the person and by using various other sources, much as the biographer does in writing a book-length life story. Like the cross-sectional and longitudinal methods, it is not a single entity but a broad approach, with many variations in research design, techniques, and aims. It, too, has inherent limitations, especially in its reliance on memory and reconstruction.

It is not ideal for all purposes and to the exclusion of other methods. Still, it has certain advantages and ought to be recovered from the limbo to which psychology has for so long relegated it. For the study of life structure development, we have no other method of comparable value. The biographical method is the only one that enables us to obtain a complex picture of the life structure at a given time and to delineate the evolution of the life structure over a span of years. It is well suited for gaining a more concrete sense of the individual life course, for generating new concepts, and in time, for developing new variables, measures, and hypotheses that are rooted in theory and are relevant to life as it actually evolves.

Issue 6. How can we bring together the developmental perspective and the socialization perspective? Different theories deal with different variables or domains, yet the differences are often blurred or ignored. By and large, psychologists study the development of properties of the person—cognition, morality, ego, attitudes, interests, or psychodynamics. When we find a basic order in the evolution of these properties, the order is assumed to have its origins in the nature of the organism. External conditions influence the specific forms of individual growth and decline and serve to facilitate or hinder the process, but the basic developmental scheme is considered organismically given. Indeed, a *developmental perspective* in psychology has traditionally meant the search for a maturationally built-in, epigenetic, preprogrammed sequence.

The social sciences, on the other hand, look primarily to the sociocultural world for the sources of order in the life course. They show how culturally defined age grades, institutional timetables, and systems of acculturation and socialization shape the sequence of our lives. What we may broadly term the *socialization perspective* (Clausen, 1972; Hareven & Adams, 1982; Lowenthal et al., 1975; Neugarten, 1968) holds that the timing of life events and the evolution of adult careers in occupation, family, and other institutions is determined chiefly by forces in the external world; forces in the individual biology or psyche produce minor variance around the externally determined norms. A balanced approach to the search for order in the life course would obviously draw jointly upon the perspectives of development and socialization. Yet this integration has rarely been attempted.

What about the evolution of the life structure? Is it determined primarily from within or from without? Is it a product more of development or of socialization? As I have already indicated, the life structure constitutes a boundary—a mediating zone between personality structure and social structure. It contains aspects of both and governs the transactions between them. The life structure is a pattern of relationships between the self and the world. It has an inner–psychological aspect and an external–social aspect. The universal sequence of periods in the evolution of the life structure has its origins in the psychobiological properties of the human species, as well as in the general nature of human society at this phase of its evolution (Levinson, 1978, Ch. 20). Each individual life structure progresses through the successive periods in its own unique way, influenced by a multiplicity of specific biological, psychological, and social conditions.

Because the life structure is not solely a property of the individual, its evolution cannot be understood solely from an intraorganismic, developmental perspective. Because the life structure is not simply a matter of externally imposed events and roles, its evolution cannot be understood simply from a socialization perspective. It is necessary, instead, *to create a new perspective that combines development and socialization* and that draws equally on biology, psychology, and social science, as well as on the humanities. Movement in this direction is not easy, violating as it does the current vested interests of each discipline involved. Fortunately, it is becoming increasingly evident that the sharp divisions among these disciplines, whatever their value in the past, are now very costly. New cross-disciplinary boundary systems must be generated if we are to progress in the study of basic individual and social phenomena—not the least of which is the human life course. The study of the life structure and its development is an effort in this direction.

REFERENCES

Campbell, J. (Ed.). (1971). *The portable Jung.* New York: Viking.

Clausen, J. A. (1972). The life course of individuals. In M. W. Riley, M. Johnson, & A. Foner, A. (Eds.), *Aging and society:* Vol. 3. *A sociology of age stratification* (pp. 457–514). New York: Sage.

Erikson, E. H. (1950). *Childhood and society.* New York: Norton.

Erikson, E. H. (1958). *Young man Luther.* New York: Norton.

Erikson, E. H. (1969). *Ghandi's truth.* New York: Norton.

Gooden, W. E. (1980). *The adult development of Black men.* Unublished doctoral dissertation, Yale University, New Haven, CT.

Gould, R. L. (1978). *Transformations: Growth and change in adult life.* New York: Simon & Schuster.

Hareven, T. K., & Adams, K. (Eds.). (1982). *Aging and life course transitions: An interdisciplinary perspective.* New York: Guilford.

Holt, J. (1980). *An adult development psychobiography of C. G. Jung.* Unpublished senior thesis, Yale University School of Medicine, New Haven, CT.

Jung, C. G., von Franz, M.-L., Henderson, J. L., Jacobi, J., & Jaffe, A. (1964). *Man and his symbols.* New York: Doubleday.

Kegan, R. (1982). *The evolving self.* Cambridge, MA: Harvard University Press.

Kellerman, B. L. (1975). *Willi Brandt: Portrait of the leader as young politician.* Unpublished doctoral dissertation, Yale University, New Haven, CT.

Kohlberg, L. (1969). Stage and sequence: The cognitive developmental approach to socialization. In Goslin, D. A. (Ed.), *Handbook of socialization theory and research.* New York: Rand McNally.

Kohlberg, L. (1973). Continuities in childhood and adult moral development revisited. In P. B. Baltes & K. W. Schaie (Eds.), *Life span developmental psychology: Personality and socialization.* New York: Academic Press.

Levinson, D. J. (1977). The mid-life transition. *Psychiatry, 40,* 99–112.

Levinson, D. J. (1980). Toward a conception of the adult life course. In N. Smelser & E. H. Erikson (Eds.), *Themes of love and work in adulthood* (pp. 265–290). Cambridge, MA: Harvard University Press.

Levinson, D. J. (1981). Explorations in biography. In A. L. Rabin, J. Aronoff, A. M. Barclay, & R. A. Zucker (Eds.), *Further explorations in personality* (pp. 44–79). New York: Wiley.

Levinson, D. J. (1984). The career is in the life structure, the life structure is in the career: An adult development perspective. In M. B. Arthur, L. Bailyn, D. J. Levinson, & H. Shepard, *Working with careers* (pp. 49–74). Columbia University, School of Business.

Levinson, D. J. (in press). *The seasons of a woman's life.* New York: Knopf.

Levinson, D. J., with Darrow, C. N., Klein, E. B., Levinson, M. H. & McKee, B. (1978). *The seasons of a man's life.* New York: Knopf.

Levinson, D. J., & Gooden, W. E. (1985). The life cycle. In H. I. Kaplan & B. J. Sadock (Eds.), *Comprehensive textbook of psychiatry* (4th ed., pp. 1–13). Baltimore, MD: Williams and Williams.

Loevinger, J. (1976). *Ego development: Conceptions and theories.* San Francisco: Jossey-Bass.

Lowenthal, M. F., Thurnher, M., & Chiriboga, D. (1975). *Four stages of life: A comparative study of women and men facing transitions.* San Francisco: Jossey-Bass.

Neugarten, B. L. (1968). Adult personality: Toward a psychology of the life cycle. In B. L. Neugarten (Ed.), *Middle age and aging: Reader in social psychology* (pp. 137–147). Chicago: University of Chicago Press.

Ortega y Gasset, J. (1958). *Man and crisis.* New York: Norton. (Original work published 1933)

Piaget, J. (1970). *Structuralism.* New York: Basic Books.

Pirandello, L. (1964). Six characters in search of an author. In R. W. Corrigan (Ed.), *The modern theater.* New York: Macmillan.

Stewart, W. (1976). *A psychosocial study of the formation of the early adult life structure in women.* Unpublished doctoral dissertation, Teachers College, Columbia University, New York, NY.

Vaillant, G. (1977). *Adaptation to life.* Boston: Little, Brown.

van Gennep, A. (1960). *The rites of passage.* Chicago: University of Chicago Press. (Original work published 1908)

Werner, H. (1940). *Comparative psychology and mental development.* New York: Harper.

White, R. W. (1952). *Lives in progress.* New York: Holt, Rinehart & Winston.

[21]

Some executives hunger for managerial promotion. Others, equally talented, reject managerial power for functional autonomy. A Sloan School of Management study suggests that companies need to know more about key executives' motivational drives and needs.

How "Career Anchors" Hold Executives to Their Career Paths

Edgar H. Schein

Certain motivational/attitudinal/value syndromes formed early in the lives of individuals apparently function to guide and constrain their entire careers. These basic combinations of needs and drives act, in effect, as "career anchors" that not only influence career choices, but also affect decisions to move from one company to another, shape what the individuals are looking for in life, and color their views of the future and their general assessments of related goals and objectives.

This concept of career anchors emerges directly from a lengthy—and continuing—study of a representative group of Alfred P. Sloan School of Management alumni who completed their graduate work in the early 1960s and are now more than a decade into their life careers. Periodic contact with these young men and analysis of their postgraduate activities has provided extensive insights and intimate

11

details of both their professional and personal lives. The evidence at hand strongly suggests that, in addition to exerting strong influences on the career paths and career satisfactions of the individuals themselves, career anchors—as a concept—also carry important implications for business, industrial, and other employing organizations. For example:

• If career anchors do indeed function as stable syndromes in the personality, it becomes important for employing organizations to identify these syndromes early. It does little good, for example, to offer promotion into management to someone who basically does not want to be a manager but whose basic goal is attainment of technical/functional competence or who is anchored instead to entrepreneurial, creative, or primarily autonomous activities. The organization stands to gain by creating career opportunities that are congruent with the basic anchor needs of its human talent.

• Within the context of the career anchor concept, organizations thus will have to learn to think more broadly about the different kinds of contributions people can make. This means development of multiple reward systems as well as multiple career paths that will permit full development of diverse kinds of individuals.

Origins and scope of the Sloan management panel study

Launched in 1961, a panel study covering the careers of 44 Sloan School graduates was initiated to assess the interaction of personal values and career events in the lives of managers in organizations. The project had the original goal of determining the mechanisms and effects of organizational socialization. Some of the key questions it was designed to answer included:

In what manner and through what means would the values of Sloan students be influenced by their organizational experiences? Would certain sets of individuals with certain sets of values be more or less socialized? Could one determine what kinds of value syndromes would lead to careers in which the individual would innovate, that is, change organizations rather than be changed by them?

Participants in the study were selected on the basis of random sampling techniques and were invited to participate in order to eliminate the bias of volunteering. The panel of 44 men who agreed to cooperate is believed to be reasonably representative of the graduating classes from which its members were drawn. (The panel originally consisted of 15 men each from the Sloan classes of 1961, 1962, and 1963, but was reduced to 44 by the withdrawal of one member after a point where it was too late to replace him.)

Beginning with interviews and various attitude and value surveys administered prior to graduation, contact has been maintained with each of the 44 panelists at various points during their subsequent careers. A major review and resurvey of the panel was completed in 1973–74, and various aspects of that effort will be spelled out in later reports. On the basis of the initial analysis, however, it was determined that the career histories of the panelists could be understood best in terms of the concept of "career anchors."

The Anchor Concept: Spotlighting common themes and needs

A career can be thought of as a set of stages or a path through time that reflects:

1. An individual's needs, motives, and aspirations in relation to work.

2. Society's expectations of what kinds of activities will result in monetary and status rewards for the career occupant.

Work careers thus reflect both individual and societal (or organizational) definitions of what is a worthwhile set of activities to pursue throughout a lifetime. In a sense, then, one can speak of two sets of "anchors" for a career.

• On one hand, a career is anchored in a set of job descriptions and organizational norms about the rights and duties of a given title in an organization. The "head of production," for example, is expected to perform certain duties; he carries certain sets of responsibilities and is held accountable for certain areas of organizational performance.

• On the other hand, the career is anchored in a set of needs and motives which the individual is attempting to fulfill through the work he does and the rewards he obtains for that work—money, prestige, organizational membership, challenging work, freedom, and other satisfactions. The rewards he seeks thus can be thought of as his job values—what he is looking for in a job. These values, in turn, also reflect an underlying pattern of needs that the individual is trying to fulfill.

Thus, as head of production, he may seek to exercise his basic need for influencing and controlling numbers of people and resources. Or he may be trying to meet the challenge of successfully building something or getting something accomplished that is proof of his competence.

For others, the underlying need serving as a career anchor is the exercise of a certain talent such as quantitative analysis; for still others it is a need to find security—to link oneself with a stable and predictable future via an occupation or an organization. The drive for money, as many previous analyses have shown, is perhaps more difficult to unravel because it often masks other underlying needs. The career anchor categories as defined here must take these needs into account.

The 44 interviews revealed a number of common themes in what people are fundamentally looking for in their careers. And these common themes can be defined as the underlying individual career anchors that function to pull a person back if he strays too far from what he *really* wants.

Anchor 1. Managerial competence

The panelists who were classified in this category made it clear that their fundamental motivation is to be competent in the complex set of activities that comprise the idea of "management." The most important components of this concept are:

1. *Interpersonal competence*—the ability to influence, supervise, lead, manipulate, and control people toward the more effective achievement of organizational goals.

2. *Analytical competence*—the identification and solving of conceptual problems under conditions of uncertainty and incomplete information.

3. *Emotional stability*—the capacity to be stimulated by emotional and interpersonal crises rather than exhausted or debilitated by them, the capacity to bear high levels of responsibility, and the capacity to exercise authority without fear or guilt.

In other words, the person who wants to rise in the organization, who is seeking higher and higher levels of responsibility, must be good in handling people, an excellent analyst, and emotionally able to withstand the pressures and tensions of the executive suite. In terms of organizational categories, he is usually thought of as a line or general manager, depending on his rank. Occasionally a senior functional manager fits this concept if he gets his prime satisfaction from managerial and related human relations responsibilities rather than from the technical part of his job.

Anchor 2. Technical-functional competence

A number of respondents left no doubt that their careers are motivated by the challenge of the actual work they do—financial analysis, marketing, systems analysis, corporate planning, or some other area related to business or management. Their anchor is the technical field or functional area, not the managerial process itself. If a member of this group holds supervisory responsibility, he is usually supervising others in the same technical area, and he makes it clear that it is the area, not the supervising, that turns him on. This kind of person is not interested in being promoted out of his technical area; his roots are in the actual analytical work he is doing. In terms of organizational titles, such people are spread over a wide range of functional managers, technical managers, senior staff, junior staff, and some external consultants and related activities. People with this set of needs will leave a company rather than be promoted out of their technical/functional area.

Anchor 3. Security

Other respondents have tied their careers to particular organizations. Although one must infer the assumption, it is reasonable to postulate that their underlying need is for security, and that they seek to stabilize their careers by linking them to given organizations. The implications are that an individual in this grouping will accept, to a greater degree than the other types, an *organizational* definition of his career. Whatever his private aspirations or competence areas, this individual must rely increasingly upon the organization to recognize these needs and competencies and do the best possible by him. But he loses some degree of freedom because of his unwillingness to leave a given organization if his needs or talents go unrecognized. Instead, he must rationalize that the organization's definition of his career is the only valid definition.

If such an individual has technical/functional talent, he may rise to a senior functional manager level; but if his psychological makeup includes a degree of insecurity, that very insecurity could make him "incompetent" with respect to higher levels of management where emotional security and stability become prime requisites for effective performance.

Length of time with a given organization is not a sufficient criterion for defining this career anchor. One must know something of the reasons why an individual has remained with a given organization before one can judge whether the holding force is insecurity or a pattern of constant success.

By the same logic, we find some individuals who are security-oriented yet who move from one company to another. In these cases strong similarities mark the types of companies and the career slots that the individual exchanges. To cite an example, one panelist's pattern of seeking security and stability expressed itself partly in seeking to remain in a given community where his family was very happy. Over a period of years he switched companies three times, but in each case he picked a similar company and started in that company at an equal or lower level in terms of rank. He is quite willing to sacrifice some autonomy in his career to stabilize his total life situation.

Anchor 4. Creativity

Some respondents expressed a strong need to create something on their own. This is the fundamental need operating in an entrepreneur, and it expresses itself in the desire to invent a new business vehicle, find a new product, develop a new service, or in some way create something that can be clearly identified with the individual.

On the Sloan graduate panel, for example, one participant has become a successful purchaser, restorer, and renter of town houses in a large city. Another, who developed a string of financial service organizations that use computers in a new and more effective way in a region where such services were not available, also is purchasing and developing large tracts of land and is co-owner of a large cattle ranch.

One gets the impression that the creativity/entrepreneurial pattern is also closely related to the need for autonomy and independence. All of the entrepreneurs strongly expressed the desire to be on their own, free of organizational restraints, but the decisive factor is that they did not leave the world of business to achieve their autonomy. Instead they chose to try to express their business and managerial skills by building their own enterprises.

This commitment to business also shows up in this group's ambition to acquire a great deal of money. But money is not sought for its own sake or for what it will buy. Instead, one gets the distinct impression that total financial assets are only a measure used to define one's degree of success as an entrepreneur.

Anchor 5. Autonomy and independence

The respondents who were primarily concerned about their own sense of freedom and autonomy had found organizational life to be restrictive, irrational, and/or intrusive into their private lives. Some left the world of business altogether, seeking careers that provided more autonomy; others became consultants operating on their own.

One became a university professor in areas related to business. Another has become a freelance writer who not only has rejected business as an arena but also has rejected the success ethic he associates with it. For him it has become more important to develop himself—he lives frugally, working as a ghost writer when he needs the money; he travels; and he works on his creative writing when the mood strikes him.

The consultants in the sample include several who are plainly in that line of endeavor because they seek autonomy although, as noted previously, not all consultants have that need. Some consultants are motivationally entrepreneurs; some are technical/functional specialists; and some are in transition toward a managerial role.

Relationship of career anchors to occupational/organizational titles

Career anchors are *personal* motivational/attitudinal/value syndromes. For that reason, the areas in which a person wants to become competent or sets the goals of his career will not necessarily be reflected in his occupational or organizational titles as shown in the summary on pages 18 and 19.

• Of the eight panelists anchored in managerial competence, not all have made it to higher levels of management. But their interviews clearly indicated that they seek higher levels and that they get their primary satisfactions out of managerial activities per se. Within that group are two career patterns—working one's way up within large organizations, and seeking larger jobs within smaller organizations.

Both pattern groups include individuals who have moved from one company to another and who sometimes have interrupted the pattern with stints in management consulting. But in the first group the individual always ended up in another large organization; in the second group there was a clear decision to move toward smaller organizations.

• Almost half of the panelists (19) were classified as anchored in technical/functional competence, reflecting their major concern that they be able to continue the kind of work they enjoy and are apparently good at. We should not assume, however, that members of the other groups are less concerned about developing their expertise or that they care less about the kind of work they do. We can say that in each person one can find a predominant concern that will function as an anchor in the sense of pulling him back if he strays too far from fulfilling that concern.

In the autonomy group, for example, the professor is certainly concerned about his area of specialization. But if given a chance to pursue that line of work in a large organization at a much higher sal-

Job Titles and Organizations of

Anchor 1—Managerial Competence

Manager of factoring systems: corporate headquarters, large financial corporation
Sales manager and part owner: family furniture business
Sales manager: industrial foods division, large conglomerate
Director of corporate plan administration: large airline
President and part owner: small manufacturing firm
Manager of marketing and assistant to general manager: large division of large corporation
Director of administration: insurance services division of large financial corporation
Vice-president for finance and administration: medium size service organization

Anchor 2—Technical/Functional Competence

Manager of data processing and part-founder: large consulting R&D firm
Research associate to vice-president for academic affairs: medium size university
Director of required earnings studies: large national utility
Manager of engineering: large product line of medium size manufacturing company
Member of technical staff: R&D division of large national utility
Principal programmer: technical unit of large systems design and manufacturing company
Market development engineer: new venture group, chemical corporation
Project manager: aero-space division of large electronics corporation
Treasurer: small growth company
Commerce officer: large government department, Canadian government
Assistant professor of operations research: management department, U.S. Naval Academy
Senior consultant: small management consulting firm
Assistant director: White House Office of Telecommunications
Plant manufacturing engineer: large consumer products division of large corporation

ary and with much better equipment or resources, he probably would not take it if he viewed that organizational setting as one in which he would have to sacrifice his autonomy.

In the technical/functional competence group, we find several middle level functional or technical managers; several people in senior or middle staff roles; some in straight consulting; and two in teaching (one at a university, the second at high school level).

It must be remembered that if the concept of career anchors is valid, the 19 men in this group are *not* in transition toward managerial roles per se. They may climb within functional/technical management, but the theoretical assumption is that they would refuse to

Panelists in Career Anchor Groups

Manager, market support systems, Europe: information services division of large corporation
Teacher and department head: regional rural Canadian high school
Project supervisor: technical division of large chemical company
Director, cost analysis group: large technical systems consulting firm
Principal in large management consulting firm

Anchor 3—Organizational Security
Manager, forward product planning research: large auto company
Marketing sales representative: large data services company
Advisory marketing representative: large computer manufacturer
Chief engineer: small family steel fabricating company

Anchor 4—Creativity
Founder of several financial, service, and real estate businesses
Founder of one firm and developer of second firm in chemical industry
Marketing development staff: overseas development of new ventures for industrial protein products of large consumer company
Marketing consultant: self-employed, searching for new enterprises to buy or develop (one previous unsuccessful venture)
Senior vice-president: media services, large advertising firm; real estate owner and developer
President and co-founder: planning and consulting firm

Anchor 5—Autonomy and Independence
Senior consultant: small management consulting firm
Communication consultant: self-employed, looking for entrepreneurial opportunity in communications field
Proprietor and owner: retail hardware and wholesale pumping equipment business
Assistant professor of business and economics: regional campus of a large state university system
Self-employed consultant: operations research field emphasizing applications to health care
Senior consultant: specialist in taxation work, large accounting firm
Self-employed free lance writer

be promoted into a role that would entail giving up the kind of work they are doing.

Many of the panelists in this group sense that they are violating the "success ethic" of the business world and feel somewhat guilty and in conflict about their lack of success and ambition. And while they talk of their work and family as being important to them and claim that they enjoy their life as it is, they wonder, nonetheless, whether they are missing something and whether they are doing as well as their peers. But our prediction is that none of these men will move out of their present orientations and will find ways to deal with their conflicts.

• Of the four men who can be classified as security oriented, three have spent most of their careers within a single organization. One has moved frequently, but he always remained within the same geographical area and always took similar types of jobs (with one exception—an abortive venture into trying to start a company with a group of associates). These men talk of their work, their families, their overall satisfaction with the geographical area where they have settled, and their sense of having achieved enough to satisfy themselves.

• The group concerned with creativity has proved to be the most interesting because it includes the entrepreneurs. Four have launched successful enterprises which have brought them fame or fortune, or both. Their activities vary greatly, but each activity is a clear extension of the person behind it.

• The autonomy group—four consultants, one owner/proprietor of a small business, one professor, and one freelance writer—resembles the technical/functional competence group in many respects—except that no functional managers or staff roles are represented in it. This group is distinguished by the fact that its members display little conflict about missed opportunities or failure to aspire higher. All are happy in their work and enjoy their freedom. All have a sense of their own professionalism and can link the results of their work to their own efforts, a feeling they share with the creativity group.

On the surface it is not easy to differentiate the autonomy and creativity group members because the entrepreneurs also enjoy autonomy and freedom. But when one listens to the entrepreneurs, it becomes obvious that they are preoccupied with building something, whereas the primary need of the autonomy oriented panelists is to be on their own, with no concerns about making money or building empires.

Background characteristics of the anchor groups

If career anchors are formed fairly early in life, even though they may not be recognized by the person, will one find symptomatic relationships between panelists' background characteristics and the anchor groups they ended up in? Several key background characteristics were considered—intellectual aptitude and performance, and parental education and occupation. Because of the small number of men involved in the study sample, it is difficult to do more than draw attention to a few trends.

The data shown do not yet permit spelling out the nature of the mechanisms in operation, though a more detailed analysis of the original interviews with the panelists should illuminate these findings. However, there appear to be consistent patterns of intellectual performance, particularly in the autonomy and creativity groups, and all groups show some biases in terms of the educational and occupational status of mothers and fathers. To summarize:

Grade point averages and business aptitude test scores (See Table 1): In terms of undergraduate grade point averages (GPA), the managerial and technical/functional groups scored highest, while the creativity group had the lowest grades. Similarly, in terms of aptitude as measured by the Admissions Test for Graduate Study in Business (ATGSB), the autonomy group scored highest and the creativity group again had the lowest scores. In terms of grade point averages at Massachusetts Institute of Technology, the groups resemble each other closely—except for the lower average of the creativity group.

This difference could reflect real intellectual aptitude differences, but it is more likely a reflection of early biases in the entrepreneurial group toward breadth of interest and creative activities. Perhaps this group put more energy into developing skills of leadership and creation of opportunities than into narrow academic pursuits.

Parental education and occupations: Motivational syndromes should be related to parental values and aspirations, and from the objective data available, several interesting patterns emerge.

The managerial competence group is average in fathers' education,

Table 1

Undergraduate Grade Point Averages, Business Aptitude Test Scores, and Graduate Grade Point Averages of Anchor Groups

Career Anchor	Under-graduate G.P.A.	ATGSB Total	Verbal	Quanti-tative	Grad-uate G.P.A.
Managerial Comp. (N=8)	4.0	574	29	39	4.4
Tech./Funct. Comp. (N=19)	3.9	590	34	38	4.2
Security (N=4)	3.7	573	31	38	4.2
Creativity (N=6)	3.2	555	31	36	4.0
Autonomy (N=7)	3.5	628	37	41	4.2
Total	3.9	587	33	38	4.2

low in mothers' education, high in business and managerial fathers, and high in percentage of housewife mothers. In contrast, the technical/functional competence group is high in parental education but is more diversified in parental occupations. The security group is low in fathers' education and high in mothers' education, high in percentage of business and managerial fathers, and average in number of housewife mothers. One can conjecture that the security orientation reflects a feeling on the part of the alumnus that once he has completed graduate school and made it into some level of management, he already has achieved success by climbing higher on the socioeconomic ladder than his father.

The creativity group shows high levels of education for both fathers and mothers and a high percentage of business/managerial fathers. Perhaps the broad interests of this group derive from the breadth that is associated with the higher level of education of *both* parents.

The autonomy group, average for parental education and level of mothers' occupation, stands out in having the lowest percentage of business/managerial fathers and the highest percentage of professional fathers. The autonomy pattern may already have been set in these families in that among the fathers' occupations were farmer, associate professor, chief engineer of a company, electrical contractor, insurance agency owner, and executive vice president of a family business. Only the latter two jobs are business and managerial, and they both involve ownership; none of the fathers was a manager in the traditional sense.

Table 2

Income of Career Anchor Groups

Career Anchor	Mean	Median	Range
Managerial Competence* (N=8)	$35,500	$31,000	$27,000–$50,000
Tech./Funct. Competence (N=19)	25,800	26,000	16,000– 42,000
Security (N=4)	23,000	24,500	18,000– 25,000
Creativity** (N=6)	29,000	26,000	17,000– 40,000
Autonomy (N=7)	19,000	17,000	10,000– 25,000
Total	26,600	25,000	

* One person has over $50,000 per year in supplemental income from real estate ventures.
** The two successful entrepreneurs report assets in excess of a half million dollars.

Measuring career success of anchor groups

Success is a complex and difficult variable to define and measure. It can be defined objectively by societal standards or subjectively by personal standards and goals. The data reported here focus on one indicator of *objective* success—the income of panelists. Table 2, which is based on incomes reported in the 1973–74 interviews, in many cases shows only baseline numbers that exclude annual bonuses, value of stock options, and other perquisites. Annual incomes of the entrepreneurs would have to be supplemented with figures on the total value of assets that they said they have accumulated.

As might be expected, the most successful in pure income terms is the managerial competence group; climbing of the managerial ladder is congruent with society's definition of success. The successful entrepreneurs are similarly high if one includes their assets, but even the most successful of them reports an annual *income* of only $40,000. For this group it perhaps is more important to build total assets than to consume what they have amassed. At the low end of one income scale we have the autonomy-oriented group who have left large organizations.

Assessing the anchor concept

In introducing and elaborating on the concept of career anchors, we have viewed them as syndromes that, while formed fairly early in life, effectively influence one's entire career. In classifying the panelists into career anchor groups, the groupings were made on the basis of reasons they gave for career choices, why they shifted from company to company and job to job, and how they assess their future work careers. Data from the earlier (precareer) interviews were not used in order to minimize bias. The relationships reported between career anchors, intellectual aptitude, school performance, parental background, current jobs, and current income are therefore real relationships because the classification into career anchor groups was made before any of the correlative data were examined.

Accepting this overall correlation as an indication of the stability of career anchors as influential syndromes in the personality underscores a need for organizations, on the one hand, to help employees recognize their anchors and, on the other hand, to create multiple paths and reward systems to permit effective utilization of managerial, technical, and other professional talents. Organizational efforts to identify underlying career anchor orientations and to channel them toward fulfillment of individuals' indicated needs and goals should generate greatly improved rewards and benefits for both the organization and its managers.

EDGAR H. SCHEIN *is chairman of the organization studies group at the Alfred P. Sloan School of Management, Massachusetts Institute of Technology where he also serves as professor of organizational psychology and management and M.I.T. undergraduate planning professor. Recipient of several awards in the field of social psychology, Dr. Schein has authored many books and studies in organization development, organizational psychology, and interpersonal dynamics. In addition to his academic work, he also serves as a consultant on management and organization development to various industrial and business organizations, including General Foods, Digital Equipment, Polaroid, General Electric, and other companies. After earning a Ph.B. degree at the University of Chicago in 1946, Dr. Schein received his B.A. and M.A. degrees at Stanford University and his Ph.D. at Harvard University. He was appointed to the M.I.T. faculty in 1956 after serving as a research psychologist at the Walter Reed Army Institute of Research.*

[22]

Journal of Applied Psychology
1984, Vol. 69, No. 2, 252–260

Stress and Strain From Family Roles and Work-Role Expectations

Robert A. Cooke
Department of Management, College of Business
Administration, University of Illinois at Chicago

Denise M. Rousseau
Department of Organization Behavior,
J. L. Kellogg Graduate School of Management,
Northwestern University

Using questionnaire and interview data from a random sample of Michigan teachers ($n = 200$), this study investigates contradictory models of the effects of family roles and work-role expectations on strain. Role theory predicts that multiple roles can lead to stressors (work overload and interrole conflict) and, in turn, to symptoms of strain. Social-support research and theory suggest that multiple roles, and in particular family roles, serve to reduce strain. The results of this study are generally consistent with role theory's predictions for work-role expectations. These expectations were found to be related to work overload and interrole conflict, and these stressors were found to be related to strain. The relation of family-role expectations to strain is more complex. Family roles were found to be related to strain in three ways: They interact with work-role expectations so that the relation between those expectations and work overload is progressively greater for single teachers, those who are married, and those who have children; they are indirectly related to strain through their relation to interrole conflict; and, finally, they are directly and negatively associated with physical strain when their relation to interrole conflict is controlled. Although both family roles and work expectations appear to exacerbate strain though their positive relationship with interrole conflict, family-role expectations seem to reduce the amount of physical strain individuals experience. Thus, although results from this study generally support role theory, the social-support model also is supported with regard to family-role expectations and health.

Research on work and nonwork has produced contradictory findings concerning the effects of family roles on the well-being of workers. On the one hand, research on stress and social support suggests that the support system implied by family roles can moderate the impact of work-related stressors (LaRocco, House, & French, 1980) or directly reduce the strain experienced by the individual (Thoits, 1982). On the other hand, research on role conflict indicates that tensions between family and work roles can lead to poor marital adjustment, inadequate role performance, and other negative outcomes (Blood & Wolfe, 1960; Jones & Butler, 1980; Staines et al., 1978). Thus, although family roles might reduce the effects of stressors, these same roles can simultaneously serve as a source of stress for the employed person. These inconsistent effects of family roles are investigated in this article on the basis of interview and questionnaire data provided by 200 teachers.

Background

The expectations associated with work and family roles can lead to physical and psychological strain in at least two ways. First, the expectations surrounding either of these roles can generate interrole conflict when they involve pressures to dominate the time of the focal person and interfere with fulfilling the

The data for this article were collected as part of a study on the Quality of Work Life of Teachers, which was funded by the U.S. Department of Labor (Contract Numbers 41-NSC-252C3 and J9-M9-0124; H. Kornbluh and R. Cooke, Principal Investigators). The analyses and preparation of this article were supported by a J. L. Kellogg Research chair.

We wish to thank Jeanne Brett and two anonymous *Journal of Applied Psychology* reviewers for their helpful comments on an earlier version of this article and Cathleen, Heather, and Jessica Cooke for the insights they have stimulated regarding the positive effects of family-role senders.

Requests for reprints should be sent to Denise M. Rousseau, Department of Organization Behavior, J. L. Kellogg Graduate School of Management, Northwestern University, Evanston, Illinois 60201.

expectations associated with the other role (Katz & Kahn, 1978). Second, these dual role expectations can lead to an increase in overall workload and to feelings of overload within the work or nonwork domain (Hall & Hall, 1982; Szalai, 1972).

Interrole confict is likely to increase as the demands of either the work role or family role increase. For example, conflict can result from pressures to expand one's work activities beyond the normal working day (Beutell & Greenhaus, 1983). Such pressures are felt by many workers. In the 1977 *Quality of Employment Survey* (Quinn & Staines, 1979), a significant number of respondents cited as problems "excessive hours" (mentioned by 8.2% of all respondents), "overtime" (10.5%), and "work schedules that interfere with family life" (26.7%). Similarly, interrole conflict can increase as one's obligations to the family expand through marriage and the arrival of children. This is particularly the case for women who, more than men, tend to assume responsibility for household management and child care (Gordon & Strober, 1978; Gutek, Nakamura, & Nieva, 1981).

Expectations to work more hours, beyond leading to interrole conflict, also are likely to produce feelings of work overload. Quantitative work overload is defined here as the feeling that there is too much to do on the job (Caplan, 1971; Katz & Kahn, 1978). Although closely related to interrole conflict, work overload should be the direct result only of work expectations (and not family roles). Family roles, nevertheless, might exacerbate or amplify perceived overload in the work domain. The stress created by pressures to work extra hours can most easily be reduced by allocating more time to work-related activities. However, this coping strategy becomes more difficult to implement as the size of one's family increases and expectations multiply. Thus, family roles are likely to moderate the relationship between work expectations and perceived overload; people who are single, married, and parents have available progressively fewer degrees of freedom for reducing the stress caused by increasingly demanding work expectations.

Both perceived work overload and interrole conflict can lead to strain and other negative outcomes. Blood and Wolfe (1960) found that as men work more, they do less at home, and

their wives report less satisfaction with their spouse's marital role peformance. Coburn (1978) identified a negative relationship between interrole conflict and the psychological and physical well-being of men. Gove and Geerken (1977) found a positive relationship between number of children and psychiatric symptoms for employed women; Haynes and Feinleib (1980) found that working women with three or more children were more likely than those without children to develop coronary heart disease; and Woods (1978) found that, in the absence of support from significant others, women's involvement in multiple roles has a deleterious effect on their mental health. Other studies have not shown these relationships, but Haw (1982) argues that many of them have lacked specificity in measurement. She suggests, among other things, that perceived work demands be more clearly measured and that role conflict be distinguished from work overload.

In contrast to the research on role conflict and overload, studies on social support suggest that family roles can reduce strain. Though results have not been consistent (Schaefer, 1982), social support from a spouse potentially can mitigate the effects of stress on certain health outcomes (House & Wells, 1978; LaRocco et al., 1980). Social support has been hypothesized to serve as a moderator and, alternatively, as a variable directly and negatively related to strain (Thoits, 1982). This latter hypothesis is consistent with studies showing that the physical and mental health of married people is better than that of single people whose health, in turn, is better than that of separated or divorced people (Doherty & Jacobson, 1982). This trend has been observed in studies using such diverse health measures as mental disorders, debilitating chronic ailments, work-limiting conditions, and self-reported happiness (Campbell, Converse, & Rogers, 1976; Gove, 1973; London, Crandell, & Seals, 1977; Verbrugge, 1979). Thus, while marriage can lead to interrole conflict, this conflict and its effects can be offset by the support and other positive contributions a spouse can provide.

The relationship between parenthood and physical and mental health is more complex. There is substantial evidence that the presence of children, particularly those under six years of age, is associated with symptoms of psy-

254   ROBERT A. COOKE AND DENISE M. ROUSSEAU

chological strain. Women with young children are more likely than others to experience incessant demands and limited freedom and to report loneliness, depression, and concern about having a nervous breakdown (Brown & Harris, 1978; Campbell et al., 1976; Gove & Geerken, 1977). Children can produce inter-role conflict with respect not only to parent versus spouse roles but also to family versus work roles. Nevertheless, Brown and Harris (1978) report that the vulnerability to health problems of women with children can be offset by employment outside the home. Such employment can be particularly beneficial when the work role is viewed as a career rather than as a job (Holahan & Gilbert, 1979). With respect to men, Bachman, O'Malley, and Johnston (1978) conclude that marriage and parenthood can have positive effects on the self-esteem and job motivation of young males. The presence of children also has been found to be related to higher job involvement and organizational identification (Gould & Werbel, 1983). Furthermore, in a recent survey, childless couples were perceived as having neither the most satisfying lives nor the most satisfying marriages (Blake, 1979, p. 249). Thus, although children are likely to produce interrole conflict for people with jobs and careers, the resulting strain can be counterbalanced by the satisfaction derived from parenthood and the complementarity of multiple roles.

These contradictory effects of marital and parental status are investigated in the study reported below. The two sources or antecedents of stress considered are as follows: work-role expectations (i.e., expectations to expand one's work activities beyond the normal working day) and family roles (i.e., number of different role senders as reflected in the presence of a spouse and/or children in the household). Interrole conflict (work versus nonwork) and perceived overload in the work domain are the two stressors measured. Finally, both physical strain (self-reported) and psychological strain (job and life dissatisfaction) are considered. Figure 1 describes the status of these variables as hypothesized here.

Using these variables, this study tests the following hypotheses:

1. The greater (a) the expectations from work and (b) the number of family role senders, the greater the interrole conflict.

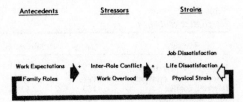

Figure 1. Hypothesized relations. (Family roles as spouse and parent are expected to be negatively related to strain when the intervening effects of the stressors are partialed out. This negative relationship is denoted by the white arrow in the figure.)

2. The greater the expectations from work roles, the greater the perceived work overload; family roles are not expected to be directly related to work overload.

3. The relationship of work-role expectations to perceived work overload is progressively greater for single workers, married workers without children, and married workers with children.

4. The stressors work overload and interrole conflict are positively associated with job and life dissatisfaction and physical symptoms of strain.

5. When the effects of intervening stressors (work overload and interrole conflict) are controlled, there is a negative relationship between family roles and strain.

The last hypothesis is intended to reconcile the conflicting research evidence regarding the relation of family roles to symptoms of strain. The hypothesis predicts that the presence of a spouse and children will be positively related to physical and mental health (as suggested by Doherty & Jacobsen, 1982, and others) *if* the stressful effects of these role senders (as reported by Beutell & Greenhaus, 1983, and others) are partialed out. We have not included a parallel hypothesis concerning the possible positive effects of work-role expectations on physical and mental health in view of the lack of previous research supporting such a relation.

Method

Sample and Subjects

This study focuses on elementary and secondary public school teachers. As professionals, teachers are likely to experience pressures to put extra time into their work and

Table 1
Descriptive Statistics

Measure	n^a	Minimum	Maximum	M	SD	α^b
Work-role expectations	179	1.00	7.00	4.22	1.22	.88
Perceived work overload	197	1.33	5.00	3.19	0.94	.80
Interrole conflict	180	1.00	4.00	2.18	0.77	.69
Job dissatisfaction	195	1.00	5.00	3.80	0.95	.73
Life dissatisfaction	200	1.00	5.00	3.55	0.95	.70
Physical strain	196	−1.44	2.95	0.00	0.87	—^{c}

^{a} Scores along each measure were generated only for respondents with no missing data.
^{b} Cronbach's alpha was used to estimate internal consistency reliability.
^{c} The measure is a factor score.

thus are subject to the stressors discussed above (Blase, 1982).

A two-stage procedure was used to obtain a sample of teachers representative of all those employed in the southeastern quadrant of the lower peninsula of Michigan. First, all schools in this geographical area were listed in a sampling frame organized by type of school (elementary, middle/junior high, and senior high) and then by county. Within each county, schools were listed by size according to number of teachers. Twenty-five schools were randomly selected with the probability of selection weighted by the size of each school. The sample selected included 11 elementary, 6 middle/junior high, and 8 senior high schools from 23 different districts.

Second, eight teachers were randomly selected in each of the 25 schools. Of the 200 teachers initially selected, 23 (11.5%) could not be contacted due to extended vacations or job changes. Another 18 teachers (9%) preferred not to participate in the study. Additional teachers were randomly selected until eight individuals could be surveyed from each school (see Cooke & Rousseau, 1981).

The final sample of teachers was 63% female and 37% male. Over 16% of the teachers were between 21 and 29 years old; 51.5% were between 30 and 44; 23.5% between 45 and 54; and the remaining 8% were 55 years or older. All but 3% of the teachers held a college degree.

Measures

Data were collected by means of a preliminary telephone interview, an extensive face-to-face interview, and a self-administered questionnaire. First, each teacher was contacted by telephone to obtain some background data (e.g., marital status, presence of children in the household) and to set an appointment for the more comprehensive interview. Next, the teachers were interviewed, usually in their homes, by a graduate student or research assistant from the Institute for Social Research or the School of Education at the University of Michigan. The interview, based directly on the 1977 *Quality of Employment Survey* (Quinn & Staines, 1979), included questions on job dissatisfaction, life dissatisfaction, and physical health. Finally, the teachers were asked to complete and return a self-administered questionnaire. The questionnaire focused on various aspects of teachers' jobs and their organizations—including expectations surrounding their work roles.

Work-role expectations. Expectations to expand one's

work role beyond normal working hours were measured by four questionnaire items specifically developed for this study. Teachers were asked to assess the accuracy of the four following statements relative to their work roles: My co-workers and superiors expect that any person doing a job such as mine should

—take on work-related duties and responsibilities, even though these activities may interfere with their free time.
—view work as the most important part of their life.
—finish job-related tasks by staying overtime or bringing work home, even if they are not paid extra to do so.
—*not* have other activities more important than work.
Responses could range from 1 (*very inaccurate*) to 7 (*very accurate*). Descriptive statistics for the index based on the mean of these four items are presented in Table 1.

Family roles. During the telephone interview, it was ascertained whether the teachers were married and had children in the household. Those who were divorced or separated were coded as single; similarly, those with children living elsewhere were coded as having no children in the household unit. This coding strategy was based on the assumption that former spouses and children living elsewere generate significantly less powerful expectations (and support) than do family members living at home. A three-level variable was constructed with 1 representing "single" (39 respondents), 2 representing "married with no children" (60 respondents), and 3 representing "married with children at home" (97 respondents).

Perceived work overload. Items from two different "card sorts" were used for this measure. The first card sort included two items: "I never seem to have enough time to get everything done on my job" and "I have too much work to do everything well." The response cards provided four options: 1 (*strongly disagree*), 2 (*disagree*), 3 (*agree*), and 4 (*strongly agree*). The second card sort included the item: "I have enough time to get the job done." The response cards were: 1 (*not at all true*), 2 (*a little true*), 3 (*somewhat true*), and 4 (*very true*). Responses to the last item were reversed, and the mean of the three items was calculated to construct an overload index. Descriptive statistics for this measure, and the measures below, are summarized in Table 1.

Work/nonwork interrole conflict. This index included two closed-ended interview items with response options ranging from 1 (*low conflict*) to 4 (*high conflict*). For example, teachers were asked: "How much do your job and free-time activities interfere with each other?" The conflict

ROBERT A. COOKE AND DENISE M. ROUSSEAU

Table 2
Factor Analysis of Physical Conditions

Condition[a]	Communality	Factor 1	Factor 2	Factor 3
Trouble breathing or shortness of breath	.15	.34	.15	.14
Pains in my back or spine	.21	.44	.09	−.06
Becoming very tired in a short time	.44	.62	.17	.18
Finding it difficult to get up in the morning	.26	.50	.11	.01
Feeling my heart racing or pounding	.38	.60	.09	.10
Hands sweating so that they feel damp and clammy	.37	.59	.06	−.15
Feeling nervous or fidgety and tense	.39	.58	.17	.17
Poor appetite	.19	.38	.20	.09
Spells of dizziness	.24	.46	.12	.10
Having trouble getting to sleep	.66	.25	.77	.07
Having trouble staying asleep	.71	.21	.81	.00
Smoking more than I used to	.24	.04	.02	.49
Drinking more than I used to	.39	.07	.03	.62
SS		2.45	1.42	.77
% variance explained		18.8	11.0	6.9

[a] Note that the conditions are not presented here in their order in the interview but are arranged to facilitate interpretation.

index also included two variables developed on the basis of responses to an open-ended question: "Could you tell me what problems or difficulties you run into concerning the hours you work, your work schedule, or overtime?" First, a work/nonwork interference variable was created. Respondents mentioning some type of interference were assigned a 4; those not mentioning any interference were assigned a 1. Second, a family-problem variable was created. Respondents mentioning any type of family problem (whether with their spouse, children, parent, etc.) were assigned a 4; those not mentioning any family problems due to their work hours were assigned a 1. The mean of these four items was used for the interrole conflict score.

Psychological strain: Job dissatisfaction. Four *Quality of Employment* interview items were used to measure job satisfaction/dissatisfaction (see Quinn & Staines, 1979, pp. 210–211). Some of these questions were direct ("All in all, how satisfied would you say you are with your job— very satisfied, somewhat satisfied, not too satisfied, or not at all satisfied?"); others were more indirect ("Knowing what you know now, if you had to decide all over again whether to take the job you now have, what would you decide?"). Responses to the four questions were averaged to generate a scale ranging from 1 (*satisfied*) to 5 (*dissatisfied*).

Psychological strain: Life dissatisfaction. Life satisfaction/dissatisfaction was measured by means of the following two items from the interview (Quinn & Staines, pp. 233–234):

—Taking all things together, how would you say things are these days? Would you say you're very happy, pretty happy, or not too happy these days?

—In general, how satisfying do you find the way you're spending your life these days? Would you call it completely satisfying, pretty satisfying, or not very satisfying?

Responses to these two items were averaged to generate an index ranging from 1 (*satisfied*) to 5 (*dissatisfied*).

Physical strain. As in the 1977 *Quality of Employment Survey,* respondents were given a list of 13 physical conditions and asked to check how often they had experienced each in the past year. Response options ranged from 1 (*never*) to 4 (*often*). Data provided by the teachers were factor analyzed (principal components analysis with varimax rotation) and, as shown in Table 2, three factors were identified. The first factor explains the greatest percentage of the variance in responses (18.8%) and includes tiredness, trouble getting up, heart pounding or racing, hands sweating, and nervousness. The second factor includes problems getting and staying asleep, and the third factor includes problems with smoking and drinking. This factor structure is somewhat different than that for the national *Quality of Employment* sample. In the national study, the items loading heavily on our first and second factors (see Table 2) loaded on a single factor and were combined to form an 11-item index of physical health with an internal consistency reliability of .80 (Quinn & Staines, p. 235). In the present study, scaled factor scores for the first factor shown in Table 2 were used to represent physical strain.

Analyses

Correlations were computed among all the variables under study. The hypotheses were tested using regression analyses. To control for the possible confounding effects of other variables with the same status in the model (see Figure 1), partial regression coefficients were used to test the significance of relations of antecedents to stressors and of antecedents and stressors to strains. Our concern here is to isolate each hypothesized relationship by controlling for the most theoretically plausible alternative explanation in the model. The regressions for the final hypothesis, concerning the direct relation of family roles to health, controlled for the intervening effects of the stressors. Work overload and interrole conflict were entered into the equation first, as fixed variables, prior to entering the family-role variable. It should be noted that though this analysis resembles path analysis, this approach to hypothesis testing is not presented as a *causal analysis* in the strict sense of the term.

Table 3
Correlation Matrix: Antecedents, Stressors, and Strains

Variable	1	2	3	4	5	6
Antecendents						
1. Family roles						
2. Work-role expectations	.11					
Stressors						
3. Perceived work overload	−.07	.21**				
4. Interrole conflict	.24**	.25**	.23**			
Strains						
5. Job dissatisfaction	−.04	.13	.24***	.17*		
6. Life dissatisfaction	−.14*	−.06	.16*	.11	.40***	
7. Physical strain	−.08	−.06	.18*	.26***	.31***	.33***

Note. $162 \leq N \leq 196$.
* $p \leq .05$. ** $p \leq .01$. *** $p \leq .001$.

Results

The correlations presented in Table 3 indicate that the three strain variables are positively intercorrelated, as are the two stressors. Work-role expectations and the number of family-role senders are not significantly related.

Hypothesis 1, concerning the relation of work-role expectations and family-role senders to conflict, was tested using regression analysis. Multiple regression of role conflict against the work and family-role variables yielded a multiple correlation of .33, $F(2, 156) = 9.5$, $p \leq .0001$. The partial regression coefficients for both these independent variables were significant ($p \leq .01$). Given that the correlation analysis showed the family and work-role variables to be essentially uncorrelated, these results suggest that separately and together high role expectations from work and family contribute to perceived role conflict. Thus, Hypothesis 1 is supported by these data on teachers.

When work-role overload is regressed on family roles and work-role expectations, only the variable work-role expectations enters the equation significantly $\beta = .24$, $p \leq .01$; $R = .25$, $F(2, 171) = 5.6$, $p \leq .01$, consistent with Hypothesis 2. Hypothesis 3 predicted that family roles would moderate the relation between work-role expectations and perceived work-role overload. Regression analysis shows that this relationship is strongest for married workers with children and supports this hypothesis: single, $\beta = .03$, $F(1, 34) = 0.03$, *ns*;

married without children, $\beta = .26$, $F(1, 50) = 3.6$, *ns*; married with children, $\beta = .34$, $F(1, 84) = 10.7$, $p \leq .01$.

Hypothesis 4, predicting a relation between the stressors (role conflict and work overload) and the strain variables, is generally supported by regression analysis. Regression of job dissatisfaction on both stressors indicates that only work overload enters significantly ($p \leq .01$). For life dissatisfaction, the partial regression coefficients for both stressors are positive but not significant. However, when physical strain is regressed against the stressors, both work overload and interrole conflict enter significantly, $R = .31$, $F(2, 170) = 9.2$, $p \leq .001$. Thus, although both of the stressors are associated with strain, work overload is more consistently related to strain symptoms measured here.

Hypothesis 5, concerning the possible direct negative relationship of family-role senders to strain, received little support, with one interesting exception. The results above show that the relationship of family roles to strain is mediated by the stressor interrole conflict. In addition, the family-role variable moderates the work-role expectation—work-overload relationship when subgroups were formed based on whether or the teachers were married and had children in the household. However, regression analysis reveals one interesting direct effect: After the intervening relations of stressors to strain are accounted for, family-role expectations maintain a direct relationship with physical strain, $\beta = -.20$, $p \leq .01$. Perhaps more interesting is the fact that this relationship is *negative,* in contrast to the other significant relations with strain found in this study, all of which were positive. This finding suggests that having a family role (spouse, parent), although associated with interrole conflict, may also be linked to better physical health. It should be noted that no direct relationship was postulated between work expectations and strain, and none was found. Implications of such findings for the nature of strain's relations with social support and multiple roles are discussed below.

Discussion

Figure 2 summarizes this study's results in terms of the basic model employed here. Results generally confirm the hypothesized intervening effects of work overload and interrole conflict in the work-expectation–strain relationship. They also support the hypothesized link between the stressors, conflict and overload, and two of three types of strain studied here (i.e., job dissatisfaction and physical strain but not life dissatisfaction).

However, the impact of family roles on strain as experienced by working people seems to be more complex. The results of this study of teachers suggest that the demands of family roles affect strain in three concurrent ways. First, as individuals marry and have children, they are subject to increased interrole conflict as their nonwork roles change and become increasingly demanding. Second, the effects of work expectations on perceived overload become increasingly stronger as workers marry and have children. Thus, the threshold separating equilibrium from overload is lower for individuals with children—parents may have lower tolerance for high work demands than nonparents. Third, there is a positive effect of family roles in the equation. After the relationship of family-role demands to the stressors is accounted for, the presence of a spouse and children is related to physical well-being. Parents tend to experience symptoms of strain less frequently than nonparents, and married teachers less frequently than those who are single.

It is possible that the causal direction is the opposite of that assumed here; good health might lead to, or at least make more feasible, marriage and child-rearing. Nevertheless, the

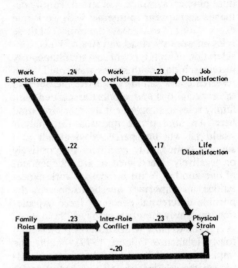

Figure 2. Summary of results. (The arrows denote partial regression coefficients significant at the .05 level. Although this diagram is not presented as a confirmatory causal analysis, it provides a model for such research.)

causal direction shown in Figure 2 is consistent with previous research on family roles and social support (Thoits, 1982). This support can be particularly meaningful when spouses hold nontraditional sex-role attitudes and are willing to share child-rearing and housework activities (Beutell & Greenhaus, 1983). Furthermore, health risks might generally be lower for socially active than for less active people (Verbrugge, 1983). There may be value in the activity levels associated with multiple roles so that busier people tend to be happier and less prone to spend time in anxious or depressed states. Similarly, the availability of multiple roles provides workers the opportunity to "compartmentalize" the stressful events and conditions associated with any particular role. Clearly, it is necessary to separate the dysfunctional conflict and overload resulting from multiple role expectations from the support, positive activity, and alternatives they provide.

The present study of teachers indicates that family roles and work-role expectations operate differently on strain. Although work-role expectations generally appear to be strain-in-

ducing, family roles can both induce and reduce physical symptoms of strain. Family demands also appear to interact with work-role
expectations to exacerbate the impact of these
roles on work overload and strain. Thus, consideration of both types of role simultaneously
in research on health seems warranted. Such
research could include subjective measures of
the expectations and support associated with
family roles to supplement the measures used
here. An appropriate question for analysis
would be whether perceived demands and
support from family members are positively
or negatively interrelated or are independent
of one another. With respect to work expectations, an important question concerns the
possible differential effects of these expectations on family members who just "hold jobs"
as opposed to those with careers or professional
roles (Holahan & Gilbert, 1979). Finally, the
implications of sex should be explored. Although the relatively small number of males
in the present sample prevented us from including this variable,[1] other studies have shown
that stress and strains from family versus work
roles are more serious for women than men
(Cooper, 1983). However, the differences in
the levels of stress and strain experienced by
these groups might be decreasing to the extent
that men are becoming more involved with
their children and women are becoming more
concerned with their careers.

---

[1] Some *trends* regarding similarities and possible differences between males and females can be reported. The
present data indicate that, for both sexes, work overload
is directly related to work expectations and not to family
roles. However, interrole conflict appears to be due more
to work expectations for males and more to family roles
for females. For both males and females, job dissatisfaction
is related to overload (but more so for females) and physical
strain to interrole conflict (but more so for males).

References

Bachman, J. G., O'Malley, P. M., & Johnston, J. (1978).
   Youth in transition, (Vol. 6), Ann Arbor, MI: Institute
   for Social Research.

Beutell, N. J., & Greenhaus, J. H. (1983). Integration of
   home and nonhome roles: Women's conflict and coping
   behavior. *Journal of Applied Psychology, 68,* 43–48.

Blake, J. (1979). Is zero preferred?: American attitudes
   toward childlessness in the 1970's. *Journal of Marriage
   and the Family, 41,* 245–258.

Blase, J. J. (1982). A social-psychological grounded theory
   of the teacher stress and burnout. *Educational Administration Quarterly, 18,* 93–113.

Blood, R., & Wolfe, D. (1960). *Husbands and wives.* New
   York: Macmillan.

Brown, G. W., & Harris, T. (1978). *Social origins of
   depression: A study of psychiatric disorders in women.*
   New York: Free Press.

Campbell, A., Converse, P. E., & Rogers, W. L. (1976).
   The quality of American life. New York: Russell Sage
   Foundation.

Caplan, R. D. (1971). *Organizational stress and individual
   strain: A sociopsychological study of risk factors in coronary heart disease among administrators, engineers,
   and scientists.* Unpublished doctoral dissertation. Ann
   Arbor, MI: The University of Michigan.

Coburn, D. (1978). Work and general psychological and
   physical well-being. *International Journal of Health
   Services, 8,* 415–435.

Cooke, R. A., & Rousseau, D. M. (1981). Problems of
   complex systems: A model of systems problem solving
   applied to schools. *Educational Administration Quarterly, 17,* 15–41.

Cooper, C. L. (1983). Problem areas for future stress research: Cancer and working women. In C. L. Cooper
   (Ed.), *Stress research: Issues for the eighties* (pp. 103–
   119). New York: Wiley.

Doherty, W. J., & Jacobson, N. S. (1982). Marriage and
   the family. In B. B. Wolman (Ed.), *Handbook of developmental psychology* (pp. 667–680). Englewood Cliffs,
   NJ: Prentice-Hall.

Gordon, F. E., & Strober, M. H. (1978). Initial observations
   on a pioneer cohort: 1974 women MBA's. *Sloan Management Review, 19,* 15–25.

Gould, S., & Werbel, J. D. (1983). Work involvement: A
   comparison of dual wage earner and single wage earner
   families. *Journal of Applied Psychology, 68,* 313–319.

Gove, W. R., & Geerken, M. R. (1977). The effect of
   children and employment on the mental health of married men and women. *Social Forces, 56,* 66–76.

Gove, W. R. (1973). Marital status and mortality. *American
   Journal of Sociology, 29,* 45–65.

Gutek, B. A., Nakamura, C. Y., & Nieva, V. F. (1981).
   The independence of work and family roles. *Journal of
   Occupational Behavior, 2,* 1–16.

Hall, D. T., & Hall, F. S. (1982). Stress and the two-career
   couple. In C. L. Cooper & R. Payne (Eds.), *Current
   concerns in occupational stress* (pp. 254–266). New York:
   Wiley.

Haw, M. A. (1982). Women, work and stress. *Journal of
   Health and Social Behavior, 23,* 132–144.

Haynes, S. G., & Feinleib, M. (1980). Women, work and
   coronary heart disease: Prospective findings from the
   Framington heart study. *American Journal of Public
   Health, 70,* 133–141.

Holahan, C. K., & Gilbert, L. A. (1979). Inter-role conflict
   for working women: Career versus job. *Journal of Applied
   Psychology, 64,* 86–90.

House, J. S., & Wells, J. A. (1978). Occupational stress,
   social support, and health. In A. McLean, G. Black, &
   M. Colligan (Eds.), (NIOSH) Publication, No. 78–140.
   Washington, DC: Department of Health, Education and
   Welfare.

Jones, A. P., & Butler, M. C. (1980). A role transition
   approach to the stresses of organizationally-induced

260 ROBERT A. COOKE AND DENISE M. ROUSSEAU

family role disruption. *Journal of Marriage and the Family, 42*, 367–376.

Katz, D., & Kahn, R. L. (1978). *The social psychology of organizations* (2nd ed.). New York: Wiley.

La Rocco, J. M., House, J. S., & French, J. R. P. (1980). Social support, occupational stress, and health. *Journal of Health and Social Behavior, 21*, 202–218.

London, M., Crandell, R., & Seals, G. W. (1977). The contribution of job and leisure satisfaction to quality of life. *Journal of Applied Psychology, 62*, 328–334.

Quinn, R. P., & Staines, G. L. (1979). *The quality of employment survey.* Ann Arbor, MI: Institute for Social Research.

Schaefer, C. (1982). Shoring up the "buffer" of social support. *Journal of Health and Social Behavior, 23*, 96–98.

Staines, G. L., Pleck, J. H., Shepard, L., & O'Connor, P. (1978). *Wives' employment status and marital adjustment.* (Working paper). Ann Arbor, MI: Institute for Social Research, The University of Michigan.

Szalai, A. (1972). *The use of time.* The Hague: Monton.

Thoits, P. (1982). Problems in the study of social support. *Journal of Health and Social Behavior, 23*, 145–158.

Verbrugge, L. M. (1979). Marital status and health. *Journal of Marriage and the Family, 41*, 267–285.

Verbrugge, L. M. (1983). Multiple roles and physical health of women and men. *Journal of Health and Social Behavior, 24*, 16–30.

Woods, N. F. (1978). *Women's roles, mental health, and illness behavior.* Unpublished doctoral thesis. Chapel Hill, NC: University of North Carolina.

Received June 20, 1983
Revision received December 13, 1983 ∎

Name Index